Called to be Holy in the World

Called by the Gospel
**Introductions to Christian History and Thought
From a Distinctly Lutheran Perspective**

Volume 1
Called to be God's People: An Introduction to the Old Testament
Andrew E. Steimann, editor

Volume 2
Called by the Gospel: An Introduction to the New Testament
Michael P. Middendorf and Mark Schuler

Volume 3
*Called to Believe, Teach and Confess:
An Introduction to Doctrinal Theology*
Steven P. Mueller, editor

Volume 4
*Called to be Holy in the World:
An Introduction to Christian History*
Timothy H. Maschke

Called to be Holy in the World

An Introduction to Christian History

Timothy H. Maschke

WIPF & STOCK · Eugene, Oregon

CALLED TO BE HOLY IN THE WORLD
An Introduction to Christian History

Copyright © 2016 Timothy H. Maschke. All rights reserved. Except for brief quotations in critical publications or reviews, no part of this book may be reproduced in any manner without prior written permission from the publisher. Write: Permissions, Wipf and Stock Publishers, 199 W. 8th Ave., Suite 3, Eugene, OR 97401.

Wipf & Stock
An Imprint of Wipf and Stock Publishers
199 W. 8th Ave., Suite 3
Eugene, OR 97401

www.wipfandstock.com

PAPERBACK ISBN: 978-1-4982-9246-7
HARDCOVER ISBN: 978-1-4982-9248-1

Manufactured in the U.S.A.

Table of Contents

Preface and Acknowledgements. vii

Introduction ix

PART ONE: The Early Church
1. The Fullness of Time 1
2. Apostolic Fathers and Apologists 13
3. Persecution and Confession 25
4. The Official Religion 37

PART TWO: Christian Growth
5. The Expansion of Christianity and the Latin World . 57
6. Gregory the Great and Mission Activities . . 73
7. A Crescent Moon Arises 87
8. Iconoclasts and the Ecumenical Councils . . 97
9. Charlemagne and the Western Church . . 107

PART THREE: The Middle Ages
10. Light in the Darkness 119
11. Dawning and Division in Christendom . . 127
12. Crusader Mentality and Growing Intellectualism . 141
13. Church Theologians and Mendicant Movements . 155
14. Scholasticism, Mysticism, Reforming Spirits and Suppression . 173

PART FOUR: Renaissance and Reformation
15. The Renaissance and Calls for Reform . . 185
16 A. The Age of Reform and Northern Humanism . 199
16 B. The Lutheran Reformation. . . . 213
16 C. The Protestant, Catholic, and Radical Reformations . 233
17. War, Orthodoxy, and Piety 249

PART FIVE: The Modern Era
18. The Age of Reason and New Awakenings . . 265
19. The Age of Change 283
20. The Ecumenical Age 307
21. Post-Modern Potentialities. 331

General Bibliography 337

Index 341

Preface and Acknowledgements

Over a decade ago, several faculty members from the Concordia University System decided to prepare a set of textbooks that could be used throughout our Lutheran Church—Missouri Synod higher education system. The first three have been well received and are regularly used by many of our colleagues in the Concordia University System. I want to express my special appreciation to Steve Mueller for his early editorial guidance and continued help on this project.

Initially conceived as a joint endeavor, this particular history book has become a personal project for me over the past ten years. I want to acknowledge the initial work of Rev. Dr. Thomas von Hagel, Concordia University Chicago, for preparing a draft of the first four chapters of this book. I appreciated his productivity in those early years and thank him for his patience.

Since then I have toiled with writing this book always desiring yet not always finding the time required to do the research and writing. I want to express my thanks to my dear wife, Sharon, who allowed me time "in my cave" (my basement office), as well as at the kitchen table, to write and review and rewrite chapters. Her patience with me is astounding and deeply appreciated.

There are several idiosyncratic elements in this book. First, the reader will notice the organization. As I explain more fully in the Introduction, each of the chapters covers a century in the history of Christianity. Some are longer and some are shorter, depending upon what information seemed important for me for a general understanding of Christianity in that century. The whole book is structured in that fashion—one chapter, one century. While many historians try to give a general sense of eras, for example, "the Dark Ages," I found it helpful to look at the history of the church as it unfolds over time century-by-century, always under the Lord's graciously patient presence.

Dates for individuals' lives or events are indicated throughout the book as a reference and reminder of the century being read. When able to be determined, the years of a person's life is given. The letter "c." (Latin *circa*, "about") is placed before those which are uncertain or approximate. The years that rulers and popes served are also given, when available, and are indicated with either "rule" or "pope" followed by the year. If a date has a "+" before it, that is the person's death year and is all that is known for sure. A few individuals are only known from their writings or in the century in which they lived and no date is given.

Readers will also notice already in the Table of Contents that the sixteenth century is actually three chapters. Because I am writing from a Lutheran perspective, I felt the need to include more information on Luther and his ideas, yet I wanted to keep them in the context of the century.

At the end of each chapter are about a half-dozen questions which can be used for discussion and application of the information of the chapter. Some questions may require further reading or research, while others can provide an opening for class or group discussions. They are arranged along the chapter structure.

Also at the end of each chapter are a list of books which either provided help to me in preparing the content of the chapter or are specific texts which would give greater background for further understanding and appreciation of the specific topics in the chapter. A general bibliography of history textbooks or resources which cover broader areas is included at the end of this book.

The pictures and maps in this book are all in "public domain" and are readily accessible from the internet. When helpful, I included information about the source or general content of the illustrations. Therefore, there is no list of illustrations in this front part of the book or specific acknowledgments of the sources.

I would be remiss if I did not acknowledge the collegial aid and encouragement I received from several of my colleagues here at Concordia University Wisconsin. Dr. William Cario (Vice President of Academics), Dr. Roland "Cap" Ehlke, Rev. Dr. Patrick Ferry (University President), and Rev. Dr. Brian German (Director of the Concordia Bible Institute) took time from their busy schedules to read several chapters of the book and made very helpful suggestions for improving the style and content of this work.

As all writing projects, I take full responsibility for any errors or inadequacies in the final version of the work. It has been a joy to see the centuries unfold on these pages, knowing that God continues to hold the world in His gracious hands and enables His people to strive to be holy in the world through the power of His Son's Spirit.

Timothy H. Maschke
Concordia University
Epiphany 2016

Introduction

The story of God's marvelous activity in the world is exciting and stimulating. The marvel is that He works through common ordinary people to do uncommon and extraordinary things. By the power of His Holy Spirit, the church has progressed through two millennia expanding, expounding, and extending Christ's kingdom. From the pen of Luke to the power-point presentations of classroom instructors, the message of God's activity in the world is being proclaimed.

Looking over one's shoulder is a habit of the historian. This is not a paranoid behavior filled with fear and apprehension, but an honorable act of respect and reconnoitering. There is so much information and research and experience that has had an effect on the present and affects our future that it is foolish to ignore it. There are several directions that we need to look, so join us as we look around and beyond our present times.

A Christian historian first and foremost looks back to the cross, recognizing that it is *"in hoc signo vincit"* ("in this sign He conquers"), as Constantine recognized in his vision in the early decade of the fourth century in the Christian era. The cross confirms our vocation as God's people and serves as a comfort in our times of need. On that cross our Savior, Jesus the Christ, offered Himself as the victor over the devil, the world, and our own sinful flesh. That Christ on the cross remains our focus throughout both troubling and triumphant times.

Throughout this history of His story, we will be looking out into the world. Not only is our focus on the cross, but also on how the message of the cross—Christ crucified and victorious—served as a beacon to draw people to know Him who is the Light of the world. Because of that Light, those who follow Christ are also light bearers who have a calling, a vocation, a mission to go into the world with that Light. We are called to carry His cross to a world which is in desperate need of stability, hope, and that peace which passes all understanding, as St. Paul expresses it (Philippians 4:7).

Finally, we will be looking forward to heaven. Although historians are often portrayed as only being interested in the past, the motivation for doing and learning Christian history is to prepare for our future. God has called us in this life for eternal life. Through the waters of baptism, we have been brought into a union which is incomplete until we experience it fully in eternity. This is also the hope of those who have gone before us.

Historical Perspective

Historians always are standing on the shoulders of those who have gone before. With the preacher of Ecclesiastes, we can say that "there is nothing new under the sun" (Ecclesiastes 1:9). The past is past, yet there is sometimes a novel or insightful perspective that the present provides that sheds light on the past and opens us up to the future more clearly. The following chapters are designed to give you a glimpse into God's activities in the past in order to bring you assurance of His presence and hope for the future.

Sometimes when we view the history of God's people, we only see those great leaders who had a significant influence on the world. Gregory Dix says it well when he describes "those innumerable millions of entirely obscure faithful men and women, everyone with his or her own individual hopes and fears and joys and sorrows and loves—and sins and temptations and prayers—each every whit as vivid and alive as mine are now. ...Each of them once believed and prayed as I believe and pray, and found it hard and grew slack and sinned and repented and fell again."[1] It is also these individuals, like you and me, who are behind the great events of the past. Those "little ones" should also be on our minds as we read.

Similarly, we can consider those who will come after us and ask ourselves how our own actions will influence them. Someone has said that Christianity is one generation away from extinction. Each generation has an obligation as well as a privilege to pass the promises of God down to the next generation in whatever way is deemed appropriate and most effective. This book is designed to help you tell the good story, His story, to those who follow you.

From 1557-1575, the Lutheran historian, Matthias Flacius Illyricus (1520-1575), prepared a thirteen-volume history of Christianity, called "the Magdeburg Centuries." Each chapter dealt with one century and the work was a standard for many years. While not a common approach recently, it is the approach of this volume, not because it is "Lutheran," but because I hope students will benefit from it. It has been my experience that students do not have a "sense of history" and so I believe readers will develop a sense of historical continuity as well as appreciation of sequential events from this centenary structure.

Called to be in the World

Called into the world is a central theme of this account of God's people. Martin Luther helpfully reminds us that the Holy Spirit has called us by the Gospel. We are people who have a special divinely created vocation, to be people of the promise. The scope of this textbook, then, is on the Christian church from Pentecost to the present, particularly as those believers lived out their vocation as God's people.

---

[1] Dom Gregory Dix, *The Shape of the Liturgy* (Westminster: Dacre Press, 1945), 744-745.

Acts 2 captures the excitement of Pentecost as God's people are filled for witnessing wholly to the world. Yet, that event was not a mere historical phenomenon. Rather, that event became a hallmark of our Lord's directives to be witnesses "in Judea, Samaria, and the ends of the earth" (Acts 1:8). Pentecost captures the vocation of the Christian community as they were moved by God's empowering Spirit and gracious love in Christ to share the good news with a world bent on destruction. Luke records the events of Pentecost and then moves out into the world with that same empowering word. A unique unity is portrayed by Luke as he describes the Christians as being "in one accord" (Acts 2:44), sharing everything with each other as they "devoted themselves to the apostles' teaching, and to fellowship, to the breaking of bread and to prayer" (Acts 2:42).

The early church was not a monolithic nor a morose institution, but a multi-faceted dynamic movement which God used mightily. As you hear the voices of those early Christians, you will recognize your own hopes and fears, your own desires for fulfillment in service and comfort in Christ. Through times of perilous persecution and artful articulation, these early believers recognized what God had called them to be, His witnesses in the world. A peculiar unity is evident even in the midst of extremely difficult and hostile times.

Within the imperial church, a designation associated with Constantine's edict approving Christianity as a viable religion of the empire, Christians blossomed into a social and political force second to none. From the beginning of the fourth century, His story expanded into a public witness to the world. Expansive constructions and expressive controversies vied for attention during these years as Christian basilicas began to dot the countryside and conversations turned to the question of how to articulate the biblical revelation most clearly and correctly. Concepts, such as "being" and "essence," "nature" and "person," were used by various spokesmen to communicate more carefully the reality of God's love for the world. Creeds were formulated which helped in this process.

The Middle Ages, sometimes called the dark ages, were never dark or even dull. The expansion of Christianity through the monastic movements brought social growth in diverse areas of the Mediterranean world and beyond. Clarification of doctrine continued as the faith was explored and expressed. A united church quickly divided, yet the confession of faith in Christ remained central to both divisions. Education continued to be a strong vehicle for the development of the faith both in the sacred realms as well as the developing secular sphere of society.

An age of change began in the early fifteenth century as new discoveries of ancient wisdom were made. Voices of concern were raised regarding the purity of teaching and practice, along with a desire to connect with the human experience more closely. Several reformations occurred. The resulting changes were far-reaching. Beginning in central Europe, they expanded into the new world through exploration and publication. Expansion also called for articulation of God's gracious plan in a way that brought hope and joy to a people oppressed and battle-weary. A divided, yet purified, church continued to bear witness to God's presence and power.

Times of transition provided opportunities for some to throw out all that was past. The modern era is marked by a strong emphasis on the present, with little appreciation for the past and a megalomanic perspective on the future. An emphasis upon the use of reason and a dependence on human emotion struggled together to draw the church away from its roots into a contemporary world of science and industry. Again individuals sought to speak words that connected the past with the present. New ideas were proposed along with a restoration of older patterns of belief bringing together a new synthesis of revelation. World events continued to influence the drive of the church into the world to witness to Christ as the hope of all. Conversations with other Christians and even non-Christians expanded as many boundaries were slowly erased or at least made less distinct.

Conversations must never cease, yet no history is adequate if it only looks at the past. Our final chapter looks beyond the present. What is beyond? What does God have planned? Upon what is our hope built? The church must continue to proclaim the message of forgiveness, life, and salvation in Jesus alone, if it tells His story correctly. And that is the plan for this book, to tell His story of His people who have been called into the world.

Called to be Wholly in the World

The church has been called to be wholly in the world. Jesus told His disciples that they were in the world, but "not of the world" (John 17:15-16). He articulated a tension worth talking about, how the community of saints can remain both a community and saints. The creeds of the church confess that the body of Christ is "one" and "holy." Yet, it is this double-emphasis that has remained a struggle throughout His story. As any duality, there is a tendency to emphasize one over the other and then to misrepresent the reality. This biblical reality of the Body of Christ is a major emphasis in this textbook project; in each era the struggle will become clear as the tension is recognized.

The Niceno-Constantinopolitan Creed (we commonly refer to it as the Nicene Creed) uses four words to describe the church—one, holy, catholic, apostolic. Each word describes a quality or characteristic of Christ's people through the ages. The first two serve as a guiding principle in this text. In all of this, the church seeks God's aid in fulfilling these qualities.

By the call to be "one," *una* in Latin, we hear an echo of Jesus's prayer to His Father "that they may be one, as We are one" (John 17:11). That desire for unity has always been on the hearts of Christ's people through the ages.

The struggle to be one is a struggle to share the same faith as the first Christians confessed. St. Paul spoke of "one Lord, one faith, one baptism..." (Ephesians 4:5). What is meant by that one-ness? Is it physical unity as a corporate institution or is it a unity of belief? Is it a common confession of faith or a common commitment to Christ?

The struggle to be one has been measured by the success or lack of success in creating a physical community as a visible body of Christ. A church body divided is an affront to the witness of love and forgiveness in Christ. The church as a community of believers lives and moves and has its being in conformity and commitment to a corporate expression of that unity as an institution, say many in the Christian church. Yet, we need to ask if this is really true.

The struggle to be ecumenically one continues to be unclear, yet desired. What does this unity involve? The Lutheran confessions repeatedly emphasize the theme of one church, united under doctrinal agreement. The concept of ecumenism, recently, has been watered down to mean merely cooperative inter-church relationships or even toleration of error so that some semblance of oneness is displayed to a doubting world. The continual tension to be one will be seen throughout the chapters of His story.

Called to be Holy in the World

By the call to be "holy," *sancta* in Latin, we hear an echo of Peter's apostolic promise "to be a holy priesthood…a holy nation" (1 Peter 1:5,9). That yearning for holiness has been heard throughout the ages as God's people desire to be what God has already declared them to be in Christ Jesus.

Holy lives display a recognition of a holy God whose blood cleanses us from all sin (1 John 1:7). Sin continues to draw us away from holiness, both in word and actions. The tension begins within each individual, yet it extends throughout the history of Christianity. Forgiveness restores us as God's people and gratitude motivates us to live holy lives in response. Some Christians have sought this holiness by their own actions and works as a response to the Spirit's activity. Others have rested in the comforting proclamation of the Gospel which announces and bestows the forgiveness of sins through the means of grace. Both perspectives need to be joined for a proper understanding of the Body of Christ.

The struggle is not merely personal either. To be pure is also a struggle to keep community and its teachings from contamination. Sometimes that meant expelling members of the community or announcing that their teachings are *anathema* (damnable; see Galatians 1:8-9). At other times, whole segments of the community broke away and followed a variety of leaders whose opinions and views they believed were more pure and holy. Reformers, as we will see, sought just such a renewal of purity through right teaching of the divine revelation; yet, they were not always able to agree with each other and the resulting groups divided further.

Because the church is always seeking to communicate to a contemporary society, some formulations of the church's teachings distorted, distracted, and even destroyed the purity of God's divine revelation. The community then needed to seek ways to restore their straight teaching and straight praising—orthodoxy—through a common confession of the faith. Creeds and symbols and statements and affirmations have abounded in the church as the faith is spoken, passed down, and expounded in a desire to tell the whole truth, and nothing but the truth of Him who is the Truth.

Called to Be

I hope that the Christian community's desire for unity and holiness will be caught in the following pages. This desire moves me to express the history of the world both as a calling out of the world as well as a calling into the world. The

Holy Spirit continues to work in the lives of God's people as they are moved to serve the Savior, Jesus Christ.

A tension, then, remains in the history of Christianity, yet it is not troublesome. If the church is to be one and holy, it must be wholly in the world, yet remain wholly united with the Lord. The unity and purity that the church experiences must always be found in its relationship with Jesus who is one with the Father and who has restored us by His blood. There is no other way. The history of the church reflects that tension between unity and purity, between oneness and holiness. It is a struggle we face today. In light of the past, we can have hope for the future as God's people called to be wholly and holy in the world.

1. The Fullness of Time

The First Century

> When the fullness of time had come, God sent forth his Son, born of a woman, born under the law, to redeem those who were under the law, so that we might receive adoption as sons. (Gal 4:4, ESV)

The first century marks a pivotal time in world history and especially for the people of God. The many prophecies in the Old Testament were being fulfilled in the New Testament: the New Testament was supplementing the Old Testament. The Son of God was born of a woman (Galatians 4), and the Holy Spirit descended upon the apostles (Acts 2). The birth of the Savior of the world was followed immediately by the birth of the Christian Church. These births took place within the Roman Empire and were the beginning of the history of Christianity. In the initial years, Christianity had to examine itself and determine its spiritual relations with Judaism and the paganism of the Roman Empire.

Luke-Acts

Luke, evangelist and historian, documented a good portion of the first century in his two-volume set: the Gospel according to St. Luke (c.5 BC to c.30 AD) and the Acts of the Apostles (c.30 AD to c.62 AD). Inspired by the Holy Spirit, the former portrayed the life of Jesus, while the latter chronicled significant events in the life of select apostles. This Gospel is one of four, while Acts is the only example of this literary genre in the Bible. Both were addressed to Theophilus (Luke 1:1-4; Acts 1:1-2), probably a well-to-do new Christian who helped support Luke's and Paul's ministries.

In volume one, Luke, the evangelist, began with the Annunciation. The angel Gabriel announced to Mary that she would give birth to a child. Even though Mary had not had sexual intercourse with a man, she would conceive by the Holy Spirit. And her child, the Son of God, was to be called Jesus (Luke 1:26-38). Luke, the historian, situated the annunciation in Nazareth and the birth of Jesus even more precisely: Jesus was born in Bethlehem during the reign of Caesar Augustus, and shepherds visited this newborn babe (Luke 2:1-20).

The bulk of this Gospel included many events of import in the ministry of Jesus. Jesus preached and taught (Luke 6, 8, 10-19). He performed miracles and forgave sins (Luke 7, 9). He disputed with the Jewish leaders and prophesied

(Luke 20:1-8). All of these in one manner or another pointed toward His imminent death.

The Gospel according to Luke reached its pinnacle with the death of Jesus and the events surrounding it (Luke 22-23). Jesus triumphantly rode a colt into Jerusalem on Palm Sunday and instituted the Lord's Supper on Maundy Thursday. Betrayed by Judas, one of the twelve apostles, Jesus was arrested and taken up before the Jewish Sanhedrin (literally, "assembly/court" of seventy-one Jewish elders who served as a Supreme Court for religious issues) and King Herod, and finally Pontius Pilate, the Roman governor. On Friday, they crucified Jesus. Upon His cross, the inscription read, "This is the King of the Jews" (Luke 23:38). At the empty tomb on Sunday morning, an angel proclaimed to Mary Magdalene, Johanna, and other women that Jesus was raised from the dead; Jesus Himself appeared to several disciples until His ascension forty days later (Luke 24).

> **The Ascension of Jesus**
>
> Jesus ascended into heaven forty days after His resurrection. Luke chronicled this event to close the Gospel according to St. Luke and open the Acts of the Apostles, connecting these two volumes with a common narrative. The Ascension further revealed Jesus' purpose and power. With His work of salvation completed upon the earth, He was free to return to heaven, and yet, He did not abandon the apostles and His church. Instead, He sent the Holy Spirit to the apostles on the Day of Pentecost (Acts 2). More specifically, Jesus ascended to the right hand of the Father. This is not a geographical locale in the heavenly realm, but rather a position of honor and glory and power over all of creation. Enthroned above the earth and heavens, Jesus continues to fill all things, watch over and work in the Christian church throughout her history. Jesus, ever before the Father, intercedes on behalf of His people (Rom 8:34; Heb 7:25).

In volume two, Luke delineated the events on the Day of Pentecost, fifty days after Jesus' resurrection (Acts 1-2). The Holy Spirit descended upon the gathered disciples and apostles. Audible and visible signs of this anointing included the sound of a powerful wind and a flame of fire flickering on each of their heads. In addition, the apostles spoke in foreign languages that were understood by those Jews from many foreign lands who were in Jerusalem for the Jewish Feast of Weeks. The apostle Peter preached to the entire assembly: Jesus' miracles, crucifixion, and resurrection showed that the heavenly Father chose Him; that He was Lord and Savior (Acts 2:14-36). Immediately following, more than three thousand were baptized in the name Jesus (Acts 2:41).

Following upon the example of the Day of Pentecost, the Christian Church reached out to others with the message of Jesus (Acts 3-6). Stephen preached Jesus to the Jews in Jerusalem (Acts 6-7). Philip preached in Samaria and showed an Ethiopian eunuch how Isaiah prophesied of Jesus (Acts 8). And Peter, directed by a vision, visited Cornelius, a gentile (Acts 10). Hearing of Jesus, Cornelius and his entire family believed and were baptized in the name of Jesus. The message of Jesus, then, was for both Jew and Gentile, for the entire world.

Luke provides the evangelical and historical basis for the beginning of the history of the Christian church. Utilizing the metaphor of a building, the Christian church is a temple in which Jesus is the cornerstone; the apostles are the foundation set in place around the cornerstone; and Christians are the stones built upon the foundation (Eph 2:19-21). Thus, the history of Christianity began on the

Day of Pentecost and continued to grow through the Church's proclamation of Jesus and its administration of baptism in God's Trinitarian name.

Paul the Missionary

While the first half of the Acts of the Apostles focused upon Peter, the second half featured the missionary career of Paul (+c.67). Not one of the original Twelve apostles who witnessed the entire ministry of Jesus, Paul initially persecuted Christianity. While Paul was traveling to Damascus, the ascended Jesus appeared to him and blinded him. Ananias then baptized Paul and Jesus commissioned Paul to be the apostle to the Gentiles (Acts 9).

The excessive energy that Paul had expended persecuting Christianity, he efficiently translated into his missionary endeavors on behalf of Christianity. Paul's missionary journeys were quite extensive in the northern portion of the Mediterranean world. On his first trip (c.46-48), he began in Antioch of Syria and traveled through Galatia and Cyprus (Acts 13-14). On his second trip (c.49-52), he again began in Antioch and traveled through Galatia. He also journeyed further west, visiting Philippi and Thessalonica in Macedonia, Athens and Corinth in Greece, and Troas and Ephesus on the west coast of Asia Minor (Acts 15-18). The destinations of his third trip (c.53-57) were similar to his second (Acts 18-21) as he revisited and encouraged these young congregations to remain faithful.

Upon entering a town, Paul would visit first the Jews and then the Gentiles. To both, he preached the message of Jesus: crucified upon the cross and risen from the dead. In addition, he performed miracles and baptized. Working with his traveling companions, e.g., Barnabas and Silas, Paul then attempted to organize a Christian community in each town and appoint a bishop as an overseer over each (Acts 15). Paul was persecuted on several occasions and forced to flee. In Philippi, he was beaten and imprisoned until an earthquake broke open his cell and loosed his chains (Acts 16). He was, however, able to establish Christian communities in numerous towns, including Thessalonica, Corinth, and Ephesus (Acts 17-20).

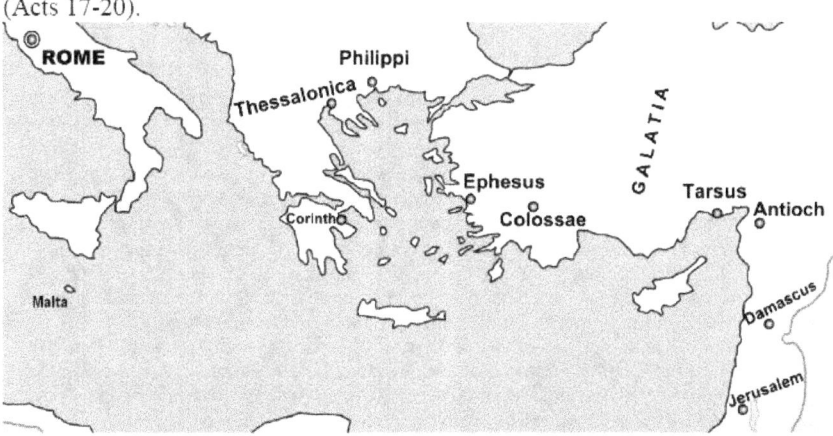

After Paul had visited these communities (see map), he often corresponded with them through personal or congregational letters. Each letter addressed relevant issues for a specific Christian community or Christian leader

(Pastoral Epistles). Paul penned one of his first letters to Christians in Corinth during his stay in Ephesus (c.55) while he was on his third missionary journey. The problems in Corinth were grave: civil suits, sexual immorality, and Eucharistic divisions (1 Corinthians). Paul, as a father to a child, severely reprimanded the Corinthians and reminded them that their actions were unacceptable among Christians. In addition, Paul proclaimed Jesus: crucified upon the cross and raised from the dead.

Following his missionary journeys, Paul was arrested in Jerusalem (Acts 21-22). He was then tried before the Jewish Sanhedrin in Jerusalem and the Roman governor Felix in Caesarea, and subsequently imprisoned (Acts 23-24). Paul was tried again in Caesarea by Festus, the new Roman governor, and Agrippa, the King of the Jews. Finally, he was sent by his own request to Rome where he was imprisoned (Acts 25-26). While the Acts of the Apostles do not describe Paul's death, he died a martyr in Rome according to the tradition of the Church.

The arch-persecutor of Christianity turned into the arch-missionary of Christianity. Though Christianity began in Jerusalem and the Promised Land, Paul's journeys spread the Christian faith into Asia Minor, Greece, Macedonia, and even as far as Italy. Through the spiritual labors of the apostle to the Gentiles, the Christian church shifted from a Jewish constituency to Gentile. His numerous letters were well received by the Christian communities he helped establish, and thus, quickly became foundational for the doctrines and practices of the Christian Church. As such, Paul was an influential figure in the early history of Christianity.

First Century Judaism

During this same time period since the time of Augustus (63 BC-14 AD, ruled 27 BC-14 AD), Judaism had been recognized as a legitimate religion in the Roman Empire. While small numerically (estimates of 5-7% of the Roman populace), Judaism's influence greatly exceeded its diminutive size. Judaism was an ancient religion with a revered tradition. Furthermore, it was the religion into which Jesus was born and from which the Christian church developed. This meant that more than a few of the beliefs and practices of Judaism carried over into Christianity, e.g., monotheism, Ten Commandments, and singing Psalms.

> *Pax Romana*
> The successive Mediterranean empires of Babylonia, Persia, and Greece, were followed by the Roman Empire that began in 64 BC. The last was vastest; it encompassed the Mediterranean Sea and stretched into Europe. The *Pax Romana*, Peace of Rome, was one of its great accomplishments. It began in the first century AD and continued well into the fourth century. Roman law, architecture, literature, and way of life influenced all throughout the empire. A network of roads connected major cities, and soldiers patrolled both highways and shipping lanes. This allowed many to travel with relative safety. Complementing this, Greek was the common language of the empire, and so, communication in commerce and among travelers from different lands was simplified. This, of course, greatly enhanced the missionary endeavors of the first-century Christians. Not only could they safely travel throughout the empire, but also of greater import, they could communicate with clarity the message of Jesus.

The Torah and the Temple were the heritage of first century Judaism. The Torah, authored by Moses in the fifteenth century BC, comprised the first five books of the First Testament, the sacred and authoritative writings of Judaism. It contained the narratives of the Creation and the patriarchs (Genesis and Exodus). It also delineated the civil, moral, and religious laws commanded by Yahweh (Hebrew, "LORD") to his people (Leviticus, Numbers, and Deuteronomy). Historically and theologically, it served as the basis for the other biblical writings. By the first millennium before Christ, the Temple was the site of ritual sacrifice whereby the Israelites atoned for their sins and became reconciled with Yahweh. Constructed by King Solomon in the tenth century BC and destroyed in 586 BC by the Babylonians, it was rebuilt in 516 BC, although not to the proportions or grandeur of Solomon's Temple. Herod the Great (74/73 BC-4 BC, ruled 37-4 BC), around 30 BC began construction of a new Temple (most often referred to in recent scholarship as "the Second Temple") which served as the center of Jewish worship until its destruction by the Romans in 70 AD.

Hellenism—humanistic ideals and classical styles associated with the Greek culture—had begun to infiltrate and influence the many cultures of the Mediterranean world by the end of the fourth century BC after the conquests of Alexander the Great (356-323 BC) and continued into the first century AD. Judaism reacted to Hellenism in one of two fashions. On the one hand, the Diaspora–those Jews dispersed throughout the Mediterranean world–was often more accepting of certain components of Hellenism. Many Jews outside of the Promised Land quickly dropped the Hebrew language and adopted Greek. As a result, these Jews began to utilize the Septuagint (LXX)–a Greek translation of the Old Testament originating in Alexandria of Egypt (c.3rd cent BC). In addition, Philo (c.25 BC-c.50 AD), a first century Jewish philosopher in Alexandria, attempted to harmonize the earlier Jewish teachings of Moses with the later Greek philosophers, suggesting that the latter had read and utilized ideas of the former.

On the other hand, many of the Jews in Palestine were much less receptive of Hellenism. Several Jewish sects began to combat Hellenism in the third and second centuries BC and were very much alive in the first century AD. The Pharisees attempted to preserve Judaism against the Greek culture through their legalistic emphasis upon moral and communal purity (see the books of 1 and 2 Maccabees). Teaching in the synagogues, they advocated a strict observance of their interpretation of the Law and segregating themselves from Gentiles. The Sadducees were the keepers of the Temple and emphasized the sacrificial rituals

> **Dead Sea Scrolls**
> The first Dead Sea Scrolls were discovered in 1947 at Qumran near the Dead Sea. Subsequent excavations unearthed more than 800 documents written in the Hebrew, Aramaic, and Greek languages. The various documents have been dated to as early as the second century BC and as late as the first century AD. They include the books of the Old Testament, biblical commentaries, and others, such as the *Community Rule* and *War Rule*. The biblical documents contain all the books of the Old Testament, except Esther. Though there are many fragments in this collection, of particular note is the Great Isaiah scroll that provides the complete text of the prophet on seventeen strips of leather. The *Community Rule* laid out the regulations for community life and distinguished between the righteous and evil, whereas the *War Rule* looked for a Messiah from the lineage of David. It is debated whether these were the libraries of the Essenes or another Jewish sect.

of the Torah. They were also the principal constituents of the Sanhedrin, the highest Jewish court consisting of 71 Jewish leaders.

Two smaller groups were known as the Essenes and the Zealots. The Essenes, a strict sect of Judaism, opposed the pagan influences of the Greek culture and viewed contemporary Judaism as totally corrupted by the Greeks. Subsequently, they migrated from Jerusalem to the desert region. In several locations around Qumran next to the Dead Sea, they established their own social-economic-religious communities. They lived extremely rigorous lives and practiced ceremonial washings. The Zealots, an even smaller minority group, yet one with influence beyond their size, were militants who sought to oust the political oppressors of the Jewish nation through military revolt. These sects attempted to preserve Judaism; however, they did so in very different fashions. As such, first century Judaism in the Promised Land was quite diverse.

Judaism and Jesus

Judaism did not receive Jesus well. Even though many Jews initially thronged after Jesus to witness and experience His miracles, they quickly fell away when they heard His difficult teachings (John 6). The Pharisees and Sadducees were particularly opposed to Jesus. They publicly questioned His theology and sought to discredit Him. Ultimately, they plotted against Him and encouraged the Jews to demand His crucifixion before Pilate (Matthew 27). Following this, the Jews, for the most part, rejected Jesus and His interpretation of the Old Testament, and persecuted the Christians who remained in Jerusalem (Acts 3-5). First century Judaism interacted quite extensively with both Hellenism and Christianity. Some Jews embraced one or the other, while others quite vehemently rejected both.

Destruction of Jerusalem

Just as with the Greek cultural influences, the relations between Judaism and the Roman Empire were tenuous at best. Rome occupied the Promised Land and taxed the Jews heavily. Because of this, the Jews vilified the Romans. Of graver concern was the religious attitude of the Romans. Rome tolerated most religions of the countries that it conquered and subsumed into its empire. Rome also expected these countries to accept at least in part the Roman civil religion into their own religious practices. Judaism, roused by the sect of the Zealots, constantly chafed at the polytheism and syncretism of the empire, and so, very much irritated Rome.

Over and again, Jewish-Roman relations were strained. In the waning years of the first century BC, according to Josephus's (37-100 AD) *Antiquities*, during the reign of Herod Archelaus (23BC-c.18 AD, ruled 4 BC-6 AD), a few Jews removed the empirical eagle from the Temple and incited riots in Jerusalem. Three legions of the Roman army were needed to restore order; they crucified 2,000 Jews. When Pontius Pilate, a Roman governor, took money from the Temple treasury to finance an aqueduct, the riotous Jews in Jerusalem were severely beaten and quickly silenced. In AD 21 and AD 51 respectively, the emperors Tiberius (42 BC-37 AD, ruled 14-37 AD) and Claudius (11 BC-54AD, ruled 41-54 AD) briefly expelled the Jews from Rome.

The most significant Jewish-Roman War broke out in AD 66 and continued until AD 73. It was preceded by more than a decade of repeated uprisings by the Jews against a series of cruel Roman governors. The Roman governor Gessius Florus (64-66) was so malicious that the Jewish uprisings turned into violent revolt: Roman soldiers were slaughtered and military buildings razed by the Jews. In 66, a Roman legion was rebuffed by the Jews and retreated. General Vespasian (9 AD-79 AD) entered the Promised Land a year later and briefly quelled the revolt. At the death of Emperor Nero (37-68 AD, ruled 54-68), a subsequent Roman civil war put this matter on hold.

Vespasian (ruled 69-69 AD) became emperor. One year later, he sent his son, Titus (39-81, ruled 79-81), to deal with the Jewish problem. With an immense army, Titus laid siege to Jerusalem. The situation quickly became bleak: food was scarce and infighting erupted. After a series of fierce attacks, the walls were breached, and the Roman army overran Jerusalem. The soldiers pillaged the town, destroyed the Temple, and much of Jerusalem went up in flames. According to Josephus' account in *The Jewish Wars*, at least 100,000 Jews died in the fighting at Jerusalem, and another 100,000 survivors were sold into slavery.

This first Jewish-Roman War came to an end with the defeat at Masada. This last stronghold of Zealots was situated on a plateau in the Judean desert with nearly 1,000 men, women, and children. The Roman army laid siege against it. Rather than surrender and be sold into slavery, they committed suicide (see box at end of this chapter).

The tensions between the Jews and Romans culminated in this Great Jewish War. The destruction of Jerusalem reinforced Rome's military stranglehold on the Jews. Moreover, it brought about an end to the Sadducees: the destruction of the Temple meant no vocation for this priestly sect. Furthermore, it increased the Christian Diaspora that had initially centered in Jerusalem, but was beginning to spread throughout the Mediterranean world (1 Peter).

The Twelve Disciples

The Bible does not give detailed information about the last years of Jesus' twelve apostles. Only the death of Judas (Matthew 27:5; Acts 1:18) and James, the brother of John (Acts 12:1-2), are described in the New Testament. Reliable traditions, particularly Eusebius's *Ecclesiastical History* provide some ideas about their influence in spreading Christianity throughout the then-known world.

All except John, the Evangelist, died a martyr's death. John, according to the Apocalypse of John the Divine (Revelation) was exiled on the island of Patmos, where he died of old age. Peter was crucified upside down in Rome around AD 66, probably around the same time as Paul was beheaded. Andrew, Peter's brother, had done missionary work in Turkey and Greece, where he was also crucified or hanged on an olive tree for three days before he succumbed to death. James, son of Alphaeus, served in Syria, where Josephus reports he was stoned and then clubbed to death.

Philip went to Scythia (present-day south Russia), Northern Africa, around Carthage, and then back to Asia Minor (Phrygia), where he converted the wife of a Roman proconsul. The proconsul retaliated and aroused hostile Jews to crucify Philip in Hierapolis, Turkey. He may have gone to present-day France, since he is the only apostle associated with Gaul.

Bartholomew-Nathanael may have accompanied one of the other disciples. One tradition says he was with Philip in Turkey, another with Thomas in India, or Matthew in Ethiopia, or with Jude in Armenia, and then to southern Arabia, where he was flayed and then crucified. His tomb is in present-day Derbend, Azerbaijan (New Testament Albanopolis) on the west coast of the Caspian Sea.

Thomas seemed to have been active in the regions east of Syria and, according to ancient Marthoma Christians of India, founded Christian communities there, where he died at the hands of several soldiers. Matthew reportedly went to Persia and then Ethiopia, being mortally wounded in Egypt as he was returning to Palestine.

Thaddaeus or Jude went to Armenia, perhaps with Bartholomew and Thomas. He probably spent time evangelizing in Syria and northern Persia, where he was beaten to death by angry pagan priests. Simon the Zealot traveled to Egypt, Cyrene, Africa, Mauritania, Britain, Lybia, and Persia, where he was killed after refusing to present an offering to the sun god. One tradition suggests he was killed and buried in Lincolnshire, Britain.

> **Johannine Literature**
>
> The apostle John penned a gospel, three letters, and an apocalypse in the waning years of the first century. His writings revealed the context of Christianity at that time. First, John utilized the term *Logos* to identify Jesus in the prologue to his Gospel: Jesus was the divine Word that took on human flesh and blood (John 1:14). This Greek term meant 'word' or 'reason,' and those knowledgeable with Greek philosophy would have been familiar with it. Second, light-dark imagery occurred in all of his writings. This dichotomy clearly distinguished between good and evil, Christianity and other religions. Third, the apocalyptic genre of the Revelation of Jesus Christ set late first century Christianity in a time of persecution that was looking to the end times when Jesus would return with the heavenly host in judgment to condemn the wicked, but raise up the righteous.
>
> John was the last of the New Testament authors. These documents were most certainly written for Christians. At the same time, John had his eye of those outside of Christianity and, no doubt, hoped that those outside of Christianity had their ears opened to his words.

First Century Pagan Religious Life

Religious life among the pagans was very eclectic. The multiplicity of religious beliefs and practices reflected the many different peoples and their religions that comprised the Roman Empire. Two important traits were polytheism and syncretism. Polytheism—two or more gods and/or goddesses within a particular religion—was quite common. Syncretism—mixing religious beliefs and practices from two or more religions—was a natural result of these polytheistic religions in the empire. As peoples and religions were brought together under the umbrella of the empire, it was not unusual for a polytheist to add deities to his current list of deities.

Popular Roman religion incorporated a myriad of deities, spiritual beings, and practices into the lives of the people. The names of the Greek deities were transformed into corresponding Roman deities, e.g., the chief Greek god, Zeus, became the Roman god, Jupiter; the Greek god of fertility and wine, Dionysus, became the Roman deity, Bacchus; and the Greek goddess of love and beauty, Aphrodite, became the Roman goddess, Venus. Each deity had a particular day when detailed rituals were utilized, led by priests or priestesses. There were also myriad lesser deities or spiritual beings—*Lares*—that were more domestic in nature, protecting home and family, road and traveler. A statue of a favored *Lar* would be placed in the home and honored in hopes that it would protect and bless that household.

In addition to the deities adapted from the Greeks, the Romans also followed several

> **Persecution of Christians**
>
> Initially, Christianity enjoyed religious toleration in the Roman Empire by its close connection to Judaism. At the same time, just as serious tensions developed between Jerusalem and Rome, leading to riots and uprisings. So also tensions arose between Christianity and the Roman Empire resulting in the persecution of Christians. Nero became emperor of Rome in 54. A decade later, flames engulfed much of Rome for more than a week. The majority of the city lay in a heap of ashes. Looking to transfer the blame from himself, Nero pointed to the Christians as the cause. Tacitus, an early Roman historian, tells us that Christians made a ready target because of their perceived immorality. Nero then persecuted Christians in Rome; they were torn apart and devoured by wild animals, crucified, and burned alive, all for the amusement of the Roman onlookers. Nero did not persecute Christians for their religious beliefs; however, this set a precedent that would not be forgotten by Emperor Domitian at the end of the first century and other Roman emperors in the second and third centuries.

"mystery religions." The mystery religions included Isis and Osiris from Egypt, Mithra from Persia, Attis and Cybele from Phrygia, and Dionysius from Thrace. Many of these religions required fertility rites and ritualistic meals. The details of their rituals were kept secret from outsiders. Only initiates were enlightened with their secret knowledge (*gnosis*; thus, the adjective "mystery"). Influenced by the syncretism of the day, many followers were initiated into more than one of these mysteries producing their own hybrid religion.

The Roman religions also had a civil dimension. Over time the Emperor had come to be viewed as a deity. While the early emperors initially dismissed this acclamation, Caligula (12-41, ruled 37-41), Nero, and Domitian (51-96, ruled 81-96) very much emphasized this self-designation in the first century AD. For polytheistic and syncretistic religious adherents, bowing in homage before an emperor or his image was of little religious concern. Jews and Christians, on the other hand, were monotheists and so would not acknowledge or revere a deity other than the one true God. Emperor worship was intended to unify the empire, but caused divisions for Jewish and Christian citizens.

This differentiation caused more than a few dilemmas for Christianity. Christians were labelled "atheists" (without gods), because they rejected the multiple gods of the empire. In addition, they were thought to be anti-social in that they were opposed to syncretism and were accused of being anti-patriotic because of their rejection of emperor worship.

Clement of Rome

Clement (c.92-101) was a head pastor or bishop of Rome, purportedly the fourth after Peter, Linus (c. 66-78), and Anacletus (c. 79-91). While little is known about his personal life, later patristic authors claim that he heard both Peter and Paul teach in Rome and was placed into his episcopal office by Peter. During his Roman bishopric, Clement wrote a letter to the Christians in Corinth, the First Epistle of Clement to the Corinthians. This was one of the earliest interpretations of New Testament theology.

The occasion of his missive was a disruptive situation in Corinth. An influential faction had deposed the presbyters (elders)—bishop and deacons—and replaced them with their own men. Clement reminded them that God orders the church: Just as the Father sent the Son and the Son the apostles, so the apostles appointed a bishop and deacons in each Christian community. As such, Christians were not to second-guess God, but rather, submit to His divine will as had the prophets and the apostles before them. This subversion of God's will was scandalous, and the guilty must repent. Such contrition was pleasing to God.

Salvation, for Clement, was rooted in the holy passion of Jesus. Sinful beings must repent of their sins, and this repentance looked to the precious blood of Jesus shed upon the cross for the forgiveness of the sins of the entire world. Relying heavily upon imagery of the prophet Isaiah, Clement portrayed Jesus as a sacrificial lamb that bore our sins and received our punishment. The grace and mercy of God that was revealed in Jesus' passion is now given and received, not through good works, but in faith (*First Clement* 32).

In commenting upon the resurrection, Clement utilized the illustration of the phoenix (*First Clement* 25). This avian myth, then thought to be real, referred to a unique bird. After five hundred years of life, it built a nest of frankincense and myrrh. Upon dying, its flesh was transformed into a small worm that grew up and became a new phoenix. Similarly, though the body of a Christian dies, it shall be raised up on the Last Day as happened with Jesus' resurrection.

Clement's advice to the Corinthians was not as a superior to a subordinate. Instead, he wrote on behalf of one stable Christian community to another that was deeply troubled. He wrote not to exert his authority, but to provide evangelical advice to the Corinthians. In so doing, Clement addressed a number of theological issues, and so, began the development of Christian theology after the New Testament.

The Christian Church was birthed and breathed its first breaths in the first century Roman Empire. The immediate concern was heritage and family. With whom or with what would this fledgling religion align? To put it another way, what family name would she take? The most obvious answer was Judaism because Jesus and the first Christians were Jewish. This, however, proved fruitless as Judaism rejected Jesus, persecuted Christianity, and cast Christians out of its Temple and synagogues. Invited by Rome, Christianity immediately and loudly rejected its brand(s) of religion. At the same time, it must be noted that the Christians refrained neither from citing the prophets of the Jewish Old Testament nor from utilizing the nomenclature of Greek philosophy. Nevertheless, the Christian Church extended her religious family and proceeded to chronicle her own unique history. The Christian Church was now ready to take her first steps in the second century.

Massacre on Masada: A Report

Eleazar said to those gathered on Masada: "Since we, long ago, my generous friends, resolved never to be servants to the Romans, nor to any other than to God himself, who alone is the true and just Lord of mankind, the time is now come that obliges us to make that resolution true in practice. And let us not at this time bring a reproach upon ourselves for self-contradiction, while we formerly would not undergo slavery, though it were then without danger, but must now, together with slavery, choose such punishments also as are intolerable; I mean this, upon the supposition that the Romans once reduce us under their power while we are alive. We were the very first that revolted from them, and we are the last that fight against them; and I cannot but esteem it as a favor that God hath granted us, that it is still in our power to die bravely, and in a state of freedom, which hath not been the case of others, who were conquered unexpectedly. It is very plain that we shall be taken within a day's time; but it is still an eligible thing to die after a glorious manner, together with our dearest friends. This is what our enemies themselves cannot by any means hinder, although they be very desirous to take us alive. Nor can we propose to ourselves any more to fight them, and beat them. It had been proper indeed for us to have conjectured at the purpose of God much sooner, and at the very first, when we were so desirous of defending our liberty, and when we received such sore treatment from one another, and worse treatment from our enemies, and to have been sensible that the same God, who had of old taken the Jewish nation into his favor, had now condemned them to destruction; for had he either continued favorable, or been but in a lesser degree displeased with us, he had not overlooked the destruction of so many men, or delivered his most holy city to be burnt and demolished by our enemies. To be sure we weakly hoped to have preserved ourselves, and ourselves alone, still in a state of freedom, as if we had been guilty of no sins ourselves against God, nor been partners with those of others; we also taught other men to preserve their liberty. Wherefore, consider how God hath convinced us that our hopes were in vain, by bringing such distress upon us in the desperate state we are now in, and which is beyond all our expectations; for the nature of this fortress which was in itself unconquerable, hath not proved a means of our deliverance; and even while we have still great abundance of food, and a great quantity of arms, and other necessaries more than we want, we are openly deprived by God himself of all hope of deliverance; for that fire which was driven upon our enemies did not of its own accord turn back upon the wall which we had built; this was the effect of God's anger against us for our manifold sins, which we have been guilty of in a most insolent and extravagant manner with regard to our own countrymen; the punishments of which let us not receive from the Romans, but from God himself, as executed by our own hands; for these will be more moderate than the other. Let our wives die before they are abused, and our children before they have tasted of slavery; and after we have slain them, let us bestow that glorious benefit upon one another mutually, and preserve ourselves in freedom, as an excellent funeral monument for us. But first let us destroy our money and the fortress by fire; for I am well assured that this will be a great grief to the Romans, that they shall not be able to seize upon our bodies, and shall fall of our wealth also; and let us spare nothing but our provisions; for they will be a testimonial when we are dead that we were not subdued for want of necessaries, but that, according to our original resolution, we have preferred death before slavery."

Josephus, *Jewish Wars*, Book 7, chapter 8, paragraph 6.

For Review and Discussion
1. How does Luke's history of Christ and the early Church demonstrate that God's plan of salvation is for the whole world?
2. What shift in focus would have occurred in Judaism after the Romans destroyed Jerusalem?
3. Why were Christians persecuted by both the Jews and the Romans?
4. What could Christians offer to Roman citizens who followed one of the mystery religions? (You may need to research one or more of these groups.)
5. Read the *First Epistle of Clement to the Corinthians* and compare and contrast it to Paul's letters to the same congregation.
6. Research the concept of the *Pax Romana* and relate it to Paul's words in Galatians 4 about the "right time".

For Further Reading
Breasted, James Henry. *Ancient Times: A History of the Early World*. Chicago: Ginn and Company, 1935.

Bright, John. *A History of Israel*. Philadelphia: Westminster Press, 1959.

Clement. *First Epistle of Clement to the Corinthians*.
   http://www.earlychristianwritings.com/1clement.html

Josephus. *Antiquities of the Jews*, and *The War of the Jews*.
   http://www.ccel.org/j/josephus/works/JOSEPHUS.HTM

Maier, Paul. *The First Christians*. New York: Harper & Row, 1976.

2. Apostolic Fathers and Apologists

The Second Century

The Christian church experienced exciting challenges in the second century. The church had to address some of the practical matters of the faith, particularly, baptism and fasting. In addition, the Roman Empire stepped up its persecution of the church. And if those were not enough, doctrinal divisions arose concerning some of the basic teachings of the faith. In the previous century, Jesus and then the apostles had the authority to address these concerns. With the ascension of Jesus and the deaths of the apostles, who or what would speak and act determinatively on behalf of the Christian church and its faith? Several authorities would rise to the occasion.

Apostolic Fathers

The Apostolic Fathers are the first generation of post-apostolic writers in the Christian church. Their lives overlapped those of the apostles, and so, their writings began at the very end of the first century and carried over into the first half of the second century. The great value of the Apostolic Fathers was their chronological and theological proximity to the New Testament era. Just as Clement of Rome (+c.100) had been a student of Peter and Paul, so also Polycarp (+c.155) studied at the feet of the apostle John. These Christians were among the first to hear and read and study the New Testament documents and write works reflecting the New Testament message of God's gift of Jesus.

The Didache

Among the initial concerns of the fledgling Christian church were catechesis, worship, and ministry. The New Testament writings clearly advocated all three, but did not provide many specifics for practical application. The *Didache* ("the Teaching"), probably written in Syria around 100 AD, is the earliest known Christian document after the New Testament which served as an instructional manual in the church.

The *Didache*, similar to Wisdom literature of the Old Testament, began with instruction on two very different paths that may be followed in life. The way of death was the way of everything that is evil and sinful, e.g., murder and adultery, greed and boasting. In contrast, the way of life was the way of the Ten Commandments and Jesus' prescriptions in the Sermon on the Mount, such as, "pray for your enemies" and "turn the other cheek" (Matthew 5-7). It was one or the other: either one was a Christian or not; one was either saved or condemned.

Concerning the rites of Christianity, the *Didache* answered the very practical questions of how and when to carry out the early sacramental acts. In baptism, running water was preferable to warm water. Prior to baptism, both the baptized and baptizer ought to fast. In fasting, Christians ought to fast on Wednesdays and Fridays, and so, distinguish themselves from the Jews who fasted on Mondays and Thursdays. Christians should pray the Lord's Prayer three times daily. Only the baptized were allowed to partake of the Lord's Supper, and Eucharistic prayers were provided, including a prayer to be prayed over the loaf:

> We thank you, our Father, for the life and knowledge that you have revealed through Jesus, your child. To you be glory forever. As this piece was scattered over the hills and then was brought together and made one, so let your church be brought together from the ends of the earth into your Kingdom. For yours is the glory and power through Jesus Christ forever. (*Didache*, 9.3-4)

The offices of the ministry mentioned in the *Didache* addressed a unique situation in the history of the church: the ministry of traveling prophets and apostles overlapped that of a bishop and deacons ministering in a specific locale. (The former pair of offices quickly disappeared in the second century.) Prophets and apostles were to be shown respect and honor. At the same time, they were not above the careful scrutiny of the local Christian community. For example, one who stayed more than one day, possibly two, was certainly not a true apostle, and a prophet was required to live according to what he preached. The offices of bishop and deacon share in the ministry of the prophet and apostle, and so, deserved the same respect and honor.

The *Didache* did not legalistically try to regulate every aspect of the Christian life and church. Instead, it simply addressed practical matters by interpreting the New Testament witness and then drawing applications from it. In so doing, it provided godly guidance for the very young Christian church in Syria, and would serve as a basis for other church manuals in the subsequent decades and centuries.

Shepherd of Hermas

A first century Christian apocalypse, similar to the book of Revelation, is among the early writings of the Apostolic Fathers. Hermas of Rome received five visions and twelve mandates. The third vision addressed repentance. In it, an elderly woman showed a tower to Hermas. The six men constructing it gathered stones; some came from land and others had been dragged out of the sea. Those from the water fit together perfectly in the construction of the tower. Those from the land were cast aside; they did not fit and were irreparably cracked. Some were thrown near the tower and others far away. Many of the latter desired to roll into the water, but fell into a fire.

This imagery was an analogy of the church. The stones from the sea were the faithful, whereas the stone from the land were the unrighteous. Some of the latter were too far removed to repent. Those lying near the tower, if they repented while there was still time, they would not be condemned eternally, but rather, would be brought into the church.

The view of Christ, in this work, is known as "adoptionism." Jesus lived as a common human being who was adopted by God the Father at His baptism at which time He received the Spirit. This view was rejected by the Council of Nicaea in the fourth century.

Ignatius

Ignatius (+c.110) was a bishop of Antioch in Syria, an early center of Christianity. There the followers of Jesus were first called Christians (Acts 11:26), and the Christian community served as the home base for Paul's missionary journeys (Acts 13 and 15). Arrested for being a Christian, Ignatius was transported under armed guard to Rome. During this journey, Ignatius was allowed to meet with church leaders and send letters to the congregations under his pastoral care. Seven letters like those of Paul addressed a variety of doctrines and practices in Christianity. Once in Rome, Ignatius, having been thrown to wild beasts, died a martyr's death.

Martyrdom, for Ignatius, was a noble calling and not to be shirked. He pleaded to the Christians in Rome not to free him from his captors, but rather allow him to be put to death in this life so that he may be with Jesus in the life to come. Ignatius saw his martyrdom as obedience to the divine command, "take up your cross and follow me" (Mark 8:34).

For Ignatius, the office of the ministry was three-fold: bishop (ἐπίσκοπος, "overseer" or "supervisor"), elder (πρεσβύτερος, "presbyter"), and deacon (διάκονος, "minister" or "servant"). The bishop represented either the Father or the Son, speaking and acting on behalf of God. As such, he was to be obeyed. Neither baptism nor the Lord's Supper was to be administered apart from his approval and presence. The elder or presbyter stood in the stead of Jesus and the apostles, while Ignatius compared the deacon to Jesus and other servants in the church. A hierarchy of offices was clear: there was only one bishop in a particular community, who held the sole authority. The elders served under the bishop, and the deacons under the elders. At the same time, all three offices worked together in a harmony like a melodious chord from the strings of a harp.

> **Martyrdom**
>
> A martyr was a witness. The term was initially used of the apostles who witnessed the baptism, ministry, and crucifixion and resurrection of Jesus. The title was quickly applied to all Christians who were put to death – beheaded, burned alive, thrown to the gladiators and wild beasts – because of their confession of Jesus and the Christian faith. Though not the first martyr, Ignatius' letters helped to develop the theology of martyrdom.
>
> Of greater import, martyrdom intimately connected the martyr to the crucifixion of Jesus. And if the Christian was connected to the crucifixion of Jesus, then he was also intimately connected to the resurrection of Jesus. Thus, martyrdom was not to be feared or avoided, but embraced and greatly honored.

The powerful words of Ignatius (see illustration) thundered loudly in the early second century Roman Empire. Christians would not be intimidated by persecution. Rather they proclaimed boldly and confidently the message of God's love in Jesus and the Gospel of forgiveness even in the face of a grisly death.

Polycarp

Persecution of Christianity persisted for several centuries. Whereas Ignatius addressed the theology of martyrdom, the *Passion of Polycarp* portrayed an actual martyr, that of the Smyrnean bishop (+c.155), and held him up as a godly model. It remains the most ancient example of this literary genre after the New Testament.

With an arrest warrant issued for Polycarp, he desired to suffer and die for Jesus, but the faithful swayed him to flee. He traveled from home to home until one of his servants was tortured and betrayed his whereabouts. Upon his arrest, Polycarp ate and drank with his captors and was then permitted a time of prayer. Following this, he rode a donkey into town where the chief of police was named Herod.

Hostile words and aggressive actions escalated. The chief of police demanded with threats of violence that Polycarp offer a sacrifice to Caesar, but Polycarp refused. At the arena, the governor commanded that Polycarp condemn the Christians as "atheists" (that is, those who did not acknowledge the pagan gods of Rome and thus were considered not being godly citizens). Instead, looking at the pagans in attendance, Polycarp condemned them as atheists. Threatened with being burned alive, Polycarp fearlessly confessed that he was a Christian, saved by Jesus, and a servant of Him as King. Standing upon the pyre, he prayed:

> Trajan and Christians
>
> Pliny the Younger, governor of Bithynia, a province in northwest Asia Minor, had to deal with Christians who would not worship the emperor and about whom swirled rumors of immorality. Arresting and torturing two deaconesses, he learned that Christians met regularly to worship Jesus whom they believed was their God. At this worship, they participated in a simple meal. They rejected criminal behavior and sought to live pious lives. Uncertain as to how he should react, Pliny sent a letter to Emperor Trajan (98-117) requesting advice. Trajan responded with this guidance: (1) the government should neither seek out Christians, nor act upon anonymous allegations; (2) if evidence was provided, Christians must be punished; and (3) apostatizing Christians (that is, those who abandoned the faith) would be acquitted.

> O Lord God Almighty, Father of Your beloved and blessed Son, Jesus Christ,... I bless You that You have considered me worthy of this day and this hour, that I might receive a place among the number of martyrs in the cup of Your Christ, to the resurrection of eternal life, both of soul and body, in the incorruptibility of the Holy Spirit. . . . For this reason, indeed for all thing, I praise You, I bless You, I glorify You, through the eternal and heavenly High Priest, Jesus Christ, Your beloved Son, through whom to You with him and the Holy Spirit be glory both now and for the ages to come. Amen. (*Passion of Polycarp*, 14.2-3)

The fire was lit, but did not consume Polycarp. Instead it produced a beautiful aroma. Finally, a soldier pierced him with a knife, and Polycarp's blood extinguished the flames. These events stunned the pagans.

Immediately following the death of Polycarp, the Jews petitioned the officials to cremate his body, lest the Christians worship Polycarp. The Christians, however, preserved his burnt remains, holding him as an imitator of Jesus' passion.

Heresies and Heretics

The word, heresy (Greek, αἵρεσις, for "choice"), came to be used specifically as a term to identify wrong choices or teachings, which countered the correct Christian faith as reported in the Bible. While they gave alternate views, they usually led advocates to depart from the centrality of Jesus as Savior.

Gnosticism

Gnosis, a Greek term that means "knowledge," came to be associated with a number of loosely related pseudo-Christian sects that claimed another *gnosis* concerning Jesus and matters of salvation. This *gnosis* was mystical and preserved in oral tradition, kept secret, revealed only to the initiated. Obtaining *gnosis* was the only means by which one's spirit could be delivered from its entrapment to flesh and soul.

Gnosticism originated outside of Christianity and had a very specific worldview: dualism. This dualism was outlined in a complex cosmology. There was a single thing, a "monad," that was considered the "first principle." Through a series of devolving replications, multiple series of aeons (or ages) were produced. At the lowest level of aeons, a dualism developed that pitted good versus evil, spirit versus matter. This dualism was declared to be the reality of this world. The general maladies of this world and of human life especially were explained as being a result of good spirits trapped in evil bodies and souls.

> **Heresy and Orthodoxy**
>
> **Orthodoxy** refers to right, correct, proper, or straight praise and teaching of divine revelation. **Heterodoxy** refers to "other" praise and teaching of divine revelation, either through addition or subtraction. In sharp contrast is **heresy**: false doctrines and practices which divide. Heresy came from both outside and inside the Christian church.
>
> In the face of heresy, a group of theologians called **apologists** defended the Christian faith. Another group, **polemicists** (often called heresiologists because they studied and critiqued heresy), attacked the opponents of Christianity and publicly confessed the Christian faith in their writings. Both clearly delineated the orthodox Christian faith for the faithful who might otherwise be ignorant or confused by heretical

Influential Christian Gnostics at the beginning and into the middle of the second century included Cerinthus (c.100-170), Saturninus or Satornil of Antioch (c.125), Basilides (c.90-138), and Valentius (c.150). Most of their writings have been lost or destroyed. A few fragments are extant and other small portions were preserved in Christian polemic writings. The *Gospel of Truth* by Valentius or one of his students was discovered in 1945 at Nag Hammadi, an ancient library in Egypt that contained almost fifty volumes of Gnostic texts. (See chapter 20)

Different groups of Christian Gnostics had diverse beliefs; however, a number of teachings can be attributed to them as a whole. First, they rejected the nature of the world as revealed in the creation narrative of Genesis. The earth was not created by the one true God, but by an evil demiurge (a Platonic-type creator). Thus, this material world was not good, but evil. Second, since the material of this world was evil, then Jesus, who is good, could not have taken on flesh and blood. Instead, they taught a form of Docetism (Greek, δοκεῖν, *Dokein*, "to seem" or "appear"). Jesus was spirit only and only "appeared to be human." Third, they rejected the Christian doctrines associated with the crucifixion and resurrection of Jesus. Salvation came not through the atoning work of Jesus upon the cross, but rather, through initiation into a mystical *gnosis*. Since Jesus did not have a physical body, He could not rise physically from the dead. Consequently, the human body would not be raised from the dead and participate in salvation.

Gnosticism began with a dualistic worldview that did not match that of Christianity, but then subsumed elements of the Christian message and Christian vocabulary into its own belief system. This proved very tempting to many Christians who could not distinguish between "Christian" Gnosticism and Christianity. "Christian Gnosticism," though, was not Christian, but Gnosticism only and soon came under Christian condemnation.

Marcion

Marcion (+c.160) was born in Sinope of Pontus (the Roman provice south of the Black Sea in Asia Minor). His father was the bishop and excommunicated him, reportedly for "seducing a virgin." Relocating in Rome, he became a member of the church there, but also studied under Cerdo (taught c.135-145), a Gnostic. As Marcion began to lean strongly toward Gnosticism, the church in Rome also excommunicated him, and he began his own church. While it is debated among scholars whether he was truly a Gnostic, he was most certainly a dualist and a Docetist.

The principle heresy of Marcion was his dichotomy between two gods—one of the Old and one of the New Testament. The god of the Old Testament corresponded to the evil demiurge of the Gnostics. This deity was legalistic, delivering multitudinous laws, and vengeful, threatening to punish the children of sinful parents. His requirements of animal sacrifices revealed that he was bloodthirsty and his desire for battle and power showed him a despot. This god reveled in the law and was not worthy of worship by Christians, said Marcion.

The god of the New Testament was wholly different; he emphasized grace and mercy. Jesus revealed this deity, the god of love. Whereas the Old Testament condemned all, the New Testament forgave all. Jesus came to overcome the god of the Old Testament. Marcion's error was not that he distinguished between the Old and New Testaments, between law and grace, but that he saw no correlation between the two.

Marcion supported his views with his edited versions of select writings from the apostle Paul and the Evangelist Luke. He rejected the Old Testament and non-Pauline epistles in the New Testament witness because they put undo stress upon the law and the Jewish religion. He utilized some of Paul's epistles when they pointed to God's grace as it was revealed in the life and work of Jesus. In addition, he produced an edited version of the Gospel according to St. Luke that removed any connection between Jesus and the god of the Old Testament.

While Marcion shared a few traits with Gnosticism, he also distinguished himself from them. He did not claim to have a secret *gnosis* that was required for salvation nor did he adopt the cosmology of the Gnostics. Because Marcion came out of the Christian church, yet was very much influenced by Gnosticism, he was able to merge the two belief-systems much more subtly than had his Gnostic predecessors. By forming another community opposed to the Christian church, Marcion was one of the most divisive heretics in the second century.

Montanism

During the last half of the second century in Phrygia, a movement erupted that attempted to revitalize the Christian church which some perceived as complacent. A key leader was Montanus (c.110-c.195), a Cybeline priest (a Roman cult which worshiped a "mother goddess"), who was converted to Christianity and was baptized around 155, although little else is known about him. This movement, known as Montanism, sought to connect Christianity back to the work of the Holy Spirit in the Old Testament prophets and in the apostles on Pentecost. It also sought to sharpen the church's focus forward with a renewed expectation of the End Times.

Following his baptism, Montanus claimed to be the mouthpiece of the Holy Spirit. He had visions and began to prophesy. Later Christians reported that, when Montanus spoke on behalf of God, he spoke in the first person: "I am the Holy Spirit" or "I am the Lord." Two female founders, Prisca and Maximilla, served as prophetesses with him. It appears that their prophecies primarily addressed morality.

According to Montanism, the Christian church had become morally lax. Widows and widowers were allowed to remarry. Fasting was not sufficiently practiced. In the face of persecution, Christians were allowed to flee. Thus, Montanism called for a renewed and vigorous morality in the Christian church. Christians must quickly turn their lives around, because the final advent of Jesus was imminent.

> **Ebionites**
>
> This second century Jewish sect of Christianity exhibited a rigorous lifestyle east of the Promised Land. Epiphanius (+410), a heresiologist, preserved in part their *Gospel According to the Ebionites* and noted a few of their heresies. According to their Gospel, at Jesus' baptism by John, the heavenly Father added, "This day I have begotten you" and a bright light shone upon Jesus. According to Epiphanius, the Ebionites denied the divine nature of Jesus, claiming Jesus was created like an archangel, though much greater. The Ebionites did not have much interaction with the Christian church and quickly faded out of existence.

The prophetic utterances of Montanus, Prisca, and Maximilla claimed that the End Times were at hand. The Heavenly Jerusalem would soon descend upon the town of Pepuza in Phrygia. Stirred up by hope of the final apocalypse, many Montanists moved to Pepuza awaiting the return of the Lord.

Rather than revitalizing the Christian church, Montanus created another sect that was only nominally connected to Christianity. The immediate revelations of the Montanists disenfranchised them from those who held solely to the prophetic and apostolic witnesses of the Old and New Testaments. Their moral rigors were legalistic and their prophecies of the End Times contradicted the words of Jesus that no one can know the day (Matthew 24:42). Consequently, Montanism, which began with good intentions, went terribly awry.

Justin Martyr

Justin (c.100-c.165), one of the more influential Greek apologists, was born into a pagan family in Samaria. Intensely interested in matters spiritual and philosophical, he studied Stoicism, then the philosophies of Aristotle, then Pythagoras, and finally Plato. After converting to Christianity, Justin became a staunch defender of the Christian faith, penning a number of apologies (literally "defenses"). He died a martyr's death in Rome.

A Jewish rabbi named Trypho (c.70-c.135) complained that Christianity had forsaken many of the Old Testament laws. For example, Christians no longer worshipped on the Sabbath (Saturday), but the Sunday of Jesus' resurrection. In his *Dialogue with Trypho*, Justin argued that the new covenant in Jesus superceded the old covenant given to Moses. Even Jeremiah had prophesied this change (Jereremiah 31:31-32). The many Old Testament laws were not the ends, but the means; they prepared for and pointed the Jews to Jesus. Trypho disagreed and held that obedience to the Old Testament law merits righteousness before God. In sharp contrast, Justin confessed that righteousness before God comes through the merits of the crucified and risen Jesus, and through faith in the gracious works of God as Abraham had believed. Justin extensively and positively cited the Old Testament in this dialogue to show that Christianity was not a religion divorced from the Old Testament, but the true fulfillment of authentic Judaism.

The Roman Empire had criticized the immorality of Christianity and violently persecuted her (see chapter 1). In his *First Apology* and *Second Apology*, Justin defended Christianity against these misunderstandings and hostilities. While admitting that some Christians were immoral, Justin argued that Christians were not only moral, but their morality exceeded that of the average pagan in the empire. Christians paid their taxes and obeyed the laws of the government. The average Roman citizens emulated the immorality of their Roman pantheon and only obeyed the law when they might be caught and punished by the temporal government. Christians, though, had much higher moral standards: they obeyed the law at all times because God was omniscient and condemned eternally.

The Roman Empire honored ancient ideas, but often spurned innovation, and so showed contempt toward Christianity as a new religion. Justin's defense was two-fold: Christianity was not a new religion, but a fulfillment of an old religion, Judaism; and the many prophesies in the Old Testament pointed ahead to the New Testament. In addition, Christianity was older than ancient Greek philosophy, so that, Justin suggested, Plato had been dependent upon the writings of Moses. (See his *First Apology* 59.)

Justin argued that Christianity was worthy neither of the condemnations of the Jews nor the persecutions of the Romans. Not only should it be tolerated, but Christianity should be recognized as the truest religion and the basis for all philosophy.

Irenaeus

Irenaeus (c.130-c.200) was a student of Polycarp in Smyrna, studied in Rome, became a presbyter, and finally served as the bishop of Lyon in Gaul. His magisterial polemic, *Against the Heresies*, provides invaluable data concerning the heresies of Gnosticism and Marcionism, and the early Christian reaction to them. After detailing the heresies of the various Gnostic sects of his day in Book One, Irenaeus rebutted them in Books Two through Five. Utilizing reason, he argued that God the Creator is the only God. The heretical claim that there is another being above or beyond the Creator creates an insatiable desire to add more and more deities at higher and higher levels. In the end, the Gnostics have no truly omnipotent God. In the last book (Book Five), Irenaeus refuted the Docetic tendencies of the Gnostics. In a Pauline fashion, he argued that if Jesus did not become a human, then how could He save humans? Instead, Jesus came to deliver both body and spirit. This occurred on the cross where Jesus' body was torn and His blood was shed for the forgiveness of sins. And then in the Eucharist, the Christian eats the body and blood of Jesus and therein receives the forgiveness of sins earned by Jesus upon the cross (Book 5.1.3).

Irenaeus cited the Word of God and the tradition of the church to refute Gnostic heresy. In no uncertain terms, Jesus spoke of the true God as one God in the four Gospels. Inspired by the Holy Spirit, the prophets in the Old Testament and the apostles in the New Testament taught no differently of God. Thus, all of the life-giving doctrines of Christianity has been carefully preserved in the Christian church like a treasure on deposit in a bank.

The heresies of the Gnostics were untenable and unbearable to Irenaeus. He was not so much intolerant of the heterodox as he was enamored with orthodoxy. The Christian faith, as revealed by the prophets and apostles, and preserved in the church, was the only message of salvation for a fallen world, consequently, the message of Jesus and the Gospel could not be silenced or tainted, but rather, must be proclaimed in its purity to all the world.

Canon

Canon is a Greek term that refers to a straight edge, a bar, or a ruler. It became a technical term in Christianity that referred to the sacred and authoritative writings recognized by the church as written by men and inspired by the Holy Spirit (2 Peter 1:21). In the first century AD, the writings of the Old Testament were considered canonical by Christianity (2 Timothy 3:16), while the books of the New Testament were being composed, read, and disseminated throughout the church. In the second century, a plethora of New Testament-like volumes, not all in harmony with the others, raised the question of the content of a New Testament canon. The Apostolic Fathers did not delineate a New Testament canon. Rather they cited as sacred and authoritative the writings of the apostles and evangelists that were recognized by the church as divinely inspired.

Marcion created the first known attempt at a New Testament canon. As previously noted, he recognized only his edited versions of the Gospel according to St. Luke and the Pauline Epistles. Another attempt was the *Diatesseron*, Tatian's (+c.180) harmonization of the Gospels into a single narrative that was used in Syria. Adding to the confusion, there were other supposed gospels, e.g., Gospel of Thomas, Gospel of Peter, Proto-Gospel of James, along with other acts, epistles, and apocalypses, e.g., Acts of John, Paul's Third Letter to the Corinthians, and an Apocalypse of Peter.

The Muratorian Fragment (late 2nd cent.) of unknown authorship provided an early and somewhat complete list. It cited Luke and John as the third and fourth Gospels, followed by the Acts of the Apostles. It included John's apocalypse and the Pauline epistles, but excluded Hebrews and the general epistles, excepting 1 and 2 John. The Wisdom of Solomon and an Apocalypse of Peter were recognized, while the Shepherd of Hermas was recommended for reading, but was not to be considered canonical.

By the end of the second century, Christian teachers not only noted volumes that belonged in the New Testament canon, but also prescribed those that did not belong. The Muratorian Fragment rejected Paul's so-called epistles to the Christian communities in Laodicea and Alexandria as forgeries by the followers of Marcion. Among the heretics, the Ebionites used only the Gospel according to St. Matthew, others only Mark, Marcion only Luke, and Valentinus only John. Concerning the gospels, Irenaeus argued that they must be four, because there are four parts of the world and four corresponding winds. Therefore, he said, it was necessary that orthodox Christians have four Gospels, no more and no less, to carry the message of Jesus and the Gospel into all the world.

The importance of a clearly delineated New Testament canon cannot be overstated. As the second century church began to discuss a variety of Christian doctrines and practices, particularly for drawing a line between orthodoxy and heterodoxy, the church needed a collection of sacred and authoritative writings. It needed a New Testament canon to complement the Old Testament canon. While not completed in the second century, the process had certainly begun.

> *Infancy Gospel of Thomas*
>
> A Gnostic text from the first half of the second century claimed to have been authored by Thomas the Israelite. Portraying the childhood of Jesus beginning at the age of five, it ends his twelfth year when Jesus and his parents visited Jerusalem. The tales were of two types: miraculous and malicious, and often overlapped. For example, a story is recorded that while Jesus was rather young, He fashioned twelve birds from clay. When a Jew complained to Joseph that his son should not have done so on the Sabbath, the youngster clapped his hands and the birds flew away. On another occasion, a young boy bumped into Jesus. Jesus struck the boy dead with mere words. When the parents of the dead boy complained, Jesus blinded them. These tales are quite interesting and they describe a time in Jesus' life of which the Gospels according Matthew, Mark, Luke, and John are silent. At the same time, this text portrays a very different Jesus than do the Gospels and thus it is not counted among the canonical gospels, but as an apocryphal gnostic text.

Tradition

Closely connected to canon was tradition as an authority in the Christian church. Tradition means "handing down" and had its basis in the Old Testament. The God of the Israelites was often referred to as the "God of Abraham, Isaac, and Jacob." The faith of one generation was preserved and handed down to the next generation (see 1 Corinthians 15:1-3). Paul instructed Timothy to "believe that which had been handed down to him" from his grandmother and mother, Lois and Eunice (2 Timothy 1:5). In 1 Corinthians 11, Paul speaks positively of tradition, since he had received the Words of Institution of the Lord's Supper from the Lord.

This emphasis upon tradition and its importance for the Christian church carried over into the second century. Although delineation of the New Testament canon was important, it did not solve all of the doctrinal and practical concerns of the day. Just as Satan quoted the Old Testament to Jesus in the wilderness (Matt 4), so the heretics often cited the New Testament to the second century Christians. Both Satan and the heretics utilized these canonical writings; however, they misinterpreted them so as to lead Christians astray.

Something called the *regula fidei* ("rule of faith") was the answer at least in part to this problem. According to Irenaeus, the most basic teachings of the Christian faith were preserved in the Christian church and believed by all Christians in a creed-like formula.

> [The church] believes in one God, the Father Almighty, Maker of heaven, and earth, and the sea, and all things that are in them; and in one Christ Jesus, the Son of God, who became incarnate for our salvation; and in the Holy Spirit, who proclaimed through the prophets the dispensations of God, and the advent and the birth from a virgin, and the passion, and the resurrection from the dead, and the ascension into heaven in the flesh of the beloved Christ Jesus, our Lord, and His future manifestation from heaven in the glory of the Father "to gather all things up into one." (*Against the Heresies*, 1.10)

These doctrines Jesus had taught to the apostles and the apostles to the bishops and the bishops of one generation to the next, but the heretics were not part of the Christian church. Their interpretations of the Holy Scriptures were invalid. The one Christian church had one *regula fidei* and Irenaeus illustrated it in this fashion: just as the rays of the one sun shone similarly throughout the world, so the preaching of the one Christian faith was not diverse but unified as it illumined all peoples.

The *regula fidei* incorporated the basic doctrines of the Christian faith and was non-negotiable and rejection of the *regula fidei* was a rejection of Christianity. While it did not supplant the biblical canon as an authority in the early church, it was based upon the biblical canon and certainly complemented it. Moreover, it served the church well in defending the Christian faith, in catechesis and confession of the Christian faith. Furthermore, it signaled the development of

---

Easter and the Quatrodeciman Controversy

The first Christians were Jewish, observing Sabbath on Saturday. Sunday, however, quickly supplanted it as the principle and most holy day of the week because it was the day of Jesus' resurrection from the dead. The Lord's Day (Rev 1.10), as it was often called, was celebrated weekly as a day of worship. Easter was celebrated annually, becoming the oldest and most venerable day in the Christian church. This annual celebration of the Resurrection coincided with the Jewish feast of Passover. The dating of the resurrection in the second century resulted in the Quatrodeciman Controversy. The Quatrodecimists (fourteen-ists) in Asia Minor observed Easter on the fourteenth day of Nissan corresponding to the Jewish calendar. When Pope Victor (+199) argued that Easter must always fall on a Sunday, the actual day of the week of the Resurrection, a controversy erupted. The controversy continued to smolder until the Council of Nicaea (325) declared that Easter be celebrated on the Sunday following the vernal equinox.

tradition, the beginning of an official orthodoxy in Christianity, which ultimately was preserved in the ecumenical creeds.

The individuals identified as apologists and polemicists often crossed categories. Justin, for example, in defending the morality of Christianity, attacked the immorality of the Roman deities. And in attacking the heresies of the Gnostics, Irenaeus defended the orthodoxy of Christianity. More significantly, they added two basic and useful literary genres to the corpus of second century Christian literature: apology and polemic. And in so doing, they greatly benefited the Christian church in protecting her from heresy and better understanding her own orthodoxy.

Thus, the second century Christian church produced a host of authorities. The words of Jesus and the inspired utterances of the apostles and the evangelists were preserved as the witness of the New Testament, while the apocryphal witnesses were rejected. The Christian church preserved the doctrines from Jesus and then the apostles. Bishops taught and apologists defended these. Martyrs publicly proclaimed these in the arena and Polemicists with their pens. These authorities powerfully confirmed, secured, and publicly proclaimed the Christian faith in the face of practical concerns, persecution, and heresy.

For Review and Discussion

1. Look at several chapters of *The Didache* (in translation) and compare its description of worship to a traditional Sunday service today.
2. Had you lived in the second century, how would you react to Ignatius' idea of martyrdom?
3. What aspects of Gnosticism seem to survive even in our present society (think about popular movies or television shows)?
4. How did Montanism drift away from basic Christian teachings? Could this happen today with other Christian groups?
5. Why was it necessary to develop a canon and a *regula fidei* at this time in Christian history?

For Further Reading

Campenhausen, Hans von. *The Fathers of the Greek Church*. Stanley Godman, trans. New York: Pantheon Books, Inc., 1959.
Cullmann, Oscar. *The Early Church*. London: SCM Press, Ltd., 1956.
Didache, The. http://www.earlychristianwritings.com/didache.html
Dunn, James D. G. *Jews and Christians: The Parting of the Ways, AD 70-150*. Grand Rapids, MI: Wm. B. Eerdmans, 1999.
Esler, Philip F. *The Early Christian World*. New York: Routledge, 2004.
Goppelt, Leonhard. *Apostolic and Post-Apostolic Times*. Robert A. Guelich, trans. London: Adam and Charles Black, 1970.
Ignatius of Antioch. http://www.earlychristianwritings.com/ignatius.html
Lightfoot, J. B. and J. R. Harmer, eds. *The Apostolic Fathers*. 5 volumes. Grand Rapids: Baker Book House, 1984 reprint of 1891 edition.
Pelikan, Jaroslav. *The Christian Tradition: The Emergence of the Catholic Tradition (100-600)*. Chicago: University of Chicago Press, 1975.

3. Persecution and Confession

The Third Century

The Christian church experienced dangerous, yet productive challenges in the third century. The Roman Empire stepped up its persecution of Christians with new and innovative methods being applied in empire-wide attempts to eradicate the church. Individual Christians suffered willingly, but the church responded in a variety of fashions. In addition, heretics did not wilt in the face of orthodoxy, but rather these false teachers again and again spewed forth their false doctrines. The Christian church counteracted persecution and heresy by responding tenaciously and continuing to develop her doctrines and practices in line with God's self-disclosure in Jesus.

Perpetua

One of the unique reports of martyrdom is the record of a young Christian woman named Perpetua (+203). Emperor Lucius Septimius Severus (193-211), who brutally ruled the Roman Empire, allowed for the chronic persecution of Christianity. Maltreatment was especially cruel in Syria and his homeland of Africa. Though he did not actively promote persecution of the church, local authorities often did. Many Christians died a martyr's death, particularly in the northern African cities of Alexandria, Madaura, and Carthage.

At the beginning of the third century, a band of Christian catechumens (those who were studying to become full members of the Christian community) were arrested and imprisoned in Carthage. Perpetua, a mother of an infant son and one of the arrested catechumens, chronicled their final days in her diary, later titled *The Passion of Perpetua and Felicitas*. Three times her father visited her and begged her to recant the Christian faith for the sake of her father, family, and son, but she refused. While in prison, Perpetua had been baptized, and so, as she said, she had a new father and family. As such, she disobeyed her earthly father, but longed to be with her heavenly Father. Consequently, she dreamed of their heavenly reunion, and she along with her fellow prisoners rejoiced when the Roman governor sentenced them to death.

Felicitas, another of the arrested catechumens, was pregnant, and so her punishment was to be postponed. Despairing, Perpetua and the others prayed for a speedy delivery so that Felicitas might participate in their godly death. Two days later she birthed a girl. Her joy was two-fold—the joy of her daughter and the joy of martyrdom. In that joy, Perpetua and her band entered the arena where they were scorned and beaten. Perpetua sang a psalm; the others shared a spiritual kiss and supported one another with comforting arms and words of hope. Wild beasts tore some of them apart. Finally, Perpetua assisted a young gladiator to pierce her throat with his sword.

The *Passion of Perpetua and Felicitas* chronicled the martyrdom of this small band of catechumens. Moreover, it held up martyrs as heroes of the Christian faith. Martyrs faithfully trusted in Jesus despite temporal suffering and pain, and desired the joys of eternal life in heaven. Furthermore, one did not have to be a bishop or apologist to "fight the good fight of faith" (1 Timothy 6:12). Women and mothers, as well, could be heroes of the Christian faith.

Fruits of Persecution

Although persecution and martyrdom were frequent throughout the Roman Empire, they created new opportunities for the Christian community. However, bishops warned their people against seeking martyrdom. While martyrs were recognized as a blessing, seeking such a death was not to be the goal of Christian life. As a result a number of doctrines and practices developed at this time.

Martyrdom of catechumens who had not been baptized raised a unique question concerning their salvation. Jesus taught: "Unless one is born of water and the Spirit, he cannot enter the Kingdom of God" (John 3:5). These catechumens had been instructed in the Christian faith, they believed on Jesus, and yet they had not been baptized with water according to the words of Jesus. The concern was raised: What was their eternal destiny? Many of the first Christians argued that a martyr was baptized in blood, and this was sufficient for salvation because in both the water and the blood (1 John 5:6) baptisms, Christians participated in Jesus' crucifixion and resurrection. Because many Christians who had been baptized in water were later martyred, the "baptism of blood" was often referred to as a "second baptism." Unfortunately, some argued that the "baptism of blood" was even greater than the baptism of water, which then detracted from the comfort of Christian baptism for "all nations" (Matthew 28:19).

Fearing persecution, Christians in the environs of larger cities worshipped in human made subterranean chambers, called catacombs. These underground caves were used both as cemeteries and as worship sites. Although they were not unknown by the Roman government, Christians were left alone in their use of these catacombs because the pagan Romans were superstitious of the dead and their Jewish opponents considered the dead "unclean." These sites became the location for annual celebrations on the anniversary of a martyr's earthly death and heavenly birth at the grave or tomb. Still today, the catacombs of Rome give vivid evidence of these early community worship sites and remembrance of martyrs. (See illustration of a depiction of an Agape meal above a catacomb tomb.) Some communities greatly revered the bones of the martyrs by placing them in the altars of their local churches. These early Christians were  familiar with the apostle John's vision of heaven wherein he saw the martyrs below the heavenly altar (Rev 6:9). Consequently, this practice was a visible and earthly manifestation of an invisible and heavenly reality—we worship with "all the company of heaven."

The Roman Empire wielded persecution and martyrdom as weapons to decimate at best and at least to impoverish the ethos of Christianity. They caused the reverse. Christians neither ignored persecution nor feared martyrdom. In fact, they embraced both and incorporated both into the Christian life style. Rather than hindering Christianity, persecution and martyrdom added to the doctrinal and practical vitality of the Christian Church. "The blood of the martyrs," assured Tertullian, "was the seed of the Church."

Monarchianism

Christianity like Judaism was monotheistic from its birth. Christianity confessed the singularity of God, and yet, recognized some type of plurality. The Old Testament writings not only identified God as *El*, the singular form of God in Hebrew, but *Elohim*, the plural form. The New Testament more clearly revealed a plurality in the one God: He is Father, Son, and Holy Spirit. This produced an obvious tension between the singularity and plurality of God's self-disclosure.

Monarchianism chose to exploit the singularity or "monarchy" (Greek, (μόνος, monos, "one, singular" + ἄρχων, archon, "ruler, chief.") of God at the expense of any plural qualities associated with God. This movement began in the second century and continued into the third. It took one of two forms: dynamic and modalistic.

Two dynamic monarchians were Theodotus (c.180, he was the earlier of two men with this same name and the teacher of the second) at the end of the second century and Paul of Samosata (c.260-268), Bishop of Antioch, in the latter half of the third century. Both espoused an adoptionist concept concerning the relation between the one God and Jesus. According to dynamic or adoptionist monarchians, Jesus was an ordinary man, though Theodotus recognized His virgin birth. At His baptism, the Spirit of God descended upon Jesus. Hence, Jesus performed miracles and prophesied, not because He was divine, but because the divine Spirit inspired Him or "adopted" Him so to speak.

Praxeas (late 2nd and early 3rd century) and Sabellius (c.215-220) were two modalistic monarchians. Both promoted what would later be called "patripassianism," the belief that the Father suffered. According to the patripassianists or modalistic monarchians, the Son of God could not suffer apart from the heavenly Father without dividing the divine monarchy, that is, the Father suffered upon the cross. Thus, the biblical terms, "Father," "Son," and "Spirit," did not describe an actual plurality within the divine unity. Instead, these were merely different names for the one God who acted in different times and places in diverse fashions or modes.

Both forms of monarchianism attempted to alleviate the tension between the singularity and plurality of God at the expense of the biblical evidence. The Christian church, though, refused to ignore the distinctness of the Father, Son, and Holy Spirit. Bishop Victor (+199) of Rome excommunicated Theodotus, and the Council of Antioch condemned Paul in 268. Pope Calixtus of Rome (217-222) excommunicated Sabellius, but Praxeas ultimately retracted his patripassianism.

Tertullian

Throughout the first and second centuries, Christians predominately employed the Greek language. There were exceptions. For example, Syrian was used in parts of the East and Latin in the West. Tertullian (c.160-c.225), born to pagan parents, a native of Carthage in northwest Africa, and a lawyer, was fluent in Greek and Latin. He wrote in both, though predominately in Latin. Having a creative intellect and a proclivity for words, Tertullian became the Father of Latin Christianity.

Key terms surfaced in Tertullian's writings that would later develop into technical theological terms and official ecclesial vocabulary. In *Against Praxeas*, Tertullian embraced both the singularity and the plurality of God, while opposing the modalistic monarchianism of Praxeas. To do so, Tertullian utilized the Latin term, *trinitas*, trinity (Latin, *tri* + *unitas*, three+unity/oneness), to explain what has been revealed by God and is believed in the church: there is one God, and the one God consists of three persons. The three persons are "distinct, but not separate" (*Against Praxaes*, 11). And so, there are not three gods, but one God who is Father, Son, and Holy Spirit.

The Latin word, *sacramentum*, oath, was another term that Tertullian borrowed from his contemporary culture and applied to the Christian faith. In *The Crown*, Tertullian contrasted the *sacramentum* that a soldier took prior to receiving a temporal crown from the state to the *sacramentum* that the Christian took in baptism and the Lord's Supper that leads to the reception of an eternal crown from God. For Tertullian, the Christian can take only one oath, either to the state or to God.

On more than one occasion, Tertullian referred to the *regula fidei*, rule of faith (see chapter 2), which embraced the doctrine of God. God was the creator. Jesus was born of Mary and crucified by Pontius Pilate. He proclaimed the Word of God and performed miracles. Jesus was raised from the dead, ascended to heaven, and will return on the Last Day in judgment. Jesus then sent the Holy Spirit to direct the church on earth. Like Irenaeus, this was the faith of the Christian church, and it was non-debatable.

Tertullian's words and writings marked a significant development in the history of the Christian church. In attacking heresy and the state, he clearly confessed the Christian faith. Doctrinally, Tertullian set the stage for Latin Christianity in the west. Practically, Tertullian was a moral rigorist. As such, he became enamored with Montanism (see chapter two), and finally joined their ranks toward the end of his life.

> Tertullian's *Advice to His Wife on Marriage*
> I have thought it meet, my best beloved fellow-servant in the Lord... to provide for the way which you must pursue after my departure from the world, if I shall be called before you; and to entrust to your honor the observance of this provision. For in things worldly we are active enough, and we wish the good of each of us to be consulted. If we draw up wills for (earthly) matters, why ought we not much more to take forethought for our posterity in things divine and heavenly, and in a sense to bequeath a legacy to be received before the inheritance be divided—(the legacy, I mean, of) admonition and demonstration touching those (bequests) which are allotted out of immortal goods, and from the heritage of the heavens? Only, that you may be able to receive in its entirety this offer in trust of my admonition, may God grant; to whom be honor, glory, renown, dignity, and power, now and to the ages of the ages!
>
> The precept, therefore, which I give you is, that you do, with all the constancy you may, after our departure, renounce nuptials; not that you will on that score confer any benefit on me, except in that you will profit yourself. But to Christians, after their departure from the world, no restoration of marriage is promised in the day of the resurrection, translated as they will be into the condition and sanctity of angels. Therefore no solicitude arising from carnal jealousy will, in the day of the resurrection, even in the case of her whom they chose to represent as having been married to seven brothers successively...nor is any (husband) awaiting her to put her to confusion. The question raised by the Sadducees has yielded to the Lord's sentence. Think not that it is for the sake of preserving to the end for myself the entire devotion of your flesh, that I, suspicious of the pain of (anticipated) slight, am even at this early period instilling into you the counsel of (perpetual) widowhood. There will at that day be no resumption of voluptuous disgrace between us. No such frivolities, no such impurities, does God promise to His (servants). But whether to you or to any other woman whatever who pertains to God, the advice which we are giving shall be profitable. *To His Wife*, Book 1, chapter 1.

Hippolytus

A contemporary of Tertullian, Hippolytus (c.170-c.236) resided in Rome. Both penned polemics against the monarchians and both had checkered ecclesial lives. Hippolytus became the first anti-pope (a rival placed in office in opposition to an officially recognized pope) during the Roman bishoprics of Calixtus (217-222), Urban (222-30), and Pontian (230-35). Hippolytus was exiled to Sardinia, but was reconciled with the Christian church prior to his death as a martyr, and his body was interred in Rome. Most noteworthy of Hippolytus is a document attributed to his authorship, the *Apostolic Tradition*.

Although more recent scholars have suggested that the *Apostolic Tradition* is a fourth century document from Egypt, it certainly reflects earlier Christian practices. What is doctrinally intriguing is that this church manual incorporated a creedal statement into its baptismal ritual. The baptizer asked three questions, and the baptized responded after each with an affirmative answer:

> Do you believe in God the Father Almighty?
> I believe.
> Do you believe in Jesus Christ, the Son of God who was born of the Holy Spirit and the Virgin Mary, who was crucified in the days of Pontius Pilate, and died and buried, and rose the third day from the dead, and ascended into heaven, and sat down at the right hand of the Father, and will come to judge the living and the dead?
> I believe.
> Do you believe in the Holy Spirit, in the Holy Church, and in the resurrection of the dead?
> I believe.

The baptized were immersed in water after each answer and ultimately anointed with oil.

While Tertullian benefited the church with his development of dogmatic vocabulary and *regula fidei*, the *Apostolic Tradition* established a sacramental norm by incorporating this Old Roman Creed into the baptismal ritual. In answering affirmatively, the baptized disconnected themselves from any previous religious convictions that they may have held. This was visualized by immersion in the sacred fount where the baptized was "drowned and died" to their old religious affiliations. It is quite obvious that the Old Roman Creed followed the Trinitarian form of earlier *regula fidei* and served as one source for the later Apostles' Creed.

> **Creed**
> A creed, from the Latin *credo*, which means "I believe," confesses what one believes, while implicitly or sometimes explicitly rejecting opposing views. For example, though some said that Jesus was the Baptist or one of the prophets, Peter confessed that He was "the Christ, the Son of the living God" (Mt 16:16). In the first two centuries, several creedal statements were developed and confessed by Christians. The principle purpose of a creed was to distinguish the faith of Christianity from other religions. As such, creeds played a key role in the identity of the early church.

The Lapsed

The Roman Emperor Decius (201-251) cruelly persecuted Christians throughout his two-year reign. He martyred Bishop Fabian of Rome (236-50) and Bishop Babylas of Antioch (c.240-c.250). Many Christians were imprisoned and tortured. Persecution was systematic and empire-wide. Those who survived but did not recant the Christian faith were called "confessors."

Decius's ultimate purpose was to appease the Roman deities by revitalizing the state religion. This meant that sacrifices must be offered to the Roman pantheon. A certificate given by the priest-official of the shrines confirmed the appropriate obeisance. Those without a certificate faced imprisonment, torture, and sometimes death. Decius did not seek so much to persecute the anti-syncretistic Christians as to force them to convert and become patriotic supporters of the state religion.

This practice wreaked havoc in the Christian church. On the one hand, many Christians remained loyal to the faith of the church: martyrs and confessors. On the other hand, some "lapsed" from the Christian faith. A few of them submitted to the demanded obeisance to receive the necessary certificate. Others obtained a certificate without actually offering sacrifices to the Roman deities. These "lapsed" were seen as denying Christ and thus were dismissed from the rolls of the Christian community and not permitted to participate in the liturgical life of the church.

When persecution subsided after the death of Decius, and many of the lapsed desired to return to the Christian church, a dispute arose. Could the lapsed return to the church? If so, what was the required penance? Should the penance be different for those who actually offered sacrifices to the Roman deities compared to those who did not offer sacrifices but purchased a certificate? Who had the authority to make these determinations?

In Carthage, this dispute erupted between the confessors and Bishop Cyprian (c.200-258). The confessors had suffered considerably for their confession of Jesus and the Gospel, and so they claimed to have the authority to address the issue of the lapsed. Because Cyprian had fled the Decian persecution, many questioned his authority. He argued, nonetheless, that the authority to forgive or retain the sins of the lapsed and assign acts of penance belonged to the bishop and no one else. Cyprian's *On the Lapsed* (251) was read at the Council of Carthage in 251. The council established the following criteria for re-admittance of the lapsed: those who had offered sacrifices were to be readmitted to the church only on their deathbed after extended penance. Those who had only purchased a certificate were to be readmitted after a time of penance. And all of this was within the purview of the bishop.

This dispute spilled over into Rome between Bishop Cornelius (251-253) and the priest and antipope, Novatian (c.200-257). Cornelius claimed that the bishop had the power to forgive all sins, even the apostasy of the lapsed. Novatian, in contrast, followed a more rigorous tradition in the church: there was no forgiveness for the most heinous sins committed after baptism. Novatian's position was rejected, and he was expelled from the church. Novatian established an extremely rigorous religious community, which was subsequently considered heterodox by the Christian church.

> **St Laurence (c.225-248)**
> Serving as a deacon under Pope Sixtus II (+258), young Laurence was responsible for managing the financial concerns of the church. Cyprian reports that with the martyrdom of Sixtus by Emperor Valerian (c.195-260), Laurence was the last of seven deacons to be martyred. Ambrose tells the story that Laurence was required to deliver the treasures of the church to an imperial guard. Laurence requested three days to gather together and inventory the wealth, during which time he sold and distributed most of the church's furnishings and funds to the poor. Standing before the Roman official, Laurence then presented the poor, blind, and crippled, explaining that these were the true treasure of the church. He was immediately martyred, but his care for the poor remains exemplary.

The Decian persecution caused more problems for the church than it could have ever imagined. At the same time, it produced two invaluable benefits. The hierarchy of the church was clearly established so that bishops were the successors of the apostles to whom Jesus had been given the authority to forgive and retain sins. The ultimate purpose of the church was to absolve the sins of the penitent.

Origen of Alexandria
One of the most brilliant and prominent theologians of the third century was also one of the most troubling. No Christian compared to Origen of Alexandria (c.185-c.254) in having an encyclopedic mind, a boldness of confession, and a uniqueness of personality.

Concerning the Christian life, Origen was exemplary. He abandoned temporal comforts in service to the church, first as a catechist in Alexandria, and then as a priest and theologian in Caesarea. In addition, he embraced persecution. While still a child, his mother hid his clothing so that he could not leave the house and join his father in martyrdom. Later in life he penned an *Exhortation to Martyrdom*, which inspired several of his students to die the death of martyrs. Origen himself was tortured during the reign of Decius and his father had been martyred under Emperor Septimius Severus (145-211).

Yet, Origen's life also caused offense in the church. According to the words of Jesus that some have made themselves eunuchs for the sake of the kingdom (Matthew 19:12), Origen castrated himself while he was still a young man. Fleeing political unrest in Alexandria, he went with Ambrose of Alexandria (c.212-250) to Caesarea and began to preach there, though still a layman. Later, he abandoned his Alexandrian church to be ordained in Caesarea.

Origen is most remembered for his biblical scholarship and commentaries. Although it has been lost, one of the greatest feats of academic biblical scholarship was Origen's preparation of the *Hexapla*. (See sidebar.) This major work influenced not only the Latin Vulgate (see chapter four) but also other extant copies of the Old Testament.

Concerning his Christian theology, Origen was a masterful exegete and preacher. Though many of his biblical commentaries and sermons have been lost, several are extant, though many only in Latin translation, many by Rufinus (see chapter four). In *On First Principles*, he spelled out his exegetical method and corollary doctrines. Origen delineated the different levels of interpretation of Bible texts. An interpretation according to the "flesh" was the most basic; the words meant what they say. The Jews followed this literal interpretation only, because they rejected Jesus, and refused to listen to any other interpretation of the Old Testament that pointed to Jesus. Even the simplest Christians were mired in this interpretation, said Origen. Since many biblical passages had no useful interpretation according to the flesh, Origen

---

> **Origen's *Hexapla***
> Six columns of biblical text were placed side by side in a codex (a book in contrast to a scroll). The Old Testament text was in Hebrew and in a Greek transliteration. Then Origen added a version by Aquila of Sinope, which was the most literal Greek translation used by Jews instead of the Septuagint. An eloquent Greek translation by Symmachus was followed by the second-century BC Septuagint version and finally the Theodotion translation, which was used by early Christian churches to fill in some Septuagint ambiguities. Scholars estimate the project took over 20 years to prepare and resulted in over 6500 pages in fifteen volumes. The one copy was held in the famous library in Caesarea until it was destroyed by the Muslims in 638.

pointed to two other levels which must be employed: for the soul (moral) and for the spirit (mystical). Both led to a deeper meaning of and provided greater insight into the divine revelation concerning Jesus, argued Origen, and so, more significantly benefited the Christian than did the literal interpretation. Origen greatly favored the interpretations of soul (allegorical) and spirit (anagogical) in his own biblical commentaries and sermons. Although not alone in this approach, his method led to many misinterpretations in later centuries.

Origen's *regula fidei* was quite orthodox as he confessed the Triune God in his book, *On First Principles*:

> The holy apostles, when preaching the faith of Christ, took certain doctrines, those namely which they believed to be necessary one, and delivered them in the plainest terms to all believers.... First, that God is one, who created and set in order all things.... Christ Jesus, he who came to earth, was begotten of the Father before every created thing.... He took to himself a body like our body, differing in this alone, that he was born of a virgin and of the Holy Spirit. And this Jesus Christ was born and suffered in truth and not merely in appearance, and truly died our common death. Moreover he truly rose from the dead,...and was then taken up into heaven.... The Holy Spirit is united in honor and dignity with the Father and the Son. (Preface, 3-4)

Thus, Origen clearly confessed the basic tenets concerning the Christian faith,

especially in the work of Jesus. Unfortunately, he strayed into heterodoxy concerning the pre-existence of souls. He speculated that a spiritual world preceded this physical world. The fallen of the spiritual world were imprisoned in this physical world. For this and other theological peccadilloes, Origen would be condemned at the Council of Constantinople (553).

Both the life and doctrine of Origen strengthened and weakened the faithful. Though he was a phenomenal churchman, teacher and preacher, his practical and doctrinal aberrations harmed the church in his day and the centuries to follow. A faithful and tireless worker in the church, Origen simply over-exceeded his own spectacular abilities.

Gregory the Wonderworker

A student of Origen (see illustration above of Gregory's sketch of Origen), Gregory Thaumaturgus (c.213-c.270) (Latinized from the Greek for "wonder worker") had an intriguing place in Christian history. While in Caesarea, Theodore (his original name) of Neocaesarea in Pontus (north Asia Minor) sat in on Origen's classes. There, Theodore was converted to the Christian faith by Origen and took the name "Gregory" at his baptism. He stayed in Caesarea and studied under Origen for five more years. These catechetical schools of the early church instructed catechumens and strengthened the faithful. They also sought to enlighten pagans who attended these schools to experience the pedagogical method of their famous teachers or to learn the basic tenets of the new and strange religion called Christianity.

In 238, Gregory was ordained bishop of the small flock in his hometown. He preached relentlessly and powerfully to the pagans converting many. Some conversions resulted from his ability to perform miracles, which were purported to be numerous and varied, and thereby provided his nickname. Reportedly, he preserved a church building during an earthquake and protected a town from a flood as well as cast out a demon. The *Life of Gregory* by Gregory of Nyssa (c.330-c.395) recounted these and other wonders. With his preaching and his miracles, a pagan land became Christian.

Gregory was also a faithful bishop. Although he fled during the Decian persecution, he did not abandon his people, but returned to help soon after. During a plague, he remained and ministered to his people and throughout a very prolonged assault by the Goths (252-254), he supported them. Theologically and pastorally, he condemned the monarchian heretic, Paul of Samosata, at the Council of Antioch I (264-65).

As a student of Origen, the orthodox theology of Origen rubbed off on Gregory. Conversely, the student did not speculate philosophically nor stray theologically as had his famous teacher. In his *Short Creed*, Gregory identified the Father as the Eternal Image and Begetter, the Son as the Perfect Begotten and Eternal of Eternal, the Holy Spirit as the Life and Sanctifier. He concluded his confession by addressing the unique unity of the Trinity:

> There is a perfect Trinity, in glory and eternity and sovereignty, neither divided nor estranged. Wherefore there is nothing either created or in servitude in the Trinity; nor anything super-induced, as if at some former period it was non-existent, and at some later period it was introduced. Neither was the Son ever wanting to the Father, nor the Spirit to the Son; but without variation and without change, the same Trinity abides ever. (*Short Creed*, attributed to Gregory)

Citing Tertullian's term, *Trinity*, more than once, Gregory underscored both the singularity and plurality of God. Without attempting to disprove rationally the obvious tension, he confessed that the one God is Father, Son, and Spirit.

Gregory was ultimately a theologian with a missionary's heart. He was not interested in theology for the sake of theology. Instead, just as the theology of Origen converted him to the Christian faith, so Gregory's theology was espoused and explained in order to convert the pagans of Pontus to Christianity. Toward the end of his life, he reminisced about his work, reporting that upon his arrival in Pontus there were only seventeen Christians. At the end of his life, he supposedly asked how many pagans remained in Pontus and was told "only seventeen." The city had become almost completely Christian.

Didascalia Apostolorum

Of unknown authorship, the *Didascalia Apostolorum*, like the *Didache*, was an early third century church manual from Syria, which addressed the Christian life, ecclesial offices, and the sacred liturgies. While the *Didache* was relatively brief, the *Didascalia* delineated much more extensively the significant practical matters of the Christian church.

Just a century after the *Didache* and the letters of Ignatius, noticeable changes and alterations had occurred among the ecclesial offices. The offices of prophet and apostle no longer existed, while the three-fold hierarchy of bishop, presbyter (or elder), and deacon remained. Akin to Ignatius's letters, the *Didascalia* assigned symbolic meanings to each office: the bishop represented God Almighty, the presbyter the apostles, and the deacon Jesus. And yet, the *Didascalia* developed their respective responsibilities much more fully. The bishop was responsible for retaining and loosing sins. He admonished the sinful, but mercifully received the penitent. For the penitent, he determined the kind and amount of penance to be performed. Most importantly, he announced the forgiveness of sins on behalf of Jesus. The bishop was to live an exemplary life and be shown due honor by the people. His honored position was displayed in the liturgy where he sat upon a throne among the presbyters at the east end of the sanctuary.

Widow and deaconess were also offices mentioned in the *Didascalia*. The apostle Paul had first noted the role of widows (1 Timothy 5:3-16) and the *Didascalia* more precisely delineated their responsibilities: they must neither gallivant nor gossip; they should speak of the Christian faith in general conversation, but they may not teach; they must be gentle and obedient toward their ecclesial supervisors, and must pray for all who petition them and meditate upon the Word of God.

Mentioned only in passing in the New Testament (Romans 16:1), the *Didascalia* explains that the deaconess' chief activity and ecclesiastical  responsibility was to assists the bishop, particularly in his ministry to women. There were places that a male bishop should not enter, but a female deaconess may. The principle service of a deaconess revolved around Holy Baptism. The deaconess anointed a woman with oil preceding her baptism. And after the baptism by a male clergy, the deaconess received the baptized woman and provided spiritual care for her.

As the Christian Church grew and expanded, older offices had to be expanded to serve better the Christian church in different times and new places. As the pattern of theology, each generation built upon that of the previous generation. While not identical to the *Didache* and the letters of Ignatius, the *Didascalia* showed development in the offices (life and liturgies) of the Christian church.

The third century was similar to the second century for the Christian church in many ways: persecution and heresy relentlessly attacked it. Yet, these early Christians responded with great faithfulness to New Testament witness of Jesus and the Gospel. At the same time, these two centuries were not identical. As the weapons of the enemy intensified, the Christian life and doctrine of the church was increasingly attacked. Rather than shriveling in the face of persecution, the church embraced martyrdom and incorporated it into its life and doctrine. In face of heresy, the church recruited a phalanx of theologians armed with their confessions of the faith. Not producing new doctrines, they carefully extrapolated upon the witness of the New Testament. In so doing, the third century theologians more clearly defined orthodoxy in relation to heterodoxy.

For Review and Discussion
1. Why was martyrdom not to be sought, yet held in high respect by the Christian community?
2. What development do you detect in the *Regula fidei* from the second to the third century?
3. How were the two types of Monarchianism problematic for the church?
4. Why was the issue of "the lapsed" a critical concern both for the church and the role of the bishops?
5. Research the role of deacon/deaconess in the third century and summarize their significance in a paragraph.

For Further Reading
Butterworth, G. W. *Origen: On First Principles*. Gloucester, MA: Peter Smith, 1973 reprint of 1936 edition.
Cruzel, Henri. *Origen*. Translated by A.S. Worrall. San Francisco, CA: 1989.
Gonzalez, Justo. *A History of Christian Thought*. Vol. 1. Nashville, TN: Abingdon, 1970.
Kelly, J. N. D. *Early Christian Creeds*. London: Longmans, 1960.
Kelly, J. N. D. *Early Christian Doctrines*. San Francisco, CA: Harper and Row, 1960.
Quasten, Johannes. *Patrology*. Vol. 2. Westminster, MD: Christian Classics, 1992.
Salisbury, Joyce E. *Perpetua's Passion*. New York, NY: Routledge, 1997.
Streeter, Burnett Hillman. *The Primitive Church: Studied with Special Reference to the Origins of the Christian Ministry*. New York: The Macmillan Company, 1929.

4. The Official Religion

The Fourth Century

The fourth century saw much turmoil and change. At the beginning of the fourth century, the Roman Empire increased its persecution of Christianity to its most severe level. Violent and widespread, many Christians were tortured and died the martyr's death. By the end of the fourth century, Christianity had become the predominate religion in the Roman Empire; persecution was now directed toward the pagans in the empire. In the midst of this change, bishops no longer addressed only those under their local episcopal charge, but supervised the church throughout the empire at large councils. Hence, the Christian faith would become more formalized in doctrine and practice. Christianity changed from persecuted to favored status and the leading figures took on more significant roles in the church and the world.

The Great Persecution (c.303-11)

Emperor Diocletian (245-311, ruled 284-305) brought stability to the Roman Empire at the end of the third century. With at least twenty emperors in fifty years, Diocletian recognized two problems: the empire was too large for one emperor, and the lack of a clear successor after an emperor's death often led to civil war. To counteract these problems, Maximian (c.250-310, ruled 286-305) was appointed the "augustus" (meaning "exalted one," referred to the emperor) in the west with Constantius (c.250-306, ruled 293-306) under him as the "caesar" (the designation for the heir to the throne).

Diocletian remained the augustus in the East with Galerius (c.260-311, ruled 305-311) named caesar for the West. Each caesar was to succeed his respective augustus. At that time, Diocletian's power was absolute. Visitors were required to prostrate themselves before him. Although they were not permitted to look directly at him, they might be allowed to kiss the hem of his robe. He rode roughshod over the Roman senate, and he changed the title of the emperor from "First Citizen" to "Lord and God." Though he was an autocrat, Diocletian was well organized and successfully held together the Roman Empire of his day.

Augustus Diocletian initially held no animosity toward Christianity. Noteworthy is the fact that his wife and daughter were confessing Christians. Caesar Galerius, however, fervidly hated Christianity. At the end of the third century, the caesar persuaded his augustus to purge the Roman army of Christians.

The Great Persecution began in 303 when Galerius convinced Diocletian to eliminate all Christians from governmental positions in the empire along with razing their churches and destroying their sacred books. Christians were also required to sacrifice to the Romans deities as in the days of Decius. When Christians refused to hand over their books and participate in pagan sacrifices, they were tortured, imprisoned, or killed. When Diocletian's palace was inexplicably set ablaze, the Christians were blamed. This led to increased persecution—initially it began with the condemnation of church leaders, but later all Christians were subject to political scrutiny.

In 305, Diocletian abdicated his authority due to illness and Galerius became the augustus in the east. He continued the policy of persecuting Christianity, which was brutally enforced by his caesar, Maximinus Daia (270-313, ruled 308-313). The Great Persecution came to an end when on his deathbed Galerius issued the Edict of Toleration: the Christian faith would no longer be persecuted in the Roman Empire on the condition that Christians petitioned their God for the benefit of the empire. Unfortunately, within months Augustus Maximinus overturned Galerius's edict and Christianity again was not to be tolerated in the eastern half of the empire.

Constantine the Great

With the abdication of Maximian and the subsequent death of Constantius (c.250-306, ruled 293-306), the Roman troops in Gaul declared Constantine (272-337, ruled 306-337) augustus. With no hesitation, Constantine moved his soldiers against Maxentius (c.279-312), the augustus in Rome. Two slightly differing narratives describe the events prior to Constantine's victory over Maxentius. According to the Christian apologist, Lactantius (c.240-c.320), Constantine was instructed in a dream to place the sign of Christ, chi-rho (XP), the first two Greek letters of Christ (ΧΡΙΣΤΟΣ = Christ), upon the shields of the soldiers. According to the Christian historian Eusebius of Caesarea (c.260-c.340), Constantine saw the chi-rho in a vision on the battlefield and heard the now famous *in hoc signo vincit* (in this sign he conquers). Fighting under the sign of Christ (see illustration), Constantine defeated Maxentius and became the western augustus.

At Milan in 313, Constantine met up with Augustus Licinius (c.263-325). They allied—Licinius marrying Flavia Julia Constantia (c.293-330), the half-sister of Constantine—and jointly issued the Edict of Milan. This decree forbade the persecution of Christians and ordered the return of the properties to the churches that had been seized by the empire. In the meantime, Maximinus Daia continued his persecution of Christianity, but only for a few months until defeated by Licinius. One year later, Constantine attacked Licinius and finally defeated him in 322, thereby becoming the sole emperor of the empire.

Constantine did not make Christianity the official religion of the Roman Empire and it is not clear when he actually became a Christian. He certainly was influenced by the Christian community and favored the church. Lactantius, the apologist, tutored Constantine's son, Crispus (c.200/305-326), and joined Constantine's entourage. Other Christian theologians advised Constantine as well. The emperor donated the Lateran Palace in Rome to the Christian church and financed the building of churches in Rome and the Holy Land. He decreed Sunday to be the official day of religious worship in the empire and reformed many laws which had harmed the Christian community. At the same, Constantine participated in pagan rituals throughout his career. He and his successors minted coins that included both pagan symbols and the Christian chi-rho (see illustration). Constantine was finally baptized on his deathbed.

Constantine thus played a pivotal role in the radically new direction of the Roman Empire and the status of the Christian church. As the first Christian emperor of the Roman Empire, Constantine completely transformed the Christian-Roman relations of the previous three centuries. In addition, Christianity emerged as a prominent religion in the Mediterranean World.

Donatism

Just as the Decian persecution had caused an unintended dilemma of "the lapsed," the Great Persecution similarly caused a crisis concerning the *traditores*. During the Great Persecution, bishops and numerous clergy had succumbed to the fear of torture and death, and "betrayed" the Christian church by revealing the names of Christians to Roman officials and turning over the sacred writings of the Christians. The name for people who surrendered church property was *"traditores"*—traitors! The return of these clergy to their ecclesial posts after the Great Persecution was hotly contested.

The majority group in northern Africa, which were later called "Donatists," emphasized the purity of the Christian church and the need to maintain such purity in the face of economic, political, and theological difficulties. Initially, the controversy was over the appointment of Caecilianus (+c.345) as bishop of Carthage. The concern was raised about his "holiness of life," since he had turned over church property (probably biblical papyrus scrolls and perhaps communion vessels) during the Diocletian persecution

In 311, Caecilianus was ordained bishop of Carthage by three local bishops, one being Felix of Apthungi who had also been a *traditore*. The more rigorous faction of Christians in Carthage would not acknowledge an ordination by a *traditore*, and so placed the lector, Majorinus (+c.315), into the office of bishop of Carthage. The issue of the church's holiness rested, in their understanding, upon the holiness of each person (particularly each leader) rather than on the imputed holiness of Christ.

As a result of what was seen as a denial of the Christian faith, the people questioned the validity of all the sacraments administered by Caecilinianus. This was true, not only of ordination, but of the sacraments. Thus, one baptized by a bishop who was a former *traditore* or a bishop ordained by a *traditore* or any bishop in the Christian church that contained a *traditore* would have to be re-baptized in joining the Donatist Church.

Constantine addressed this African schism at first by recognizing Caecilianus as the bishop. Caecilianus and his congregation would continue to receive the generous benefices of Constantine for the Christian church in Carthage. Later, Constantine summoned a council at Arles in Gaul (314) which then amended his position and found the Donatists heretical. Although the Donatist community was deemed schismatic and heterodox, those of the more rigorous Donatist position did not immediately disband, but rather created their own church. The successor of Majorinus (the actual founder of the group who died shortly after being declared bishop) was Donatus (bishop 313-355, exciled 347) in 313, for whom the movement would be named.

Constantine persecuted the Donatist Church until 321 after which it briefly flourished in North Africa. The actual schismatic controversy in the church continued for almost a century in northern Africa. Although several church meetings condemned the Donatists, their numbers, particularly in northern Africa, continued to grow because of their rigorous orthodoxy and emphasis upon personal piety. Bishop Augustine of Hippo (354-430, bishop c.395-430) in North Africa penned acidic polemics against it in the fifth century. (See chapter five) Donatism finally disappeared after the incursion of Islam in the seventh century.

Council of Nicaea (325)

A second and much more volatile predicament erupted during the fourth century regarding divergent teachings concerning the doctrine of God. Throughout the second and third centuries, Christians had debated the nature of God. The heterodox monarchians emphasized the unity of God, while the orthodox Christians clearly confessed that there was only one God who was at the same time Father, Son, and Holy Spirit. We saw how Tertullian had popularized the term "trinity" to teach that God was both three and one. This debate came to a head in the fourth century when the Christian church initially addressed the divinity of Jesus at Nicaea and later at Constantinople (381), the divinity of the Holy Spirit.

Arius (c.250-c.336), a deacon and later a priest at Alexandria in Egypt, was highly regarded for his preaching and moral rigor. Many believers were devoted to him and his teachings. Though he

> *Ecclesiastical History*
> Eusebius (c.260/265-339), bishop of Caesarea and "the father of church history," recorded the first centuries of Christianity in his *Historia Ecclesiastica*, in Greek. He was not the first historian, since he mentioned a work (now lost) by Hegesippus. Providing detailed accounts and primary materials from the persecutions and Constantine's establishment of the church, Eusebius is properly credited for his careful historiography. This prolific author also wrote a *Life of Constantine* and several other treatises on Gospel witnessing.

was not strictly speaking a monarchian, Arius assumed the singularity or monad of God and then argued that there can be only one which is truly and fully God. He declared that the "Son has a beginning" (*Letter to Eusebius of Nicomedia*), and the Son "was not before he was begotten" (*Letter to Alexander of Alexandria*). Arius asserted that the Son of God was created before time by God the Father and so was not coeternal with God the Father, nor completely God like the Father. He used the term, *homoiousios* (ὁμοιούσιος), meaning "similar being," to describe this distinction. Thus, Arius subordinated the Son to the Father attempting to preserve the monotheism of the Christian faith.

Alexander (c.250-328), the bishop of Alexandria, on the other hand, confessed that the Son of God was coeternal with God the Father. Jesus was fully God and, thus, was to be worshipped as God. The bishop quarreled with his priest until a council in Alexandria deposed Arius from his office. Arius instigated local disturbances among his loyal followers and wrote to other bishops, including Eusebius of Nicomedia (+341) who had baptized Constantine, seeking their support. What had began as a local concern quickly escalated throughout the empire. Having just dealt with the Donatist schism, Constantine forged ahead with this controversy concerning the doctrine of God.

Constantine first sent Hosius (256-359), bishop of Cordova, to calm the situation. When this failed, the emperor summoned the bishops of the Mediterranean world to a council at Nicaea in northern Asia Minor. At least two hundred bishops attended the council, the great majority from the east.

A small faction of bishops, led by Eusebius of Nicomedia, fully supported Arius's views. Alexander of Alexandria led an equally small troupe of bishops in complete opposition to Arius. The vast majority began the council rather ambivalent toward the issue. After the presentation of an Arian creed and hearing the arguments of Eusebius of Nicomedia, the majority of the assembled bishops sided with Alexander. The creed of Eusebius of Caesarea was presented to the council. Since it predated the Arius-Alexander controversy, the second article on the Son of God had to be amended to address the issue at hand. The bishops at Nicaea confessed that Jesus was:

> God of God,
> Light of light,
> True God of true God,
> Begotten, not made.

They further confessed that Jesus was *homoousios* (ὁμοούσιος), "of the same substance," with the Father, in contrast to Arius' *homoiousios* (ὁμοιούσιος). In no uncertain terms, the Creed of Nicaea, as it would become known, clearly identified the Son of God as fully divine and equal with God the Father (though it did not include a specific article on the Holy Spirit). If this statement of the creed was not clear enough, its conclusion clearly rejected Arius' opposing view: "those who say that there was when He was not…or that He is created, or mutable, these the catholic church anathematizes." (The Greek word, ἀνάθεμα, Latinized *anathema*, means to condemn eternally.)

The council adopted this creed as the official statement of the church along with twenty canons (official rules adopted by church councils). Constantine enforced the creed as a key element in the official theology of the Christian church, exiling Arius and two bishops who rejected the creed. Though the council and the emperor championed the creed and its doctrine, the controversy would continue well into the fourth century. Athanasius (c.296-373), then deacon of Alexander of Alexandria and future bishop of the same church, attended the council and would become the standard-bearer of Nicene theology in the subsequent decades.

Athanasius

Athanasius (c.296-373) was the single most heroic figure in the fourth century Christian church. Only a deacon at the Council of Nicaea (325), he died eight years prior to the Council of Constantinople (381). During the interim period, Athanasius faithfully confessed the Christian faith, despite relentless persecution.

The theological genius of Athanasius was that he understood the salvific error related to the Arian controversy. The Arian Jesus was not fully God. This meant, as Athanasius realized, that Jesus could not redeem this fallen world. In sharp contrast, Athanasius argued that to be truly the savior of the world, Jesus must be fully God in human flesh:

> Because He is God, being Son of God, and is everlasting King, a reflection and likeness of the Father, on account of this, He is with reason the expected Christ, whom the Father announces to men in the revelation to His holy prophets–in order that, just as through Him we came into existence, thus in Him a redemption of sins might occur for all, and all things might be ruled by Him. (*Orations against the Arians*, 1.49)

Hence, *homoousios* was not merely theological hair-splitting, but was the touchstone of salvation.

The Council of Nicaea confessed the orthodox term, *homoousios*, which defined the divinity of Jesus, but unfortunately did not exterminate Arianism. While Constantine expelled the three Arian teachers, others with varying degrees of Arian tendencies remained in their bishoprics keeping quiet until opportunity arose. The winds began to shift in 328 when Athanasius became the bishop of Alexandria.

In the same year that Athanasius was ordained bishop, Constantine released Arius from exile and demanded that Arius be returned to his former ecclesial position in Alexandria. Eusebius of Nicomedia publicly agreed to the Creed of Nicaea, but had remained a closet Arian, and so, became a fierce opponent of the *homoousios* bishop. He and other Arian sympathizers prepared false reports that Athanasius was involved in the occult and had murdered a bishop. Athanasius was accused of exhibiting a domineering behavior toward the Christians in Egypt. Worse yet, Athanasius was rightly accused of threatening to withhold Egyptian corn from Constantinople if it did support the orthodox faith of Nicaea. In 335, the Council of Tyre excommunicated Athanasius, and Constantine exiled Athanasius to Trier in Gaul.

With the death of Constantine in 337, his three sons, Constantine II (316-340), Constantius (317-361), and Constans (323-350), allowed all exiled bishops to return, including Athanasius. Constantius ruled the east and favored Eusebius of Nicodemia who became the bishop of Constantinople. Within three years, Athanasius again was forced out of Alexandria, but found refuge in Rome, only to return to Alexandria in 346.

After his two brothers died, Constantius became the sole emperor. Now favoring the Arian bishop, Valens of Mursa (c.300-375), Constantius furtively maneuvered the western Councils at Arles (353) and Milan (355) to excommunicate and exile Athanasius and other *homoousios* bishops, along with Hosius of Cordova (257-359), Hilary of Poitiers (300-368), and the pope, Liberius of Rome (+366). This time Athanasius found refuge among the ascetics in the Egyptian desert.

Under the leadership of radical Arians such as Valens of Mursa and George of Alexandria (+361), the *homoousios* of the Creed of Nicaea was renounced. The extreme Arian position confessed that the Son was *anomoios* (ἀνόμοιος, "unlike") the Father. The Son was confessed, more commonly by the Arians, to be *homoios* (similar) to the Father. A third view was at the forefront: the Son is *homoiousios* to the Father (sometimes called, semi-Arian).

Homoousios was reaffirmed at the Council at Constantinople in 360. With the death of Constantius in 361, Julian (331/332-363) became emperor and inexplicably recalled all exiled bishops, including Athanasius, to their previous positions.

Athanasius immediately rallied the supporters of *homoousios* along with the *homoiousios* theologians against the Arians. Previously, the *homoousios* theologians condemned *homoiousios* as semi-Arian, the Father and the Son were not equal. Similarly, the *homoiousios* theologians rejected *homoousios* as Sabellian, stating that there was no distinction between the Father and the Son. In light of the current Arianism—*homoios*—both parties accepted *homoousios* as long as it was understood not to tolerate Sabellianism.

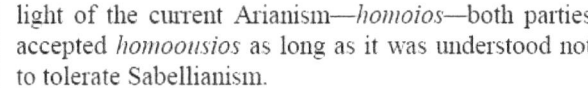

The extraordinary career of Athanasius ended as it began. He was exiled once again by Emperor Julian (331/2-363, ruled 361-363), known as "the Apostate," after rejecting Christianity, but was reinstated by Emperor Jovian (331-364, ruled 363-364). Though Emperor Valentinian (321-375, ruled 364-375) wished to exile him, Athanasius remained in Alexandria until his death. Through all of this, Athanasius never wavered in his profession of the *homoousios*, steadfastly confessing the Creed of Nicaea, that Christ is "of one substance" with the Father.

Asceticism

An ascetic (Greek, ἄσκησις, "exercise" or "training") was one who exercised his or her Christian faith in a very strict manner. These Christian "exercises" included but were not limited to prayer and fasting and almsgiving, which were expected of all Christians. In the ante-Nicene (before the Council of Nicaea in 325) church, all Christians more or less lived an ascetic life. This developed in part from the Christian-pagan dichotomy in the Roman Empire: Christians lived exceedingly moral lives in contrast to the immorality of the pagans. The moral rigor of Christians was especially acute as persecution weeded out hypocrites. With the toleration of Christianity and then full-fledged support, the church grew numerically. At the same time, many new Christians lacked the moral intensity of their spiritual ancestors. As the morality of the church grew lax, asceticism turned "professional" and moved outside of the local church and developed into two forms: an eremitic form (Greek, ἔρημος, "desert" or "uninhabited"), living a solitary life as a hermit and a cenobite form (Greek, of Rome (+366). This time Athanasius found refuge among the ascetics in the Egyptian desert.

Under the leadership of radical Arians such as Valens of Mursa and George of Alexandria (+361), the *homoousios* of the Creed of Nicaea was renounced. The extreme Arian position confessed that the Son was *anomoios* (ἀνόμοιος, "unlike") the Father. The Son was confessed, more commonly by the Arians, to be *homoios* (similar) to the Father. A third view was at the forefront: the Son is *homoiousios* to the Father (sometimes called, semi-Arian).

Homoousios was reaffirmed at the Council at Constantinople in 360. With the death of Constantius in 361, Julian (331/332-363) became emperor and inexplicably recalled all exiled bishops, including Athanasius, to their previous positions.

Athanasius immediately rallied the supporters of *homoousios* along with the *homoiousios* theologians against the Arians. Previously, the *homoousios* theologians condemned *homoiousios* as semi-Arian, the Father and the Son were not equal. Similarly, the *homoiousios* theologians rejected *homoousios* as Sabellian, stating that there was no distinction between the Father and the Son. In light of the current Arianism—*homoios*—both parties accepted *homoousios* as long as it was understood not to tolerate Sabellianism.

The extraordinary career of Athanasius ended as it began. He was exiled once again by Emperor Julian (331/2-363, ruled 361-363), known as "the Apostate," after rejecting Christianity, but was reinstated by Emperor Jovian (331-364, ruled 363-364). Though Emperor Valentinian (321-375, ruled 364-375) wished to exile him, Athanasius remained in Alexandria until his death. Through all of this, Athanasius never wavered in his profession of the *homoousios*, steadfastly confessing the Creed of Nicaea, that Christ is "of one substance" with the Father.

Asceticism

An ascetic (Greek, ἄσκησις, "exercise" or "training") was one who exercised his or her Christian faith in a very strict manner. These Christian "exercises" included but were not limited to prayer and fasting and almsgiving, which were expected of all Christians. In the ante-Nicene (before the Council of Nicaea in 325) church, all Christians more or less lived an ascetic life. This developed in part from the Christian-pagan dichotomy in the Roman Empire: Christians lived exceedingly moral lives in contrast to the immorality of the pagans. The moral rigor of Christians was especially acute as persecution weeded out hypocrites. With the toleration of Christianity and then full-fledged support, the church grew numerically. At the same time, many new Christians lacked the moral intensity of their spiritual ancestors. As the morality of the church grew lax, asceticism turned "professional" and moved outside of the local church and developed into two forms: an eremitic form (Greek, ἔρημος, "desert" or "uninhabited"), living a solitary life as a hermit and a cenobite form (Greek, κοινός, "common" + βίος, "life"), where individuals resided in a community of like-minded ascetics. These cenobites were called monks (Greek, μοναχός, "single, solitary") and their community a monastery.

The *Life of Anthony*, chronicled by Athanasius, portrayed this early hermit as a faithful hero of the Christian faith. Anthony (c.251-356) was an Egyptian who had been raised in a Christian family. At twenty years of age, both of his parents died. Attending the Divine Service, he heard the words of Jesus,  "sell everything and give it to the poor" (Matthew 19:21). Immediately, Ahntony sold all of his parents' possessions, placed his sister with a community of Christian virgins, and set out to live an ascetic life. Initially, he learned this life from a local hermit. Following this, Anthony took up residence in some nearby tombs that were considered the habitation of demons and evil spirits. Their attacks upon Anthony were ruthless and unrelenting: they appeared as wild beasts and uttered unbearable sounds and shook the walls of the tombs. Athanasius reports that Jesus watched over Anthony and delivered him from this torture.

Antony rigorously exercised his Christian faith throughout his life. His sparsity of food was contrasted by his multitudinous prayers. He sought an eremitic solitude, but often he was sought out by or led into the company of other Christians, for whom he performed miracles and provided spiritual guidance. During the Arian controversy, he marched a troop of Egyptian ascetics into Alexandria to condemn Arianism and confess that Jesus was the "Eternal Word."

Another Egyptian, a military officer named Pachomius (c.290-346), was converted to Christianity when he was twenty years old. Initially, he also became an eremite, but was frustrated with its lack of order. Consequently, he became a cenobite, forming a community along the Nile River in southern Egypt. His first attempt failed dismally when the monks complained that his ascetic demands were too rigorous. Dismissing the lot, he began anew, increasing his ascetic requirements for the monks.

Pachomius developed the first "rule" or set of instructions for an ascetic community. His rule detailed the many components of the ascetic's life, and it was to be followed by all in the community. The structure of the community was a familial-like hierarchy: an abbot (Latin, *abba*, "father") was the father-figure of the community and the monks were seen as brothers. Their clothing was a simple uniform: white, sleeveless garments that were sewn from a coarse material, including a hood or cowl. General activities were regimented: individuals cooked, cleaned, and cared for sick in service the community; food and possessions, speech and sleep were kept to a minimum. Spiritual activities were strictly ordered: daily reading and memorization of Holy Scripture, regular prayer both communal and private, reception of the Lord's Supper on Saturday evening in town and on Sunday morning at the monastery.

Pachomius's cenobitic monasticism ultimately fared well with his general principles of obedience, devotion, and useful labor. By the end of his life, he oversaw nine monasteries of men and two of women.

Asceticism replaced martyrdom as the premier office in the Christian church. While there was more variation among the lives of the eremites and more order for the cenobites under a rule, both were highly revered among Christians because, just as the martyrs had sacrificed their lives in the confession of the Christian faith, so now these ascetics sacrificed their lives in the rigorous exercise of the Christian faith.

Cappadocian Fathers

Athanasius handed on the theological baton to the Cappadocian Fathers. Basil of Caesarea (c.330-379), Gregory of Nyssa (c.330-395), and Gregory of Nazianzus (c.329-389) were so named "Cappadocian Fathers" because of their births and bishoprics in Cappadocia, an eastern province in Asia Minor. These three bishops were all related: Basil and Gregory of Nyssa were siblings; Basil and Gregory of Nazianzus were classmates; both Gregories attended the Council of Constantinople (381). Of greater import, all three defended the orthodox teachings of the Christian church.

All three favored the ascetic life. Basil penned a *Shorter Monastic Rule* and a *Longer Monastic Rule*, which followed a question-answer format that addressed many aspects of asceticism. Both were quite influential in eastern monasticism. The times, though, were theologically troubled and did not allow for their spiritual repose. Instead, all three theological philosophers were eventually called to proclaim Jesus publicly and the message of the Gospel in clear and certain terms.

Basil was the most prominent theologian of the three and the first to leave the seclusion of the monastery for the public office bishop. During the reign of the Arian Emperor Valentinian, Eusebius of Caesarea (c.260/265-339) ordained Basil priest, and five years later Basil succeeded Eusebius. Looking for theological allies, Basil appointed his brother as bishop of Nyssa and the other Gregory, bishop of Sasima.

The Cappadocians played a vital role in the development of Trinitarian terminology. Although they initially adopted the term *homoiousios*, they quickly recognized that their actual biblical belief concerning the relation between the Father and Son did not differ from the *homoousios* of Nicaea. Thus, they participated in the alliance of the *homoiousios* and the *homoousios* parties to battle against the heresy of Arianism.

More significantly, they formalized the use of two key terms to define the Holy Trinity. During the fourth century, Trinitarian terminology was still fluid and indecisive. For a time even Athanasius used the Greek terms οὐσία (*ousia*) and ὑπόστασις (*hypostasis*) interchangeably to refer to the "being" or "essence" of God. The Synod of Alexandria (362) acknowledged that it was appropriate to say God is either one *hypostasis* or three *hypostases*. The Cappadocians distinguished these terms. According to Basil, the Holy Trinity was one *ousia* ("being") and three *hypostases* (persons). Gregory of Nazianzus explained the Holy Trinity in this fashion

> Three in individualities or hypostases, if any prefer so to call them, or persons, for we will not quarrel about names so long as the syllables amount to the same meaning; but One in respect of the substance—that is, the Godhead. For they are

divided without division, if I may so say; and they are united in division. For the Godhead is one in three, and the three are one, in whom the Godhead is, or to speak more accurately, Who are the Godhead. Excesses and defects we will omit, neither making the unity a confusion, nor the division a separation. (*Oration*, 39.11)

With this language, the Cappadocians attempted to show how the Triune God was one essential being who was composed of three distinct persons: Father, Son, and Holy Spirit.

Rather symmetrically, the Cappadocian Fathers set the theological table for the Council of Constantinople in 381. Though Basil died before the council, the Gregories would attend the council at least briefly.

Council of Constantinople (381)

The Trinitarian controversy instigated by Arius mutated logically through the machinations of the Macedonians or Pneumatomachians (Greek, "combatants against the Spirit"). Just as Arius had denied the full divinity of the Son of God, the Macedonians denied the divinity of the Holy Spirit. There were two variations. Some were Arian, and so rejected the divinity of both the Son and the Spirit. Others, such as Eustachius of Sebaste (c.300-c.377) in Pontus, confessed that the Son was fully God according to the Creed of Nicaea, but denied the same of the Spirit.

Basil of Caesarea defended the divinity of the Holy Spirit against the Macedonians in his brief and insightful booklet, *On the Holy Spirit*. He noted the older doxology in the Greek East: "Glory to the Father through (διά, *dia*) the Son in (ἐν, *ev*) the Holy Spirit," but added another: "Glory to the Father with (μετά, *meta*) the Son together with (σύν, *sun*) the Holy Spirit" (*On the Holy Spirit*, 3). He argued that the older phrase was sufficient, except when used to subordinate the Son and/or Spirit, as though they were not worthy of being worshipped as fully God. The Cappadocian favored the newer doxology because by using it Christians could clearly and unambiguously worship the Son and the Holy Spirit as God.

Much more caustically, Basil attacked the Macedonian Pneumatomachians in relation to the sacred rite of baptism:

> How are we saved? Obviously through the regeneration of baptism. How else could we be? We are confirmed in our understanding that salvation comes through Father, Son, and Holy Spirit. Shall we cast away the standard of teaching we received? This would surely be grounds for great sorrow; if we now reject what we accepted at baptism, we will be found further away from our salvation than when we first believed. (*On the Holy Spirit*, 26)

Rejection of the divinity of the Holy Spirit was not a mere issue of theological hair-splitting, but a rejection of the salvation given in baptism by the Father, Son, *and* Spirit; a rejection of the very Christian faith.

Like Constantine, Emperor Theodosius (347-395, ruled 379-395) summoned the bishops to a council in Constantinople to address the Trinitarian controversy. Gregory of Nazianzus was the bishop of Constantinople and the president of the council until it was argued that he had previously been the bishop of Sasima, and so was ineligible according to ecclesial law. Rather than fighting, Gregory resigned both positions. The 150 bishops, primarily from the East, condemned the Macedonian heresy and appended the Creed of Nicaea. At Nicaea, the second article on the Son concluded with the terse reference to the Spirit: "I believe in the Holy Spirit." At Constantinople, the third article of the Holy Spirit was expanded:

> We believe in the Holy Spirit,
> The Lord and Giver of Life,
> Who proceeds from the Father,
> Who with the Father and the Son together is worshipped and glorified,
> Who spoke by the prophets.

While this article did not explicitly state that "the Holy Spirit is God," it strongly implied the same affirmation, giving to Him the divine titles of "Lord" and "Giver of Life." In addition, the Spirit was to be equally worshipped as God, along with the Father and Son. Thus, the three articles that are commonly called the Nicene Creed are more appropriately termed the Niceno-Constantinopolitan Creed.

Ambrose and the Arians

While heroes of the faith–Athanasius and the Cappadocian Fathers–defended the Christian church in the East, the battles on the other end of the empire were no less fierce. Orthodoxy in the West was championed by an unexpected and reluctant hero. When the bishop of Milan died in 373, Ambrose (c.339-397) was chosen to become the bishop, though he was a trained and talented rhetorician, a popular and gifted city governor, and also an unbaptized catechumen. Ambrose, for obvious reasons, initially refused the position and sought to flee, but finally acquiesced. Eight days later he was baptized and made bishop. Trusting that this was the will of God, Ambrose underwent extensive theological training.

The new bishop's principle enemies were at first political, but later were theological. Shortly after his episcopal appointment, the Germanic tribes, known as Goths, swept down from northern Europe. When they took several captives from Milan, Ambrose (see illustration) exchanged the sacred and valuable vessels of the church for their release. Arian adversaries condemned the actions of Ambrose, but Ambrose defended himself stating that Christian lives were much more valuable than ecclesial vessels.

With the death of the orthodox emperor, Valentinian (375), the western portion of the Empire was divided between his two sons, Gratian (359-383, ruled 375-383) and Valentinian II (371-392, ruled 375-392). The latter was a very young boy and under the supervision of his mother. When two Arian bishops, Palladius of Ratiaria and Secundianus of Singidunum, requested a council to address the doctrine of God, Gratian summoned the western bishops to Aquileia (381) on the Adriatic Sea. The thirty-two bishops chose Ambrose to chair the council. When Palladius was called upon to defend himself, he rejected the validity of the council. The council deposed Palladius and Secundianus from their ecclesial offices and condemned Arianism.

However, Valentinan II and Justina (c.340-391), his mother, were Arians. Residing in Milan, Justina demanded that Ambrose set aside one of the churches in Milan for Arian worship, but the bishop of Milan refused.

Consequently, she sent imperial soldiers who laid siege around the desired structure and threatened physical assault, but the faithful led by Ambrose remained in the church and the congregation sang orthodox hymns to God. Finally, Justina withdrew her troops.

Although Arius spawned his virulent heresy in the East, it also quickly propagated throughout the West. Emperor Constantine was very much responsible for its condemnation at the Council of Nicaea; however, his successors greatly varied in their theology, which worked against the elimination of Arianism. As the struggle between orthodoxy and heterodoxy waged on, Ambrose proved a mighty warrior.

Cyril of Jerusalem

Cyril (c.315-386) was the bishop of Jerusalem and a fourth century catechist extraordinaire. Following considerable instruction of the catechumens in the Christian faith, Cyril preached a procatechetical (introductory) homily, followed by a series of eighteen catechetical homilies during the Season of Lent. During the week of Easter, he delivered five mystagogical homilies, dealing with the "mysteries" of the faith, that is, the sacraments.

In these catechetical homilies, Cyril informed the catechumens on the most basic tenets of the Christian faith. For example, his fourth catechetical homily followed a creedal outline—briefly addressing God and Christ; he spoke of Jesus' birth, cross, burial, resurrection, ascension, and judgment; then he explained the person and work of the Holy Spirit; and finally, he concluded with remarks on the soul and body, the resurrection of the body, and the Holy Scriptures. The subsequent homilies went into greater detail about these and other doctrines. In the thirteenth catechetical homily, he clarified the all-encompassing merit of Jesus's crucifixion:

> *Catechesis*
> The Greek word for instruction was an integral part of the Christian church from its beginning. For example, Philip interpreted the prophet Isaiah for an Ethiopian eunuch showing how it pointed to Jesus (Ac 8.26-40), and Origen (185-254) instructed many, including Gregory Thaumaturgus (c.213-270), at his catechetical schools in Alexandria and Caesarea. Catechesis for adult converts included intensive and extensive study of the doctrines and practices of the Christian faith. Ultimately, these years of study resulted in Holy Baptism and membership in the Christian community.

> The Catholic Church glories in every action of Christ, but her glory of glories is the Cross.... It was not a mere man who died for us, but the Son of God, God made man. If under Moses the lamb kept the destroyer away, did not "the Lamb of God, who takes away the sins of the world," all the more deliver us from our sins? The blood of a brute sheep accorded salvation; shall not the blood of the Only-begotten much more save us? (Cyril, *Catechetical Homilies*, 13.1,3)

In addition, he helped them to understand their present catechesis in relation to their future baptism. The catechumens were to be actively involved in the catechetical process. They were like runners running a race or fighters fighting a battle, he said. They were to leave behind their old lives apart from God and approach a new life in the one, true God. God was the active agent in baptism uniting the baptized with the crucified Christ and clothing the baptized in the glorious attire of his resurrected Son.

In the mystagogical homilies, Cyril debriefed the newly baptized. Even though they had received extensive catechesis prior to their baptism, anointing, and reception of the Lord's Supper, they could never be fully prepared for what they would experience and receive in these sacred rituals. Having been submerged in divine mercy through baptism, Cyril sought to explain what had just happened to them:

> For as in the night one no longer sees, while by day one is in the light, so you during your immersion, as in a night, saw nothing, but on coming up found yourselves in the day. In the same moment you were dying and being born, so that saving water was at once your grave and your mother. (Cyril, *Mystagogical Homilies*, 2.4)

Cyril masterfully preached the Christian faith to catechumens. He both explained the biblical content and utilized vivid imagery to paint pictures of spiritual realities that transcend explanation. Of greatest import, Cyril preserved the doctrine and practices of Christianity through his faithful proclamation of Jesus and the message of the Gospel.

The Latin Theologians

While there was much work done in the East, two significant theologians arose toward the end of this century—Augustine and Jerome. Both of them had a great influence on the theology of Western Christianity as they wrote predominantly in Latin. We will look at their work in the next chapter, but we conclude this chapter with a review of their early lives.

Augustine's Early Life

From a seeker to a saint describes Augustine's incredible transformation at the close of the fourth century. Born on November 13, 354, in Tagaste, a small town in northern Africa, to a pagan Roman official, Patricius, and a Christian

mother, Monica, Aurelius Augustinus (354-430) became one of the most influential theologians of early Christianity since the time of Saint Paul. Some say his conversion to Christianity was nothing short of miraculous. (See illustration of Monica taking Augustine to school.)

Augustine was not baptized as a child, since in those days it was felt that baptism should be saved until after one "sowed his wild oats." This Augustine certainly did. In observing little children, Augustine noted the selfishness of an infant, which he considered as clear and obvious evidence of original sin. He also told of how with some friends he had stolen some unripe fruit in an orchard, illustrating the human enjoyment of wanton destruction. Something not even animals do, noted Augustine.

> I stole a thing of which I had plenty of my own and of much better quality. Nor did I wish to enjoy that thing which I desired to gain by theft, but rather to enjoy

the actual theft and the sin of theft…We took great loads of fruit, not for our own eating, but rather to throw to the pigs; we did this to do what pleased us for the reason that it was forbidden. Behold my heart, O Lord, behold heart upon which you had mercy in the depths of the pit. (*Confessions*, Book 2:5, 9)

Before his conversion, Augustine was an avid student of rhetoric in the great northern African city of Carthage. Rhetoricians of the time sought eloquence over insight and persuasiveness over truth. Yet, Augustine read the Greek rhetorician and philosopher, Cicero (104-44 BC), who in his *Hortensius* advocated truth-seeking, too. Augustine was soon teaching rhetoric there and met a young woman whom he could not marry, because she was of a lower class, yet with whom he fathered a son, Adeodatus (Latin for "gift from God").

Rejecting the Christianity of his mother as too simplistic, he became attracted to Manichaeism for several years. Mani (c.215/216-c.276/277), the founder of this philosophical religion from Persia, taught that the things of this material world (a realm of darkness) were evil and only the spiritual (the realm of light) was good. Sexual intercourse was obviously evil because it was physical, and having children was even worse. After encountering the most famous living leader of the Manichaeans, a man named Faustus of Milan (+399), Augustine found him pious, but unable to answer his own more profound questions.

After this disappointment, Augustine continued his philosophical searching and conversations. Quietly moving to Rome at the age of twenty-nine with is son and concubine, Augustine began to study the Greek philosophical concepts of Neoplatonism (the Latin translations of Plotinus by Victorinus were available to him in Rome). Plotinus had taught that evil was not a substance, but merely the absence of good. Neoplatonism helped Augustine move away from a purely materialistic view of the world and begin to understand a spiritual dimension. The Neoplatonic goal was to experience contemplative ecstasy. Yet, his experience in Rome did not bring him anything close to ecstasy, since his students often failed to pay him and he began to suffer financial concerns for his family (his mother had joined them soon after he had left Carthage).

In 384, Augustine was provided a position as a professional rhetorician in Milan. There, he heard about a very successful and popular orator, named Ambrose of Milan. Ambrose actually was a pastor and faithful preacher of the gospel. Initially, Augustine visited the church to learn of Ambrose's rhetorical style, but soon he was listening to the gospel message. Augustine was impressed with the fact that an intelligent man, a former civil servant, could grapple with issues of faith as a Christian. More particularly, he found the allegorical interpretations of Scripture, which were compatible with his Neoplatonic perspective, to eliminate many of his earlier difficulties with what the Manichaeans had taught were biblical crudities.

Still he clung to his pagan ways. (See *Confessions* 5.14) His mother finally convinced him to send his concubine back to Africa, and marry a girl of noble status. Unfortunately, the girl was too young to marry, and Augustine began living with another woman of the community. Around that same time, he was exasperated when he heard that the great Neoplatonist, Marius Victorinus (c.300-c.375), had become a Christian.

Then one day, as he tells his story in his *Confessions*, he was reading the book of Romans but put it aside. As he meditated on his life, he heard a child's voice say "take and read; take and read" (*tolle, lege*). He took up the book of Romans again and opened it to this passage: "Not in reveling and drunkenness, not in debauchery and licentiousness, not in quarreling and jealousy, but put on the Lord Jesus Christ and make no provision for the flesh, to gratify its desires" (Romans 13:13-14).

> No further wished I to read, nor was there need to do so. Instantly in truth, at the end of this sentence, as if before a peaceful light streaming into my heart, all the dark shadows of doubt fled away. (*Confessions*, Book 8:12, 29)

He was shocked to see his own life described there and realized his need for a savior, Jesus Christ. He continued:

> Who am I, and what am I? Is there any evil that is not found in my acts, or if not in my acts, in my words, or if not in my words, in my will? But you, O Lord, are good and merciful, and your right hand has had regard for the depth of my death, and from the very bottom of my heart has emptied out an abyss of corruption. This was the sum of it: not to will what I willed and to will what you willed. (*Confessions*, Book 9:1, 1)

Augustine's relationship with God had changed; Jesus had spoken to his heart; his vocation was now clear.

Augustine was baptized with his son, Adeodatus, on Easter Sunday, 387, by Ambrose and dedicated his life to serving Christ and His people. Planning to return to Tagaste with his mother and son, he suffered immediate disappointment. Both of them died unexpectedly within a short time of each other. Augustine then set up a monastic-type community, something he had done on a more secular basis earlier with friends in Italy near Cassiciacum. In 391 he became a presbyter to Valerius (+396), the bishop of Hippo, who needed a Latin-speaking assistant. Upon the bishop's death in 396, Augustine was installed as the head of the church in Hippo, where he remained for the rest of his life. We will see more of Augustine in chapter five.

Jerome's Early Life

Born in an unknown town in northern Italy about the middle of the fourth century, Eusebius Hieronymus Sophronius (c.347-420), his full name, had his greatest impact in the fifth century and beyond. His Christian parents came from the region of Dalmatia of somewhat noble stock which allowed Jerome to attend school in Rome. He was an ardent reader and a ferocious polemicist, trained in the great Ciceronian prose of classical Rome. He excelled in both Greek and Latin, although he had been raised in the Illyrian dialect. A few years after his Roman training, he traveled with his friend Bonosus and became acquainted with Rufinus of Aquileia (c.344/345-410). Soon he would share an appreciation with Rufinus for the work of Origen as well as Rufinus' major task of translating some of Origen's writings into Latin. (These translations became an invaluable source for many of Origen's works which were composed in Greek but were lost when he was declared a heretic.) In the meantime, Jerome wrote his first biblical commentary, *On Obadiah*, in 403.

Although they never met face to face, Augustine and Jerome were aware of each other's work and corresponded on occasion—usually criticizing the other for a theological statement or perspective which the other found incongruous with their own understanding of the Christian truth.[1]

Jerome's personality more than his piety was renowned. He had the uncanny verbal ability to speak and write harshly almost to the point of being insensitive; yet he also could write the most eloquent prose. Old before his time, yet respected among his peers, Jerome associated with few because of his stormy personality, sometimes calling his opponents "two-legged asses." He was involved in the various controversies of the era—especially continuing Arianism (see above) and the Pelagian controversy (see chapter five).

Frustrated by the sexual temptations he experienced in Rome, in 372 he fled to a remote desert hermitage in Syria for several years. In a self-revealing letter, Jerome reports that, while recovering from a fever, he had had a dream in which Jesus appeared to him as Judge and asked him who he was. Jerome replied that he was a Christian, but Jesus accused him of lying and instead being a self-righteous Ciceronian. Almost immediately, Jerome sought to divest himself of Roman paganism—although the eloquence and diction of Cicero remained in his Bible translation. On another occasion in a letter to Eustochium, he reported on his dessert experiences, "I seemed to myself to be in the midst of the delights and crowds of Rome.... In this exile and prison to which I had voluntarily condemned myself, I many times imagined myself watching the dancing of Roman maidens as if I had been in the midst of them." As a result of these sensual temptations while living a very ascetic life, he began to learn biblical Hebrew. As he noted in a letter to Rusticus (*Epistle* 125) from 411, "When my soul was on fire with wicked thoughts, as a last resort, I became a pupil to a monk who had been a Jew, in order to learn the Hebrew alphabet. From the judicious precepts of Quintilian, the rich and fluent eloquence of Cicero, the graver style of Fronto, and the smoothness of Pliny, I turned to this language of hissing and broken-winded words" (¶12).

Around 380, because of his irritation with his associates in Antioch, Jerome moved to Constantinople, where he had resided after his desert experiment had failed. While in Constantinople, he met Gregory of Nazianzus and was further introduced to the works of Origen. He began to work as a translator, amplifying Eusebius of Caesarea's *Chronicle*, a history of the world from Abraham to the Council of Nicaea, and also Origen's sermons on Jeremiah and Ezekiel. God was forming him for his vocational contribution to the church's life.

Returning to Rome in 382, under the encouragement of Pope Damasus (305-384, pope 366-384), he began the work that would make his name renowned—a revision of the Old Latin version of the Bible. Working on the New Testament, he completed the Gospels in Rome, but several months after the death of Damasus he fled from Rome to Bethlehem; or as he said, "from Babylon to

---

[1] For example, Augustine (*Epistle* 28.2) questioned Jerome's translation from Hebrew, believing that the Greek was superior and had stood the test of time by many translators. Jerome's tardy reply was merely that Augustine was too young to understand and shouldn't seek to debate with his elder who was obviously superior to him intellectually.

Jerusalem." His sense of purity was still from an outward understanding rather than seeing the purity of Christ within.

While still in Rome, Jerome had promoted a very rigid form of the monastic and ascetic life. There he became a spiritual leader, teacher, and spiritual counselor for a group of wealthy and aristocratic women—Albina (+387), whose palace they used, and her daughter, Marcella (325-410), Ambrose's sister Marcellina (c.330/335-c.398), and Paula (347-404). With them he studied and commented on Scripture, a practice which he continued for the rest of his life (see illustration).

One of the reasons for his abrupt departure from Rome was his rigid insistence that a rigorously ascetic life, particularly virginity, was superior to marriage. He argued in *Against Helvidius* and later *Against Jovinian* that Mary, the mother of God, was a model ascetic, because she maintained her virginity throughout her life. He also boldly attacked the comfortable life of the Roman clergy and nobility. On one occasion, he preached against the worldly women of Rome, saying that they "paint their cheeks with rouge and their eyelids with antimony." He continued:

> Their plastered faces, too white for human beings, look like idols; and if in a middle of forgetfulness they shed a tear, it makes a furrow where it rolls down the painted cheek. Women to whom years do not bring the gravity of age, load their heads with other people's hair, enamel a lost youth upon the wrinkles of age, and affect a maidenly timidity in the midst of a troop of grandchildren.[2]

Is it any wonder that the nobility of Rome, particularly the wealthy women, were happy to see him depart?

Jerome echoed the fears and frustrations of Christianity's new-found and already-entrenched acceptance of the culture of his day, recognizing that the softness of Christianity was also its potential downfall. Therefore, he sought to return to what he thought was the purity of earlier Christian living. After his flight to Bethlehem in 388, he established two small monastic communities for himself and several women, Paula (+404) and her daughters Blesilla (363-384) and Eustochium (c.368-419/420). Paula supervised the monastery for women and Jerome headed the men's monastery. In a letter to Eustochium laying down some severe rules for women, Jerome includes this telling paragraph:

> I praise wedlock, I praise marriage, but only because they produce virgins for me. I gather the rose from the thorns, the gold from the earth, the pearl from the shell. *Does the plowman plow all day to sow?* (Is. 28:24) Shall he not also enjoy the fruit of his labor? Wedlock is more honored, when what is born of it is more loved. Why, mother, do you envy your daughter? She has been nourished with your milk, she has been brought forth from your womb, and she has grown up at

---

[2] From *Butler's Lives of Saints*, cited in www.catholic.org/saints/saint.php?saint_id=10.

your bosom. Your watchful religious faith has kept her a virgin. Are you angry with her because she wishes to be the wife not of a soldier, but of a king?[3]

Jerome's monastic discipline was extreme. We will see more of Jerome's work in the next chapter.

    The fourth century commenced with the Great Persecution under Emperor Diocletian. It continued with Emperor Constantine's tolerance of and favor toward the Christian Church. It concluded with Emperor Theodosius establishing Christianity as the official religion of the Roman Empire at the expense of the pagans. This development brought great numerical growth to the church, but was also the context of controversy, particularly concerning the doctrine of God.

    The one Christian church had to be united in the one Christian faith. Divergent views on the Son of God and the Holy Spirit could not be countenanced. Consequently, Christian emperors summoned the bishops of the Christian church to Ecumenical Councils to confess the Christian faith and condemn heresy. The Niceno-Constantinopolitan Creed was the product of two Ecumenical Councils and became the fourth century touchstone of the Christian faith because it faithfully confessed Jesus and the message of the Gospel.

    In addition, this century saw the early lives of two of the most influential Christian writers of the West—Augustine and Jerome. It is to their lives and social contexts that we now turn.

For Review and Discussion

1. What significant role did Athanasius play in the Council of Nicaea?
2. Why were the Cappadocian fathers so helpful in their philosophical/theological distinctions?
3. Describe the influence of monasticism in this century.
4. What is memorable in Augustine's early years that undoubtedly affected his understanding of God?
5. How do you think Jerome would have related to you and your friends, if he lived in our time?

For Further Reading

Brown, Peter. *Augustine of Hippo: A Biography*. Oakland CA: University of California Press, 2000.

Chadwick, Henry. *The Early Church*. New York, NY: Penguin Books, 1990.

Davis, Leo D. *The First Seven Ecumenical Councils (325-787)*. Collegeville, MN: Liturgical, 1983.

Ehrman, Bart D. and Andrew S. Jacobs. *Christianity in Late Antiquity: 300-450 C. E.: A Reader*. New York: Oxford University Press, 2004.

Kelly, J. N D. *Jerome: His Life, Writings, and Controversies*. New York: Harper and Row, 1975.

---

[3] From *Handmaids of the Lord: Contemporary Descriptions of Feminine Asceticism in the First Six Christian Centuries*, trans. Joan M. Petersen (Kalamazoo, MI: Cistercian Studies, 1996). "Letter to Eustochium" (20).

Maier, Paul L., trans. *Eusebius: The Church History*. Grand Rapids: Kregel, 2007.
Quasten, Johannes. *Patrology*. Vol. 3. Westminster, MD: Christian Classics, 1992.
Rusch, William G. *The Trinitarian Controversy*. Philadelphia, PA: Fortress, 1980.
Williams, Megan Hale. *The Monk and the Book: Jerome and the Making of Christian Scholarship*. Chicago: University of Chicago Press, 2006.

5. Expansion of Christianity and the Latin World

The Fifth Century

Christianity was experiencing phenomenal growth during the first four centuries. But as with anything that grows, the church faced uncertainties and disappointments. The fifth century was marked by strong convictions and strong controversies. Purity of teaching was essential for the church's growth, yet the desire to communicate that teaching to a new age and to new peoples and in new languages created a theological tempest.

John Chrysostom and God's Voice

Among the strongest voices proclaiming the gospel was John of Constantinople (c.345-407). Surreptitiously made bishop in 398, he was soon

extremely popular with the common folk and just as unpopular with the wealthy clergy and notable politicians. John clearly and boldly preached messages of Law and Gospel, often pointing out specific sins of the wealthy and the powerful. Trained as a lawyer in his hometown of Antioch, he lived as a monk for several years before being ordained a deacon and then a presbyter. He brought to his pulpit, initially at Antioch and later as bishop of Constantinople at Saint Sophia, the rhetorical gifts of persuasive communication with the spiritual depth of a true follower of Christ. His powerful preaching would later result in his being known as John Chrysostom ("the golden-mouthed" in Greek).

Commenting on Hebrews 11:1, "Now faith is the assurance of things hoped for, the conviction of things not seen," Chrysostom preached the following in a sermon on baptism:

> What is the meaning of these words? Why have I said that one must not attend to the visible but develop spiritual eyes? I will tell you. I said it so that when you see the font with its water and the hand of the priest touching your head, you will not think that this is mere water or that it is simply the hand of the bishop that is laid upon your head. It is not a man who performs the rites, but the gracious

> presence of the Spirit who sanctifies the natural properties of the water and who touches your head along with the hand of the priest. I was right, then—was I not?—to speak of the need to have the eyes of faith if we are to believe in what is unseen instead of despising what our sense perceives.[1]

John Chrysostom's preaching brought comfort to many as he expounded on the biblical texts and proclaimed the forgiveness of sins through Christ alone. His *Homilies*, sermons on the Bible, are still studied by scholars and pastors. Yet, his preaching also provoked one of the most powerful persons of his day, the empress Aelia Eudoxia (c.365/375-404), who expelled him from Constantinople. Although rioting in his support ensued, Chrysostom left the city.

The actual cause of his exile was a combination of political and theological controversies. During this time, the issue of Origen's orthodoxy was being questioned. Jerome (345?-420) (see below) although translating many works of Origen from Greek to Latin, joined others in questioning the correctness of Origen's philosophical Christianity. Supporting some of the Origenists who came from Egypt to Constantinople for refuge, Chrysostom was deposed by a church meeting held in 403 under Bishop Theophilus of Alexandria (bishop 384-412). Hearing of this theological response, the empress quickly concurred.

During this initial exile, Chrysostom gained much support from the greater church, including a letter from the pope in Rome, Innocent I (pope 401-417), and was allowed to return for a while by the empress. However, when he began to compare her to Herodias (Matthew 14) and to the wicked queen Jezebel (1 Kings 21), she re-imposed her ban on him. Deported again, he died quietly on his final journey to the site of his intended exile near the Black Sea.

The involvement of Pope Innocent I is noteworthy at this point, since under his papal leadership, his position as the bishop of Rome acquired greater power and influence. Earlier, Pope Julius I (pope 337-352) had claimed the right of appeal over other bishops. That meant that if a dispute arose, he expected to serve as arbitrator. Innocent I, however, took that claim and insisted that all major disputes be adjudicated in Rome. The worldly power of papal authority was slowly but surely on the rise.

Christology in Conflict

The fourth century, so thought the leaders at that time, had resolved the burning issue of who Christ was. The Niceno-Constantinopolitan Creed had delineated the nature of Christ and his relationship to the Father—"of one substance with the Father." The creed was being spoken in the liturgy of the great basilicas weekly. Yet, there was still an undercurrent of uncertainty.

Theodore of Mopsuestia (c.350-428) was a well-known and highly respected exegete. He sought to articulate the theological view held in Antioch, where he had studied as a monk before becoming bishop of Mopsuestia in 392. He rejected the view that Christ had one composite nature and argued from Scripture that Christ had two natures or "hypostases"—the divine Logos (Greek

---

[1] From *The Awe-Inspiring Rites of Initiation: The Origins of the R.C.I.A.*, 2nd ed., trans. Edward Yarnold. Collegeville, MN: Liturgical Press, 1994. John's Second Baptismal Instruction homily (10)

for "Word") and "the Man." He said that the Logos of God indwelt the Man from the moment of conception, giving the Man divine status. His views, however, while maintaining a biblical focus, gave rise to a potential dualism of persons, although that does not seem to have been his intent. The issue of Christ's natures, however, was raised again and again controversy developed.

Nestorius's Error

Nestorius, the patriarch of Constantinople (c.385-451, patriarch 428-451), took Theodore's ideas to a more concrete expression. In his desire to be orthodox and to affirm the true humanity of Christ, Nestorius demanded in a sermon that his people not speak of Mary as the mother of God (*Theotokos*, Greek Θεοτόκος, "God-bearer"). She was, after all, only a person and should be referred to only as the mother of Christ (*Christotokos*, Greek Χριστοτόκος, "Christ-bearer"). That subtle distinction in terminology had theological implications which went beyond the city of Constantinople. As other people heard of Nestorius' pastoral injunction, they questioned the theological accuracy of such a distinction. Wasn't Jesus also God? If Jesus is God, then shouldn't we be able to call Mary, "the mother of God"? Letters soon were sent to Nestorius, reprimanding him for his inaccurate statement.

Cyril of Alexandria was one of Nestorius's most articulate opponents. A politically astute theologian, he secured support for his opposition from western Christian leaders, including Pope Celestine I (pope 422-432) in Rome. He warned Nestorius of his potential error. In response, Nestorius wrote an explanation of his position by showing how he was trying to avoid earlier heresies:

> Therefore, it is right and worthy of the Gospel traditions to confess that the body is the temple of the Son's divinity and a temple joined to the divinity according to a certain sublime and divine union, and that his divine nature makes his own the things of his body. But in the name of the relationship to attribute also to his divinity the properties of the united flesh, I mean birth, suffering, and death, is, my brother, the act of a mind truly led astray like the pagans or diseased like the minds of that mad Apollinarius, Arius, and the other heresies, but rather more grievously than they. For it is necessary that such as are dragged into error by the word relationship make the Word of God partake of the nourishment of milk through the relationship and have a share in growing, little by little, and of fear at the time of his Passion, and be in need of angelic assistance. And I pass over in silence that circumcision, sacrificing, sweat, hunger, and thirst, which happened to his body on account of us, are worshipfully united to the divinity. If these are taken with reference to the divinity, and falsely, there is a cause for just condemnation against us as slanderers.[2]

Read carefully, his view seemed to separate the person of Christ into two distinct natures and even persons. Later followers would argue that he merely wanted to distinguish the uniqueness of each nature, but the questions were critical.

---

[2] From *Saint Cyril of Alexandria, Letters 1-50*, ed. and trans. John I. McEnerney. (Washington, D.C.: Catholic University of America Press, 1987) "Letter to Cyril of Alexandria" (8).

A church wide (ecumenical) council was again called, this time by the emperors Theodosius II (401-450, ruled 408-450) in the East and Valentinian III (419-455, ruled 425-455) in the West. Held in Ephesus in June of 431, the assembled church leaders reiterated the theological position articulated at Nicaea and Constantinople that Christ had two natures in His one person. However, Nestorius's supporters were delayed and Nestorius refused to appear until they arrived. His opponents swiftly and specifically addressed the view of Nestorius. In one day's session they declared Nestorius' views heretical and approved the use of the term *Theotokos* in reference to Mary.

As a result of this controversial situation, Canon 5 of that Council stated:
> Those who have been condemned by the holy council or by their own bishops for culpable actions and those whom Nestorius (contradicting the canons with the indifference that characterizes him) or his followers sought out or may seek out to return to communion or to their rank. We have judged that these persons should in no way profit from these actions and should remain deposed.[3]

Nestorius's position was condemned. Yet, that was not the final answer, nor a complete answer. Christians in Persia, Assyria, Arabia and India continued to hold to the views of Nestorius (some into the twenty-first century).

Eutyches's Overstatement

An opponent of Nestorius, another monk from Constantinople named Eutyches (c.375/380-454/456), who had a significantly influential connection to the imperial court, attacked Nestorius's views as being inaccurate, yet Eutyches overstated his own position. Rather than arguing that Christ had two natures, Eutyches said that Christ had a new and different nature—different from God and also distinct from humanity. Jesus was "of one substance with the Father," he said, but not "of one substance with us." More disconcerting was his statement that Christ was "of two natures before the union incarnation, but in one nature after the union." This view is called "monophysite" (from the Greek word for "one nature") because it emphasizes that Christ has only a unique divine nature.

After some years of political and theological intrigue and controversy, Pulcheria (398/399-453, ruled 450-453), the sister of Theodosius who had suddenly died as a result of an accident, succeeded her brother and called another church wide meeting, which Pope Leo I (c.400-461, pope 440-461) suggested be held in Rome. Both Nestorius's and Eutyches's views were addressed at this fourth church wide meeting held at Chalcedon in 451. Once again the church leaders sought to articulate the pure biblical truths so that the gospel of God's actions in Christ was sufficiently clear and intelligible. Leo, in the meantime, submitted a carefully written letter, his *Tome*, in which he appealed to the baptismal creed of Rome. Because of his timely letter and its acceptance by the theologians and rulers, Leo's prestige in the East rose significantly and, in the West, he is often identified as the first real pope in the later medieval sense. In his

---

[3] From *The Church of the Ancient Councils: The Discplinary Work of the First Four Ecumenical Councils*, ed. and trans. Archibishop Peter L'Huillier (Crestwood, NY: St. Vladimir's Seminary Press, 1996), 154-164.

Tome, which was actually a letter to the patriarch of Constantinople, Flavian (patriarch 446-449), Leo wrote:

> Without detriment to the properties of either nature and substance (the divine and the human), which came together in one person, majesty took on humility, strength weakness, eternity mortality, and for the payment of the debt belonging to our condition inviolable nature was united with the suffering nature, so that, as suited the needs of our case, one and the same Mediator between God and men, the man Jesus Christ, could die with the one and not die with the other. Thus in the whole and perfect nature of true man was true God, born, complete in what was his own, complete in what was ours....[4]

The resulting doctrinal statement from this meeting at Chalcedon is sometimes called the Chalcedonian Creed, although it is more accurately named the Chalcedonian Definition, since it specifically and carefully defines only one aspect of the Niceno-Constantinopolitan Creed. The "definition" stated that only one person was united "unconfusedly, unchangeably, indivisibly, inseparably" in two natures. While not a complete or thorough definition, the statement was a delimitation beyond which orthodox Christians should not go.

The Definition of Chalcedon included the clarifications and reaffirmations of the Niceno-Constantinopolitan Creed (see box below). Clearly both the views of Eutyches and Nestorius are rejected in the third paragraphs as well as Arius's views. (Some Coptic, Abyssian and Armenian churches remain confessionally Eutychian, and many Protestant Christians today still hold a Eutychian view in their own piety.) The bishops and leaders also give equal status to Constantinople and to Rome, calling Constantinople the "New Rome."

Definition of Chalcedon

We teach and confess one and the same Son, our Lord Jesus Christ, at once complete in divinity and complete in humanity, truly God and truly man, consisting also of a reasonable soul and body; of one substance (*homoousios*), consubstantial, with the Father as regards his divinity, and at the same time of one substance (*homoousios*), consubstantial, with us as regards His humanity; like us in all ways, except for sin. As regards His divinity, begotten of the Father before the ages, but yet as regards His humanity born, for us men and for our salvation, of Mary the Virgin, the God-bearer (*Theotokos*), One and the same Christ, Son, Lord, Only-begotten, made known in two natures without confusion/mingling, without change, without division, without separation. The distinction of natures being in no way taken away by the union, but rather the characteristics of each nature being preserved, and uniting in one person (*prosopon*), and substance hypostasis,, not as divided or separated into two persons (*prosopa*), but one and the same Son and Only-begotten God the Word, the divine Logos,, Lord + Jesus Christ.

Unfortunately, the hope that a church council had "settled" the matter did not settle the matter. The Monophysite proponents rallied political support, particularly in Alexandria. For example, when a new patriarch named Proterius (patriarch 451-457) was appointed to succeed Dioscorus (patriarch 444-451), who had opposed Chalcedon, troops were called in to control the protesting mod. Proterius was lynched, and then in retaliation a new patriarch named Timothy "the Cat" (patriarch 457-477) was installed, since he supported the Monophysite position. Shortly thereafter he was exiled, but he was later reinstated to his office when a new emperor came into power.

---

[4] "Letters and Sermons of Leo the Great," in *Library of Nicene and Post-Nicene Fathers*, series II.

The Latin Church

Two contemporaries, as noted in chapter 4, share a common ground in being foundations for the developing edifice of the Latin church. Both of them are commonly referred to as saints of the church—Saint Augustine (354-430) and Saint Jerome (345?-420)—yet both of them also showed that they recognized their own "feet of clay." Their influence was felt most strongly among Christians living under the western regions of the Roman Empire, since both men wrote in Latin, rather than in Greek. Because of their significance for western Christianity, their lives and works will be explored in more detail here.

Augustine's Writings

First, as a teacher, then as a bishop and leader, Augustine articulated the Christian faith as it faced new theological questions and practical situations. Dealing with such theological topics as the character of God, the nature of humanity, the redemptive role of Christ, and the role of Church and state, Augustine articulated a profoundly biblical, yet philosophically nuanced view of Christian doctrine which remains strongly influential into the present. The wealth of Augustine's writings included not only doctrinal statements growing out of controversy, but letters of encouragement and innumerable sermons, preached from his *cathedra* in the north African city of Hippo.

Augustine's energies were directed less to philosophical questions than to pastoral issues. His early writings as bishop of Hippo dealt with Scripture and its authority as well as the origin of evil and the limits of human will to deal with spiritual matters. Augustine argued that humans had free will to deal with life's circumstances, yet this was not total or even real freedom. The question of evil grew out of his Manichaean misunderstanding of evil being matter. When he realized that evil was not material, he developed the idea that evil was the absence of good and more particularly the absence of God.

Augustine's *Confessions* (probably written around 395) tell the story of his life through the time of his conversion in 386. This spiritual autobiography is written as a prayer to God and is a confession in two senses—a confession of sins and a confession of faith in God's grace and providential love. He begins with this statement:

> You are great, O Lord, and greatly to be praised; great is your power and to your wisdom there is no limit. And man, which is a part of your creation, wishes to praise you, man who bears about within himself his mortality, who bears about within himself testimony to his sin and testimony that you resist the proud. Yet man, this part of your creation, wishes to praise you. You arouse him to take joy in praising you, for you have made us for yourself, and our heart is restless until it rests in you. (*Confessions,* Book 1:1.1)

Yet, this is more than a confession; Augustine articulated clearly the reality of human sin, not only his own, but that of all human beings, as well as the glorious power and effective results of God's grace, especially as evident in the life, death, and resurrection of Jesus Christ. Perhaps more than any other work, this book has remained influential for Christian thought and devotional life as Christians realize the possibilities of living in the world, but not of the world.

Augustine's writings deal with more than human experiences of sin and grace. When Augustine became bishop he brought his rhetorical skills to deal with pastoral and ecclesiastical concerns. Among these were the increasing conflicts between the catholic Christians in northern Africa and a dissident group known as the Donatists. (See chapter 4)

Augustine felt compelled to write against the Donatists as he served as bishop in the prominent African city of Hippo. In a series of tracts and treatises, he first sought to strengthen the Catholic community in northern Africa. He argued that the validity of the sacraments rested in the Word of God which gave them their effective power. Without such divine assurance, Christians could never be certain of the efficacy of their baptisms, since they could not know the spiritual condition of those who had administered the sacraments. Similarly, the church was holy not because of its members lives, but because of Christ's forgiveness and the presence of the Holy Spirit. Violence against the Catholic believers by the Donatists continued as Augustine sought reconciliation. Finally, Augustine engaged the political powers. The Council of Carthage in 411 condemned the Donatists. The fervor of the movement was weakened, but it remained a concern in northern Africa until the Muslims conquered the region in the seventh century.

A few years after Augustine became bishop, one of the most devastating events occurred in western Christianity; the Germanic tribe of the Visigoths under Alaric (c.370-410) invaded Rome in 410 (see below). Quickly and unexpectedly, the Christians were blamed. The majority of Romans concluded that with the rise of Christianity the pagan Roman deities were no longer "guarding" the city and so it was lost to the invading hoards. Similarly, Christians wondered where God's protective providence was. In response, Augustine penned his *City of God* in which he showed how Christianity actually builds society for the good of all. More than merely answering the immediate question of the fall of Rome, Augustine's *City of God* presents a Christian philosophy of history. Beginning with a critique of pagan philosophy and religion, Augustine shows that the highest goal should be service to God. Contrasting the church (the city of God, built on the love of God) with the world (the city of Satan, built on the lust of self-serving power), Augustine shows that all events are finally governed by God and that even evil is used by God for good. The struggle throughout world history is between these two realms—a struggle for purity or power.

In addition, Augustine opined that both church and state were part of society and each had a responsibility to the other—the church was to inform the state of the good and the right; the state was to provide security and opportunity for the free exercise of its spiritual guidance:

> The City of God we speak of is the same to which testimony is borne by that Scripture, which excels all the writings of all nations by its divine authority, and has brought under its influence all kinds of minds, and this not by a casual intellectual movement, but obviously by an express providential arrangement. For there it is written, "Glorious things are spoken of thee, O city of God." And in another psalm we read, "Great is the Lord, and greatly to be praised in the city of our God, in the mountain of His holiness, increasing the joy of the whole earth." ... From these and similar testimonies, all of which it were tedious to cite, we have learned that there is a city of God, and its Founder has inspired us with

a love which makes us covet its citizenship. To this Founder of the holy city the citizens of the earthly city prefer their own gods, not knowing that He is the God of gods, not of false, i.e., of impious and proud gods, who, being deprived of His unchangeable and freely communicated light, and so reduced to a kind of poverty-stricken power, eagerly grasp at their own private privileges, and seek divine honors from their deluded subjects; but of the pious and holy gods, who are better pleased to submit themselves to one, than to subject many to themselves, and who would rather worship God than be worshipped as God. But to the enemies of this city we have replied in the ten preceding books, according to our ability and the help afforded by our Lord and King. Now, recognizing what is expected of me, and not unmindful of my promise, and relying, too, on the same succor, I will endeavor to treat of the origin, and progress, and deserved destinies of the two cities (the earthly and the heavenly, to wit), which, as we said, are in this present world commingled, and as it were entangled together. And, first, I will explain how the foundations of these two cities were originally laid, in the difference that arose among the angels. (*City of God*, Book XI:1)

Thus, Augustine dealt with the question of why Rome fell in theological terms. The sins of the Romans can be the only answer to why the barbarians finally overcame the city. As any corrupted nation, Rome had provided many great benefits and therefore Christians should defend it in the face of hostile pagans. After all, Christ had come "at the fullness of time" (Galatians 4:4), which was during the *Pax Romana* (Peace of Rome), a time of order, and the Gospel was facilitated by their vast transportation and communication systems. In addition, Augustine condoned warfare as the government's responsibility to its people particularly because it was a God-desired tool to provide peace. Rulers, not the soldiers, bore the moral burden of proof for a just war—that is, said Augustine, a war that was motivated by love for those being defended and that opposed a clearly defined unjust enemy.

One Christian doctrine which has the mark of Augustine, but was not a result of controversy, was his writing *On the Trinity*, which he began shortly after becoming bishop but which he did not finish until near the end of his life. Augustine did not contribute the same kind of philosophical insights into the understanding of the Trinity as did the earlier Cappadocian fathers or even Athanasius and Tertullian (see chapter 4). Rather, Augustine's contribution came in the form of his analogies for the Trinity. He believed that once one understood the Trinity, other Trinitarian images become apparent in one's life. Initially, he described the internal relationship of the Trinity as analogous to a Lover, the Beloved, and Love (*On the Trinity*, Book VIII, 14, x). Augustine thought his analogy would help humans understand God as the source, the object, and the power. This comparison would then enable them to live more God-like lives. After a recess of several years, he continued to explain the Trinity and turned to other analogies, including his famous "psychological analogy," in which he compared the human ability to remember, know, and will (*On the Trinity*, Book XIV, 15, xii) to the three persons. Another analogy, following from human experience, was the tripartite human nature—body, mind, and spirit (1 Thessalonians 5:23). These images of the triune God have remained in the vocabulary of Christian writers ever since.

The last twenty years of Augustine's life were spent in bitter opposition to a British ascetic named Morgan, Latinized as Pelagius. Pelagius had acquired a significant following both in Rome (around 390) and in north Africa (shortly thereafter) with his teaching that people by their own efforts could be perfect without the assistance of God, since the commandments showed that God expected such perfection from humans. He claimed that there was a "spark" of good in everyone, a kind of "Adamic" condition, which merely needed to be tapped and then utilized for one's own salvation. Jesus was the ultimate example to be followed for such a life directed toward perfection.

Beginning cautiously in 412, Augustine wrote *On the Reward and Remission of Sins* and *On the Spirit and the Letter*, in which he argued against Pelagius' follower, Caelestius (c.+430), that infant baptism implied the church's recognition of original sin, but more importantly he argued for the necessity of God's grace in the life of all Christians. Finally, in 415, Augustine asserted that Pelagius erred in at least three ways from the biblical revelation, particularly from the words of St. Paul. First, Pelagius rejected the biblical truth that people have original sin. Secondly, Pelagius failed to see that the human will was thereby corrupted in spiritual matters. And, finally, Pelagius asserted that people could be saved by following the law, thus rejecting (in effect) the purpose of Christ's life, death, and resurrection. These errors needed to be confronted and corrected. Ultimately, Pelagius' views were condemned by at least five church councils, including the Council of Ephesus in 431. Augustine's strongest statements were made against Pelagius; yet, his most comforting words were also spoken as he reiterated the marvel of God's grace in sending Christ as the world's redeemer.

Curiously, in spite of the church's rejection of Pelagius's views, his teaching remained an influence in the Roman Catholic Church as well as among some evangelical Protestant denominations into the present. A modification of his view was articulated by John Cassian (c.359/360-c.435/440)) (see chapter 6) and, forty years later, stated most clearly by the abbot and rhetorician, Faustus of Rhegium (c.405/410-c.490/495). Cassian spoke of "seeds of goodness implanted in every soul by the Creator." Faustus stated that human free will begins the process of salvation which is supplemented by grace as a divine promise or warning.

Later known as semi-Pelagianists, those who held to this position claimed that humans can and must make the first move toward God and only then will God act by giving sufficient grace for people to work out their own salvation. Roman Catholic sacramental theology thus requires people to go to the sacraments as a work rather than as a gift; a significant group of Protestants, following the late 16th century teacher, Jacob Arminius (1560-1609) (see chapter 17) resurrected the same idea with what has popularly become known in the United States as "decision theology"(see chapter 20). Both of these semi-Pelagian views take the emphasis away from God's grace and focus on human efforts.

During the last years of his life, Augustine continued his pastoral concerns. About five years before he completed his *City of God*, he wrote a short catechetical resource for an otherwise unknown associate, Lawrence. In response to his request for spiritual guidance, Augustine prepared an *Enchiridion ad*

Laurentius, structuring this simple guide around the three great virtues of faith, hope, and love, as he explained:

> Now if I should answer, that God is to be worshipped with faith, hope, and love, you will at once say that this answer is too brief, and will ask me briefly to unfold the objects of each of these three graces, namely, what we are to believe, what we are to hope for, and what we are to love. And when I have done this, you will have an answer to all the questions you asked in your letter.

Beginning with faith, Augustine expounded the Apostles' Creed. Continuing with hope, he explained the Lord's Prayer. Concluding with love, he described the Christian's life that leads to eternity.

Similarly, he wrote a doctrinal exposition of Scripture, *De doctrina christiana* (on Christian teaching). Begun in 396 soon after Augustine became bishop, it was not completed until 427. The major theme of this work was that education should be Christian and that Christians can create a new culture through the biblical language of faith. In some ways, this was one of his most innovative essays.

The last years of Augustine's life, as mentioned above, also witnessed the rise of several Germanic peoples. The Visigoths (the western or noble Goths), under Alaric had sacked Rome in 410 and then moved on to Spain. The Vandals had crossed the Rhine about the same time from Scandinavia and entered northern Africa, laying siege to Hippo in 429.

Augustine died on August 28, 430 and was buried in Hippo. For several years near the end of his life he had returned to his study, reviewing his many writings. He prepared a chronological catalogue of his major works, giving explanatory comments on each of them. In the preface to these *Retractiones*, Augustine wrote: "Therefore, what remains for me to do, is to judge myself under my single Master, whose Judgment I desire to escape, for all my offences" (Prologue 2).

During these events, the western church was wrestling with many ideas promoted by Augustine of Hippo. Four years after his death, a monk from southern Gaul, Vincent of Lérin (+450), attacked Augustine's position, saying that it was not part of the larger Catholic tradition. Vincent crafted an expression in his *Commonitorium* which became the standard definition of tradition: "what has been believed everywhere, always, and by all" (*quod ubique, quod semper, quod ab omnibus creditum est*). A decade or so later, a follower of Augustine, Prosper of Aquitaine (c.390-c.455), coined another phrase in support of his teacher, when he argued that the church's practice, particularly in worship, creates a clearer expression of the church's faith. In support of infant baptism, he said that the law or rule or pattern of prayer or worship creates the law or rule or pattern of belief (*lex orandi, lex credendi*[5]). Both these ideas were later instrumental in helping the church deal with theological issues that potentially could divide the Christian community. The intent of each was to go back to the biblical roots of the church, yet over time, the church's tradition slowly became as authoritative as the Bible.

---

[5] Prosper's actual formula is *legem credendi lex statuat supplicandi*: the law of believing is established by the law of supplication.

Jerome and Scripture

Jerome's monastic life was one of selfless service, albeit quite extreme (see chapter 4). He not only supervised the monasteries, but he also kept up a voluminous correspondence with Christian leaders throughout the Christian world. From the depths of his cell poured a vast collection of commentaries and treatises. In addition, his Bethlehem monastery became a home for throngs of visitors and, after the fall of Rome, for refugees seeking comfort and security in this Christian site. The harlot-like city of Rome from which Jerome had fled with anger and fear had been raped by the plundering pagans and Jerome mourned her demise as he continued to expound and apply the biblical texts daily to the Christian community.

Through his writings, he had great influence. Besides his emphasis upon virginity and advocating the non-biblical teaching that Mary was a perpetual virgin, Jerome also encouraged the veneration of relics, which he claimed were not worshiped but only used as a way of paying respect for those martyrs who gave their lives. Coupled with the relics, he also continued to encourage people to pray to the saints. The roots of Jerome's opinions bore fruit in later Roman Catholic beliefs and practices.

A war of words also developed over the writings of Origen. His friend, Rufinus (340/345-410), had moved to Jerusalem and continued to translate Origen's sermons and commentaries into Latin. Jerome became vehemently opposed to Rufinus, when he learned that some monks had been introduced to erroneous thinking from Origen's words. The argument became so harsh that even Augustine became involved for a time. Shortly thereafter, Rufinus and Jerome went their separate ways.

Jerome's greatest influence came not from his theological work, though it was quite significant, but from his translating ability. Closeting himself in the bowels of the earth in a cell-like cave just beyond the traditional grotto of the Holy Nativity, Jerome spent years translating the Hebrew scriptures into the florid rhythms of Latin rhetoric. Until then, the Latin translations had been made from the Septuagint (the Greek translation of the Hebrew Old Testament with some additional material)—in other words, a translation from a translation. Jerome's final product, completed about 405 after over twenty-two years of labor, was known as the Vulgate, since it was a translation into the "vulgar" or common language of the people. This Latin version became the established and universally sanctioned translation of the Church for over a thousand years. In 1456 Gutenberg printed Jerome's text as the first Bible produced from a moveable press and one hundred years later, the Council of Trent (in 1546) declared the Vulgate as the official and only Bible translation for the Roman Catholic Church.

The last years of Jerome's life were almost completely consumed by his writing of commentaries on the Old Testament. Writing on the Minor Prophets (406), Daniel (407), Isaiah (410), and Ezekiel (414), he also opposed the Pelagian views, writing a *Dialogue against the Pelagians* in 416. In a letter to Ctesiphon, an advocate of Pelagius's views, Jerome wrote with a concern similar to Augustine:

> In order to deceive those people, you have also tacked on this phrase—"not apart from God's grace"—which deceives readers up front but cannot deceive when examined and very carefully poured over. Even as you establish God's grace...you mean by it free will and the precepts of the law, laying out that saying of Isaiah: "God indeed established the law as a helper" (Is. 8:20 LXX), such that in this are thanks to be conferred to God, because he established in us the ability to choose good and to avoid evil by our own will. You don't even understand that when you say this, the devil hisses intolerable blasphemy against your mouth. If indeed God's grace is merely this, that he established in us our own volition and we are content with free will, then we require no more of his assistance, unless we should demand that free will be abolished. Such people annul prayer and boast that through free will, they have been made not persons of their own volition, but even of Godlike powers, who require no support.[6]

Jerome died on September 30, 420 in his Bethlehem cell after two difficult years of remarkably ill-health, but his legacy lives on in his translation work.

Expansion and Exposure

During this same time, territorial tribes from the north and east were moving into the Mediterranean coastal lands occupied by the Roman Empire. These "invaders" were seeking more territory for their expanding powers and agricultural needs; and they also were experiencing the push of the Christians into their lands. A clash was inevitable.

The area first to experience this pagan invasion was the region around Constantinople. Yet that was not the only area of the world to suffer an Asian assault. Rome soon was feeling the hostility of the Vandals from northeastern Germany and the Goths from the Black Sea region or Scandinavia. These Indo-European peoples were gifted horse-riders and excelled in military stamina. By the turn of the fifth century, they had come to the doors of the great city of Rome. How shocking it was to have that noble and ancient city come under attack from barbarians, much less become a war-torn community. Yet, that is exactly what happened. When Rome was "sacked" in 410 by the Goths under Alaric (c.370/375-410), the whole Christian world was stunned. As mentioned above, Augustine tried to explain it as God's judgment. Others saw it as a result of Christianity's weakening of the polis and the anger of abandoned pagan deities.

The next years were distressing for all the people in the crumbling empire. After the Visigoth (western Goths) invasion and sack of Rome, the Huns, led by Attila (406-453), devastated the city of Aquileia, near Rome, and attacked the western region of the empire, known as Gaul. The Vandals soon followed, traveling through France (Gaul) into Spain and then south and east into northern Africa, capturing Carthage in 439. From there they moved back up through the islands of Sicily, Sardinia, and Corsica, from where they returned to conquer Rome in 455. In the meantime, the Huns forced some Saxon tribes along with the Angles (from the region of Angeln in northern Germany) to move across the channel into the British Isles to populate England (Angle-land).

---

[6] From *Hieronymus; Epistulae, pars III*, ed. I. Hilberg (Vienna: Verlag der Österreichischen Akademie der Wissenschaften, 1996). "Letter to Ctesiphon" (5); translated by Andrew S. Jacobs. TM changed "they" to "you" for effect.

The last emperor to hold sway over the city of Rome was Romulus Augustulus (c.460-c.500), ironically named after the mythical founder of the great city-empire. His unremarkable deposition in 476 by Odoacer (c.433-493) ended the thousand-year domination of the Romans over the vast Mediterranean region. No less than nine men had assumed the title and role of emperor after the last strong emperor, Valentinian III (423-455). The end of the Roman Empire in the west also marked a recognition that the Germanic tribes were new forces to be contended with. Odoacer had established the Goths as the new rulers of the empire.

The church, however, benefited from these barbarian invasions. Particularly under Pope Leo I (pope 440-461), known as "Leo the Great," the church centralized political as well as religious control over the people. His deputies had a great impact on the Chalcedonian Definition with his *Tome*, as mentioned above, defining the orthodox belief and also consolidating his own claim that the apostle "Peter has spoken through Leo." Strategically, he was able to persuade the Eurasian, Attila the Hun, nicknamed *Flagellum Dei* (Scourge of God), to leave Italy and secured cooperation from the Vandals not to destroy Rome after they laid siege to it. Emphasizing his Petrine authority (Matthew 16:18-19), Leo formed a secure stronghold for Christianity in uncertain times. The unity of the church would rest in his authority.

Unfortunately, Leo's successors began to draw powerful distinctions between Constantinople and Rome, setting the scene for later divisions between the two Christian centers. Felix III (pope 483-492) excommunicated the patriarch of Constantinople, and Gelasius I (pope 492-496), only added to the discord by claiming for himself the title, "Vicar of Christ," based upon the theory that the papacy held "two powers" or "two swords"—spiritual and temporal. The unity of the church was based more and more on earthly power than on the unity of faith in Christ.

Monastic Developments

Among the monastic movements which had risen during the previous century, two fifth century individuals are worthy of mention—Simon and John Cassian. Each of these men was seeking a dimension of purity which was not present in the world and each tried to create a holy environment on earth.

Probably one of the most famous of the eccentric monks who practiced extreme forms of ascetic self-denial was Simon the Elder (390-459). He is often called "Simon Stylites" because he spent the last thirty years of his life living on a platform atop a pillar in Syria where he preached to the people who came to visit him. Simon was respected as an authority and was even consulted prior to the Councils of Ephesus and Chalcedon. His influence, however, was less from his holy living than through his exotic behavior. The holiness of one's life should draw the observer to see Jesus, not oneself.

John Cassian (360-435) had a lasting influence on popularizing monasticism with his *Institutes* and *Conferences*. He prepared these two works as guidance for western Christians who were seeking to follow the Egyptian style of the ascetic life. John supposedly wrote the following poem in which he notes the various hours of prayer observed by the monks, which correspond to the life of Christ:

> At Matins bound, at Prime reviled, Condemned to death at Terce.
> Nailed to the Cross at Sext; At None His blessed side they pierce.
> They take Him down at Vesper-tide, In grave at Compline lay,
> Whence thenceforth bids His church observe Her sevenfold hours alway.[7]

Regrettably, John Cassian opposed Augustine and was a significant voice in the view which became known as semi-Pelagianism (see chapter 7).

Missionary Opportunity

Historian Justo González solicitously described the missional situation this way: "Many of the invaders were pagan, and therefore the conquered felt the need to teach their faith to their victors. Slowly, through the unrecorded witness of thousands of Christians, the invaders accepted the Christian faith, and eventually from their stock came new generations of leaders for the church" (I, 218). However, the invaders also brought their own form of Christianity into the West. Many of the Goths had had contact with an Arian form of Christianity a century earlier when Ulfilas (c.311-383) translated the Bible into his own native language. These Gothic Christians had lived and worked in Constantinople for several generations and Christian traders had frequently traveled into their territories.

Christianity had already spread to Great Britain in the south through the influence of the Roman Empire. When the Romans left the island because of the pagan invasions on the continent, the Christian population diminished considerably. Yet there seems to have remained a faithful core of Christians who followed their various vocations in the world and whose legacy would be revived in future generations.

Expansion of Christianity is most evidently marked by the work of missionary monks. Originally settling in isolated locales away from the populace, these monastic organizations saw their apostolate as outreach into the world. They would go into an isolated region and begin farming the land and conversing with the peoples of the area. After a significant group of monks and their lay neighbors had developed in one area, the monks would send a core group to a more remote region so that this very practical and effective process would continue.

---

[7] John Cassian, *The Twelve Books of the Institutes of the Coenobia*, Book III "On the Canonical System of the Daily Prayer and Psalms," trans. by E. C. S. Gibson, in *Nicene and Post-Nicene Fathers of the Christian Church*. Second series, vol. 1 (New York: 1894). The source of this English translation is unknown.

St Patrick

Patrick (c.385/9-460/1), an intriguing historical figure and missionary, became associated with Ireland as he brought the gospel to that isle of green. Little  is known of his early years, although in his autobiography he reports that his father, a Roman official named Calpurnius (c.350-c.400), was also a deacon. As the Roman legions were departing to defend the continent, Irish pirates (called Scots) began to attack settlements along the English (British) or French (Brittany) coast, plundering the lands and securing slaves for their lands. Among the slaves was the young sixteen year old lad, Patrick (probably named Maewyn Succat until his ordination), who was forced to serve as a swine herder. As he watched over the pigs he prayed for deliverance. Escaping the herd of pigs, he reports that he came to the coast where a cargo ship needed someone to care for their cargo of dogs when they sailed to France. Volunteering to assist, Patrick fled his captors. After gaining his freedom and coming in contact with some French monks, he returned home to England. However, he had a dream about unborn Irish children needing the Gospel. He returned to a French monastery for training, remaining there fourteen years. Finally, he secured approval from Pope Celestine (pope 422-432) and was ordained as a bishop, enabling him to return to Ireland around 432. There he baptized many of the inhabitants, establishing congregations in the north and west. He found strong opposition from the traditional religious leaders, the Druids.

Among the famous works attributed to Patrick is his Christo-centric affirmation of the Trinity in his famous "Breastplate":

> I bind unto myself today the strong name of the Trinity
> By invocation of the same, the Three in One and One in Three.
> I bind this day to me forever, by power of faith, Christ's incarnation,
> His baptism in the Jordan River, His cross of death for my salvation,
> His bursting from the spiced tomb, His riding up the heavenly way,
> His coming at the day of doom, I bind unto myself today.
> Christ be with me, Christ within me,
> Christ behind me, Christ before me,
> Christ beside me, Christ to win me, Christ to comfort and restore me.
> Christ beneath me, Christ above me, Christ in quiet, Christ in danger,
> Christ in hearts of all that love me,
> Christ in mouth of friend and stranger. (*Lorica*)

The faith of Patrick was clearly directed to Christ as the one who saved by grace alone. It was faith in Christ alone that he proclaimed wherever he traveled. Patrick died quietly around 461 at one of the monasteries he founded in Ireland.

Near the end of the century, the date was Christmas Day in 496 to be precise, the leader of the Franks, Clovis, was baptized into the Christian faith. As

Gregory of Tours (538-594)[8] reported a century later (see chapter 6). Clovis (466-511) had promised his wife, Queen Clothilde (475-545), that if he would be victorious in battle with the Alamanni he would convert to her God. With him were baptized 3000 of his army. In the next few years he would settle them in northern Gaul, where they would establish an agricultural people intermarried with the remaining Romans and adopt Latin culture and government, along with the orthodox form of Christianity.

For Review and Discussion
1. Review three of Chrysostom's *Homilies* and report on how he speaks the Law and the Gospel. Would Chrysostom's style of preaching be popular today?
2. Describe the errors of Nestorius and Eutyches.
3. What is the significance for the future of the church of the phrases espoused by Vincent of Lérin and Prosper of Aquitaine?
4. Why did the destruction of Rome have such an impact on the empire?
5. Of the many contributions made by Augustine, what insight do you find especially helpful for your own understanding of living "holy in the world"?
6. What is especially remarkable about the character of Jerome?
7. How did monasticism assist in the expansion of Christianity?
8. Who had preceded Patrick in Christianizing Ireland? Who followed him?

For Further Reading
Augustine. *City of God*. V. J. Bourke, ed. New York: Doubleday, 1958.
Augustine. *The Confessions of Saint Augustine*. E. B. Pusey, trans. https://www.gutenberg.org/files/3296/3296-h/3296-h.htm
Baur, Chrysostomus. *John Chrysostom and His Time*. Trans. by M. Gonzaga. 2 volumes. Westminster, Md: Newman Press, 1959-1960; reissued
Cahill, Thomas. *How the Irish Saved Civilization*. New York: Doubleday, 1995.
Chrysostom, St. John. *Homilies on Genesis, 1-17*. Ed. by Robert C. Hill. Washington, D.C.: Catholic University of America Press, 1999.
Cochrane, Charles Norris. *Christianity and Classical Culture: A Study of Thought and Action from Augustus to Augustine*. New York: Oxford University Press, 1957.
Duckett, Eleanor S. *Latin Writers of the Fifth Century*. New York: Archon Books, 1930.
Grillmeier, Aloys. *Christ in the Christian Tradition, Vol. 1: From the Apostolic Age to Chalcedon*, revised ed. Trans. by John Bowden. Louisville: Westminster John Knox, 1975.
Lienhard, Joseph T., Earl C. Mueller, and Roland J. Teske, eds. *Augustine: Presbyter Factus Sum*. New York: Peter Lang Publishing Inc., 1993.
Sellers, R. V. *The Council of Chalcedon: A Historical and Doctrinal Survey*. London: S.P.C.K., 1953.

---

[8] Gregory of Tours, *History of the Franks* (New York, 1927): II, 30-31.

6. Gregory the Great and Mission Activities

The Sixth Century

In spite of the conflicts and controversies which swirled around the centers of Christianity, there was also an awareness of others who needed to know of Christ. Perhaps second only to the first century, the sixth century brought a real expansion of the Christian faith. The people of God were reaching out with God's holiness wholly into the world.

Germanic Tribes

The Germanic tribe known as the Franks settled in northern Gaul (France) and later gave their name to that region. Under their brutally cruel leader, Clovis (c.466-511), they established a strong government by combining Germanic customs and Roman law. Soon after conquering the region, Clovis was baptized as a Christian (Christmas Day, 496) and the Franks for future generations would be supportive of orthodox Christianity, including the papacy in Rome. Clovis honored the Christian God as superior to the Germanic gods, who had held a juridical sway over the people's lives. Christ was often depicted as the victorious Christ (*Christus Victor*), the One who had conquered the hearts of these Germanic peoples. The message of the gospel changed hearts. The Burgundian king Sigismund (ruled 516-524), who held another part of Gaul, converted to orthodox Trinitiarian Christianity in 516. This kingdom was conquered by the Franks in 534 and finally all of Gaul was under Frankish Christian rule.

Around the same time, the Ostrogoth (eastern Goths) leader, Theodoric (454-526, ruled 475-526), took control of Italy, but followed an Arian form of Christianity. Theodoric had the great church of St. Apolinnarius built in his capital, Ravenna. After Theodoric's death, armies from Constantinople defeated the Ostrogoths as well as the Vandals in North Africa, but could not maintain control for long. Another tribe, the Lombards (literally, "long beards") from Scandinavia, invaded Italy in 568, and left their mark through their name on northern Italy to this day.

A touch of paganism remained to influence the Catholic Church's teachings, however. For example, the concept of repayment was strong among the German tribes. Compensation was paid to a family whose member was murdered and the loss of limbs required compensatory payments. (Eyes and feet were more costly losses than an ear; fingers were twice as costly as toes; even the loss of a fingernail required a minimum payment.) This practice would have later consequences for the Catholic teachings on penance.

Boethius and Christology

Theologically, the issue of Christ's natures continued to be of concern. One of the great philosophers and writers of this century was Anicius Manlius Severinus Boethius (480-524). He wrote a treatise *Against Eutyches and Nestorius* (see chapter 4) in which he not only emphasized the biblical understanding of Christ, but also affirmed the creedal mystery of the Trinity. His most renowned work, however, was *The Consolation of Philosophy* in which he argued that a Christian's soul can arrive at a vision of God (the "beatific vision") through philosophical study. This acceptance of Greek philosophy was promoted for centuries through this work as it became a standard text in the church for a millennium. Boethius wrote the following in order to clarify the distinction between fate and divine providence:

> The engendering of all things, the whole advance of all changing natures, and every motion and progress in the world, draw their causes, their order, and their forms from the allotment of the unchanging mind of God, which lays manifold restrictions on all action from the calm fortress of its own directness Such restrictions are called Providence when they can be seen to lie in the very simplicity of divine understanding; but they were called Fate in old times when they were viewed with reference to the objects which they moved or arranged. It will easily be understood that these two are very different if the mind examines the force of each. For Providence is the very divine reason which arranges all things, and rests with the supreme disposer of all; while Fate is that ordering which is a part of all changeable things, and by means of which Providence binds all things together in their own order. Providence embraces all things equally, however different they may be, even however infinite: when they are assigned to their own places, forms, and times, Fate sets them in an orderly motion; so that this development of the temporal order, unified in the intelligence of the mind of God, is Providence. (*Consolation of Philosophy*)

Such philosophical distinctions became foundational for later theological discussions.

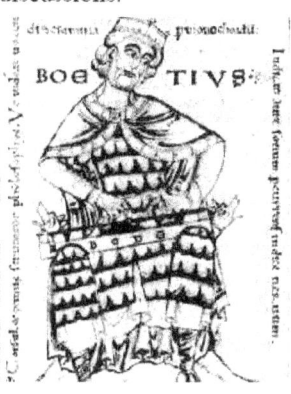

Boethius's life (see illustration) was not easy, in spite of his great learning. During his lifetime, the Arian Ostrogoths ruled Italy and often persecuted the orthodox leaders. As a result of contrived political charges of conspiracy, Boethius and his father-in-law, Pope Symmachus (pope 498-514), were imprisoned, where Symmachus died. In 524 Boethius was executed and, two years later, Pope John (470-526, pope 523-526), who had also been imprisoned, died suspiciously. As a result the three were considered official martyrs of the Roman church. Only after the invasion by Justinian's general Belisarius (c.500-565) in 544 were the Ostrogoths evicted from the region.

Synod of Orange (529)

After many years of controversy with the semi-Pelagians, particularly in Gaul, several voices remained strongly Augustinian, particularly Fulgentius of Ruspe (462/7-527/533) and Caesarius of Arles (468/70-542). The latter presided at a gathering (synod) of fourteen bishops and produced the first theological document from the area of Gaul. The twenty-five canons prepared at the synod brought the semi-Pelagian controversy to a sound conclusion. Using quotations from Augustine prepared by Prosper of Aquitaine (c.390-c.455), this synod affirmed Augustine's view of original sin and the fact that everything in humanity's salvation is attributable to God's grace alone. This grace will bring about works, which do not merit salvation, but are only an expression of gratitude to God. Pope Boniface II (pope 530-532) received the report of the council and approved it early in 531. This same document was used against Luther during the Council of Trent a millennium later.

Justinian I (483-565)

In the East, the tribal migrations had less an impact as the Empire grew stronger and stronger until the reign of Justinian I (c.482-565, ruled 527-565) and his wife, Theodora (c.497-548). Pope Hormisdas (450-523, pope 514-523) had settled the misunderstandings and tensions between Constantinople and Rome through a series of subtle, yet significant negotiations

Most important among Justinian's many accomplishments in his vocation as emperor was the publication in 529 of what commonly is called "the Justinian Code." Known as the *Corpus Juris Civilis* (body of civil law), this document established an enduring definition of Roman law both for the East and the West. Among the ideas explicitly articulated, besides an introductory section on the Trinity, was the assertion of the state's power over the church (a term somewhat inaccurately associated with this idea is *caesaro-papism*). While there remained a degree of cooperative concord between the spiritual and civil authorities, this relationship has shaped the Orthodox churches of the East ever since.

Already in 529, two years after assuming the imperial crown, Justinian (see mosaic portrait) closed the Academy in Athens, a center for Platonic learning and pagan practices. Around the same time, he required all unbelievers to be baptized and persecuted Samaritans and Jews along with outlawing Manichaenism, Arianism, and other heresies in his attempt to bring a Christian unity to the Empire.

Justinian also enhanced the architecture of Christian churches through his rebuilding of Hagia Sophia in Constantinople in the great basilica style. According to Procopius (c.490/507-c.560/565), a noted Byzantine historian of that era, the dome of this magnificent edifice "hangs as from a golden chain from heaven." Dedicated on Christmas Day, 538, this impressive building served as a model for generations of Christian congregations.

Between 548 and 565 Emperor Justinian was also instrumental in the construction of what is now the oldest Christian monastery, Saint Catherine's Monastery at the base of Mount Sinai in Egyptian peninsula. This monastery has remained active ever since, although it was briefly captured by Muslims.

Fifth Ecumenical Council (553)

Under Justinian's leadership a second Council of Constantinople was called (553) to deal with the continuing question of Christ's natures. Thinking that he could draw together dissident groups who had rejected Chalcedon, Justinian planned to attack, not the definition, but three Antiochene theologians in the controversy of the "Three Chapters." The "three chapters" were actually three authors' works—Theodore of Mopsuestia (see chapter 3), and his two students, Theodoret of Cyprus (c.393-c.458/466) and Ibas of Edessa (bishop 435-457) who sent a letter explaining their understandings of Christology to Maris of Persia. Ibas' strongly stated writings about Christ's two natures had been used and affirmed in Chalcedon. By condemning these works, Justinian intended to mollify the Monophysites and bring them into closer agreement with him.

> **Ecumenical Councils**
>
> During the first centuries of the Christianity, special meetings were held to discuss theological (and sometimes political) issues. These assemblies were legally convened by either the Emperor or one of the church leaders and were composed of members of the church hierarchy. Their purpose was to carry out judicial and/or doctrinal functions, through careful deliberation so that regulations and decrees would have the authority of the whole assembly. The first seven, which are recognized by most mainline Christian groups, are the following:
> First Council of Nicaea (325)
> First Council of Constantinople (381)
> Council of Ephesus (431)
> Council of Chalcedon (451)
> Second Council of Constantinople (553)
> Third Council of Constantinople (680)
> Second Council of Nicaea (787)

This Fifth Ecumenical Council tended to confuse the issue further by giving some concessions to Monophysite views. That approach did not draw the empire together as intended. At this council, a proposed compromise between the orthodox position and the Monophysite position was presented and accepted. Known as *"enhypostasis,"* (ἐνυπόστασις) the view is that Christ had two natures in one hypostasis or person. Leontius of Jerusalem (485-543) suggested that, following a kind of Aristotelian philosophy, Christ had one hypostasis (distinguishable and identifiable existence), which came from the Logos. Thus, Christ's human nature was not independent but rather was incorporated by the Logos. Although not a Monophysite position, there was a degree of understanding and acceptance by the bishops at the Council; however, the Monophysites were not content with this proposed solution and so formed their own churches during the end of this century—Armenian, Coptic, Syrian-Jacobite (named after the monk Jacob Baradaeus (+578), bishop of Edessa, who became a traveling missionary after being named patriarch of Antioch), and (later) Abyssinian (Ethiopian) communities.

In the West, a similar response resulted. Although Justinian brought the weak pope, Vigilius (pope 537-555) to Constantinople where he consented to Justinian's views, a synod of bishops in Africa excommunicated the pope and Justinian's actions were declared to be tantamount to a repudiation of Chalcedon and the Council's decisions unrecognized by several western sees.

Soon after Justinian's death, the pagan hordes once again entered Europe. The Scandinavian Lombards invaded northern Italy after 568 and Constantinople was besieged by other Asiatic peoples, particularly the Avars from central Asia and the Slavs from the Balkan region. Among these European invaders was the Visigoth (western Goth) ruler, Recared (586-601) who publicly converted to Christianity at the Council of Toledo in 589, embracing the Nicene form of orthodoxy rather than that of Arianism, which many of the other invaders had brought with them.

Much of the work of missions and evangelism grew out of a vibrant restoration of the Catholic Church under Pope Gregory I (c.540-604, pope 590-604). But prior to his influence there were several scholars and prolific writers and inexhaustible missionaries.

Benedict and Monasticism

Benedict of Nursia (c.480-c.550) has been called the "patriarch of western monasticism," since he established one of the strongest monastic orders to survive into the present. At first living only as a hermit in a cave near Subiaco, Italy, Benedict soon had drawn together a group of like-minded followers. This small community grew and moved to Monte Cassino, between Rome and Naples.

Initially designed to help organize these communities, Benedict's *Rule* was written in order to set forth in simple and clear language guidelines for a common community life. Members were required to renounce personal possessions (vow of poverty), to practice celibacy (vow of chastity), and to remain in their community for life (vow of stability)—thus eliminating wandering monks or isolated hermits. This last rule provided the Benedictine order with one of its greatest strengths in difficult times.

Obedience to the abbot (Latin, *abba*, "father") was to be unquestioned, unless a monk was incapable of performing the task assigned. He was also encouraged to consult the other brothers in the monastery on issues of grave concern. Breaking of the rule resulted in reprimands, first privately, but if repeated infractions occurred, publicly. Excommunication was the next step, which meant not only not being allowed to take Holy Communion, but also not eating with the rest of the monks. Whipping and expulsion from the community could follow, yet even these were not permanent and a repentant monk could return to the community up to three times.

Besides these three vows, the *Rule* designated three activities which were to occupy the monks' lives: the daily office (seven devotional services throughout the day and one at night), manual labor (usually in their vast farm holdings), and scriptural reading and meditation (called in Latin, *lectio divina*). Believing that "idleness is the enemy of the soul" (*Rule* 48), Benedict gave form to the life of the monks. All of this was under the general Benedictine principle of *ora et labora* ("prayer and work").

A daily schedule for a Benedictine monk would be something like this, with its particular emphasis on the devotional *opus dei* (work of God): Arising at about 2 a.m. the monks would assemble for Matins (a night service of the Word which included the chanting of several psalms) then go to their cells for private meditation until around sunrise when they would assemble to sing Lauds (a simple service of praise). For the next four hours they would study, perhaps stopping briefly for Prime (in which they would pledge their loyalty to God). At around nine in the morning, after a brief devotion (Terse) they would go out into the fields for three hours of agrarian labor. At noon (our English word comes from the Latin term for the ninth hour, *nona*, although technically this was the sixth hour, *sext*), the monks would eat one meal after a short devotional time recalling Jesus' suffering on the cross. (The actual ninth hour was 3 p.m., since the day began at 6 a.m., but Benedict realized men could not labor effectively without food earlier in the day.) An hour of rest was allowed after which manual labor was once again required. At three another brief devotional break was allowed for prayer (the actual office of None), along with a second meal during the winter months. The day ended in the late afternoon with a service of Vespers, which followed the evening meal in summer months. After preparing for sleep, a service ending the day (Compline) was conducted and the monks would silently go to bed soon after sunset.

Monasteries were self-sustaining, having their own tillable fields, a clean well for drinking water, and sufficient areas for poultry or rabbits or fish. Food was somewhat meager, even for these communities, since they would normally eat only bread and wine, vegetables and some meat (usually fish or poultry). Beef was reserved only for the weak. Benedict, however, did not promote an extreme asceticism, since he allowed for two meals a day with two cooked dishes at each, along with fresh fruit and vegetables as available. Bathing was a luxury and property was held in common. These institutions were not established for the comfort of the community, but for the glory of God.

Along with their land holdings, the Benedictine order established schools which were necessary for instructing the novices interested in prayer and Scripture. Benedict died in 550 after predicting his own death six days earlier. The death of King Totila (ruled 541-552), the last great Ostrogothic ruler, occurred two years later, as predicted by Benedict. When the Lombards plundered the Monte Cassino monastery in 586, most of the monks fled to Rome where the future Gregory the Great would come under their influence. The lasting legacy of Benedict is in his *Rule*, which is still used today in many monastic communities.

Cassiodorus, the Statesman Monk

Cassiodorus (c. 485-580) was a statesman turned monk and contemporary of Benedict, who also wanted to establish a monastic life. After serving King Theodoric as a statesman (senator), he founded a monastery in Vivarium in extreme-southern Italy as a center for biblical and humanistic learning.

The illustration at right is from an eighth-century Bamberg manuscript of Cassiodorus's *Institutions* and depicts the site of this ideal world. Cassiodorus described the monastery rather vividly:

> The site of the monastery of Vivarium conduces to making provision for travelers and the poor, since you have irrigated gardens and the nearby river Pellena full of fish--its waves threaten no danger, but neither is it despicable for its size. It flows into your precincts, channeled artificially where it is wanted, adequate to water your gardens and turn your mills. It is there when you want it and flows on when no longer needed; it exists to serve you, never too roisterous and bothersome nor yet again ever deficient. The sea lies all about you as well, accessible for fishing with fishponds [*vivaria*] to keep the caught fish alive. We have constructed them as pleasant receptacles, with the Lord's help, where a multitude of fish swim close by the cloister, in circumstances so like mountain caves that the fish never sense themselves constrained in any way, since they are free to seek their food and hide away in dark recesses. We have also had baths built to refresh weary bodies, where sparkling water for drinking and washing flows by. Thus it is that your monastery is sought by outsiders, rather than that you could justly long for other places. These are the delights of temporal things, as you know, not the things the faithful hope for in the future; these things shall pass away, but those shall abide without end. But placed here in the monastery, let us be in the power of those desires that will make us co-regents with Christ. (*Institutions* 1.29.1)

Among the emphases of Cassiodorus's monastery was academic transcription of the classic works by Cicero, Ovid, and Virgil. The copying of manuscripts required not only the self-discipline of the monk, but a significant financial cost—a single treatise written on parchment (animal skin) sheets would require a whole flock of sheep or goats. While his monastic model was not successful in his lifetime, his ideas as expressed in his book *Institutions* set a vision for future monasteries in the West which would follow his model of scriptural study with classical education.

Emphasizing the grace of God in Christ, Cassiodorus described the Christian's continuing vocation—not merely monastic, but throughout one's life, in his work *On the Spirit*: "In Christ's service no heart which gives itself wholly up to Him is ever found untouchable, nor can it fail to see what it seeks, nor can it lose what it is given in reward for loyalty." (*De anima* 17.33-36). Similarly, Cassiodorus interpreted the Psalms as being centered in Christ—either speaking of Him or His speaking through them.

Dionysius the Areopagite and John of the Ladder

Two curious figures from this century need to be introduced. Taking the name Dionysius (c.470-c.532) (also spelled Denis or Dennis), an Athenian disciple of Paul mentioned by St. Luke (Acts 17:34), this monk's Greek compositions were considered authentic products from the hand of a prominent disciple of Paul. In the ninth century, his works on hierarchy were translated into Latin, when they became a standard by which various bishops and popes claimed their superior authority over other clergy and, certainly, over the laity (see chapter 9). Because of its later origin, the incorrect attribution to the first century Dionysius is usually clarified by calling this monk, pseudo-Dionysius (the false Dennis).

This prolific Syrian monk prepared several detailed descriptions of angels and their orders and their application to the church life of his era. These influential works were entitled, *On the Divine Names*, *On Mystical Theology*, *On the Ecclesiastical Hierarchy*, and *On the Heavenly Hierarchy*. The latter two became standard works among mystical thinkers in the high middle ages. Gregory the Great accepted them as being authentic works from the first century. Dionysius' basic premise was that as monks contemplated the three triadic ranks of angels, they could acquire an ever-increasing closeness to God. Following a Neoplatonic way of thinking, he described a negative way of coming into God's presence—the Greek word is *apophatic*—by which one does not seek to understand qualities or characteristics of God, but rather one emptied simself of knowledge so that he experiences only spiritual things and

ultimately God Himself. This path of "unknowingness" speaks of "rays of divine darkness," and is sometimes called "mysticism of darkness."

Another monk of Syrian origin was John Climacus (525-606), who wrote a book on the ascent to heaven on a ladder (*climax*, thus his name, or a *scala*) (see illustration on previous page). Eastern Orthodox Christians still use his book, *Ladder of Ascent*, as a guide to their own spirituality during Holy Week as John describes thirty steps toward divinity. After presenting a variety of virtues to pursue and vices to flee, John concludes that the ultimate virtue is *apatheia*, a kind of dispassionate acceptance of all that one experiences in life. He is commemorated in Catholic and Orthodox churches on March 30, the date of his death.

Gregory the Great

Born in Rome to an aristocratic family in about 540, little is known of Gregory's (540-604) early years other than the city was in great disrepair and the glory of the city was no more. The conditions in Rome had become devastating after Justinian's rule broke down and the Goths left it in ruins. The ancient, yet effective aqueduct system had been breached so that sections of Rome had no water and other sections, because of the leaking water, had become marshlands rife for malaria. After the death of Justinian in 565, the Lombards were no longer held back by the Byzantine rule and frequently moved against the emperor's representative (called an exarch) in Ravenna.

Made governor ("prefect") of Rome around 573, Gregory left this wealthy position in Rome to become a monk according to the Benedictine *Rule*, establishing seven monasteries in the area with his family inheritance. Soon he was consecrated as one of seven deacons of Rome by Pope Benedict (pope 575-579). In that role Gregory was given many opportunities to work in the administrative area of the church. When the next pope, Pelagius II (pope 579-590), named him as his ambassador to Constantinople, Gregory was privileged to work for six years in the midst of several theological and political controversies which were centered in that city. He returned to Rome in 585 to serve as abbot of his monastery, St. Andrew, from where he assisted the pope in sanitation efforts and feeding the hungry.

On one occasion, Gregory, then still a deacon, led a procession of penitents through the streets of Rome. As he approached the Hadrian mausoleum, he had a vision of Michael, the Archangel, with a flaming sword which he placed in his sheath to indicate the ravishing plague would soon end. (The sepulcher has ever since been called the Castle of the Holy Angel, *Il Castello di Sant'Angelo*, and became a fortress sanctuary for several medieval popes.) Pope Pelagius (520-590), however, died in the plague and Gregory, against his will, was declared his successor.

Gregory (pope 590-604) assumed the administrative tasks necessary to restore order in Rome, including the purchase, importing, and distribution of food and the restoration of the aqueducts. As pope, he also encouraged the military stability of the region, acting as the political leader of that part of the Italian peninsula. Seeing the vast land holdings of the church, he also insisted that these estates be utilized to aid the poor. Another noteworthy political accomplishment of Gregory was establishing a treaty with the Lombards in Italy, enhancing the influence and power of the Roman see over against the ever-weakening Byzantine patriarch.

As bishop of Rome, Gregory preached regularly in the numerous churches of the city. He also extended his pastoral and political influence through correspondence with leaders in Spain, Gaul, and even Africa (over 850 letters have survived). Although these efforts were not always successful, his prolific writing has resulted in his being called "the Great."

Gregory (see illustration) is counted among the "Doctors of the Church." As a teacher (*doctores*) he wrote several influential books, particularly his *Book of Pastoral Care,* directing the bishops to be especially faithful in their watching over their spiritual flocks. The work, which described the bishop as a physician of souls whose main responsibility was to preach and enforce church discipline, became a standard guide for the bishops of the medieval church. His *Morals on Job* explored the monastic life of work and contemplation. Likewise, his *Dialogues on the Life and Miracles of the Italian Fathers* described the work of Benedict of Nursia and other monks. In both these latter works, Gregory's theological ideas took concrete form.

A strong promoter of monasticism, Gregory saw the potential in using monks to help expand the church's influence in the world. He himself had loved the monastic life, yet when he became pope he was shocked into action. In one of his sermons on Ezekiel, he recounts the biblical patriarch Jacob in Genesis 29. Jacob had two wives; Rachel was beautiful (depicted as the contemplative life) and Leah was fertile (depicted as the active life). In one of his sermons on Ezekiel, Gregory said he thought of himself as being married to Rachel when he was a monk, but said that being pope was like waking up in the night to find oneself in the arms of Leah...a shock, but a necessary and productive shock.

An oft repeated story about Gregory's early years is perhaps apocryphal, but it recounts his first experience of seeing three young blond men from England. Gregory asked the nationality of these boys and was told, "They are Angles." He continued, "They are accurately named, since they have faces like angels." In response to his question of their country of origin, he was told, "De Ire" (from Ireland). "*De ira* (Latin for "from wrath") they are indeed," said Gregory, "for they have been called from God's wrath to His mercy. Who is their king?" "Aella," was the answer he received. "Alleluia? Then God's name must be praised in that land." Thus, Gregory became concerned with those who were outside the general contact of Roman citizens.

In 597, seven years after his accession to the papal throne, Gregory sent forty monks under the leadership of the prior of Gregory's own monastery,

Augustine (bishop 597-605), to the isle-kingdoms. Experiencing many obstacles, Augustine requested that he return, but Gregory insisted that he and his companions continue to work with these Angles. Eventually, they met the king of Kent, Ethelbert (c.560-616), who was soon converted to Christianity (probably through the influence of his Christian wife, Bertha) and was baptized on Easter, 601. Augustine then set up a religious center for the kingdom in the capital city of Canterbury, where he became the first archbishop. He was thereafter known as Augustine of Canterbury to distinguish him from Augustine of Hippo.

In response to an inquiry from Augustine about how to deal with the various customs in the different churches, Gregory replied: "Select from each of the Churches whatever things are devout, religious and right; and when you have bound them, as it were, into a Sheaf, let the minds of the English grow accustomed to it" (Bede, *A History of the English Church*, Book 1, 27). In addition, Gregory organized the various churches in England into provinces (called diocese) which were supervised by a bishop. Over these bishops was an archbishop, who after some political disputes, was placed in Canterbury instead of London. The archbishop was ultimately responsible to the pope. The success of this system let to its expansion throughout the church.

Unfortunately, some of Gregory's writings influenced several doctrines of the Roman Catholic faith which had a negative impact on the church's biblical teachings in future centuries. Affirming Augustine's view of human nature being contaminated and corrupted by sin, Gregory correctly preached that Christ alone rescued people from sin through the waters of baptism, which brought forgiveness and the Spirit. However, he added the idea that sins committed after baptism had to be satisfied as well, through acts of penance. Penance became much more of a commercial procedure under Gregory by which one felt sorrow over sin (contrition) and then confessed the sin to a priest. The priest, besides speaking a word of absolution, would require that some kind of physical punishment or satisfaction (usually in the form of some work) be performed to prove the genuineness of the confession.

Gregory also emphasized the mass as a sacrifice for guilt incurred by venial sins or sins of weakness. These venial sins could be removed in purgatory if sufficient penance had not occurred in this life. Thus, purgatory served as a place to continue the satisfactions if they had not been completely fulfilled before death. Although the formulation of this teaching of purgatory was rather new, Gregory thought he was merely affirming the teaching of Augustine. However, whereas Augustine was speculating, Gregory insisted that there was such a place in fact.

Masses could be purchased in the name of a deceased relative, too, claimed Gregory. These masses were more than mere recollections of Christ's death, the priests were re-offering Christ as a sacrifice to God in payment for sins committed.

In addition, he formalized the liturgy and established schools for teaching proper conduct of the liturgy, called *schola cantorum*, evident in the attribution "Gregorian chant" to the stylized singing which actually predates his papacy. He also encouraged the veneration of relics of those recognized as "saints." His use of allegory in interpreting the Bible helped to make it the standard approach to Scripture for almost a millennium.

Gregory died on March 12, 604, but because of the impact Gregory had on the future strength of the Roman Catholic Church in the West, he is often identified as "the father of the medieval papacy." Although the title "pope" was used earlier by several bishops, both in the East and the West, the bishop of Rome gradually appropriated that title as his exclusive prerogative. Gregory's place in the rise of papal authority was sealed by his acquisition of temporal power over significant areas in Italy and over kings in more distant lands.

Gregory of Tours' *History*

Another Gregory should be mentioned here. Gregory of Tours (539-594, bishop 573-594) wrote a *History of the Franks* in which he reported on the powerful influence Christianity had on the inhabitants of the region. Raised in a Christian family of long-standing wealth, he was trained by clerics after his parents died and soon found churchly life appealing. Upon the death of the bishop of Tours, Gregory was elected to that position in 573. Experiencing the great suffering of the people because of the political uncertainties and inequities of the various princes, Gregory tried to maintain a political aloofness while serving the people of his community. Much of the information we have on the Frankish people comes from Gregory. Gregory reports: "I have written ten books of *historia*, seven of miracles, one on the lives of the Fathers, a commentary in one book on the psalter, and one book on ecclesiastical liturgy." He died on November 17 in Tours, experiencing the gracious patronage of the king and queen in his last years.

Eastern Concerns

During this era, the Greek Church continued to grow and expand, too. Yet, the Greeks' emphasis was theological and not political. They sought to further clarify their theological positions rather than to expand their political landholdings. Among the theological issues which the Eastern Church faced was the Monothelite controversy. A development of the earlier Christological controversies, this dispute had a more limited scope, yet a more vital concern in the East. Related to the Monophysite issue of the previous century, Monothelites taught that Christ had only one will. Coupled with some unsavory political intrigues, the controversy was not resolved until the later seventh century. (See chapter 7)

One seemingly insignificant issue occurred near the end of this century, but it would ultimately be a factor which led to the schism between the East and the West. The little word, "*filioque*" (Latin, "and the Son") was officially added to the Niceno-Constantinopolitan Creed at the Synod of Toledo in 589 (later sanctioned by the Synod of Aachen in 809). The desire in the West was to demonstrate that each of the persons of the Trinity was equal. In the East, however, to change the creed without an ecumenical council was a brash and disrespectful act. In addition, the Eastern prelates feared that the phrase had a potentiality of distorting the work of the Holy Spirit. The tension between the two churches began to increase significantly in the next centuries.

Monastic Outreach

Monastic activities continued in the British Isles after the work of Patrick (see chapter 5) and Augustine of Canterbury. In Ireland, Finnian (c.495-589) established a monastery from where his student, Columba (521-597), and twelve companions conducted missionary work on the Scottish island of Iona around 563. Both of these men were instrumental in expanding the Christian faith throughout the British Isles and beyond. These monastic communities were organized as religious as well as cultural centers and their structure resulted in a kind of church hierarchy which was more tribal than episcopal.

Born into an Irish Christian family, Columba was educated in the ways of the land and the people he would serve for over fifty years. While completing his training in Dub Linn (later Dublin), a devastating plague forced him to go out into the world to conduct the priestly ministrations for which he had been trained. Having an eloquent voice and a poetic heart, Columba crafted inspiring sermons and songs for his congregants. After a dispute with both his teacher, Finnian, and with his king, Columba left Ireland for Iona, where his monastery became a missionary center for future generations. Columba returned to Ireland periodically, particularly for ecclesiastical meetings. The day before he died, he had been copying biblical texts and had completed the verse, "They that love the Lord shall lack no good thing." He looked up and said, "Here I must stop; let Baithin do the rest." Baithin (c.536-c.599), his successor, continued the missionary and educational work begun at Iona.

Another monk from the Irish abbey of Bangor (which means "monastery"), Columbanus (543-615), founded a new monastery in Gaul around 590. In Gaul his rigorous Irish Catholic faith countered the more lax faith of the Frankish clergy. In a controversy over the date for the celebration of Easter, Columbanus insisted on an older dating system. As a result he had to flee to Italy, where he founded another monastery in Burgundy and from which his disciple, Gall (c.550-c.646), later founded a monastery in Switzerland (St. Gall).

Throughout this century, God's people worked to develop a greater contact with the world. Although distortions and errors crept into the official dogmas of the church, the Gospel was being carried out into the world through a variety of enterprising individuals and communities.

For Review and Discussion
1. What connection can you detect between the Germanic tribal idea of repayment and Gregory the Great's advocacy of penance and purgatory?
2. Considering the work of Boethius, Benedict, and Cassiodorus, which had the greatest impact on Christianity? Give three reasons or examples.
3. How would you defend the fact that Pope Gregory I was called "the Great"?
4. What is the theological problem with Dionysius' idea of a ladder to heaven?
5. Why was monasticism a blessing for Christianity throughout this century?

For further reading
Cahill, Thomas. *How the Irish Saved Civilization.* New York: Doubleday, 1995.
Daly, Lowrie J. *Benedictine Monasticism: Its Formation and Development through the 12th Century.* New York: Sheed and Ward, 1965.
Duckett, Eleanor Shipley. *Monasticism: The Gateway to the Middle Ages.* Ann Arbor: University of Michigan Press, 1938.
Mack, John. *Ascending the Heights—A Layman's Guide to* The Ladder of Divine Ascent. Chesterton, IN: Conciliar Press, 2000.
Marenbon, John. *Boethius.* New York: Oxford University Press, 2003.
Meisel, Anthony C. and M. L. del Mastro, trans. *The Rule of St. Benedict.* Garden City, NY: Image Books Doubleday, 1975.
O'Donnell, James J. *Cassiodorus.* Berkeley: University of California Press, 1979-93; postprint 1995, available from
http://ccat.sas.upenn.edu/jod/texts/cassbook/toc.html
Straw, Carole. *Gregory the Great: Perfection in Imperfection.* Oakland, CA: University of California Press, 1991.

7. A Crescent Moon Arises

The Seventh Century

While Christianity was growing stronger in western Europe under the papacy of Gregory the Great (c.540-604, pope 590-604), the once-vibrant communities in Egypt and Africa were no longer centers of Christianity. The gospel message had become side-lined by survival concerns and internecine fighting. Into this void came a new religious leader and a new religion, Muhammad and Islam. The Muslim crescent moon would gradually gain a dominant hold throughout that region.

Although Christians today are aware of the presence of Islam, less is known or understood of its origin and beliefs. This chapter will recount the growth of Christianity in western Europe, the British Isles, and the unique evidence of Christianity in China. A historical overview of Islam will precede a discussion on a theological issue which disturbed Christianity throughout this century, Monothelitism.

Isidore of Seville and Education

In the West, the most gifted theologian of the seventh century lived among the Visigoth (west Goths) peoples, Isidore of Seville (560-636). He was born into a prestigious family in Cartagena, Spain. His family had been influential in directing the Visigoth rulers to reject Arianism in favor of Roman Catholicism. Isidore was educated in the *trivium* and *quadrivium* at the cathedral school of Seville, perhaps by his older brother, Leander (c.534-600/601) who was bishop of Seville. Isidore became bishop of Seville around the turn of the century and presided over the Second Council of Seville in 619. His stress on education was motivated in part by a desire to unite the Gothic peoples in Spain as well as a desire to spread the truths of Christianity. In his old age, he presided at the Fourth Council of Toledo (633), where his educational reforms were accepted and promulgated. Among his educational innovations was the requirement that all bishops were to establish seminaries in their diocese. He was also a prolific writer.

> **Liberal Arts**
> To foster a free society (*liberal*), educators in classical antiquity promoted seven areas of studies (ars)—three in the area of human studies and four in the sciences. The three human studies—grammar, logic, and rhetoric—were called the *trivium*. The four sciences—arithmetic, geometry, astronomy, and music—were called the *quadrivium*.

His encyclopedic *Etymologies* provided a collection of ancient and current understandings of agriculture, astronomy, medicine, and religion. Through this twenty-volume work, Greek philosophical thinking was preserved (until the Arabic sources brought them back through translation in the twelfth century) along with much understanding of the shape of the world. Isidore was the first to propose, for example, that the earth was round—or at least disc-like. From his understandings, a map of the world was developed which is sometimes called the T-O map, since the Mediterranean Sea was drawn so that it divided the world like a T (see illustration). In his *Etymologies*, he cited over 150 authors, including Greek and Roman classical writers. The work remained an important textbook for almost a millennium.

Similarly, his *History of the Goths, Vandals and Suebi* (the latter were a Germanic people who had swept into France and Spain) along with his *Chronicle*, which covered world events from Creation to 616, laid the groundwork for future historical records of these early Middle Ages. Although his biblical and dogmatic works were merely compilations of previous materials, they exhibited a selective approach exemplary of life in Spain at that time. Isidore is also credited with preparing the final form of the Hispanic liturgy, which became known as the Mozarabic Rite after the Muslims took over the Iberian peninsula.

Growth in Christianity

The successors of Pope Gregory I were not as powerful or spiritual as Gregory. Boniface III (pope 604-607), for example, assumed the title "universal bishop," which Gregory had rejected as antichristian and blasphemous and which the patriarchs of Constantinople also claimed.

The Merovingian (Gallic) dynasty (named after Merovech [+453/457] a barbarian warlord of the Salian Franks and father of Clovis—see chapter 6) of the Frankish kingdom remained strong for the first part of this century. With the death of Dagobert I (c.502-639), however, the Merovingian line slowly degenerated. In the next century, a new political power arose in the person of Pepin II (c.714-768) and his illegitimate son, Charles (see Charlemagne [c.742/748-814] in chapter 8). This new dynasty was interested in reunifying the Frankish lands and defending their various frontiers from pagan raiders.

In the East, Emperor Heraclius (ruled 610-641) led Byzantine Christians in several victorious battles between 622 and 628 against hostile forces encroaching upon Constantinople from the East and the West. His highly trained army withstood the attack on his capital by two kingdoms, the Persians and the Slavic Avars, but they were not able to check the advance of the Muslim hordes which gradually encroached upon the Empire (see below). He did, however, rebuff the Persians sufficiently to regain Syria, Palestine, and Egypt for his imperial rule.

Christianity in the British Isles

Christianity in England began to thrive in this century. On Easter Sunday, 601, Augustine of Canterbury (c.550-604, bishop 597-604) baptized the king of Kent, Ethelbert, according to papal plans conceived by Pope Gregory the previous century. After Augustine of Canterbury's successes, the next forty years provided some stability for Catholicism in the British Isles. Around the same time, an Irish monk named Aidan (+651) was brought to England from Scotland by King Oswald (c.605-642) in order to christianize his kingdom of Northumbria. According to Bede (see chapter 8), Aidan developed a unique mission tactic, recruiting young men to be sent out as missionaries to carry on conversations with local peoples, engaging them in doctrinal discussions, including Cedd (c.620-664), later bishop of East Saxons, and his brother, Chad (+672).

This Irish-Celtic form of Christianity was competing with the Roman form—distinguished in part by ecclesiastical concerns such as the date of Easter and in part by civil concerns between the Angles and Saxons and Britons. King Oswig (c.612-670), brother of Oswald, finally called a council to seek a settlement between the Celtic and English perspectives. Only after the Synod of Whitby in 664 was the Roman influence secured when Oswig heard that the papacy had roots back to St. Peter.

Less than a decade later, at the Synod of Hertford, the Archbishop of Canterbury, Theodorus of Tarsus (c.602-690, bishop 668-690), was given primacy over all other bishops and church holdings. Given his Greek training, he was instrumental in developing a culturally diverse community by drawing from his Graeco-Roman background together with the Celtic and the Anglo-Saxon ideals. His reorganization of the English church helped develop a more secular form of government as well as an educational system which flowered in future generations (see Venerable Bede in chapter 8).

Because of his opposition to Theodorus, a British Benedictine monk named Wilfrid (c.633-709), who had helped in establishing the Roman form of Christianity, departed from England for Rome. Enroute to Rome, he began to do mission work in the region which would later become Denmark, an endeavor which his successor Willibrord (657-739) would expand and solidify. In 690, Willibrord took twelve associates and spread Christian ideas among the Frisians in what is now Holland. Five years later, he was ordained bishop and established his cathedral at Utrecht.

Muhammad and the Rise of Islam

Arabia at this time was a vast desert land surrounding the southern expanses of the ancient "fertile crescent." Inhabited by a wandering people, known as Bedouins or nomads, the word *arab* is derived from this wandering lifestyle. Tracing their lineage to Abraham's son, Ishmael (Genesis 17-21), this Semitic people group was loosely organized by family, clan, and tribe, headed by an elder (sheik). Tribal warfare and commercial trade worked together to create a dynamic social context.

Little is known of Muhammad's childhood and early years. He seems to have had some contact with both Christians and Jews and their Scriptures. In addition, the influence of a monotheistic movement in Arabia, known as Hanif, is apparent in his spirituality. His father died before Muhammad was born. He and his widowed mother resided in the Arabian city of Mecca, approximately forty miles east of the Red Sea. They were members of the prominent Quraysh tribe,  which served as custodians of a sacred shrine, the Ka'abah (cube). This pagan temple, which housed a supposedly sacred black stone (perhaps a meteorite) and several hundred idols, has continued to be held as sacred by Islam (see illustration). The *Qur'an* (literally, "the reading" or "the reciting") provides Muhammad's moral injunctions, but gives almost no information on his life. His most reliable biographers wrote over a hundred years after Muhammad's death, leaving much room for speculation and exaggeration. As a youth, Muhammad tended sheep and goats outside of Mecca and developed a deep appreciation for the poetic aspects of the Arabic language. At some point, he participated in caravan travel to Palestine, Syria, and Yemen. From that experience, he was invited to manage the caravan trade of a wealthy widow named Khadija (558-620). Because she was a distant relative, she asked him to marry her, although she was fifteen years his elder. This provided him with ample time to spend in contemplation and ultimately to receive his call.

Around the beginning of the second decade of this century, he claimed to have received a call from the archangel Gabriel and began to preach, declaring himself to be a new prophet. Muhammad's message was simple: God, or Allah, is one. He is all-powerful and all-knowing. Unconditional submission to Allah is the essence of this religious system, and thus the name of the religion is Islam (which means "submission" to Allah's will). Muhammad received several more divine revelations which were subsequently recorded in the *Qur'an* (also spelled *Koran*). These revelations told of good and evil angels and the immortality of the soul, which would be judged and rewarded or punished according to one's obedience to the five obligations ("pillars of Islam")—confession of faith, prayers five times daily, various forms of fasting (including the holy month of Ramadan), almsgiving for charities, and a once-in-a-lifetime pilgrimage (*hajj*) to Mecca. Islam also teaches that other prophets had come before Muhammad, including Adam, Noah, Abraham, Moses, and Jesus, but Muhammad was the final messenger who provided God's last and ultimate word. The *Hadith*, a collection of traditions from Muhammad, along with a body of laws (*Ijma*) are also part of the *Qur'an*. The religious actions and comments by Muhammad as recorded by his companions make up a second source of religious truth in Islam, called the *Sunna* or Path. One of the major sects of Islam, the Shiites, disputed the authority of this source in favor of additional guidance from Muhammad's successors.

After inciting severe opposition in Mecca because of his monotheistic views in a polytheistic culture, Muhammad fled north 250 miles to Medina (known as the *Hegira* [hijirah] or flight) on July 15, 622, the date most Muslims identify as the beginning of the new religion. At Medina, Muhammad organized a theocratic system in which he served as prophet, lawgiver, judge, and king. He negotiated a tribal alliance between two warring tribes in the area and solidified his support there, creating a community that was unique to the Arabic people, based upon religion and not blood lines. Here, after the death of his beloved Khadija three years earlier, he practiced polygamy and concubinage. By the end of his life, he had married a total of twelve women.

Returning to Mecca in 630 with a military entourage of over 40,000 Muslims, he quickly gained control not only of that city, since the Meccans offered no resistance, but in less than seven years he dominated the whole Arabian peninsula. Along with the decapitation of more than 600 men from the Jewish banu-Qurayzah tribe, one of the most famous stories of Muhammad is his night journey to Jerusalem. According to the *Qur'an*, Sura 17:1, "Glorified be He Who carried His servant by night from the Inviolable Place of Worship [Mecca] to the Far Distant Place of Worship [Jerusalem] the neighborhood whereof we have blessed, that We might show him of our tokens [signs]." Tradition says that a winged horse took him to Jerusalem where he met the angel Gabriel, who accompanied him to heaven and then returned to Mecca. The Dome of the Rock in Jerusalem marks the place where this event occurred. Over a period of twenty-two years (610-632), Muhammad composed the *Qur'an*.

> Quotations about Christianity from the *Qur'an*
>
> Christ Jesus, the son of Mary, honorable in this world and in the world to come, and one of those who approach near to the presence of God [3:45] ...Christ the son of Mary is no more than an apostle [5:74]. ...Jesus is no more than a servant....The Christians say, Christ is the Son of God...May God resist them....Kill them wherever you find them, and turn them out of that whereof they have dispossessed you [2:191]. ...strike off their heads, until you have made a great slaughter among them [47:4]. ..Those who fight in defense of God's true religion...he will lead them into Paradise...and there shall accompany them fair damsels having large black eyes; resembling pearls hidden in their shells [56:23]. ...They who believe not shall have garments of fire fitted to them, boiling water shall be poured on their heads [22:19].

Upon his rather painful death of a fever in 632, Muhammad was succeeded by various caliphs (literally "successors") who were more military than theological leaders. The continuing strife among Muslims in modern times stems from the various claims to legitimate leadership. Caliph Abu Bakr (632-634), the father of Muhammad's favorite wife, Aisha (613/614-678), consolidated the lands of Arabia and conquered the first Byzantine area. His successor, Caliph Omar [*Umar b. al-Khatttab*] (634-644) invaded Syria, conquering Damascus the following year and capturing Jerusalem in 638. He also proclaimed that only Muslim rule would be allowed in the Arabian peninsula, which included both Mecca and Medina. Uthman ibn Affan (644-656) then became caliph, establishing the official version of the *Qur'an*. After his assassination by the son of the first caliph while reading the *Qur'an* in his home, Uthman was succeeded by Ali ibn Abi Talib (c.600-661), the prophet's cousin and son-in-law (married to

Muhammad's youngest daughter Fatima [c.605-632]). His caliphate was much contested and many battles resulted from the power struggle between him and other tribesmen. The ultimate split between Sunnis and Shiites came with Ali's son, Hussai.

Among the characteristic features of this new religion was the use of force. Muhammad had purportedly asserted that "the sword is the key of heaven and hell; a drop of blood shed in the cause of Allah, a night spent in arms, is of more avail than two months of fasting or prayer; whosoever falls in battle, his sins are forgiven, and at the day of judgment his limbs shall be supplied by the wings of angels and cherubim." The idea of a holy war (*jihad*) against all infidels served to motivate many Arab followers as these military leaders became civil governors of the occupied areas. By the middle of this century, three of the five centers of Christianity—Antioch, Jerusalem, and Alexandria—were seized by Islamic forces.

During the initial century of their existence, Islam's dramatic conquest of many Christian regions, including Palestine, Syria, and Mesopotamia and the African lands that bordered the Mediterranean Sea from Egypt to the Atlantic

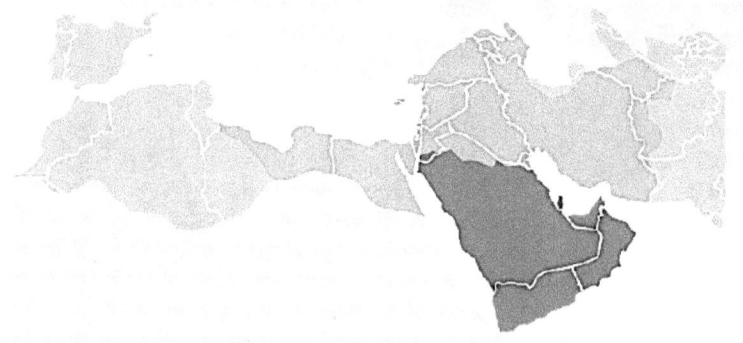

Ocean, caught most Christians by surprise. (Map displays expansion: dark gray: 622-632; medium gray: 632-662; lighter gray: 661-750.) The weakness of the Persian and Byzantine kingdoms coupled with the strong military solidarity of the Muslims explains some of these conquests. The territory conquered or controlled by Muslims was known as "the house of Islam" (*dar al-Islam*) in contrast to the *dar al-harb* ("the house of war") which meant that warfare was encouraged for the expansion of Islam. Thus, within a few decades most of the centers of Christianity—Antioch (638), Alexandria (641), Carthage, Damascus (635), and Jerusalem (638)—were under the control of Islamic caliphs. A major geographic shift was occurring in Christianity.

Internal strife among the various Muslim leaders continued throughout the final years of this century. Upon the death of Ali, his eldest son, Hasan (625-670), was poisoned after abdicating his power. Ali's youngest son, Husain (626-680), was killed shortly thereafter, but established a rift in Muslim rule. The followers of Ali are known as Shiites (*Shi'a* means "party" or those belonging to Ali) and continue to hold sway predominantly in southern Iraq and Iran.

Christianity in China

Although Christian tradition suggests that the apostle Thomas brought Christianity to India and some also claimed he came to China and even preached in Xi'an, no evidence of a Christian presence was evident that early in Chinese history. However, in the early seventeenth century a large stone monument was discovered, which describes events from the second quarter of the seventh century. Known as the "Nestorian Stele," (see illustration) this ten foot high limestone block was erected in 781 and describes 150 years of Christian activity. During the Tang Dynasty (618-877), China seems to have been open to Christian missions. The inscription on the stone tells how Nestorian Christian monks from the Assyrian Church of the East came to the area and were given a public hearing by officials, who approved of the general principles of this "illustrious religion."

In the year 638, a public proclamation acknowledge the work of a bishop Alopen (or Olopun), known only from this stele. Alopen brought the Christian Scriptures and, apparently, some icons. He was given administrative responsibilities for several congregations which the emperor sponsored. In addition, Alopen prepared a Chinese book about Jesus, which recent historians have given the title, *The Sutra of Jesus the Messiah,* a mixture of Christianity and some Buddhist philosophy.

The presence of Christianity in China continued throughout the Tang Dynasty, but subsequently disappeared, most likely through the strength of Buddhist philosophy and Islamic pressures.

Sixth Ecumenical Council (680-681)

As noted above, Emperor Heraclius (610-641) had resolved a major issue for the Empire by defeating Slavic raiders who had attacked the very walls of Constantinople, and regained land from Persian forces in Syria, Palestine, and Egypt. Through several brilliant campaigns between 622 and 628 these lands were once again restored in the eastern Empire. Feeling the blush of victory, Emperor Heraclius proposed a compromise position between the Monophysites and the Orthodox Christians in order to build a more solid political and theological union against the increasingly hostile Islamic forces. Although seemingly settled at Chalcedon and subsequently at the fifth ecumenical council, the Third Council of Constantinople, in 553 (see chapter 6), this Monophysite view continued to trouble the church, a position which claimed Christ had one nature.

In the East, this compromising view was promulgated by Patriarch Sergius I (patriarch 610-638), and in the west by Pope Honorius I (pope 625-638).

Emperor Heraclius used the term that Christ had "one energy" or "one operation" (that is, the two natures acted together in all activities and thus Christ had only one power—a form of Eutychianism) which corresponded not to His two natures, but to His being one person. This position was accepted by Sergius and Honorius, but unfortunately, Honorius changed the term from "energy or operation" to "will." He suggested that Jesus, although He had two natures, only had one united and divine will (the Monothelite error). Thus, Pope Honorius I, who had supported Sergius's and Heraclius's idea, confused the issue by failing to distinguish between "energy" and "will." In his so-called *Ekthesis* (exposition), Heraclius forbid any talk of "energy" and instead insisted on "will." The result was that he appeared to be saying that Christ's divine will took the place of a human will. This view, seemingly similar to that of Apollinarius of Laodicea (+390) (see chapter 4), raised the concern that a person without a human will cannot be fully human. Shortly after Honorius' death, Heraclius was opposed by Maximus the Confessor (580-662), an Orthodox theologian from Palestine who argued that both Christ's human and divine natures were involved in all of His saving work for humanity. In 648, Emperor Constans II (630-668, ruled 641-668) banned further discussions of the issue, concluding that Christ has two wills which correspond to His two natures.

In the meantime, Honorius introduced the festival of the Elevation or Exaltation of the Cross on September 14. He was also instrumental in sustaining the mission work in the British Isles. He helped resolve the conflict between the Irish and Romans over the date of Easter, in favor of the Roman dating of Easter.

By the end of the century, the imperial successor of Constans II, Constantine IV (c.652-685, ruled 668-685) called a sixth ecumenical council at Constantinople in 680-681. Honorius was anathematized posthumously by this Third Council of Constantinople for his position as a Monothelite along with other advocates of that view. The Council concluded:

> Christ had two natures with two activities: as God working miracles, rising from the dead and ascending into heaven; as Man, performing the ordinary acts of daily life. Each nature exercises its own free will....The two distinct natures and related to them activities were mystically united in the one Divine Person of our Lord and Savior Jesus Christ.

The great Christological controversy finally came to an end, but was also a triumph for western Christianity. The Niceno-Constantinopolitan Creed entered not only the baptismal liturgy of the church, but the Eucharistic services as well.

Curiously, Emperor Justinian II (669-711, ruled 685-695,704-711) called another meeting at Constantinople in 692 to complete the work of the Eastern prelates in establishing clearer disciplinary rules. Called either the Trullan  Council (from the domed room or *trullus* where they met) or the Quinisext Council (literally, "fifth-sixth" council, completing the work of the fifth and sixth councils), several decisive rules or canons were established at this time which showed a greater divide between the eastern and western Christians. In contrast to Gregory the Great's usurpation of the title, "universal bishop," the council stated that the bishops of

Constantinople and of Rome were equal. While bishops were required to be celibate, it permitted deacons and presbyters to marry and went so far as to condemn the Roman Church for imposing celibacy on all its clergy. The council also forbade the use of a lamb to depict Christ, insisting that a human figure be used to emphasize the reality of the Incarnation. In defiance of this, the Roman pope, Sergius I (c.650-701, pope 687-701) introduced the singing of the canticle, *Agnus Dei* (Latin, "Lamb of God") into the communion liturgy in order to counter this Eastern practice.

Perhaps no century had a greater impact on world affairs than did this century with the rise of Islam. While Christian education continued, especially as envisioned by Isidore of Seville, the breach between the East and the West seemed to become wider and more politically charged. Christianity was on the move, but it was also on several collision courses as will be seen in the next chapters.

Christianity or Islam?

But what a difference in the means employed and the results reached! Christianity made its conquest by peaceful missionaries and the power of persuasion, and carried with it the blessings of home, freedom and civilization. Muhammadanism conquered the fairest portions of the earth by the sword and cursed them by polygamy, slavery, despotism and desolation. The moving power of Christian missions was love to God and man; the moving power of Islam was fanaticism and brute force. Christianity has found a home among all nations and climes; Muhammadanism, although it made a most vigorous effort to conquer the world, is after all a religion of the desert, of the tent and of the caravan, and confined to nomad and savage or half-civilized nations, chiefly Arabs, Persians, and Turks....

And yet it is not hostile only. It has not been without beneficial effect upon Western civilization. It aided in the development of chivalry; it influenced Christian architecture; it stimulated the study of mathematics, chemistry, medicine (as is indicated by the technical terms: algebra, chemistry, alchemy); and the Arabic translations and commentaries on Aristotle by the Spanish Moors laid the philosophical foundation of scholasticism. Even the conquest of Constantinople by the Turks brought an inestimable blessing to the West by driving Greek scholars with the Greek Testament to Italy to inaugurate there the revival of letters which prepared for the Protestant Reformation.

Philip Schaff, *History of the Christian Church*, Vol. IV (New York: Charles Scribner's Sons, 1910), 150-152.

For Review and Discussion
1. Describe Isidore of Seville and his contributions to Christian thought and living.
2. What signs of deterioration in Christianity do you see in this century?
3. How was Celtic Christianity a benefit for the European Christians?
4. Why was Islam able to establish itself so quickly after the death of Muhammad?
5. Describe the missionary activities that were hallmarks of this century.

For Further Reading
Barney, Stephen A. W. J. Lewis, J. A. Beach, and Oliver Berghof, trans. *The Etymologies of Isidore of Seville.* Cambridge: Cambridge University Press, 2006.

Ehlke, Roland Cap. *Speaking the Truth in Love to Muslims.* Milwaukee: Northwestern Publishing House, 2004.

Fletcher, Richard. *The Conversion of Europe: From Paganism to Christianity, 371-1386.* New York: HarperCollins, 1997.

Kelly, J. N. D. *Early Christian Creeds.* New York: Longman, 1960.

Qur'an. Trans. by Muhammad Marmaduke Pickthall. http://islam101.com/quran/QTP/index.htm

8. Iconoclasts and the Ecumenical Councils

The Eighth Century

Political unrest, missionary expansion, and theological debates all came together in this century. With the incursion of Islamic forces and various Germanic tribes along with the increased tension between the Eastern and Western Christian leadership, several controversies erupted, particularly in the East. In the West, Christian mission developed in a unique way, as political and religious figures vied for power.

Battle of Tours

Islam extended its influence and political power to the borders of Constantinople in the north and to the southern borders of Spain and France. In 711, a marauding band of Muslims (later known as "Saracens") crossed the Straits of Gibraltar. (The name Gibraltar comes from the Arabic "Jebel Tarik" or Mount of Tarik.) These Islamic militants overthrew the weak Visigoth-controlled region of Spain, entering Europe for the first time. Under Islamic control, Spain developed a syncretistic cultural perspective made up of Christian, Jewish, Arabic, and Berber (a North African tribe) influences, often referred to as the Moors. (The names of the countries of Mauritania and Morocco retain this cultural connection.) Within the next few years, the aggressive and militarily-oriented Muslim empire would extend all the way to the borders of China.

In 732, a Frankish military leader, Charles Martel (c.680/688-741) ("the Hammer"), defeated the Muslim attacks on Frankish Gaul in a battle between Tours and Poitier, thus preventing further conquest of western Europe. Rejecting papal requests to pursue the Lombards in Italy, who had been his allies against the Muslims, Charles refused to return ecclesiastical lands which he had confiscated as payment for his military support. Thus, Charles laid the foundation for a stronger Christian presence in Europe, but also created a power struggle with the papacy. Both he and his father, Pepin of Herstal (c.635-714), sought to reunify their realms and strengthen the weak and deteriorating Christian influence in the region through military and missionary endeavors.

Boniface and His Mission

During the previous century, Christianity had reached a low point in spirituality as well as in social influence. With a weak papacy struggling against the patriarchs of Constantinople, the clergy were in a survival mode and were ineffective in keeping the focus on their mission to bring Christ to their communities.

Anglo-Saxon missionaries arrived from England in order to restore the Christian culture as well as establish a stronger papal connection through the political support of Frankish Gaul. Boniface (680-754), known in his homeland of England as Wynfrith of Crediton, was most effective in carrying the gospel back to central Europe. Initially working with Willibrord (c.658-739) around 716, Boniface was discouraged by his lack of success, but returned to Europe several years later. After consulting with papal authorities, he took the name of the Roman martyr, Boniface, and was consecrated as a bishop in 722 by Pope Gregory II (669-731, pope 714-731). Instead of being given a specific city to oversee, he was named "bishop of the German church" and so his mission opportunities expanded. With the political support of Charles Martel, he successfully evangelized much of southern Germany through his powerful and Christ-centered preaching.

> **Boniface and the Oak**
> A story associated with Boniface recounts his confrontation of paganism. Approaching a sacred grove at Geismar, ner Fritzlar, Boniface felled the oak sacred to the thunder-god Thor. After Boniface came to no harm, he proclaimed Christ as being superior to Thor and converted many.

For Boniface, ecclesiastical authority was exemplified by servanthood as demonstrated by Christ washing His disciples' feet. As bishop, Boniface received many gifts. No matter how insignificant or grand the gift would be, Boniface always responded in appreciation with a linen towel, reinforcing his own episcopal authority and servant mindedness.

Around 725, a bishop from England named Daniel of Windsor (+745) wrote to Boniface giving him advice on how to convert pagans. The gist of his argument was simply to point out the God of creation as being superior to the various Germanic deities. Propitiation was a key concept in the Germanic tribes' relationship to their gods. Each god had specific needs to be satisfied, yet the people were never certain what to sacrifice and to which deity. Particularly poignant, said Daniel, was the fact that because the pagans were unsure of their salvation, they could find true comfort in Christ's sufficient sacrifice. In addition, Boniface should ask them why Christians had the richly productive lands and they only had the frozen north. He sought to demonstrate the effectiveness of Christ's presence in his contemporary world.

In a noteworthy letter, Boniface wrote: "Let us not be dumb watch-dogs or silent spectators. Let us not be hirelings that flee at the approach of the wolf. Let us preach to great and small alike, to rich and poor, preach all that God has decreed to men of all degrees and ages, in so far as God gives us the power. Let us preach in season and out of season" (*Epistle 78*).

After the death of Charles Martel and Pope Gregory III (pope 731-741), both in 741, Boniface sought ecclesiastical (through the pope) and political (through the emperor) support for the German churches. Several synods—gathering of bishops—were held in Germany thereafter, culminating in Boniface being made Archbishop of Mainz and Primate of Germany. Near the end of his life in 754, Boniface resigned his ecclesiastical office and returned to Frisia as a missionary. There the following spring, after gathering several dozen candidates for a Christian confirmation, which included baptisms, he was martyred by Frisian bandits, who had hoped to acquire gold, but only found Boniface's manuscripts and books.

Venerable Bede's *History*

The original chronicler of England, Venerable Bede (673-735), studied in Northumbria and wrote on chronology, grammar, biblical exegesis, and history. For the most part, he lived his entire life from age seven to his death exclusively in the monasteries of St. Peter in Wearmouth and St. Paul in nearby Jarrow. Following a devastating plague in which all the monks of the monastery died, only the young lad, Bede, and the abbot survived. Bede reports that Abbot Coelfrid (or Coelfrith, c.642-716) and one boy (Bede?) conducted all the services of the Divine Office together until more monks could be enlisted. Ever since, Bede found the regular routine of daily worship stimulating for his own spiritual life (see illustration from the *Nuremberg Chronicle*). He was ordained a deacon and later a priest by John of Beverley (+721), whom Bede reports taught a deaf person to speak (*Ecclesiastical History*, Book 5, chapter 2).

His *Ecclesiastical History of the English People* remains a classic exposition of the early years of Christianization and missionary work as it coalesced in England. Noted for citing his sources, Bede sought facts rather than legends as the basis for his history. His calendric interest led him to date events on the basis of Christ's birth, *anno domini* ("in the year of our Lord"); the first to do so. In Book 1, chapter 2, he dates the Roman contact with England both from the founding of Rome, the usual way of dating events at that time, and also in relation to the birth of Christ.

Adoptionism

A seeming recurrence of an earlier heresy, known as Nestorianism, arose in this century in central Spain around the major city, Toledo. The Archbishop of Toledo had responsibility to oversee the theological teachings in his region. Having rooted out a heretic identified as a certain Migetius, the Spanish archbishop, Elipandus of Toledo (c.715/717-805/808), proceeded to argue that the man Jesus was united with the second person of the Trinity by way of "adoption" (*filius adoptivus*). This understanding may perhaps have been proposed as a way to explain the incarnation to the Muslim invaders and to maintain the oneness of God. Elipandus had used this term from the "Mozarabic" (Spanish) liturgy to emphasize the unity of Christ with all of humanity. The question was whether Christ was the divine Son of God in human form by nature or by adoption.

Elipandus suggested that, as Christ was adopted as the Son of God at his baptism, so each believer was adopted into God's family at baptism. Elipandus's views were supported and articulated most clearly by the Frankish bishop of Urgel, Felix (+816).

The problem with his explanation is that he made Christ into two distinct persons—one divine and one human, one from the Father and the other by adoption. The other problem is that the divinity of Christ was questioned along with the actual humanity of the Son of God. The first to raise concerns about this view was a monk, Morgan Beatus of Liebana (c.730-c.800), who wrote a two-volume work with his friend, Etherius (c.750-c.800), bishop of Othma, condemning Elipandus. Elipandus responded with threats to banish them both. When Charlemagne (742/47-814) heard that this view was held by Felix of Urgel in his newly acquired region, he convened a meeting in Regensburg in 792. Although initially recanting his position, Felix returned from Regensburg by way of Rome, where his recantation was accepted, and then to Spain, where he repented of his recantation! Several Spanish bishops then sent letters to the Emperor and Pope Hadrian I (or Adrian, c.700-795), requesting that they endorse the Adoptionism of Felix and Elipandus.

Most significantly, the English scholar, Alcuin (735-804), opposed Elipandus and Felix. Initially absent from his post in Frankfurt, Alcuin sent letters encouraging Felix and Elipandus to change their views for the sake of Christian love. He composed a treatise against the adoptionist view, which Charlemagne sent to various religious leaders, including the pope. Officially, adoptionism was condemned in 794 at the Council of Frankfurt. However, Felix was brought to a Synod at Aachen (Aix) in 799, called by the emperor, where Alcuin persuaded him to cease using the term, although privately he held this view until his death. Alcuin stated what would become the accepted formulation, "when God assumed fleshly form, the human person disappeared, but not the human nature."

Iconoclastic Controversy

The last ecumenical council, which is recognized by nearly every Christian group, dealt with a topic which had heated up and nearly boiled over for almost a century—icons. An icon (see illustration) is a stylized two-dimensional tempura painting on wood of a biblical figure, saint, or of Christ. Little objection to such drawings was evident in the early church, especially when one considers the many drawings and paintings in the catacombs depicting the sacraments and biblical stories, including pictures of Christ.

However, over time, questions had been raised whether icons were being worshipped or were merely adored. With the rise of Islam and the continuing influence of Judaism with their rejection of any depictions of humans, Christian leaders debated the appropriateness of such paintings, especially in Christian churches.

The iconoclastic (Greek, εἰκονοκλάστης, "icon/image" + "breaker") issue came to a head in the second decade of this century. After the horrific onslaught of the Muslim troops on the Byzantine Empire, Emperor Leo III (717-740) and his son, Constantine V (741-775) founded the Isaurian dynasty (named after the region around Mt Taurus in Asia Minor). Leo defeated Caliph Omar II (717-720) at Constantinople, reasserting Roman control of Asia Minor. But, in so doing, he also abolished all veneration of icons—whether painted or sculpted—of Mary or Christ or saints. He also removed the patriarch of Constantinople, Germanus (c.634-733), who opposed Leo's ban. Pope Gregory II resisted the mandate and rejected the emperor's policy as exceeding lay authority; a move which was both political and theological. Because Leo's military control over the Italian peninsula was weak and ineffectual, Gregory could take such a contrarian stand. His successor, Gregory III (pope 731-741), holding the same respect for icons, declared that anyone who profaned a sacred image should be excommunicated; in effect he was excommunicating Leo. Because of his distance from Rome, the emperor could do little with Rome itself, but finally confiscated the papal estates in Sicily and southern Italy.

Gregory III sought political support against the domination of the emperor in Constantinople and pleaded (albeit unsuccessfully) for the support of Charles Martel against the Emperor in Constantinople. However, another form of support arose.

Around the middle of the century, an unusual document suddenly but quite appropriately appeared, the *Donation of Constantine*. This document was based upon a popular legend that Emperor Constantine had been cured of leprosy by Pope Sylvester (+335). In gratitude for this miracle, Constantine is said to have given over all the patriarchates of Antioch, Alexandria, Jerusalem, and Constantinople, declaring that "more than our empire and earthly throne, the most sacred seat of St. Peter shall be gloriously exalted... [and] the city of Rome and all the provinces, districts and cities of Italy or of the western regions" be given

to the papacy. This forgery would have an enormous influence on papal powers over political leaders for almost a millennium. Not until the fifteenth century was this document finally recognized and identified by Lorenzo Valla (1407-1457) as a forgery prepared by an early medieval papal secretary.

In 754, Leo's iconoclastic son, Emperor Constantine V (718-775, ruled 741-775), at the Synod of Hieria, not only forbade the use of all icons in church, condemning anyone who defended their use, but also destroyed an image of Christ above one of the gates to the imperial palace in Constantinople. (See illustration from the 9th century psalter *Clasm Chludov*.) Such an act of desecration was condemned by the Patriarch Germanus and brought on a violent reaction among both laity and monks throughout the region. Among the condemned by that synod was John of Damascus.

John of Damascus and Icons

One of the greatest theologians in the Eastern Church, John of Damascus (c.675/676-749), was raised in Muslim communities. His father had held a high position under several caliphs, although he was a Christian, a position which John inherited for a period of time. He left that political post and entered the monastery of St. Sabas near Jerusalem where he wrote his great work, *The Foundation of Knowledge*. Parts one and two dealt with Aristotelian and Neoplatonic philosophical questions and earlier heresies. The third part of this work, "On the Orthodox Faith," gives a systematic presentation of the Trinity and the Incarnation and has served as a doctrinal source for Eastern Orthodoxy ever since.

In a series of discourses, John insisted that images may be "venerated" (προσκύνησις, *proskunesis*), but are not to be "worshipped" (λατρεία, *latreia*). Yet, he also noted that icons were not even objects of veneration, since they were merely portrayals or likenesses which conveyed to the mind what the artist had drawn. (People at that time considered light to be emitted from an object, so that light conveyed the object to the eyes and then to one's mind and heart.)

> **John of Damascus**
> To depict God in a shape would be the peak of madness and impiety.... But since God...became true man...the fathers, seeing that not all can read nor have the time for it, approved the descriptions of these facts in images, that they might serve as brief commentaries.
> *On the Orthodox Faith* IV.16

The real issue or concern related icons had to do with a proper Christology. John argued that "the hypostasis of God's Logos is perpetually one." He spoke of a "mutual penetration" (Greek, περιχώρησις, *perichoresis*, literally "a dancing together") of the human and divine natures in Christ in such a way that both natures retain their uniqueness and distinctiveness yet are united in the person of Christ. He also stated that the divine gave qualities to the human nature, but not vice versa. Thus, even in the icons of the church, the Lord's transcendent and majestic qualities are clearly evident. These works of the human hand mediated divinity, making the divine accessible to the senses. While not worshiped, icons may be adored because they bring the divine into the presence of the individual. Thus, the issue of icons had a theological foundation for devotional practices among Christian believers.

Liturgical Innovations

During this century, several liturgical innovations were introduced or became nearly universal. As a sign of their authority yet service, priests in Rome began to wear clerical stoles (the practice was followed earlier in other areas, particularly in the East). Reception of both kinds (bread and wine) in the Lord's Supper diminished among the laity as communion was considered something especially holy. At the same time, private masses increased as priests performed their duty in the confines of their private chapels, usually for specific causes or people and for a financial fee. Slowly a distinction between the laity and the clergy became more and more apparent.

The first evidence of the modern version of the Apostles' Creed is recorded by the missionary monk, Pirminius (c.700-753), in his collection of quotations from Scripture and Church Fathers. The first report of a church organ occurred when the Byzantine emperor, Constantine V (718-775), sent an organ to King Pepin III (714-768), in 757 for use in his chapel. In the next century, Charles [Charlemagne] would request that a similar organ be placed in his Palatine chapel in Aachen in 812. In 826, a priest from Venice named George built a calliope-sounding organ at the palace chapel of Louis the Pious (778-840, ruled 814-840)

at Aachen. (The illustration above is from the *Utrecht Psalter*, c.830.) Chanting, usually attributed to Gregory the Great (540-604), probably developed during this century as a combination of Gallic and Roman worship practices and spread through France, Germany, and England. Under Bishop Chrodegang (bishop c.742/8-766), a close political advisor to Charles Martel, a monastic rule for cathedral clergy was prepared which featured chanting of the Daily Office.

Pepin prescribed the Roman liturgy for his realm in 754 and Charles the Great (747-814) made the Roman Rite standard for his whole empire in 789. That same year, Pope Hadrian (c.700-795, pope 722-795) sent a Gregorian sacramentary (texts used by priests for various worship services) to Charles. Charles added several liturgical texts from Gallican-Frankish liturgies, since he noted in his preface that Hadrian's was deficient. Gradually, the liturgical life of the community became increasingly elaborate and formalized.

The Seventh Ecumenical Council: Council of Nicaea (787)

Returning to the issue of icons, some important distinctions were being made toward the end of this century. Serving as co-regent with her son, Constantine VI (771-c.804, ruled 780-797), Empress Irene (c.752-803, ruled 797-

802) convened a council at Nicaea in 787 in her son's name. An attempt to meet the year before in Constantinople had failed because of military opposition. Through the great influence and theological acumen of John of Damascus, the bishops gathering in Nicaea distinguished between worship (λατρεία, *latreia*), the kind of worship that is due only to God, and reverent service (δουλεία, *dulia*), a pious veneration which may be given to images. Although a helpful distinction, Pope Hadrian I and the Latin West did not find it completely acceptable, but did agree that images were beneficial objects because they enabled the laity to grow in their faith. The Council, the last of those recognized as "ecumenical," denied that icons were idols. Instead, they asserted that images could be venerated (*dulia*). In addition, the monastic properties which had been confiscated under Constantine V were restored. At a subsequent synod in Frankfurt in 794, Charlemagne's theologians held that pictures should not even be objects of adoration but only understood as pedagogical devices or decorative pieces for the God's people.

The Eastern theologian, Theodore of Studios (759-826), continued John of Damascus's Christological argument in favor of icons, saying that since Christ was human, God had "pictured" Himself. Similarly, he argued, the Gospels depict Christ in words, which was still an acceptable form for accessing God. Although the iconodules "won" the argument, iconoclasts regained some power for a time and only in the ninth century was the final victory able to be celebrated with the "Feast of Orthodoxy" (see chapter 9).

Politics and the Papacy

Returning to the political scene, in 739 Charles Martel came to the aid of Pope Gregory III, defending Rome against the surrounding Lombard dukes and princes. Two years later both died within two months of each other, as noted above. Negotiations between the papacy and the dominant ruling authority in Europe once again resumed. Boniface, the apostle to Germany, had worked closely with the Frankish successors of Charles Martel, Carloman (c.706/710-754, ruled 741-754) and Pepin III (c.714-768, ruled 751-768), both of whom had been raised in the Parisian monastery of St. Denis. Carloman and Pepin (also called "the Short") divided their father's realm, as was the Frankish practice, and served as "mayors" (*majordomo*) of their respective areas (see illustration). After several years, Carloman renounced his position in favor of a monastic life in Rome.

Meanwhile, the Lombard kings sought to conquer Rome. Pope Zacharias (679-752, pope 741-752) appealed to Pepin I, who was recognized as an experienced statesman and warrior. But in order to legitimize his rule, Pepin felt he needed papal recognition. After deposing the last Merovingian king, Childeric (c.717-754), Pope Zacharias delegated Boniface to anoint Pepin as king in March

751. The Merovingian rule was thus replaced with the Arnulfing house (later named Carolingian, after Charlemagne).

Five years later, the papal successor, Pope Stephen II (c.715-757, pope 752-757), placed Rome under Pepin's protection after the Lombards were defeated by his Frankish army. The pope then crowned and anointed Pepin and his two sons, Charles (c.742/748-814) and Carloman I (751-771), in the church of St. Denis in Paris and then declared Pepin to be the "Patrician of the Romans." ("Patrician" was the title given by Constantine the Great to the next highest ranking ruler; and, up until this time, the title given to the Byzantine ruler of Italy.) A few years later, Pepin came to Italy by invitation of Pope Stephen II and confiscated the land of the Lombardian king, Aistulf (749-756), forcing him to return it to the papacy.

This 754 land grant to Pope Stephen became known as the "Donation of Pepin," and created the first "papal states," land exclusively operated and owned by the Roman pontiff. The possession of this territory indicated that the papacy had powers over temporal as well as spiritual matters. Pepin was crowned the king of the Franks by Pope Stephen II as a reward for his gift as well as for providing aid against a Lombard blockade of Rome. This donation provided the papacy with an independence from political rule unknown for centuries.

Stephen II was succeeded by Pope Paul I (c.700-767, pope 757-767). Paul I was weak politically and lived in constant fear that the Eastern Roman Emperor would bring military forces against Rome. Following his death, several antipopes tried to gain control over the office of the papacy, including Constantine II (pope 767-768) and Philip (pope 768), who only served for one day. Finally, with political and ecclesiastical supporters, Stephen III (c.720-772, pope 768-772) was elected.

Upon the death of Pepin III in 768, his two sons, Charles and Carloman, received the divided kingdom, as was the Frankish practice. However, within three years, Carloman died and the whole kingdom came under the strong rule of Charles, who quickly established himself as "the Great." Concerned with Charles' alliance with the Lombards, the successor of Pope Stephen III, Hadrian I (or Adrian, c.700-795, pope 772-795), acquired more papal lands through the personal diplomacy and military tactics of Charles, who would crown himself king of the Lombards in 774. Thus, a new struggle was portended between the church and the state; a solution which would be realized tenuously on Christmas Day, 800 (see chapter 9).

This century ends with the powerful empress, Irene (797-802), ruling over the last vestiges of the Holy Roman Empire in the East. After deposing, blinding, and finally killing her son, Constantine VI (780-797), she continued to wield power until she was exiled to Lesbos, where she died the following year. In the West, Charlemagne would become the new figure for the future growth and expansion of Christianity.

For Review and Discussion
1. How did Charles Martel play a key role in several events during this century?
2. What makes Venerable Bede a noteworthy historian?
3. Describe the nuanced distinction made regarding the use of icons as objects of spirituality.
4. What liturgical innovations arose during this century?
5. Why did the papacy desire and acquire political territories?

For Further Reading
Bede, Venerable. *A History of the English Church and People*. Translated by Leo Sherley-Price. New York: Penguin Classics, 1955.

Giakalis, Ambrosios. *Images of the Divine: The Theology of Icons at the Seventh Ecumenical Council*. Leiden: Brill, 2005.

Lupton, Joseph H. *St John of Damascus*. London: SPCK, 1882.

Williamson, James M. *The Life and Times of St Boniface*. London: Henry Frowde, 1904.

9. Charlemagne and the Western Church

The Ninth Century

Christmas Day 800 was one of the most significant dates in the Middle Ages for both the church and the state. Charles, king of the Franks, became emperor over all western Christendom when Pope Leo III (795-816) placed a royal crown upon his noble head in Rome. Charles the Great (742/747-814), or as we are more familiar with the French form of his name, Charlemagne, created a legacy of power and prestige for both church and state. Because he wielded universal power over the church, Christianity established a strong foothold throughout his expanding empire.

Eastern Christians, in the meantime, were seeking to clarify several issues, particularly the proper use of icons and the relationship between the Eastern patriarchs and the Western papacy. Throughout this century, God continued to make sure that the gospel was being delivered to the ends of the earth.

Charlemagne's Revival

Before becoming emperor, Charlemagne, eldest son of Pepin the Short (see chapter 8), had gained hard-won control of lands held by the Frisians and the Saxons. By 785, after a series of bloody campaigns, which included the savage  "massacre of Verden," in which Charlemagne's troops killed 4,500 captured Saxons, Charlemagne had conquered and forced these Germanic tribesmen to become Christians. Offering them either baptism or death, thousands of pagans were "converted" to Christianity. Realizing that baptism was a sign that they had rejected their traditional gods, these pagan peoples had recourse only the Christian God as a source for their continuing existence. Unfortunately employing similar methods, they in turn went out to "convert" their neighbors, a practice which gave Christianity an ominous prospect for the future.

Approaching the western edges of his territory, Charlemagne (see illustration) invaded the Spanish peninsula, expecting support from the then-ruling Muslim leaders. Unable to conquer the city of Sarabossa, Charlemagne planned to leave Iberia. As he escaped, his troops, led by Roland, were ambushed and almost destroyed. Yet, as the eleventh-century epic poem, "Song of Roland" (*Chanson de Roland*) notes, God's will was still accomplished.

> Then say the Franks: "Lord God, be Thou our Guide!
> Charles we must not fail; his cause is right."
> ...
> Next of his flesh he has undone the seam,
> All his ensign thrust through the carcass clean,
> So flings him dead, let any laugh or weep.
> Upon that blow, the Franks cry out with heat:
> "Strike on, baron, nor slacken in your speed!
> Charles's in the right against the pagan breed;
> God sent us here His justice to complete."
> (*Song of Roland*, verses CCLXI and CCXLII, lines 3358, 3362-3368)

The poem recalls the 781 defeat at Roncevaux in northern Spain of Charlemagne's rearguard, led by Roland. In spite of this defeat, Charles had established a significant hold of the western lands and continued to work with several Moorish leaders to consolidate that control.

Indeed, already a decade earlier, in response to a request by Pope Hadrian I, Charles defeated the Lombard ruler, Desiderius (ruled 756-774, +786), and extinguished that kingdom in Italy in 774. As a result, Hadrian gave Charles the title, "the king of the Franks and Patrician of the Romans by the grace of God." Thus, Charles understood himself as an instrument of God for the good of both the church and the state. To rule was to fulfill his divine calling in the world.

While the pope was nominal head of the church, Emperor Charlemagne was its chief administrator, especially after his ecclesiastically approved coronation by Pope Leo III. For the next fourteen years, the papacy was directly under the emperor. Clergy were enlisted to assist the expanding government in the newly conquered territories. Laws were enacted which supported the work of the church, including the collection of tithes by the political officials. Yet, Charlemagne also had a spiritual sensitivity for his people. Among the laws he promoted was one which required that preaching be done in the language understandable by the people. In addition he ordered that Sunday be held as a day of rest and worship for all. He himself attended mass and vespers daily in his Romanesque chapel at Aachen. Rather than following the more elaborate Gallican rite, he asked Alcuin of York (c.735-804) to prepare a standardized version of the Roman liturgy in the Gregorian Sacramentary, which Charlemagne then promoted throughout his empire. Alcuin made an updated revision of Jerome's *Vulgate*, wrote several Bible commentaries, and contributed to the growing regulations of the church.

The revival of learning associated with Charlemagne is known as the "Carolingian renaissance." (*Carolus* is the Medieval Latin form of Charles with the Germanic suffix, *ing*, indicating parentage.) The classical academic curriculum once again was centered in the seven liberal arts—the *trivium* of grammar, logic, and rhetoric, and the *quadrivium* of arithmetic, geometry, astronomy, and music. Early Christian sources became the subject of monastic and ecclesiastical study. Under Charlemagne's patronage, Warnefrid (c.720-799), known as Paul the Deacon, wrote a *History of the Nation of the Lombards* in six volumes, covering over two hundred years of Lombardian culture and life. The

court scholar and historian, Einhard (c.776-840) wrote a comprehensive biography, *Vita Karoli Magni*, detailing Charlemagne's personal and professional life and his noble character. In addition, many nameless monks copied and embellished exquisite manuscripts in their scriptoriums (see illustration). These copyists of classical authors provided the only access later generations would have of the original thinking of these masters.

Much of the educational reform in the empire was a result of the able leadership of Alcuin who had come from Northumbria (England) and whom Charlemagne had met in Italy. Alcuin was a careful Christian thinker, who wrote several commentaries and philosophical treatises, including a work dealing with the nature of God, entitled *On the Trinity* (*De Trinitate*). He also wrote convincingly *Against Felix*, a Spanish priest who argued for "Adoptionism," a heresy which alleged that Jesus' humanity was only adopted by the Son of God (see chapter 8). He joined Charlemagne's court in 781 and remained a strong influence throughout Charlemagne's reign. As a result of Charlemagne's support, many scholars seeking to use their Christian vocations in a Christian context moved into the empire.

Noteworthy is the Benedictine monk, Hrabanus Maurus (780-856), who later became the Archbishop of Mainz. Hrabanus began his studies at Fulda, but was recognized for his intelligence and was sent away to Tours to study with Alcuin. Around 804, he returned to Fulda after studying with Alcuin for two years

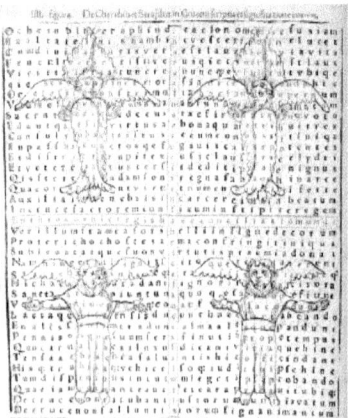

and, then, a decade later was ordained into the priesthood. After traveling to Palestine, he returned to Fulda and from 822-842 served as abbot, where he prepared commentaries on many biblical books. Near the end of his life, he was elected Archbishop, but felt his greatest service was in his literary production, such as his *De rerum naturis*, "of the things of nature." He is remembered for a peculiar form of poetic-art in which poems were composed of 36 letters and 36 lines on a grid often superimposed with a religious image (see illustration at the left). Among the poems were those honoring the holy cross, *In honorem sanctae crucis*. His hymn, "Come, Holy Ghost, Creator Blest," is still sung in many Christian churches.

Charlemagne's Successors

Charlemagne's second son was named Carloman (770/773-810) after two of his relatives, but, when he was crowned king of Italy in 781, he changed his name to Pepin, after his grandfather and older half-brother (c.767-811), who had been banished to a monastery in 792. Several months after a long, but unsuccessful siege of Venice in 810, he died, always ruling under the imperial authority of his father.

Pepin Carloman's younger brother, Louis the Pious (778-840), was given Aquitaine in 781, but then was named co-emperor in 813 by his father, sustaining the power and growth of Charlemagne's empire. One of Louis's noteworthy acts, besides continuing his father's political and educational endeavors, was to receive a copy of Pseudo-Dionysius' writings from the Byzantine emperor, Michael II (770-829), and send it to the abbot of the French monastery of Saint Denis, who claimed its author was their patron. This gift was translated thirty-five years later into Latin by John Scotus Eriugena (c. 810-877), although it was not widely used until the twelfth century.

Another policy, begun by Louis's father, was the restoration of monastic discipline. Through Benedict of Aniane ([751-821] not to be confused with the earlier Benedict of Nursia [480-547]), Louis restored order as well as a sense of piety in the monasteries. Benedict promoted his regulations in the *Concordia regularum* (Harmony of Rules) and *Codex regularum* (Book of Rules) over the next few years. The resulting monastic presence in which all the monks followed the same Rule provided a sense of peace and concord in a very troubled and socially disordered world.

After a series of internecine wars, the weakening of the empire became increasingly apparent. Upon his death according to Frankish tradition, Louis's three sons divided the kingdom, diminishing the Carolingian influence and power further. After a series of legal and military disputes, the Treaty of Verdun was formally accepted by the sons in 843. This date is often used to mark the beginning of the separate histories of Germany and France. Louis (804-876) received the eastern area by which he was given the nickname, "the German"; the youngest son, Charles the Bald (823-877), was given the western region (present day France); and the eldest son, Lothair I (795-855), took the strip of land between them, from the Netherlands to northern Italy. Subsequently at his death, Lothair's land was subdivided into three more regions and eventually the area became a string of insignificant principalities (see map below).

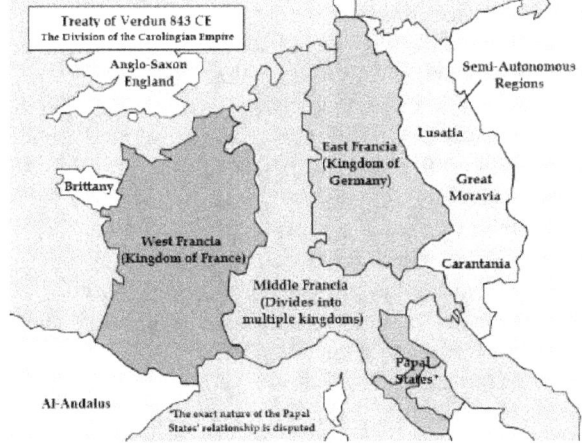

Around 840, raids by the Norsemen (or Vikings) began along the coasts of Europe and along the main rivers of the continent. Sailing swiftly with their sleek boats, which were up to 60 feet in length and could held as many men, these prowling pirates raised a major concern for the empire. Within twenty years they had penetrated Russia and in another ten years had occupied a portion of England north of the Thames. In 880 the Vikings from Denmark had dispatched an entire army of Saxons. By the end of the century, the land was reacquired by King Alfred the Great (849-899, ruled 871-899) in England, but "Danelaw" was officially accepted for central and northern England. By God's grace, many of the Vikings were Christianized, which resulted in a stronger church although a weakened empire.

The Triumph of Orthodoxy

In the East, the iconoclastic controversy had not been completely settled. Strong opposition to icons continued in parts of Asia Minor and particularly among the professional military class. They had suffered innumerable defeats for the first quarter of the ninth century and surmised that the "idolatry" of icons was the cause. With the ascension to the imperial throne in 813 by Leo V, the Armenian (775-820, ruled 775-870), the official policy of iconoclasm was re-established. The newly appointed patriarch, Theodotos I of Constantinople (patriarch 815-821), who was selected to replace the iconodule, Nikephoros (c.758-828, patriarch 806-815), called a synod which reaffirmed the anti-icon position of the previous century.

During the seventeen years following the death of Leo V, little persecution of the iconodules occurred. However, in 837, John VII (c.790-867, patriarch 837-843), known as Grammaticus, became patriarch and he persuaded the Emperor Theophilos (813-842, ruled 829-842) to take a strong iconoclastic position, including the mandate of capital punishment for anyone possessing an icon. Theophilos also restored the university in Constantinople where a lay theologian named Photios (c.810-c.893), later to be made patriarch of Constantinople, served as its distinguished scholar. At this time in history, theological purity was perceived as outward actions instead of faith in Christ alone. How one regarded icons was more important that what one believed. Although the iconoclastic controversy would soon end, the Eastern Empire had become extremely weak both politically and theologically.

Finally, the Byzantine Empire slowly began to expand with the reign of Emperor Michael III (840-867, ruled 842-867), who repudiated the iconoclastic issues of the previous century. In 843, the Empress Theodora (c.815-c.868, regent 82-855), holding the imperial authority for her young son, Michael, called a synod at which the patriarch John Grammaticus was deposed and iconoclasm was fully and finally condemned. This act confirmed the rulings of the seventh Ecumenical Council. The first Sunday in Lent is still celebrated among Orthodox Christians as the "Triumph of Orthodoxy" to commemorate this political conclusion of the iconoclastic controversy. Under the domination of Michael's mother, Theodora, and his uncle, Bardas (+866), Emperor Michael III built a strong navy and military force which defeated several Saracen caliphs between 853 and 863.

Photios and a Papal Power Play

In Rome, Pope Nicholas I (c.800-867, pope 858-867) reestablished papal power as he intervened in the affairs of both Eastern and Western Christian controversies. Nicholas had come to the papal throne just one year after the Saracen raiders had boldly entered the very basilica of Peter and Paul in Rome. One factor which elevated and empowered Nicholas was the discovery of the *Decretals*, consisting of early papal statements along with several forged documents including the *Donation of Constantine* (see chapter 8). These documents claimed to have the authority of Isidore of Seville (560-636). The *Decretals* (now known as the *Pseudo-Isidorian Decretals*) strongly suggested that the pope of Rome had supreme authority over all churchly and political powers already in the second century because of a direct apostolic connection through previous popes to Christ Himself. In addition, the documents required civil rulers to avoid interfering with the church's internal functions. Papal power was given considerable support and Nicholas boldly took it upon himself to use it to his own political advantage.

One aspect of Nicholas's increasing power grew out of his communication with the Eastern Church during the Photian controversy. The Archbishop of Constantinople at the time, Photios (c.820-893, patriarch 858-867, 877-886), had come to power after a revolution had deposed the conservative patriarch, Ignatios (c.798-877, patriarch 847-858, 867-877). Ignatios turned to Pope Nicholas I for support, which he secured as a result of Nicholas's excommunication of Photios in 863. Learning of Nicholas's support for Ignatios, Photios declared the entire Western church heretical, citing as theological grounds the introduction of the *filioque* (Latin, "and the Son") in the Nicene Creed. The earlier Councils had understood the relationship of the Holy Spirit in the Trinity as proceeding from the Father *through* the Son. The *filioque* was included in the Creed used at Charlemagne's chapel at Aachen and, when some Frankish monks visited Constantinople, they created a scandal among the Eastern Christians by including that term as they confessed the creed. They were immediately questioned regarding who had authorized the amending of this ecumenical creed. In answer to Photios' accusation and excommunication, Nicholas resurrected the old Roman Creed (the Apostles' Creed) and replaced the Nicene Creed with it in the liturgy of the West. Back at Constantinople with the installation of a new emperor, Basil I (811-886, ruled 867-886), Ignatios was restored to his patriarchate and Photios was promised to be made his successor upon his death, but the bitterness between the East and West persisted.

Although the controversy was quelled, the *filioque* issue would remain a divisive issue between the two churches. In addition, tensions would escalate as Latin theologians criticized the Eastern practice of dating Easter according to the Jewish dating, rather than a more general lunar calendric approach. Eastern clergy countered with their own criticism of the hypocritical requirement of celibacy for all clergy (in the East only monks were to be celibate, clergy could marry unless they aspired to be bishops).

Evangelistic Movement

The gospel's power continued to influence God's people. In 862, King Rastislav of Moravia (ruled 846-870) wrote to Photios requesting orthodox teachers for his Slavic people. Several Christian groups—Germans, Greeks, and Italians—had already made some significant, yet contradictory contacts with them. Aware of the political advantage being offered, Photios sent two brothers whose names are synonymous with missionary work to the Slavic countries, Cyril (c.827/828-869) (or Constantine, to use his given name) and Methodius (815/820-882). These brothers had been raised in the Balkan region near Thessalonika and could speak the Slavic language. In Moravia, Cyril developed a writing system which was later named after him, "Cyrillic," using elements of both Greek and Latin lettering (see illustration). Translating the Bible, the liturgy, and several

А Б В Г Д Є Ж Ѕ Z И І К Л М Н Ѻ П Р С Т ОУ Ф Х Ѡ Ч Y Ш Щ Ъ Ы Ь Ѣ Ю ІА ІЄ Ѧ ІѦ Ѫ ІѪ Ѯ Ѱ Ѳ V

other theological works using this alphabet brought a wealth of material for this Christian nation. Christianity was given a solid foundation with God's Word in the language of the people.

Shortly after they had completed their work on the liturgy, some German missionaries claimed that only Latin and a few Greek and Hebrew words were acceptable for the liturgy. Traveling to Rome, Cyril and Methodius sought the pope's support. In so doing, they also acceded to his ecclesiastical jurisdiction. The Moravian church was thereby torn between Rome, Constantinople, and Germany. Cyril died in Rome in 869, but Methodius returned as archbishop with the papal approval to use the Slavonic language. In 906, Hungarians took control of the land and the Moravian kingdom was lost. In the meantime, Serbia came under Byzantine domination with the founding of the Macedonian dynasty by Basil 1 (811-886, ruled 867-886). Territorial disputes instead of the more important theological goals of expanding Christ's kingdom and communicating the Christian faith began to rise.

Pope Nicholas I added to the tension between the East and the West as a result of an issue which was not his initial making. Boris, king of Bulgaria (ruled 852-889, +907), was baptized in 864 after being defeated by Emperor Michael III. He then requested that Photios send an archbishop to his region. After some questions and hesitancy on Photios's part, Boris appealed to Nicholas, who immediately sent him two bishops. Not to be outdone, Photios's successor consecrated an archbishop and sent several bishops to form the Bulgarian Orthodox Church. The two rulers were visibly competing for the same privileges and responsibilities over Bulgaria.

Politically, Nicholas exerted his power when he discovered that Lothair II (835-869) had dismissed his wife, accusing her of incest and infertility, and then naming his concubine as his new queen. Nicholas immediately excommunicated Lothair at a synod held in Germany in 863 and, despite Louis the German's troops moving to attack Rome, the excommunication remained in force until Lothair reinstated his wife. Whether the king was moved by spiritual concerns for his soul by being removed from the sacrament or whether he was aware that his subjects' allegiance would waver, he capitulated, providing the pope with an increasing sense of political power and prestige.

Two Theological Controversies

In the meantime, Nicholas became embroiled in a controversy of his own making in the West, when he disagreed with the Archbishop of Reims and Metropolitan of France, Hincmar (c.806-882, bishop 845-882). Known more as a politician and student of canon law than as a philosophical theologian, Hincmar had opposed the monastic theologian, Gottschalk (c.805-866/870). Gottschalk had taught what he thought was an Augustinian teaching of "double predestination"—saying that some were chosen by God for salvation and some were chosen from eternity for damnation. Hincmar opposed Gottschalk and asserted that only the former was true from a biblical perspective. John Scotus Eriugena (c.810-877) agreed with him, but in such an abstract and philosophical way that his own orthodoxy was questioned.

At the time, John Scotus Eriugena was the greatest, albeit one of only a few theologians of the century. He never had a significant following since he worked directly under the private patronage of Charles the Bald (823-877), one of Louis's three sons. As a respected scholar from Ireland (his last name means "born in Erin" and "Scotus" indicates his Irish roots), he served most of his life in the French court. His unrivaled knowledge of Greek resulted in his promulgation of a long philosophical tradition, known as Neoplatonism. He also translated from Greek into Latin the *Heavenly Hierarchy* by Pseudo-Dionysius, a work which encouraged the political and ecclesiastical hierarchy of his society (see chapter 7). Eriugena wrote a work called *Periphyseon: On the Division of Nature*, stating that God was incapable of doing evil and therefore Gottschalk's concept of double predestination was not correct even from a philosophical point of view. Eriugena later wrote *On Predestination* to clarify his own position against Gottschalk's erroneous views.

John Scotus Eriugena and Hincmar were also involved in a more significant controversy toward the end of this century. Paschasius Radbertus (c.790-860), the Abbot of Corbie, had prepared a study *On the Body and Blood of the Lord* for the monks in his monastery, one of the first treatises ever prepared specifically on the medieval understanding of the sacrament of the altar. He taught, along with Eriugena and Hincmar, that Christ was physically present in the sacrament in a miraculous manner—a sacramental presence of the very body born of Mary and the blood shed on Calvary. Not only was Christ really present, he said, but there was actually a transformation of the substance of bread and wine into the body and blood at the words of institution. He added that believers were incorporated into the mystical body of Christ, the church, through their participation in the sacrament.

Opposing Radbertus was his monastic colleague, Ratramnus (+868), who along with the Archbishop of Mainz and Abbot of Fulga, Hrabanus Maurus (c.789-856), and Gottschalk, taught that in the sacrament Christ was truly present, but not in the same sense as a physical body, since that body was sitting at the right hand of the Father (a view not unlike that of the sixteenth century non-Lutheran reformers). Ratramnus also agreed with Gottschalk on double predestination in a work he prepared for Charles the Bald, *On Predestination*. Ratramnus would later be declared a heretic and Radbertus a saint, although echoes of their positions on the real presence of Christ in the sacrament of the Lord's Supper would again appear during the sixteenth century.

The predestination and Eucharistic controversies quickly subsided after the death of their chief proponents. Yet, these two debates illustrate the beginning of theological sophistication and the rebirth of serious theological discussions which would eventually be raised again during the Protestant Reformation.

The Empire Weakens

With the weakening of political power under Charlemagne's successors and the increasingly limited exercise of commerce due to both the Viking control of the northern seas and the Muslim dominance of the southern and eastern Mediterranean, a unique form of society began to develop. Known by its eighteenth century label of "feudalism," landholdings became the chief source of power and economic wealth. Subsistence farming had been the major means of economic survival for several centuries.

This developing hierarchical, and later hereditary, system was structured so that those who held land possessed power. A lord held land and his vassal (from the Latin, *vassus*, servant) was required to pay homage (honor or allegiance) for the privilege of working the land. Oftentimes, a lord was granted land from a greater lord to whom he owed homage or vassals acquired land from various lords. In one sense, everyone was a lord, except the lowliest slave, and everyone was a vassal, except the emperor (and pope). The result was much fragmentation economically and politically, yet the system provided a certain sense of continuity as contractual relationships were based upon mutual obligations. Included in this system was one of the greatest land holders of the Mediterranean world, the Roman Catholic Church.

The last pope to hold any semblance of order in this century was John VIII (pope 872-882). During his pontificate, Emperor Louis died, resulting in renewed assaults in Italy by the Saracens. Preferring to work individually with these Muslim infidels, the local Lombardian and southern Italian princes permitted these invaders to gain a permanent foothold in Italy, just outside the city of Rome. John's assassination by a close relative or associate, the first in the history of the papacy, marked the beginning of a century of discord, degradation, and disorder in Rome and papal authority.

The last decade of this century saw no less than a half-dozen popes, several for only a few weeks! Pope Formosus (c.816-896), a pope of questionable repute, held office from 891-896, under a cloud of illegalities. His successor, Boniface VI (pope 896), died of gout within two weeks of his own problematic election—he had been defrocked twice for unbecoming conduct of a clergyman and never reinstated. After his death, Stephen VI (+897) called for a synod of bishops, known as the Cadaver Synod, at which they exhumed the body of Formosus, propped it on a papal throne in full pontifical vestments, and put him on trial for perjury, coveting, and several other acts against Catholic canon laws. The three fingers of his right hand, by which he had sworn oaths and gave blessings, were cut off and his body reburied, only to be exhumed a second time and thrown into the Tiber River, from where it was retried by a hermit monk and reburied a third time. The popular outrage at this action resulted in Pope Stephen VI being deposed and strangled to death in prison. His successor, Romanus (pope 897) served for less than a year and was succeeded by Theorore II (840-897, pope 897) who held office merely for twenty days. Finally, Pope John IX (pope 898-900) served for the final two years of the century, dying in January 900.

Missionary Moments

Christian missionary work continued throughout this century, despite the floundering of the political powers in the latter half of the century. Several popes and many monasteries remained vigilant, although at times corrupted by their own wealth. Benedictine reforms had been adopted by many monasteries between 813 and 817, giving a new sense of divine purpose and Christian service.

Notable among the monastic missionaries sent to the North was Ansgar (801-865), who went to Denmark at the request of the exiled king, Harald of Jutland (c.785-c.852, ruled 812-814, 819-827). Ansgar then traveled to Sweden as the "Apostle to the North" and built the first Christian church there. Ansgar's activities in Birka, Sweden, became more difficult when pagan merchants opposed his introduction of another deity, particularly one who warned against offering sacrifices to other gods. Fortunately, traders with the Carolingians recognized the blessings of Christianity and supported Ansgar's work. Ansgar would later become Bishop of Hamburg and Archbishop of Bremen (now Germany), providing guidance for others to extend the message of Christ to the world.

Although this century saw the dominance of the Carolingian rulers, the theological debates at this time would have immense consequences in the future, particularly on the use of images and the understanding of the presence of the Christ in the Lord's Supper. Clarification of doctrine is always a necessary end so that the gospel can be clearly and boldly proclaimed throughout the world.

For Review and Discussion
1. What was Charlemagne's greatest contribution to Christianity?
2. How did the controversy between Patriarch Photios and Pope Nicholas create a greater divide between Eastern and Western Christians?
3. Where was evangelist missions done during this century? How successful were they?
4. Describe one of the two theological controversies of this century and explain how it might affect future discussions of the same topic.
5. Why was the gospel message effective in non-Christian communities?

For Further Reading

Carabine, Deirdre. *John Scottus Eriugena.* New York: Oxford University Press, 2000.

Ginther, James. *Westminster Handbook to Medieval Theology.* Louisville, KY: Westminster John Knox Press, 2009.

Tachiaos, Anthony-Emil N. *Cyril and Methodius of Thessalonica: The Acculturation of the Slavs.* Crestwood, NY: St. Vladimir's Seminary Press, 2001.

White, Despina Stratoudaki. *Patriarch Photios of Constantinople.* Brookline, MA: Holy Cross Orthodox Press, 1981.

Wilson, Derek. *Charlemagne.* New York: Doubleday, 2005. (Reprint 2015)

10. Light in the Darkness

The Tenth Century

Although most people did not anticipate the millennial change in the year 1000, remarkable events were occurring the previous century, especially among the political and ecclesiastical powers of the western world. With no strong military power after the Carolingian era, the empire devolved into political chaos and civil war. Muslim invasions proliferated and new groups threatened the Christian empire—the Magyars (Hungarians) from the East and Vikings (Scandinavian Norsemen) from the North. The intellectual and cultural life subsided even in the monasteries as they were sacked and destroyed by the marauding hordes. At the same time papal powers were elusively eroding as spirituality and morality declined. These were indeed the dark ages for European Christianity.

The only real light in the darkness of this medieval world was emanating from the East, as a result of the strong legacy of Patriarch Photios of Constantinople (c.810-c.893). Mission work continued to progress during the middle of the century when Russia officially became a Christian land. Although baptized by German missionaries, the queen of Russia, Olga of Kiev (c.870/890-969), provided a strong direction for future Russian kings as will be noted later in this chapter. Two other gospel lights beamed brightly from monasteries at Cluny in France and the monastery of Stoudios near Constantinople.

A New Era of Papal and Imperial Power

The last Carolingian king in Germany, Louis II, "the Child" (893-11), died in 911, and almost immediately tribal rivalries among the chiefs in Bavaria, Swabia, Saxony, and Franconia erupted. The loss of strong imperial leadership left a vacuum of power until the German Emperor Otto I (912-973, ruled 962-973) came to power fifty years later. He moved his throne to Rome, after conquering the kingdom of Italy. But even he faced diplomatic struggles with the Byzantine emperor and the Roman papacy during the last years of his reign. By the end of this century, the last Carolingian king in France, Louis V (c.967-987, ruled 986-987), had so little power during his brief reign that, for all practical purposes, his reign was merely the nominal ending of the great Carolingian era which had ceased almost a century earlier. (The map below gives approximate locations of the various kingdoms toward the end of the tenth century.)

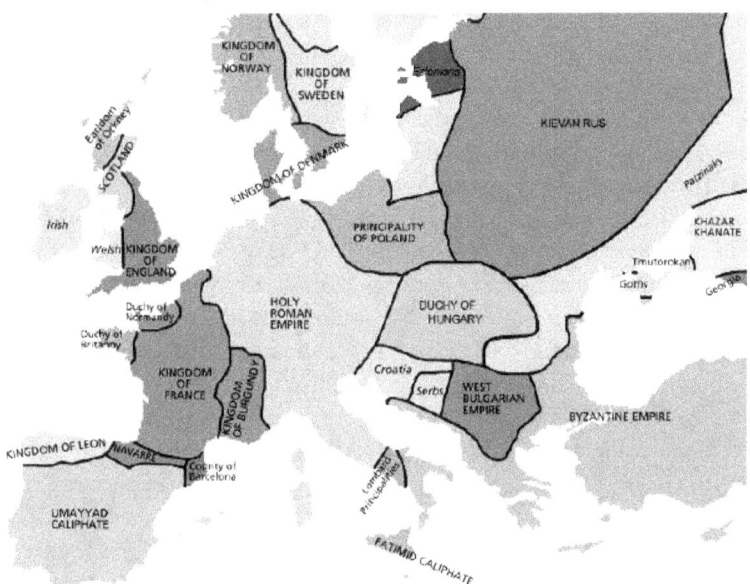

Emperor Otto I had expanded the German territories a few years earlier, following the election of his father, Henry the Fowler (919-936), as the first German emperor. Otto worked very closely with the German bishops and abbots, providing land, special privileges, and military protection. In return, these ecclesiastical leaders supported his expansion of the empire against the various hereditary noble families in and around Saxony. He also initiated a renewed sense of liturgical worship and ecclesiastical art, evident in his establishment of a very important monastic scriptorium for manuscript illumination at Quedlinburg Abbey. As his kingdom extended, he wielded greater control over the papal lands which had suffered under the Roman and Italian political chaos.

In 951, Otto entered Italy and declared himself king of Lombardy. He also acceded to the request to marry Adelaide of Italy/Burgundy (931-999), who had succeeded her husband, Lothar I of Arles (c.926/8-950), as ruler over Italy. This alliance proved extremely beneficial to the church, since they now had military support, which though somewhat distant was sufficiently strong to protect it from local interference. However, because of political intrigues, Pope Agapetus II (pope 946-955) did not declare Otto emperor; something Otto had to await for another ten years, during which time his own soldiers acclaimed him emperor as a result of his defeat of the Hungarians in 955.

In 961, Otto returned to Italy. This time he came at the invitation of Pope John XII (c.930/937-964, pope 955-964), a much weaker pope than those before. In February of 962 in St. Peter's Basilica, Pope John crowned Otto successor to

Charlemagne and Emperor over the Holy Roman Empire along with Empress Adelaide. From this date (until 1250), every German ruler would receive the crown from the hands of the pope in Rome. This recognition of the papacy was at the cost of the papacy losing its sole ecclesiastical power in the election of future popes. Every pope had to be approved by the emperor before being elected. This practice is known as *lay investiture*.

Shortly after his coronation, Pope John XII was deposed by Emperor Otto for turning against the emperor. The pope was then summarily replaced by a layman, Leo, whose consecration remained suspect. Pope Leo VIII (pope 964-965) was installed into his papal office through an unusually swift and highly dubious process. Normal procedures would be that a man was ordained into the various "ordered ministries"—porter, exorcist, lector, subdeacon, deacon, priest, bishop—over a series of years or at least months of on-the-job training or at least some practical experience. Leo, as a layman with no ecclesiastical training (although he had worked in papal administration for several years), was made pope by Otto within one twenty-four hour period. No sooner had Otto left Rome, but Leo was deposed and John was restored. When John XII died in 964, Pope Benedict V (964) was placed in the papal office, but without imperial consent. Therefore, Otto returned to Rome, banished Benedict to Germany, and restored Leo and his successor, John XIII (c.930/935-972, pope 965-972). These personal appointments by the emperor continued until the great Investiture Controversy (see chapter 11) in the next century.

Papal Pornocracy

Perhaps the hallmark of this century is the concept of *pornocracy*, which literally means "the rule of the illegitimates/prostitutes." Also known in Latin as *saeculum obscurum* ("dark age"), it refers to the papal office holders of almost half the century in which papal power was wielded by the mistresses and

concubines of the popes, particularly by the noblewoman, Theodora (c.870-916), and her daughter, Marozia (890-937).

Corruption of the papacy had been going on for several decades, but under Pope Sergius III (c.860-911, pope 904-911), the papal quarters declined to an extremely low moral plane. Gaining control of the Lateran Palace with armed troops, after being deposed and exiled in 897, Sergius was acclaimed pope early in 904. Denying the validity of several of his predecessors, he immediately had his predecessor, Pope Leo V (pope 903-904), and his opponent, an antipope named Cardinal Christopher (antipope 903-904), strangled in prison. His sexual liaisons with fifteen year old Marozia, produced at least one son (later to become Pope John XI, see below). Sergius III was succeeded by two puppet-popes, Anastasius III (pope 911-913) and Landus (pope 913-914), whose pontificates were undistinguished, because the papacy was under the powerful noble family of Theodora.

John X (pope 914-928) tried to distance himself from the powerful families of Rome, although he was known to be a lover of Theodora. He was finally deposed, imprisoned. An elderly priest was chosen by Marozia as Pope Leo VI in 928 (serving only seven months), while John was still alive. However, after the death of John X under the suspicious conditions (purportedly suffocated with a pillow) and Leo VI, Pope Stephen VII (pope 929-931) was also selected by Marozia, in anticipation of the election of her twenty-year old son, John (910-935), to the papacy as Pope John XI (pope 931-935).

The next succession of popes all were directly elected as a result of the absolute ruler of Rome, Alberic II (c.912-954, ruled 932-954). Alberic II's son and Marozia's grandson became Pope John XII (937-964, pope 955-964), but he only held the papal throne for ten years, having been elected when he was only eighteen years old. He brought the papacy to a new low—converting the Lateran Palace into a brothel and dying of a stroke while in bed with a married woman. A nephew of Marozia was elected as John XIII (930/935-972, pope 965-972), whose brother, the antipope Boniface VII (pope 974-983), killed Benedict VI (pope 973-974). John XIV (pope 983-984) was poisoned in his dungeon cell at Castel Sant'Angelo, where he had been sentenced by the returned exile, Boniface VII, who was poisoned himself. In all, there were over twenty-two men who sat on the papal throne during this century, most of whom were so corrupt that few official records of their ecclesiastical activities even survived.

In the latter half of the tenth century, Liutprand (922-972), Bishop of Cremona, wrote a devastating account of his experiences with the papal court. His *Antapodosis* (Revenge) relates many accounts of papal sexual escapades after hunting expeditions and the marriages and divorces of bishops and other church leaders. Much of the corruption was kept quiet officially, even though the papal power was so weak. However, the papacy remained strong enough to survive the degradation through its chief governing body, the chancery or curia.

Cluniac Movement

While devastating evil was rampant in the papal chambers, others recognized a great need for spiritual reform and ecclesiastical renewal among the monastic communities. Around 910, a new order of monks was established by the pious patron, Duke William of Aquitaine (875-918). When the duke and the new abbot, Berno (c.850-927, abbot 910-925), set out to find a suitable spot for a monastery, Berno chose the duke's favorite hunting ground, the richly wooded valley of Cluny in the Burgundian area of southern France.

What made the Cluniac organization unique was its administrative structure. Each monastery was tied not only by history but also by vows of obedience to the mother house. Each new or reformed house was under a prior, second-in-command to the abbot of Cluny. In just over two centuries, there were only six abbots who ruled over Cluny. Their allegiance was to the papacy alone, being given a papal exemption from local influences by clergy and laity. In turn, they stood as strong papal supporters and advisors throughout the next turbulent century.

After the death of the first abbot in 927, a series of notable abbots succeeded him. Recognized by the papacy for his pastoral and spiritual insights, Odo (c.878-942, abbot 927-942) was summoned on several occasions to provide guidance to Alberic II. As a reforming movement among Benedictine monasteries, Odo's approach focused on restoring the traditional monastic ideals of celibacy and communal property, encouraging art and caring for the poor. Chief among the responsibilities of the monks was prayer and worship. Odo helped the order strengthen its influence on the church by emphasizing autonomy from lay intervention. The Benedictine life was portrayed again as the only authentic fulfillment of the Christian vocation.

Cluniac reforms were designed to re-establish a strict Benedictine *Rule* which centered on devotional worship. The rigorous observance of the Divine Office—the performance of a regular schedule of prayers and Scripture readings established by Benedict—resulted in the neglect of manual labor, for which later reforms were again instituted. Such a departure from the balanced work-and-prayer schedule of the original Benedictine *Rule* was justified, according to the reformers, because the emphasis upon the spiritual vocations would result in purer piety if it was not tainted by the soil of the fields. This spiritual direction and the community's strong administrative structure provided a beam of light in this dark century.

Expanding Christ's Kingdom

In spite of the difficulties of the age, mission endeavors continued, particularly through the military conquests of Christian rulers. In one sense, the conversion of a nation did not occur until after it was Christianized politically.

Although Christians had settled in Denmark and Sweden a century before, the Viking assaults diminished the Christian influence to such an extent that it was nearly non-existent in Sweden. Only after the Danish king, Harald Bluetooth (930-986, ruled c.958-c.986), was baptized around 960 was there a resurgence of Christian influence in that region. King Harald not only allowed Christian missions, but expanded his rule briefly into Norway. The power of the Gospel continued.

Haakon the Good (c.920-961, ruled 934-961), who had been trained by English clergy, tried to reintroduce Christianity to Norway after his father's death. Because of political concerns and his English upbringing, his attempt was suspect and unsuccessful. It was not until Olaf Tryggvasson (c.960-1000), a Viking who had converted to Christianity after conquering the Isles of Scilly southwest of

England, became king of Norway in 995 that Christianity was fully established in his realm.

Probably the most significant missionary achievement in this century was the conversion of the Russian people, centered in its capital city, Kiev. Swedish Vikings had taken control of the waterways between the Baltic and the Black Sea and their descendants now ruled the region. As traders continued to come to Byzantium with their western goods, Christian missionary work was also progressing into the territory.

After her husband Igor's (ruled 912-945) death by an eastern Slavic tribe, the Drevlians, Princess Olga (c.879/890-969) was converted to Christianity in mid-century (see illustration by Roerich). Prior to her conversion, the *Primary Chronicle*, a Slavic history of this era, indicates that she took drastic steps to avenge her husband's death— burying some Drevlian ambassadors alive, burning others in a bathhouse, and finally killing several thousand at a feast given in her husband's honor. After her conversion she rejected missionary envoys sent by Bishop Adalbert (c.956-997) from Otto I probably recognizing them as having political implications for her own rule. Her son, Svyatoslav (942-989), with whom she served as co-regent from 945 until 963, rejected her Christian faith, but allowed her to practice it privately. Her grandson, Vladimir I (989-1015), on the other hand, expanded Christianity from Kiev into the northern area of his realm and continued his grandmother's legacy.

After the Magyars were defeated by Otto I in 955, the Great Prince of the Magyars, Géza (c.940-997), allowed Christian missionaries to work among his people. He was baptized sometime within the last quarter of the century, but continued several pagan practices as well, claiming he was wealthy enough to sacrifice to both old and new gods. His son, Stephen (c.970-1038), who became the patron saint of Hungary, advanced beyond his father's toleration of Christianity and worked hard to evangelize his people with the assistance of Slavic missionaries from Poland and Bohemia. These Slavic missionaries had undoubtedly been converted as a result of the work of Cyril and Methodius (see chapter 9).

Around this same time, Otto I had brought Bohemia under his rule and within several decades Duke Boleslav II (967-999) established Prague as a center for Christianity in Poland. Clearly, the light of Christianity was beginning to enlighten the darkness of paganism.

Symeon the New Theologian

Born to a well-to-do aristocratic family of Galatia around 949, Symeon (c.949-1022) was sent to Constantinople for his early education as an imperial officer. As a teen, he met a monk, Simeon the Pious (918-986/987) from the monastery of Stoudios, near Constantinople, who became his spiritual director. Spending time in the royal courts was not satisfying for this spiritual young man and he entered the Orthodox monastery of Stoudios. In order to avert any appearance of a homosexual relationship with his spiritual director, he moved to another nearby monastery. Here he led a spiritual movement of silent prayer which blossomed the following century (see *Hesychasm* in chapter 14). He is especially remembered for a hymn to the Holy Spirit (see below) which is still sung in Orthodox churches and his writing on Divine Love. His designation as "the New Theologian" is misleading in that he was not a "new theologian," but he wanted to be called "Symeon the New" to distinguish him from his spiritual director. Only later was he given the official Orthodox title of "theologian," along with Gregory Nazianzus and John, the author of Revelation.

On the eve of a new millennium, no one really noticed a change. Concerns for survival dominated the humble peasants and poor farmers. The nobility were not much better off, seeking only to maintain some semblance of security in the face of hostilities all around. Even the church seems to have ignored the millennial shift. Yet, throughout these years, the gospel message of God's love and His forgiving grace changed hearts and lives for eternity.

For Review and Discussion
1. Why was the period known as "papal pornocracy" so offensive for the gospel and living "holy in the world"?
2. How did the Cluniac reform change monastic life?
3. What methods for missions was most effective in this century?
4. What signs of gospel light in this "dark age" can you identify?
5. Describe the contributions made by Eastern Christians in this century.

For Further Reading
Brooke, Zachary Nugent. *A History of Europe from 911 to 1198*. London: Methuen & Co., 1938.
Lopez, Robert Sabatino, ed. *The Tenth Century: How Dark the Dark Ages?* New York: Holt, Reinhart and Winston, 1959.
Sitwell, Dom Gerard, ed. and trans. *St. Odo of Cluny: Being the Life of St. Odo of Cluny by John of Salerno and the Life of St. Gerald of Aurillac by St. Odo*. London: Sheed and Ward, 1958.

Symeon the New Theologian's
Hymn to the Holy Spirit

Come, O True Light!
Come, O Eternal Life!
Come, O Hidden Mystery!
Come, O Indescribable Treasure!
Come, O Ineffable Thing!
Come, O Inconceivable Person!
Come, O Endless Delight!
Come, O Unsetting Light!
Come, O True and Fervent Expectation of all those who will be saved!
Come, O Rising of those who lie down!
Come, O Resurrection of the dead!
Come, O Powerful One, who always creates and re-creates and transforms by Your will alone!
Come, O Invisible and totally intangible and untouchable!
Come, O You who always remain immobile and at each moment move all, and come to us, who lie in Hades, You who are above all heavens.
Come, O desirable and legendary Name, which is completely impossible for us to express what You are or to know Your nature.
Come, O eternal Joy!
Come, O unwithering Wreath!
Come, O purple of the great King our God!
Come, O Crystalline Cincture, studded with precious stones!
Come, O Inaccessible Sandal!
Come, O Royal Robe and Truly Imperial Right hand!
Come, You whom my Wretched soul has desired and does desire!
Come, You who alone go to the lonely for as You see I am lonely!
Come, You who have separated me from everything and made me solitary in this world!
Come, You who have become Yourself desire in me, who have made me desire You, the absolutely inaccessible one!
Come, O my Breath and life!
Come, O Consolation of my humble soul!
Come, O my Joy, my glory, and my endless delight!

11. Dawning and Division in Christendom

The Eleventh Century

With the dawning of a new millennium, European Christians living in the proverbial dark ages began to see a glimmer of light. The reforming movements of the Cluniac monasteries had an impact not only on the church, but on society as a whole. As an era of greater political peace ensued, time allowed for greater scholarship and the church increasingly became a political force to be reckoned with.

Imperial Reformers

In the first decades of this century, political and religious conflicts dominated the scene. Emperor Otto III (980-1002, ruled 996-1002) died in Italy under suspicious circumstances (either by poisoning or of malaria) after dealing with rebellious citizens of Tivoli. His son and successor was Henry II (973-1024, ruled 1002-1024). During the early years of Henry's reign over the Holy Roman Empire, the Muslim caliph, al-Hakim (985-1021) ordered the destruction of the Church of the Holy Sepulcher in Jerusalem in 1009. A cause for concern began to be voiced regarding the Muslim invasion and devastation of this devotional site.

Conrad II (990-1039, ruled 1024-1039), successor of Henry II, continued the policies of his father, giving political power to bishops rather than secular lords. Yet, he allowed the Italian papacy to fend for itself. As a result, Benedict VIII (c.980-1024, pope 1012-1024) and John XIX (pope 1024-1032), both sons of the Roman nobleman, Gregory of Tusculum (count 954-1012), consolidated their family control of the region around Rome.

Henry III (1017-1056, ruled 1039-1056) was recognized for his piety and dedication to reformation. During the year of his accession to the throne, the Church of the Holy Sepulcher was rebuilt by Byzantine Christians, especially supported financially by Eastern Emperor Constantine IX Monomachos (c.1000-1055, ruled 1042-1055), along with Muslim support, since the Muslims recognized much financial gain from the Christian pilgrims. Henry's military prowess was evident in his numerous campaigns in Hungary and various regions in Burgundy and Italy. Securing their allegiance, he strengthened the political hold on the papacy.

In the northern Europe, Olaf II Haraldsson of Norway (St. Olaf) (995-1030, ruled 1015-1028) desired to unite the whole Scandinavian region under Norwegian control. After a decade of pagan resurgence, he is credited with re-establishing Christianity in the land, particularly in the interior regions.

The papacy, on the other hand, had returned to a despicable condition of low morals and high living. Benedict IX (c.1012-1056), nephew of his two predecessors, grew weary of his papal responsibilities, although he enjoyed the perquisites. He is the only pope to serve at three different times (1032-1044, 1045, 1047-1048). Escaping Rome after a rebellious group set up a rival pope, Sylvester III (1000-1062/63, pope for three months in 1045), Benedict was reinstated shortly thereafter, but chose to pursue a marriage along with a pension instead. He then abdicated the papal office. His godfather succeeded him as Gregory VI (pope 1045-1046, +1048). When Henry came for the imperial coronation of Gregory, he was distressed to see the ecclesiastical chaos and invoked a synod of clergy at Sutri. Declaring Benedict IX, Sylvester II, and Gregory VI deposed, he established the bishop of Bamberg, Germany, as Pope Clement II (pope 1046-1047), who in turn crowned Henry "emperor." After only nine months, Clement died and the Italian ruling nobility reinstated Benedict IV. Shortly thereafter, Damasus II (1048) was named pope by imperial edict, but he died within the month of his enthronement, reportedly of lead-sugar poisoning.

Approaching the city of Rome as a barefooted pilgrim, the German nobleman, Bruno of Egisheim-Dagsburg (1002-1054) and the future Pope Leo IX (pope 1049-1054), entered Italy amidst popular acclamations and reported miraculous acts. Prior to receiving the papal tiara, he had been a notable German canon and bishop of Toul, whom Henry III had appointed to the papal office at a synod in Worms. Concentrating on reforming the papacy, he gathered like-minded men as his counselors and assistants who promoted clerical celibacy and sought to abolish simony. Among these men, whom he called "cardinal" clergy, were Hildebrand (c.1015-1085, later Pope Gregory VII 1073-1085) and the Benedictine reformer, Peter Damian (1007-1072), who as prior and theologian served as a prophetic voice condemning clerical marriage, simony, and ecclesiastical worldliness. After attacking these issues in Italy, Leo went through Germany and France, where he was fairly successful in personally expanding his

---

Celibacy and Simony

The connection between these two ecclesiastical concerns is not obvious to us in the 21st century, yet they formed a vital link for the feudal system in which the Church existed at this time. Simony, the buying and selling of church positions, was named after Simon in Acts 5:18. The practice resulted in only the rich occupying ecclesiastical offices. If these clergy were married, their heirs could hold these offices perpetually, creating an ecclesiastical dynasty open to corruption. Thus, celibacy (remaining unmarried) was not only promoted, but finally became mandatory for all ecclesiastical offices, seemingly following Paul's advice in 1 Corinthians 7-8.

reforms of the church and establishing the authority of the Roman see. After these successes, he was emboldened to attack the adventurous Norsemen who had settled in southern Italy and Sicily. Marching at the head of his papal troops, Leo was captured and imprisoned until shortly before his death.

The Great Schism (1054)

Although seemingly precipitated by a small issue, the breach between eastern and western Christianity had been slowly but surely widening over several centuries. From the time of Patriarch Photios (see chapter 9), theological distinctions had begun to separate the two major realms of Christianity. Political rivalry and ecclesiastical jurisdiction following the fall of Rome increased the sense of acrimony and ill-will between the leaders in Rome and Constantinople.

When Leo of Ohrid (+1056), archbishop of Bulgaria, noticed that western clergy were forbidden from marrying, fasted on Saturdays, and celebrated the Lord's Supper with unleavened bread, he accused western Christians of error, preventing any unity between them. The ambassador from Pope Leo IX, Cardinal Humbert (c.1010-1061), came to Constantinople not with an olive branch of peace, but with an axe to grind. Knowing no Greek, he openly advocated clerical celibacy and was loath against the Byzantine emperor's influence on the church. After exchanging insults with Patriarch Michael Cerularius (patriarch 1043-1059), Humbert produced a bull of excommunication against Cerularius and all the eastern Christians who followed him. He placed it on the high altar of St Sophia on June 16, 1054, and returned to Rome. Patriarch Michael responded with an equally harsh excommunication of the cardinal and the pope. (The actual bull was invalid because Pope Leo had died several months earlier.) The split between Rome and Constantinople—between western Christians and eastern Christians—was now officially sealed. (Later, while serving as an abbot in Lotharingia, Humbert prepared a vicious treatise *Three Books against the Simoniacs*, which furthered the animosity between the East and the West.)

Population Explosion and Agricultural Developments

During these ecclesiastically troubling times, Europe's population was expanding rapidly. As a result, forested and poorer farming lands began to be utilized. Loggers would move in and clear the land and then peasants would be invited by the lord of the land to make it somewhat productive. Arab invasions had also introduced new crops of sorghum and hard (durum) wheat, which was not suitable for bread, but was well-suited to pasta.

During this time farm implements were improved technically with the moldboard plow and the horse collar. The moldboard plow is composed of a wedge-shaped surface attached to the plow's metal cutting blade allowing the plow to cut the soil and flip it over as well as to plow deeper. This innovation (see illustration) greatly reduced the time required to plow a field, since previously the fields had to be crisscrossed in order to accomplish the same effect. Wheels also increased productivity in the northern regions with heavier soils. Oxen were used for millennia in plowing.

Horses, not having as large a shoulder for harnessing a plow, were not used until the invention of the horse-collar. Horses were twice as fast as oxen and were capable of a variety of farming functions.

Crop cultivation had become more efficient as the Arabs also introduced summer irrigation. Instead of only planting during the spring and fall, lands which had normally lain fallow for the summer were able to be used for more production of grains and leafy vegetables. Fertilization from animal manure aided in this expanded use of the lands. Wheat, barley, peas and oats, along with vegetables, vineyards and fruit orchards were the mainstay of this agrarian economy. Medieval monasteries experimented with various techniques for improving crop production, although the communication of these techniques and the suspicion of changing practices did not influence farming to any great extent. The church, while requiring a tithe from its landholders, also stored excess grains and in times of drought or famine, regularly opened its storehouse for the poor and needy.

Towns were growing as more and more people were able to be sustained by surplus food. Fulltime artisans were able to survive in these towns as others exchanged food and produce for the specialized work of leather workers, blacksmiths, thatchers, bakers, butchers and carpenters. Trade was expanding, too, as surplus food was exchanged for handcrafts in other cities. London and Brussels, for example, became significant trading centers.

After the Norman's captured England at the Battle of Hastings (see below), the arable land on local estates shifted their farming techniques. Previously, they had farmed one area near the villages during the summer, allowing their cattle to roam in more distant areas. In the winter, they would bring their animals nearer their village or estate (a natural source of fertilization). The new method was to leave one of three fields fallow for each of three years, allowing the sheep and cattle to graze the land and the soil to regain its fertility. On the other two fields, wheat (for bread), barley (for beer), oats, or other crops such as peas or beans could be grown in a simple rotation. The grains were normally planted in the fall and, if the winter was not too severe, harvested in the spring. A second crop was then planted in spring as early as possible and harvested in the fall. Flax and hemp were planted for clothing and rope production. Normally, a bushel of grain was planted with the hopes that up to a half-dozen bushels could be harvested of the same grains.

Medieval fields were divided into strips of roughly an acre, which was about the area one could plough in a day. Each villager would farm a few of these strips scattered around the three fields. The heavy, iron-shared plough, pulled by a team of oxen, could cut a furrow of roughly a furlong (a term derived from the joining of "furrow" and " long") before the team had to stop to rest.

Reforming Papacy

The election of Pope Victor II (1018-1057, pope 1055-1057) was rather unusual in that he was elected by the Roman clergy, but was German and the obvious appointee of Henry III. His election removed the Italian families from wielding control over the papacy as they had in the past. But it did not completely eliminate the interference of the emperor, something the reforming movement had been working for. After the death of Henry III, Victor cared for Henry's six-year old son, Henry IV (1050-1106), so that he had power over both church and state. But that convenient arrangement was short-lived with the death of Victor.

Young Henry IV (king of Germany 1056-1106, emperor 1084-1105) (see illustration), under the regency of his mother, Agnes of Poitou (c.1024-1077), was powerless to become involved in the election of the next pope. As a result, the Italian clergy, once again having the power, elected Frederick of Lorraine (c.1020-1058) as Pope Stephen IX (1057-1058). Cardinal Humbert's treatises against simony were published at this time. Although not everyone agreed with Humbert (including Peter Damian (1007-1072), who still favored lay investiture), his positions on reforming the church prevailed. This became evident at the death of Stephen when the Roman nobility, headed by Count Gregory of Tusculum, elected John of Velletri (+1073/1080) as Benedict X (antipope 1058-January 1059). Prior to his death, Stephen had secured from the Roman clergy a promise not to elect a successor until Hildebrand had returned from his negotiations with the German imperial court. Upon Hildebrand's arrival in Rome, the reformist clergy elected

Gerard of Florence (c.1000-1061), who took the name Nicholas II (pope 1059-1061), and declared Benedict X's election invalid.

Shortly after his election, Pope Nicholas II called a council at his Lateran Palace in 1059 which determined that only cardinals could elect a pope, who in turn would name new cardinals. This procedure removed lay involvement completely in the selection of the pope and remains in place to the present time. As a result, reforming of the church continued, but papal power was being solidified in the Roman curia. To support this ecclesiastical power, Nicholas secured the perpetual support of a Norman army (at the time, serving in southern Italy) under the pope's direct command.

The Battle of Hastings in 1066

When Pope Alexander II (pope 1061-1073) was duly elected by the cardinals, he was opposed by powerful Roman families as well as the German nobles, including Empress Agnes (c.1025-1077), who helped set up a rival pope, Honorius II (antipope 1061-1072). A revolution against Agnes gave political power to the archbishop, Anno I of Cologne (c.1010-1075, bishop 1056-1075), who sided with Alexander. However, in order to gain greater political support, Alexander sanctioned the historically monumental invasion of England by Duke William of Normandy (c.1028-1087).

At the decisive, Battle of Hastings in 1066 (see illustration from the Bayeaux Tapestry, with the Latin words "William, Leader, the Great"), England fell under French rule. Papal influences spread throughout the English church, particularly when the pope's appointment, Lanfranc (c.1005/10-1089), became Archbishop of Canterbury. As

"the Conqueror," William acknowledged the spiritual superiority of the bishop of Rome; however, he said such rule was by royal approval. In the meantime, Henry IV came of age and was crowned king in 1065. Securing the support of the German clergy through his own selection of bishops, he presented land holdings to them as repayment.

Shortly after this significant invasion and change of power in western Europe, Muslim forces under the Seljuk Turks defeated the Byzantine forces of Emperor Romanus IV of Constantinople (1032-1072, ruled 1068-1071) at Manzikert in Armenia in 1071. Having lost much land to the Muslims over the preceding decade, this battle is most memorable in the fact that it set a series of destabilizing losses for the Christian East. After appealing to Rome for help,

Constantinople had to wait another twenty-five years until the pope proclaimed the First Crusade.

Pope Gregory VII

Hildebrand (c.1015/28-1085), the powerful papal counselor, cardinal, and advocate of reform for a quarter of a century, was finally elevated to the office of the papacy as Pope Gregory VII (pope 1073-1085) by popular acclamation when the Roman citizenry enthroned him almost in spite of himself and only then did he receive the approval of the cardinals. His papal reign is characterized by his near-obsession with reform. Peter Damian is said to have described him as a "holy Satan." Reform, as he conceived of it, entailed gaining political control over all of Christendom. He aspired to overthrow Islamic forces in the East and in Spain, but that desire was of no avail. In 1075, he prepared his *Dictatus papae*, which proclaimed papal power as absolute and condemned simony, marriage of the clergy, and lay investiture.

> **Gregory VII's *Dictatus papae***
> ...the Roman pontiff alone can with right be called universal.
> ...he alone may use the imperial insignia.
> ...his name alone shall be spoken in the churches.
> ...it may be permitted him to depose Emperors.
> ...he himself may be judged by no one.
> ...the Roman church has never erred; nor will it err to all eternity, the Scripture bearing witness.

When Michael VII (1050-c.1090, ruled 1071-1078), the emperor of Constantinople, appealed to Gregory for help against the encroaching Seljuk Turks, Gregory laid out plans for an expedition in 1074. He perceived this as a unique opportunity to reunite the East and West, but his plans were short-lived as he became sidetracked by more regional issues—lay investiture and rebellious clergy.

Gregory VII's reform movement was not as successful as he had envisioned. French clergy, especially those in smaller parishes, although recognizing the danger of simony and supporting its reform, refused to give up their wives. But, more critical was his clash with the emperor, Henry IV. Already on Easter 1075, Gregory had officially and absolutely prohibited lay investiture.

After Henry had replaced a bishop of Milan, whom Henry felt was extreme in his reforming demands, Gregory immediately summoned Henry to Rome for public admonition. Meanwhile, Henry called a council of German bishops at Worms (January 1076), at which he deposed the pope calling him "no pope, but a false monk." On the date set by the pope for Henry's public admonition, Gregory excommunicated Henry, declaring that he should no longer be obeyed as king of Germany. After losing face and some support, Henry sought a private resolution and reconciliation with the pope.

As Henry traveled through northern Italy, supporters rallied behind him as a hero and the pope feared for his life. Escaping to his more fortified residence in Canossa, Pope Gregory VII demanded a public penance from Henry IV. For three days in early 1077 (see illustration on previous page), Henry stood in the snow outside the papal residence as a penitent until Gregory had to admit him and grant him pardon. In some ways, this was a political triumph for Henry, since he would regain his imperial power. On the other hand, the event has remained a symbol of the empire bowing before the church.

Returning to Germany, Henry found that rebellious nobles had elected a new emperor, much to the pope's delight and benign support. After being excommunicated again, Henry set up a rival pope, Clement III (c.1029-1100, antipope 1080-1100), and killed his imperial opponent, Rudolf of Swabia (c.1025-1080), in battle. In spring of 1081, Henry returned to Rome with a military retinue and, after a short, but valiant battle with papal troops, the citizens of Rome opened the gates and welcomed Henry. Gregory fled to Monte Cassino and Henry enthroned Clement III as pope in Rome. However, the Normans in southern Italy, who had refused to support Gregory, saw an opportunity to gain lands and took control of the city, killing and looting thousands of Roman citizens. Gregory died in exile in Solerno in 1085.

Acquiescing to Gregory's dying wish, the aged abbot of Monte Cassino was appointed Pope Victor III (c.1026-1087, pope 1086-1087). His successor, Pope Urban II (c.1042-1099, pope 1088-1099) regained control of Rome and expelled the antipope, Clement III. Urban's greatest claim in the annals of the church was his proclamation of the First Crusade. In many ways, Urban's proclamation symbolized and solidified Gregory VII's desire for papal supremacy and complete leadership of all Christendom. Through his legate, Urban would serve as the physical leader of the troops as they marched to Jerusalem.

The First Crusade

The idea of a crusade to liberate Jerusalem was not originally conceived by Urban II. Gregory VII had already broached the subject after the appeal from Michael VII, but Gregory VII could not carry it out during his pontificate. A new and stronger emperor in Constantinople, Alexius I (c.1048/56-1118, ruled 1081-1118), appealed to Urban II for assistance in defeating the Seljuk chieftains in March of 1095. In November at the Council of Claremont, Pope Urban II urged his audience to take up a decisive battle in defense of Christianity, not merely as an aid to the eastern realm. Jerusalem, symbol of the church and heaven, was to be restored to Christian control.

Although Muslim invaders had captured Jerusalem's holy shrines in the seventh century (see chapter 7), pilgrims had been allowed to visit until the Seljuk Turks took over most of Asia Minor in 1071. (See map of the Seljuk Empire on the next page.) Those who undertook this new military pilgrimage (for so it was designated by many) were promised remission of all their sins as well as the prospect of keeping all that they plundered, including the land and property reclaimed in the Holy Land.

Pilgrimages had always been popular. Since the seventh century they had been imposed as penance for wealthy sinners. With the Seljuk Turkish control of Jerusalem, the prospect of such a spiritual pursuit had ceased, particularly with the destruction of significant holy sites. Yet, those so moved by the greater spirituality of penance, desired to continue the pathway of penance. This coincided with the Muslim accumulation of significant income earned through pilgrimage activity. Such a promise of a holy war against the infidels seems also to have mirrored the Islamic ideal of *jihad*.

The response to Urban's proposal, as recorded by the chroniclers of the time, was almost immediate. The crowds reportedly shouted, "*Deus lo volt*" (medieval Catalan, "God wills it!"). Among the initial responses was the popular preacher, Peter the Hermit (c.1050-1115), a monk from Amiens, France, who mobilized large groups of peasants in the spring of 1096 in what is sometimes called the Peoples' Crusade. Although these reckless bands often took recourse to plundering the German and Hungarian countryside through which they travelled, they got as far as Nicaea where the Turkish troops destroyed them completely.

The real First Crusade began in 1096 and was conducted by the feudal nobility of Europe. Four individual armies were mustered by French, English, and Italian knights. They arrived at Constantinople in the winter, causing Alexius I concern, since they would not swear allegiance to him. In the spring of 1097, they laid siege to Nicaea. After severe losses to hunger and thirst during the summer, the Crusaders laid siege to Antioch in the fall. Not until June of 1098 was Antioch taken by the Crusaders, only to suffer a severe setback when the Turkish troops tried to regain the city. Finally, in June of 1099 they approached Jerusalem and, in the middle of July, recaptured it for the Christian community.

The Cluniac reforms and Cistercian movements played a key part in the success of this first crusade. The knighted nobility were encouraged to take up Christ's cross and follow a "higher spirituality" as had the monks, yet maintain their own lay vocation and military prowess. They were able to follow a form of lay monasticism.

During the latter half of this century, Spanish rulers, Ferdinand I of Leon (c.1015-1065), also known as "El Magno" ("the Great"), and Alfonso VI of Castile (1035-1109), known as "El Bravo" ("the Brave"), defeated some of the Muslim land-holders in the southern Iberian peninsula. The recapture of Toledo in 1085 was a significant event. Yet, the Muslims fought back strongly. Their only defeat came at Valencia in 1094, due to the actions of Rodrigo Diaz de Vivar (c.1043-1099), the chief general of Alfonso VI. Rodrigo Diaz was given the honorific title, "El Cid" ("the Lord" by the Moors) and "El Campeador" ("the Champion" by the Christians). Thus, the prospect of reclamation (*reconquista*) of Spain from the Moors became more attractive and impelling and, as a result, emboldening their northern Christian comrades.

Anselm of Canterbury

Born in northern Italy to a noble family in 1033, Anselm's studious nature and religious sensitivities combined to make him desire the monastic life at the age of fifteen. In spite of his mother's support, his father refused permission and as a result Anselm took to travelling. Finally, around 1060, he entered the Benedictine abbey of Bec in Normandy (the northwestern coast of what is now France) as a novice to study under the Benedictine abbot and theologian, Lanfranc. Shortly thereafter he was named prior and, at the death of the abbot in 1078, Anselm became the new abbot of Bec.

During the next years, the monastery became a center of learning. It was during the following decade that Anselm wrote his first philosophical meditations, the *Monologion* and *Proslogion: Fides quaerens intellectum*. These were followed by his dialogues *On Truth*, *On Free Will*, and *On the Fall of the Devil*. The quality and depth of these works resulted in him being considered the first philosophical theologian of the middle ages.

> *Proslogion:*
> *Fides Quaerens Intellectum*
> "Discourse: faith seeking understanding" is Anselm's philosophical explanation for the existence of God. He proposed that God's existence can be proven merely by thinking logically about existence (Greek, *ontos*). Here is a selection from chapter 3:
> "God cannot be conceived not to exist—God is that, than which nothing greater can be conceived—that which can be conceived not to exist is not God. And He assuredly exists so truly, that He cannot be conceived not to exist. For, it is possible to conceive of a being which cannot be conceived not to exist; and this is greater than one which can be conceived not to exist. Hence, if that, than which nothing greater can be conceived, can be thought of as not existing, it is not that, than which nothing greater can be conceived. But this is an irreconcilable contradiction. There is, then, so truly a being than which nothing greater can be conceived to exist, that it cannot even be conceived not to exist; and You are this Being, O Lord, our God."

Anselm penned one of his most original works on the existence of God, *Proslogion* (see selection on previous page). The treatise was originally a monastic meditation and a mental exercise for his students. Known as "the ontological argument" for the existence of God, Anselm used natural reason to postulate God's being. Basing his approach from Scripture, his subtitle was "faith seeking understanding." He concluded that God is "that than which a greater cannot be thought." His line of reasoning is that a person can always think of something bigger or greater. Finally, with this line of reasoning, there is ultimately something (or Someone) so great that nothing greater can be thought, and that being is God. If one can conceptualize such a Being, he argued, then He must exist, at least in the mind. If He exists in the mind, He must also exist in reality, he concluded.

Because of its close proximity to England, the monastery at Bec gained considerable land holdings after the Norman Conquest. Required to visit his abbey's lands, Anselm traveled occasionally to England where he became a popular figure among both the clergy and laity. After the death of the archbishop of Canterbury, Lanfranc, many citizens expressed a desire to have Anselm named archbishop. However, the king, William II (c.1056-1100), son of William the Conqueror, was collecting the tithes and revenues from the church and so was slow in selecting a new archbishop. When he became seriously ill, he felt this was God's judgment on himself and he quickly appointed Anselm as the new Archbishop of Canterbury in 1093 (serving until his death in 1109). A dispute between Anselm and William II resulted in Anselm's departure from England around 1098 to reside in a little village outside of Rome. There Anselm wrote another of his famous works, *Cur Deus Homo?* (Why did God become human?), a presentation of the atonement known as "the satisfaction theory" (see selection on the next page). Upon the death of William II in 1100, Anselm returned to England (see chapter 12).

> *Cur Deus Homo*
> Book I, section 11: There is a debt which man and angel owes to God. No one who pays this debt commits sin; but everyone who does not pay it sins. This is justice, or the righteousness of the will, which makes a being just or upright in heart, that is, in will. This is the only and complete debt of [feudal] honor which we owe to God, and which God requires of us…. He who does not render this honor which is due to God, robs God of His own and dishonors Him; and this is sin.
>
> Moreover, so long as he does not restore what he has taken away, he remains in fault. It will not suffice merely to restore what has been taken away, but, considering the contempt offered, he ought to restore more than he took away. For as one who imperils another's safety does not do enough by merely restoring his safety without making some compensation for the anguish incurred; so he who violates another's honor does not enough by merely rendering honor again, but must, according to the extent of the injury done, make restoration in some way satisfactory to the person whom he has dishonored.
>
> We must also observe that when any one pays what he has unjustly taken away, he ought to give something which could not have been demanded of him, had he not stolen what belonged to another. So then, everyone who sins ought to pay back the honor of which he has robbed God; and this is the satisfaction which every sinner owes to God.
>
> *Anselm concluded that, therefore, the only one who can repay God for our sin is Jesus Christ, who had to become human to make an acceptable and satisfactory payment to God.*

New Monastic Orders

It was in the mid-eleventh century that an Augustinian order, known as the Black Canons or the Canon Regulars, was formed as a monastic order of communal clergy. *The Rule of the Canons Regular* was adapted from the writings of St. Augustine. In contrast to monks, canons did not live in cloistered communities, but were engaged in liturgical and sacrament ministries in their chapels. Sometimes called "Augustinian Canons," they are not to be confused with the Order of the Hermits of Saint Augustine, which was founded in 1244 and which Luther would join in the sixteenth century.

Following the Cluniac reforms of the previous century, another new order was founded near the end of this century. Around 1080, Bruno of Cologne (c.1030-1101) left his post as head of a cathedral school in Reims to join a group of hermits in Burgundy and within a few years founded a monastery in Chartreuse, from which they derived their name, Carthusians. The order followed a very strict discipline prepared by Bruno, known as the *Statutes*, which required a vow of silence and the eremitic lifestyle (living as isolated hermits), although they did meet together in community (the cenobitic life) for worship and meals.

Shortly thereafter, a French monk, Robert of Molesme (c.1028-1111), and an English monk, Stephen Harding (+1134), founded a new order in 1098, determined to follow the original Benedictine *Rule* as extremely literally and strictly as possible. Called Cistercians after the Latin name of the village, Cîteaux (Latin, *Cistercium*) in eastern France, they built their first monastery in that region. The desire for the simplest and plainest is evident even in their habits, made of cheap undyed wool (because of their habits, they are often referred to as "White Monks" in contrast to the Benedictine "Black Monks," whose habits were made from wool of black sheep). In a sense their desire for purity was a reaction against the abuses witnessed earlier in the century. This order had a significant impact on the next century (see chapter 12).

The century ended in both triumph and defeat. Pope Urban died at the eve of the century and was succeeded by Pope Paschal II (c.1050/55-1118, pope 1099-1118), a former Cluniac monk and papal legate for Pope Gregory VII. However, in the same year, the crusaders took control of Jerusalem after a ferocious battle with Muslim forces and re-established Jerusalem as a Christian city. This is the same year that El Cid (1040-1099) died quietly in his palatial residence in Valencia, his last conquest.

The crusader movement, however, had only begun. As travel opportunities increased, greater intellectual vigor followed as will be evident in the next century.

For Discussion
1. Looking over some of the previous chapters, identify several factors which led to the breach between Eastern and Western Christians.
2. Why did the agricultural innovations aid in the population expansion as well as increase the wealth of the church?
3. How did Gregory VII secure a stronger rule for the papacy?
4. What distracting features were present in fulfilling the ultimate goal of the first Crusade?
5. Describe two lasting beneficial insights provided by the writings of Anselm of Canterbury for contemporary Christianity.

For Further Reading
Anselm of Canterbury. *Proslogion, Monologion, An Appendix In Behalf of the Fool By Gaunilon, and Cur Deus Homo.* Trans. by Sidney Norton Deane. (Chicago: Open Court Publishing, 1903). Available from http://www.ccel.org/ccel/anselm/basic_works.titlepage.html
Harris, Matthew Arnold. *The Life and Times of Hildebrand, Pope Gregory VII.* London: Francis Griffiths, 1910.
Lawrence, C. H. *Medieval Monasticism: Forms of Religious Life in Western Europe in the Middle Ages.* New York: Longman, 1984.
Posnov, M. E. *The History of the Christian Church until the Great Schism of 1054.* Bloomington, IN: Author House, 2004.
Tyerman, Christopher. *The Crusades: A Very Short Introduction.* New York: Oxford University Press, 2005.
Whalen, Brett. *Rethinking the Schism of 1054: Authority, Heresy, and the Latin Rite.* New York: Traditio, 2007.

12. Crusader Mentality and Growing Intellectualism

The Twelfth Century

Religious and political conflict dominated this century. There is also a new sense of theological discussion as papal power claims greater political influence. Throughout these hundred years, the desire to be holy in the world ebbs and flows as human ideas vie with the gospel for clarity.

New Kinds of Monastic Orders

The First Crusade was immediately successful with the reclamation of Jerusalem, but the hostile relationship between Muslims and Christians was not ameliorated. As this century begins, Baldwin of Bouillon (c.1058-1118) assumed the title King of Jerusalem, following his recently deceased brother, Godfreyk's (1060-1100) precedent at having been named "Protector of the Holy Sepulcher." Baldwin established several kingdoms, including a claim on the region of Edessa. For all practical purposes, these were fiefdoms independent from Jerusalem. They were supported by the military orders which had developed at this time—the Knights of St. John (Hospitalers) founded already in 1070 as a hospice for pilgrims and, sometime after the crusade, the Knights of the Temple (Templars), who were founded in 1119 and officially recognized by the papacy in 1128.

These new monastic orders brought together two seemingly contradictory occupations—the monks who were not allowed to shed blood and the knights who were trained for fighting and killing. In addition to their three traditional monastic vows of poverty, chastity, and obedience, these new orders added a vow of perpetual warfare against infidels. Although a gradual change of opinion was occurring over the past century, the papal indulgence granted by Urban II in 1095 sealed the idea of a holy war. Killing an enemy of Christ was not a sinful requiring penance, but a meritorious act which guaranteed forgiveness of temporal punishments. Bernard of Clairvaux (see below) confirmed this view when he wrote in *De Laude Novae Militiae* (In Praise of New Knights), "The knight of Christ need fear no sin in killing the foe; he is the minister of God for the punishment of the wicked. In the death of a pagan a Christian is glorified, because Christ is glorified."[1]

Other monastic communities began to thrive, following the Gregorian reforms at the same time as the twelfth-century society experienced a kind of "evangelical awakening." The abbey of St. Victor in Paris is established early this century. Being founded in 1113, it produced several great thinkers in the next centuries, particularly Hugh of St. Victor (1096-1141). Although of noble birth, he entered the order of the Canons Regular of St Augustine. Before completing his novitiate in 1115, he entered the monastery of St. Victor, where he remained for the rest of his life, writing treatises on the mystical life of a contemplative.

The Investiture Issue

A few years after the turn of the century, Henry V of Germany (1086-1125, rules 1111-1125) came to the throne under unusual circumstances. As a rebellious youth, he had forced his father to abdicate his imperial throne in 1105. Nevertheless as head of the Holy Roman Empire, he retained his father's royal control over the German bishops and abbeys.

Five years later, Henry V marched to Rome to confront Pope Paschal II (c.1050-1118, pope 1099-1118). Paschal, because of his reforming ideas and his monastic training, saw a point of compromise between the civil and the spiritual powers. He proposed that Henry give up all rights to invest bishops with spiritual authority. In exchange, the church would surrender all temporal rights to the king, including control of the feudal lands and political powers of abbots and bishops. The proposal pleased no one and was later repudiated. Yet, this distinction between spiritual and temporal authority would later prove to be extremely beneficial for the later investiture controversy. (The term, investiture, is used to describe the authority or power for vesting or placing someone in a political or spiritual office.)

Prior to Paschal II's proposal, two French bishops—Ivo of Chartres (c.1040-1115) and Hugo of Fleury (+1118/20), had argued similarly that the church had spiritual authority and the crown had temporal powers. This issue of the differing areas of power and authority would continue to be raised in the next centuries, but a temporary solution was imminent.

Concordat of Worms (1122) and First Lateran Council (1123)

Henry V worked out an official agreement with Pope Calixtus II (c.1065-1124, pope 1119-1124), a successor of Paschal. This official agreement was known as the Concordat of Worms. Based upon that historical document, no king would ever be asked to place a ring on the pope's or a bishop's hand and give him a staff (symbols of ecclesiastical authority). On the other hand, the king would always be required to give a scepter to each pope or bishop as a symbol of their temporal rights (*regalia*). Although the king could be present at the election of a pope, if there were any disputes, the archbishops and administrative clergy would

---

[1] Bernard of Clairvaux, *De Laude Novae Militiae* in *S. Bernardi Opera*, ed. J. Leclercq, C. H. Talbot, and H. Rochais (Rome 1959), III, 217, cited by C. H. Lawrence in *Medieval Monasticism* (New York: Longman, 1984), 168.

be consulted and come to the final determination of the papal office holder. This was a major shift in powers and, for all practical purposes, this ended the investiture issue for the time being.

The following year, a ninth ecumenical council was called by Pope Callistus II, who hosted it at his Lateran palace in Rome (making it the First Lateran Council). This was the first assembly made up solely of western clerics. Following the pope's success with Henry, the council officially formalized the Concordat from the church's perspective. Other activities included reconfirming the ban on clerical marriage, opposing lay investiture and simony, punishing thieves and robbers of persons making pilgrimages, as well as providing solutions to several local issues. During this same century, two other councils were held—in 1139 under Pope Innocent II (pope 1130-1143) and in 1179 under Pope Alexander III (c.1100/5-1181, pope 1159-1181). The Second Lateran Council (1139) reaffirmed the clerical marriage ban and excommunicated an opponent of Innocent who had set himself up as an alternate pope. The Third Lateran Council (1179) established the papal enclave of cardinals as the only proper institution of the church able to elect future popes by a two-thirds majority and condemned the heretical Albigenses and Waldenses (see below and chapter 13).

Stephen Harding's Cistercian Rule

In the area of monastic reforms, the influence of the Cistercian Order grew rapidly under its third abbot, an Englishman named Stephen Harding (c.1050-1134, abbot 1109-1134). Besides the motherhouse at Cîteaux, four other monasteries were founded during the next decade and by mid-century, when Bernard of Clairvaux died, there were over 300 houses and by the end of the next century almost 700. In contrast to the close control practiced by the system of Cluny, the Cistercians organized more as a federation of equal and autonomous monasteries, each abbot having a voice in the annual meeting at Cîteaux.

Some of the credit for this growth rested with Stephen Harding's charter, *Carta Caritatis* (Charter of Charity). His rule, besides acknowledging a simple return to a strict Benedictine regimen, emphasized the collegial care with which the order was governed. Yet, the most striking feature in the order was its return to manual labor, especially work in the farmlands, which became a special characteristic of Cistercian life. Many of their new monasteries were settled in remote and often difficult areas to farm. Because the Benedictine Rule emphasized worship and prayer, the Cistercians engaged a significant number of lay workers who assisted them in their agricultural endeavors. As a result, the Cistercians became the main force of technological diffusion throughout medieval European agricultural settings.

Bernard of Clairvaux

More influential than Harding's charter was the fact that around this same time Bernard of Clairvaux (1090-1153) entered the monastery at Cîteaux with thirty companions. The most influential figure of this century, Bernard was a strong, yet humble servant of Christ. Born near Dijon, France, both his parents were of noble society—his father was a knight and his pious mother was the daughter of a nobleman. Because of his mother's untimely death during his childhood, Bernard resolved to enter a monastery early in his life. When given the opportunity to enter the Cistercian monastery in 1098, he not only took his vows quickly and confidently, but he brought several friends and family members. When a new monastery was founded at Clairvaux, Bernard was immediately appointed abbot.

Bernard served as the conscience of the church. Strongly affirming the necessity of rigorously obeying the Cistercian Rule, Bernard influenced many other abbeys as well as bishops to reform their monasteries or congregations from their worldly emphasis on wealth and to reinvigorate a spiritual fervor for the Lord's kingdom-work. Among the Cistercian practices which influenced Bernard was the replacement of the *Christus Victor* image (the Lord in majesty) with a corpus of a suffering Savior. As a result, one of the most cherished meditations in western contemplative Christianity was penned by Bernard in 1127, entitled "The Love of God" (*De Diligendo Deo*), which depicts the soul's desire for God (see text box below). He composed this while serving as abbot at Clairvaux after settling several political disputes, particularly one between the pope and the city of Milan.

Bernard: *On Loving God*

In this life, I think, we cannot fully and perfectly obey that precept, "Thou shalt love the Lord your God with all your heart, and with all your soul, and with all your strength, and with all your mind" (Luke 10:27). For here [on earth] the heart must take thought for the body; and the soul must energize the flesh; and the strength must guard itself from impairment; and by God's favor, must seek to increase. It is therefore impossible to offer up all our being to God, to yearn altogether for His face, so long as we must accommodate our purposes and aspirations to these fragile, sickly bodies of ours. Wherefore the soul may hope to possess the fourth degree of love, or rather to be possessed by it, only when it has been clothed upon with that spiritual and immortal body, which will be perfect, peaceful, lovely, and in everything wholly subjected to the spirit. And to this degree no human effort can attain; it is in God's power to give it to whom He wills. Then the soul will easily reach that highest stage, because no lusts of the flesh will retard its eager entrance into the joy of its Lord, and no troubles will disturb its peace. May we not think that the holy martyrs enjoyed this grace, in some degree at least, before they laid down their victorious bodies? Surely that was immeasurable strength of love which enraptured their souls, enabling them to laugh at fleshly torments and to yield their lives gladly. But even though the frightful pain could not destroy their peace of mind, it must have impaired somewhat its perfection.

From chapter X: *"Of the Fourth Degree of Love: Wherein Man Does Not Even Love Self Except for God's Sake."*

At about the same time, the monastic order of the Knights Templars were recognized by the Synod of Troyes in 1129 due to Bernard's strong advocacy of their function as well as his own composition of their rule. The men in this new order took vows of chastity and obedience. Poverty was their symbol and providing food for the poor was their vocation, along with the practice of fasting for great lengths of time. The seal of the Knights Templar (see illustration) was an image of two knights on a single horse, emblematic of their vow of poverty. The text combines Greek and Latin characters, *Sigillum Militum Xpristi* ("Seal of the Soldiers of Christ") followed by a cross.

With the death of Pope Honorius (1060-1130; pope 1124-1130), two rival factions set up their own preferences for the position, one group electing Anacletus II (antipope 1130-1138) in opposition to Innocent II (pope 1130-1143). At a synod convoked by Louis IV "the Fat" of France (1081-1137, ruled 1108-1137) in April, Bernard showed how Innocent's claims were most valid. Thus the end of a potentially troublesome schism was averted, a feat which can be attributed to Bernard's careful and pastoral leadership. Travelling between centers of political power in Germany and France and Italy, Bernard slowly strengthened the papal power in Rome, especially after the death of Anacletus in 1138.

Sometime around 1140, Bernard was drawn out further from his monastic duties to serve the greater church. Perhaps more than any other figure in this century, the young scholar and monastic theologian, Peter Abelard (see below), gave voice to his eloquent teachings, yet problematic expressions, which needed to be addressed. Bernard's clarity and force of logic in pointing to Abelard's errors ultimately led Abelard to retire in Cluny.

The Second Crusade

After almost half a century of nominal coexistence between Christians and Muslims in Palestine, a new crusade was called for by Pope Eugenius III (c.1080-1153, pope 1145-1153) and strongly supported by Bernard through his persuasive preaching. The crusader state of Edessa, founded by Baldwin (ruled Edessa 1100-1118 and Jerusalem 1118-1131), was recaptured by infidel Muslim forces in 1144. The kings of France (Louis VII, 1120-1130, ruled 1137-1180) and Germany (Conrad III, 1093-1152, ruled 1138-1152) were enlisted to fight, but travelled different routes. In addition, several northern German nobles were diverted to fight the Slavs and Wends.

Inspired by the fervor for defeating the Muslims, a group of crusaders stopped in Muslim-controlled Portugal and retook Lisbon in 1147. Bernard, who had encouraged the crusade, continued to preach, but this time condemned the unnecessary violence which was carried out also against Jews who were living in Germany. With significant distrust among the various armies, troops finally arrived in the Holy Land in 1148 to support the inhabitants of Jerusalem against the Muslim forces in Damascus. Following a failed siege of Damascus, the crusaders departed the Holy Land in defeat, much to the embarrassment of Bernard, who claimed the disaster was caused by the sinful behavior of the participants.

In the early 1150s, after the death of several of his close friends including Pope Eugenius, Bernard felt that his own life was coming to an end, too. He died in Cluny in August of 1153, having spent over two-thirds of his life in the cloister. He was canonized as a saint in the Roman Catholic Church soon afterward (1174).

Anselm of Canterbury's Later Activities

We now return to the activities of Anselm of Canterbury (see chapter 11). After the death of William the Conqueror in 1100, Anselm was invited by the new king of England, Henry I, to return to his homeland. But almost as soon as he came into the royal courts, the king demanded that homage be paid to the king for the privilege of occupying the Canterbury estates and that Anselm be installed as archbishop by the king (thus insisting on lay investiture). Anselm refused and shortly thereafter was exiled from England.

Around this time, Anselm finished writing several noteworthy treatises: *De Processione Spiritus Sancti* (*On the Proceeding of the Holy Spirit*, 1102), *De sacramentis ecclesiae* (*On the Sacraments of the Church*, 1106-7), and *De Concordia Praescientia et Praedestinationis et Gratiae Dei cum Libero Arbitrio* (*On the Harmony of the Foreknowledge, the Predestination, and the Grace of God with Free Choice* 1107-8). The first of these works was specifically designed to satisfy the concerns of the Orthodox bishops in Italy over the *filioque*, although whether or not it did was unclear.

Anselm came back to England in 1107 and served the remaining two years of his life as a strong and pastoral archbishop. He enforced several rules which had been ordered in 1105, particularly the prohibition of clergy marriages (and concubinage for those in holy orders). He died during Holy Week in 1109. His greatest influence was in his writings, which resulted in his being called "the Father of Scholastic theology."

Peter Abelard

One of the most self-centered clerical scholars in Christian history, Peter Abelard (1079-1142) was always living on the edge. In his autobiography, *The History of My Calamities*, he related his early years as a precocious monk. Never finding satisfactory teachers, he was dismissed from one monastic school after another until he finally entered the newly founded cathedral school of Paris. There an unscrupulous and otherwise unknown canon, named Fulbert, invited Abelard to tutor his niece in his home. In exchange for Abelard's tutelage, Fulbert provided Abelard with free housing and complete access to his niece. Over the next months, Abelard's plan to seduce Heloise (c.1098-1163) succeeded and she became pregnant. After being emasculated by Heloise's uncle, Abelard returned to his academic life and established a monastic community as a residence for Heloise. Their son, Astrolabe (c.1118-c.1150?), rarely mentioned, was raised by Abelard's sister. His burial is recorded at the cemetery of his mother's convent, the Paraclete.

Peter Abelard's academic career was erratic and vitriolic as was his moral life. As a young student of the renowned scholar, William of Champeaux (c.1070-1121), Peter quickly departed over a theoretical disagreement and tried to start his own school outside of Paris. Unsuccessful, he returned to study rhetoric and dialectic with William, who agreed to work with him until William's retirement. Sometime around 1113, Abelard began studying theology and managed again to acquire a teaching position in Paris. In 1121, he published a book on the Trinity in which he used philosophical dialectics to "prove" the Trinity. The work was almost immediately banned and burned. Over time, he entered and departed from several monasteries and schools, almost always in disgrace, yet always rising again with a new project.

Sic et Non, literally "This and Not" (or "Yes and No"), is Abelard's greatest contribution to theology. Organized around 158 theological themes, Abelard set Scripture passages and quotations of patristic authors "for" and "against" these doctrinal opinions. His first five questions are: *Quod fides humanis rationibus non sit abstruenda, et contra. Quod fides sit de non apparentibus tantum, et contra. Quod sit credendum in deum solum, et contra. Quod agnitio non sit de non apparentibus sed fides tantum, et contra. Quod non sit deus singularis, et contra.* (That human faith must be completed by reason, or not? That faith deals only with unseen things, or not? That there is any knowledge of things unseen, or not? That one may believe only in God alone, or not? That God is a single unitary being, or not?) His goal was to show that truth was the result of dialectics, that is, debating—a skill which he possessed to the highest degree. The work, though criticized immediately, became a standard textbook for medieval scholasticism. His motto and his approach to education can be summarized by a quotation from this work: "By doubting, we come to inquiry; by inquiry, we grasp truth" [*Dubitando ad inquisitionem venimus; inquirendo veritatem percipimus.*]. His approach along with his attitude gave voice to eloquent teaching, yet resulted in problematic expressions of the Christian faith, which needed to be addressed. Into such a context, Bernard's clarity and force of logic pointed to Abelard's errors.

> From *Sic et Non*
>
> Doubtless the fathers might err; even Peter, the prince of the apostles, fell into error: what wonder that the saints do not always show themselves inspired? The fathers did not themselves believe that they, or their companions, were always right. Augustine found himself mistaken in some cases and did not hesitate to retract his errors. He warns his admirers not to look upon his letters as they would upon the Scriptures, but to accept only those things which, upon examination, they find to be true.
>
> All writings belonging to this class are to be read with full freedom to criticize, and with no obligation to accept unquestioningly; otherwise the way would be blocked to all discussion, and posterity be deprived of the excellent intellectual exercise of debating difficult questions of language and presentation. But an explicit exception must be made I the case of the Old and New Testaments. In the Scriptures, when anything strikes us as absurd, we may not say that the writer erred, but that the scribe made a blunder in copying the manuscripts, or that there is an error in interpretation, or that the passage is not understood. The fathers make a very careful distinction between the Scriptures and later works. They advocate a discriminating, not to say, suspicious, use of the writings of their own contemporaries.

Abelard's influence, though great, was tarnished not only by his own arrogant and pugnacious behavior, but by the hostility he drew from Bernard of Clairvaux. Serving as a prosecutor for Peter Abelard's heresy trial at Sens in 1141, Bernard presented fourteen charges of anti-scriptural heresy from Abelard's writings. Not only his philosophically-tainted Trinitarian views, but his view of the atonement as expressing God's love was criticized by Bernard and condemned by the Council at Sens. Although Abelard sought to have the trial moved to Rome, Bernard had the condemnations immediately publicized at Rome. On the way to Rome, Abelard collapsed at the monastery of Cluny, where he stayed a few months until his death was imminent. Through the efforts of Peter the Venerable

(1092-1156), he and Bernard were officially reconciled and Abelard was taken to St. Marcel where he died.

Monastic Theologians

Although not as well known or as notorious as Bernard or Abelard, Hugh of St. Victor (1096-1141) left a lasting legacy in Christian theology. Around 1134 he published his *De sacramentis Christianae fidei* (On the sacraments of the Christian Faith) in which he discusses over thirty sacraments and sacramentals for the Christian believer. Although the work focuses on sacraments, it became the first complete scholastic text which utilized the dialectical method to present topics from creation to the last things. Hugh has been called one of the most influential theologians of the twelfth century. His biblical commentaries straddled the fine line between mystical allegory and literal application of texts.

About the same time, a Benedictine abbess, Hildegard of Bingen (1098-1179), established several convents in Europe and built her own convent in Bingen, Germany (1147-1151). Hildegard is best known for her musical compositions and mystical poetry. She wrote the first extant morality play, *Ordo Virtutum* (Order of Virtues), in which the human soul is depicted as struggling between the devil and the divine virtues. Her writings included a wealth of letters to various leaders throughout the church and government, corresponding with kings, prelates, and at least one emperor. Yet, she was much more than a writer. Hildegard also was a visionary, claiming to see visions of heaven [see illustration], which she dictated to her loyal scribe. In addition to her spirituality, she was very interested in holistic healing and the effects of a variety of natural herbs and plants for medical purposes.

Muslim and Jewish Philosophers

Just before the Second Crusade, the Cluniac abbot, Peter the Venerable (c.1092-1156), had prepared a translation of the *Qur'an* into Latin (1143). Two centuries earlier, an Arab philosopher, Ibn Sina (Latinized as Avicenna, 930-1037), had introduced Greek learning, particularly Aristotle's metaphysics to Islamic scholarship. Near the end of the eleventh century, the Muslim philosopher and *Mujaddid* (renewer of the faith), al-Ghazali (1058-1111), tried to reconcile faith and reason. But, prior to his death, he wrote *The Destruction/Incoherence of Philosophers* in which he argued that the two ways of thinking were truly antagonistic. A half-century later, a young Muslim scholar in the Iberian peninsula, Ibn Rushd (Latinized as Averroes, 1126-1198) proposed a kind of "double truth" in which theology and philosophy are on parallel tracks. It was through the work of Avicenna and especially Averroes that Aristotelian philosophy again entered into western thinking. Within a century, Aristotle would dominate most academic studies in the West as we will see in the next chapter.

A Jewish philosopher, Moses Maimonides (1135-1204), was also instrumental in promoting Aristotelian philosophy among Christian scholars. He served as a prominent rabbi and successful physician in Spain, Egypt, and Morocco, where he read Aristotle in Arabic. His commentaries on the Torah and Mishnah (Jewish code of law) are still held in high regard. He is best known for his work on Jewish ethics and law (Torah), particularly his essay *The Guide to the Perplexed*, which he wrote in Arabic.

> Maimonides's
> *13 Principles of Judaism*
> 1. God's existence
> 2. God's unity
> 3. God's spiritual incorporeality
> 4. God's eternity
> 5. Worship only God
> 6. God's revelation through prophets
> 7. Moses as preeminent prophet
> 8. God's Mosaic law
> 9. God's Torah is immutable
> 10. God foreknows human acts
> 11. God rewards good and punishes evil
> 12. Jewish Messiah is coming
> 13. The dead will be raised

Architectural Innovation

One of the major medieval architectural innovations was the use of the ribbed vault (see illustration). Thin ribbings of stone were placed diagonally, transversely, and longitudinally, running from the pillars to the second innovation, the pointed ceiling arch. To support the walls, side pillars, known as "flying buttresses," were constructed outside the building. These architectural approaches enabled the walls to be thinner and the ceilings higher. The overall effect was that these grand buildings were much brighter and provided greater openness of space. The name for this style was labeled "Gothic" (a pejorative term suggesting it was barbarian) in the fifteenth century because it had been a departure from the classical style of earlier Greeks and Romans, which the Renaissance was seeking to restore.

During this century, construction began on the Cathedral of Notre Dame in Paris (1160), the Laon Cathedral (1160) and the Chartres Cathedral (1194).

Gratian's Decretals of Canon Law

Known as the "Father of Canon Law," an almost unknown monk and jurist named Gratian (c.1100-c.1165) assembled a concordance of various ecclesiastical laws from the earliest Christian era to the Lateran Council. The book, *Concordia discordantium canonum* (a harmony of discordant canons), followed a principle of harmonization. Gratian sought to unify the interpretation of several thousand seemingly contradictory laws by classifying the different explanations which had been presented. The result was a textbook for church lawyers to analyze church law and formalize the various practices associated with church discipline. It was used in the Roman Catholic Church until 1918 as the basis for all church legal decisions.

Peter Lombard

Coming from a very humble and obscure background, Peter Lombard (c.1095/1100-c.1160) studied at various cathedral schools, finally coming to Paris in the middle 1130s as a result of Bernard of Clairvaux's recommendation. While at the Cathedral School of Notre Dame, he studied with Peter Abelard, whom he respected greatly. About 1145, he became a full professor, a *magister*, at the cathedral school.

His most famous work, *Libri quatuor sententiarum (Four Books of Sentences)*, which he composed around 1150, gives evidence of his dialectical method. Within these four volumes, Lombard gathered quotations from the Bible and earlier church fathers, setting them beside each other in a way which would allow them complement each other and be used as a resource for discussion, debate, and further theological exploration. This format provided engaging opportunities for students to investigate the various topics creatively. The first book dealt with the Trinity, including God's attributes. He also included the topics of providence, predestination, and evil. The second volume addressed issues related to the six days of creation, angels and demons, the fall, grace, and sin. The third book focused on the incarnation, redemption and the spiritual virtues, along with the Ten Commandments. The final book included the sacraments in general and the seven sacraments in particular (Lombard was the first to limit the number), as well as the last things—death, judgment, hell, and heaven. From this incredibly thorough work, Lombard became known as the *Magister Sententiarum* (Teacher of the Sentences). From the twelfth century through the sixteenth century, almost every theologian was required to comment on these sentences as part of his training, including Martin Luther.

Besides teaching, Peter Lombard pursued the various ranks of clergy from sub-deacon until he was finally ordained as a priest in 1156. In 1159, he was elected as Bishop of Paris, a position he held only for about a year prior to his death in July 1160. Besides his sentences, he is remembered for his commentaries on the Psalms and some of the Pauline epistles, although the style was not unique.

Glossa Ordinaria

From earliest Christian times, biblical texts were the subject of innumerable commentaries. Over the centuries, these comments took on a more authoritative quality. During the twelfth century, marginal and interlinear comments on the Bible became a standard educational resource. As a teacher commented on a biblical text in his lecture, students would write his explanations of terms and the various senses of Scripture in their text. Occasionally, a longer discussion of a theological question would be given, too. The short interlinear comments and clarifications of Bible terms in the biblical text were known as the *glossa interlinearis* (interlinear comments). Slightly larger marginal notes were called *glossa marginalis*, although together they were often referred to simply as *Glossa* (or *Glossa ordinaria*). Among several other writers, Peter Lombard had prepared glosses on various books of the Bible along with his marginal quotations from earlier Christian authors.

By the end of this century, and drawing on the work of many anonymous theologians, the *Glossa ordinaria* became a standard text for theological study. As the biblical explanations lengthened and as longer discussions of theological topics were introduced, the *Gloss* gradually took the form of a biblical commentary. The biblical text would be situated in the middle of the page (see illustration of a page from Genesis) and the comments of various theologians would be placed around it.

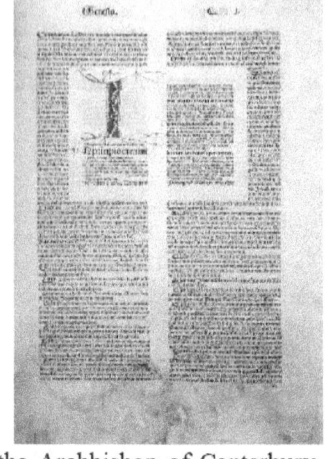

Thomas Becket

As a very gifted young man, Thomas Becket (c.1118/20-1170) was educated in England and France. Attracting the attention of the Archbishop of Canterbury, Thomas was enlisted for several important political and ecclesiastical missions. Because of his administrative skills, he began service to King Henry II (1133-1189, ruled 1154-1189) as Lord Chancellor in 1155. In 1162, Becket became archbishop of Canterbury. His amicable relationship with the king quickly deteriorated, as he withstood attempts by the king to diminish clerical autonomy. Within two years he had to flee to France after refusing to follow the Constitutions of Clarendon, a set of sixteen articles designed by Henry II to restrict the power of the church. (See the 14th century illustration of Henry II and Thomas.) Eight years after becoming archbishop, he was assassinated by four French knights in the Canterbury Cathedral (whether or not they were under orders from Henry has remained uncertain). Three years later he was declared a saint of the church and his grave became an important site of pilgrimages.

Heresiarchs

During the first half of this century, unrest among both clergy and laity began to increase. Strange teachings began to be promulgated. Many of the teachers were labelled heretics, religious teachers or leaders who firmly held and defended teachings contrary to Roman dogma. (The originators of these teachings were identified with the term, *heresiarch*.)

A popular preacher, Peter de Bruys (c.1087-c.1131), for example, attacked devotion to the cross and images; he suggested that infant baptism was useless; and he taught that communion bread and wine only represented Christ's body and blood in the Sacrament. Much of this concern came as a result of the corruption of the clergy and the privileges and property rights usurped by the church. Although such teachings were not widespread, the Benedictine abbot, Peter the Venerable (c.1092-1156), was compelled to write a tract in 1139 against de Bruys, who had promoted his views for almost two dozen years. De Bruys was labelled a heresiarch, an originator of erroneous doctrines and heresy, by the Roman Catholic Church.

Joachimites

Another popular preacher was Joachim of Fiori (c.1132-c.1202). As Abbot of a Cistercian monastery, he had a great influence on his order as he professed to have had unique spiritual insights After making a pilgrimage to the Holy Land, he claimed to have experienced a celestial vision on Mount Tabor. He then declared the establishment of a "spiritual church" to supersede the present institutional church.

He published three books, which set forth his understanding of this new age. He believed that three states of the world corresponded to the three Persons of the Trinity. During the Father's age, corresponding to the Old Testament, the world was ruled by fear and power. The Son's age revealed the wisdom long hidden, but present in the Catholic Church of the New Testament. The final period, the Kingdom of the Holy Spirit, would provide a new dispensation of universal love, which proceeded from the Eternal Gospel in which there will be no need for institutions, particularly the church. Although Joachim was never convicted of heresy, subsequent to his early death, Joachim's followers, called Joachimites, mostly Franciscans in the next century, greatly exaggerated his teachings. These teachings associated with Joachim were condemned at the Synod of Arles in 1263. They also succeeded in creating a deeper awareness of and appreciation for the Holy Spirit's activity in the world.

Waldensians

About the same time, another preacher began gathering followers in the region of Lyon, France. His name was Peter Waldo (c.1140-c.1205), a wealthy layman who around 1175 renounced his possessions, giving his money away in the streets of Lyon and became an itinerant preacher. Preachers at that time were required to be licensed by the local bishop, but the bishop of Lyons refused to grant Peter such permission. At the Third Lateran Council (1179), Peter approached the pope, Alexander III (c.1100-1181), who appreciated Peter's enthusiasm and advocacy of poverty, yet felt obligated to defer to the concerns and critique of the local bishop. By 1180 Peter and his followers, who became known as Waldensians, were expelled from Lyon. In 1184 they were declared heretics of the Catholic Church for not submitting to ecclesiastical authority. Their continuing struggles will be noted in the next chapter.

Cathars

Originating in the early years of the twelfth century, this group of medieval Puritans (Greek, *Katharoi*, "pure ones") held views similar to the early Manicheans (see chapter 2). They taught a dualistic view in which two gods ruled—an evil Old Testament god and a good New Testament god. Matter, they said, was evil because the physical world was ruled by the evil god. The physicality of Christianity was greatly questioned as they denied the incarnation (how could the true God contaminate Himself with a physical body?) and the sacraments (why would there be any benefit in consuming bread and wine?). Christ, the son of the good god, came only to be an example of how a life-giving Spirit could transcend his body. Sexual intercourse was considered evil as was the consumption of milk, meat, and eggs—all products of intercourse. By 1140 their teachings had spread throughout much of western Europe, especially northern Italy and southern France, where they were called Albigensians after the region of Albi where they settled (see chapter 13).

Third Crusade (1187-1192)

Perhaps one of the more remarkable, albeit unsuccessful, crusades was conducted near the end of this century. Saladin (Salah ad-Din Yusuf), the sultan of Egypt (1137/8-1193), had overwhelmed the Christian troops in the famous battle at the Horns of Hattin in the Galilee northwest of Tiberias. He then recaptured Jerusalem in 1187. The cross atop the Dome of the Rock was removed and Saladin's army plundered the churches and convents of the city. In response to the news of this event, Pope Gregory VIII (c.1105-1187, pope 3 months) called upon several of the most well-respected military leaders, King Philip II of France (1175-1223; ruled 1180-1223), Emperor Frederick I (Barbarossa, "red beard") of the Holy Roman Empire (1122-1190, ruled 1155-1190), and King Richard the Lionhearted of England (1157-1199, ruled 1189-1199).

In 1191, on his way to the Holy Land, Richard captured the Byzantine-held Isle of Cyprus, which remained a significant base for all future crusades. Later that year, the city of Acre was recaptured, although Philip returned to France to engage in his own political pursuits. The final battle was thirty miles north of Jaffa where Richard along with the knight-monks, Hospitalers and Templars, succeeded in defeating Saladin's army. Frederick Barbarossa had drowned after being thrown from his horse, so Richard was dubious of taking Jerusalem with a diminished army. Negotiations with Saladin resulted in an agreement that unarmed Christians could be allowed to visit the holy sites in Jerusalem. Returning home, Richard was captured by several political enemies, including Henry VI, who held him for a time for ransom. Richard finally returned to England in 1194, where he died five years later as a result of a severe wound from a crossbow bolt.

A new military order developed at this time, the Teutonic Knights, founded in Acre in 1190 under the official title of "The Order of Brothers of the German House of St Mary in Jerusalem." Originally part of the Order of German Hospitallers, they were reorganized as a military order to protect the port of Acre.

The century ends as vigorously as it began. Theological and political issues swelled the conversations of academicians, prelates, and nobles. Monastic influences increased as did the preaching and teaching of key figures, such as Bernard. Just as architectural structures reached new heghts, so the Christian gospel impelled the faithful to greatere interest in clearer communication of divine truths. With Pope Innocent III's (1160/61-1216; pope 1198-1216) election by the College of Cardinals at the age of 37, the stage was set for a major change in the hierarchy of the Roman Catholic Church as we will see in the next chapter.

For Review and Discussion
1. How was the Investiture Controversy settled?
2. Recognizing Bernard's many accomplishments, which one would you consider his greatest and why?
3. What makes Peter Abelard such a distinguished, yet distasteful scholar?
4. Which of the monastic orders mentioned in this chapter do you find most attractive?
5. How would you characterize the crusades that were conducted during this century?

For Further Reading
Asbridge, Thomas. *The Crusades: The Authoritative History of the War for the Holy Land.* New York: Harper Collins ECCO, 2018.
Fairweather, Eugene R., ed. and trans. *A Scholastic Miscellany: Anselm to Ockham.* Library of Christian Classics series. Philadelphia: The Westminster Press, 1956.
Flanagan, Sabina. *Hildegard of Bingen: A Visionary Life.* London: Routledge, 1989.
Mabillon, John, ed., and Samuel J. Eales, trans. and ed. *Life and Work of Saint Bernard.* London: John Hodges, 1896.
Maimonides, Moses. *The Guide for the Perplexed.* Trans. by Schlomo Pines. Chicago: University of Chicago Press, 1974.
Phillips, Jonathan. *The Crusades: 1095-1204.* Second Edition. New York: Routledge, 2014.
Posset, Franz. *Pater Bernhardus: Martin Luther and Bernard of Clairvaux.* Kalamazoo, MI: Cistercian Publications, 1999.
Rosemann, Philipp W. *The Story of the Great Medieval Book: Peter Lombard's "Sentences".* Toronto: University of Toronto Press, 2007.

13. Church Theologians and Mendicant Movements

The Thirteenth Century

With the enthronement of Pope Innocent III (1161-1216, pope 1198-1216) at the end of the twelfth century, the Roman Catholic Church's power became firmly established in medieval society in the thirteenth century. This century also marks one of the high points for scholastic theology. Yet, the mendicant (begging) orders come of age in this era as reforming agents not only for the monasteries but also for the church itself. The century opened with a call by Innocent II for another crusade.

Innocent III

Probably one of the most powerful popes of the middle ages, Lotario de Segni (1160/61-1216, pope 1198-1216) was made a cardinal-deacon at the age of

twenty-nine by his uncle, Pope Clement III (1130-1191, pope 1187-1191), and upon the death of Celestine III (1106-1198, pope 1191-1198) was elected pope at the age of thirty-seven, taking the name Innocent. His papacy was noteworthy both for his political powers as well as his desire for reform. He asserted that as the moon is related to the sun, so the political system is related to the universal church. After securing a strong power-base in Rome, he became involved in one of the first major political coalitions. With the death of Henry VI of Germany (1165-1197), Otto of Brunswick (1175-1218, ruled 1209-1215) and Frederick of Sicily (1194-1250, ruled 1220-1250) vied for the position. Because Otto promised to support the expanded papal area which Innocent had acquired, the pope chose Otto. Once in power, Otto reneged on his promise and Innocent deposed him, giving the political authority to Frederick.

Innocent was anything but innocent. He initially became involved in England, excommunicating King John (1166-1216, ruled 1199-1216) for not acknowledging Stephan Langdon (1150-1228) as archbishop of Canterbury. When the king later relented and gave land to the papacy. For that act of papal support, Innocent declared the *Magna Carta* void, since it had been executed without papal approval. Only France seemed to have been strong enough to withstand the pope's political encroachment. Other countries as extent as Poland, Scandinavia, Armenia, and Portugal experienced direct papal control and political involvement.

> *Magna Carta*
> "The Great Charter of the Liberties of England" was presented to King John by the noble barons of England in 1215, declaring their freedom from arbitrary royal decisions. This basic document led to the possibilities of rule by strong constitutional law in the English-speaking world for future centuries.

Besides the reforms carried out in the Fourth Lateran Council (see below), Innocent was involved in a variety of negotiations between political and civil authorities. He died of a fever in July 1216, after an expedition between the Italian cities of Pisa and Genoa.

Fourth Crusade (1201-1204)

Early in the thirteenth century, a fourth crusade, was proposed by Innocent III to expand the Christian holdings in the Holy Land. The venture commenced with French and Italian militia and sailors embarking from Venice early in 1202. After a less-than-expected number of crusaders rallied in Venice, local leaders sought financial remuneration for "hosting" these mercenaries by diverting the ships to the nearby Dalmatian port of Zara. That community had owed the citizens of Venice a debt which had gone unpaid. Although the pope censured an attack on fellow Christians, Zara was besieged and fell to the Venetian "crusaders" almost immediately.

In the meantime, several Byzantine princes were vying for control of Constantinople. One prince, Alexios IV Angelus (c.1182-1204, coregent 1203-1204), deceitfully offered the crusaders a great sum of money as well as several thousand men to help secure and then maintain Christian control of the Holy Land, if they would overthrow his uncle, Alexios III Angelus (c.1153-1211, ruled 1195-1203). The crusaders were initially rebuffed by the Greek armies, but after a little while the crusader armies laid siege to Constantinople. In July 1203, Constantinople fell to the crusaders who established the "Latin Kingdom of Constantinople," which lasted until 1261. Needless to say, the rift between the Eastern and Western Christians of 1054 was sealed and any possibilities for political and theological recognition were eliminated.

Children's Crusade (1212)

Although not technically a crusade, after the failure of the Fourth Crusade to regain possession of the holy sites in the Holy Land, an estimated 10-30,000 children from France and Germany set out to recapture Jerusalem, led by a shepherd boy named Stephen. Claiming a vision of Christ, Stephen approached Philip (1165-1223), King of France (1180-1223)), requesting his assistance in organizing a crusade to free the Holy Land from the Muslim occupiers. Children gathered in the northwestern French city of Vendôme and traveled to Marseilles, where they awaited the parting of the Mediterranean Sea which Stephen had predicted. After several disappointing days, some merchants agreed to take the children by ships to the Holy Land.

About the same time, an eloquent German lad named Nicholas preached a similar message and gathered a throng of children at Cologne. Traveling across the Alps to Genoa, Italy, this group similarly expected to walk on dry ground to the Holy Land when the Mediterranean divided. Again, the sea did not open for them and most returned home.

While modern scholarship has questioned the historical accuracy and veracity of a Children's Crusade, early accounts existed already in the thirteenth century confirming some of these facts.[1] Whatever the origin or even the make-up of these groups, the expeditions failed. According to later accounts, either the would-be crusaders, particularly those who were from France, were either drowned at sea on several of the ships or they were sold into slavery in Tunisia.

Mendicant Orders

Early in the thirteenth century, a new development in monasticism arose. Rejecting the materialism of many contemporary and very wealthy communities, these new orders of religious eschewed possession of property and relied only on begging (Latin, *mendicans,* means "beggar") for their sustenance. As a result, these orders were of necessity not bound to their monasteries, but travelled throughout much of Europe with the gospel. A new era of evangelism and evangelical activity began to shine in the darkness.

Franciscans: The Order of Friars Minor

In the latter decades of the previous century, a son had been born into a wealthy Italian textile-merchant family and, at his baptism, was given the Christian name, Giovanni (1182-1226), after John the Baptist (his mother's name was Pica Giovanna). His father, out of devotion to his wife's homeland of France and his own attraction to that country, changed it to Francesco (Francis). Attending classes at St. Giorgio, Francis learned to speak and read both Latin and French. He was a natural leader among his peers. One year, on the eve of the Feast of St. George, he heard the story of St. George and the Dragon, which inspired him to be a military warrior like St. George.

In 1202, a border dispute between the Italian city-states of Assisi and Perugia erupted. Volunteering for his city's militia, Francis was imprisoned for a year after the military excursion failed. Returning home, he spent some time in solitude and prayer at a grotto near Assisi. There Francis had a vision of Christ,

---

[1] Peter Raedts, "The Children's Crusade of 1212," *Journal of Medieval History*, Vol. 3, No. 4 (December 1977): 279-323, has argued rather convincingly that the actual crusaders were not children, but bands of poor people (often referred to as "children" (Latin, *pueri*), since they were dependent upon society for their welfare) who believed God had empowered them to do what the military were unable to do in re-acquiring the Holy Land for Christianity.

who instructed him to wait for direction for a new knighthood. Francis traveled to Rome, where he observed true poverty for the first time in his life. While in Rome, he dressed as a beggar in front of St. Peter's basilica and begged for alms. He then gave the alms he had collected to a leper and kissed the leper's hand, rationalizing that perhaps this was Christ Himself (as Jesus said in Matthew 25:40).

Upon his return home, he visited the chapel ruins of San Damiano at Portiuncula. There he heard the Christ-figure on the crucifix tell him to restore the chapel: "Go, Francis, and repair My house which you see is nearly in ruins." He stole a horse and several bolts of cloth from his father's textile supply and sold them in the nearby town in order to obtain funds to begin the restoration project. Francis' father swiftly summoned civil authorities to punish his son for thievery.

When Francis refused to submit to civil authorities, his father demanded that Francis report before the bishop of Assisi. Francis there renounced his family and finances and took up a life of humble service, working to repair the San Damiano chapel. On the Feast of St. Matthias, February 24, 1208, the Gospel account of the commission of Christ to the apostles was read (Matthew 10:7-19). Francis determined to establish such a mission for himself and anyone who would follow. In 1209, twelve individuals began to follow Francis and on April 16th of that next year, Pope Innocent III approved a simple Rule for the new order.

The Franciscans (known as the Gray Friars for the color of their habits or the Friars Minor, *fratres minores*, "little brothers") ordered their lives in a flexible style around Francis's ideals of imitating Christ through voluntary poverty and service. The three vows of poverty, chastity, and obedience were taken as marks of the ideal Christian servant.

> **Friar**
> The word is derived from the Latin, *frater*, "brother," and is used by mendicant orders to distinguish themselves from "monks" who are generally cloistered.

In 1212 Francis, along with his wealthy friend, Clara of Assisi (1194-1253), established an organization for women, the Poor Clares, which was housed at San Damiano, following Francis' simple rule, *Regula primitive*, and was given papal approval in 1223.

Hoping to convert the Moors (north African Muslims who had taken over the Iberian peninsula), Francis traveled to southern France and Spain between 1214 and 1215, but illness prevented his completion of the task. In 1219 Francis, with several associates, traveled to Eastern Europe, the Holy Land, and down to Egypt on a preaching ministry, leaving the administration of the new Order to others.

In 1221 a third order (Tertiary) of "brothers and sisters of penance" was established for lay people who had to stay "in the world" and work, yet who desired to become "more spiritual." Withdrawal from the world and religious vows were not demanded for these Tertiaries. By the end of the year 1221, there were over 3000 friars.

In 1224, Francis went to Mount La Verna (Alverno) in the northern Apennines of Italy to meditate more deeply on Christ's sufferings. During this

time of nearly complete isolation, only one colleague, Brother Leo, had contact with him, bringing him food occasionally. On September 14, the Feast of the Holy Cross, a seraph (Isaiah 6:2 describes such an angel as having six wings of fire) presented an image of the crucified Christ before Francis, which imprinted on Francis Christ's marks of crucifixion and the lance wound. Brother Leo claimed he saw a "ball of fire" come down to Francis and return to heaven (an angel?) and the *stigmata* (simulations of Christ's wounds) appeared on Francis' body. (See illustration of a fifteenth century painting by Bernardo Strozzi.)

Upon his return to Assisi, Francis visited the Poor Clares, but experienced some kind of a terrible eye disease along with severe headaches. The story continues that he went into seclusion and darkness for fifty days and was tormented by mice during the whole time. Finally, cauterization was tried (a hot iron was inserted into his sinuses), but this failed to cure his eye pain and headaches. Francis died on October 3, 1226 and within two years was canonized by Pope Gregory IX.

Popular legends surrounding Francis' life are recorded in the *Fioretti* ("little flowers"), a fourteenth century composition. Among these anecdotes are several about his care for all of creation, where Francis would refer to animals and even the sun and moon as "brothers" or "sisters." (His "Canticle of the Sun"—*Laudes Creaturarum*, "Praise of Creation"—appears in many church hymn books as "All Creatures of Our God and King.") Thus Francis was named the "patron saint of ecology" by the Roman Catholic Church in 1979.

The overall goal of Francis was to seek Christian perfection in this life. Three approaches were taken by Francis: (1) to unite with God through prayer, (2) to take up the apostolate—missionary work, and (3) to imitate Christ literally and perfectly. The Franciscan life was simple: become like Christ by imitating Francis. As wandering evangelists, the Friars Minor also practiced their respective trades—often taking the role of teachers. The Rule required that the friars give up all possessions. Modeling themselves after the description of Christ in Philippians 2:7 which says that Christ "emptied Himself," the Franciscans became exemplary illustrations of the mendicant movement.

The Dominicans: Order of Friars Preachers

In contrast to the Franciscans, yet consistent with the mendicant movement, a young priest named Dominic de Guzman (1170-1221) followed the *vita apostolica* (apostolic life) by rejecting possessions for the sake of spreading the gospel. His newly founded order, named after him, was focused on study and eradicating heresy through proclamation of the truth. Born to a well-to-do family around 1170 and trained in the Augustinian order as a canon regular in Castilian Spain, Dominic was moved to preach against the Cathari and Albigensian heresies early in the thirteenth century (see below).

Recognizing the need for an educated clergy, Dominic established several monastic schools. In 1206, he established a female convent to safeguard  the women of the region from heretical teachings and crusader contact. In 1215, the community which had formed around him was recognized by the papacy at the Lateran Council specifically for the propagation of true doctrine, good morals, and the extinction of heresy. A year later, Dominic provided an official rule for his Order of Friars Preachers but more commonly known as Dominicans. The "Black Friars," as they were also known from their habit made of black wool, were placed directly under the pope of Rome, rather than under local bishops or abbots. (See illustration by Fra Angelico illustrating Dominic's black habit over his white cassock.) A pun on their name in Latin, *Dominicanus,* was that they were the "Lord's watchdogs" (*domini + canis*).

The following year, Pope Honorius III (1150-1227, pope 1216-1227), who succeeded Innocent III, sent several Dominicans to Paris to supervise the university faculty. In order to keep Dominic at the Lateran, Honorius appointed him as his theological advisor with the title, "Master of the Sacred Palace," a position traditionally held by Friar Preachers ever since. Around this time, tradition suggests that Dominic developed the prayers used for reciting the Rosary. Somewhat later Dominic sent the members of his small community to various schools not only to supervise, but also to become better educated. In the meantime, he himself traveled throughout France, Spain, and Italy, helping the poor and preaching repentance. By 1220, the Order had grown to eight provinces: Spain, Provence, France, Lombardy, Rome, Germany, Hungary, and England.

As mendicant preaching-friars, the Dominicans relied heavily on financial and physical support by residents of the growing cities. This new class of urban citizens had sufficient wealth to supply the needs of these itinerant preachers, who were developing the art of sermon-making. An early master general of the Dominicans, Humbert de Romans (c.1190/1200-1277) provided useful advice for the preaching task in his book, *On the Formation of Preachers.* Key to the sermon, he asserted, was an emphasis upon life-applications and a positive recognition of various vocations which carried out their Christian responsibilities in the world.

Although Dominic died on August 6, 1221, his administrative ability created a strong, yet efficient organization through representative governance. In addition, the colleges and seminaries which the order founded, served not only their members, but also produced some of the great medieval theologians, such as Thomas Aquinas (see below). This is in line with their rule, which stated, "Study is not the end of the order, but is most necessary to secure its ends, namely preaching and the salvation of souls, for without study neither can be accomplished." Dominic was canonized in 1234.

Other Mendicant Orders

The thirteenth century saw more mendicant orders than merely the Franciscans and Dominicans. Over a half-dozen other groups were formed during this spiritually vibrant era. Unique among the orders of friars was the strong encouragement of lay involvement. Through the Tertiaries, lay members of confraternities (brotherhoods) were formed in which the members, living outside the monasteries, agreed to attend mass at churches of their order and also to recite the daily devotional hours. The financial support of the mendicant movements by these Tertiaries increased the orders' fiscal strength as well as their political and religious influence.

Order of the Holy Trinity for the Ransom of Captives

The Order of the Holy Trinity for the Ransom of Captives, although founded at the end of the twelfth century and approved by Pope Innocent III in 1198, was established as a way to free those Christians held captive by the Muslims during the Crusades. However, by the middle of the thirteenth century their duties expanded to include caring for the sick and poor, particularly by establishing sites for hospitality and education.

Friars of the Cross

The Friars of the Cross, also known as the Crutched Friars, were founded in Italy sometime in the twelfth century to serve the sick, although they claimed to originate in Palestine a millennium earlier. The name of the group grew out of the fact that the friars used a walking stick topped with a cross and had a red cross on their habits, although their habit was changed to a blue cross by papal decree in the fourteenth century. They became a strong force in England from the thirteenth century through the fifteenth century. The Crosiers, or the Order of the Holy Cross, are members of a thirteenth century off-shoot of this order.

Carmelites

Carmelites, known officially as "The Order of Our Lady of Mount Carmel," also claimed Palestinian origins. Apparently, with the hostility to Christian settlements in the Holy Land under Muslim rule, groups of hermits abandoned their mountainous caves on Mount Carmel in northern Palestine near the coast of the Mediterranean Sea and resettled in Italy and Spain. Approved as an order by Innocent IV (1195-1254, pope 1243-1254) in 1250, they followed a Dominican model, thereby reconciling the activities of the mendicant orders with the contemplative lives of the hermits.

The Order of Friar Hermits of St Augustine

The Order of Friars Hermits of St Augustine, known in England as the Austin Friars, unified several hermitages in the Italian countryside and moved into the cities and universities of Europe. They were officially recognized by Pope

Alexander IV (c.1185/99-1261, pope 1254-1262) in 1256 under the *Rule of St Augustine*, although they followed a mendicant model of organization. Martin Luther would join this order which had spread to Germany several centuries later.

These mendicant orders nevertheless proved to be a threat to the local parishes. The successes of the preachers and their papal alliances created a serious conflict both in the cities and in the universities. Because the mendicant orders were able to move about with impunity, they were able to keep pace with the growing urban populations of wealthy merchants and university elites.[2] Around the middle of the thirteenth century, this conflict came to a head. A Burgundian secular priest, William of St. Amour (c.1200-1266), challenged the right of the friars to exercise pastoral responsibilities, claiming that the existing hierarchical structure of the church with priests at the apex was of apostolic origin. Bonaventure (1221-1274), still a student at the University of Paris, defended the friars as being under the pastoral supervision of the pope, who could delegate his pastoral duties to whomever he desired. Several years later in 1281, a Franciscan pope, Martin IV (c.1210/20-1285, pop3 1281-1285), granted the mendicant orders the privilege of performing any pastoral functions in any diocese or parish without seeking the consent of the local priests. As a result, the conflict between these two groups escalated throughout the rest of this century.

Heretical Harassment: Albigenses/Cathari and Waldenses

The Dominicans were particularly focused on eradicating errors in the church under the pope's directive. Two reform-minded groups became the object of strong measures from the church which sought to eliminate their reforming influence on medieval society. Each had their own history, yet they come together during this century for ecclesiastical condemnation.

Four years after the conquest of Constantinople (1203), Pope Innocent III proclaimed another crusade, but this time it was not against the Muslims in the Holy Land, but against two growing reforming movements—the Albigensians (as they were known in southern France) or Cathars and the Waldensians.

As introduced in chapter 12, the followers of Peter Waldo fled Lyon, France, early in the thirteenth century. Settling in the French regions of Lombardy and Provence, they organized themselves as a church with their own bishops, priests, and deacons. Among the doctrinal distinctions held by the Waldensians were the rejection of papal authority and the preaching of the Bible as the sole authority for their faith. Many of the developments of medieval Catholicism had no biblical basis and so were rejected by the Waldensians as being man-made and not in line with a New Testament church.

The Albigensians held views similar to the Waldensians, although they were located around Toulouse in the southernmost region of France, known as

---

[2] By some estimates, the cities of Europe nearly doubled between the turn of the millennium and the end of the thirteenth century. See Wim Blockmans and Peter Hoppenbrowuwers, *Introduction to Medieval Europe 300-1550*, translated by Isola van den Hoven (New York: Routledgem 2007), 218. However, the plague would devastate that population and it would not recover for another 300 years.

Languedoc. The term Albigensians came from the neighboring community of Albi, which in the mid-twelfth century the Catholic Church considered the Albigensian stronghold. Membership among the Albigensians included both men and women, but an elite group of *perfecti* lived extremely ascetic lives. Although the Albigensians served in manual trades, particularly as weavers, they remained a powerful influence on the society and church. Theologically, they were closer to the ancient Gnostic groups (see chapter 2). The Albigensians held a dualistic view of the world in which all physical things of the world were evil. The teachings of Christ's incarnation as well as of the materiality of the sacraments were offensive to them, since both involved the physical world. The *perfecti*, they claimed, were capable of finding heaven within themselves and were responsible for communicating that knowledge (Greek, *gnosis*) to their disciples. One explanation for the other designation of the group, the *Cathars*, is that the term comes from the Greek word, καθαροί (katharoi), for "pure ones," but the Albigensians never used the term themselves. For all practical purposes, the Albigensians was obliterated from Languedoc by the end of the thirteenth century, but the name Cathar lived on, particularly in Germany, where their Germanized name, *Ketzer*, still means heretic.

In 1226, Louis VIII of France (1187-1226, ruled England 1223-1226) celebrated the victory of his crusade against the Albigensians with a high mass at which the sacramental bread was adored rather than received. This is the first instance of such adoration of the host. Subsequently, Pope Innocent III at the Fourth Lateran Council denounced both of the Waldensians and Albigensians as heretics, setting in motion the Inquisition (1231-33).

Fourth Lateran Council (1215)

The first three Lateran councils (see previous chapter) decreed a number of reform measures which gave the church increased power over medieval society. However, the Fourth Lateran Council convoked by Pope Innocent III in 1215 marked a pinnacle in the power and prestige of the medieval papacy. Funding for this council required the clergy to contribute one-twentieth of their income while the papacy gave a tenth. Well over 1,000 churchmen from throughout Christendom, including two Eastern Orthodox patriarchs and several hundred secular princes, attended the sessions as the council deliberated over and passed 70 decrees. Most significantly, the council sanctioned a definition of the Eucharist in which the word "transubstantiation" (see sidebar) was used officially for the first time. It also called for a new crusade to the Holy Land and encouraged expanding the crusading efforts against the heretical groups of the Albigenses/Cathari and Waldenses. Reforms, including the simplicity of life, were required for the Roman Curia and honest business practices were to be observed. The church leaders also forbade the formation of any new monastic orders, although that was a short-lived

> **Transubstantiation**
> [Christ's] Body and Blood are truly contained in the Sacrament of the Altar under the appearance of bread and wine, after the bread has been transubstantiated into the Body, and the wine into the Blood, through the power of God. Only the rightly ordained priest can perform this sacrament.
> *Part 1. Confession of Faith*

ordinance. Many of the other precepts adopted at this momentous council are still binding on Roman Catholics (such as the Easter obligation of making a confession and receiving Holy Communion at least annually).

Inquisition

Begun as a measure to control heretical teachings of specific groups in 1231, Pope Gregory IX (1145-1241, pope 1227-1241) placed the inquisitors, mostly Dominican and Franciscan friars, directly under his jurisdiction. He collected earlier papal decretals and canonical decisions, following the style of the Gratian *Decretals* (c.1140), to create a definitive statement of canon law for the church. Gregory's papal bull, *Excommunicamus*, initially required that heretics be banished and their earthly goods confiscated, although the death penalty was also carried out on occasion. The institution of inquisitors was permanently established in 1252 by Pope Innocent IV (c.1195-1254, pope 1243-1254). Among the sanctions encouraged by him was the use of torture. The death penalty by burning at the stake was required for persons holding heretical views considered dangerous. Later inquisitions, particularly the Spanish (from 1478-1520s) and the Protestant (from the 1560s through the mid-seventeenth century), followed a similar goal of wiping out an opposing heretical religious group.

Theological Philosophy

The thirteenth century is marked as one of the greatest theological centuries since the era of the apostolic fathers. With the rediscovery of Aristotle (chapter 12), a new interest was raised in explaining the Christian faith in philosophical terms. In addition, the rise of universities provided a venue for promulgating such new teachings. These schools were originally formed as guilds of scholars—students and teachers—who sought to standardize and certify professional competencies in their several academic fields. Most schools offered basic education in the liberal arts, but some schools tended to specialize. For example, medical students would go to Montpelier (1220) or Salerno (9th century), law students attended Bologna (1088) and Cambridge (1209), and the centers of theological studies were Oxford (1167) and Paris (1150).

The method of learning was mostly lecturing and disputations. Disputations were technical questions (*quastiones disputatae*) posed by a

---

A Medieval University Education:
An aspiring theologian would be required to begin his studies in philosophy and the humanities with the Faculty of Arts and then proceed to the Faculty of Theology where he would become an "auditor" (hearer). He would then progress through the following levels: first as a "Bachelor of the Bible," then a "Bachelor of the Sentences." He would move on to become a "Formed Bachelor," and a "Licensed Master," who could teach underclassmen, and finally he would achieve the highest level, a "Doctor of Theology" (Teacher), giving him ecclesiastical responsibility for teaching the faith. Similar steps would be required in medicine and law.

---

professor, which the student was then required to answer, based upon a reasoned and logical presentation of Scriptural evidence and the support from ancient writers. Such an approach reached a high level in the *summae*, most particularly by Thomas Aquinas (see below).

Earlier in this century at the University of Paris, Alexander of Hales (1185-1245) introduced the *Sentences* of Peter Lombard as a teaching tool in his classroom to augment biblical study. His academic comments were recorded by his students as marginal notes, known as glosses, similar to the interlinear comments on the biblical texts (see chapter 12). As students (bachelors) were preparing to become teachers (masters) themselves, they would develop their own comments on the *Sentences*, although by the end of this century, Lombard's actual text was neglected and even his topics were expanded into the *summae*. A *summa* was a larger often multi-volume work in which the teacher (doctor) sought a coherent and studied organization of all theological topics, analyzing each topic rigorously in the form of a disputation. The incorporation of Aristotelian philosophical thought added a greater level of profundity to the questions raised and an apparent clarity to the answers proposed.

Thomas Aquinas

Perhaps the greatest medieval Catholic theologian, Thomas Aquinas (1225-1274) is known for his monumental work, *Summa Theologiae*, a compendium of scholastic theology structured around Aristotelian philosophical formulations. Thomas's teacher, Albertus Magnus (c.1193-1280), beginning in 1241 had interpreted Aristotle's writings chiefly through paraphrasing those works, thus popularizing Greek thought in the West. Ten years earlier in 1231, Pope Gregory IX (1145-1241, pope 1227-1241) lifted the ban on studying and promoting Aristotelian thought. The result of Thomas's work was a renewed philosophical approach to theological questions which utilized Scripture and early Christian writers, but in a way that placed human reason at the center. For Thomas, faith was supported by reason and even when teachings seemed beyond reason, they could be explained rationally (for example, transubstantiation).

Thomas was born in 1225 to wealthy parents in the region of Monte Cassino, where he was sent for his early education in the influential Benedictine abbey. In 1239, he began to study at Naples, where in 1244 he entered the Dominican Order, much to his family's dismay. After abducting him and confining him to the family estate for a year, Thomas escaped and went to the University of Paris as a Dominican novice. Studying with Albertus Magnus at Cologne (1248-1252), he acquired the philosophical structure for his new approach to theology. He was ordained into the priesthood around 1250 and returned to Paris in 1252.

Thomas' academic preparations continued in Paris as he lectured for four years on Lombard's *Sentences* and then in 1256 on the Scriptures. During this time, he conducted academic disputations, including defending the mendicant orders against their opponents, and began the composition of his *Summa Contra Gentiles* (An Explanatory Summation of Christian Truth for Gentiles), which he completed sometime later. Between 1259 and 1268 he taught at Naples, Orvieto, Rome, and Viterbo, and then returned to Paris. Asked to teach at the newly founded university at Naples in 1572, he suffered some kind of a head injury on December 6, 1273, and ceased to write, saying, "After what I have seen, all is straw!" On his way to the Council of Lyons in 1274, he became ill and died on March 7.

Summa Contra Gentiles was designed as an introductory textbook for aspiring theologians. In the first three books, Thomas deals with God, creation and humanity, and divine and human governance, based upon Aristotelian philosophy. Thomas asserts that these doctrines are accessible by human reason alone. The final book is a biblical exposition of the central Christian doctrines: the Trinity and Christ's incarnation, the seven sacraments, and the resurrection and final state of the dead.

His *Summa Theologiae* is considered to be by far the most influential work by any Catholic theologian, although it was initially not considered fully orthodox. The structure was based upon Thomas' understanding of moving from the general to the particular, from the abstract to the concrete, from God as the "first cause" to God as the final goal. (See the sidebar with the topics in each of the parts.)

Among the doctrinal distortions formulated by Aquinas is his teaching that in purgatory both the guilt and the punishment incurred during one's life are purged. While extremely logical and fulfilling a necessary gap in understanding salvation, he eliminated the full and free grace of God in Christ.

Summa Theologiae
FIRST PART: Sacred Doctrine, The One God, The Blessed Trinity, Creation, Angels, The Six Days, Man, and The Government of Creatures.
First Part of SECOND PART: Man's Last End, Human Acts, Passions, Habits, Vice and Sin, Law, and Grace.
Second Part of SECOND PART: Faith, Hope, Charity, Prudence, Justice, Fortitude, Temperance, and Acts Which Pertain to Certain Men.
THIRD PART: The Incarnation, The Life of Christ, Sacraments, Baptism, Confirmation, The Holy Eucharist, and Penance.
SUPPLEMENT TO PART THREE [incomplete at Aquinas's death]: Penance (continued), Extreme Unction, Holy Orders, Matrimony, and The Resurrection

---

Some scholars have suggested that the Festival of Corpus Christi (Body of Christ) was instigated by Thomas. While there is little explicit evidence, a communion hymn is attributed to him, which celebrates the institution of the Lord's Supper on Maundy Thursday.

The Ultimate Authority

To the Supreme Pontiff, who has this authority, major difficulties are submitted.... One faith should be held by the whole Church, *that ye all speak the same thing, and that there be no divisions among you,* cannot be ensured unless doubts about the faith be decided by him who presides over the whole Church, and whose decision will be accepted by all. The publication of articles of belief is like the convocation of a General Council for any other commitment affecting the Universal Church: no other power is competent but that of the Pope.

Summa Theologiae I.10.2a-2ae

Thomas Aquinas's teachings did not initially receive a ready acceptance and his work was actually replaced by the teachings of Duns Scotus (1266-1308) and William of Ockham (1287-1347) (see chapter 14) until after the Reformations. Many of his views were officially condemned by the University of Paris in 1277 as an attempt to limit the use of Aristotelian philosophy in theological studies. Yet, fifty years after his death, Pope John XXII (1244-1334, pope 1316-1334) declared Thomas a saint of the church.

Bonaventure

Often called the second founder of the Franciscans, Bonaventure (1217-1274) was born in 1217 to a physician's family near Viterbo, Italy and baptized as Giovanni (John) di Fidanza. As a child he was cured of a severe illness and, through a vow to Francis, was turned over to the order upon regaining his health. While studying with the Franciscans, he felt that if he did not sing God's praises, he would be showing ingratitude.

In 1234, he studied at Paris under Alexander of Hales, who had also recently joined the Order. Bonaventure's brilliance caused the order to be recognized as academically prominent. He was also a gifted preacher, who straddled the middle ground between Aristotelian philosophy and the mystical path of faith. Both Bonaventure and Thomas Aquinas received their doctorates in 1257 from the University of Paris.

Bonaventure wrote several scholastic treatises which underscored Scripture as the chief theological authority and opposed the new Aristotelianism which was emerging. His spiritual writings are just as influential. Three of them are famous: *The Soul's Journey Into God* (*Itinerarium mentis in Deum*) describes the presence of God in creation and involves meditation on nature, the soul, and God through Christ as Francis may have experienced it on Mt. Laverna; *Tree of Life* is a meditation of Christ's humanity and the blossoms of the gospel in Christ's passion; *Life of St. Francis* is the official biography of the Order's founder, which Bonaventure was commissioned to write in 1263. This is the same year in which the Feast of the Visitation of the Blessed Virgin Mary was introduced into the Franciscan order. Ten years later, in 1273, Bonaventure was made a cardinal by Pope Gregory X (1210-1276, pope 1271-1276). Bonaventure died July 15, 1274, shortly after Thomas Aquinas's own death.

The Emergence of Modern Science in the Church

One of the first truly scientific scholars, the Franciscan friar, Roger Bacon (1214-1292), proposed a method of experimentation which remains a hallmark of science to this day. His major work was an encyclopedic volume covering not only the *trivium*, but also physics, experimental science, and moral philosophy. His approach to God's creation caused some concern, particularly among his Franciscan colleagues, who finally condemned him for "suspected novelties" and "dangerous doctrine." However, one of his students, Duns Scotus (see below), took up the task of restoring theology as a biblically-based discipline.

Another Franciscan friar with scientific interests, Robert Grosseteste (c/1175-1253), was from an Anglo-Norman family in England. He advocated a strong emphasis upon training clergy for their pastoral ministries. Elected chancellor of the newly founded Oxford University (1214), he guided the early years of that school for several decades. In 1235 he became the bishop of Lincoln, serving for eighteen more years as a church leader and critic of its increasingly centralized power. He died in early October, 1253.

Although most of his writings have not been translated from the Latin or Anglo-Norman (early French), Grosseteste was a prolific author on a great diversity of topics. He is known both for his scientific research as well as his philosophical works, writing and commenting on Aristotle's *Ethics*. His sermons and pastoral writings, particularly toward the end of his life, demonstrate his strong faith in God's redemptive love in Christ. He spent a significant amount of time writing theological books, both in biblical studies as well as translations from Greek into Latin or his Anglo-Norman mother tongue.

An unintended, yet influential contribution by Robert Grosseteste was his translation of the mystical author known as Pseudo-Dionysius. This anonymous sixth century work (as noted in chapters 6 and 9) was attributed to a follower of St Paul (Acts 17:43) and provided a hierarchical system of angels and, by way of comparison, the whole Christian church. Grosseteste's translation enabled later medieval churchmen with a supposedly-valid basis for establishing a rigid structure for the church with the papacy at the top.

Both these Franciscan theologians feared that the emphasis on philosophy, even as evident in the commentaries of Lombard's *Sentences,* would distract students from real biblical study. For them, theology should be scriptural study exclusively. Their fears were in fact fulfilled as seen in the emphasis upon the *summae,* which incorporated Aristotelian philosophical categories.

Scholarly Prospects for the Next Century

Never a dunce, John Duns Scotus's (1265/1270-1308) name has unfortunately been associated with ignorance in common parlance. His birthplace and early life are unknown, but the moniker of *Scotus,* suggests that he came from the British Isles (Scotland, Ireland, or England). He taught at the University of Oxford in England around 1300 and then went to study in Paris for a few more years, finally being transferred to Cologne, where he died in 1308. We will hear more of Scotus in the next chapter.

Around the same time as Duns Scotus, Nicholas of Lyra (c.1270-1349) was born in southern France. In the next century, he produced the first printed Bible commentary in a style used later for the *glossa ordinaria,* basing his interpretations on the literal text of Scripture.

Cathedral Construction

In 1194 in the burgeoning city of Chartres' construction of the bishop's church commenced. The construction of the Cathedral of Reims began in 1210. Bishop's official seat or throne, known from the Greek word, *kathedra,* were placed in these city churches and thereby the bishop's church was called a *cathedral.* The Chartres Cathedral became a standard for many other European cathedrals with its immense clerestory above the grand arcade on the main floor. Also characteristic of this new "Gothic" style building are high pointed arches, lighter stone vaulting, and tall towers. The thinner walls were supported by flying buttresses (exterior supports) which also allowed for larger stained glass windows.

Besides the Chartres Cathedral, representative of this period include Notre Dame in Paris; Reims Cathedral, Strasbourg Cathedral in France, Antwerp Cathedral in Belgium, Cologne Cathedral in Germany, Salisbury Cathedral, Canterbury Cathedral and Lincoln Cathedral in England, and several in Austria, Italy, Spain, and Portugal.

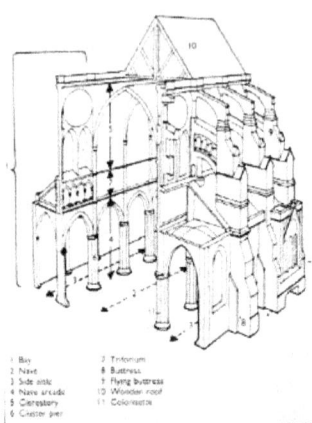

The Last Crusades?

Pope Honorius III (1150-1227, pope 1216-1227), who had come to the papal throne in 1215, authorized the last official crusade (the Fifth) to receive papal approval. Crusaders were sent against the Muslim stronghold in Egypt in 1217. Four years later, in 1221, they had to flee Cairo after severe flooding of the Nile prevented their continued military activities.

In 1228, Emperor Frederick II (1194-1250, ruled 1220-1250) of the Holy Roman Empire led a sixth crusade to the Holy Land. Having knowledge of the Arabic language, he was able to gain jurisdiction over most of Jerusalem (except for the Temple Mount which the Muslims considered sacred). As a result, he assumed the title, King of Jerusalem. Frederick was subsequently excommunicated at the First Council of Lyons (1245) for trying to make the church part of his imperial territory. This same Council instigated a crusade (1248-1254) led by Louis IX of France (1214-1270, ruled 1226-1270), which failed miserably. Initially relying upon diplomatic maneuvering, Saladin (see chapter twelve) and his allies moved from northern Iran into the center of Jerusalem to the Church of the Holy Sepulcher, where innocent victims who were seeking asylum were murdered.

Louis IX of France (1214-1270, ruled 1226-1270) set out in 1248 to eradicate the Muslims in Egypt, but was captured at Mansura, so that seventh crusade also failed. His armies had suffered both financial and physical decimation due to an exorbitant ransom demanded by the Muslims and severe dysentery experienced by thousands of his soldiers. His second crusade, the eighth crusade, ended with his death in 1270. As a result Islamic troops slowly but surely overpowered the last of the Latin territory, the city of Acre.

For the next several centuries, crusades were invoked against the Muslims or Turks until the sixteenth century. Only occasionally were they carried out with any actual military endeavor. Thus, for all practical purposes, the thirteenth century saw the last of the crusades.

Holy Land Abandoned

After the fall of the city of Acre to the Muslims in 1291, the last crusaders departed from the Holy Land. The consequences of the crusading centuries are mostly negative. The Holy Land was lost to Muslim control for another seven centuries. Hostile relations between Jews and Muslims and Christians were only exacerbated by the warfare. Even Christian relations, particularly between the East and the West, were damaged beyond repair. Two positive effects of the crusade were the development of several military tactics and recognition of the benefits of trade relations with the East, which helped stimulate the European economy.

    This century could be called the century of the movements. With the significant support of such a strong Christian proponent as Bernard, who apparently perceived the possible spiritual benefits of having access to the holy sites, the crusades continued in ways which can be described only as misdirected. Much rhetoric and many lives were spent on what finally was an unsuccessful drive to regain the land of the Lord. Movement also characterized the new mendicant orders as they travelled throughout Europe in their spiritual desire for Christ-like living. Finally, there was a profound movement in theology, with the introduction of Aristotelian philosophy and scientific investigation.

    The scholarly interests in theology and the growth of mendicant orders continued in the next century, but with a twist! Calls for reform began to arise as people sought a deeper spirituality of holiness in the world.

For Review and Discussion
1. Describe the crusades as they waned throughout this century.
2. What unique practices and goals did mendicant orders bring to medieval monasticism?
3. How were the Albigensian and Waldensian heresies dealt with by the Roman Church?
4. Why was Thomas Aquinas's work so profoundly detailed?
5. Explain the contribution in scientific study provided by several theologians in this century.
6. How did cathedral construction mimic the theological development of this age?
7. Why can this century be characterized by the idea of movements?

For Further Study
Baldwin, Marshall W. *The Mediaeval Church*. Ithaca, NY: Cornell University Press, 1953.
Caner, Daniel. *Wandering, Begging Monks: Spiritual Authority and the Promotion of Monasticism in Late Antiquity*. Oakland, CA: University of California Press, 2002.
Chenu, M.-D. *Toward Understanding Saint Thomas*. A.-M. Landry and D. Hughes, trans. Chicago: Henry Regnery Company, 1964.
Chesterton, G. K. *Saint Thomas Aquinas: The Dumb Ox*. New York: Image, 1974.
Cullen, Christopher. *Bonaventure*. New York: Oxford University Press, 2006.

Dillard, Peter S. *A Way into Scholasticism: A Companion to St Bonavengure's The Soul's Journey to God.* London: James Clarks & Co., 2012.
McEvoy, James. *Robert Grosseteste.* Great Medieval Thinkers series. New York: Oxford University Press, 2000.
Runciman, Steven. *A History of the Crusades.* 3 volumes. New York: Cambidge, 1951.
Weisheipl, James A., OP. *Friar Thomas D'Aquino: His Life, Thought, and Work.* New York: Doubleday, 1974.

14. Scholasticism, Mysticism, Reforming Spirits and Suppression

The Fourteenth Century

The fourteenth century saw several polarizing or at least paradoxical activities vying for prominence which significantly affected the future of Christianity. Scholasticism was expanding its impact at the same time as a rise in spiritual mysticism occurred. While reforming spirits were raising concerns with the church and its leadership, these same ecclesiastical leaders were seeking ways to suppress any divergences in the official expressions of the Roman dogma.

Papal Powers Rise and Fall

Papal power drastically increased in the person and pontificate of Boniface VII (c. 1235-1303, pope 1294-1303). Boniface, an accomplished canon lawyer (having studied at Bolgna and served in the Curia), declared in his papal bull *Clericis laicos* (1296, "Clergy laity") that no clergy could be taxed by a political power unless approved by a pope. In response, Philip IV of France (1268-1314, ruled 1285-1314) immediately forbade the export of precious metals to Rome. Boniface quickly, although only temporarily, retracted his bull. In the meantime, Philip had imprisoned several bishops, demanding income from them, at which time Boniface reissued *Clericis laicos* and added another bull *Ausculta fili* (1301, "Listen son") which summoned Philip to Rome to be reprimanded. Philip was unmoved.

In 1302, Boniface promulgated a momentously crucial document, known from the first words, *Unam sanctam* ("One Holy"), which declared that the pope was the supreme head of the Christian church. Even more lasting was the teaching that salvation is impossible outside of membership in the church (the Latin phrase used was *extra ecclesium nulla salus*, "outside the church there is no salvation"). Both these ideas had already been embodied in the papacy of Pope Innocent III (see chapter 13), but they had not been officially adopted as church dogma. Boniface also declared that he possessed a superior "sword," a spiritual power, which held greater authority than the temporal powers of the various kings.

Within the year, King Philip of France not only denounced the pope's claims to political authority, but he attacked Rome and had the pope imprisoned and threatened to have him killed. Boniface was released from prison after a few days without food and water, but never regained his strength—or personal prestige. Shortly thereafter Boniface developed a fever and died a broken man on October 11, 1303, yet he left a lasting legacy. His less skilled successors saw diminished powers for the remainder of the century, yet the foundation had been laid by Boniface for increasing papal potentialities.

Opposition to the dogmatic assertion of papal supremacy was voiced by several individuals, including the Dominican philosopher, John of Paris (c. 1250-1306). In his treatise "Concerning the Power of the Royal Court and the Papacy" (*De Potestate Regia et Papali*), which he composed around the same time as the pope's *Unam sanctam*, John maintained that a church Council, which included lay participants, could indeed depose a pope. Similarly, Marsilius of Padua (ca. 1275-1342) argued in his *Defensor Pacis* (*The Defender of the Peace*, 1324) that the lack of world peace was a result of papal ineptitude. Instead, the world should be governed by the people, that is, by the more standard and universally recognized Roman law and Aristotelian philosophy. In this most profound work, Marsilius also argued that the New Testament knew of no domination by clergy, but rather that the believers who gathered together could determine legitimate legislation. Church and state each had their respective areas of responsibility as God's representatives. Even the renowned Italian poet, Dante (1265-1321) wrote against the papacy both in his famous *Divine Comedy* and in a lesser known work, *On Monarchy*, in which he said the church should abandon temporal authority and wealth and submit to the emperor.

The successors of Pope Boniface were not as strong or as politically astute as he or his predecessors. Boniface's immediate successor, Benedict XI (1240-1304, pope 1303-1304), was only in office for a few months, to be succeeded by a French archbishop and friend of the King of France, Clement V (c.1264-1314, pope 1305-1314). Clement after several years of open hostility between Rome and France, finally acquiesced to the French king's demands and moved his papal court, the Curia, to the French city of Avignon. Noteworthy is the fact that in 1314 Clement V condemned the practice of selling indulgences which claimed to absolve a sinner of both the penalty and the guilt of sin.

> **Petrarch**
>
> Born as Francesco Petracco, "the Father of Humanism" was destined to write when most people of his era were illiterate. He felt compelled to record his inner thoughts and ideas, which were disseminated over Europe. His father, a lawyer, moved the family to France when the papacy moved to Avignon. Rejecting Scholastic thought, he turned to the classical authors of antiquity. In 1342, he was declared "poet laureate" in Rome. Francesco's prolific writing renewed interest in classical Latin authors as he travelled across Europe. His collection of personal and professional letters and his Italian poetic songs and sonnets emphasizing anthropocentric ideals remain objects of scholarly appreciation to this day.

The culmination of this episode was what became known as "The Babylonian Captivity," a term coined by the Italian poet, Francesco Petrarch (1304-1374), recalling the seventy years during which the people of Israel lived in Babylon (2 Chronicles 36, Jeremiah 25, 29, and Daniel 1, 9). It was for nearly seventy years that the papacy resided in Avignon (1309-1377). While not a real

Scholasticism
John Duns Scotus

At the same time as these political and ecclesiastical intrigues were occurring, there was a renewed interest in the academic study of theology. Among the brighter lights of this century was John Duns Scotus (ca.1265-1308), or "the Scot" (see chapter 13). Little is known of his early years, except that he began lecturing in Oxford in 1300 and then moved to Paris the following year. Trained as a Franciscan, he was a transitional theologian between his *via antiqua* (old way) of the Dominican method of Thomas Aquinas, and what would be known as the *via moderna* (modern way) of later Scholasticism, led by another Franciscan, William of Ockham (see below). During his relatively short academic life, Scotus wrote mainly philosophical commentaries.

Known as "the Subtle Doctor," Duns Scotus disagreed with earlier theologians, including Thomas Aquinas, who believed that doctrines could be proven true by the use of reason alone. In contrast to Aquinas's high view of human reason, Duns Scotus argued that God was not bound by reason and could do whatever He wanted. It was not God's reason, but His will that brought about creation. God's actions are not subject to human rationality, but should be accepted merely because they are God's decisions.

> **"Dunce"**
> The term purportedly comes from Duns Scotus' name, whose followers in the sixteenth century were criticized for not accepting the new scholarship under King James of England. They were accused of not being scholarly. Scotus was also accused by his critics of hair-slitting and subtle distinctions.

Christians must believe whatever the church taught, whether reasonable or even absurd, he said.

While he agreed with the traditional teachings of the church, Scotus relied more on scriptural revelation as the basis for those teachings. For example, the Thomistic proofs for God's existence were not convincing to him, since, Scotus argued, God's existence belongs in the realm of revelation and faith. Instead of the mind, he emphasized the necessity of the will as being free to act on its own—this was true both for God and for humans. Salvation was a result of God's absolute sovereign will, something which was ultimately beyond human comprehension.

Among the notable teachings of Scotus was the proposition that Mary was probably born sinless (the "immaculate conception"), the result of her Son's most perfect form of redemption. Although he died at a relatively young age, his influence through his writings was significant, particularly in opposition to the teachings of Aquinas.

William of Ockham

William of Ockham (c. 1280-1349), an English Franciscan, studied at Oxford in 1309 or 1310 and completed his degree as a *magister* ten years later (see illustration on next page). Although he lectured on Lombard's *Sentences*, he

never was granted full teaching privileges as a doctor. In 1323, a couple of years after his graduation, the chancellor of Oxford filed charges of heresy against him and Ockham was summoned before the pope in Avignon to defend himself. No formal action developed from the charges, but he remained in Avignon, becoming involved with the dispute among the Franciscans over whether they should possess property or not. Finally in 1329, he publicly opposed Pope John XXII's (1224-1334, pope 1316-1334) toleration of property ownership by the Franciscans. The Pope excommunicated him and Ockham fled Avignon for Munich. He died twenty years later, probably of the Black Death.

Ockham was a fiercely independent scholar and original thinker who followed in the Franciscan tradition, although was a critic of both Aquinas and Scotus. He is most exemplary of the philosophical view known as "nominalism," from Latin word for "name." Nominalists believed that ideas are only names of concrete things. Truth is attained only by investigating those specific things, using reason.

Advocating Scripture as the single and sufficient source and norm for church teachings, he attacked transubstantiation as a rationalization of something which should be accepted by faith alone. Also parting ways with Aquinas who taught that God necessarily followed the dictates of high reason, he followed Scotus' idea that God's freely ordained plan of salvation included some human participation. God will save everyone who does their best (*facere quod in se est*, "do what in you is"). As a result, he said that a person could perform works which God could consider good; that is, they were congruent with natural human abilities (*de congruo*). God would then reward such actions with the gift of grace (*de condigno*), thus enabling believers to do the good works which earned salvation. Ockham also rejected Scotus' idea of predestination, arguing that predestination was always based upon God's foreknowledge of the works (or lack of good works) which a person performed. These teachings would remain in Roman Catholic piety and dogma.

> Ockham's "Razor"
> The simplest version of his decisive statement, also known as the economy of explanation, states: *Numquam ponenda est pluralitas sine necessitate*, "Plurality is not to be postulated without necessity." In other words, one should always strive to consider or accomplish something using the least number of assumptions. The simplest explanation is best. All knowledge is intuitive, he believed. One knows something because it is either observed or revealed in Scripture. There are no independent "universals" as earlier Christian theologians had postulated, following the ancient Greeks.

Although never forming a specific theological "school," Ockhamist thought continued in Europe for several more centuries under the "nominalist" perspective. Advocates included the French theologians Pierre d'Ailly (1350-1420) and Jean de Gerson (1363-1429) and the German scholar, Gabriel Biel (1420-1495), whose teachings would influence Martin Luther in the sixteenth century (See chapter 16 B). More will be discussed about these theologians in the next chapter.

Ockham's teaching on works and merit was one of the critical issues that gave rise to Luther's rejection of scholastic doctrine. Luther said that this idea of meriting salvation offered no consolation for the anxious conscience, since it depended upon human actions and not on God's gracious mercy in Christ.

Gregory of Rimini

In the midst of this scholastic revival, another voice was heard. Gregory of Rimini (c. 1300-1358) was an Augustinian friar who spent much of his later career opposing Ockhamist doctrine, although maintaining a nominalist interpretation of theological issues.

> A Century of Universities
> In many ways, the 14th century is the century of universities. Although Oxford and Paris were established sites of academic studies, the growth of universities as such bloomed in the 14th century. The following universities were founded or organized at this time: Prague (1348), Vienna (1365), Heidelberg (1386), Erfurt (1392), Leipzig (1409), and Louvain (1425).

After studying and teaching at the University of Paris, he became General of the order in 1357 and publicly taught a radical interpretation of Augustine's predestination of the elect, wherein God's foreknowledge of human activity played no part. Luther would praise Gregory for emphasizing the Augustinian teaching on grace.

Mysticism
Dante Alighieri

Expressing the Christian faith in a more personal and spiritual manner was not new. We have seen such spirituality in St. Francis and his student, Bonaventure. Although not necessarily considered a mystic as such, Dante Alighieri (c.1265-1321), had a great influence on mystical thought during this fourteenth century. His *Divine Comedy* explored the depths of hell (*Inferno*), the purifying fires of purgatory (*Purgatorio*), and finally the glories of heaven (*Paradiso*). This poetic journey of the soul finally leads to the mystic's greatest goal, the beatific vision, that is, a personal encounter with divinity and union with God. He died in 1321, after living in exile due to his active involvement with a faction of Florentine politicians (some supporting the papacy and a desire for greater freedom).

Meister Eckhart

The most famous mystic of the fourteenth century was John "Meister" Eckhart (c. 1260-1327). He was a Dominican friar who became extremely popular as a provocative preacher. While he emphasized faith as a heavenly gift, he nevertheless resorted to pantheistic ideas ("God is all things," he said, "and all things are God."). He taught that the human soul had a "spark" (*scintilla, Fünklein*) which is like God and where God was physically dwelling. To attain the mystical union with God, the soul needs to return to or be transformed into its pre-existence in the divine state of divinity (*Gottheit*). By 1326 he was accused of heresy and made his appeal to Pope John XXII, seeking to defend his ideas as orthodox using Augustinian and Thomistic terms. Unfortunately, the pope found twenty-eight heretical ideas among Eckhart's sermons and he was ultimately condemned two years after his death.

Johannes Tauler

Another German Dominican and disciple of Eckhart, Johannes Tauler (ca.1300-1361) was more cautious in his preaching, although just as popular, especially in light of the devastating consequence on society of the Black Plague (see below). As Eckhart, Tauler also emphasized faith and the working of the Spirit to create that faith. Even the sacraments require faith to be beneficial, he proclaimed. Tauler did emphasize the idea of the "spark" in one's soul, but he differed from Eckhart in that he identified it as being God-given. Tauler asserted that clergy and laity were equal before God and the elevation of priestly authority was unscriptural. He is credited with elevating the role of Mary as a mediator before God and her Son, Jesus. Two centuries later, Martin Luther found Tauler's sermons attractive as a source of "pure theology," but not his mysticism. In Tauler's stress on self-denial and suffering, he demonstrated the human need for God's grace.[1]

Henry Suso

Another mystic of this century was Henry Suso (c. 1295-1366). His *Little Book of Eternal Wisdom* was printed in Germany around 1325. In this practical guide, Henry presented a mystical treatise on how to meditate on Christ's Passion.

Such meditations became popular sources for personal devotions, especially among the cloistered nuns and Beguines (See sidebar below) who had spiritualized the ideal of absolute poverty by emphasizing interior self-sacrifice. Henry's sermons accentuated God's love which motivated people to return that love back to Him. Such expressions of love, he said, were in the form of suffering, which he practiced throughout his life by starving himself and even administering bloody flagellations. (See medieval illustration of flagellants.)

---

[1] Martin Luther referred to Tauler early in his teaching ministry; the phrase is from his letter to Spalatin. See LW 25 "Lectures on Romans: Glosses and Scholia," ed. Hilton C. Oswald (St Louis: Concordia, 1972), 366; LW 31 "Explanation of the Ninety-Five Theses," ed. Harold J. Grimm (Philadelphia: Fortress Press, 1957), 128-129, 178; as well as LW 48 "Letters," ed. Gottfried Krodel (Philadelphia: Fortress Press, 1963), 35-36 "Letter to Spalatin, December 14, 1516."

Theologia Deutsch

Communities of mystics also appeared during this century. One group, known as the Friends of God (*Gottesfreunde*), was founded by Rulman Merswin (1307-1382). In this community, both lay people and priests studied Scripture together and developed close spiritual relationships. One of their members wrote a pamphlet, known as *German Theology* (*Theologia Deutsch*), which Martin Luther published twice (1516 and 1518) because it emphasized the gospel so clearly and personally.

Brethren of the Common Life

Another community, also having an impact on Martin Luther, was the Brethren of the Common Life, or the Brothers of the New Devotion (*devotio moderna*) in the Netherlands. The founders, Geert de Groote (1340-1384) and Florentius Radewyn (1350-1400), stressed the simple piety which led to union with God. They rejected the material extravagance of the church and were alarmed by the low morality of the clergy. They sought to foster a deeper spiritual life among both clergy and laity. Toward the end of his life, Radewyn founded a community of strict Augustinian canons, which later led to the "Observantine" movement in the next centuries.

The major contribution of the Brethren, besides their own piety, was the establishment of many free schools throughout Europe. By the end of the next century, there were over a hundred lay communities devoted to practical Christian living and holiness. Most likely Luther was taught at one of their schools in Magdeburg, as was Erasmus of Rotterdam (1466-1536).

English Mystics

Mystical writers and communities were not limited to northern European males. Among the English mystical writers were several hermits—Richard Rolle (c. 1300-1349), who wrote *Fire of Love*; Walter Hilton (c. 1320?-1396), who authored *The Scale of Perfection*; and one of the most well-known woman mystics, Julian of Norwich (1342?-1416), who recorded her *Revelations of Divine Love*, perhaps after losing both her husband and child to the Black Death. Margery Kemp (1373-1438) fits better in this century than the next, since she met Julian and, after hearing Julian's mystical messages, determined that she was "of God," since Julian's communications led to acts of charity. Margery's autobiography, considered one of the first in the English language, provides details about her own mystical visions of Christ, her experiences in English society, and her later pilgrimages to the Holy Land and various sacred sites in Europe.

Catherine of Sienna

In Italy, the female mystic, Catherine of Sienna (1347-1380), had visions throughout her life of personal piety. When she was seven she claimed she saw Jesus with Peter, John, and Paul. Vowing to live a celibate life, she became a Dominican tertiary, living in solitude at her home. In 1368, she experienced a

"mystical betrothal" to Christ (see illustration of Giovanni de Paolo's painting of her mystic marriage) and began to devote her activities to care for the poor. She is most remembered for her letter writing campaign to most of the European leaders from around 1374 until her death. She claimed to have received the "stigmata" as had Francis of Assisi, but only invisibly. During the Babylonian Captivity, she decried the activities of the church as "stink in my nose with the stench of mortal sin."

Bridget of Sweden

Bridget of Sweden (c.1303-1373), a wealthy widow, who after her husband's death in 1344 claimed that she received many visions of Christ. These "heavenly revelations," as they were called, were written down in Latin. Performing great acts of charity in Rome, she worked for the return and restoration of the papal seat in Rome. In 1370, shortly before Pope Urban V's (1310-1370, pope 1362-1370) return to Avignon, he recognized a new community of nuns which followed Bridget's Order of the Most Holy Savior for their works of mercy and service to the poor.

Hesychasm

Mystical ideas were not limited to European Christianity. Orthodox Christians in the East also experienced an increase in mystical writings and practices. Most significant in this century was a controversy over a special form of meditation, *hesychasm* (Greek, ἡσυχασμός "quietness, inner stillness, or silence"). This experiential prayer practice may involve body postures and quiet breathing, similar to some yoga methods, although the prayer is never to

> The Jesus Prayer
> This simple prayer, "Jesus Christ, Son of God, have mercy on me a sinner," continues to be prayed, along with quiet breathing and meditation. It is a popular model for *hesychastic* prayer.

be considered a mindless mantra. Gregory Palamas (1296-1359), a monk from Mt. Athos and later archbishop of Thessalonica, defended the monastic practice during a decade of controversial synods held in Constantinople between 1341 and 1351. *Hesychasm* is an official dogma of Orthodox Christianity. The "Jesus Prayer" is one of the most popular forms of *hesychasm* still practiced by many Christians.

Call for Reform

A fifteenth Ecumenical Council, the Council of Vienne (1311-1313) was called by Pope Clement V (c.1264-1314, pope 1305-1314) to respond to the cries for reform both from within and from outside the church. One of the decrees issued by the council was against the "abominable sects" of Beguines and Beghards, who were accused of three major errors: "antinomianism" (repudiating divine law), "spiritualism" (eliminating any outward aids for worship), and "autotheism" (identifying one's soul with God). Among other significant decisions of that Council was an emphasis upon reforming the clergy. These reforms included a review of certain monastic groups, including the Fraticelli (extreme Franciscans who embraced absolute poverty) and the Knights Templars. Five years later, the Fraticelli officially broke from the Franciscan order, which had been given the right to ownership by the second Avignon pope, John XXII (c. 1244-1334, pope 1316-1334). Leaders of the Beghards and Beguines were also called to explain their views before the Council. A noteworthy side issue was the mandate that universities have chairs of biblical languages.

Pope John XXII, while seeking to reform aspects of the church, provided a financial boon for priests and bishops. Besides canonizing Thomas Aquinas in 1323, he determined that those who held ecclesiastical posts could tax the parishes and dioceses under them, providing lucrative opportunities for simony among the more wily ecclesiastics. In the final year of his pontificate (1334), John XXII provided a lasting, although little recognized, legacy by establishing the celebration of Trinity Sunday as a universal practice in the church. He is noted as one of the few popes to be accused of heresy for denying that saints can see God (in what was known as the "beatific vision") prior to Judgment Day.

> **Beguines and Beghards**
>
> Already in the thirteenth century, groups of lay women lived in convents or in their homes, observing the monastic rule (without actually taking vows) of poverty, chastity, and charity. The name, Beguines, seems to come from their association with Albigensians, although that is not certain. The Beghards were a similar association of non-monastic men, following the spiritual life and practices monastic communities. The Fourth Lateran Council specifically named them as being unauthorized and therefore prohibited. Yet, their existence demonstrates the spiritual void which the church had not recognized or met. By the beginning of the fifteenth century, most of the individuals and communities involved were absorbed by monasteries or convents.

His successor, Benedict XII (pope1334-1342) tried to establish reforms of a variety of papal abuses, but they were realized only during his eight-year pontificate. Among his most significant documents was *Fidem Catholicam* (Catholic Faith) in which he proclaimed that the authority of the emperor came directly from God, not from the popes.

During Benedict XII's pontificate, a defining event between England and France began, known as the Hundred Years' War—from 1337-1453. With papal approval, the French King, Philip VI (1293-1350, ruled 1328-1350) sought to confiscate Aquitaine, a region ruled by the English in southwestern France. For over a century, these two nations besieged, plundered, and raided each other, interspersed with truces of often uneasy peace.

In the meantime, Benedict XII's successor, Clement VI (1291-1352, pope 1342-1352), was easygoing and very French. Declaring 1350 a Jubilee year in his bull, *Unigenitus* ("only-begotten"), he solicited funds to help repair impoverished Rome, but also used the collection to purchase the region around Avignon for papal palaces. In this announcement, he included his understanding of a "treasury of merits," which was to become Catholic dogma. This treasury was filled by the extra-merits earned by Christ and the saints, which he declared could be applied to individual Christians. The method for such application of merits became known as "indulgences," a teaching which gave much fodder for the Reformation two centuries later.

Reform was once again in the heart of the next pope, Innocent VI (1282-1362, pope 1352-1362), although he failed in several such attempts. In addition, he was unable to prevent England and France from resuming their on-going military conflicts. Similarly, he tried to reunite the East and West and to liberate the holy sites in Palestine from Islamic control, but these all failed to materialize.

In the meantime, Eastern Christianity was being overcome by the Mongols of central Asia. An Islamic warrior, Timur or Tamberlane (1336-1405), led Mongol forces throughout that region, destroying Dominican and Franciscan missions as well as nearly eliminating the various Nestorian, Jacobite, and Armenian Christian minorities. His capital was Samarqand (in present day Uzbekistan) and he was the most powerful Muslim ruler of the time.

Innocent VI's successor, Urban V (1310-1370, pope 1362-1370), was a Benedictine monk, who continued his predecessor's goals and strongly emphasized reform. He set about to halt the abusive luxury in the papal court and used the papal treasury to finance university students and artists, establishing several universities in France, Italy, and Poland. Repairing the papal buildings in Rome, he considered returning to that city, but after several military defeats, remained to Avignon. Finally, Pope Gregory XI (1329-1378, pope 1370-1378) reclaimed the papal throne in Rome.

> **The Plague**
>
> Appearing in Europe around 1347, the bubonic plague or "black death" not only decimated the major city populations of Europe (an estimated 25 million people died in three years), but had significant economic and political effects. Often blamed on Jews or witches, persecutions of both occurred along with an increasing obsession with death and penitence. Yet, the actual cause was the uncleanliness of society—fleas on infested rats carried bacteria, causing a highly contagious fever.
>
> This experience of wide-spread death led to an increased interest in the penitential season of Lent, which then gave rise to outlandish practices associated with pre-Lent, especially carnival (carni = meat; + vale = farewell). During the several days before Ash Wednesday, especially Shrove Tuesday (in French, *Mardi Gras*, "Tuesday Fat"), the sins of the community were given public display (and often acceptance), particularly those associated with over-indulgence of food and sexuality. Bands of flagellants (penitents who whipped themselves) increased throughout Europe in response to the Plague, but Pope Clement VI condemned the practice of flagellation in 1349.

The Great Western Schism

Ironically, a dispute over Gregory's successor led to the election of rival popes by the College of Cardinals. While Gregory's successor, Urban VI (1318-1389, pope 1378-1389), remained in Rome, the cardinals elected a person who was less concerned with reform, Clement VII (1342-1394, antipope 1378-1394), who returned to the papal palace in Avignon. This began the Great Western Schism (1378-1417), which led to a greater split in European politics as Germany, Hungary, England, Scandinavia and Poland followed Urban and his successors and Scotland, Aragon, Castile, Navarre and France looked to Avignon.

The subsequent pope, Boniface IX (1350-1404, pope 1389-1404), only exacerbated the need for reform. His pontificate was renowned for its corruption—nepotism (granting political favors to relatives) and simony (buying and selling ecclesiastical offices) were not only tolerated, but they were perpetuated. During the last decade of this century, he began the sale of indulgences during the so-called "Holy Years" of 1390 and 1400.

Biblical Scholar and Advocate of Reform

In England, John Wycliffe (c.1320/1330-1384) gave voice to an increasingly recurring concern for reform, not merely correcting corruption, but by removing the spiritual causes that had limited any real reform. Details of his early life are non-existent, except for his birth to a propertied family in Yorkshire. He earned his bachelor's (1356) and master's (1362) degrees from Oxford University, where he continued to teach as a brilliant lecturer and respected philosopher. His philosophical views followed a more traditional view—he was a "realist," in contrast to the "nominalists" popularized by Ockham. In the early 1370s, he accepted an appointment as a theological advisor to King Edward III (1312-1377, ruled 1327-1377), after earning his doctorate in 1372, but failing to gain an ecclesiastical appointment (possibly because of papal objections).

Chaucer
A British writer, diplomat, scientist, and philosopher, Geoffrey Chaucer was born in 1343. He wrote prolifically throughout the last half of the century until his death in 1400. Best known for his *Canterbury Tales*, he is considered the "Father of English literature."

Summoned to Rome in 1377 for theological condemnation, Wycliffe stayed in England thanks to the support of the English court. Earlier in the decade, Wycliffe had penned two significant works, *On Divine Lordship* (1375) and *On Civil Lordship* (1376), in which he asserted that if church leaders abused their powers, they lost their right to temporal possessions, since they were only stewards of God, the supreme Lord. He distinguished between the church's spiritual authority and the government's physical or temporal authority. He questioned the wealthy property holdings of monastic communities which claimed to follow the rule of poverty. After the death of Edward, Wycliffe was excommunicated by Pope Gregory XI, but remained protected by the English Parliament and his political allies.

The following year, 1378, Wycliffe (see illustration) prepared two more significant treatises—*On the Truth of the Holy Scriptures* and *On the Church*. Appealing to the laity rather than the clergy, Wycliffe asserted that the Bible was the only source for Christian doctrine and life. Therefore, he encouraged the production of the first complete Bible in English, which was published over a period of years (1382-1395). In spite of not being directly involved, this English translation is one of his lasting legacies for world Christianity.

Wycliffe held many doctrines which were further clarified and upheld at the time of the Reformation, especially that individuals were justified by faith in Christ as Savior from sin, not by one's own works. In his treatise, *On the Eucharist*

(1380), he rejected transubstantiation as being unbiblical and unfounded in early Christian thought. He went so far as to declare the pope the Antichrist. He remained active as a theological writer and preacher until his death at his home in Lutterworth in 1384.

Wycliffe's influence went beyond the British Isles. Nine years before Wycliffe died, a young Bohemian lad was born, named Jan Hus (c. 1373-1415). He would take Wycliffe's call for reform to a new level. We will look at his influence in the next chapter.

The fourteenth century ended as it began, in the midst of uncertainty and spiritual struggles. The Roman papacy struggled for its own identify and direction, yet created a foundation for subsequent gains in spiritual as well as political power. Theological thought saw a move away from more traditional methods along with an increased personal piety through mystical contemplation. As the century ended, the need for reform in the church became more and more evident. The time was approaching for renewal.

For Review and Discussion
1. Using some on-line resources, describe the differences between the *via antiqua* and the *via moderna* which arose during this century.
2. Why did Dante place a pope in one of the lower levels of the Inferno?
3. What error do you see in the idea of "doing one's best" (*facere quod in se est*) to earn salvation?
4. How did the mystics of this century seek to attain salvation?
5. What issues in the church began to arise and elicit calls for reform?

For Further Reading
Adams, Marilyn McCord. *William Ockham*. 2 vols. Notre Dame: University of Notre Dame Press, 1987.

Chaucer, Geoffrey. *The Canterbury Tales* in *The Complete Works of Geoffrey Chaucer*, ed. by W. W. Skeat. Oxford: Clarendon Press, 1899.

Hoffman, Bengt, trans. *The Theologia Germanica of Martin Luther*. The Classics of Western Spirituality series. Mahwah, NJ: Paulist Press, 1980.

Jacoff, Rachel, ed. *The Cambridge Companion to Dante*. New York: Cambridge University Press, 2007.

Levy, Ian C., ed., *A Companion to John Wyclif: Late Medieval Theologian*. Leiden, Brill, 2011.

Vos, Antonie. *The Philosophy of John Duns Scotus*. New York: Oxford University Press, 2006.

15. The Renaissance and Calls for Reform

The Fifteenth Century

The fifteenth century may be designated the blossoming of the Renaissance, a term which merely refers to a "rebirth" of culture. While many historians say the rebirth began in Florence, Italy in the middle of the fourteenth century, the real blooms of this revival of classical Greek and Roman culture increased significantly in the fifteenth century after the fall of Constantinople (1453). Both for the church as well as for the world, there was an increased attention paid to humanity as an object of study and appreciation for individualism. But always in the background were increasing calls for reform.

The Human Spirit

The Renaissance focus on humanity begins with the recognition of humanity's unique spirit. We can get a sense of that spirit in the dedicated missionary and Dominican priest originally from the Spanish city of Valencia, Vincent Ferrer (c.1350?-1419), who set out to reform society. During the first two decades of the fifteenth century, he preached thousands of sermons across France, Spain, and the northern regions of Italy and southern Switzerland. Reportedly, he converted many Jews and Moors to Christianity, too. His powerful message was to trust in Christ and His cross, because the Last Days were indeed at hand. He urged his fellow Dominicans to observe the ideals of St. Dominic strictly, especially that of poverty and service. He worked hard to reconcile the two papal offices during the western schism, a goal which he was able to see accomplished (see below).

In 1399, another young man, who had been trained in a school run by the Brethren of the Common Life in Deventer (in the Netherlands), visited an Augustinian house of canons in Zwolle (northeast of Amsterdam). His name was Thomas and he was from the town of Kempen. He could not officially join the order because his brother, Jan, was serving as prior. Upon Jan's transfer to another monastery in 1406, Thomas à Kempis (c. 1380-1471) became a canon

> From *Imitation of Christ*
> by Thomas à Kempis
> Not everyone can have the same devotion. One exactly suits this person, another that. Different exercises, likewise, are suitable for different times, some for feast days and some again for weekdays. In time of temptation we need certain devotions. For days of rest and peace we need others. Some are suitable when we are sad, others when we are joyful in the Lord.

regular and remained there until his death. A prolific writer, Thomas is most remembered for his four-book devotional treatise, *The Imitation of Christ*. Taking its title from the first chapter of the first book, the work provides guidelines for a spiritual life of self-examination and humility, self-denial and discipline, acceptance of one's station in life, and a deep love and trust for God. The human spirit and God's Spirit were being brought together.

The Lollard Persecution

The followers of John Wycliffe (see the chapter 14) were called "Lollards," a term derived from their quiet praying style (our English words, "lull" and "lullaby" are of similar derivation). Although frequently criticized and persecuted at the end of the fourteenth century, under Henry IV (1367-1413, ruled 1399-1413) an anti-heresy law was passed in England in 1401, but was not implemented. His son, Henry V (1387-1422, ruled 1413-1422) enforced this law ruthlessly, particularly against the followers of Wycliffe. Most notable was the execution of Sir John Oldcastle (c.1360/78-1417), a nobleman and Lollard preacher, who had become notorious for first befriending the king and then, after being accused of rebellion, for scheming to kidnap the king. Thereafter, the Lollard movement almost completely disappeared in England, although a few followers remained into the sixteenth century.

Jan Hus

A few years before John Wycliffe died, Jan Hus (c.1370-1415) was born in Husinecz. Although he never studied with Wycliffe, Wycliffe's works were brought to Bohemia (approximately the present day Czech Republic) when a local princess married an English nobleman and students from Bohemia went to study in Oxford. While teaching at the University of Prague, where he had earned both a bachelor's and a master's degree, Hus was ordained into the priesthood in 1400/1401. As a priest and professor in Prague, Hus found Wycliffe's ideas biblically sound and theologically accurate and began to share them with his students and colleagues.

In 1409, after a dispute between two factions of the faculty, Hus became rector of the University of Prague, where his preaching of reform at the Bethlehem Chapel stirred many. He taught that God's church was founded on Christ, not Peter. All believers were saved by grace through faith in Christ, he affirmed; works do not save. The Bible, not the papacy, was the ultimate authority for the Christian life and teachings. The true church consisted of all the predestined, who were to exhibit simple Christ-like lives of poverty.

> **Hus on Clerical Celibacy**
> Many centuries have passed since the foundation of Christianity and bishops and priests have wedded and permitted themselves to be wed in honor and decency, until some Primates, Gregory VII (also called Hildebrand) and Innocent III, thousand years after the death of Jesus the Nazarene, conceived the thought to forbid marriage to priests, so that they would not love their families, would not honor their home and would be compelled to seek salvation under the wing of Rome only, remembering the protection which was to come from there against worldly powers. And what shall I say about the unnatural trend of such a request?

Exacerbating Hus's concerns over papal improprieties, Pope John XXIII (c.1370-1419, antipope 1410-1415) implemented the sale of indulgences to finance a "crusade" against the city of Naples. Such inappropriate use of churchly power and exploitation of Christian donations raised the ire of Hus and his close colleague, Hieronymus of Prague (1379-1416), who had studied in Oxford. Together they condemned such actions, coupling their concerns with a nationalistic cry against Czech monies being sent to Italy. Hus proclaimed that indulgences were unnecessary, since Christ's forgiveness was always freely given to all who were penitent (a theme picked up by Luther in his *95 Theses*).

Hus had to leave Prague as a result of this protest, having upset both key supporters at the University as well as King Wenceslas IV (1361-1419, ruled 1376-1419). After taking refuge with several friendly nobles in southern Bohemia in a self-imposed exile from Prague, Hus spent his last years writing. He would have one more opportunity to give witness to his theological understandings. (See below)

Councils to End the Great Western Schism

A church council was proposed by various university professors of Paris and Bologna to settle what had become a great offence to the Christian community—two popes! With the support of the majority of cardinals of both popes, a meeting was called. Both rival popes refused to come to Pisa in 1409, so the Council elected a third pope, Alexander V (1339-1410, pope 1409-1410). Allegiances to the three papal leaders now divided the various regions and no consensus was possible. A stalemate ensued.

An ecumenical council, regarded as the sixteenth by some, was called by the brother of Wenceslas IV, the soon-to-be Holy Roman Emperor, King Sigismund of Germany (1368-1437, king of Germany 1410-1437, emperor 1433-1437), to meet in Constance (1414-1418). A summons by an Emperor followed precedent from the early church. Pope John XXIII presided. The most significant action of this council was the deposing of Pope John XXIII and accepting the resignation of Pope Gregory XII (c.1326-1417, pope 1406-1415) in Rome. The third pope, Pope Benedict XIII (1328-1423, antipope 1394-1403, claimant 1394-1423) in Avignon, refused to resign, but was also deposed, although he persisted to claim his office with little support from church leaders. In effect, this ended the western schism, although the necessary spiritual and administrative reforms of the church were not enacted.

An interesting feature of this Council was the fact that national leaders voted as "nations," rather than individually, thus, countering the Italian influence which had come under papal control. One bright spot in the proceedings of this Council was the acknowledgement of a need for reform and two proposals that general church councils were to be called on a regular basis, instituting what came to be called "the conciliar movement," and that such councils have authority over the Pope. The newly elected pope, Martin VI (1369-1431, pope 1417-1431) complied with a call for a council five years later in Pavia, albeit not enthusiastically. His major goal was to establish the papal state as a political power among the several Italian city-states—Florence, Milan, Naples (known as "the Kingdom of the Two Sicilies"), and Venice.

Regrettably, the other significant action taken by the Council was the condemnation of Jan Hus. After hearing the case against him, he was handed over to civil authorities and burned at the stake on July 6, 1415 (see illustration from the 1485 *Spiezer Chronik* manuscript), in spite of having been given safe passage to and from the Council by Sigismund. As a result, he remains a national hero of the Bohemians. Wycliffe was also condemned posthumously and his bones were disinterred and burned.

Five years after the Council, the Bohemian followers of Hus prepared a common statement to be implemented by several conflicting groups. The "Four Articles of Prague" demanded that God's Word be the basis of all preaching; the laity be given the communion cup along with the bread; apostolic poverty be practiced; and both clergy and laity live a strict life in conformity with Scripture. The three groups which joined together were known as the Utraquists (*utraque*, Latin for "both," indicating that both bread and wine were used in communion), the Calixtines (*calix*, Latin for "cup," for those who only wished to receive the chalice), and the Taborites (named for the fortress of the more political group of Wycliffe and Hus disciples). The Taborites and Utraquists, along with a group of Waldenses formed the *Unitas Fratrum* (United Brethrens of Bohemia), which became the spiritual ancestors of the Moravians.

Humanistic Scholars
Nicolas of Cusa

Born to lowly peasants, Nicolas of Cusa (1401-1464) studied canon law, mathematics and astronomy at the University of Padua. Although not an actual humanist, he did not follow the traditional scholastic approach to knowledge either. His views have been called "Neoplatonic mysticism," and first appeared in his 1440 philosophical treatise, *De docta ignorantia* (On Learned Ignorance). There he stated that God unites all things in Himself and all things come from Him. This unity of all things is not recognized by using discursive reasoning, but is only a result of a kind of intelligent-intuition, which he called "learned ignorance." He asked, "How is it that knowing is not-knowing?" By use of a variety of metaphors and mathematical analogies, he believed humans could appreciate God, although not understand Him.

Gabriel Biel

Born in Speyer Germany, Gabriel Biel (c.1425-1495) began his education in Heidelberg and continued in the universities of Erfurt and Cologne. Receiving training in both the *via antiqua* of Thomas Aquinas and Duns Scotus as well as the *via moderna* of William of Ockham, he sought an amalgam of them, with some preference toward Ockham. In 1460, he joined the Brethren of the Common Life, which allowed him to incorporate a more devotional dimension to his intellectual endeavors. His academic abilities resulted in his becoming the first professor of theology at the University of Tübingen in 1484, where he served as rector until 1490. Near the end of his teaching career, Biel prepared *Sacri Canonis Missae Expositio* (1488), an explanation of the Roman canon of the Mass, a lengthy communion prayer which included the Words of Institution. As a young friar, Luther considered this work very moving.[1] Biel died a few years later, having served as provost for a new Brethren house in his retirement years.

> Biel's *Exposition on the Sacred Canon of the Mass*
> The sacrament of the eucharist, as a sacrifice offered to the Most High Father, takes away not only venial but also mortal sin. I do not say only of those who receive it, but, of all those for whom it is offered, so far as concerns guilt and penalty....and therefore this service is offered for the living and the dead.

Biel's teaching and writing focused upon the earned grace of God, a concept which the teachers of Martin Luther had learned as Biel's students. Drawing upon Ockham's phrase "to do what is in you" (*facere quod in se est*) or doing one's best, Biel taught a form of semi-Pelagianism. Sinners need to take the first step in the way of salvation, turning to God and loving Him to the best of their abilities. This action then merits God's grace as a reward (not, he declared, as a wage, although the distinction is unclear) which then enables one to do good works. Works merit God's justification, which God then owes to the faithful believer. Although it would appear that Biel taught justification by works, he argued that God was still gracious in that He could have demanded perfection rather than merely doing one's best.

Johannes Reuchlin

Humanism was evident early in Germany in the person of a young peasant's son, Johannes Reuchlin (1455-1522). His parents sent him to school where he acquired great facility in Latin and was sent to the University of Paris as a companion of a local nobleman's son. After studying Greek in Paris, he returned to Basel where he received his master's degree and began his teaching career in 1477, having already published a popular Latin dictionary. He continued his scholarly pursuits by studying law in France. Visiting Florence, he was admired for his abilities in Greek and was regarded as one of the outstanding scholars of that language. However, his interests also were biblical, so he became the first non-Jewish scholar in Germany to learn Hebrew as an aid to his study of

---

[1] Martin Luther, *Luther's Works* 54:264. WA, TR 3, no. 3722. Luther said, "When I read in it my heart bled."

the Old Testament. We will come back to Reuchlin's influence on the Reformation in the next chapter.

Desiderius Erasmus

Born in Rotterdam as the illegitimate son of a local priest, Desiderius Erasmus (1466?-1536) was schooled at Deventer where he was introduced to the *devotia modern* of the Brethren of the Common Life. Entering an Augustinian monastery, he studied classical authors and Italian humanists in addition to their devotional practices. Although ordained in 1492, he left the monastery the following year in order to serve as a bishop's secretary. In 1495, he began studying in Paris, where he became disenchanted with scholastic thought. In 1499, he had his first opportunity to visit England and two humanist scholars, John Colet (1467?-1519) and Thomas More (1478-1535). Colet was lecturing on Romans and encouraged Erasmus to study in the original language, so Erasmus returned to Paris in order to perfect his knowledge of Greek. Concerned with the superstition, corruption, and barren theological dialectic practiced by most of his teachers, he used his wit and command of Latin rhetoric to castigate both clergy and civil leaders in a little booklet entitled, *In Praise of Folly* (1509). His influence on Luther and the sixteenth century reformers will be discussed in the next chapter.

During the latter years of the fifteenth century, notable figures for the sixteenth century were born, whom we will consider in the next chapter. Martin Luther (1483-1546) was born in Eisleben, Germany, on November 10th, 1483 (or perhaps 1482). His family moved shortly thereafter to Magdeburg, where he began his schooling, transferring to Eisenach for a stronger educational foundation. Ulrich Zwingli (1484-1531) was born in Switzerland during a time of increasing nationalistic tendencies. His humanistic studies at the Universities of Vienna and later in Basel were formative in his theological thinking.

Renaissance Influences

With the stronger connection to Greek Christianity, and the continuing study of the ancient Latin authors, the Renaissance emphasis on human subjects continued to expand. The study of Greek led to the study of ancient church fathers and grammatical and philological studies of the more ancient texts following the theme of *ad fontes* ("to the sources")

Ad fontes
The Latin phrase means "to the sources" and was an attitude, more than a motto, which characterized the Renaissance humanist movement. Already with Francesco Petrarch (14th century), European scholars had turned their attention to ancient sources. The ancient languages of Greek and Latin, along with the biblical language of Hebrew, were revived and used to rediscover the truths which humanity desired.

Critical Scholarship and Dissemination

In 1440, a scholar named Lorenzo (Laurentius) Valla (1406-1457) analyzed an important document, *the Donation of Constantine* (see chapter 8), which had been used by the papacy to support the validity of its political powers and land holdings in Rome for centuries. Using philological and historical methods, Valla proved without a doubt that this supposed fourth century document was a forgery from around the 8th century. He also proved that the writings attributed to Dionysius the Areopagite, the supposed follower of Paul, were unauthentic. He demonstrated that the Apostles' Creed was not a composition dictated section by section by each of the apostles, but rather a product of early Christian baptismal formulations.

Perhaps no one invention has been more accurately credited with creating an all-encompassing transformation in culture than the moveable type  printing press (see illustration) of Johannes Gutenberg (c.1398-1468). It was in 1450 that he produced the first Bible, the Latin Vulgate, on such a press. Within a half-century over two hundred printing establishments had arisen in Europe, providing opportunities for the dissemination of Renaissance learning and (later) Reformation teaching in large quantities and at reasonable prices. Estimates suggest that more than thirty thousand publications were issued before 1500. By the end of the century, ninety-two editions of the Vulgate were printed, in addition to complete Bibles in German (1466), Italian (1471), French (1478), Spanish (1478, although initially burned, 1492 republished), and Czech (1488 and 1489).

Art and Artists

Artistic expressions are perhaps the most visible characteristic of the Renaissance, especially as this was disseminated from the heart of Renaissance thought in Italy. Painting expressed a grander presentation of true perspective, anatomical accuracy of human forms flourished, impressive sculptures, which reflected earlier Greek and Roman influences, were produced on an extravagant scale, and architectural advances transformed the great cities of Europe.

Florentine Artists

Consider the following artists who came into prominence during this century: Donatello (1386-1466) sculpted and painted in Florence and was a key  in making that city a center of humanistic art. Botticelli (1444-1510), born as Alessandro di Mariano di Vanni Filipepi, characterized the golden age of Florentine art. Most of his works were religious in character, although his most popular work, the "Birth of Venus" (*La Nascita di Venere*, 1486) was commissioned by the Medici. Leonardo da Vinci (1452-1519) born near Florence, Italy, was the epitome of the "Renaissance man." Besides several scientific inventions, he was a mathematician and creative designer. He began painting one of his most famous works, *The Last Supper*, in 1495 for a local monastery's dining area. He was also active in scientific investigation, both of the human anatomy (which he employed carefully in his painting and as seen in his *Vitruvian Man*; see illustration on the previous page) and in engineering (producing designs for both military and civil projects).

German Artists
Albrecht Dürer (1471-1528) grew up in the Nuremberg, Germany, one of the centers of commerce. Skilled as a draftsman, painter, and writer, he is best known for his print-making. Having visited Italy toward the end of the century, his artwork is characteristic of northern European humanism. One of his greatest works, *Apocalypse*, a series of woodcuts illustrating the book of Revelation, was begun at the end of the century.

Lucas Cranach the Elder (1472-1553) was also a print-maker and painter, although he served the city of Wittenberg in several capacities (see chapter 16 A). Born in the Franconian town of Kronach, he was trained by his father, a local painter. By the close of the century, he had demonstrated a very high degree of artistry and would serve in the court of Frederick the Wise in the next century.

Artists of Rome
Michelangelo (1475-1564) was renowned as a painter, sculptor, and architect. His statue of David and the painting in the Sistine Chapel remain objects of the highest humanistic ideals. Raphael (1483-1520), born to a painter in the ducal court of Urbano, Italy, served under several popes to decorate the Vatican with numerous frescoes and tapestry designs.

All these artists, exhibiting classical techniques, used their skills in service to the church. Many of the popes of the latter half of the fifteenth century were patrons of letters and artists, supporting the adornment of Rome as "the City."

Papal Impediments

After the Council of Constance, several more councils were called, although with little accomplishments to note. In Basel (1431), the conciliar position was condemned by Pope Eugenius IV (1383-1447, pope 1431-1447), who declared the decisions void and the council dismissed. They continued to meet in his absence, even electing a successor, but the council's influence waned in protracted business until 1449. In the meantime, the pope transferred the Council to Ferrara and then Florence (1439), where he preferred to reside, under the excuse that he could meet with Eastern Orthodox prelates in hopes of reuniting Christendom. Although proclaimed an accomplishment, these Greek representatives were not well received upon their return. The Council had required that the Eastern Christians accept the insertion of *filioque* in the Nicene Creed, the doctrine of purgatory, and the supremacy of the pope. The only compromise from the West was the allowance of leavened bread in the Eucharist. When the Turks captured Constantinople in 1453, the reality of union was permanently lost. Attention to and the influence of Eastern Christianity slipped away until it reemerged in Russia two centuries later. One other feature of the Ferrara-Florence Council was an agreement in 1439 with the Armenian Orthodox Church in which, for the first time, the Roman Catholic Church officially listed the seven sacraments—baptism, confirmation, communion, penance, last rights, ordination, and marriage.

Pope Nicholas V (1397-1455, pope 1447-1455) among his many humanistic endeavors, founded the Vatican library and desired to make Rome the center of humanistic culture and art. His plans for St. Peter's basilica represented the full flowering of papal powers and humanistic grandeur. His successor, Calixtus III (1455-1458), ignored the humanistic tendencies of his predecessor and focused, however briefly, on trying to organize a crusade to remove the Turks from Constantinople.

Wars, Nationalism and Spirituality

The Hundred Years' War (1337-1453) (see chapter 14) between England and France ended in somewhat of a stalemate, yet feudalism had significantly faltered and finally failed. Before the end of this series of wars, France, under King Charles VII (1403-1462, ruled 1422-1461) had secured relief from papal interference and especially taxation. His successor, Louis XI (1423-1483, ruled 1461-1483), secured sovereign rule over the lower nobles, thereby eliminating feudalism in France and establishing a centralized state for his successor, Charles VIII (1470-1498, ruled 1483-1498). The church in France was largely under royal control.

Joan of Arc (1412-1431)
A French peasant girl with visionary messages aroused the French people to a national fervor. Known as "the maid of Orleans," she captured the hearts and ideals of her compatriots. After leading a victorious battle against English and Burgundian troops to save her city, she was captured by them, tried as a heretic, and put to death for witchcraft and false teachings.

For thirty years between 1455 and 1485 two royal families in England claimed the throne, each with an insignia of a rose. The House of York (white rose) and the House of Lancaster (red rose) vied for control. Thus, the name of this conflict is "the War of the Roses." When Henry VII (1457-1509, ruled 1485-1509) came to power, the English people sought stability through a strong government in order to avoid further civil war. Indeed, the Catholic Church had come under the English sovereign's authority.

In the latter quarter of this century, two key political figures were born—Machiavelli and Thomas More. Niccolo Machiavelli (1469-1527) was born in Florence during the tumultuous times of papal rule. As a humanistic writer, historian, and diplomat, he was extremely knowledgeable of political machinations in Italy. His sixteenth century work, *The Prince* (1513), was an instruction manual for political ruthlessness, immoral intrigue, and self-glorifying leadership (see illustration of the cover page). Thomas More (1478-1535), son of an English judge, was born in London. After wrestling between a career as a lawyer or as a Carthusian monk during the last years of the fifteenth century, he felt compelled to serve his country as a statesman. His humanistic ideals for a perfect political system are expressed in in his sixteenth century work, *Utopia* (1516).

In Spain, a consolidation of political power was realized with the marriage of Ferdinand of Aragon (1479-1516) with Isabella of Castile (1474-1504). These two kingdoms now united, in addition to Portugal and Navarre, dominated the Iberian peninsula after the Moorish conquest several centuries earlier. Establishing an efficient bureaucracy, Spain became a leader, particularly after the discovery of the New World, with its potential for great wealth. After the French invaded Italy, Spanish troops moved into Naples and in the early sixteenth century slowly moved up the whole Italian peninsula. The pious queen, Isabella, while supporting the spiritual authority of the papacy, promoted a "Spanish awakening" as she encouraged a moral and zealous clergy. Already in 1482, the king and queen had forced Pope Sixtus IV (1414-1484, pope 1471-1484) to accept royal control over the election of the highest ecclesiastical posts. Clergy were taxed and papal bulls required royal approval. In 1492, the queen appointed a politically astute, yet extremely pious lawyer and theologian, Francisco Jiménez de Cisneros (1436-1517). Earlier he had become an ascetic Franciscan friar and changed his name to Francisco. At the turn of the century, he was the chief ecclesiastical administrator of Spain and set about to reform both the secular and monastic clergy in line with his Franciscan Observant convictions.

As Spain experienced this spiritual renewal, orthodoxy and patriotism coalesced. In 1478, an Inquisition was established by Pope Sixtus IV which give royal authority for the appointment of all inquisitors. This Spanish Inquisition was especially directed against those Jews and Muslims who had claimed to become Christians (known as Marranos and Moriscos, respectively) but now had "lapsed from the faith." Practicing Jews were expelled from Spain in 1492, unless they reconverted to Christianity. Similarly, Muslims faced conversion or expulsion at the end of the century. This Inquisition would deal with Protestants and suspected "Lutherans" in the next century.

In Germany a similar inquisitorial movement was occurring. While the ecclesiastical leaders, particularly the bishop-princes were wielding their political authority over the laity, the people themselves were earnestly desiring a sense of security—both physically and spiritually. Popular devotional practices often expressed a great fear of death and the devil in the face of the lingering results of the plague. Witchcraft increased as superstitious spirituality spread throughout Europe. In 1484, Pope Innocent VIII (1432-1492, pope 1484-1492) produced a bull declaring that Germany was full of witches. In 1489, two self-proclaimed inquisitors prepared a celebrated work, *The Hammer of Witches* (in German, *Der Hexenhammer*), which argued for the existence of witches and then told how to overpower them.

Renaissance Papacies

With the papacy of Pope Pius II (1405-1464, pope 1458-1464), a reclamation of papal powers occurred. Although prior to being elected pope, he had been an advocate of the conciliar movement, early in his pontificate, he promoted his bull *Execrabilis* (1460), which prohibited any further appeals to church councils over against papal powers. Any such proposal for a council by a non-pope would be considered heresy. Pope Paul II (1417-1471, pope 1464-1471) continued the humanistic tendencies of the age, particularly as an avid collector of antiquities. A semblance of sanctifying sanity is seen in his papacy, as he sought to curb simony (selling church positions for money), restore a more conservative life-style among the Curia, and only appoint men of high spiritual caliber to papal offices.

A Franciscan friar and scholar was elected pope in 1471, Sixtus IV. However, he had greater political interests and sought to make Rome the center of Italian life. As a scholar, he reorganized the Vatican library and attracted many scholars and artists to Rome. His Sistine Chapel (named after him) is only one of many building projects which he funded through higher taxes during his extravagant pontificate. He was also known for his political ambitions and his unabashed practice of nepotism. In 1476, he introduced as the official article of faith that indulgences could be purchased for souls even in purgatory.

Innocent VIII (1432-1492, pope 1484-1492), the next pope (see illustration), was anything but "innocent." Prior to his ordination as a priest, he had been married and fathered several illegitimate children along with one son (some scholars suggest he had fathered sixteen children in all). His appointees as cardinals lived as worldly princes—hunting, gaming, and womanizing. His political activities included receiving generous "gifts" from a Turkish sultan for keeping a rival brother imprisoned in Rome.

In 1492, the successor of Innocent VIII was Alexander VI (1431-1503, pope 1492-1503). Intimately acquainted with papal administration and intrigue, Rodrigo Borgia, was an extremely wealthy Spanish nobleman who had purchased the chair of Peter. He did much to improve the city and culture of Rome, encouraging an expansion of the already wide-spread development of the city. He was also notorious in his personal conduct and used his children as pawns in ecclesiastical procurements and national alliances. His son, Cesare Borgia (1473-1507), was similarly unprincipled, having been appointed cardinal as a teenager, a position he later rejected in order to develop his political ambitions of leading Italy. Caesar's sister, the pope's daughter, Lucrezia Borgia (1480-1519), was given in marriage several times, all for political purposes.

While embodying the fatal flaws of the papacy, these popes did represent the Renaissance of Italy.

An Italian Reformer

From the city of Florence came an interesting itinerant preacher, Girolamo Savonarola (1452-1498) (see illustration). After studying to become a  medical doctor, he entered a Dominican monastery in 1475 where he experienced some kind of mystical vision. He became prior of the Florentine monastery, San Marco, which he restored as an "observant" congregation. Feeling compelled to be an itinerant missionary, his superiors gave him leave of the monastery, although he had little initial success on his missions. After several more years of preaching and teaching, his message settled on three key themes—the church needed to be punished for its corruption, the church will be renewed, and such reforming events are imminent. In 1480, the great Florentine nobleman, Lorenzo de Medici (1435-1488), "the Magnificent," called him back to Florence. In spite of his own scandalous life-style as a "Renaissance man," Lorenzo failed to reverse Savonarola's reforming movement and died in 1488 with Savonarola's blessing.

When Charles VIII of France drove Piero Medici (1472-1503) from Florence in 1494, Savonarola's popularity increased, since it appeared to be the apocalyptic tribulation he had predicted. Savonarola tried to turn the city into a Christian democracy. The new republic of Florence, freed from French domination, provided him with a great opportunity to carry out his reform. During the carnival seasons of 1496 and 1497, Florence experienced "the bonfires of the vanities"—the public burning of games and cards, extravagant wigs and colorful cosmetics, gaudy baubles and ornate jewelry, lewd pictures and bawdy books. Upon hearing of Savonarola's activities, Pope Alexander VI placed him under a papal ban, particularly because of his denunciation of papal authority. The following year, Savonarola was falsely condemned as a heretic, hanged, and then burned at the stake and his ashes thrown into the river. Luther would later commend Savonarola for his piety and evangelical teaching.

The Century Ends in Explorations

In 1488, Bartolomeu Dias (c.1451-1500) named the tip of southern Africa, the Cape of Good Hope, as he sought a navigational route to India. Exploration of the world continued to expand as the now famous "discovery" of the Americas by Christopher Columbus (1451-1506) in 1492 and excursion of

Vasco da Gama's (c.1460-1524) exploration of a sea route to India (1497-1498). The English explorer, John Cabot (c.1450-1499), sailed from the British Isles to North America. The world was becoming larger and the opportunities for good and evil expanded.

The rebirth of society experienced severe birthing pains throughout this century. Humanistic studies gave a new vitality to academic and artistic expressions. While the human spirit was celebrated, the evil dimensions of that same spirit came to the fore also. Emerging nationalism, abuse of papal prerogatives, and a restive uncertainty about the future left room for reforming voices. The time was ripe for reformation.

For Review and Discussion
1. Describe the Renaissance as an academic, cultural, political, and theological movement.
2. Why was Jan Hus perceived as a dangerous preacher, worthy of execution by the Roman Church?
3. What was the "conciliar movement" and why would it threaten papal power?
4. Research one of the Renaissance artists in light of his contributions to the Christian faith.
5. How were Hus and Savonarola forerunners of the sixteenth century Reformation?

For Further Reading
Carpenter, Christine. *The War of the Roses: Politics and the Constitution in England, c. 1437-1509.* New York: Cambridge University Press, 1997.
Goffen, Rona. *Renaissance Rivals: Michelangelo, Leonardo, Raphael, Titian.* New Haven, CN: Yale University Press, 2004.
Manchester, William. *A World Lit Only By Fire: The Medieval Mind and the Renaissance.* New York: Hachette Book Group, 1992.
Oberman, H.A. *The Harvest of Medieval Theology.* Cambridge, MA: Harvard University Labyrinth Press, 1963.
Sellery, George Clarke. *The Renaissance: Its Nature and Origins.* Madison: The University of Wisconsin Press, 1965.
Setton, Kenneth M. *The Papacy and the Levant (1204-1571).* Volume II: The Fifteenth Century. Philadelphia: The American Philosophical Society, 1978.
Spinka, Matthew, ed. *Advocates of Reform: From Wyclif to Erasmus.* Volume XIV in The Library of Christian Classics series. Philadelphia: The Westminster Press, 1953.

16 A. The Age of Reform and Northern Humanism

The Sixteenth Century: Part 1

The sixteenth century marks one of the most outstanding epochs in the history of Christianity. The struggles for unity resulted in further divisions within Christendom. The process of purifying the church's doctrines brought about a solidifying of some of the most horrific heretical teachings associated with Christianity. Internal concerns for spiritual security seemed to weigh heavy on the leaders as well as the individual believers throughout Europe. Yet, during this time, one of the greatest expansions into the world occurred. In this first part of chapter sixteen, we will take a panoramic view of the century and then in the next two sections of this chapter look at more specific events which transpired in the midst of these political, social, and cultural changes of the Renaissance.

Ripe for Reform

The church was ripe for reform. Northern European city-states were beginning to experience the first flush of power over their own lives. Political power was slowly being drawn away from the church. New worlds were beckoning from beyond the edges of the existent maps and exploration provided new opportunities for political and economic and religious influence and expansion. And a new way of looking at the world, later known as humanism, was rising throughout Europe.

Humanism, with its roots in Italy, gradually spread north into and among the Germanic and Scandinavian peoples. Humanism, in contrast to a medieval scholastic mindset, was centered in the appreciation of this world and human abilities. The beauty of nature, the wonder of past cultures, the perfection of the human form, and the limitless prospect of the future were all the subjects of an elevated eloquence in literature and artistry. In addition, a sense of nationalism and economic autonomy were essential components of this humanist time of discovery.

In all of this, Christian individuals struggled with their understanding of the church, which seemed ever more corrupt, and with its teachings, which seemed ever more irrelevant, irreverent, and obscure. Yet, the reality of the Gospel of Jesus Christ began to escape its enormous encrustation which had developed over the centuries. Exploration provided opportunities for mission work. The age of reformation was beginning to be evident on the surface as well as the soul of society.

Nationalism

No one form of government existed throughout the sixteenth century. From loosely connected federations of villages to local principalities under a duke or prince; from kingdoms to free imperial cities, a diversity of political constellations held sway over the growing populations of what later became Europe.

The Holy Roman Empire was slowly disappearing. What remained in name of the feudal rule which had dominated the scene for centuries was disintegrating as peasants, merchants, and princes began to grow stronger. The Holy Roman Empire was more Germanic than it was European—emperors were chosen by seven electors, all but one from Germany, and almost all emperors after the thirteenth century were chosen from the Hapsburg dynasty in Vienna. Through political and marital alliances, these emperors had consolidated much of European political control.

Five emperors served as dynastic rulers during the sixteenth century of the Holy Roman Empire. Beginning his reign in the late fifteenth century, Maximillian I (1459-1519, ruled 1493-1519) was succeeded by his son, Charles V (1500-1558, ruled 1519-1530). Charles's tumultuous imperial rule is noteworthy both in the person of Martin Luther and the rise of the Reformation as well as the fact that the Ottoman Turks besieged his capital in 1529, giving greater need for unity among the European nations, and the rise of Protestantism. We will read more about his Reformation connection in the next section of this chapter. Charles was succeeded by Ferdinand I in 1556 (1503-1564, ruled 1556-1564) and Maximillian II (1527-1576, ruled 1564-1576), who ruled only a dozen years and was followed by Rudolph II (1552-1612, ruled 1576-1612).

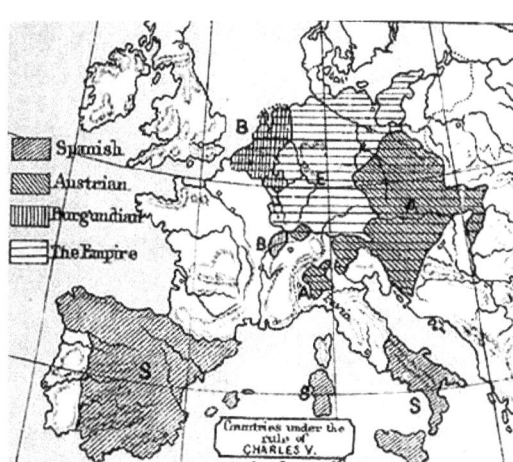

Although a political reality first in the nineteenth century, several nascent nation-states were emerging during the sixteenth century—France, England, Spain, Portugal and the Netherlands. Each of these nation-states developed a professional army, equipped with new fire-power in the form of recently imported gunpowder. France had experienced strong dynastic leadership for almost a half-millennium and only in the sixteenth century did it lose some of its influence to Spain. In contrast, following the War of the Roses (1455-1485) and the consolidation of political power under Henry VII (1457-1509), who had married a son to Catherine of Aragon (1485-1536, queen 1509-1533) and a daughter to the king of Scotland, his successor, Henry VIII (1491-1547), inherited a prospering English empire. Charles V also ruled as Charles I in Spain, succeeding Ferdinand and Isabella, until abdicating to his son, Philip II (1527-1598, ruled 1556-1598) in 1556, thereby continuing the Spanish hegemony over the seas, particularly in the New World. Italy remained divided into numerous city-states and Germany struggled to unite several strong feudal states as the Holy Roman Empire grew weaker by the decade. Yet, the process was set in motion for greater national autonomy.

Cities grew in population and a new urban middle class arose, the *bourgeoisie* (French, "borough-dwellers," as distinct from the rural peasants). These city-dwellers were very much aware of what was needed politically, economically, and culturally. Merchants and guilds of craftsmen became prominent community leaders, often competing with various ecclesiastical bureaucrats for revenue and influence. Cities such as Lisbon and Seville, Brussels and Antwerp became more important than the great Italian cities of Venice, Florence, and Genoa, which had been reduced by Turkish incursions.

The Ottoman Empire (see map) posed a decisive danger throughout most this century. Holding lands around the south and eastern shores of the Mediterranean Sea, these Muslims maintained a constant threat to the remaining Christian regions of Europe. In 1571, at the Battle of Lepanto, the papal fleet reduced the Turkish power permanently.

Discovery

Humanism and nationalism were at the heart of the great geographic discoveries of the century. The Portuguese had long been the leaders in exploration, particularly moving down and around the African coast as well as crossing the Atlantic to a new world. Coupled with the humanist desire for discovery, these navigators established Christian outposts at many of their trading sites which were built around the western coast of Africa and, finally after 1497, in India.

Exploration of the New World began in earnest during the first years of the sixteenth century. In 1500, the Portuguese nobleman and explorer, Pedro Cabral (1468-1520), sailed to South America and claimed the region which would later be Brazil. Around 1510-1513, the Spanish explorer, Vasco de Balboa (1475-1519), crossed the Panama isthmus and reached the Pacific Ocean (see illustration). Another Spaniard, Ponce de Leon (1474-1520) arrived in Florida around 1513, seeking the proverbial "fountain of youth." By 1541, Hernando de Soto (1497-1542) explored much of South America for Spain and then directed his attention to what became southern United States, particularly the region around the Mississippi River, where he died. By 1555, the Portuguese had established a significant number of trading posts in Brazil and along the coast of Africa. In addition, they founded settlements all the way to India and what became known as the East Indies and then further East to Japan.

The Spanish discoveries in the New World, following the initial successes of Christopher Columbus (1451-1506), provided a unique development in the life of the church. One of the objectives of his exploration into the New World, claimed Christopher Columbus, was the conversion of the Amerindians. During the first years of the sixteenth century, the popes allowed the Spanish sovereign to have enormous authority. In a little more than a decade, Hernán Cortés (1485-1547) overthrew the Aztec state and founded Mexico City (1521). Francisco Pizarro (1478-1541) entered Peru (1532) and established a base for Spanish conquest in South America.

These Spanish conquests ignored papal influence and the colonial church instead came under the appointees of the Spanish crown. As a result, many of the bishops sent to the New World were politicians with little spiritual strength or pastoral concern to direct the development of this mission field. Enslavement and cruelties were not only tolerated by the church, but often were carried out in her name.

Yet, in the New World there were monastic missionaries accompanying the explorers. The Franciscans, Dominicans, and later Jesuits, who came with each ship, often stayed with the indigenous people in the New World, living with them and helping them develop in the face of disastrous European settlements. For example, Dominican Antonio Montesinos (+1545) in Santo Domingo preached a sermon against the European exploitation of the indigenous peoples there. As Justo Gonzalez reports:

> The system of *encomiendas*—trusts—was the main abuse against which the Dominicans protested. It was forbidden to enslave the Indians. But, supposedly in order to civilize them and to teach them Christian doctrine, groups of them were "entrusted" to a settler. In exchange for the settler's guidance, the Indians were to work for him. The result was even worse than outright slavery, for those who held trusts—the *encomenderos*—had no investment in the Indians, and therefore no reason to be concerned for their well-being. (*The Story of Christianity*, 1:382)

After hearing Montesinos's sermons, Bartolomé de Las Casas (1474-1566), the first priest to be ordained in the New World, realized that the Christian faith was incompatible with holding individuals as "trusts." He released the enslaved Indians under his care and began a lifetime of protest against the practice. He died at the age of ninety-two, having failed to make a significant change in the actual colonial culture, but at least protesting the handling of the native peoples.

In New Spain, the name given to the Aztec empire known now as Mexico, the Spanish conquistador, Cortés, introduced a Catholic presence. After seeing how the non-monastic priests often looked only for the comforts of home, he requested a dozen Franciscan priests from Emperor Charles V. Although these priests sometimes performed mass baptisms with little instruction, they lived among the people and provided contact points for the people.

In 1536, the first bishop of New Spain was ordained, Juan de Zumárraga (1468-1548). Recognizing the need for reform through education, he brought the first printing press to the western hemisphere to publish Christian material for the communities. In 1539, he opened the minor orders of the Catholic Church to Amerindians, although not those of deacon, priest, or bishop. In 1588, the king of Spain issued an order declaring that Amerindians could enter priestly and monastic orders. Bishop Zumárraga, later to become archbishop, became concerned with heresy and in a period of less than ten years, almost 150 people were tried for false doctrine. In 1573, Spain adopted a policy of pacifying rather than conquering the New World peoples. Conversions to Christianity were to be voluntary and peaceful, not coerced.

Two Italian Jesuit missionaries traveled from India to the Portuguese colony of Macau in the latter quarter of this century. From that peninsula of China, Matteo Ricci (1552-1610) and Michele Ruggieri (1543-1607) entered mainland China around 1582, settling in Zhaoqing in southern China. There they prepared a Chinese catechism and a Portuguese-Chinese dictionary for future mission workers. (See illustration depicting Ricci with Xu Guangqi, who helped establish Christian work in China.)

Along with the practical, political, and mercantile causes associated with the magnificent land acquisitions by the European nation states, the Gospel was being carried "into all the world." Yet, as the historian, Kenneth Latourette, noted about this century, "If a Christian motive entered into the initial voyages, results followed which were a tragic contradiction of that motive" (*Christianity Through the Ages*, 164).

Commerce

Coupled with nationalism and discovery was the increase in commercial activities during this century, sometimes referred to as "the Commercial Revolution." Feudalism as an economic system (as well as a form of governance) declined as both peasants and townspeople gained some fiscal independence.

Guilds of merchants, associations of like-minded skilled workers and businessmen, formed larger leagues, or *hanses*, to ensure mutual protection and efficiency of trade. The Hanseatic League, for example, formed around the North Sea, quickly dominated northern European commerce for most of this century. This commercial expansion included a rise in the use of capital—products or services used to produce new income. Banking increased under the Medici family in Italy and later the Fuggers in Germany.

This rise in commerce gave clearer evidence of the great disparity between the wealthy land-holding nobles and the impoverished land-bound peasants. Poverty was ubiquitous throughout most of Europe following the Black Death of the fifteenth century. Throughout most of the middle ages, the church had stepped in to aid those who could barely survive, yet the monastic system itself extoled poverty as a Christian virtue. Peasants began to acquire more land and, although still vulnerable to natural disasters and poor weather, they soon became a significant voice in society, especially in this sixteenth century.

In 1525, a major Peasants' Revolt occurred in Germany, sometimes blamed on Luther's own writings (see chapter 16 B). However, this was not the first peasant revolt. Already in 1381, English peasants had revolted and several years earlier an uprising among French peasants had to be addressed. Most of these protests were over unusually high taxation by the governing kings or landlords. In the sixteenth century, the Peasants' Revolt was accelerated by pamphlet printing of their manifesto, *The Twelve Articles of Memmingen*. The serfs and local citizens demanded the right to make both commercial as well as religious decisions in their own territory. Unfortunately, the German princes took harsh steps to suppress the revolt, resulting in the death of nearly 100,000 citizens.

Christian Humanism

Growing out of the Italian Renaissance, humanists in the rest of Europe exhibited a stronger Christian component in their scholarship. Along with classical antiquity, they returned to the Christian sources. Key to their understanding of Christianity was a sense that understanding would lead to piety, particularly understanding the writings of early Christians in their context of classical antiquity. Such understanding required education. Thus, the vernacular languages began to supplant Latin, although Latin remained the scholars' tool of trade. In addition, the use of the printing press grew exponentially during this century.

Spain saw the first printed Greek New Testament in 1514 (although it was not published until 1520). Two years later a six-volume Bible (see illustration) was published, known as the "Polyglot Bible" (Greek, "several" + "languages"), containing Hebrew, Latin, and Greek texts of the Old Testament, an Aramaic Targum of the Pentateuch with a Latin translation, and the entire New Testament in the Greek with the Latin Vulgate.

Perhaps one of the most outstanding teachers at the University of Paris, Jacques Lefèvre d'Étaples (1455-1536), advocated the Scriptures as the sole authority for Christian doctrine and life. As a Bible teacher, he encouraged his students to return to a more primitive New Testament style of Christianity along with a revived Aristotelianism and restored Platonism. To that end, he worked tirelessly to translate the Latin Vulgate into French, producing a commentary on the Psalms with five different Latin versions in 1509 and a complete French New Testament by 1523.

Another Parisian-born humanist was the printer, Robert I Estienne (Robertus Stephenus) (1503-1558), who late in life converted from Catholicism to Calvinism. Besides his print shops' extremely high quality typography, he is remembered as the first printer to introduce verse numberings into the Greek New Testament in 1551.

Desiderius Erasmus of Rotterdam (1466-1536), undoubtedly the most gifted Renaissance scholar of the century, was recognized as the humanist's

humanist. An exceptional linguist, he loved Latin, but also worked proficiently in Greek and Hebrew. His publication of a critical edition of the New Testament in Greek in 1516 provided a magnificent resource for the Protestant Reformation. In 1511, he prepared a satirically critical social commentary, *In Praise of Folly*. The Greek title, *Moria Encomium*, was a pun on his friendship with Thomas More. (See below and chapter 15.) Erasmus's humanistic qualities led him to reject the amassing of scholastic details. Instead, he advocated an emphasis on Christian morality as the key to a revitalized Christianity. Eschewing the superstitions which had enveloped the piety of the church, Erasmus saw true piety as resting in the ethical teachings of Christ. We will discuss Erasmus more in the part B of this chapter.

In 1526 William Tyndale (c.1494-1536) published an English translation of the New Testament, using Luther's 1522 Testament as a guide. Because he was declared a heretic, it had to be printed in Germany. He was assisted by Miles Coverdale (1488-1568) in translating the Old Testament and a complete Bible was printed in 1535. The following year, Tyndale was kidnapped from Antwerp, which was then a "free city," that is, a non-aligned city-state, and taken to a castle in present-day Belgium where he was tried as a heretic, and condemned to death by strangulation. His body was then burned.

Tyndale's strongest opponent was Sir Thomas More (1478-1535), another English humanist. More never joined a monastic order, but was always a strong proponent of papal authority and Roman Catholic doctrine. Although a friend of Erasmus, he took strong actions against Tyndale and the rise of any potential Lutheran influences. As a lawyer and statesman, he held political positions under King Henry VIII, but opposed the king when he ventured too far away from papal authority. More was beheaded for high treason in 1532. His major contributions were political, particularly his creatively imaginary, *Utopia*, a land with an ideal political system and no lawyers, since the laws were simple and self-evident.

A German humanist with more political than theological interests was Ulrich von Hutten (1488-1523). Trained in a Benedictine monastery, he fled that environment and sought a less sedate humanistic lifestyle. Recognized for his poetic ability, he wrote satirical poems against many social, political, and religious individuals and circumstances. Most recognized was his contribution (if not authorship) of *Letters of Obscure Men* (*Epistolae Obscurorum Virorum*), which supported Reuchlin against his scholastic and monastic opponents.

Architecture and the Arts

Under the pontifical aegis, art and architecture found significant patrons. Pope Alexander VI (1431-1503, pope 1492-1503) supported architectural and civic improvements in Rome, especially encouraging many artists through patronage from his vast personal and ecclesiastical wealth. Having fathered several children most of whom were illegitimate, he openly gave preferential treatment to his sons, especially Caesar Borgia (see chapter 15). Alexander's successor, Pius III (1439-1503) died after less than a month in office. His successor, Julius II (1443-1513, pope 1504-1513), led the efforts to construct a new St. Peter's Basilica in Rome in 1506. This masterpiece of humanistic architecture was finally completed 120 years later, having been underwritten by twenty papacies. Other architects of this era include Donato Bramante (1444-1514), recognized in Milan for his unique adaptation of ancient classical Roman style and also in Rome for his exquisite design for Julius II's basilica and several other churches.

Michelangelo

Combining architecture and art are the three great masters of this age—

Leonardo da Vinci (1452-1519) (see chapter 15), Michelangelo (1475-1564), and Raphael (1483-1520). Flowing with the vigor of Italian humanism, Michelangelo grew up in Florence, where he often returned, and was a recognized rival of Raphael. Michelangelo combined the versatile skills of a sculptor, painter, inventor, and architect. He also wrote over 300 sonnets in Italian. His *Pieta* (see illustration) and *Statue of David* are classical in style, yet exemplify the high

Renaissance humanism of his day with their emotive content and physical dimensions. Having been commissioned to produce forty statues for Pope Julius II's tomb (a project which covered over forty years and was never completed to Michelangelo's satisfaction), he was constantly interrupted for other projects, including the painting of the Sistine chapel. Fifty years after the construction of St. Peter's Basilica began, Michelangelo was commissioned to take over the architectural work and nearly saw its completion in his lifetime (the dome was completed shortly after his death). Six years after St. Peter's was begun, Michelangelo completed his fresco work on the pope's personal chapel, the Sistine.

Raphael

Although Raphael died at the relatively young age of 37, he was extremely productive both in his artistic contributions and in his architectural designs. He was well-known throughout Europe through his prodigious printmaking and his prolific workshop team. His greatest artistic contributions are still evident in several rooms of Vatican, where he worked for the final twelve years of his life.

Science

A new awareness of human ability and a new willingness to look beyond the present marked the new humanistic studies. We have already mentioned Leonardo da Vinci (chapter 15), with his investigations and inventions in anatomy and engineering. Astronomers, such as Copernicus (1473-1543), Galileo (1564-1642), and Kepler (1571-1630) had their eyes opened through the development of new ocular skills and the invention of the telescope.

Nicolaus Copernicus

Nicolaus Copernicus (1473-1543) was born in the fifteenth-century Polish province of Prussia. In 1491, he began his studies at the University of Krakow, which was known for its mathematical and astronomical scholarship. These studies fostered his further humanistic explorations in Italy at the end of the century and later resulted in his earthshaking conclusion of a heliocentric universe. Sometime around the middle of the first decade of the sixteenth century, Copernicus prepared a brief forty-page manuscript in which he described his ideas for some of his friends. About twenty years later, an associate of Philip Melanchthon from Wittenberg, Georg Rheticus (1514-1574) studied with Copernicus for two years from 1539-1541. At that time Rheticus encouraged his teacher to publish the work and provided a brief treatise in which he summarized Copernicus's ideas. Rheticus brought the book to Germany where he oversaw its publication in Nuremberg. The Lutheran theologian, Andreas Osiander (1498-1552), prepared a preface for the work in which he suggested that new theories are certainly worthy of consideration as long as they have scientific support. Copernicus's major work, *De revolutionibus orbium coelestium* (On the Revolutions of the Heavenly Spheres) (see illustration) was finally completed and, according to some biographers, the final pages were given to Copernicus on the day he died at the age of 70.

Galileo Galilei
Galileo Galilei (1564-1642) has been called "the father of modern observational astronomy." Although coming from a pious Catholic musical family, his father allowed him to study mathematics after a few years of medical training. As we will see in chapter 17, his discoveries supported a heliocentric understanding, which resulted in serious controversies with the church.

Johannes Kepler
Johannes Kepler (1571-1630), although not a direct student of Copernicus, was an astronomer and an assistant to Tycho Brahe (1546-1601), who himself advocated a geo-heliocentric universe. As a child, Kepler was intrigued by a great comet (1577) and a lunar eclipse (1580). As a university student at Tübingen, he was convinced that Copernicus's view was correct. After studying for the pastoral ministry, he received a teaching position in mathematics and astronomy at the Lutheran school in Graz, where he published his first astronomical work, *Mysterium Cosmographicum*, (Cosmographic Mystery or Secret of the Universe) in 1595. Later, he introduced a key concept, his laws of planetary motion, which in turn influenced Isaac Newton's (1642-1727) concept of universal gravitation.

Francis Bacon
Besides these astronomers, Francis Bacon (1561-1625) encouraged the use of observation of God's creation through the natural sciences. As a British philosopher and scientist, Bacon advocated a careful and meticulous scientific method of inductive experimentation rather than merely following the philosophical assumptions of the ancients. He had three goals for his life—to uncover truth, to serve his country and to serve his church. He sought

Parliamentary positions, which he held for several years until he was knighted by the new king of England, James I (1566-1625).

Although each of these early scientists brought significant change, the real scientific revolution blossomed in the next century and will be explored more in chapter seventeen.

Eastern Orthodoxy

In the East, the time was also ripe with reform. However, the reform did not come from humanistic influences but from the monasteries. The monasteries had been leaders in colonization. Although the monks settled in remote sites, as in the West, communities soon developed around them. In addition, these monks cared for travelers, the sick, the young, and the aged. Particularly among this last group, monasteries became centers for culture and the arts as wealthy business owners retired to the security of these monastic havens.

Early in the sixteenth century, two conflicting monastic communities were vying for influence among the Orthodox. Joseph Volotzky (1440-1515) and his Josephites emphasized hard work and study along with elaborate worship services with costly vestments in ornate buildings. Many young men of aristocratic families were trained in his monastery and later served as abbots and bishops and prominent public figures. The other group, known as the Non-possessors (rejecting monastic landownership), led by Nilus Sorsky (1433-1508), emphasized the eremitic life of seclusion or small communities in remote locations seeking union with God rather than political or earthly power. In 1503 the Non-possessors lost a critical conflict over secularizing land holdings, and the Josephites extended the close association between church and state.

Politically, after the strong Josephite leadership of the Metropolitan Macarius I (1482-1563), who was a significant teacher and advisor to the great

Tsar, Ivan IV "the Terrible" (1530-1584), Moscow became known as "the third Rome," since Constantinople, the second Rome, remained under Muslim control. Moscow became the center and guardian of the apostolic faith among the Slavonic peoples as they continued to hear the service and the reading of Scripture in their own language. In 1572, the Peace of Constantinople brought an end to Turkish attacks on Europe. In 1589 Moscow was recognized as an independent patriarchate under Patriarch Job (+1607, patriarch 1589-1605) (see illustration) and the Russian Orthodox Church became the "master of the East."

Spirituality

In spite of the humanistic reforms and expansive explorations of new worlds, a vacuum was occurring in the life of the church during this time. In the

West, monastic communities were losing influence and power and prestige, because of their laxity, lethargy and lasciviousness. Christian ideals were being repudiated both by intellectual humanists and by those who sought reform. From the papacy to the nobility to the common folk, people did what they thought they could get away with. An encroaching secularism with its concomitant nationalism was rising in attraction. The morality at this time would have shocked many of the earlier pagan cultures. Rather than standing up for a Christian worldview, the world was being viewed through humanistic eyes and the New Testament simplicity was being abandoned for cultural diversity.

The Holy Christian Church was still united at the beginning of the sixteenth century. Increasingly, the superficial unity was more political than theological, as the papal state vied with the rising national groups for power and prestige. The Hapsburgs and the Fuggers in Germany and the Medici in Italy, along with the wealthy Portuguese and Spanish nobles, weighed in heavily on the side of the papacy, yet the spiritual powers of the papacy were overshadowed by their political and economic influence.

Theologians and politicians, monks and maidens, had decried the abuses occurring in the Roman Church for over a century, yet little had seemed to effect a necessary change. Nepotism (granting political and ecclesiastical favors to relatives) and simony (the selling of ecclesiastical positions to the highest bidder) were rampant. Unbridled sexual misconduct was widespread among the clergy, including the immoral misbehavior of several popes themselves. Stories about the Borgia popes' exploits and escapades are exceptionally lewd and risqué. Economic concerns and political suspicion among the German peoples were continually rising as the papacy raised its gluttonous head and feasted upon the general populations of Christendom. Roman opulence had become a hallmark of the church. Religious activities were central for most communities, more for their social value than for the spiritual depth they provided. This was an era ripe for reformations and reform was emerging in many ways and places, but none as significant as northeastern Germany in the early sixteenth century.

For Review and Discussion
1. What were the political consequences of the demise of the Holy Roman Empire?
2. How did the "age of discovery" help in the advancement of the gospel into all the world?
3. We saw the *ad fontes* theme in chapter 15, how did that theme continue in the sixteenth century, especially among Christian humanists?
4. What humanist themes were emphasized in the artistic expressions of this century and how did they relate to Christianity?
5. Describe the scientific contributions made by Christian thinkers in this century.

For Further Reading

Cameron, Evan. *The Sixteenth Century.* New York: Oxford University Press, 2006.

Dannenfeldt, Karl H. *The Church of the Renaissance and Reformation: Decline and Reform from 1300-1600.* St. Louis: Concordia Publishing House, 1970.

Dickens, A. G. *Reformation and Society in Sixteenth Century Europe.* New York: Harcourt, Brace, and World, Inc., 1966.

Gonzalález, Justo L. *The Story of Christianity: Volume 1: The Early Church to the Dawn of the Reformation.* San Francisco: Harper & Row, 1984.

Green, V. H. H. *Renaissance and Reformation: A Survey of European History between 1450 and 1660.* New York: St. Martin's Press, 1974.

Harbison, E. Harris. *The Age of Reformation.* Ithaca, NY: Cornell University Press, 1955.

Hillerbrand, Hans J. *Men and Ideas in the Sixteenth Century.* Chicago: Rand McNally & Company, 1969.

Hunt, Jocelyn. *The Renaissance.* New York: Routledge, 1999.

Latourette, Kenneth Scott. *Christianity through the Ages.* New York: Harper & Row, 1965.

Lindberg, Carter, ed. *The Reformation Theologians: An Introduction to Theology in the Early Modern Period.* Malden, MA: Blackwell Publishers, 2002.

MacCulloch, Diarmaid. *The Reformation: A History.* New York: Penguin Books, 2003.

Mazzoco, A. *Interpretation of Renaissance Humanism.* Leiden: Brill, 2005.

McGrath, Alister E. *Reformation Thought: An Introduction.* Third Edition. Malden, MA: Blackwell Publishers, 1999.

Oberman, Heiko A. *The Reformation: Roots and Ramifications.* Andrew Colin Gow, trans. Grand Rapids: Wm. B. Eerdmans Publishing Company, 1994.

Ozment, Steven. *The Age of Reform 1250-1550: An Intellectual and Religious History of Late Medieval and Reformation Europe.* New Haven, CN: Yale University Press, 1980.

Smith, Preserved. *The Age of the Reformation.* New York: Henry Holt and Company, 1920.

Spitz, Lewis W. *The Renaissance and Reformation Movements.* Two volumes. Revised Edition. St. Louis: Concordia Publishing House, 1987.

Tanner, Emmeline M. *The Renaissance and the Reformation: A Textbook of European History, 1494-1610.* Oxford: Clarendon Press, 1915.

Thulin, Oskar, ed. *Illustrated History of the Reformation.* St. Louis: Concordia Publishing House, 1967.

16 B. The Lutheran Reformation

The Sixteenth Century: Part 2

The history of Western Christianity would be forever changed as a result of the life and work of Martin Luther. Certainly there were significant events and individuals throughout this century that had an impact on society and the church, but the name of Luther remains a hallmark of this century. Luther's experiences of conflict and profound proclamation of God's grace in Christ grew out of a context of the need for the assurance of God's love and the hope of eternal life for the whole world. In this second section of chapter sixteen, we will explore Luther and the movement which grew out of his own appreciation of God's revelation.

Martin Luther's Early Years

Near the end of the fifteenth century in a small town in north-central Germany, a young woman, Margarethe (1460-1531), gave birth to a son, Martin (1483/4-1546). She and her husband, Hans Luder (c.1459-1530), named him after Martin of Tours, whose festival was November 11, the day following Martin's birth and the date of his baptism. As an industrious copper miner, Hans soon moved his young family from Eisleben to the larger community of Mansfeldt, where the mining business was flourishing. The influence of Margaret's and Hans's son would be world-changing. Martin Luther (he spelled it several different ways throughout his lifetime) became God's instrument for a new era of Gospel-oriented living.

At the turn of the century, in 1501, Luther entered the University of Erfurt to begin his studies in Law, considered an entry point to patronage by wealthy nobility. Luther was slightly above average—out of fifty-two classmates to graduate with his bachelor degree, Luther was thirtieth; for his master's diploma, he came in second place among the seventeen graduates. More than his academic abilities, Luther struggled with a sensitive heart for spiritual issues. After a university friend was killed and Luther himself suffered a leg injury after a knife fight, he was travelling back to the university from his hometown during a storm. The popular scene of Luther falling to the ground in the midst of a thunderstorm is real. Luther cried out to the patron saint of miners and the supposed mother of the Virgin Mary, "Anne, save me! I will become a monk!"

In July, 1505, Luther entered the Black Cloister of the Order of the Hermits of Saint Augustine in Erfurt as a novice (see portrait). He continued his academic studies at the University of Erfurt after his novitiate, but changed his focus from law to theology. He was ordained into the priesthood in April of 1507 in the Erfurt cathedral of St. Mary and celebrated his first Mass the following month. In 1508, he was sent by his superior, Johann von Staupitz (c.1460-1524), to teach philosophy at the fairly new university in Wittenberg. After another year in Erfurt, Staupitz sent him back to Wittenberg in 1511, this time with the added responsibility of earning a doctorate (1512) and becoming an official teacher of the church [1] The following year, the affable Pope Leo X (1475-1521, pope 1513-1521) was elected to the chair of Peter in Rome.

The Ninety-five Theses

Recognizing his own spiritual needs and having a gift for communicating clearly and winsomely, Martin Luther spoke to the hearts of thousands of people when he raised the issue of indulgences (a process whereby sins were forgiven through an act of mercy or a gift of money) in sermons he preached toward the end of 1516 and early 1517. Nailing his "Ninety-five Theses" or propositions to the door of the Castle Church in Wittenberg on October 31st of that year, Luther broached the question whether the papacy had the power and right to extort money from the laity for forgiveness. He drew the attention of the people to the full and free forgiveness assured by God through Jesus Christ as reported in the Scriptures. Addressing a spiritually vexing need among the laity, this document,[2] and the consequent communications that it enlisted, became the precipitating event for the Protestant Reformation. As Erasmus stated later, "Luther sinned in two respects, namely, that he attacked the crown of the Pope and the bellies of the monks."

> **Indulgence Sales**
>
> A Dominican friar, Johann Tetzel, was an outstandingly successful salesman of indulgences and was engaged by Albrecht, Archbishop of Mainz. His method was to enter town with a fanfare and preach three sermons—on hell, on purgatory, and on heaven. Without the purchased indulgences, he proclaimed, individuals and family members would suffer the torments of hell or purgatory. For the simple purchase of indulgence document, forgiveness was granted from a theoretical storehouse of merits. "When a coin in the coffer rings, a soul from purgatory springs," he claimed. Luther's protest over such arrogant claims was sent to the Archbishop, whom Luther incorrectly thought was unaware of Tetzel's activities.

---

[1] Martin Luther, *Luther's Works* 49:48. Luther said of Staupitz, "It was through you that the light of the gospel first began to shine out of the darkness into my heart."
[2] The official title of Luther's academic proposal was "A Disputation on the Power and Efficacy of Indulgences." Such a disputation was apparently never held, but the subsequent consequences were earth- and church-shaking.

Luther's "breakthrough" had come as a gradual clarification for Luther over several years, contrary to some scholarly proposals. Sometime during his class preparations for his biblical lectures on Psalms (1513), Romans (1515-1516), Galatians (1516-1517), and Hebrews (1517-1518), Luther came to realize that the phrase of Paul in Romans 1, "the righteousness of God," was not only a characteristic of God and a requirement of humanity, but it was a gift which God bestowed on all who believed and trusted in the life, death, and resurrection of Jesus, the Messiah and God's Son. With that understanding, heaven opened for him, he said.[3] Salvation was not something earned, but a free gift of grace, received through faith, because of Christ. Luther thereby reversed the longstanding medieval idea that good works made a person acceptable to God. Rather, because one is declared acceptable by God because of Christ, one can perform good works. Salvation is not achieved but received.

In May of the next year, 1518 (the same year Leonardo da Vinci was born), Luther met with his Augustinian brother-friars at Heidelberg for their chapter meeting. He was asked to defend his theses. Instead of defending them, which he had done in print, he presented a completely new set of theses, later known as *The Heidelberg Theses,* in which he spoke more clearly about a

distinction between a theology of glory—which sought the hidden things of God and elevated the manifestation of God's goodness in people's lives—and the true theology of the cross—God is always present in our sufferings. Later that year and almost a year after the posting of his *Ninety-five Theses,* the Roman Catholic theologian and papal legate, Cardinal Thomas de Vio Cajetan (1469-1534), met with Luther for three days in Augsburg. Cajetan demanded that Luther recant, that is, withdraw his teachings from public discourse, and his condemnation of indulgences and the questioning of papal infallibility (see illustration, with Cajetan at the table and Luther standing). Luther refused and left town. But Cajetan had uncovered the sensitive issue of ecclesiastical authority, one which would become more central to the papacy than the morality of selling indulgences.

In early January of 1519, Luther was visited by another papal representative, Karl von Miltitz (c.1490-1529), who orchestrated Luther's agreement to support papal authority in temporal matters. The short-lived concord disintegrated when Emperor Maximillian (1459-1519, ruled 1486-1519) died and his replacement became a political issue throughout the continent. In early

---

[3] Martin Luther, *Luther's Works* 34:337. "I felt that I was altogether born again and had entered paradise itself through open gates."

summer of 1519, deliberations began for Maximillian's replacement as the electors were enticed by the chief candidates, Francis I (1484-1547, ruled 1515-1547) and Charles V (1500-1558, ruled 1519-1556). On June 28, Charles was elected, much to the dismay of Pope Leo, who had supported Francis, but also had delayed in dealing with Luther.

The day before Charles's election, a debate was held between Luther and the Roman Catholic theologian, Johann Maier von Eck (1486-1543), in Leipzig. Originally scheduled to be between Luther's colleague, Andreas Bodenstein von Carlstadt (c.1480-1541), on the topics of grace and free will, Luther quickly stepped into the fray as the topics touched on the critical issues of indulgences and then penance, purgatory, and papal authority. Along with 200 students, Carlstadt and Luther were accompanied by a new Wittenberg faculty member, Philip Melanchthon (1497-1560). Although both sides claimed victory, Luther demonstrated most clearly his commitment to Scripture alone as his ultimate authority—neither Councils nor popes were infallible, he declared.

Significant Documents of 1520

The following summer, on June 15, 1520, Pope Leo X published his papal bull (an official statement from the Vatican marked with a lead seal known as a *bulla*), *Exurge domini* ("Rise, Lord") (see illustration of the cover page) condemning over forty teachings attributed to Luther or drawn from the *Ninety-five Theses*, and requiring that he recant all these teachings. About this same time, Luther wrote his treatise on *The Papacy in Rome* in which he asserted that the papacy's claim to divine origin based upon Matthew 16:18-19 was a faulty interpretation and that, because of such self-acclaimed status, the papacy was indeed "the true Antichrist" and the "scarlet whore of Babylon."

That same year, three significant documents stated Luther's position most clearly—*To the Christian Nobility of the German Nation*, *On the Babylonian Captivity of the Church*, and *On the Freedom of a Christian*. Each of these works, produced at this critical time in the course of the Reformation, illustrated a significant idea in Luther's thinking and emphasized an important aspect of the Gospel, which was the sole motivation for Luther's call for reform.

In the first treatise, *To the Christian Nobility*, Luther emphasized the right and responsibility of the Christian nobles to live out their vocations as spiritual priests. Papal authority was limited, he stated, to spiritual things and even Scripture itself was to be recognized as being over the pope. He concluded that document by requesting a church council to address the ecclesiastical problems recognized by so many.

The second work used the seventy-year captivity of the people of Israel in Babylon and also the fiasco of the papal duplication in the fourteenth century as its starting point, known as *The Babylonian Captivity*. Luther argued that the church itself had held the people captive through its sacramental system, which required access to God's grace solely through priests. He decried the decrepit understanding of Scripture, which he believed should be open to all Christians. Finally, he rejected the idea of the "sacrifice of the mass," which seemed to infer that Christ had to be re-sacrificed by priests in order to earn salvation. He concluded by accusing the pope of being the very Antichrist warned about in the New Testament.

The third work was more specifically addressed to the common laity and explained how the concept of justification by grace through faith because of Christ can be a liberating doctrine. The key phrase in *On the Freedom of a Christian* seemed almost paradoxical: "A Christian is a perfectly free lord of all, subject to none. A Christian is a perfectly dutiful servant of all, subject to all." In this treatise, the great distinction between Law and Gospel was given clear and understandable application for the evangelical communities.

During the nineteen months between the Leipzig Debate and the Diet of Worms, Luther preached over 116 sermons, wrote sixteen treatises, published his first Galatians Commentary, and completed his daily classroom lecturing on the Psalter.

The Diet of Worms and Consequences

Unlike the previous productive years, 1521 marked a more perilous time in Luther's life and the Reformation movement. A bull of excommunication, *Docet Romanum Pontificem* ("It is Fitting that the Pope") was prepared on January 3, 1521 and delivered by Jerome Aleander (1480-1542) to the Diet of Worms. The Diet, an official meeting between the German nobility and the Emperor, was held over a period of several months. Luther had been invited to appear at the Diet already in November, but the invitation was removed and reissued several times, because of papal pressures. Finally, in a document dated March 6 (and sent on the 11th), Luther was invited to present his case before the imperial meeting in Worms.

During the early months of the summer of 1521, Luther was preparing to stand in the city of Worms face-to-face before the new emperor, twenty-one year old Charles V, who was to ascertain Luther's orthodoxy. On April 17th, Luther was asked by Eck, who served as the church official overseeing the confrontation, whether the books assembled by his accusers were indeed his and if they were, would he disavow them because of their anti-Catholic views. Luther, overwhelmed by the occasion, asked for a day to consider his answer. The following day, Luther stood before the assembly of nobles and

> HERE I STAND?
> Before the Imperial Diet of Worms, Luther stated: "Unless I am convinced by the testimony of the Scriptures or by clear reason (for I do not trust either in the pope or in councils alone, since it is well known that they have often erred and contradicted themselves), I am bound by the Scriptures I have quoted and my conscience is captive to the Word of God. I cannot and will not recant anything, since it is neither safe nor right to go against conscience. *Here I stand, I can do no other.* May God help me. Amen." Because the italicized sentence is only in Rohrer's report and not in eye-witness records, scholars have questioned its authenticity.

theologians and, again in response to the three questions, divided his answer carefully. If he disavowed some of his writings, he would be going against the very words of Scripture; so he could not speak categorically against them all. Other works represented the traditional positions of the Catholic Church, certainly he could not reject them. Finally, he agreed that some of the statements that he had written were not as considerately written as they could have been in pointing out errors that needed correcting. However, he held that these were legitimate concerns. Therefore, he concluded, he could not recant any of these writings because they were supported by Scripture and sound reason.

Luther as Outcast

After Luther left the city of Worms, anticipating a dubious safe-conduct, he was "kidnapped" and taken to the Wartburg Castle, just outside the city of Eisenach. Shortly thereafter, in an official declaration, *The Edict of Worms*, Emperor Charles V declared Luther a *Vogelfrei* (literally a "free bird," able to be killed by anyone) and anyone harboring him was subject to severe punishment. There at the Wartburg under the protective custody of Elector Frederick II "the Wise" (1463-1525), Luther took on the disguise of a knight, Knight George (*Junker Georg*). To keep himself busy, he began translating the Greek New Testament into German—a remarkable fete completed in less than half a year.

In the meantime in England, Henry VIII (1491-1547, ruled 1509-1547) took up some of Luther's treatises and declared them banned from his kingdom. He also had several documents prepared which promoted the teachings of the Roman Catholic Church. The following year, Luther prepared a vicious response to Henry's work on the seven sacraments, *Contra Henricum Regem Anglicum*. During the same year 1521, the Muslim military leader Suleiman the Magnificent (1494-1566, ruled 1520-1566) invaded Hungary. His Islamic Turkish forces advanced toward central Europe. This threat and a continuing fight between Charles and Francis I of France resulted in the Edict of Worms not being enforced.

Luther returned to Wittenberg secretly in December of 1521, but openly in March, 1522, in order to oversee the reformation from his pulpit and classroom podium. Almost immediately, Luther sought to calm the iconoclastic and radical reforms promoted by his colleague, Carlstadt. He also began to lecture in the university classroom. In September of 1522, Luther's fresh translation of the New Testament was published, known as the *September Testament*. Earlier that year, the more amicable Pope Adrian VI (Hadrian) (1459-1523, pope 1522-1523) was elected, although his pontificate was only two years. He was succeeded by Clement VII (1478-1534, pope 1523-1534).

July 1st of 1523 saw the death of the first Lutheran martyrs, Johann Esch and Heinrich Voes. These two Augustinian friars from Brussels refused to recant their Lutheran faith and were burned alive in the marketplace. In honor of these young men, Luther composed his first hymn, "A New Song We Raise," (*Ein neues Lied wir heben an*).

Also in 1523, Gustavus Eriksson (1496-1560) was elected the first king of Sweden (ruled 1523-1560), Gustavus I (also known as Gustavus Vasa). Shortly thereafter he declared independence from Denmark-Norway. Influenced by the

Petri brothers, Olavus (1493-1552) and Laurentius (1499-1573), who had studied with Luther in Wittenberg, Gustavus I broke with Rome over political and economic concerns, although Lutheran theology had already been preached and taught in several communities. Officially severing ties with Rome toward the end of the 1520s by becoming a state-church, Sweden officially became a Lutheran nation in 1544. Other Scandinavian students also studied in Wittenberg at this time.

After several requests, Luther published his first order of worship, *The Formula of the Mass and Communion for the Wittenberg Congregation* (1523). He began his lectures on Deuteronomy in the Augustinian monastery, but was soon preoccupied with revising the university's curriculum.

A Revolting Revolt

Unfortunately at the same time, Luther's life took on a darker hue as unrest between the peasantry and nobility increased. Warning against bloodshed, Luther advocated swift suppression of any rebellion by the peasants as well as a plea to the nobles to treat the peasants properly. The tensions between the two groups escalated. In 1524 bloody conflicts erupted. Known as the Peasants' Revolt (see illustration), Luther was later blamed for the hostilities that occurred throughout many communities in Germany after writing a pamphlet in 1525, "On the Murdering and Thieving Mobs of Peasants." However, other voices, such as

those of Thomas Müntzer (c.1490-1525), fueled apocalyptic hopes of the peasantry into an economic and social fervor that ended in disaster in Frankenhausen.

Later in 1524, the great humanist, Desiderius Erasmus of Rotterdam (1466-1536), attacked Luther regarding whether or not mankind has true freedom of the will. As Luther noted in his subsequent response, *On the Bondage of the Will*, Erasmus clearly identified the central issue in Luther's theology. In the very detailed style of academic discourse. Luther critiqued Erasmus's ideas with stronger evidence, demonstrating from Scripture that Erasmus had adopted the humanist view which was neither biblical nor even Christian. Luther concluded that humans were indeed bound by sin and only Christ could loose them from this bondage. Although Erasmus responded again to Luther, Luther refused to continue the debate. Their previously cordial relationship had ended.

Practicing the Faith

Luther's protector, Elector Frederick the Wise, died in late spring of 1525 and was succeeded by his brother, Johann (1468-1532), known as John "the  Steadfast" (ruled 1524-1532). Fearing for his life and acknowledging his own inadequacies as a husband, Luther reluctantly yet confidently entered into marriage on June 13, 1525 at the age of forty-one. His new wife was Katherine von Bora (1499-1552), a twenty-six year old nun who had escaped from her Nimbschen convent with a dozen others a year earlier. "Dr. Katie," as he often affectionately referred to her, provided the strength and stability that Martin needed to be free to carry on his academic and theological pursuits, calling her "Katie, my rib," in reference to Eve's complementary role. Their first child, Hans (1526-1575), would be born a little more than a year later.

Early in 1526, Luther issued his *German Mass and Order for Public Worship*, which he had prepared for the Wittenberg worshipers the previous December, entirely in German. During the busyness of teaching and preaching, Luther prepared several commentaries on the Old Testament books of Jonah, Habakkuk, and Ecclesiastes. In the meantime, Emperor Charles and Francis I signed a peace treaty ending their five-year conflict and Charles turned his attention to Germany. Toward the end of June, an imperial diet was held in Speyer, although Charles could not attend. This allowed the Lutheran princes to form an alliance, the League of Torgau, and suspend the earlier Edict of Worms and decide the religious allegiance of their region, thus providing a great advantage for the reformation movement.

Further Unrest

Controversy between several of the reformers began to erupt around this time. Swiss theologians, Ulrich Zwingli (1484-1531) and Oecolampadius (1482-1531), did not always agree with Luther's scriptural interpretations, particularly on the Lord's Supper. In 1526, Luther published a strong pamphlet against the views espoused by Oecolampadius in *The Sacrament of the Body and Blood of Christ—Against the Fanatics*. "Fanatics" for Luther were those who denied the real presence of Christ and only held a spiritual view. In seeking to ameliorate the issue, Luther actually exacerbated the situation for the next several years.

By the beginning of 1527, political issues began to emerge again as a significant influence on the reformation. The Islamic forces of Sulieman defeated King Louis (ruled 1516-1526) in Hungary as the Turkish threat extended further into European consciousness. At about the same time, Francis I with the support of the papacy moved against Charles V, but the Charles's imperial armies not only defeated him, but also sacked the city of Rome. A treaty was negotiated between Charles and Pope Clement VII toward the end of the year.

Forging a Stronger Church

During this same year Luther composed his famous Reformation hymn, "*A Mighty Fortress Is Our God*," perhaps in light of the political and theological unrest of the time. Luther began to experience severe health issues, which would become more chronic over the next years as he worked tirelessly to forge a stronger church. Through a series of pastoral and ecclesiastical "visitations," Luther and his colleagues promoted a critique of the evangelical congregations, ascertaining what they needed as well as how to address those needs. The key to a strengthening the church, Luther recognized, was better educated pastors and laity. The following year, Philip Melanchthon (1497-1560) prepared (with Luther's encouragement and approval) a series of "Visitation Articles" by which clergy and congregations could be evaluated. It was in that same year, 1528, in Scotland that Patrick Hamilton (1504-1528) was burned at the stake for advocating Luther's teaching, an event which only fueled the Reformation in that country.

Along with the Visitation Articles and regular preaching on the central doctrines of the Christian faith, Luther finally completed a task he had proposed earlier—the preparation of a catechism for both pastors and parents. In 1529, Luther published both his *Small Catechism* for the heads of the households and his *Large Catechism* for pastors. The *Small Catechism* came out in the form of a set of posters (see illustration), which families could use as a household teaching aid. Around that same time, a second Diet was called at Speyer, but this time the Catholic leaders prevailed. When the reformers protested the actions of this diet and appealed to the Emperor, the term "Protestant" was first applied to them.

It was later in this same year that the Sacramentarian Controversy was addressed during the Marburg Colloquy from October 1st to the 4th. Philip I (1504-1567, ruled 1518-1567), Landgrave of Hesse, desired political stability and unity in his region and so called the meeting of the leading reformers at his castle in Marburg. Among the dozen representatives, Ulrich Zwingli and Martin Luther were the chief spokesmen for the two groups. Consensus was attained on fourteen of the fifteen issues in discussion, later known as the *Marburg Articles*; however, over the understanding of Christ's presence in the Lord's Supper, Luther maintained that Christ was present in the bread and wine, while Zwingli continued to hold that the elements were only symbolic representations. As Luther left the meeting, he stated: "We are not of the same spirit."

The 1530s and the Augsburg Confession

At the end of 1529, Emperor Charles had defeated Francis I and received a papal promise to be recognized as the head of the Holy Roman Empire. At the same time, Suleieman was marching toward Vienna with a force of almost a quarter of a million soldiers. Charles saw the need for political unity and called for a meeting to be held in Augsburg to settle the religious disputes and form a military alliance against the Turks.

In March 1530, Elector John "the Steadfast" of Saxony received word of the diet at his castle in Torgau and called upon Luther, Melanchthon, Johannes Bugenhagen (1485-1558) and Justus Jonas (1493-1555) to prepare a statement which reflected both agreements and disagreements with the Roman Catholic Church. Known as the *Torgau Articles*, these doctrinal statements served as a basis for the subsequent diet. In the meantime, Johann Eck had sent Charles *404 Articles*, which he claimed were held by Luther and were heretical.

Because he was still under the imperial ban, Luther had to stay in the castle at Coburg from April through August, rather than attend the assembly at Augsburg. In June, Luther learned of the death in May of his father, who had been ill since February and to whom Luther had sent a letter of encouragement. From Coburg, Luther relied on Philip Melanchthon to prepare and present a clear statement of the doctrinal positions to the Emperor and princes at this diet and

corresponded with him frequently. (Luther wrote over 70 letters during those months.) Two previous statements, the *Torgau Articles*, and another document written just after the Marburg Colloquy, known as the *Schwabach Articles* which more clearly stated what it meant to be "Lutheran," were used by Melanchthon. On June 25, 1530, the Lutheran chancellor, Gregory Brück (1485-1557), read to the assembly the confession of the Protestant princes in Justus Jonas's German translation. (See illustration on the previous page.) During the diet, four Protestant cities—Strassburg, Constance, Memmingen, and Lindau—asked Martin Bucer (1491-1551) and Wolfgang Capito (1478-1541) to prepare a statement of their own, known as the *Tetrapolitan*, articulating a Zwinglian perspective, particularly of the Sacrament of the Altar.

Although the Emperor seemed pleased with the result, he asked for a Catholic response. After several revisions, a Roman Catholic response, known as *The Confutation*, condemned most of the Lutheran teachings. It was only presented orally on August 3rd and no manuscript was given to the Lutherans. Remarkably, by September 22nd, Melanchthon, with only his notes and those from several others who had heard the Catholic reply, prepared a defense (*Apology*) to the Augsburg Confession. Key to this defense was a strong and thorough defense of Article IV "On Justification," the central teaching of the Lutheran theologians. In December, meetings at Schmalkald resulted in the formation of a defensive military alliance by the Lutheran princes against the Catholic states and the Emperor.

Luther's Personal Life

During the next years, Luther's students began to copy down his remarks at their evening meals, thus providing source material for the publication of Luther's *Table Talk*. While some of the material cited by students has been questioned by scholars, the conversational notes provide much helpful material and personal viewpoints about family and academic life in the sixteenth century and perceptive insights into the Lutheran Reformation.

In the summer of 1531, Martin Luther's mother died while Luther was at the elector's Torgau residence, a place of respite on several occasions over the next years. A few months later, Melanchthon responded to a request by Henry VIII, who had occasionally expressed interest in Luther's work, to approve of Henry's divorce by saying such an act, though unfavorable, is more acceptable than polygamy for the sake of a successor. Luther denounced divorce on such grounds, although he also left open the question of polygamy.

Upon the death of his father in August, 1532, John Frederick I "the Magnanimous" (1503-1554) served as the new Elector of Saxony (1532-1547). Throughout this period, Luther's pastor, Johann Bugenhagen, had made connections with clergy in various cities in northern Europe, preparing administrative manuals (known as Church Orders) for several communities, thus extending the influence of the Reformation. In Denmark (which included Norway, Iceland, sections of Sweden and the German duchies of Schleswig and Holstein), the newly elected King Christian III (1503-1559, ruled 1534-1559) who had attended the Diet of Worms, officially introduced Lutheranism in 1534. A two-year civil war erupted between the Danish Catholics and the ruling German Lutheran nobles, which ended with an official Danish Lutheran state church in 1537. Between 1537 and 1539, Bugenhagen ordained seven Lutheran bishops and helped restructure the University of Copenhagen along the lines of Wittenberg.

Struggling with the fanatics, the Peasants' Revolt, the Sacramentarian controversy, his pastoral responsibilities of the Visitation, the Diet of Augsburg, and his own health, Luther had placed his work of the complete German Bible in hiatus. Finally in 1534 the complete German translation of the Bible was published. This is the same year that Ignatius Loyola (1491-1556) first conceived the Society of Jesus (the Jesuits) in France in order to defend the Catholic faith. Early October, Pope Clement VII died and was succeeded by Paul III (1465-1549, pope 1534-1549), who officially approved the Jesuit order in 1540.

A Growing Consensus

As the Smalcald League continued to grow in its political power, it experienced some greater theological clout. Toward the end of 1535, they received acknowledgement from Henry VIII that he was interested in their doctrinal statements. Earlier he has sent Philip Melanchthon a significant gift in appreciation for a copy of his *Loci Communes*. Negotiations continued over several years with several English students in Wittenberg.

In May of 1536, Martin Bucer and Luther carried on a very animated discussion of their theological and biblical understandings of Holy Communion. Particularly at issue not only was their interpretation of the real presence, but also whether even an unworthy recipient received the body of Christ in the Lord's Supper. A resulting agreement, known as the "Wittenberg Concord," was later rejected by the Reformed, although Luther, Melanchthon, Bugenhagen and others as well as Bucer and Capito signed it. At the end of that year, Pope Paul III, under pressure from the Emperor, announced that a Council would be held in Mantua the following year, although it would be postponed again later that year. While at the same time in England, the great English translator, William Tyndale (1494-1536), was burned at the stake.

In February 1537, the *Smalcald Articles* were received at a meeting in the town of the same name. Luther had prepared this document late in 1536 as requested by his prince, Elector John Frederick, in preparation for the church council, but it also served as a personal statement of faith. The document had both political and theological import, since it united the Lutheran princes. Melanchthon also prepared a treatise, *On the Power and Primacy of the Pope*, which strongly affirmed the Lutheran right and biblical responsibility to ordain their own pastors, claiming that papal authority was not divine but only of human origin. Luther could not attend the meetings in person because of ill health, and, from some accounts, nearly died there.

Around this same time, Melanchthon (see illustration) became embroiled in a long-lasting controversy with a fellow student of Luther, Johann Agricola (1492-1566). Melanchthon had argued that the Law needed to be preached to avoid misunderstanding God's grace in Christ. Agricola disagreed and argued that the Law was no longer required for Christians and even the Old Testament Law should be ignored. Luther prepared a set of propositions against Agricola's teachings, entitled "Against Antinomians," which was published the next year as a popular pamphlet.

After several years of contact and negotiations and instructions, the Danish Diet of Odensee in the summer of 1539 officially committed itself to the Reformation and designated the University of Copenhagen as the school for preparing their Lutheran pastors. Around this same time, a Finnish student who later was a prominent Lutheran reformer in Finland, Mikael Agricola (c.1510-1557), lived with Luther from 1536-1539. That autumn a severe plague hit Wittenberg and most of the students left the city to study in Jena.

During 1541, a conference was held in Regensburg (Ratisbon) between Lutherans and Catholics and the Reformed. At first a seeming breakthrough and agreement was worked out on the doctrine of justification, but both Wittenberg and Rome rejected the final outcome. At the end of that same year, Carlstadt died in Basel, after being exiled from Wittenberg (although he was reconciled with Luther in the end).

Luther's Later Years

Early in May of 1542, Luther began a second series of lectures on Genesis, which he continued for almost a decade until nearly the end of his life. Sadly, Luther's young thirteen year-old daughter, Magdalene (1529-1542), died on September 6, a tragedy from which Luther never fully recovered, especially after losing little Elizabeth (1527-1528) a year before Magdalene had been born. The next year, Luther published two harsh works against what he perceived as an obstinacy he observed among the Jews for rejecting the Christian gospel. His ire was also meted out upon the Wittenbergers during these years, since he said they had had the gospel, but seemed to live only for the world.

In 1544, Luther preached for the dedication of a new chapel for the Elector John Frederick in Torgau, the first "Lutheran" church. Around that time, Pope Paul published another announcement for a council to be held in Trent the following year, although that was again delayed until March of 1545 (not actually convened until the end of September; see section C of this chapter). That same year, Luther produced one of his most vitriolic works against the papacy using

Scripture and church history, *Against the Roman Papacy, An Institution of the Devil.*[4]

The fall of 1545 saw a young man enter the University of Wittenberg named Martin Chemnitz (1522-1586). Born near Wittenberg, he went to high school in Wittenberg at fourteen. There he heard Luther speak, but did not have the opportunity to study with him. Instead at the University, he became close friends with Luther's colleague, Philip Melanchthon, who invited him back to teach at the university almost a decade later.

In mid-January, 1546, Luther was asked to come to Eisleben, the town of his birth, to settle a petty inheritance dispute between two prominent brothers. By mid-February, after several conversations, the dispute was resolved, but Luther's health had deteriorated. Taking up residence across the street from St Andrew's Church, he continued to preach there several times. On the evening of February 17, friends of Luther along with his three sons—Hans (1526), Martin (1531), and Paul (1533)—gathered at his bedside. He did not sleep well and awoke several times, surprised that his family was still there. Early on February 18th, the doctors announced that Luther had died (See illustration of Luther's death mask.).

The following day, Justus Jonas preached the first of several funeral sermons for Luther at St Andrew's Church in Eisleben. The next day Michael Coelius (1492-1559), the court preacher at Mansfeld, preached a second sermon, after which Luther's body was brought by procession to Wittenberg, arriving on February 22nd. Luther's funeral was held in the Castle Church and his funeral sermon, based upon 1 Thessalonians 4:13-14, was delivered with difficulty by Bugenhagen. Melanchthon then delivered a eulogy in which he both praised Luther and acknowledged his flaws and need for Christ and the pure doctrine centered in justification by grace through faith.

Later that year, 1546, Katherine had to flee from Wittenberg to Magdeburg because of the Smalcaldic Wars, returning only for a brief time in 1547. Her property was ransacked after a brief but bloody battle between the Smalcaldic League and the imperial forces. On March 1, 1547, Charles V took control of Wittenberg and a few months later, John Frederick was taken prisoner and surrendered most of his lands to the Emperor. In 1552, a plague again hit Wittenberg and most of the inhabitants, including the university students, fled to Torgau. En route to Torgau, Katherine experienced a debilitating fall from which she never recovered. She died in Torgau on December 20th, 1552, and was buried at St Mary's Church there.

---

[4] He summarized his position, "He who wants to hear God speak should read Holy Scripture. He who wants to hear the devil speak should read the pope's decretals and bulls" LW 41:332.

After Luther

After an imperial meeting was held in Augsburg in 1548, an official statement, *The Augsburg Interim*, offered several concessions to the new Evangelicals—clergy could marry and laity could receive both bread and wine in communion—however, the Evangelical Lutherans were required to accept most of the traditional Catholic teachings, including the seven sacraments. While Melanchthon's irenic spirit saw this as a beneficial solution, most of the Lutheran theologians and princes rejected this "compromise." An alternate position was drawn up the following year and was known as the *Leipzig Interim*. This time, the Catholic position was compromised; Lutherans could retain their teaching on justification by grace through faith because of Christ, but were required to give up some of their less central practices. Those who supported this Leipzig Interim became known as "Philippists," followers of Philip Melanchthon, while those who opposed it were known as "Gnesio-Lutherans" (Greek, "genuine").

From the fall of 1553 through most of 1554, Martin Chemnitz again was in Wittenberg, teaching philosophy and serving as an assistant to Melanchthon. He began to study theology on his own and was ordained by Bugenhagen as a Lutheran pastor in 1554, being recognized for his theological acumen. Shortly after the Council of Trent was concluded (see the third section of this chapter), Chemnitz prepared a four-volume critique of those proceedings, showing carefully and critically the biblical basis for Lutheran positions.

Also in 1554, Luther's student, Mikael Agricola (1510-1557), was named Bishop of Turku, Finland, but his influence on Finnish Lutheranism had already begun with his preparation of a basic catechism in 1543. Agricola published prayer books, liturgical books, and a New Testament in Finnish a few years later. Work on the Finnish New Testament, *Se Wsi Testamenti* (see illustration of the cover page), had taken his team of scholars a little more than a decade to complete. Respected by the Swedish King, Gustav I (1496-1560, ruled 1523-1560), he was sent on several diplomatic missions to Sweden and Russia. It was on such a trip to Russia that he fell ill and died in 1557. Besides being instrumental in bringing Lutheranism to Finland, he is considered the founder of Finnish literature because of his prolific translation work.

Finally, a lasting political and theological peace was worked out in 1555 in the city of Augsburg. Emperor Charles granted to all princes the right to determine the religion of their own region—Catholic princes would enforce Catholicism and Lutheran princes could establish Lutheran lands. The principle, "whose rule, his religion" (Latin, *cuius regio, eius religio*), was thereby introduced. The *Peace of Augsburg*, as it became known, also promised that religious issues would no longer be grounds for political battles.

On April 19, 1560, Philip Melanchthon died. His legacy as a teacher of Germany remained for centuries. His death marked the end of the first generation of Wittenberg reformers.

Reforming Lutheranism in the Latter Half the Century

Over the next half-century, controversies between Lutherans erupted, particularly over issues of understanding what the key distinctions were in Lutheran doctrine and practice. Most of these issues were faithfully resolved and carefully articulated in the *Formula of Concord* in 1577.

The Synergistic Controversy

One of the earliest and longest lasting issues had to do with the place of the human will in regards to salvation. Melanchthon had taught that there were three cooperating powers at work—God's Word, the Holy Spirit, and the human will which did not resist God's approach. The Gnesio-Lutherans opposed this synergistic view, stating that humans are never capable of "working with" (synergism) God for their salvation.

The Antinomian Controversy

As mentioned earlier in this section, Melanchthon and John Agricola had already demonstrated different views of the place of the Law in the Christian life—Luther's own *Against the Antinomians* explained the need for both Law and Gospel in the life of Christians. After Luther's death, the issue was again raised by some who said that the Law even as a guide for Christians was unnecessary, while some of Melanchthon's students argued that the Gospel included preaching of repentance (thus, confusing Law and Gospel). The issue was finally resolved in saying that both the Law and the Gospel were scriptural and that both were part of the necessary proclamation of God's Word.

The Crypto-Calvinist Controversy

A similar situation arose over Melanchthon's understanding of the real presence in the Lord's Supper. Some of his students adopted a moderate Zwinglian interpretation, which became known as a Crypto-Calvinistic ("secret" or "hidden" Calvinist) view. In trying to become attractive to various other Protestant groups, the Lutheran clarity of Christ's real presence was lost by saying Christ was present "spiritually," but not "bodily." Relying upon an early Christian clarification of Christ's two natures, the Lutheran position was that Christ's ascended body could also be present in the sacramental elements because of His shared divine-human natures.

The Adiaphoristic Controversy

The church historian and biblical theologian, Matthias Flacius Illyricus (1520-1575), raised a concern regarding those practices or ceremonies which were neither commanded nor condemned in Scripture (called *adiaphora*). Melanchthon had argued that such "Catholic" practices should be tolerated, since they brought peace. Flacius insisted along with the Gnesio-Lutherans that when such practices were forced upon people, they were no longer *adiaphora* and must be rejected.

His view was more in line with Scripture and therefore was accepted. Flacius (see illustration) authored a history of Christianity entitled *The Magdeburg Centuries* in which he detailed century by century the distortions introduced to Christianity and tolerated by the Roman Church.

The Flacian Controversy
 Flacius was not exempt from error. Using philosophy, rather than Scripture, he argued that human nature after the Fall into sin had become the very substance of sin. The problem with that idea was two-fold. First, God would have created sin and, second, Jesus would have been sinful. After some strong and heated debates, the Lutheran theologians agreed to keep the two concepts separate—human nature and sin—pointing out that sin had indeed so corrupted human nature that only Jesus, the perfect Son of God and son of man, could redeem humanity.

The Osiandrian Controversy
 A German Lutheran mystic, Andreas Osiander (1498-1552), drew attention among some of the theologians at the time as he tried to redefine justification as a process of sanctification (that is, one gradually becomes holy through an infusion of Christ's righteousness as Christ dwelled in a person). Although seemingly an attractive idea, Lutherans from various perspectives all opposed him, saying that the two doctrines needed to be carefully distinguished. Justification was not a process, but a forensic (a judicial declaration), instantaneous act of God, whereby Christ's perfect righteousness is imputed (placed upon) the believer. To his credit, Osiander prepared a preface in 1543 for Copernicus's *Concerning the Revolution of the Heavenly Orbs*, which kept that book out of the Roman Catholic *Index of Forbidden Books* for the rest of the century.

The Majoristic Controversy
 Another leader of the Gnesio-Lutherans, Nicholas von Amsdorf (1483-1565), had overstated his understanding of the Lutheran position on the place of good works against another theologian, George Major (1502-1574). Major, after whom the controversy was named, taught that good works were absolutely necessary for salvation, but Amsdorf made the outlandish case that works were detrimental to salvation. Flacius stepped into the fray, pointing out the biblical position that good works are the fruit of faith. The focus should be on the root of the Gospel and the fruit would naturally follow.

A Plan for Concord
 Around the mid-1560s, Jakob Andreae (1528-1590) from Swabia in southwestern Germany prepared a conciliatory document pointing out the various

controverted issues and possible solutions, which he had learned in part from his teacher, Johann Brenz (1499-1570). Since the early years of the Reformation, Brenz had spent considerable effort to meet with Calvinists over controversial issues. Martin Chemnitz encouraged Andreae to publish his conclusions, which he prepared in a series of sermons in 1573. Shortly thereafter, a professor from the University of Rostock in northern Germany, David Chytraeus (1530-1600), revised Andreae's document with the guidance of Chemnitz and prepared the *Swabian-Saxon Concord* in 1575. The following year, a colloquy was called by Elector Augustus I (1553-1586) of Saxony and Württemberg in the town of Maulbronn to resolve a Calvinistic view of the Lord's Supper being taught in Wittenberg. The resulting document was known as the *Maulbronn Formula*.

The documents from Maulbronn along with the *Swabian-Saxon Concord* were revised by Andreae, Chemnitz, Chytraeus, and others in 1576 in the town of Torgau and became known as the *Torgau Book*. It was accepted as the *Bergen Book* and became the expanded version of the *Formula of Concord*, called either the *Solid* or *Thorough Declaration*. A summary had been adapted from Andreae's work as a short extract or *Epitome* for the *Formula of Concord*.

Finally, in 1580, at the fiftieth anniversary of the reading of the Augsburg Confession, the Lutheran doctrinal statements were gathered together into the *Book of Concord* (see illustration). Over eight thousand pastors and fifty political leaders attached their names to the work as a distinct witness to the Lutheran tradition.

Two years later, Johann Gerhard (1582-1637), one of the most influential Lutheran theologians of the next century, was born in Quedlinburg, Germany. After a critical illness as a youth, he found great comfort from his pastor, Johann Arndt (1555-1621). Shortly thereafter, in 1599, he entered the University of Wittenberg to study theology. We will investigate these two men in greater detail in the next chapter.

For the last quarter century, Catholic presence remained weak in German lands, although Jesuit activities gradually led to the physical hostilities in the next century. For Protestants, advances in southern Germany were more in favor of Calvinism, especially as the Lutherans experienced their inner doctrinal conflicts. Secular authorities had followed many of the Protestant teachings, although Catholic prelates continued to dominate the German Reichstag (parliament). As the century ended, unrest seemed to be about to boil over into public displays of hostilities.

For Review and Discussion
1. How did Luther's early years prepare him for his call for reform?

2. What was significant about each of Luther's three major writings in 1520?
3. Describe Luther as a biblical theologian.
4. Why was Luther's involvement limited, yet active during the Diet of Augsburg?
5. How did Lutherans manage their theological differences after Luther's death?

For Further Reading:

Bainton, Roland H. *Here I Stand: A Life of Martin Luther.* New York: Abingdon-Cokesbury Press, 1950.

Booth, Edwin P. *Martin Luther: The Great Reformer.* Philadelphia: Chelsea House, 1999.

Brecht, Martin. *Martin Luther: His Road to Reformation 1483-1521. Martin Luther: Shaping and Defining the Reformation 1521-1532. Martin Luther: The Preservation of the Church 1532-1546.* Translated by James L. Schaaf. Minneapolis: Fortress Press, 1985, 1990, 1993.

Chemnitz, Martin. *Loci Theologici.* Two volumes. J. A. O. Preus, trans. St. Louis: Concordia Publishing House, 1989.

Chemnitz, Martin. *The Two Natures in Christ.* J. A. O. Preus, trans. St. Louis: Concordia Publishing House, 1971.

Froude, J. A. *Life and Letters of Erasmus.* New York: Charles Scribner's Sons, 1912.

Grimm, Harold H. *The Reformation Era: 1500-1650.* Second edition. New York: Macmillan Publishing, 1973.

Kittelson, James M. *Luther: the Reformer.* Minneapolis: Augsburg Publishing Houlse, 1986.

Kolb, Robert. *Martin Luther As Prophet, Teacher, Hero.* Grand Rapids, MI: Baker Books, 1999.

Lull, Timothy and William R. Russel, eds. *Luther's Basic Theological Works.* Minneapolis: Fortress Press, 2012.

Luther, Martin. *The Table Talk of Martin Luther.* New York: World Publication, 1952.

Maschke, Timothy, Franz Posset, and Joan Skocir, eds. *Ad fontes Lutheri: Toward the Recovery of the Real Luther.* Milwaukee: Marquette University Press, 2001.

Oberman, Heiko A. *Luther: Man Between God and the Devil.* New York: Image Book/Yale University, 1989.

Schwiebert, E. G. *Luther and His times: The Reformation from a New Perspective.* St Louis: Concordia Publishing House, 1950.

Spitz, Lewis W., ed. *The Reformation: Basic Interpretations.* Lexington, MA: D. C. Heath and Company, 1972.

Stjerna, Kirsi. *Women and the Reformation.* Malden, MA: Blackwell Publishing, 2009.

Taylor, Henry Osborn. *Erasmus and Luther.* New York: Collier Books, 1962.

16 C. The Protestant, Catholic, and Radical Reformations

The Sixteenth Century: Part 3

Luther and his colleagues in Wittenberg were not the only ones working on reforming the church. Voices had been raised both within the Roman Catholic Church and outside of it for over a century. In this section of chapter 16, we will look at the several reformations which were occurring simultaneously among European Christians. Three particular areas will be presented—the Protestant reformers, the Radical reformers, and the Roman Catholic reformers.

John Calvin

John Calvin (1509-1564, baptized "Jehan Cauvin"), probably the most outstanding systematician of the Protestant cause, was trained as a humanist  lawyer at various French universities. As a result, his understanding of Christianity sought to organize his biblical ideas, particularly about God's sovereign will, as well as ecclesiastical practices, into clear categories. After a conversion experience of some kind, he left the University of Paris in 1534 when he became aware that his evangelical views were unacceptable in that environment. Moving to Basel, he became acquainted with the reformer, Johannes Oecolampadius (1482-1531). Around that same time he began to prepare his theological masterpiece, *The Institutes of the Christian Religion*, published in 1536, a work which increased in size with each edition.

On a journey to Strassburg, Calvin was sidetracked through the Swiss city of Geneva, which had recently been emancipated from France. There he met William (Guillaume) Farel (1489-1565), a local reformer, who had read Calvin's work and effectively demanded his help to establish the reformation in that city. Because of his legal training, Calvin proposed a legislated reformation there, emphasizing the need for true believers to demonstrate their faith or be excommunicated. This disciplined approach, while well-intended, was not accepted by the citizens of Geneva and he and Farel were banished in 1538.

Fleeing to Strassburg, Calvin spent time with Martin Bucer (1491-1551) and developed his organizational skills there.

In 1541 under a new theocratic-type city government, Calvin and Farel were invited back to Geneva. In this same year, a French version of *The Institutes* was published. Unfortunately, Calvin inaugurated even stricter rules of a Zwinglian nature—obligatory church attendance, elimination of any ostentation in formal attire and social activities, but retaining some simple music for worship. Over the next years, Calvin continued his preaching and writing, although experiencing conflict with various leaders in the city, particularly over the power to excommunicate.

An exemplary event demonstrating Calvin's principles in Geneva centered upon a gifted Spanish physician and amateur theologian, Michael Servetus (1509-1553). In 1531, Servetus, trained as a Dominican friar, wrote a tract, *Errors of the Trinity*. Subsequently, he criticized Calvin for believing Jesus was the eternal Son of God. Insolent and contentious, Servetus argued that Jesus was only a son of the eternal God. He also held pantheistic views, which several Roman Catholic inquisitors had verified. As a result, he fled to Geneva where he publicly denounced Calvin as an imposter. The Genevan Council swiftly tried him for his anti-Trinitarian teaching and denunciation of Calvin. He was burned at the stake shortly thereafter.

Calvin was a prolific writer and a very powerful preacher. He wrote commentaries on most of the biblical books and corresponded with Melanchthon and political and religious leaders throughout Europe. His *Commentary on Romans* (1540) became a model for many later commentaries, with its original Latin translation and expository style. (See sidebar) For several years until he was

> Calvin's Bible Commentaries
> Harold Grimm, *The Reformation Era*, notes: "His mastery of philology, his knowledge of the history of the Church, his practical and logical approach, and his direct, grammatical interpretation of each Scripture passage help explain the wide use of his commentaries and his reputation as one of the outstanding theologians of his day."

near exhaustion, he preached every day and twice on Sundays. Around the mid-1540s, Calvin published the *Geneva Catechism* in French and Latin, which set forth the basic tenets of the Reformed faith. He limited congregational worship practices by forbidding polyphonic song and instrumental music, stating that polyphony was detracting from the words and instrumental music was an Old Testament practice which should not be continued.

During the last years of his life, Calvin approached the English reformer, Thomas Cranmer (1489-1556), but no final ecumenical agreement was achieved. He established a school for children as well as an Academy for more advanced study, engaging Theodore Beza (1519-1605) as rector. Becoming ill with a fever in late in 1558, Calvin worked with greater fervor on his final edition of *The Institutes*, which had grown from the original six chapters to 80 chapters, about five times the original version. After suffering from a voice-lung condition, he died on May 27, 1564. Thousands of followers flocked to view his mortal remains, so that he was buried shortly thereafter in an unmarked grave.

Calvinism

Without Beza, Calvin's legacy would not have been as strong or enduring. Born and trained as a lawyer in France, Beza practiced law for several years in Paris until a "conversion experience" led him to seek out Calvin in Geneva in 1548. After almost a decade of spreading Calvin's reformation in several parts of Europe, especially among the French Huguenots (a name of uncertain origin for the French Protestants), Beza returned to Geneva in 1559 and upon Calvin's death assumed his pastorate there. Although he was in conversation with some Lutherans, including Jakob Andreae (1528-1590), no amicable doctrinal accord could be agreed upon. Even more than Calvin, Beza emphasized obedience to divine will, ecclesiastical discipline, and a stronger view of predestination than Calvin (he is sometimes referred to as a "hyper-Calvinist"). Besides his biblical commentaries and translations, as a Greek scholar, he donated an early 5th century manuscript (D, *Codex Bezae*) to the University of Oxford.

As a result of these reformers in France, Protestantism had a viable, although never easy existence. Under Francis I, the Huguenots experienced some toleration (1529-1533), then suppression (1533-1534), then again toleration (1535) and again repression (1540-1546). The first national meeting of French Protestants met in Paris in 1559, adopting a statement of faith which had been adapted from Calvin's *Gallican Confession*, modified in 1571, and remains an official statement of the Reformed Church of France.

Particularly pertinent was the political struggles between Catholics and Huguenots, known as the Wars of Religion, beginning in 1562, but continuing well into the seventeenth century. Most notable was the extremely bloody St. Bartholomew's Day Massacre of 1572, when Huguenot supporters of Henri de Navarre (1553-1610), who had married the Catholic, Margaret de Valois (1553-1615), were attacked by her Catholic supporters in Paris, supposedly by orders of the boy-king Charles IX (1550-1574, ruled 1560-1574). The initial slaughter spread out from Paris into the countryside, so that after several months of hostilities an estimated 10-20,000 citizens, mostly Huguenots, died. (See the illustration on next page by François Dubois depicting the massacre.) After that tragic event, Henri de Navarre was released and ascended the French throne as Henry IV (ruled 1589-1610). For political reasons, he converted back to Catholicism in 1593, but five years later, in 1598, he issued the Edict of Nantes, granting French Protestants the right to be an independent church, distinct from the Catholic majority.

One of Theodore Beza's most distinguished students was Jacob Arminius (1560-1609). Orphaned as a young teen, Arminius (his Dutch name was Hermanszoon) was given an opportunity to study at the University of Leiden, where he would become a famous instructor. He learned to be critical of some of Calvin's teachings, but when went to Geneva to study under Beza he almost immediately disagreed with him. In the late 1580s he began a fifteen year pastorate in Amsterdam, where his sermons on Romans raised questions about the orthodoxy of some of his views. We will look at the controversies surrounding Arminius's teachings in chapter 17.

Calvin's teachings began to spread quickly. Most significantly, John Knox (1514-1572), born near Edinburgh, Scotland, converted from Catholicism to Protestantism over a period of years. Influenced by significant reforming preachers in the early 1540s, he was released from a brief imprisonment and travelled to England, where he met Thomas Cranmer. With the regency of the Catholic Queen Mary (1516-1558, ruled 1553-1558) in 1553, he fled to Europe and came in contact with John Calvin. Returning to Scotland in 1559, he remained there, advocating the evangelical faith of Calvin. In 1560, he issued the *First Book of Discipline*, establishing an austere form of Calvinism and a presbyterian form of church governance (presbyter, Greek, "elder."). He was the most famous of the Scottish Reformers and his legacy is in the present-day Presbyterian churches.

Ulrich Zwingli

Ulrich Zwingli (1484-1531) or Huldrychus Zwinglius as he preferred to be called, younger and more revolutionary than Calvin, had read Luther, but insisted that his own reformation ideas came independently through his careful reading of Scripture.

For Zwingli only a radical shift in one's life and a re-interpretation of Scripture which removed the "Catholic" substance of the faith were acceptable. Trained as a humanist prior to his ordination in 1506, his study of Scripture led him to reject papal authority, along with monasticism, purgatory, and many other practices associated with his Catholic upbringing. After serving for a decade as a parish priest in the Swiss town of Glarus, and around the same time as Luther's *Ninety-five Theses* were publicized, Zwingli declared that papal authority was only of human origin. Then in early 1519 he moved to Zurich where he denounced indulgences and monastic vows from the pulpit. That date is often given for the beginning of the Swiss Reformation. A few years later, he defied his local bishop and began to live in a common-law relationship with a wealthy widow, whom he married two years later.

In the meantime, Zwingli assured the Zurich city council that they had the authority to decide doctrine. He presented them with *Sixty-Seven Articles* (1523), which clearly explained the biblical teachings of salvation by grace alone through faith in Christ. He described the true church as those who had faith in Christ, not merely holding membership in the ecclesiastical organization of the Roman Catholic Church. With the council's support, he proceeded with a more radical reformation the following year, particularly in the area of worship—removing all art work and statues, forbidding all music, and eliminating church festivals from congregational calendars. He found himself in conflict both with his Catholic bishop, Hugo von Hohenlandenberg, Bishop of Constance (1452-1532), who had jurisdiction over Zurich, and with the more extreme Anabaptists, led by Conrad Grebel (1498-1526).

Huldricus Zwingli, Theol. Tigurinus

His views of the sacraments echoed Luther's evaluation in his *Babylonian Captivity of the Church* (1520), but went further to deny the presence of Christ in the Lord's Supper. Zwingli's ideas on infant baptism differed from Luther's too, in that Zwingli thought baptism was unnecessary, since he believed infants were not born sinful. Encouraged by Carlstadt's pamphlets on the Lord's Supper, published in Basel, Zwingli published his interpretation that "is" in the *Verba* meant "signifies." His headstrong views led to a showdown between him and Luther in 1529 at the Marburg Colloquy. (See chapter 16 B). Submitting a twelve-article private confession a year later to the Diet of Augsburg, known as the *Fidei ratio*, Zwingli voiced his strong anti-Catholic as well as anti-Lutheran views.

Zwingli's reformation in Zurich relied on the civil government's strong support. (Unlike Luther, he did not have an elector to support his efforts and had to rely on local entities.) As a result, Zwingli tried to force his ideas on other Swiss cantons (counties). This political dimension led to military confrontations between the Catholic "five cantons" and a confederation of Zwinglian cantons. After an attempted embargo on food for the Catholic cantons, Zwingli himself, serving as an armed military chaplain, went into battle at Kappel, about thirty miles west of Zurich, where he was killed on October 11, 1531. This civil war ended in a stalemate, although the Catholic cantons claimed victory. Switzerland would remain a split nation—half Catholic and half Protestant.

Zwingli's successor, Heinrich Bullinger (1504-1575), was of a more irenic spirit and was able to unite with Calvin's followers for a strong Reformed theological stance toward the end of the 1540s, the *Consensus Trigurinus*. In 1561, he prepared the *Second Helvetic Confession*, which became one of the key doctrinal statements for Reformed churches throughout Europe, along with the *Heidelberg Catechism* (1563).

Anabaptists

Another Protestant group, known as the "radical" reformers, are worthy of mention. They were called radical, not because of their politically violent or disrupting behavior, although some did act that way. The label "radical" comes from the Latin word for "root," *radix*, and recalls that these reformers felt that Luther and the other reformers had not gone far enough to root out all Catholic contaminations of Christianity, nor had they returned to the taproots of the New Testament faith. These leaders insisted that the root of the problem was interior and that only a total separation from the Catholic past was acceptable.

The origin of this movement is clearly drawn from a literalistic biblical perspective. This approach led these reformers to reject all but God's authority, even governmental authority. Conrad Grebel had been a strong supporter of Zwingli until the mid-1520s. At that time, Grebel communicated with Carlstadt and Luther. Carlstadt had even visited him in Zurich. One doctrine which Grebel and his small band of supporters, known as the Swiss Brethren, found unacceptable was the teaching of Christ's real presence in the Lord's Supper. They went further theologically after conversations with rebellious leader, Thomas Müntzer (1489-1525). Based upon a reading of Jesus' Sermon on the Mount (esp. Matthew 5:34-37), they rejected all oaths. Similarly, they understood baptism to be only for persons who could confess with their mouths (Romans 10) and insisted that those baptized as infants needed to be baptized again. A year after Grebel's unexpected death after a brief imprisonment, another leader, Michael Stattler (1495-1527), prepared the first confessional statement for the Swiss Brethren at Schleitheim. Stattler was executed in a most gruesome manner for his Anabaptist views in May 1527, but his *Schleitheim Confession* remained a key document for Anabaptists.

Re-baptism (Greek, ἀνά- [*ana-*] "re-" + βαπτισμός, [*baptizmos*] "baptism") became a hallmark practice for these reformers. For example in 1534, a very militant group of Anabaptists took control of the city of Münster, expelling all who refused to be baptized again. They then set up a communal-styled organization modelled after the first chapters of Acts and went so far as to allow the Old Testament idea of polygamy. Shortly thereafter, both Catholic and Protestant forces united to regain control of the city, but at the cost of slaughtering many Anabaptist inhabitants.

In the early 1530s, Menno Simons (1496-1561) (see illustration), a Roman Catholic priest in the Netherlands, heard about a person being beheaded for being re-baptized. After a period of biblical research, he rejected infant baptism himself and sometime later was re-baptized. His theological studies led him to see the church as a separated group of believers and his Dutch Anabaptist followers became known as Mennonites.

Two other radical reformers should be mentioned. Sebastian Franck (1499-1543) rejected all forms of organized church. He espoused a strong humanist tendency with an equally vivid mysticism.

Although ordained a priest, he soon left the priesthood and married. Influenced by Luther and then by the Anabaptists, he was intrigued by the more spiritual reformers and finally settled on "inner experience" as the foundation for one's faith.

Kaspar Schwenkfeld (1489-1560), a Silesian nobleman, was initially attracted to Luther's reformation rhetoric, too. However, he followed Carlstadt and Müntzer more closely, and soon became a popular preacher under their influence. During the Sacramentarian Controversy, he parted company both with Zwingli and Luther, proposing a "heavenly flesh" idea, which resulted in a weakened Christology. Although closely associated with Anabaptists, his followers, who were exiled from Silesia, formed a new denomination named after him.

The Anglican Reformation

Unusual was the reform that occurred in England, since it had much more of a political than a theological basis. Reformation, and particularly Lutheran, ideas had come to England early in the 1520s.

When Henry VIII wrote a book against Luther's view of the Lord's Supper, Pope Leo X (1475-1521, pope 1513-1521) awarded him the title, "Defender of the Faith." By the end of that decade, Henry had also rejected papal authority and, partially because of his desire to marry a second wife, declared himself head of the English church.

In 1532, Thomas Cranmer was named Archbishop of Canterbury and two years later Parliament passed the "Act of Supremacy," whereby all English citizens had to acknowledge Henry as head of the Church of England. Thomas More (1478-1535), longtime humanist statesman, social philosopher, and councilor to Henry, was subsequently beheaded when he refused to back Henry's "reformation" in defiance of papal authority. After a three-year hiatus of the Parliament, Henry called for a committee to decide on doctrinal issues in light of a visit by several Lutheran theologians. The result was Parliament's passing *The Six Articles* in 1539, which affirmed the Catholic teachings on transubstantiation, clerical celibacy and vows of chastity, private masses, auricular confessions, and withholding the communion chalice from the laity.

For the next ten years, a slow development of a protestantized Catholicism emerged. Monasteries and other church properties were turned over to the English crown. Thomas Cromwell (1485-1540), Henry's faithful political advisor was executed by beheading, presumably for his failure to support the *Six Articles* and his perceived support of several "Lutheran" heretics. Cromwell had encouraged Bible reading in 1536, but Henry changed that law in 1543, limiting Bible reading only to the nobles. Around the middle of 1540, Henry had his marriage to Anne of Cleve (1515-1557) annulled in order to marry Catherine

Howard (c.1521-1542), whom he beheaded a few years later. As noted in chapter 16 B, he also had Robert Barnes (c.1495-1540) burned at the stake.

Upon Henry's death in 1547, his nine-year-old son, Edward VI (1537-1553, ruled 1547-1553), exhibited a stronger Protestant attitude and promoted reform from a Calvinist orientation. A Reformed iconoclasm soon spread through much of the English countryside. A real reformation was in the air. In 1549, the first *Book of Common Prayer* was released, but was not widely accepted. Within three years a revised version was issued which completely eliminated any "Catholic ideas," especially that of the sacrifice of the Mass. The "black rubric" in the *Book of Common Prayer* remained, which directed people to kneel for communion, in order to provide an orderly distribution of the sacrament, yet many considered it overtly Roman. It was removed in the 1559 edition.

Edward's reign was short-lived. When Henry's only surviving daughter by Catherine of Aragon, Mary Tudor (1516-1558), came to the throne, her Catholic proclivity returned much of England temporarily to the Catholic fold (ruled 1553-1558). Besides having Cranmer burned at the stake, many other leaders with Protestant allegiances left England for Europe. After 1555, the so-called "Marian persecutions" broke out and almost 300 Protestants were executed, giving Queen Mary I the well-known moniker of "Bloody Mary." Although she thought she was pregnant with her successor, she died during a severe influenza outbreak, with her younger half-sister, Elizabeth, assuming the throne.

Upon her accession to the throne in 1558, Queen Elizabeth I (1533-1603) (see illustration) provided a restored structure to the church under the queen's governance and mediating position. Two acts of Parliament re-established the church's independence from Rome and restored Edward's *Book of Common Prayer*. In 1563, the *Thirty-Nine Articles,* an adaptation of Thomas Cranmer's *Ten Articles* (1536), were published, delineating doctrines which were distinct from the Roman Church, as well as from the radical reformers, as a kind of middle way—a stance which remains to the present in the Anglican communion. Denying Roman Catholic transubstantiation and Zwinglian symbolism, Anglicans remained open to a range of interpretations regarding Christ's presence in the Lord's Supper between Luther and Calvin. That same year John Foxe's (1516-1587) *Christian Martyrs of the World* came to print, which gave vividly detailed accounts of the Protestant executions under Mary as well as many that had occurred during the early Christian persecutions.

While the English reformation was "complete," there remained those who felt the reformation had not gone far enough. This group became known as Puritans, for their desire to have a "pure" and completely restored church free from anything "Catholic," such as vestments and liturgy. We will see more of this movement in the next chapters.

The Counter- or Catholic Reformation

The Reformation among Roman Catholics took on a very different shape, particularly as a result of the great upheaval caused by the various other reformations during this century. Even before Luther, several voices of reform had been heard. In the previous chapter, we read about the Italian reformer, Savonarola (1452-1498). In Spain, Ximenes de Cisneros (1436-1517), supported by Ferdinand and Isabella, sought reform of his Franciscan order and, as cardinal, encouraged a higher spiritual life both among all the clergy and laity alike. Ximenes was both a biblical scholar (recall his *Complutensian Polyglot* in chapter 16 A) in Hebrew, Latin, and Greek, and an ecclesiastical-statesman, using the Inquisition to "convert" Jews and Muslims. Most noteworthy is the work of Jacques Lefevre d'Etaples (1455-1536), Latinized as Faber Stapulensis. As a French biblical humanist, he sought to reform the church from within although he had sympathies for several reformers, including one of his students, William Farel. His work on the Psalter and Paul's epistles are credited with having some influence on Luther's own understanding of justification by grace through faith alone.

The same year Luther was appointed professor of Scripture in Wittenberg, the Roman Church held the Fifth Lateran Council (1512-1517). Designed to deal with several disciplinary issues as well as to plan a crusade against the Turks, it did little in the way of reforming the church. Five years later, after Luther posted his theses, Pope Leo X outlined in his bull, *Cum Postquam*, the church's theological argument for the sale of indulgences.

The Society of Jesus

Reform was possible through other means. In 1534, Ignatius Loyola (1491-1556) (see chapter 16 B), a Spanish soldier who had been severely wounded in France, founded the Society of Jesus, known more commonly as the Jesuits. A military-styled spirituality was devised by Ignatius in his *Spiritual Exercises*, which required a fourteen-week cycle of meditations on one's sin, then on Christ and His passion, and finally on Christ's resurrection. As a newly recognized order, they were directly responsible to the papacy, offering him total and blind obedience. (See sidebar) Focusing upon higher education and global missions, the members of this order did much to reclaim Europe from Protestant reforms. Francis Xavier (1506-1552), cofounder of the order, began to do missionary work under Portuguese sovereignty in India in 1542. Traveling further east to other Portuguese colonies, he arrived in Japan during the summer of 1549.

TO HAVE THE TRUE SENTIMENT WHICH WE OUGHT TO HAVE IN THE CHURCH MILITANT

Let the following Rules be observed: **Thirteenth Rule**. To be right in everything, we ought always to hold that the white which I see, is black, if the hierarchical Church so decides it, believing that between Christ our Lord, the Bridegroom, and the Church, His Bride, there is the same Spirit which governs and directs us for the salvation of our souls. Because by the same Spirit and our Lord Who gave the Ten Commandments, our holy Mother the Church is directed and govern.

From *The Spiritual Exercises*

Working hard to learn the Japanese language and culture, his efforts were met initially with very little success. He died in December of 1552 just before a planned journey to mainland China, where Matteo Ricci (1552-1610) and Michele Ruggieri (1543-1602) carried out mission work thirty years later (See chapter 16 A).

New Monastic Orders

Besides the Jesuits and the attempted reforms among some of the major orders, such as the Dominicans and Luther's Augustinian Hermits, over a half-dozen new orders were given papal approval during this century.

The Theatines

The Theatines (1524) or the Congregation of the Clerks Regular of the Divine Providence was founded by Cajetan of Tiene (1480-1547) to combat Lutheran influences in Italy through preaching, along with the reorganized and strengthened Inquisition. The order emphasized prayer and established the famous Oratory of Divine Love as well as several hospitals and mission sites in the next century.

The Capuchins

The Capuchins (1528), a strict order of Franciscan friars, first arose in the early 1520s as a reform of the more lax order of Franciscans. After being given refuge by a group of monks in central Italian mountains, they adopted the hood (Italian, *cappuccio*) worn by those hermits as a mark of their order.

The Clerics Regular of Saint Paul

The Barnabites (1530) or the Clerics Regular of Saint Paul were founded in Milan by three nobles in protest of the moral laxity in the church. The popular name was derived from their first church, St Barnabas.

The Carmelites

Teresa of Ávila (1515-1582) entered the Carmelite Convent of the Incarnation in 1535, where she suffered from a variety of ailments. During those episodes, she developed her mystical discipline, beginning with "mental prayer," which she claimed provided direct access to visions of God. (See detail from 18th century depiction by François Gérard.) Among her writings, *The Way of Perfection* and *Interior Castle,* have remained popular devotional materials for Catholic spirituality. Influenced by both Dominicans and Jesuits, she formed a new reformed order, Discalced Carmelites, initially for nuns, but expanded to include men, most notably her co-founder, St John of the Cross (1542-1591), who wrote of "the dark night of the soul."

The Ursulines

The Ursulines (1546) were officially recognized by the papacy as the first teaching order for women, after Angela Merici (1474-1540) organized a mission to educate young girls in central Italy. These communities all had reform of the church in mind and heart.

The Papacy and the Council of Trent

The variety of proposed solutions to the recognized need for reform was part of the problem for the Roman Catholic Church. As noted, several of the religious orders saw the need as being purely spiritual. The more vocal humanist theologians desired a more Erasmian approach by instilling pious practices, while those of the scholastic tradition wanted a revival of Aristotelian philosophy in the schools. Others considered the Renaissance emphasis on human dignity as requiring greater recognition. While still others rejected any reform, since their political and social status was dependent upon ignoring the corruption among the clergy at the highest level. Few recognized that the root of the problem was theological.

Although the papacy suffered from extremely immoral leadership during these years, there were several popes who sought to make changes in the church. Unlike the Borgian popes, Alexander VI (1431-1503, pope 1492-1503), and his two main successors, Julius II (1443-1513, pope 1503-1513) and Leo X (1475-1521, pope 1513-1521), Pope Hadrian VI (1459-1523, pope 1522-1523) tried unsuccessfully to reform the Curia in Rome, where he died under suspicious circumstances after only a year-long pontificate. His successor, Clement VII (1478-1534, pope 1523-1534) was well intentioned, but found the political dimensions dominating his papal agenda, especially when Rome was sacked and he was imprisoned by the Emperor. Pope Paul III (1468-1549, pope 1534-1549), who had fathered several illegitimate children early in life, was presented with a document, *On Emending the Church,* by a group of reform-minded cardinals in 1537, a move which did not go unrecognized by many Protestant leaders. Although he realized the need for reform, his method was to revive an Inquisition-style suppression of Lutheran teachings, especially in Germany, under the enigmatic title of "the Holy Office" in 1542.

Emperor Charles V (1500-1558, ruled 1519-1556), who sacked Rome in 1527, and with whom Pope Paul III had maintained a weak alliance, did more to restore Catholic domination in southern Germany than did the papacy. His continuing conflicts with Francis I of France (1494-1547, ruled 1515-1547) in a series of Hapsburg-Valois wars included several battles with the Turks (1542-1543). Proposing a council in 1537, for which Luther wrote his *Smalcald Articles,* the pope finally succumbed to imperial pressure and opened an ecumenical meeting to deal with reform in 1545.

The Council of Trent (1545-1563) was one of the most significant general or ecumenical councils by the Roman Catholic Church, with its impact felt for centuries. Initiated by Emperor Charles V, it was called to resolve the theological issues which had had political ramifications in the Holy Roman Empire. Although ordered by the Emperor with the support of Pope Paul III, continued by Popes Julius III (1487-1555, pope 1550-1555) and Pius IV (1499-1565, pope 1559-1565), no pope ever attended in person.

The three assemblies, held between 1545-1549, 1551-1552, and 1562-1563, dealt with significant doctrinal as well as practical issues facing the Roman Catholic Church at this time. After procedural matters were addressed in the first three sessions, session four took up Scripture and tradition as being equally authoritative for the church and the Latin (*Vulgate*) translation as the only authorized text. The doctrines of original sin and the sacraments of the church were also clarified at that time. The key issue during this first assembly was the doctrine of justification. In six sessions, over a dozen decrees and 33 canons were approved by the council in clear and deliberate opposition to Lutheran teachings. While asserting that sinners are justified through Christ by grace and by faith (chapters 3, 7 and 8 of the Decree on Justification), such faith is only the beginning. Faith "cooperating with good works" (chapter 10) increases one's justification. As far as the Roman Catholic Church was concerned, the Lutheran "heresy" was forcefully and finally condemned (the Greek word, *anathema*, means "cursed" or "condemned to hell") as evident in several of the official canons of the Council. (See sidebar on the next page with canons 9 and 14.) The "chapters" of the decrees stated the Catholic doctrines in positive terms and the "canons" were formed in the negative. These canons of the Council have never been rescinded and are the official teaching of the Roman Church to the present time. (See illustration from a session.)

During the second assembly, under the scandalous pontificate of Julius III (1487-1555, pope 1550-1555), the Catholic sacraments of communion, penance, and last rites were discussed and over two dozen decrees and thirty canons approved, including a reaffirmation of the teaching of transubstantiation and the Mass as a sacrifice. In the meantime, the short-lived three-week pontificate of Marcellus II (1501-1555, pope 1555) was followed by the enthronement of Pope Paul IV (1499-1559, pope 1555-1559), who almost immediately declared as dogma the perpetual virginity of Mary, the mother of our Lord. He refused to assemble the Council, claiming he could do more personally as exemplified by his *Index of Forbidden Books* (1557). A revised version of the *Index* was promulgated by the next pope the same year that Michelangelo died (1564). The final assembly at Trent, called by Pius IV, formulated teachings on communion, marriage, veneration of saints, purgatory and indulgences.

How well the counter-reformation succeeded remains a subject of much discussion. Noteworthy is the fact that no major council was called for almost 400 years, until the 1960s with Vatican II (See chapter 20). Doctrinal issues were solidified in the publication of *The Roman Catechism* (1565) and the official liturgy for all Roman Catholics was established through the *Missale Romanum* as the Tridentine Mass (1570).

Decrees on Justification at the Council of Trent

Canon 9 - If anyone says that the sinner is justified by faith alone, meaning that nothing else is required to cooperate in order to obtain the grace of justification, and that it is not in any way necessary that he be prepared and disposed by the action of his own will, let him be anathema.

Canon 14 - If anyone says that man is absolved from his sins and justified because he firmly believes that he is absolved and justified, or that no one is truly justified except him who believes himself justified, and that by this faith alone absolution and justification are effected, let him be anathema.

Responses to Trent

One of the most significant responses to the council was produced by the Lutheran theologian, Martin Chemnitz (1522-1586), in his *Examination of the Council of Trent*. In this four-volume work, Chemnitz addressed the various decrees of the Council with biblical evidence to demonstrate the errors which remained.

On the other hand, the brilliant Roman Catholic theologian, Robert Bellarmine (1542-1621) did much to sustain the Tridentine teachings in the face of continuing Protestant growth. As a young man of eighteen, he joined the Jesuits and began to study at the Jesuit school in Rome, the Roman College. Invited to teach at the University of Louvain, he was ordained the following year, 1570. He was called back to the Roman College in 1576, where he taught and wrote. During that time, he produced his most significant work, *Disputations about the Controversies of the Christian Faith against the Heretics of this Time* (1586-1593). In this three-volume work, he meticulously set forth the established position of the Roman Church. Various administrative duties were conferred upon him toward the end of the century. Finally he was made a cardinal in 1599 and an archbishop in 1602. At the death of Pope Sixtus V (1521-1590, pope 1585-1590), Bellarmine's name was suggested as a possible successor, but he was considered too spiritual for the position.

Besides Bellarmine, another Catholic theologian should be mentioned (more in chapter 17). Francis de Sales (1567-1622) was born to be a leader. Of noble birth, he was educated to become a magistrate. After studying at a Jesuit school and wrestling with the then-popular doctrine of predestination, he went through various "conversion experiences," finally deciding to join a religious order. Although his father had arranged for him to take several political positions as well as a potential wife, Francis rejected them all. The Bishop of Geneva, living in exile from that city which was under Calvinist control, appointed Francis to a high office, from which he was deployed to try to bring many back to the Catholic Church. He is most remembered for his gentle, yet persistent reconversion of Swiss Calvinists and French Huguenots to Catholicism.

The sixteenth century was truly a century of reforms. The renaissance context gave much strength to individual voices and the printing press provided a greater vehicle for disseminating the ideas to the general populous. Although toward the end of the century, confessionalization began, the next century would bring greater clarity and also opportunity for doctrinal distinctions and gospel witnessing.

For Review and Discussion
1. How did Calvin's reform methods differ from that of Luther?
2. What doctrinal distinctions are particularly noteworthy in the teachings of Ulrich Zwingli?
3. Who were the Anabaptists and why were they so-named?
4. Why did Henry VIII break with Rome, yet not follow Luther's reforms?
5. Describe the reforming movements in the Roman Catholic Church which culminated in the Council of Trent?

For Further Reading
Ackroyd, Peter. *The Life of Thomas More.* New York: Doubleday, 1998.
Bainton, Roland H. *Studies on the Reformation.* Boston: Beacon Press, 1963.
Bireley, Robert. Refashioning of Catholicism, 1450-1700. New York: Palgrave Publishers, 1998.
Bossy, John. *Christianity in the West: 1400-1700.* New York: Oxford University Press, 1985.
Bouwsma, William, J. *John Calvin: A Sixteenth Century Portrait.* New York: Oxford University Press, 1988.
Calvin, John. *Institutes of the Christian Religion.* 2 volumes. Translated by Ford L. Battles. Louisville, KY: Westminster John Knox Press, 1960.
Carlson, Eric Josef, ed. *Religion and the English People: 1500-1640: New Voices New Perspectives.* Kirksville, MO: Thomas Jefferson University Press, 1998.
Chemnitz, Martin. *Examination of the Council of Trent.* 2 volumes. Translated by Fred Kramer. St Louis: Concordia Publishing House, 1971.

Foxe, John. *Fox's Book of Martyrs: A History of the Lives, Sufferings and Death of the Early Christian and Protestant Martyrs*. William Byron Forbush, ed. Grand Rapids: Zondervan Publishing House, 1967 reprint of 1923 edition.

Jones, Rufus M. *Spiritual Reformers in the 16th and 17th Centuries*. New York: The Macmillan Company, 1914.

McNally, Robert E. *The Council of Trent, the "Spiritual Exercises," and the Catholic Reform*. Philadelphia: Fortress Press, 1970.

McNeill, John T. *The History and Character of Calvinism*. New York: Oxford University Press, 1954.

Mullett, Michael. *The Catholic Reformation*. New York: Routledge Ltd, 1999.

Williams, George H. *The Radical Reformation*. 3rd edition. Kirksville, MO: Sixteenth Century Journal Publishers, 1992.

Wright, A. D. *The Counter-Reformation: Catholic Europe and the Non-Christian World*. New York: St. Martin's Press, 1982.

17. War, Orthodoxy and Piety

The Seventeenth Century

The seventeenth century began quietly, but such tranquility was more like "the calm before the storm." Political disputes and religious intolerance continued to smolder until they erupted in violent encounters. In the midst of these monumental disturbances appeared new expressions of the Christian faith and life as well as clarification of confessional positions and expansion of the faith into the New World. Already in 1607, the Jamestown Colony is founded in the "new world" as the first permanent European settlement. Along with these settlers came the Church of England to North American lands, joining the strong Spanish missions in the west. By the end of the century, much of the land in this continent was not only claimed by Europeans, but also became the site of significant missionary endeavors.

Confessionalization

A process of building denominational identity occurred during the early years of century between the Peace of Augsburg and the end of the Thirty Years War. Labelled "confessionalization," the approach solidified the positions of each of the major denominations at the end of the sixteenth century. The idea and ideal of a uniform and unified state church was envisioned, yet quickly evaporated in reality. Many Catholic princes suppressed expressions of Protestantism (whether Lutheran or Calvinist), while disputes between the various Protestant groups, as well as within them, resulted in little resistance to the political powers. For example, shortly after the turn of the century, the Catholic takeover of some Protestant lands became more aggressive, thanks in part to strong prince-bishops and active Jesuit leaders, particularly in the archdioceses of Cologne, Mainz, and Trier. The tensions between Catholics and Protestants increasingly elevated.

In the midst of these religio-political tensions, the Roman Catholic Church experienced instability at the highest level. Roman Catholics saw three popes in 1605, as successor to Pope Clement VIII (1536-1605, pope 1592-1605), Leo XI (1535-1605) assumed the pontificate on April 1st, only to die unexpectedly twenty-seven days later. He was succeeded by Pope Paul V (1552-1621, pope 1605-1621). Twelve years later in 1617, Paul V decreed as official Roman Catholic dogma that Mary was conceived without original sin. Gregory XV (1554-1623, pope 1621-1623), the first Jesuit-trained pope, was elected for a brief two-year pontificate and was followed by Pope Urban VIII (1568-1644, pope 1623-1644).

Personal piety began to overshadow doctrinal concerns. Already in 1605, the Lutheran theologian, Johann Arndt (1555-1621), published the first book of his four-volume work, *True Christianity*, in which he emphasized a more interior piety and personal introspection. During the next decades following Arndt's publication, an emphasis on individual spirituality continued to expand among several confessional groups. Francis de Sales (1567-1622) published a work in 1608 which would become one of the most popular works of Catholic spirituality, *Introduction to the Devout Life*. He later founded a religious order for persons with disabilities which had kept them from membership in other orders.

The following year, 1609, saw the publication of the first part of the English translation for Catholics of the Latin Vulgate, the Douay-Rheims Bible. The same year, John Smythe (c.1570-1612), an exiled Englishman in Amsterdam, baptized himself and established the Baptist churches as distinct from both Catholics and Protestants. Another Englishman, Lewis Bayly (1565-1631) published *Practice of Piety* in 1611, which was translated into German in 1628 and by 1636 had seen 36 English editions. Several Baptists returned to England in 1611, following the teaching of Jacob Arminius (1560-1609) and established a congregation there as "General Baptists." Two decades later a group of these English Baptists began to teach the Calvinist idea of limited atonement and were called "Particular" or Calvinistic Baptists. Such diversity in religious expression only led to further explorations in non-dogmatic experiences.

1611 marks the date of the first edition of the King James Version of the Bible (see illustration of front page), the culmination of a seven-year project. King James I (1566-1625, ruled 1603-1625) had authorized this translation in 1604 as a revision of the Bishops' Bible in consultation with other English translations as well as the Hebrew and Greek manuscripts. As a scholarly project it involved over fifty scholars and continues to be praised for its literary beauty.

Perhaps one of the most significant events in the early years of the seventeenth century was an initial inquisitorial investigation of Galileo (see below) by Robert Cardinal Bellarmine (1542-1621). This occurred in the year, 1616, the same year Shakespeare died. Although no definitive condemnation was given against Galileo, ecclesiastical concerns were officially raised. Twelve years after Bellarmine's death, Galileo was again summoned before the church and was forced to recant his theories of a heliocentric universe.

Lutheran Orthodoxy

After the formulation of the *Book of Concord*, Lutheran theology became more focused on purity and correctness, "orthodox" (Greek, ὀρθός, *orthos*, "correct" or "true" and δόξα, *doxa*, "belief" or "doctrine") of doctrine, the uniting factor for Lutherans as they addressed their Catholic and Reformed rivals. Now, in the seventeenth century, such doctrinal concern led to greater theological clarity under the capable skills of Johann Gerhard (1582-1637).

Born in Quedlinburg, Germany, Gerhard began his theological training in Wittenberg, but shifted his academic focus to medicine for two years at the University. (A similar academic path was taken by his mentor, Johannes Arndt.) In February 1603, he returned to his theological education and transferred to the University of Jena, where he would remain for much of the rest of his professional life. His ardent attitude toward academics, particularly his exhaustive study of Scripture and the Church Fathers, resulted in his receiving a master's degree in just four months. He then studied at Marburg and completed his doctorate at Jena in 1606. He was called by Duke Johann Kasimir of Coburg (1564-1633) to serve as bishop in Heldburg, a position he held for almost a decade. The duke, after several earlier requests, released Gerhard from his academic and ecclesiastical responsibilities and allowed him to accept a professorship at the University of Jena, where Gerhard remained until his death.

Johann Gerhard taught a great variety of courses in Jena, particularly in biblical and systematic theology. He lectured on Galatians, Ephesians, and 2 Corinthians as well as the Gospel of John, in addition to his favorite book, the Psalms. He began writing devotional messages as a young man. Already at the age of 24, he produced *Sacred Meditations*, a set of edifying Christian reflections, the same year as he earned his doctorate. His most famous and influential work was his *Theological Commonplaces* (*Loci Theologici*). That work was published in nine volumes between 1610 and 1625. This voluminous work demonstrated Gerhard's careful, almost scholastic style of organizing biblical doctrine. His commitment to Scripture as the infallible Word of God and only authority for Christian teaching and living is clearly evident throughout this work. A later edition of the work came out in 23 volumes.

Much of Gerhard's writings were a defense of Lutheran theology against both Reformed and Roman Catholic positions. Adopting the practice at the time, Gerhard answered many attacks against Lutheran theology in Aristotelian philosophical terms coupled with clear Scriptural expositions. One of his chief interlocutors was the Jesuit theologian, Robert Bellarmine. Gerhard's method was to proceed from cause to effect or from biblical principles to theological conclusions. From 1633 until his death, Gerhard worked on a four-volume defense of Lutheran theology, *Confessio Catholica,* in which he demonstrated from

Roman Catholic writers that Lutheran doctrines were indeed in line with earlier Catholic theologians.

Gerhard's personal life was one of great difficulty. He had suffered a critical illness as a boy and, later in life, had faced several debilitating episodes in which he was near death. When he was 27, he married a charming young 13-year old, Barbara Neumeier (1594-1611), who died a few years later after giving birth to their only child, who also died shortly after that. That year he prepared a special devotional piece, *The Manual of Comfort*. Gerhard remarried Maria Mattenberg (1597-1660) in 1614 and had ten children with her, several of whom also died as infants.

During these years of teaching in Jena, the Thirty Years War had a great impact on his life. In 1631, for example, the commander of the Catholic Leagues' forces, Count Tilly (1559-1632), had gathered his army at the gates of Jena, planning to plunder the city. Gerhard and his colleague, Johann Major (1564-1654), approached the general, pleading for mercy not to destroy the city. Tilly, so impressed, left Jena with only a modicum of harm.

This same colleague, Johann Major, along with the "third John," Johann Himmel (1581-1642), was at Gerhard's bedside when he died in the middle of August, 1637. Gerhard's influence was significant for Lutheran dogmatic theology as well as for his prolific writing of devotional and homiletical literature for lay people and local clergy.

Lutheran Orthodoxy, which began with the *Book of Concord* in 1580, continued for another century. Besides Johann Gerhard were several noteworthy theologians. Leonhard Hutter (1563-1616), who wrote most forcefully against Calvinist incursions into Lutheran teachings; the Wittenberg theologian, Aegidius Hunnius (1550-1603), a signer of the *Formula of Concord*; and his son, Nicolas Hunnius (1585-1643), who prepared works against both Calvinists, Catholics, and Socinians. Following Gerhard was Johann Dannhauer (1603-1666), teacher of Philipp Spener; Abraham Calov (1612-1686), who prepared a 12-volume dogmatic text for his Wittenberg students; and Johann Quenstedt (1617-1688), the nephew of Johann Gerhard, who taught in Wittenberg for over thirty years.

Lutheran orthodoxy was not only evident in the writing of theologians. One of the greatest musicians of the century was the organist and composer, Heinrich Schütz (1585-1672). Schütz served as organist in Dresden for most of his adult life, although he travelled extensively in Europe, from which he drew thematic and stylistic motifs for his mostly sacred music. His most notable works were for church choirs and included "Passions" from each of the gospels as well as "The Seven Last Words" of Christ. In addition, Paul Gerhardt (1607-1676)—not related to Johann—composed many hymns which were solidly doctrinal, yet extremely popular with his parishioners in Berlin and environs. Both these orthodox Lutheran musicians would greatly influence the work of Johann Sebastian Bach in the next century.

Calvinist Concerns

In 1618, the Synod of Dort began. Designed to settle the increasing distinction between the Calvinists and the followers of Jacob Arminius, the Dutch

Reformed assembly approved the Canons of the Synod. The followers of Arminius, under the leadership of Johannes Uitenbogaert (1557-1644) had drawn up a statement, called a "Remonstrance," which set forth Arminius's views in contrast to those of Calvin. Arminius's unique view of election was that God chose people in view of their faith. He made this very clear in his *Declaration of Sentiments* (1608). He rejected the Augustinian and Calvinist view of predestination and unconditional election. At the Synod, the two key disagreements centered around two questions. One was whether the teaching of once-saved-always-saved was valid or whether salvation can be lost because of sin after one was converted. The second issue was whether the human will was still free to know and choose God or was it impaired because of the Fall into sin as Calvin and Augustine taught. The most noteworthy conclusion at the Synod was the "Five Points of Calvinism" in the Canons, which was later summarized with the acronym TULIP. (See sidebar above.) The Arminian break with Calvinism was clear and decisive.

> The Five Points of Calvinism According to the Canons of Dort:
> 1. Total depravity of humanity,
> 2. Unconditional election,
> 3. Limited atonement,
> 4. Irresistibility of grace,
> 5. Perseverance of the saints.

Thirty Years' War (1618-1648)

We have noted the continuing political and religious struggle between Protestants and Catholics at the beginning of this century. The first outbreak of actual hostilities marking the beginning of the so-called "Thirty Years' War" happened in Bohemia. The Holy Roman Emperor, Ferdinand II of Bohemia (1619-1637, ruled 1619-1637), tried to limit the religious activities of the Protestants under his rule, mirroring the activities of the Catholic duke of Bavaria, Maximilian (1573-1651, ruled 1597-1651). Maximilian had repressed Protestant worship in his region beginning in 1606 and encouraged Catholic retrieval of ecclesiastical lands confiscated after 1555. On May 23, 1618, several Protestant nobles threw two Catholic regents from a castle window in Prague (the so-called "Defenestration of Prague") after the Archbishop had ordered the destruction of a Protestant church. Recognized as an act of rebellion, the next thirty years saw unprecedented battles in Germany between Protestants and Catholics which had both political and religious implications.

A major victory was won at the White Mountain in 1620 by Ferdinand II and his Catholic supporters who came from Bavaria in southern Germany, Spain, and the papacy. The following years, his general, Albrecht of Wallenstein (1583-1634), moved against the Protestants in northern Germany and the Netherlands, ultimately taking control of Germany and parts of Denmark by 1629. In March of that year, Emperor Ferdinand issues his "Edict of Restitution," which required all Catholic properties under Protestant control since 1555 to be returned to Catholic possession, as well as the expulsion of all Protestants from Catholic lands. The recognition of Lutherans as being the only legitimate Protestant group was one positive move, but it also resulted in depriving Calvinist of any landholding rights.

Finally, in 1630, Gustavus Adolphus of Sweden (1594-1632) landed in northern Germany and, with the help of some French and many of the Protestant German states, drove the imperial armies out of Germany in 1631. Unfortunately, he was killed in a victorious battle against Wallenstein. In addition to these national military conflicts, the plague continued to devastate citizenries in much of Europe. One Bavarian town, Oberammergau, in gratitude for divine protection from the bubonic plague instituted a celebrative event, a city-wide production of the *Passion Play*, in 1634.

Three years later, Spain moved against the Swedish armies in Nordlingen and defeated them, forcing the Protestants out of southern Germany. This could have resulted in the end of the war. However, fearing political encirclement, France re-entered the fray in 1635 and declared war on Spain. From this point, the battles had lost their religious nature and were motivated purely for political reasons.

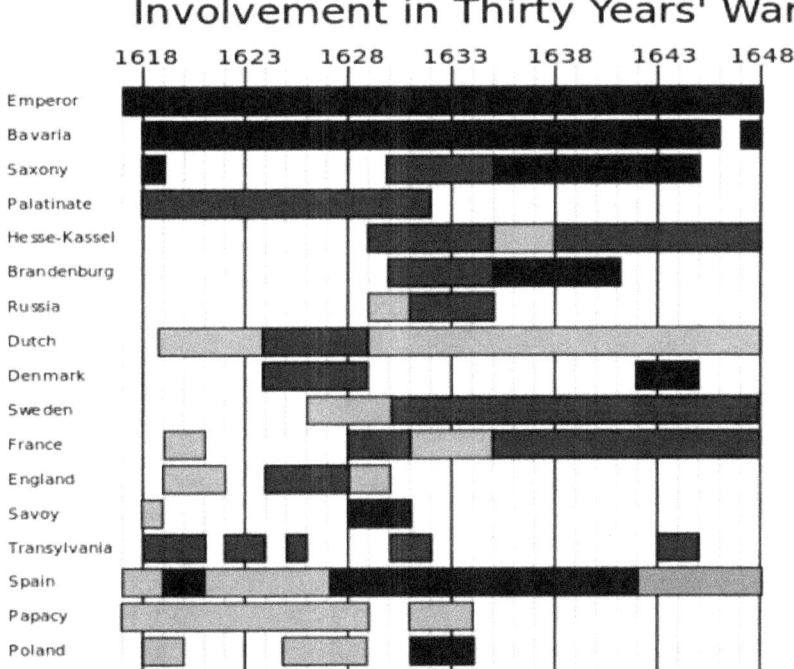

For the next dozen years, the great political powers of Europe—Spain, Sweden, France, and Austria—were contending for control of German lands. The military maneuvers were characterized by their astoundingly horrific atrocities as the mercenary troops sought to appropriate confiscated resources as payment for services. By some estimates, half the population living between Pomerania in the northern Baltic region of Germany and the Black Forest were killed in battle or died as a result of hostilities. Finally, in 1643, the French won a decisive victory over Spain in Rocroi. Two years later, the Swedes defeated the imperial armies in

Jankau. These military activities marked the ending of the major battles and the final determinations for peace.

In 1648, the Peace of Westphalia ended the Thirty Years' War. Establishing the principle of *cuius region illius religio* ("whose region, his religion"), Germany's devastating war came to an uncertain, yet definitive conclusion. The sovereignty of the German princes was recognized in this treaty, weakening the power of the Emperor. Holland and Switzerland were given independent status. The Hohenzollern elector of Brandenburg garnered great land territory, eventually leading to control over the kingdom of Prussia at the end of this century. Besides the war, famine and plague had decimated the population by over five-eighth of its citizenry. Spain was weakened significantly. France became much stronger and more influential, which may have contributed to the French Civil War (1648-1652), which began the same year.

New World Advances

In the meantime, in North America, the Mayflower Compact was drafted in 1620 as the Mayflower landed in Plymouth, Massachusetts. This colony was founded by Puritan Separatists, known as "pilgrims." Fifteen years later, in 1635, the Massachusetts Bay Colony Congregationalists founded Harvard College. Five years after the pilgrims settle in Massachusetts, the Jesuit missionary, Jean de Brébeuf (1593-1649) traveling with the French explorer, Samuel de Champlain (1574-1635), brought the Christian message to the Huron peoples in Québec. Regrettably, he died a martyr's death at the hands of some Iroquois raiders, who destroyed their Huron mission village.

In 1626, the Dutch explorer and colonial governor, Peter Minuit (1580-1638), purchased Manhattan Island from a Native American tribe, the Lenape, for 60 guilders (under $1000 today). Lutherans from Germany and other European countries were already living in the surrounding territory. Ten years later, in 1636, Roger Williams (1603-1683) founded Providence, Rhode Island, as a community for religious refugees. That same year the Puritans published the first hymn book ever printed in America, *The Bay Psalm Book*. More emigrants came to Massachusetts by 1638, under the leadership of John Cotton (1584-1652) and Richard Mather (1596-1669). Later, Thomas Hooker (1586-1647) helped establish religious services in Connecticut under the congregational polity of Puritanism.

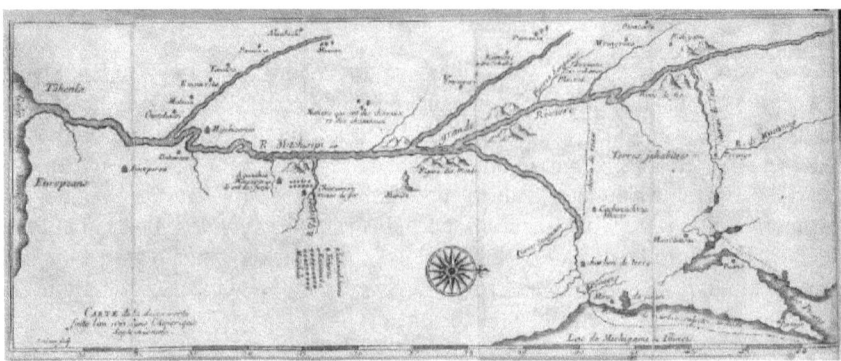

In 1675, a Jesuit priest, Pére (Father) Jacques Marquette (1637-1675), joined a French-Canadian explorer, Louis Jolliet (1645-1700), to expand his missionary and educational work with the Huron to other Native Americans. As the first Europeans to explore the northern areas of Mississippi River (see 1673 map of their expedition on the previous page), Marquette also introduced over a dozen Native American tribes to basic Christian teachings in the central mid-west and territory around Lake Michigan and Lake Superior.

In the last quarter of the century, the British entrepreneur, William Penn (1644-1718), came to the New World seeking religious freedom. Although born to a prominent Anglican family, he was drawn to the teachings of George Fox and the Quakers (see below). After experiencing religious persecution in England, he was granted a large land tract in 1689 by King Charles II (1630-1685) east of New Jersey. He named it Sylvania (Latin, "forests"), but Charles renamed it, Pennsylvania, in honor of William's father. Penn decreed that this territory would have complete religious freedom for all who believed in God, thus opening the land to a great diversity of religious groups seeking freedom of expression, including many Lutherans.

Diversity in the British Isles

In 1634, Archbishop William Laud (1573-1645) mandated that all Anglican altars in England be placed against the east wall, altar rails restored, and pulpits moved from their central focus to a less obtrusive location. As a result, the Puritans become increasingly incensed with such partisan and idiosyncratic regulations. Eleven years later in 1645, Laud was executed for "popery" and political intrigue and, in the meantime, civil war had erupted between the British Parliament and the King Charles (1601-1649).

In the following year, 1646, the Westminster Confession was drafted and ratified by a synod of Scottish and English presbyters (lay and clergy), providing English Puritans with a clear doctrinal statement for all Presbyterians in the British Isles. Among the key features was the teaching of "covenant theology" (also known as "federal theology") which presents the relationship between God and humanity as a covenant or mutual agreement. Along with the Westminster Larger and Shorter Catechisms, the Presbyterians established a common doctrinal foundation.

The erstwhile opponent of these Presbyterian confessions was the Puritan military leader, Oliver Cromwell (1599-1658). The political fallout of the civil war was the beheading of King Charles I and the usurpation of Parliamentary powers by the non-Presbyterian minority. Until 1660, a kind of tolerant democracy existed under Cromwell (Lord Protector, 1653-1658), known as the Commonwealth of England, and a significant number of religious minorities developed and grew.

George Fox (1624-1691) was a young Anglican who felt disassociated from his church. He was very much of a loner, seeking solitude in a variety ways. Although his family suggested he become a priest, he claimed to have received several visions and conversations with Christ. In 1647, he began his public ministry by emphasizing "Christ within" and "the inner Light" of the Holy Spirit in his preaching (see illustration). Although he did not intend to form a new denomination, his followers joined together during the period of the

Commonwealth to form what eventually became the Society of Friends, more commonly known as the Quakers. In 1689, the British Parliament passed the Toleration Act, which allowed nonconformist groups (such as Congregationalists and Baptists, although Catholics were not included) to worship in their own ways, as long as they pledged allegiance to the British crown. Through this act, Quakers were allowed to practice their religion in public and grew quickly thereafter.

Two decades earlier than the Toleration Act, the British parliament had passed the Five-Mile-Act of 1665 prohibiting non-Anglican clergy from speaking against the state-church unless they were five miles away from any villages or towns. That was the same year that over 75,000 people died in London during the Great Plague, followed by the Great Fire of London the following year in which London's St. Paul's Cathedral was totally consumed. Many citizens saw these tragedies as acts of God meted out upon the city for suppressing religious freedom.

In the midst of such physical devastation and reconstruction came a renewed interest in missions with the formation in 1698 of the Society for Propagation of Christian Knowledge by Thomas Bray (1658-1730). The goal of the SPCK, as it was known, was to extend the Christian faith, particularly through publication and distribution of library materials. This was especially effective in the next century as they provided a wealth of resources for American missionaries as well as publishing Bible translations (including a Tamil Bible prepared by Lutheran missionaries in India around 1715).

Pietism

The Moravians were predecessors of the Radical Reformation (see chapter 16 C) and even to Luther's own work, but their ideas exerted far greater influence on Lutheran Christianity in the several centuries following the Reformation. Johann Amos Comenius (1592-1670), for example, was a student of Arndt and, as bishop of the Moravian Brethren, promoted renewal not only of individuals, but society as a whole, particularly through educational reforms.

Not since Luther's *Ninety-five Theses* had a document such an overwhelming effect on Christian life than one penned by Philipp Jakob Spener (1635-1705). Entitled *Pia Desideria* (Pious Desires), this short work gave voice to the growing concern for "dead Orthodoxy" by emphasizing personal experience and holy living over doctrine. Published in 1675 as a forward to an edition of Arndt's sermons, the work took on a life of its own and was quickly published as a separate and unique booklet. Known as the "Father of Pietism," Spener proposed several features which became hallmarks of Pietism—a "deeper" reading of the Bible in devotional assemblies, known as "little churches in the church" (*ecclesiolae in ecclesia*), realization of the priesthood of all believers in practicing the Christian life, a limitation on confessional polemics, a reforming of the traditional pastoral training toward piety instead of doctrine, and parish preaching for edification of the inner person instead of indoctrination.

It was during his theological studies in Strassburg between 1651 and 1659 that Spener (see his portrait below) first expressed his concerns for what he saw as the rigidity of orthodox theology as well as the less-than-exemplary discipline of Lutheran clergy. He visited several Calvinist communities, where he found the regulatory nature of the teachings and a more mystical dimension of religion attractive. In 1666, Spener was named senior pastor in Frankfurt, where he developed a strong social program for the poor and introduced a more thorough catechetical program for the young by introducing the practice of confirmation instructions. He became the head preacher in the Dresden court in 1686 and in 1691 was called to Berlin, where he served Frederick III of Brandenburg (1657-1713; later Frederick I of Prussia) and influenced the new University of Halle. Hostility to Spener's views increased over the years, so that by 1695 the Wittenberg faculty prepared a list of almost 300 errors attributed to Spener. He died in Berlin in 1705 after preparing a defense of his teachings in his *Theologische Bedenken* (Theological Reflections, 1700-1702).

Hermann Francke (1663-1727), student and successor to Philipp Spener, personified Pietism as he embodied the goals articulated most ardently by Spener. Having experienced a crisis of faith as a student, such a "conversion experience" became a key element in subsequent Pietist practices. Francke was an incredible organizer. After having been placed by Spener as a language professor in the new Prussian university of Halle, Francke established an orphanage, a publishing house, an apothecary and science laboratory, along with various academic institutions—a school for Scripture study and translation, a teachers college, a seminary-type institute, and a variety of schools for students of different abilities and skills. His entrepreneurial nature led him to develop a strong missionary movement. (See chapter 18.)

Pietist Influences

The influence of Pietism was trans-denominational, affecting both Roman Catholic mysticism and Puritan devotional piety. Even the eighteenth century Jewish movement, Hasidism (Hebrew, "pious ones" promoting a mystical spirituality), was influenced in some ways by the personal, individual spirituality of Pietism.

Although Jesuit influence on the Counter-Reformation was significant, a Pietistic-type counter-movement, known especially in France as Jansenism, showed some marks and tendencies similar to Pietism. Originating as a reaction to the Tridentine opposition to Lutheranism's strong emphasis upon grace alone, Cornelius Jansen (1585-1638) sought to reaffirm the Augustinian ideal of grace. The Jansenists advocated an emphasis upon personal regeneration, a desire for small-group conventicles, a rejection of dogmatic theology and ecclesiastical hierarchy, and a return to biblical studies led by the laity. In spite of the fact that both Pope Urban VIII (1568-1644, pope 1623-1644) and Pope Innocent X (1574-1655, pope 1644-1655) condemned Jansenism, it continued to have a significant impact on Catholic communities for several decades, especially in France and northern Europe. This became evident in the pontificate of one of the outstanding popes of the century, Innocent XI (1611-1689, pope 1676-1689), who manifested both anti-Jesuit and anti-Jansenist views.

John Bunyan

Although claiming only to be "a Christian," the Puritan preacher, John Bunyan (1628-1688), seems to have taken many themes of Pietism into his most famous work, *The Pilgrim's Progress*, published in two parts in 1678 and 1684. The power of the Word of God and the struggle to maintain one's personal faith in the face of unexpected diversions and even violent confrontations are key elements in this extended allegory. With these themes, Bunyan's influence continued even in the face of the rationalist thinkers of the next century, particularly in the New World.

> Bunyan's *Apology* for the book's length:
> When at the first I took my pen in hand / Thus for to write, I did not understand
> That I at all should make a little book / In such a mode; nay, I had undertook
> To make another; which, when almost done, / Before I was aware, I this begun.
> And thus it was: I, writing of the way / And race of saints, in this our gospel day,
> Fell suddenly into an allegory / About their journey, and the way to glory,
> In more than twenty things which I set down. / This done, I twenty more had in my crown;
> And they again began to multiply, / Like sparks that from the coals of fire do fly.
> Well, so I did; but yet I did not think / To shew to all the world my pen and ink
> In such a mode; I only thought to make / I knew not what; nor did I undertake
> Thereby to please my neighbor: no, not I; / I did it my own self to gratify.
> Neither did I but vacant seasons spend / In this my scribble; nor did I intend
> But to divert myself in doing this / From worser thoughts which make me do amiss.
> Thus, I set pen to paper with delight, / And quickly had my thoughts in black and white.
> For, having now my method by the end, / Still as I pulled, it came; and so I penned
> It down: until it came at last to be, / For length and breadth, the bigness which you see.

Art, Literature, and Architecture

The arts also demonstrated Pietistic influences as the human experience became a greater focus even for religious art. Rembrandt van Rijn's (1606-1669) paintings, such as *Jacob Blessing the Sons of Joseph* (1656) and *The Return of the Prodigal Son* (1665); Isaac Watts's (1674-1748) hymn, "When I Survey the Wondrous Cross," and "Our God, Our Help in Ages Past;" Giovanni Bernini's (1598-1680) dramatic sculptures, and Christopher Wren's (1632-1723) architectural designs called "monumental, yet humane," reflect a sense of inspiring, yet very personal and emotional faith.

Global Missions

While European exploration of the New World in both North and South America was accompanied by mission efforts, there were others concerned with the Orient. At the turn of the century, the first Japanese priest were ordained by the Roman Catholic Church. Yet, within a few years a ban on Christianity was imposed and in 1614 over 40,000 Christians were killed.

China had experienced a slow acceptance of some Christian practices. In 1616 a major conflict between the traditional Chinese and the Roman Catholic Church resulted in the deportation of several Catholic missionaries. Apparently these missionaries had advocated the syncretistic practice of allowing ancestor worship along with traditional Catholic teachings. Almost immediately after their expulsion, a Jesuit missionary was sent to China, followed by several other Jesuits later in the century.

In the early 1660s, George Fox sent Quaker missionaries to China, although little was accomplished until the following century. A Russian Orthodox Church was established in China by the end of the century after the first Orthodox missionaries arrived around the mid-1680s.

Most of these missionaries struggled to make an impact because of the cultural and language differences. In spite of such difficulties, they persisted and over the next centuries would see new opportunities to bring the Gospel to the ever-expanding world.

Flickers of Enlightenment

Pietism's emphasis upon human emotion and religious experience eroded confessional demarcations and elevated the individual. It is probably no accident of history that many of the major Enlightenment figures (see chapter 18) came from Pietist families—Goethe, Schleiermacher, Kant, Schiller, and Lessing. In the meantime, there were new understandings in science and philosophy which began to raise critical questions about faith.

Galileo Galilei

One of the fathers of modern science, Galileo Galilei (1564-1642), was required to reject the Copernican theory of a heliocentric universe in 1633, yet within five years, he published his *Discourses Concerning Two New Sciences*, in which he refined his earlier studies of motion and applied mathematics to the formulations of scientific laws.

Galileo was a brilliant inventor, providing new or improved instruments for experimentation—a thermometer, the pendulum, and the telescope. Already in 1609, with the creation of his own telescope, he had found proof that the moon was not flat and that Venus had phases, which corresponded to a heliocentric universe. That was the same year that another astronomer, Johann Kepler (See chapter 16 A), defending Copernicus's views, published his three laws of planetary movement.

By 1616 Galileo had been warned by Bellarmine to desist from his perceived anti-Catholic teachings, although Galileo had affirmed that the biblical narrative was true from a perspective of that time. In 1633, he was called before a papal inquisitorial board. After this inquisitorial investigation proved him guilty of holding a Copernican viewpoint, he was declared a heretic of the Roman Catholic Church. His major crime was to deny the Roman magisterial interpretation of Scripture. His sentence of imprisonment was commuted to being placed under house arrest for the remainder of his life.

Isaac Newton

In the year that Galileo died, another scientist of the modern era was born, Sir Isaac Newton (1642-1727). Newton's mathematical work on the motion of heavenly bodies and his understanding of gravity led to his publication of *Principia* (1687) in which he demonstrated the plausibility of Copernicus's theory of a heliocentric universe. Although deeply religious and an ardent student of theology, his work would be used in the next century to deprecate Christianity.

Rene Descartes

The great French Catholic thinker, Rene Descartes (1596-1650), contributed to mathematics through his analytical geometry, but more importantly he made significant contributions to philosophy. In his *Discourse on Method*, published in 1637, Descartes argued for the existence of the perceived world along with a divine world. He based this on one's ability to conceive of both of them in one's mind. In order to determine what was real, he advocated one must doubt everything until the mind could comprehend it.

Following Augustine and Anselm, his principle, *cogito, ergo sum* ("I think, therefore I am"), has remained a hallmark of modern thinkers. Descartes concluded that a person would not even consider the idea of God, if He had not caused it to be formed in the human mind and consciousness. Unfortunately, that conclusion was outlived by his idea of doubt and self-awareness.

John Milton

After championing Cromwell's Commonwealth and nearly going through a divorce, John Milton (1608-1674), wrote one of the most famous blank-verse epic poems in the English language, *Paradise Lost* (1667). Although he had become completely blind in the early 1650s, his poem exudes an extraordinary emphasis upon human potentiality in overcoming physical and emotional obstacles. His religious views were not in line with the Anglican or even Puritan forms of Christianity, being anti-Trinitarian and advocating a kind of no-fault divorce, yet, he affirmed in *Paradise Regained* (1671) that salvation comes through Christ alone who overcame Satan's temptations.

Robert Boyle

The Irish-born Robert Boyle (1627-1691), using the scientific method espoused by Francis Bacon (1561-1626) although denying being his follower, single-handedly brought chemistry out of the dark ages of alchemy. His commitment to Scripture translation resulted in his personal financing of a complete Bible in Irish (1680-1685) as well as funding Christian missionary work with the East India Company, for which he served as director.

Blaise Pascal

Blaise Pascal (1623-1662) was one of the great thinkers of the seventeenth century. He was a precocious mathematician, inventing a type of calculator to assist his father's tax collecting profession. During the 1650s he turned his attention to atmospheric pressure and geometric theorems. In conversation with another mathematical philosopher, Pierre Fermat (1601-1665), he worked out his theory of probability.

Pascal had a conversion experience in 1654, as a result of working with two Jansenist brothers after his father died three years earlier. In his most influential work on Christian philosophy, *Pensées* (1657-58), a collection of personal thoughts on human suffering and faith in God, he presented his wager—If God does not exist, one will lose nothing by believing in Him; while if He does exist, one will lose everything by not believing.

> **Pascal's Wager**
> Let us weigh the gain and the loss in wagering that God is. Let us estimate these two chances. If you gain, you gain all; if you lose, you lose nothing. Wager, then, without hesitation that He is.
> From *Pensées*, #233

John Locke

John Locke (1632-1704) profoundly affected the future of philosophy and politics, particularly through his idea of the mind and one's self-identity. As a result, he provided foundational ideas for the Enlightenment writers in the eighteenth century. Influenced by several Baptist writers, he advocated religious tolerance, claiming that no one's conscience could be forced to believe something. However, he rejected atheism as being fundamentally destructive of society in general.

Although raised in a Calvinist tradition, he moved toward a Socinian anti-Trinitarian position for much of his life. He seemed to return to a more biblical view in one of his final works, *The Reasonableness of Christianity* (1695). He argued for a reasonable morality which humans could readily recognize because it was in actuality clear evidence of a divine law.

Leibnitz

Gottfried Wilhelm von Leibnitz (1646-1716) followed Pascal in mathematical creativity and philosophical speculation. He wrote that philosophy and religion cannot be contradictory, since both are gifts from God. He, along with Descartes and the Dutch monistic pantheist, Baruch Spinoza (1632-1677), were the rationalist leaders which gave impetus to the fuller expression of the Enlightenment in the eighteenth century, which is the subject in our next chapter.

As the century progressed, religious differences became more clearly stated and defended. A sense of personal spiritualty increased among the Anglican Puritans as well as among many Pietist-influenced movements. All this laid a foundation for the next century as more and more individuals sought to resolve religious and social questions on the basis of their own thoughts and perspectives.

For Review and Discussion
1. What evidence of confessionalization can you identify among the various religious traditions in this century?
2. How was Lutheran Orthodoxy a vibrant contribution to a Christian witness in the world?
3. What contributions did Pietism make and what problems did it create during this century?
4. Why was mission work in the New World difficult, yet effective?
5. How did John Bunyan exemplify being "holy in the world"?
6. What shift in thinking toward the end of this century gave opportunity for the Enlightenment?

For Further Reading:
Clouse, Robert G. *The Church in the Age of Orthodoxy and the Enlightenment: Consolidation and Challenge 1600-1700.* St Louis: Concordia, 1980.

Gerhard, Johann. *Theological Commonplaces.* St Louis: Concordia Publishing House, 2009-present.

Milton, John. *Paradise Lost.* New York: Penguin, 2009.

Parkman, Francis. *The Jesuits in North America in the Seventeenth Century.* Boston: Little, Brown, and Company, 1879.

Preus, Robert. *The Theology of Post-Reformation Lutheranism.* 2 Volumes. St Louis: Concordia Publishing House, 1970-1972.

Spener, Philipp. *Pia Desideria.* ed. and trans. Theodore G. Tappert. Philadelphia: Fortress Press, 1964.

18. The Age of Reason and New Awakenings

The Eighteenth Century

No era had higher expectations for the future of humanity than the eighteenth century, yet this century ended with less than glorious conclusions. Scientific discoveries, enlightened thinking, global consciousness, and a renewal of spiritual vitality all marked the first decades of this period.

In one sense the architectural style known as Rococo characterized this century (see illustration of the Bavarian Ottobeuren Abbey basilica). Its elaborate ornamentation came into vogue with King Louis XV of France (1638-1715) and disappeared with the French Revolution (1789-1799). In the midst of high hopes and ample possibilities, troubles and difficulties persisted as many Christians wavered in striving to be wholly holy in the world. Wars and rumors of wars raged as theological ideas were wrested from the church by the academy.

A New World

Although the events in Europe would be significant, our attention in this chapter will begin to focus more on the religious life in the "new world," particularly in North American lands. Two important events, occurring on opposite sides of the Atlantic Ocean, marked the opening of the century in 1701. After the Bishop of London, Henry Compton (1632-1713, bishop 1675-1713), heard a report by Thomas Bray (1658-1730) describing the deplorable spiritual and organizational condition in the American colonies, the Society for the Propagation of the Gospel in Foreign Parts (SPG) was founded for the explicit purpose of spreading Anglicanism throughout the British colonies.

In the New World, Yale College, named in 1718 to honor a generous donor, Elihu Yale (1649-1721), was established in 1702 by Cotton Mather (1663-1728) and several other conservative Congregationalists, who desired to provide a liberal education for their young people and, according to its charter, "through the blessing of Almighty God may be fitted for Publick employment both in Church and Civil State." Forty-five years later, a group of revivalistic Presbyterians, known as "New Light" Presbyterians, founded a College of New Jersey in 1746, later to be renamed, Princeton University. Several other universities with Christian roots were founded in the New World including Columbia University (known initially as King's College, started in 1754 by Anglicans with strong Presbyterian support) and Rutgers University (founded in 1766 as Queens College by Dutch Reformed church leaders). Dartmouth College (founded by another Congregationalist pastor, Rev. Eleazar Wheelock [1711-1779], in 1769) according to its charter was established for "the education and instruction of Youth of the Indian Tribes in this Land...and also of English Youth and any others."

One other significant contribution to education came from a less than expected avenue. Concerned for the poor and unschooled in his community, Robert Raikes (1735-1811), an Evangelical layman, established what he called "Sunday Schools." Since Sunday was the only day children were not working (there was no public education for children, especially of the poor), he established several home-schools and then a Society for Promoting Sunday Schools in London in 1785. As a newspaper proprietor, he drew many supporters into the movement. Within five years, Sunday Schools were established in the American colonies. Nathaniel Hawthorn (1804-184) immortalized Raikes in his 1844 essay, "A Good Man's Miracle."

The Enlightenment Darkens

Human progress and critical thinking marked a significant change in Christianity during the eighteenth century. Emphases upon human dignity and freedom were coupled with human achievements in science and exploration. The phrase, "man is the measure of all things," dominated the focus of this era. With this emphasis upon humanity, the pursuit of virtue led to greater humanitarian concerns, but a diminishing of a heaven-oriented spirituality.

Although the Enlightenment began in mid-seventeenth century, it peaked in the mid-eighteenth century. The term, Enlightenment (in German, *Aufklärung*), became the dominant worldview for most of the cultural intellectuals. Characterized by its emphasis upon human abilities, particularly the ability to use rational thought or reason as the sole authority and source of knowledge, this era is also known as the Age of Reason. Such a system of thought provided the French with the concept of the Goddess of Reason. In England, this way of thinking was known as Naturalism or Deism (not atheism). Divine revelation and church tradition were set aside. The oft-quoted English poet, Alexander Pope (1688-1744), described the era succinctly: "the proper study of mankind is man." With such an outlook, it is no surprise that Daniel Defoe (1660-1731) would pen his classic, *Robinson Crusoe* (1719), in which the hero survived numerous adventures through his own ingenuity for almost thirty-five years. What is sometimes forgotten is that Crusoe became a professed Christian and converted his companion, Friday.

> **The Gregorian Calendar**
> Although proposed centuries earlier and used in many European nations, the calendar was adopted in Great Britain and her colonies first in 1752. Communities in the United States found themselves in a quandary in early September, when the official calendar went from September 7-11th in order to "catch up" with the solar calendar of Pope Gregory XII, which he introduced in 1582.

David Hume

Perhaps no one individual represented better the role of rationalism than the Scottish empiricist, David Hume (1711-1776). His *Treatise of Human Nature* (1740) claimed that human beings possessed no innate ideas and that even cause-and-effect is a learned perspective. His *Essay on Miracles* (1746) dismissed the possibility of miracles, asserting that misinterpretation or even deceit could explain such unprecedented contrary-to-nature occurrences. He argued that ancient polytheistic religions were anthropomorphic and lacked high ethical practices. Even in his own time, he said, religious controversies made people bigoted and narrow, lacking in true moral behavior.

Voltaire and Diderot

No name epitomizes the early Enlightenment better than Denis Diderot (1713-1784), a French philosopher who published seventeen volumes of text and eleven volumes of engravings in his *Encyclopédie* in 1771. In these volumes was an article by the prolific writer, philosopher, and historian, Voltaire (1694-1778, his given name was François-Marie Arouet). Voltaire described the Enlightenment view of history as more than mere presentation of facts, but interpretation of the breadth of detail with cultural implications or consequences. Although his intellectual contributions were numerous, his spiritual life was turbulent, rejecting

> **Voltaire "On History"**
> One demands of modern historians more details, better ascertained facts, precise dates, more attention to customs, laws, mores, commerce, finance, agriculture, population.
> From Diderot's *Encyclopédie*

many scriptural accounts as well as much of his French Catholic upbringing. For Voltaire, the concept of God was a necessary presupposition for moral behavior and explains his comment, "If God did not exist, it would be necessary to invent Him." Morality became the major focus for those with deist-views.

Edward Gibbon

Another famous Enlightenment thinker was the historian, Edward Gibbon (1737-1794), who wrote one of the most massive accounts of *The Rise and Fall of the Roman Empire* in six volumes between 1776 and 1778. Although his historiography was of a very high quality, he was most remembered for his criticism of all organized religions, especially Christianity for its supplanting of other cultures and reliance on doctrinal authority.

A lesser known event in this century, yet one which had profound consequences, was an act by the still surviving Holy Roman Emperor, Joseph II (1741-1790, emperor 1765-1790). In 1780, he set forth a series of reforms by which both church and state were brought into a more Enlightenment mode. For the church, religious toleration was required for both Protestants and Roman Catholics. In addition, the liturgy of the Catholic Church was simplified, monasteries were closed, and papal power in Austria was limited. For the state, discriminatory laws, especially against serfs and Jews, were removed and a new law code was enacted.

Emmanuel Kant

In 1781, Emmanuel Kant (1724-1804) (see illustration) produced *Critique of Pure Reason* in which he said that all knowledge comes from  experience (empiricism) based upon deduction (rationalism). Such a critique of deism caused the Enlightenment's Age of Reason to begin to sputter toward the end of the century. Having been raised in a pietistic home and attending Pietist schools, he had seen the hypocrisy of religious emotion. Rather than emotion, he said, religion should focus on behavior, especially good, moral actions. In his *Grounding for the Metaphysics of Morals* (1785), he delineated what became known as his "categorical imperative" (*kategorischer Imperativ*): "Every rational person must act as if his behavior was legislating a universal law." In 1788, he published his *Critique of Practical Reason*, which looked not only at behavior, but also at one's motivation and the methods used to teach proper rational morality or the experience of moral "oughtness." Thus, Kantian moralism became a central focus for much of the theology in the next century.

Frederick Schleiermacher

Frederick D. E. Schleiermacher (1768-1834) was born in Silesia, in what is now Poland, into the family of an army chaplain. In 1794, he left the Moravian Church with its Pietist roots to become a minister in the Reformed Church. In

1799, his *On Religion: Speeches to Its Cultural Despisers*, addressed the educated elite (as he saw them) with a new definition of religion, not as dogma or even revelation, but as a universal human sense of being dependent upon a greater being ("the infinite in the finite"). We will see his influence more in the next chapters.

Gotthold Lessing

Gotthold Ephraim Lessing (1729-1781), better known as a drama critic, had a lasting impact on religious thought in the Enlightenment. He had argued that there was a "great ugly ditch" that existed between history and eternal truths which cannot be crossed (see sidebar). Revelation, he claimed, which was reported as history was not possible for such "historical truths" as the resurrection of the dead were not able to be demonstrated. He was convinced that rationalism could be the only universally acceptable mode of understanding the world. The Bible should not be trusted as a source or description of any truth, let alone the truth of God.

Lessing's Ditch
If no historical truth can be demonstrated, then nothing can be demonstrated by means of historical truths. That is: accidental truths of history can never become the proof of necessary truths of reason…That, then, is the ugly broad ditch which I cannot get across, however often and however earnestly I have tried to make the leap.
From *On the Proof of the Spirit and of Power*

The Pietist Impact

Pietism had its roots in the context of a spiritual awakening in Lutheranism and other religious groups in the seventeenth century (see chapter 17). Yet, Philipp Spener's influence continued in the person and work of his colleague and student, Herrmann Francke (1663-1727).

Hermann Francke

While serving as a parish pastor in a suburb of Halle, Francke established a philanthropic foundation for a variety of charitable programs. At the turn of the century, he was serving 100 orphans and over 500 students in his schools. By the time of his death, over 2,000 children in his orphanage were being served by over a hundred teachers (mostly from his college) as part of an enterprise with over twenty-five different educational, publishing, and entrepreneurial programs—including a pharmacy and a scientific museum.

Throughout those years, Francke's spirit (and Spirit) motivated over five dozen men to go into mission work, especially through the Danish-Halle Mission. It was in 1706, that two of Francke's students, Bartholomäus Ziegenbalg (1683-1719) and his colleague, Heinrich Plütschau (1678-1747), reached the region of Tranquebar in India. As the first Lutheran missionaries to serve in India, they worked very deliberately and intensively. Unfortunately, they faced harsh opposition from the local Hindu leaders and (for political reasons) the Danish authorities there. In spite of these obstacles, their first Indian converts were baptized on May 12, 1707. One of their chief legacies was the translation and printing the New Testament in the Tamil dialect of southern India. (Ziegenbalg completed a translation of the Old Testament books through Ruth.) Throughout this century, over sixty missionaries were sent from Halle. Herrmann Francke also served as a significant model for another of his students, Nikolaus von Zinzendorf.

Count von Zinzendorf

Count Nikolaus Ludwig von Zinzendorf (1700-1760), the god-son of Philipp Spener, exhibited a deep spiritual sensitivity even as a child. Raised by his grandmother after his mother's death, Nikolaus studied at Halle for a half-dozen years and then entered the University of Wittenberg in 1716, where he studied law until 1719. After a two-year trip during the early 1720s, he arranged to have several exiles from the United Brethren (the Hussite *Unitas Fratrum*) who had come to Germany from Bohemia and Moravia, reside on his home estate. There they formed a pietistic village, named Herrnhut, which was officially organized at a communion service in 1727 under Zinzendorf with several "elders." Zinzendorf soon envisioned this village to be a kind of separatist Protestant monastic community. He did not require vows or celibacy, but they followed strict observances of corporate prayer and worship (see 1765 illustration below). Zinzendorf maintained his Lutheran connections, although the Moravian constituents desired a greater degree of separation from the state church. Zinzendorf was also a hymn writer and is most remembered for "Jesus, Thy Blood and Righteousness," and "Jesus, Lead Thou On." The common table prayer, "Come, Lord Jesus, be our Guest, and let these gifts to us be blessed," is sometimes attributed to him.

The Moravians were extremely eager to participate in missionary activities. When Zinzendorf attended the coronation of the Danish king, Christian VI (1730-1746), he encountered inhabitants from the Danish West Indies and Greenland. Almost immediately, his Moravian colleagues took up mission work there and a few years later sent a large group to the American colony of Georgia as well as to the Baltic region, England, and later several countries in the Caribbean. Shortly thereafter, Zinzendorf experienced conflicts with the Saxon and Austrian authorities and left Herrnhut. He traveled extensively, several times to the new colonies in America where he organized congregations for native Americans as well as European colonists. In 1747, he returned to Saxony, where the Moravians accepted the Augsburg Confession and were considered part of the state church, a kind of *ecclesiolae in ecclesia*, as Spener had envisioned, although the Moravians assumed a more churchly polity.

Henry Melchior Muhlenberg

Another disciple of Francke was Henry Melchior Muhlenberg (1711-1787), who studied at Halle with Francke's son, Gotthilf August (1696-1769). In 1742, he was among two dozen men sent from Halle to America to conduct missionary work with German Lutheran settlers. Lutheran immigrants had been settling in North and South Carolina, New York, and Pennsylvania and had begun organizing themselves into congregations and even a synod. Six years later, Muhlenberg, who became known as the "Patriarch of the Lutheran Church in America," had organized sufficient clergy to form a Pennsylvania Ministerium. Muhlenberg lived by his personal motto, *Ecclesia Plantanda* ("The Church must be planted"). Most of these pastors brought pietistic tendencies with them from Germany, although as a whole, Lutherans were not affected by the Awakening (see below). By the middle of the century, Lutherans were the largest religious denomination in Pennsylvania. In 1797, the first Lutheran seminary, Hartwick Seminary, was founded in New York to train missionaries.

Catholic Missions

Such missionary efforts were not uniquely Protestant. Work in China by the Jesuits continued in this century, although in 1742, Pope Benedict XIV (1675-1758, pope 1740-1758) placed a restriction on activities with other religious groups, thereby thwarting much of the Jesuit methods. In 1773, Pope Clement XIV (1705-1774, pope 1769-1774) succumbed to political pressure from several European leaders, who saw the Jesuits as being too strong and too international, and dissolved the Jesuit order. This suppression of the Jesuits removed one of the great mission arms of the Catholic Church. Yet, some work among Catholics continued in the New World. Expansion of Catholicism coincided with the Spanish and Portuguese explorations, especially of North America. For example, San Francisco was colonized in 1776 and Los Angeles in 1781, enabling Catholic missionaries to expand their influence from these communities into the western regions of the continent.

Orthodox Missions

For centuries, the Greek Orthodox Church had focused its missionary work with the Slavic countries and, as a result of the Great Schism, had little contact with western Christians. In 1768, Greek Orthodox mission work began in the New World in a small colony established south of present-day St. Augustine,

Florida, known as New Smyrna. In 1794, Herman (later called St. Herman of Alaska, c.1750-1836) came to Kodiak Island from Russian with the message of Christ. Such work among Greek, Slavic, and Russian peoples continued in various ways in the Americas throughout the next centuries.

William Carey and World Missions

Mission work expanded globally in the nineteenth century, but was initially influenced greatly by the Baptist preacher, William Carey (1761-1834). He was a gifted linguist with a zealous heart for "the conversion of the heathens," as he titled his book in 1792. He helped found a missionary society among his colleagues and in 1793 he expanded his mission efforts to India. One of the significant issues in India was how to deal with the caste system as Christians, which he repudiated.

> Carey's Motto
> Expect great things from God and attempt great things for God.

An interdenominational mission society was formed in New York in 1796 to bring spiritual and moral influences to the American frontier. In England, the Church Missionary Society was founded in 1799 under strong evangelical Anglican leaders.

The Methodists

Methodism, a term originally used derisively for a pietistic Anglican movement, sought to achieve higher ethical behavior through religious activities. One of the key elements in its success was its strong evangelistic nature and dynamic organizational system. Doctrinal issues were less important than Christian living—"deeds not creeds" would be a later rallying cry.

The Wesleys

In 1729, John Wesley (1703-1791) formed a study group of young Anglican colleagues from Oxford known as "the Holy Club." His father, Samuel Wesley (1662-1735), had initiated a pietistic-type religious society in 1702, although it did not long survive. John was ordained a deacon in 1725 and assisted his father until his ordination to the Anglican priesthood in 1728. His Holy Club was ridiculed by some classmates for their zealous and methodical emphasis upon works, which resulted in being called "Methodists" and the name soon stuck. In 1735, the son of an innkeeper, George Whitefield (1714-1770), and John's younger brother, Charles (1707-1788), joined the group, sought ordination in the Anglican Church, and began a career as a gifted preachers and missionaries.

In 1736, the Wesley brothers were sent as missionaries by the Church of England to the British colony of Georgia in the New World. There they experienced little success and returned home within two years. During that first trip, they encountered a group of Moravians who exhibited and embodied a personal faith unknown to the Wesleys. Two years later, Charles claimed he was "converted" while attending a Moravian meeting in London on Whitsunday; three days later his brother, John, claimed a similar experience while listening to a discourse from Luther's *Romans Commentary*. He described his experience on

May 25, 1638, (see sidebar)) as a change from believing that Christ is his salvation to feeling it and thereby committing himself wholly to the gospel. Charles was a prolific hymn writer. He published his first collection of hymns in 1739, producing over 5,000 texts during his life time. Among his hymns are "Hark! The Herald Angels Sing," "Christ the Lord Is Risen Today," and "Oh, for a Thousand Tongues to Sing." Two other hymn writers grew out of these Methodist roots—John Newton (1725-1807), author of "Amazing Grace," and Augustus Toplady (1740-1778), who wrote "Rock of Ages."

> **John Wesley's Conversion**
> "About a quarter before nine, while he [Luther] was describing the change which God works in the heart through faith in Christ, I felt my heart strangely warmed. I felt I did trust in Christ, Christ alone, for salvation; and an assurance was given me, that He had taken away my sins, even mine, and saved me from the law of sin and death."

George Whitefield and the Wesleys

At that same time, George Whitefield began preaching in outdoor gatherings in the coal mining region of Kingswood, England, extending his work to Bristol. He invited John Wesley to join him there. Although initially apprehensive about such an open setting for preaching, John accepted and began his fifty-year ministry of public proclamation of the gospel. As a gifted organizer, John gradually adapted the Anglican religious "societies" (again a type of Pietist gathering) into specifically Methodist groups, while trying to remain within the Anglican communion. For much of his public ministry, John insisted that only ordained men could administer the sacraments, although lay preachers were employed almost from the beginning of the movement.

The Break from Anglicanism

Two theological issues became determining factors in the final break with Anglicanism after John's death. John taught a kind of "perfectionism," whereby true believers could love God and others to such an extent that they would be free from sin. He also disagreed with the Church of England regarding predestination, holding instead to an Arminian position.

In 1769, John sent the first Methodist missionaries to America; among them was Francis Asbury (see below). John had prepared a set of rules and regulations for Methodists in the *Deed of Declaration* (1784), which would become a decisive document for an independent Methodism in America. In spite of these differences, he and his brother remained priests of the Anglican Church throughout their lives.

The First Great Awakening (mid-1720s to mid-1740s)

As Methodism and the mission activity were occurring in Europe and the British Isles, a rapid wave of evangelistic revivals spread across the American colonies, beginning in the second quarter of this century. Partially a reflection of Pietism in Germany and the evangelical movement in England, the American colonies gradually, yet inexorably, experienced what was called a "Great

Awakening." Although human nature was viewed pessimistically, holiness was emphasized as a result of God's grace and one being "born again."

Early revivals in local communities began among the Dutch Reformed under the Pietist preacher, Theodore J. Frelinghuysen (1691-1748). In 1736, this American movement was strengthened when William Tennent, Sr. (1673-1745) founded a "Log College," which was established to train Presbyterian ministers in revivalistic and pietistic Christianity. Already present at the turn of the century, Scotch-Irish immigrants had moved out of the original colonies into the frontiers of Kentucky and Tennessee. Needing spiritual connections and stronger religious ties, the Awakening drew these unchurched, yet Christian, laypeople together for fellowship, Christian nurture, and spiritual support.

In New England, Jonathan Edwards (1703-1758), a Congregationalist minister and revival preacher, delivered his famous sermon, "Sinners in the Hands of an Angry God," in 1742. Prior to that, he had described the events of 1734-1735 in Massachusetts as "the surprising work of God in the conversion of many hundred souls" (part of the title of a book he published in 1737). Concerned with the over-emphasis of Arminianism upon human decisions, Edwards emphasized justification by faith alone. His movement spread along the coast to the southern colonies, particularly among Baptists and Methodists. At the same time, some of the Presbyterians were divided about the proper evangelistic methods that were being employed, and the Congregationalists began to split between the "Old Lights," who were suspicious of most revival methods and centered in traditional Boston, and the "New Lights," who pressed for greater revival activities.

Ultimately, it was George Whitefield (1715-1770), (see illustration) the Anglican preaching deacon and Methodist evangelist, who gave voice to this Great Awakening through his ardent American preaching tours. Not only did he support the Puritan "New Side" Presbyterians (the "Old Side" adhered to a strict subscription to the doctrines of the Westminster Confession for their ministers), but his preaching spread the revival practices into other colonies. He was an eloquent preacher, whose enthusiasm for the gospel resulted in a rapid spread of this Awakening.

The Awakening movement peaked in the early 1740s. But southern colonies continued to be affected by the Awakening, particularly as the New England Presbyterians moved southward. By the 1750s, many Baptists had caught the stirrings and expanded the revival themes with those believers under their spiritual influence. However, as concerns for American independence were increasingly being raised, spiritual concerns diminished among colonists toward the end of the century. In addition, some extravagant practices including dramatic expressions of loud groans and fits of fainting, physical convulsions and assertions of ecstasies, gave pause to the camp meeting revivals among the more established denominations.

New Denominations

While the Awakening was somewhat short lived, a general increase in religious life and thought became noticeable throughout the rest of this century. Mission work among Native Americans and new immigrants expanded and personal religious activities led to greater church membership and the establishment of denominational educational institutions.

Among Native Americans, Christian missionary efforts led to several results. Some tribes accepted European Christianity outright, although most followed the practice known as "syncretism," drawing some Christian elements into their own tribal spirituality. The result was an increasing plurality of religious practices among these indigenous peoples. Exemplary of such an attempted synthesis was "the Prophet," Tenskwatawa (1771-1836). (See chapter 19.)

Early colonial Christian groups—Anglicans, Baptists, Lutherans, Presbyterians, Quakers, and Congregationalists—were soon joined by other groups which developed either as new forms of European denominations or as new religious expressions of spirituality in the New World. In the early 1720s a group of German Baptists established themselves in Germantown, Pennsylvania, and were known as "Dunkers" because of their practice of total immersion. Another group of Swiss Baptists became known as River Brethren because of their practice of settling in close proximity to rivers. Each had European roots but expressed themselves slightly differently in the American colonial setting.

Episcopalians, after the War of Independence (see below), decided that a new association was required which was distinctly American. William White (1748-1836) prepared *The Case of the Episcopal Church Considered* in 1782 in anticipation of the war's end. The resulting "Protestant Episcopal Church in the United States," formulated their doctrine the following year in line with their Anglican roots, but proposed a more democratic polity which was not under state influence. Two years later, Samuel Seabury (1729-1796), was consecrated as the first bishop in the new Episcopal Church by several Scottish bishops. In 1789 a General Convention was held in Philadelphia where they declared their independence, yet their commitment to remain Anglican "in any essential point of doctrine, disciple, or worship." This Episcopal Church then revised the *Book of Common Prayer* slightly for its American context.

The same year that John Wesley prepared regulations for an evangelical Anglican Methodist group, the Methodist Episcopal Church in the United States separated itself from the English Methodist system in December, declaring Francis Asbury and Thomas Coke (1747-1814) as their new bishops.

Francis Asbury (1745-1816) had already been commissioned as a Methodist missionary in 1771. The next year he instituted a program of itinerant pastors, called circuit riders, who were sent to the scattered and isolated settlers in the American frontier. This practice became a hallmark of early American mission work for the next century.

The French and Indian War (1754-1763)

Known in Europe as the Seven-Years' War (which actually extended for nine years), the political struggle between Britain and France and Spain was fought in the New World over territories north, south, and west of the colonies. In Europe, the focus initially was on restricting Prussian hegemony, but with the growth of colonization, British influences increased and began to spread into what had been considered French and Spanish territories. Although the French population was not large in the New World, they enlisted several indigenous tribes to ward off further expansion into the lands north of the colonies. With a strong military, the British ultimately overcame the French and gained access to the lands in Canada, along with acquiring Florida from the Spanish. To pay for this war the British Parliament expanded their taxation practices in the colonies, resulting in increased hostilities between the Americans and the British. Further conflict was inevitable, influencing greatly the religious commitment of congregations to separate themselves from European domination.

The American Revolution (1775-1783)

The "Boston Massacre" occurred in 1770 when British soldiers killed five American colonists for throwing snowballs, sticks, and stones at them. Three years later a group of colonists dumped imported British tea into the Boston harbor to protest British import and tea taxation; this is the Boston Tea Party (1773). The following year the first American Continental Congress was assembled. The War of Independence began in 1775 and the *Declaration of Independence* was drafted, signed, and passed in 1776. Although remaining neutral for several years, the French finally sent troops to aid the American revolutionary army against the British, followed by the Spanish.

Three principles proclaimed by the Declaration were equality, national self-sovereignty, and liberty—both civic and religious. Although the Continental Congress was constituted chiefly by members of the Established Church (the Church of England), the colonial pulpits influenced the opinions of the masses toward resistance and self-rule. The preamble to the *Declaration of Independence* illustrates this politico-religious philosophy which gave voice to the American popular view of this new institution (see below).

When war broke out, many clergy were vocally committed to the cause of freedom. One of the more noteworthy episodes in American Lutheranism is the account of John Peter Gabriel Muhlenberg (1746-1807), the son of Henry. Having formed a close relationship with several leaders in the Continental Congress, including George Washington (1732-1799) and Patrick Henry (1736-1799), John Peter preached a farewell sermon on January 1776. After pronouncing the benediction, he threw back his clergy robe and stood with the uniform of a continental officer. Reportedly, he stated: "In the language of Holy Writ, there is a time for all things. There is a time to preach and a time to fight; and now is the time to fight!" Having been made a Major General toward the end of the war, he never returned to parish life, but became a respected statesman, serving both in the House and Senate.

The Constitution of the United States was ratified between 1787 and 1788. Three key features relating to religious life were also established there: government neutrality in confessional matters; the free exercise of religion; and the separation of church and state. The following year, George Washington was elected the first President. In 1791, the Bill of Rights went into effect, allowing for religious freedom for all. One result was the disestablishment of existing state churches in the colonies—voluntary denominational membership became the norm, instead of the earlier practice where citizenship was equated with membership.

> **The Preamble to the *Declaration of Independence***
> We hold these truths to be self-evident, that all men are created equal, that they are endowed by their Creator with certain unalienable Rights, that among these are Life, Liberty and the pursuit of Happiness. That to secure these rights, Governments are instituted among Men, deriving their just powers from the consent of the governed, That whenever any Form of Government becomes destructive of these ends, it is the Right of the People to alter or to abolish it, and to institute new Government, laying its foundation on such principles and organizing its powers in such form, as to them shall seem most likely to effect their Safety and Happiness. Prudence, indeed, will dictate that Governments long established should not be changed for light and transient causes; and accordingly all experience hath shewn, that mankind are more disposed to suffer, while evils are sufferable, than to right themselves by abolishing the forms to which they are accustomed. But when a long train of abuses and usurpations, pursuing invariably the same Object evinces a design to reduce them under absolute Despotism, it is their right, it is their duty, to throw off such Government, and to provide new Guards for their future security. Such has been the patient sufferance of these Colonies; and such is now the necessity which constrains them to alter their former Systems of Government. The history of the present King of Great Britain is a history of repeated injuries and usurpations, all having in direct object the establishment of an absolute Tyranny over these States. To prove this, let Facts be submitted to a candid world.

After the War

The first African American Episcopal congregation was started in 1787 by Richard Allen (1760-1831) after being frustrated by the limitations placed upon black members by a Methodist Episcopal church in Philadelphia. Ordained in 1799 by Francis Asbury, Allen (see illustration) established several black Methodist Episcopal congregations in Pennsylvania. Finally, with several other black pastors, he formed a new denomination in 1816, the African Methodist Episcopal Church.

Mother Ann Lee (1736-1784), a visionary and self-proclaimed prophetess, set up her first Shaker colony in 1770, known as the United Society of Believers in Christ's Second Appearing. As an offshoot of the Quaker movement in England, they followed the revivalist tendencies along with utopian ideals. Four years later she brought her millenarian communal group to New York, where the movement grew and influenced the frontier revivals of the next century in Kentucky.

Within the last quarter of this century, a Universalist congregation was formed in Massachusetts and a related group, the Society of Universal Baptists, was formed in Philadelphia. Both of these groups sought to unify believers under a non-Trinitarian understanding of God. By 1790, there were over two dozen distinct Protestant denominations among the states of the new nation.

Musical Masters

The musical period known as "classical age" is another key element of this century. Most noteworthy among the classical composers is the first B of the three Bs—Bach (1685-1750), Beethoven (1770-1827), and Brahms (1833-1897), who spanned the cultural shift from Baroque to Romanticism.

Johann Sebastian Bach (1685-1750) (see illustration) was born into a very musical Lutheran family in Eisenach, Germany, where Luther had studied as a young boy. Recognized as a master organist, his reputation in other musical genres was less appreciated until after his death. For example, he was also a prolific composer of vocal and instrumental music. Although living in a strongly Pietist environment, the theological content of Bach's music was clearly drawn from Lutheran Orthodoxy. While serving as Kantor in the St. Thomas Church of Leipzig, he composed over 300 cantatas, musical compositions usually based upon biblical texts for Sunday services enlisting choirs, soloists, and several instruments, including the organ. His Brandenburg Concertos were composed in 1721; the St Matthew's Passion in 1729,

and in 1738, the *Mass in B Minor*, a landmark work of the Baroque period, although it was too long for regular worship settings and considered too Catholic for Lutheran congregations. Bach is now recognized to be one of the most gifted musicians in the world. He communicated his strong Lutheran faith as a teacher as well as through his numerous compositions, frequently placing "SDG" (*Soli Deo Gloria*; "To God be the Glory") at the end of his cantatas.

George Frederic Handel (1685-1759), born the same year and within 100 miles of Bach, never met him. Yet, their Lutheran heritage influenced their compositions greatly. Although a German, Handel lived most of his professional life in London, England, where he elevated a modified form of opera, known as the oratorio, a non-theatrical musical work, to greater prominence. In addition to his vocal music, Handel's orchestral compositions included the *Water Music* (1717), *Music for the Royal Fireworks* (1749). Handel is most remembered for his well-known, familiar, recognizable, and frequently performed work, *Messsiah*, in 1741.

Wolfgang Amadeus Mozart (1756-1791) brought classical music to new heights. A child prodigy, he began composing musical works at the age of four or five. Known more as a court composer, he wrote over sixty sacred compositions, including a dozen and a half masses. Most well-known was his *Mass in C minor* (1782-83) and his unfinished *Requiem Mass* (1791). Mozart was prolific in a variety of other genres—symphonies, sonatas, string quartets, serenades, and especially operas. He received a Catholic burial, although he had also joined the Freemasons near the end of his life.

Franz Joseph Haydn (1732-1809), who became a close friend of Mozart, said that the world would not see such a talented musician as Mozart for another hundred years. Haydn is best known for his chamber music and his symphonies, such as his *London Symphonies* in the 1790s (including the *Surprise*) and *The Creation* in 1799. He also composed over a dozen masses, although they are not well known.

Ludwig van Beethoven (1770-1827) only wrote two masses—*Mass in C Major* and a *Mass in D Major*—yet both of them show not only the influence of rationalism, but also a deep piety. As a young man, he prepared several compositions based upon liturgical texts or hymns. He was not actively involved in church activities later in his life and had little significant influence, except for his "Ode to Joy," which is familiar to this day because of its use in the last movement of his *Ninth Symphony*.

Already mentioned was the work of Count Nicholas Zinzendorf as a hymn writer, but no one was more prolific (and perhaps famous) than the Congregational theologian and hymn writer, Isaac Watts (1674-1748). Watts's hymns helped cross denominational divides as well as temporal barriers over the next centuries. Many of his over 750 hymns were based on biblical texts, especially the Psalms. For example, his 9-stanza paraphrase of Psalm 90 "Our God, Our Help in Ages Past" (see sidebar) and his hymn, "Joy, to the World," is based upon Psalm 98. Having a gift for composing rhymed couplets, he also

> "Our God, Our Help in Ages Past"
> Stanzas generally omitted from modern settings:
> *Thy Word commands our flesh to dust,*
> *Return, ye sons of men:*
> *All nations rose from earth at first,*
> *And turn to earth again.*
>   *The busy tribes of flesh and blood,*
>   *With all their lives and cares,*
>   *Are carried downwards by the flood,*
>   *And lost in following years*
> *Like flowery fields the nations stand*
> *Pleased with the morning light;*
> *The flowers beneath the mower's hand*
> *Lie withering ere 'tis night.*

introduced the use of highly poetic texts, rather than merely arranging translations of biblical passages, giving his work a greater ecumenical acceptance and use. Trained in Greek, Hebrew, and Latin, he declined ordination as an Anglican priest, but served as a preacher for a Nonconformist congregation outside London until his health limited his service. He then lived with a wealthy Dissenter, teaching and writing not only musical texts but works of logic.

The Industrial Revolution

Although not directly a by-product of any religious awakening, a transformation began around the last quarter of the eighteenth century. Inventions were being introduced which expanded the manufacturing industries and populations moved from an agricultural to an industrial enterprises. Social changes would soon follow in the following century.

> Inventions of the late 18th century
> 1768-Spinning machine by Richard Arkwright (1752-1792)
> 1769-Steam engine by James Watt (1736-1819)
> 1770-Spinning jenny by James Hargreaves (-1778)
> 1784-Power loom by Edmund Cartwright (1743-1823)

The French Revolution

The fall of the Bastille on July 14, 1789, marked the outbreak of the French Revolution with its emphasis on "liberty, equality and fraternity." This remarkable event brought the history of this century to a fitting conclusion. The revolution was sparked by the ideological writing of Jean Jacques Rousseau (1712-1778), *The Social Contract* (1762), in which he asserted that governance of a nation resided with the people, as a civil religion. A newly prepared civil constitution ordered a reorganization of the Catholic Church and, shortly thereafter, the papal states were annexed to the nascent republic. Pope Pius VI (1717-1799, pope 1775-1799) died as a French prisoner and his successor, Pius VII (1742-1823, pope 1800-1823), was also imprisoned by Napoleon for a short time. The first Republic of France began in 1792 and the "Reign of Terror" began two years later. Finally, in 1799, the revolution ended as Napoleon Bonaparte (1769-1821) gained domination over the whole of French society. Unfortunately, the end of the revolution marked the beginning of the Napoleonic Wars (until 1815) between France and several other European nations.

The end of the Holy Roman Empire in 1806 serves as an appropriate concluding date to the early modern period of Christian history. Although technically (and chronologically) it occurred in the first decade of the 19th century, new movements and new ideas were setting a new stage and agenda throughout Europe and the Americas in the next century. Coming was a time of change.

For Review and Discussion
1. Why do you think church-related educational institutions were considered important for the settlers in the New World?
2. How did the Enlightenment emphasis gradually shift as a result of Kant's "critique"?
3. What lasting influence did Pietism have on world Christianity and especially in the American colonies?
4. Describe the connection the Wesley's Methodism had on the First Great Awakening.
5. What evidence can you detect for the influence of Christianity upon several famous musicians of this classical age?

For Further Reading

Cragg, Gerald R. *The Church and the Age of Reason 1648-1789.* Baltimore: Penguin Books, 1970.

Kidd, Thomas. *The Great Awakening: The Roots of Evangelical Christianity in Colonial America.* New Haven: Yale University Press, 2009.

Manuel, F. E. *The Eighteenth Century Confronts the Gods.* Cambridge, MA: Harvard University Press, 1959.

McLoughlin, William. *The Cherokees and Christianity, 1794–1870: Essays on Acculturation and Cultural Persistence.* Athens: University of Georgia Press, 1994.

Nichols, J. H. *History of Christianity, 1650-1950: Secularization of the West.* New York: The Ronald Press Company, 1956.

Pelikan, Jaroslav. *Bach Among the Theologians.* Philadelphia: Fortress Press, 1986.

Richard White, Richard. *The Middle Ground: Indians, Empires, and Republics in the Great Lakes Region.* New York: Cambridge University Press, 1991.

Willey, B. *The Eighteenth-Century Background.* Third edition. Boston: Beacon Press, 1964 reprint of 1941 edition.

19. The Age of Change

The Nineteenth Century

The nineteenth century was a tremendously transformative era. Politically and theologically, clashes between various conflicting viewpoints gave rise to divergent views and policies in church and state. Religious questions continued to be asked, but secular answers often vied for equal acceptance. As world travel became more accessible, the gospel proclamation entered new lands with fresh and invigorating results. This chapter will begin to focus on the North American scene to a greater degree than in the past.

Revolution in the Air
The century began with Napoleon Bonaparte (1769-1821) as a key political figure in Europe, yet that fact had significant effects on Christianity. Already in 1801, Napoleon established a Concordat with the papacy, returning confiscated lands to the church, but also assuming nominating or veto rights to clerical appointments. Two years later, the Huguenots were given legal status throughout France. In 1804, he declared himself "emperor" of France, extending the concept of the Holy Roman Empire to the French nation. The next year, Napoleon crowned himself in the Milan Cathedral. The following year, the last Emperor of the Holy Roman Empire, Francis II (1768-1835, emperor 1792-1806), dissolved the empire as an attempt to reduce Napoleon's impact on all of Europe. This official ending of the Holy Roman Empire serves as an appropriate beginning point for the modern times, whatever that finally means for historians of Christianity. In 1809, after a dispute with the papacy, Napoleon annexed the papal states and imprisoned Pope Pius VII (1742-1823, pope 1800-1823) for half a decade. The War of 1812, sometimes called the British-American War, was perceived as an arena of the Napoleonic Wars, although it served as a way to resolve several issued between Britain and the United States.

The French Revolution's cry for liberty, fraternity, and equality gave voice to severe criticism of the church and religion in general (see chapter 18). The dominance of humanistic and atheistic "dame Reason" had demanded critical evaluation of all traditions and authorities. Yet, that cold and unemotional intellectualism shifted in this century in an unexpected way. The replacement of reason with romanticism's revival of revelation—even if only in nature—led to an unusual and unanticipated emotional shift in society and culture and a new kind of religious fervor, known as Romanticism.

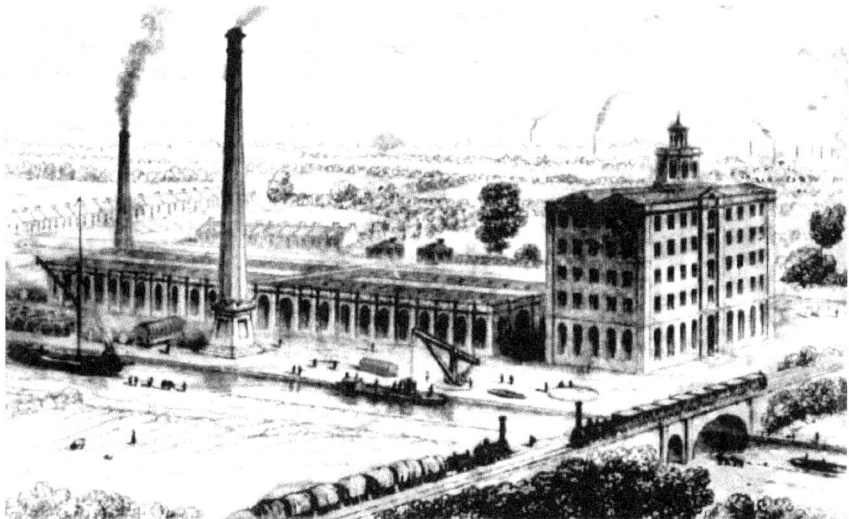

The Industrial Revolution (see chapter 18 and illustration above) took on greater significance in this century. Both positive and negative social consequences became evident. For example, Charles Dickens (1812-1870) gave names and voices to the horrific urban conditions in *Oliver Twist* (1838) and *David Copperfield* (1850). In Germany, Johann Hinrich Wichern (1808-1881) organized what became known as "inner mission work," helping the homeless and poor in the large cities. Similarly, a Lutheran pastor, Theodor Fliedner (1800-1864), founded an organization of deaconesses in Kaiserwerth, Germany, in 1836 to work with recently released women prisoners, a nursery to care for children, and medical facilities for local communities. Florence Nightingale (1820-1910) took her initial training at Kaiserwerth.

Liberalism and Romanticism

The word "romanticism," which is associated with this period of thought, began in Germany but spread throughout Europe and North America. Emphasizing individual freedom, romanticism rejected the mechanical formality of earlier rationalism as well as orthodox theology. Such freedom of the individual led to a greater focus on feelings in religious thought (similar to Pietism of the previous century), yet it had a broader perspective in the sense of a celebration of diversity. Friedrich Daniel Ernst Schleiermacher (1768-1834), for example, wrote in *On Religion: Speeches to Its Cultural Despisers*: "I find that multiplicity of the religions is based on the nature of religion…The whole of religion is nothing but the sum of all relations of man to God, apprehended in all the possible ways in which any man can be immediately conscious in his life…." Thus, a theme of a more personal concern for what was labelled "subjectivity" bore fruit throughout this century in many ways, including the religious.

According to Schleiermacher (see illustration), neither morality nor doctrine alone were sufficient to understand the realm of religion. Rather, he said, one needed to feel the faith as well. Religion as he redefined it was about human experience, thereby removing it from the rational sceptics of the previous generation. But his approach also eliminated its divinely revealed content in Scripture.

A little over twenty years later, he wrote a complete systematic theology based upon his new approach called *Christian Faith According to the Principles of the Evangelical Church* (1821-1822). Here he explained that human experience or faith is being in a relationship with God which he described as "the consciousness of being utterly dependent" (*schlechthin abhängig*). He read the Bible as a human record of human dependency upon God, not as a revelation from God to humanity. Similarly, his view of Jesus was that He recognized most perfectly His dependence upon the Father. Christ's sacrificial death, miraculous resurrection and ultimate ascension were inconsequential to humanity as long as humans experienced a sense of dependency on God, concluded Schleiermacher.

Haugian Piety in Scandinavia

The elements of a spiritual awakening were not only experienced in Europe and America. Scandinavian Protestants soon rejected the cold rationalism of the state churches and adopted a deeper and more personal piety. Noteworthy was Hans Nielsen Hauge (1771-1824), a lay evangelist from Norway, who was committed to spreading the revitalizing message of the Gospel as a personal message. Hauge travelled extensively in Norway, wrote prodigiously (thirty-three books in eighteen years), and revived Lutheranism there. His zeal for personal piety resulted in a missionary movement which spread through the subsequent migration of Norwegians to the American Midwest.

Speculations in Theology and Philosophy

One of the major movements in this century of change, was in the area of speculative theology and philosophy. Besides the work of Schleiermacher, several other individuals had an impact beyond this century into the twentieth century.

Georg Hegel

Although a philosopher of religion by training and productivity, Georg Wilhelm Friedrich Hegel (1770-1831) influenced philosophy and theology quite profoundly in the nineteenth century. He believed that his Lutheran heritage and the Lutheran church (which he called a sect) was the best belief system available in his day. Recognizing the great paradoxes of the ancient faith, Hegel strove to reconcile the various polarities of life into an ideal. These views led to what became known as "philosophical Idealism". Hegel proposed that instead of mere dialectics (whereby views were opposed to each other), two contrasting ideas should result in a movement toward an ideal synthesis of these ideas, creating something new. Applying the terminology of thesis, antithesis, and synthesis from another German philosopher, Johann Gottlieb Fichte (1762-1814), Hegel sought to bring all experiences together. Such a movement could be recognized, he believed, in philosophy, history, and theology. Even the Trinity, he said, could be explained as God's self-consciousness—God is aware of Himself, through objectifying Himself He recognizes His Son, and the resulting desire for a return to unity is the Spirit. He concluded that the incarnation was necessary because God is the thesis and humanity the antithesis, which required a God-man as synthesis.

> **Hegelian Idealism**
> In various philosophical works, he proposed a form of "philosophical idealism" claiming that history is absolute reality whereby all events unfold over time in a specific pattern of thesis, antithesis, and synthesis. He spoke of "Spirit," in the sense of a guiding power over all time, a rational understanding of God.

Ludwig Feuerbach

Another Lutheran, Ludwig Andreas von Feuerbach (1804-1872) grew up in the home of a very successful German jurist in Bavaria. After attending seminary, his studies led him to Hegelian philosophy, which he would critique

and later disavow. His view of theology was such that he reduced it simply to a kind of religious anthropology. God is ultimately nothing more than a projection of human ideals and desires. Later in life, as an avowed atheist, he did not have a significant influence on European Christianity, except to serve as the last member of the German philosophical school started by Kant. His popularity rose with the criticism of his work, *The Essence of Christianity* (1841), by Karl Marx (see below). His book, *The Essence of Faith According to Luther* (1844), reflected his Lutheran heritage as Feuerbach (see illustration) drew upon Luther's idea of God being "for me" (*pro me*), an idea which he claimed became the self-projection of an ideal in his *Lectures on the Essence of Religion* (1848).

F. C. Baur

Born into a Lutheran parsonage, Ferdinand Christian Baur (1792-1860) was greatly attracted to historical studies. Influenced by Hegel, Baur asserted that real Christianity could be found only in Jesus' words—the Sermon on the Mount and His parables and discourses. He claimed that primitive Christianity was Jewish and Paul's theology was its antithesis. The synthesis was Catholicism, but not true Christianity. The success of his teaching at the University of Tübingen from 1826 led to the formation of what became known as the "Tübingen school" in the 1840s, where he and his students questioned the Pauline authorship of most of the epistles except Romans, 2 Corinthians, and Galatians. These three letters reflected what they thought was the struggle of early Christianity with Judaism, so he dated them as the earliest New Testament books. The rest of the New Testament he asserted grew out of second century Christian communities. In his five-volume *History of the Christian Church* (1853-1863), published after his death, Baur demonstrated his long-time emphasis upon all theology requiring critical historical analysis.

David Friedrich Strauss

After several years at a Lutheran high school in Blaubeuren, Germany, where he had studied with Bauer, David Friedrich Strauss (1808-1874) matriculated at Tübingen and, after a brief teaching job at his high school, he went to Berlin, where he began studies with Schleiermacher. He hoped to study with Hegel, but Schleiermacher died shortly after Strauss's arrival in Berlin. Taking an Hegelian approach to Christianity, Strauss asserted that a synthesis of Christian thought was only possible when the biblical narratives were understood as "myths," that is, religious stories which had no basis in history, but were created to teach lessons. In his most notorious work, *The Life of Jesus Critically Examined* (1836), he asserted that Jesus Christ as a so-called "Son of God" could only be so mythically, since such an event as the incarnation of a deity is beyond human experience. At the end of his life, he had rejected any idea of a personal God and immortality. His views led to the later liberal distinction between the "Jesus of history" and the "Christ of faith," as well as to scientific materialism, a Darwinian form of understanding humanity.

Charles Darwin

Born to a wealthy English family of Unitarians, Charles Darwin (1809-1882) was never strongly religious. Later in life, he would describe himself not as an atheist, but as an agnostic. He did not set out to disprove God's creation, but only to explain the *Origin of the Species by Means of Natural Selection* (1859), the title of his most famous work, without the need for divine involvement. As a result of his scientific investigations, he concluded that a divine Designer was unnecessary and that the slow natural processes of nature are sufficient to explain all of life. He combined this view with his rejection of biblical authority. His popular writing style and financial support from the wealthy scientific community made his work one of the most influential works of the century.

Søren Kierkegaard

The Danish Lutheran philosopher and theologian, Søren Aabye Kierkegaard (1813-1855) (see illustration on the next page), was a prolific author in both theology and philosophy, and was a key figure in nineteenth century Danish literary work. Sometimes called the "gloomy Dane," Kierkegaard exhibited a deeply Pietistic sense of guilt and an awareness of his own temporal existence. He acknowledged faith as a gift, in contrast to many of the Enlightenment philosophers before him. Kierkegaard spoke of "the leap" both to sin and to faith. Because of Adam and Eve's sin, there is a separation between humanity and God. Only because of God's gracious forgiveness can one make "the leap" to faith, which is not a rational act, but a leap made "by faith" alone.

In one of his early publications, *Fear and Trembling* (1843), he uses the story of Abraham being commanded to sacrifice his son, Isaac. Seeing the anxiety and horrendous leap of faith required of Abraham, Kierkegaard described a process of "infinite resignation" before one takes a leap to faith.

This focus on the personal existence of a Christian believer produced the philosophical view known as "existentialism." The term later was used to designate the perspective that human experience and the human subject was key to finding meaning in a meaningless or at least absurd world. The Existentialist view became very popular especially in psychology, but also on the theological work of Karl Barth in the next century (see chapter 20).

Toward the end of his life, Kierkegaard critiqued the Danish state church in his *Attack on Christendom* (1854-1855). He vehemently decried the church leaders for allowing and even encouraging members to be lax in their commitment to Christ. For him, the Christian faith was much more individualistic and active, not a mere membership in an organized rigid community. Jesus Christ came to renew each person through His own life, death, and resurrection.

> Kierkegaard's *Purity of Heart is to Will One Thing*
>
> To will one thing could not mean to will the world's pleasure and what belongs to it, even if a person only named one thing as his choice, since this one thing was one only by a deception. Nor could willing one thing mean willing it in the vain sense of mere bigness which only to a man in a state of giddiness appears to be one. For in Truth to will one thing, a man must will the Good.

Karl Marx

The Communist Manifesto (1848) by Karl Heinrich Marx (1818-1883) and Friedrich Engels (1820-1895) not only critiqued religious "myths," but called religion itself "the opiate of the people," something which deadened the minds of the proletariat masses into brain-less submission to power-hungry bureaucrats. Growing from his views, socialist ideals and communal organizations began to be promoted as a means to order society instead of the church.

Although his parents were Jews, his father had "converted" and joined a Prussian Lutheran congregation, where Karl was baptized at age 6. Struggling academically, he finally earned a doctorate from the University of Jena. Influenced initially by Hegelian philosophy, he was drawn to Feuerbach's critique of Hegel, replacing Hegel's idealism as being impractical with a more materialist orientation.

A few months after his marriage in 1843, he moved to Paris, where he became involved with the social protests of the workers, known already as "communists." Over the next years, his association with such groups in Europe and England resulted in the *Manifesto* which described ten initial steps toward a communist philosophy and revolution. This document proposed a progressive income tax, the abolition of inheritances, and free education for all children. Its closing words have become famous: "The proletarians have nothing to lose but their chains. They have a world to win. Workingmen of all countries, unite!" Expelled from Paris, Marx moved to London where he continued his revolutionary writing. Although he and his family suffered economic hardships, he maintained that economic value was primary over any kind of spiritual or religious concerns.

Albrecht Ritschl

Influenced by Schleiermacher and Kant, Albrecht Ritschl (1822-1889) sought to restore a Lutheran emancipation from philosophical theology, particularly from the Hegelian ideas he had learned from the Tübingen School. In so doing, he eliminated key Christian and Lutheran teachings, such as forensic justification. His *Christian Doctrine of Justification and the Atonement* (1870-1874, *Die Christliche Lehre von der Rechtfertigung und Versöhnung*) provided the best example of his systematic and historical-critical approach. There he articulated the major doctrine of the Christian faith using the imagery of relationships which are broken and need restoration. Born in a Lutheran parsonage, he prepared a thorough, three-volume, *History of Pietism* (1882-1886, *Die Geschichte des Pietismus*). Ritschl's positive approach to theology led to his greater influence into the next century, particularly against those who sought a purely rationalistic approach to the Christian faith.

Friedrich Nietzsche

Raised in a Christian family, Friedrich Wilhelm Nietzsche (1844-1900) became an archetype of atheism, declaring that God did not even exist. He viewed Christianity as the source of a kind of slave mentality which rotted the minds and bodies of humanity. As a philosopher, he declared that humanity needed to come to its own self-realization without any transcendent claims. Life itself had no real purpose for Nietzsche, for whom the idea of nihilism is often associated. He suffered from severe mental illness over the last decades of his life.

> From *The Anti-Christ*
> I call Christianity the one great curse, the one great intrinsic depravity, the one great instinct of revenge, for which no means are venomous enough, or secret, subterranean and small enough,--I call it the one immortal blemish upon the human race..."
> Friedrich Nietzsche

Julius Wellhausen and Karl Graf

Another son of a Protestant minister, Julius Wellhausen (1844-1918) proposed a theory regarding the creation of the first five books of Moses, asserting that they were not by Moses but were a product of post-exilic editors. He augmented his views to conform to an order suggested by Karl Heinrich Graf (1815-1869), sometimes called the JEDP theory (J= used Jehovah as the divine revealer, E=emphasized Elohim as creator God; D=favored the Deuteronomic regulations; P=focused upon priestly practices) named after the supposed editorialized sources, formed the basis for the biblical studies through most of the next century. This evolutionary approach followed the liberalizing tendencies of the last part of this century and had a major impact on biblical studies into the twentieth century.

Westcott-Hort and Bishop Lightfoot

Two biblical scholars, Brooke Foss Westcott (1825-1901) and Fenton John Anthony Hort (1828-1892), published a complete edition of the Greek New Testament in 1881, known as the Westcott-Hort text. Using a system of manuscript study called "textual criticism," based upon a Darwinian idea of textual development, they sought to identify the earliest Greek text as could be determined from the oldest manuscript fragments and most ancient existent texts. While their assumptions were not always accurate, they concluded that the minor differences in biblical manuscripts amounted to only one-sixtieth of the New Testament and all of them are insignificant theologically or doctrinally. Their work continues to be the basis for much biblical translation into the present.

Around the same time, the early Christian studies of Joseph Barber Lightfoot (1828-1889), bishop of Durham (1879-1889), exemplified the challenge of modern historical scholarship, while trying to remain faithful to biblical truths. His sermons and commentaries continue to be helpful resources as is his multivolume editorial work on the Apostolic Fathers.

Religious Changes

During the first half of this century, several missionary societies were formed. Along with these organizations came the recognized need for Bibles in a variety of languages. A hundred years after the organization of such a group in Halle (see chapter 18), the British and Foreign Bible Society was founded in 1804 and a little more than a decade later, the American Bible Society was organized. Unfortunately, a conflict broke out in 1827-1828 over the benefit of including the Apocrypha in Bible translations. From that point on, most Bibles were printed without those texts, except for Catholic publishers and the German Bible Society, which was formed in opposition to this decision.

Among Anglican clergy in the early years of this century, there arose several movements that had theological implications. Ever since the restoration of the British monarchy, most people considered the British church to be "high," that is, having a high respect for the traditions of the church, including the historic vestments and ritual liturgies. Early in the eighteenth century, influenced by the strong Evangelical movement in England, questions were raised by those who advocated a simpler style of worship or "low church," such as John Newton (1725-1807) and William Wilberforce (1759-1833). They encouraged stronger preaching and promoted humanitarian efforts to alleviate the effects of the Industrial Revolution. A third movement originated in mid-century as the "broad church." As a result of the successful work of the advocates of this movement, Anglicanism regained its middle-of-the-road status, accepting many of the more liberal trends in society, yet claiming historic roots and working for social reforms.

The Oxford Movement

Arising from questions about the nature of the church, several young clergy in Oxford began to study the practices of primitive Christianity. Sometimes called "the Oxford Movement," the members began to emphasize fasting, prayers to the saints, celibacy, and other "Catholic" practices. Among the leaders of the group was John Henry Newman (1801-1890), who published a series of *Tracts for our Times* between 1833 and 1841 (the group members were therefore called "Tractarians"), and Edward Bouverie Pusey (1800-1882), who sought to restore primitive Christianity to what he called "Anglo-Catholicism." Newman, after several more years of doubting the necessity of Anglicanism's *via media* role between Protestantism and Roman Catholicism, joined the Catholic Church in 1845, taking many followers with him and, as such, ended the movement.

Vatican I (1869-1870)

Roman Catholicism had continued fairly uneventfully over the centuries following the Council of Trent in the sixteenth century. After several decades of anti-Christian sentiments, particularly in France, Roman Catholicism gradually re-established its presence as a viable institution. Known as "ultramontism" (that is, "beyond the mountains," referring to Italy), papal powers were exalted above national or local authorities. By the middle of the nineteenth century, Pope Pius IX (1792-1878, pope 1846-1878) called an ecumenical council, set to meet at the Vatican (thus it is referred to as Vatican I) from late 1869 to late 1870. This meeting was to address many of the concerns over the past century related to rationalism, liberalism, socialism, and materialism. Most significant in their doctrinal decisions was the affirmation of the infallibility of the pope (*Pastor aeternus*, "eternal shepherd"). (See selection in sidebar) Fifteen years earlier, Pope Pius had declared as official Roman Catholic dogma, the "immaculate conception of Mary," that Mary herself was without original sin as a consequence of her own miraculous conception.

> *Pastor aeternus*
> The Roman Pontiff, when he speaks *ex cathedra*, that is, when in discharge of the office of pastor and doctor of all Christians, by virtue of his supreme apostolic authority, he defines a doctrine regarding faith or morals to be held by the universal church, by the divine assistance promised to him in blessed Peter, is possessed of that infallibility with which the divine Redeemer willed that His church should be endowed.

A year after the Council, political problems arose as Victor Emmanuel of Sardinia (1807-1882) established a kingdom of Italy which included most of the papal lands. When war broke out in 1870 between France and Germany, Emmanuel captured Rome itself, granting sovereignty only of the Vatican, the Lateran, and Castel Gandolfo, thus ending the secular sovereignty of these lands. Besides Italy's unification, the aftermath of the Franco-Prussian War (1870-1871) resulted in a new German Empire.

In addition to papal authority, the Roman Catholic saw a revival of missionary work similar to that among Protestantism. Based mainly in France, members of many religious orders joined the newly restored Jesuits in supporting a worldwide spread of Catholicism. Nuns were especially involved in these activities, providing more than half the workers sent out by the Capuchins, Dominicans, Franciscans, and many others by the end of the century. Much of the rest of Catholic mission work was a result of immigration to the New World in both North and South America. German Catholics also began working in Africa, particularly in Uganda in the late 1870s.

Spurgeon and the Booth's "Salvation Army"

While the common British Christian was nominally Anglican, over the first half of this century, the non-conformist movement (those groups which rejected the state-church, such as Baptists, Congregationalists, Quakers, and Methodists) grew in both numbers and influence through their preachers and scholars. Among the most famous Baptist preachers of the century was the London orator, author, and biblical expositor, Charles Spurgeon (1834-1892), who opposed the increasing liberalism of the churches.

Inspired by Spurgeon's open-air preaching methods, William Booth (1829-1912) rejected the traditional view of the pastoral ministry with an established congregation housed in a church building. After receiving his training as a Methodist minister, he felt called to preach the Gospel to those who were outside the established Christian community—the poor, the homeless, the destitute, the outcasts of society. He began as an iterant preacher in 1852. Setting up a tent in the East End of London in 1865, he began a successful Gospel outreach in the community. Within a decade he had trained 42 fellow evangelists with over a thousand volunteers. At the time, the organization called itself "The

Christian Mission" and Booth was the general superintendent, known as the "General." A couple of years later, in reading the proof of a newspaper article, he changed the description of the mission from "a volunteer army" to the "salvation army," and the name stuck. Using military language for their activities, the leaders were identified by military rank and the members were "soldiers" of Christ. While William Booth worked with the poor, his wife and cofounder, Catherine (1829-1890) developed strong relationships with women and acquired significant financial support from the wealthy (see illustration).

The movement quickly spread from the British Isles to the Americas. In 1886, President Grover Cleveland not only received a delegation, but warmly endorsed their program of spiritual and social action. Booth had described their mission by the three-"S's"—soup, soap, and salvation. Holding basic Reformed Christian beliefs, they rejected the sacraments as only of human origin, emphasizing active service over doctrine. By the end of the century, they were established globally, with organizational bases in Canada, Australia, France, Switzerland, India, South Africa, and Iceland, in addition to the American scene.

The American Scene

An American historian of Christianity, Susan Peterson, noted that "before the nineteenth century, religion in America was largely imported from Europe. In the nineteenth century, however, the Second Great Awakening, the debate over slavery, unprecedented multiculturalism, and increasing sectarianism gave American Christianity a distinct, indigenous tint."

In 1801, as Thomas Jefferson (1743-1826) assumed office, Congregational and Presbyterian congregations in Connecticut made plans to unite in order to better evangelize the American frontier. Their "Plan of Union" allowed them to choose their minister from either denomination. A similar move towards unity occurred the following year among Lutherans as Jacob Albright (1759-1808), a farmer and tile-maker in Pennsylvania organized an evangelical association (which took that name in 1816). In the same year, Lutherans in North Carolina organized themselves as the Evangelical Lutheran Synod and Ministerium of North Carolina.

During these same years, several universities established church-related seminaries on their campuses, along with hundreds of denominational colleges. Most well-known are Princeton Seminary initiated by Presbyterians in 1812, the Harvard Divinity School in 1819 started by Unitarians, and Yale Divinity School founded by Congregationalists in 1822. Princeton Seminary, for example, was specifically established upon a traditional Reformed theological foundation, advocating a strict Calvinist theology. Other schools and seminaries were started by Baptists, Lutherans, and Moravians so that by mid-century there were over fifty church-related institutions spreading from the East coast to mid-America and by the end of the century over 100 Protestant theological schools had been established.

Homeland Wars: 1846-1848 and 1861-1865

The expansionist program of the United States took on a decided concrete form in the war against Mexico, known as the Mexican-American War (1846-1848), a decade after Texas gained its independence. President James K. Polk (1798-1849), under the overall banner of "manifest destiny," authorized several border attacks near the Rio Grande. Over the next year, major battles ensued until the final Treaty of Guadalupe Hidalgo set the border between the United States and Mexico at the Rio Grande and nearly a third of the lands under the Mexican flag were sold to the United States—California, Arizona, New Mexico, Nevada, and Utah. Among the religious dimensions of this movement was a decidedly anti-Catholic bias in the eastern United States and the consequent fear that a Catholic population would seize power.

Although not a war about religion, religious issues were involved during the Civil War (1861-1865), particularly the place of slavery. The view of slavery among most Christian groups in America, reflecting biblical statements, was that holding slaves was an acceptable practice. Where the real issue became problematic was in the treatment of these slaves—treating them as sub-human property, rather than as brothers and sisters in Christ (Ephesians 6:5-9). For most of Christian history, the use of household slaves was recognized as both an economic necessity and a spiritual responsibility (Philemon). Denominations in the United States were divided over the place of slavery and the role of abolitionism. The War-between-the-States had devastating consequences for some Christian groups, yet for others it provided a greater opportunity to expand into new areas of the nation.

C. F. W. Walther and the Saxon Immigrants

In order to celebrate the three-hundredth anniversary of the Reformation in 1817 (and for political expedience), Kaiser Frederick Wilhelm III of Prussia (1770-1840) had determined to form one Protestant church to counter the political strength of his Catholic constituents. He decreed that a common order of service and pastoral handbook be prepared for this Evangelical-Reformed Church, which tended more toward Calvinist than Lutheran teachings. The training of these pastors was conducted in the universities and was strongly influenced by the Rationalism of the day, moving away from the basic tenets of orthodox Christianity.

At this same time, there was a movement in Germany for confessional orthodoxy, originating with Claus Harms (1788-1855) and promoted by Ernest Wilhelm Hengstenberg (1802-1869) in Berlin. Asserting a vigorous return to the

sixteenth century confessions of the Lutheran church along with biblical authority and inspiration, they resisted both rationalism and romanticism. They are often identified as "repristinaters," returning to sixteenth century Lutheran foundations. Closely related to Hengstenberg were other confessionally orthodox leaders, particularly Wilhelm Loehe (1808-1872), who stressed the spread of the gospel through missionary programs within high-church liturgical practices.

Although his father and grandfather were pastors, C. F. W. Walther (1811-1887) (see illustration) was initially inclined toward music. After attending the University of Leipzig, where his older brother, Otto (1809-1841), also was studying, he became disenchanted with much of the liberal thought. During a serious illness which kept him from his university studies for half-a-year, he voraciously read Luther's writings along with the Lutheran Confessions in his father's library. Convinced that the church needed a stronger confessional stance, he struggled with his early ministerial responsibilities after his ordination in 1837.

Seeking solace for his soul, Walther had become influenced by some Pietist students who led him to meet a Reverend Martin Stephan (1777-1847) from Dresden. Stephan had a strong personality and a gift for preaching convincing Gospel-centered messages along with a compassionate counseling style. At about the same time, Stephan was organizing a group of confessional

Lutherans to flee the oppressive Prussian Union Church. The Walther brothers expressed interest and joined the group. In late 1837, five ships set sail for the New World, four of which arrived in New Orleans in January 1838 and, within a few months, settled in St. Louis and Perry County, Missouri.

Shortly thereafter, Stephan was dismissed from his duties for several acts of misconduct and C. F. W. Walther was left as one of the chief leaders of the group. A determined theologian, Walther sought clarification of the status of the congregations under his care: Were they indeed church or not? Convinced of their legitimacy, Walther set out to establish a strong confessional stance in the midwest.

Through a series of publications, particularly a weekly journal, *Der Lutheraner*, he not only set a clear direction for the Perry County and St. Louis congregations, but became a leader in gathering like-minded confessional

---

C.F.W. Walther's introductory statement from
Der Lutheraner, vol.1, no. 1, p. 1

...The German Lutherans here are greatly tempted to abandon the faith of their fathers, to give up their concern about church, worship and the like, to seek to free themselves from their religious obligations by joining other churches that are already established here. So above all, our precious brothers in faith in these parts of our new homeland need to be encouraged to remain true to their faith. They need to be warned of the danger of apostasy which threatens so many of them here. They need to be armed to defend themselves against those who challenge them as to whether their faith, which they have learned in their youth from the Catechism, is right. They need the comfort that the church which they profess has not yet vanished, so they have no reason whatsoever to seek refuge in any other fellowship. This definite need, experienced by so many, and the conviction that it must be our obligation to present in our day to our fellow citizens the reason why our church believes and teaches as she does, and according to which principles therefore these teachings are handled by us; this has moved the undersigned in conjunction with several of his brothers in the Office and faith in Missouri and Illinois to publish a paper under this masthead. That is, that it should also serve: 1.To make known the doctrine, the treasures and the history of the Lutheran Church; 2. To prove that this church is not to be lumped in with the Christian sects, and is not a new church, but the ancient, true church of Jesus Christ on earth, so that she has in no way died off, yes, that she cannot die off according to Christ's promise: "Behold I am with you every day until the end of the world." Further, our paper shall also serve, 3. To show how, as a true Lutheran, a person can rightly believe, live as a Christian, be patient in suffering, and have a blessed death. And finally, 4. To uncover the false misleading doctrine popular in our day, to oppose it and sound the warning against it, and especially to unmask those who falsely call themselves Lutheran, spreading errant faith, unbelief and enthusiasm under that name and therefore most wickedly being the cause of prejudice against our church amongst members of other groups.

---

churches throughout the Midwest. In 1847, after several meetings, an organization was finally established in St Paul Lutheran Church in Chicago, Illinois. Incorporated as the German Evangelical Lutheran Church of Missouri, Ohio, and Other States, these congregations committed themselves to faithful biblical and confessional doctrine as well as a strong educational program and mission outreach.

Besides doctrinal integrity and missional consciousness, one of the distinctive features of these evangelical Lutherans was their form of governance. Having fled Germany's state-church system and having experienced a failure in an episcopal model with Bishop Martin Stephan, Walther looked at the American scene. Appreciative of the democratic processes and yet affirming the significance of the local congregation as the embodiment of the true church, he proposed a unique form of synodical polity. The word, *synod*, from the Greek for "walking together," described the ideal structure. Walther proposed that this new Lutheran denomination seek a balance between lay and clergy leaders, between congregational and denominational authority.

Publishing his ideas in *The Voice of Our Church in the Question of Church and Office/Ministry* (1852) and *The Proper Form of an Evangelical Lutheran Congregation Independent of the State* (1863), Walther spelled out clearly his ideas and ideals. Synod, as an organizing agency, is advisory to congregations who have voluntarily joined the synod. While being somewhat influenced by his historical context, Walther was a faithful student of the Scriptures and Martin Luther's understanding of the gospel. It was the Word of God which was the final authority for faith and life for this group of New World citizens.

Camp Meetings, Revival, and the Restoration Movement

The first significant assembly of evangelical Christians met in a Kentucky frontier setting in 1800 under the "pastoral" leadership of James McGready (1763-1817). Trained as an evangelistic preacher in the 1780s, he assumed pastorates in several south-eastern states, where he emphasized a need to revive the spiritual lives of these frontier communities. The next year what became known as "the Second Great Awakening" began at the Cane Ridge Revival, particularly in response to the steady secularizing of society and the rampant rationalism of the Enlightenment. Characteristic of this movement was an emphasis on a personal conversion experience. Growing out of a Presbyterian practice of outdoor worship services (known as "the sacramental season"), these camp meetings drew ever increasing crowds together, many travelling several days and then expecting to stay for a week of worship and "supernatural" experiences. (See illustration.)

A significant theological divide occurred as a result of these activities. The mainline churches (Anglicans, Catholics, Lutherans, and the New England Congregationalists) rejected the claim that conversion could be determined by a specific event in one's life, accompanied by special signs manifesting the outpouring of the Holy Spirit, as the revivalists promoted. Others hailed these events as an indication of the Spirit's movement over the frontiers of the new world.

Barton Stone

Barton W. Stone (1772-1844), a Presbyterian minister who orchestrated a revival larger than the Cane Ridge event, along with several other followers, began to call themselves "Christians" in order to express their denunciation of denominational labels. They were part of an increasingly popular approach toward Christianity in America, known as "primitivism" or "the restoration movement." Their desire was to go back to New Testament Christianity without all the historical accretions or subsequent traditions.

The Campbells

A father-and-son team, Thomas (1763-1854) and Alexander Campbell (1788-1866), founded the Christian Association of Washington in 1809, calling themselves "Disciples of Christ," and set forth the simple statement: "Where the Bible speaks, we speak; where it is silent, we are silent." In the 1830s these two groups merged into what was called the Restoration Movement. However, as the issue of slavery became more prominent, they sought unity through silence on the subject. By the end of the century, the group had divided into three strains—known as the Church of Christ, the Christian Church, and Disciples of Christ.

A Native American Prophet

In response to the encroaching advance of European Christians, Tenskwatawa (1771-1836), the younger brother of the famous Shawnee leader, Tecumseh (1768-1813), claimed to have his own religious experiences. Moving from his home in Ohio, Tenskwatawa and Tecumseh founded a Shawnee village in Indiana. After a series of visions in the early decade of this century, Tenskwatawa achieved a significant following after predicting a solar eclipse in 1806, much to the dismay of the Indiana territory governor who had called him a fraud. Tenskwatawa, known now as "the Prophet," called for a pan-Indian coalition of tribes which rejected many of the white man's ways, particularly alcohol and Christian teachings. He claimed to follow "the Great Spirit," identifying and eliminating several witches who had contaminated the true spiritual practices of the tribe.

The large multi-tribe community which developed at the convergence of the Tippecanoe and Wabash Rivers was called Prophetstown. In 1811, Governor Harrison (later to be President) engaged and defeated the Native American confederation in the Battle of Tippecanoe. The Prophet's prediction of victory left him bereft of community support. Escaping to Canada, he fought with his brother against the United States in the War of 1812, only to return and establish a community near Kansas City late in life, where he died.

Charles Finney

Another Presbyterian minister, Charles Finney (1792-1875) (see illustration), known as "the Father of Modern Revivalism" because of his gift for preaching, placed a new emphasis upon revival practices. Raised in upstate New York, he served as an apprentice in a law office until he had "a conversion

experience" in 1821. Studying under a Presbyterian minister, he questioned some of the traditional doctrines and moved to New York City, where he attended a Manhattan church known for its revivals. Adapting and expanding the revival techniques he saw there, Finney returned to upstate New York and led revivals throughout the northeastern states between 1825 and 1835. He then moved to Ohio, where he taught at Oberlin College and became a strong advocate of the school's abolitionist movement. From 1851-1866 he was president of the college, which served a key link in the Underground Railroad.

In 1835, Finney described his techniques in *Lectures on Revivals of Religion*, known as "New Measures." Among these activities were women in leadership roles, the "anxious bench" where persons who desired to be converted could "make their decision," using music to prepare people for the message, and employing common, emotional, and persuasive language in preaching. Conversion, he asserted, was less of a miracle and more of a decision of one's free will. Worship should be entertaining and draw people into the assembly. His doctrinal views were published in 1846, *Lectures on Systematic Theology*, demonstrating his Arminian form of Calvinism.

Dwight L. Moody

Toward the end of the century, Finney's techniques were expanded by the lay evangelist, Dwight Lyman Moody (1837-1899), who also understood the need for educational programs. With little formal education, yet a natural ability to communicate, Moody became a leading force for evangelistic work at the end of the century. Born into a Unitarian family in Massachusetts, he became a Christian in 1855 under the influence of an uncle in Boston. Moving to Chicago, he started a Sunday School with a particular focus on the slums and then he began to lead a local YMCA. After losing his home, church, and the YMCA in the Chicago fire of 1871, he resolved to work globally while on a fund-raising trip to New York City. In the next years, as a tireless preacher and aggressive organizer, he set out on many international evangelistic trips, using some of Finney's techniques and adding his own—house to house visits prior to his preaching "crusades," an ecumenical involvement of various church bodies, and musical attractions during the event. In the 1880s he added educational conferences and an institution of higher education, Chicago Bible Institute, renamed in his honor as the Moody Bible Institute.

New Religious Expressions and Inventions

At the end of the Civil War another period of religious revivalism occurred in frontier America, resulting a plethora of novel expressions and organizations. Many of them developed from a renewed sense of living in the End Times or on the last days before Christ's imminent return, a theme which echoed from the Second Great Awakening. Except for the Christian Science, the other three cults continue to outpace mainline Christian groups in membership growth into the present. We can only briefly provide a historical overview of them in this chapter.

The Church of Jesus Christ of Latter Day Saints

Rejecting the religious fervor of the second great awakening, Joseph Smith (1805-1844) sought to find a true denomination. Claiming to have a vision from the angel Moroni in the early 1820s, he unearthed golden plates which he subsequently translated from a supposed ancient Egyptian hieroglyphic script. This translation, which Smith dictated from behind a screen, was written down and became known as *The Book of Mormon*. It reveals that Jesus, prior to His ascension, visited North America. The lost tribes of Israel had settled in the New World and then, through infighting, lost the true Gospel until Smith rediscovered it.

With several friends, he founded a new denomination which claimed to be a restoration of the original church of Jesus. The group grew slowly in New York and then, fleeing opposition from various communities, moved to Ohio, Missouri, and then Illinois. (See map of LDS movements) Suspicious of the

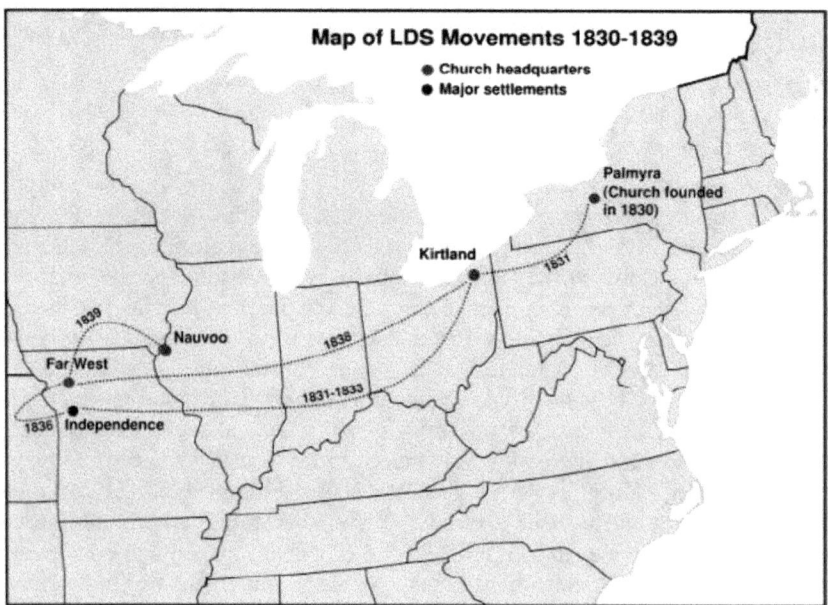

politics of the group, Smith was assassinated in 1844 while incarcerated in Carthage, Illinois. Fearful of further attacks, Brigham Young (1801-1877), close friend and successor to Smith, led a group to the territory around the Salt Lake in Utah. There they formed an independent community, later to become the Utah Territory (1850). They joined the United States in 1896, after repudiating their practice of polygamy.

Although the Church of Jesus Christ of Latter Day Saints, their official title, claim to be a Christian group and use the name of Jesus, they developed their own interpretations of biblical teachings. They reject the Trinity and the sacraments, but espouse peculiar practices based on obscure biblical texts (baptism for the dead and hierarchical priesthood), or from non-biblical sources (God the Father's wife, Jesus's brother as Satan, pre-mortal existence). Their strongest asset is the obligatory two-year missionary activity required of all Mormons and their emphasis upon family ministry.

Seventh Day Adventists

Following a similar historical context as Mormons, the Adventist movement (named for the second coming or "advent" of Christ), was begun by William Miller (1782-1849) in 1844. His followers were first known as "Millerites." Miller, a Baptist farmer and self-proclaimed prophet, predicted Christ would return on October 22, 1844. Although many adherents waited expectantly in his farm field, there was no evident return. That date was subsequently known as "the Great Disappointment," although some followers claimed that Christ did return, but only spiritually. Despite this weak beginning, several Millerites met the following year to continue his teachings. Miller himself never joined any of these new denominations. However, in the early 1860s, four distinct groups emerged, of which two remain—the Advent Christian Church and the Seventh-Day Adventists. The latter group has maintained many Old Testament regulations—particularly observing the Sabbath Day and keeping health laws (many are vegetarians)—as well as a strong emphasis on conservative biblical studies and a global mission and medical outreach.

In 1863, the Seventh Day Adventist church was organized in Battle Creek, Michigan. Ellen Gould White (1827-1915) had followed Miller with her husband, James (1821-1881). Shortly before their marriage, she began to have visions which supported the Millerite hopes. As her prophetic visions increased, transcriptions were made and published. Although some consider the denomination a cult, the teachings of the Adventists follow mainline evangelical doctrines with a pre-millennial and Arminian emphasis. Justification by grace through faith in Christ is central to the Adventist understanding of salvation.

Jehovah's Witnesses

Charles Taze Russell (1852-1916) fell under the influence of similar Adventist thinking. In 1870, he formed "the Millennial Dawn Bible Study" group. Sixteen years later, the group started the Watchtower Bible and Tract Society, the publishing arm of the Russellite group, and later their official body for interpreting the Bible. Judge J. F. Rutherford (1869-1942) assumed the leadership of the group in 1917 after Russell's death. After an internal split among the membership, the main body would take the name, "Jehovah's Witnesses," in 1931.

Most noteworthy of the group is their door-to-door witnessing and their refusal to accept blood transfusions and serve in the military. Among their witnessing tools are the publications of *Awake* and *The Watchtower*. The group is nontrinitarian. Claiming that Jesus is not God, but another name for the archangel,

Michael, the group also denies Christ's substitutionary atonement, but assert that Jesus died only for Adam's sin. Holding a premillennial perspective, they want to establish God's kingdom on earth, where the majority of Witnesses will return and rule after the resurrection on the Last Day.

Christian Science

Mary Morse Baker Eddy (1821-1910), a widow and then divorced spiritualist, gathered friends together after her third marriage and professed to them that she had special spiritual powers (see illustration).  She published *Science and Health with Key to the Scriptures* (1875), claiming to have special insights from God about healing. Suffering as a child from frequent illnesses, she sought alternate healing methods. A disciple of Phineas Quimby (1802-1855), she adapted his mesmerism (also known as "animal magnetism") to elements of Christianity and created a kind of spiritual do-it-yourself religion. Rejecting clergy, she emphasized that all members of the Church of Christ, Scientist (founded in 1879) were equally capable of teaching and instructing. She taught that the material world is a "mist" and does not really exist; therefore, illnesses can be overcome by prayer and mental discipline (a metaphysical ideal). While claiming to be a "Christian" organization, Eddy taught that Jesus was a divine healer, but He was not God. God is Father-Mother or the Divine Mind, which alone can cure all through prayer and right thinking.

Christian History and Denominationalism

Philip Schaff (1819-1893), a Swiss-born, German-trained, historian of the Christian church, prepared an eight-volume *History of the Christian Church* (1858; revised 1882 and 1890). Coming to the United States in 1844, he served as a professor at a German-Reformed seminary in Mercersburg, Pennsylvania, until it closed during the Civil War. There at Mercersburg, along with John Nevin (1803-1886), Schaff was instrumental in promoting what became known as "Mercersburg Theology," a combination of historical ecclesiology and sacramentality (more in line with Lutheranism than Calvinism). The latter emphasis resulted in severe criticism of Schaff by his Reformed Church of the United States. Subsequently, he taught at Union Theological Seminary, New York, from 1870 until his death.

In 1857, Schaff reported on "Christianity in America," noting especially that a great variety of denominations coexisted in the context of American religious freedom. Although he would later work toward unity among all Christians, he saw denominational distinctions as a blessing, something he compared to the blessing of having four distinct accounts in the Gospels. Reflecting their historical origins in European Christianity, many American denominations developed as a result of geographic or national distinctions—whether they settled in the East or Midwest or South; or, in what language they worshiped or taught (see below). Others, as evident above, had roots in the American revivalism and post-Civil War millennialism. These denominations would greatly influence the next activities in the next century and will be discussed under ecumenism (chapter 20).

Lutherans in America

What were Lutherans doing during the turbulent times of this century? As noted earlier in this chapter and in the previous chapters, there were a significant number of Lutherans in the American colonies before the Revolutionary War. The Muehlenbergs (see chapter 18) had created a strong Lutheran presence in the East. As more and more immigrants from Denmark, Sweden, Norway, and Germany moved to the Midwest and western territories in the early nineteenth century a diversity of Lutheran expressions were evident. By the beginning of this century, over twenty distinct national Lutheran groups had organized, usually using resources from their European homelands and retaining their national language in particular geographical or regional areas.

Samuel S. Schmucker (1799-1873) was born in a Lutheran parsonage in Maryland, where his father was a member of the Pennsylvania Ministerium (see chapter 18). Showing academic ability, he attended a local university/academy in York, Pennsylvania, at the age of 15 or 16 and then, after a missionary trip in Appalachia, he attended Princeton Seminary and was ordained into the Lutheran ministry in 1820. That same year, he helped organize the General Synod of the Evangelical Lutheran Church of the United States. For almost thirty-five years from 1826-1864, he

> **Lord's Supper**
> In his *Evangelical Lutheran Catechism* (Baltimore: T. Newton Kurtz, 1871), Schmucker answered Q. 299: "By faith they [worthy communicants] spiritually feed on the body and blood of the Redeemer...."

served as a professor at the Lutheran Theological Seminary at Gettysburg, founded under his leadership by the General Synod. His theology was strongly affected by his Calvinist training at Princeton, especially in his understanding of the Lord's Supper (see sidebar), and striving for a greater ecumenical posture by discarding the Augsburg Confession. He was a staunch abolitionist and was instrumental in the early seminary education of Daniel Alexander Payne (1811-1893), a leader in the newly formed African Methodist Episcopal Church.

Strong opposition to Schmucker was voiced by Paul Henkel (1754-1825) and, subsequently, his son, David (1795-1831). Both men were supported by the family printing business, the Henkel Press, which published the first English language *Book of Concord* in North America in 1851. Paul became a strong evangelistic preacher and missionary after his ordination in 1792, supporting confessional Lutheran theology.

Between 1840 and 1875 more than fifty new Lutheran groups were formed in the United States. By the end of the century there were over 150 distinct national or geographical groups of Lutherans. In the early decades of the following century, several of these groups merged to form larger *American* Lutheran denominations.

In 1867, the General Council of the Evangelical Lutheran Church in North America was organized by the Pennsylvania Ministerium under the leadership of C. Porterfield Krauth (1823-1883) and William Passavant (1821-1894) in order to counter the effects of Schmucker and the General Synod's move toward liberalism and to enhance the growing revival of a confessional Lutherans. Although initially twelve groups joined together, "four points" became key issues for continued discussion (and division) among American Lutherans—millennialism, altar fellowship, pulpit fellowship, and secret fraternal organizations (such as the Masonic Lodge).

> **Galesburg or Akron Rule**
> In response to an inquiry of the General Council about altar and pulpit fellowship, C. Porterfield Krauth in 1875 articulated a general rule in Akron, Ohio as follows: "I. THE RULE is: Lutheran pulpits are for Lutheran ministers only. Lutheran altars are for Lutheran communicants only. II. *The Exceptions* to the rule belong to the sphere of *privilege*, not of *right*. III. *The Determination* of the *exceptions* is to be made in consonance with these principles by the conscientious judgment of pastors, as the cases arise." Three years later at convention in Galesburg, Illinois, the Council added the words: "The rule, *which accords with the word of God and with the confessions of our Church*, is:"

In the early 1870s, several Midwest synods began discussions about joining together in order to form a federation which was confessional both in doctrine and in practice. By mid-year 1872, the synods of Ohio (which had been a leader in this conference), Illinois, Minnesota, Missouri, Norwegian, and Wisconsin formed a federation of synods, known as the Evangelical Lutheran Synodical Conference of North America. They agreed to work together in educational, evangelistic, and missionary enterprises. However, in less than a half-dozen years, the Ohio and Norwegian Synods separated from the conference over the teachings on predestination (see sidebar).

> **Predestination Controversy**
> Two members of the Synodical Conference, the Ohio and the Norwegian Synods disagreed with the other members regarding the cause of election. They asserted that God chose people in view of their faith (*intuitu fidei*), while the other members affirmed the biblical view that divine election was purely a result of God's grace in Christ.

Liberalism Comes of Age

Back in Germany, Adolf Carl Gustav von Harnack (1851-1930) exemplified liberalism at its apex. The son of a Lutheran pastor and professor, he came under the influence of F. C. Baur (1792-1860), who claimed that Christianity was more of a historical than a spiritual or religious phenomenon, and Albrecht Ritschl (1822-1889), whose "new theology" rejected all established historical approaches to theology. After earning his doctorate and teaching license, Harnack taught at several German universities. He authored a three-volume (seven in English translation) work, *History of Dogma* (1894-1899), which brought him into conflict with his confessional Lutheran father and the Evangelical Church of Prussia. As a historian, he questioned many of the biblical events and early Christian historical accounts. He believed that all history needed to be re-evaluated according to modern sensibilities about history and reality. As a result, he argued that John's Gospel and many biblical events, most of Jesus's miracles, and several early Christian doctrines, were overly influenced by Hellenistic philosophy and did not represent true Christianity. In spite of his controversial views, Kaiser Wilhelm II appointed him to academic position in the University of Berlin, although he never again served in the church. We will read more of Harnack's influence in the next chapter.

High hopes filled those who saw the end of this century. National hostilities seemed to be subsiding and economic prosperity was on the rise for many. Religious sensitivities were raised as missionary activities were burgeoning throughout the world. Yet, there was a need for something more…something to unite the voices into one harmonious symphony. The turn of the century would bring many surprises.

For Review and Discussion
1. Describe "romanticism" as a religious phenomenon with examples from this century.
2. How was the gospel focus undermined by the speculative theology and philosophy of this era?
3. What new denominations in the American scene because of European liberalism? …because of millennial/Adventist expectations?
4. Compare and contrast the revival movements with the rise of the Salvation Army and the work of D. L. Moody.
5. Why were Lutherans in America not able to unite as one major denomination?

For Further Reading
Gallagher, Eugene V. and W. Michael Ashcraft, ed. *Introduction to New and Alternative Religions in America.* Westport,CT: Greenwood Publishing Group, 2006.

Hoekema, Anthony A. *The Four Major Cults.* Exeter, England: Paternoster Press, 1975.

Kierkegaard, Søren. *Purity of Heart: Is To One Thing.* Translated by Douglas V. Steere. New York: Harper & Row, 1938.

Krauth, Charles Porterfield. *The Conservative Reformation and Its Theology.* Minneapolis: Augsburg Publishing, 1963. Reprint of 1871 edition.

Latourette, Kenneth S. *Christianity in a Revolutionary Age.* 3 volumes. New York: Harper & Row, 1958, 1959, 1961.

Nelson, Clifford E. *Lutherans in North America.* Philadelphia: Fortress Press, 1975.

Peterson, Susan Lynn. *Timeline Charts of the Western Church.* Grand Rapids, MI: Zondervan Publishing, 1999.

Schleiermacher, Friedrich. *Brief Outline on the Study of Theology.* Translated by Terrence N. Tice. Richmond, VA: John Knox Press, 1966.

Schleiermacher, Friedrich. *On Religion: Speeches to its Cultured Despiser.* Translated by John Oman with an Introduction by Rudolf Otto. New York: Harper & Row, 1958.

Welch, Claude. *Protestant Thought in the Nineteenth Century*. 2 vols. New Haven: Yale University Press, 1985.

Wentz, Abdel Ross. *A Basic History of Lutheranism in America*. Revised Edition. Philadelphia: Fortress Press, 1964.

20. The Ecumenical Age

The Twentieth Century

From Charles Parham (1901) and the Azusa Street revival (1906) to the *Joint Document on the Doctrine of Justification* (1999) and the papal proclamation, *Dominus Iesus* (2000), no century provides the student of Christian history with a greater diversity of perspectives on what Jesus means for the life of the world and how Christians are to live wholly and holy in the world. If there is one word to describe many of the events of the twentieth century it would be ecumenism.[1] The word itself is a transliteration of a Greek word (οἰκουμένη, *oikoumenē*) meaning "habitable world," with a basis in the word for "house" (οἶκος, *oikos*). Although the term was applied originally to an approach for Protestant unification, the concept soon became synonymous with the programmatic movement toward unity among all Christians throughout the world. In this chapter, we will see how various events drew churches together...and apart. Over this ecumenical hope lies a pall of war and international tensions which affected Christians throughout the world.

Charles Parham, Azusa Street and Pentecostalism

An itinerant evangelistic preacher and teacher, Charles Fox Parham (1873-1929) encouraged students at his newly founded Bethel Bible College in Topeka, Kansas, to seek manifestations of the Spirit. In January 1901, thirty-year old Agnes Ozman (1870-1937) and several other students claimed to speak in a foreign language (*xenoglossolalia*). Shortly thereafter Parham experienced the phenomenon himself which he then asserted professed was the necessary evidence of the Spirit's presence. He began to teach others about this experience, including a young African-American preacher, William Seymour (1870-1922). Seymour was invited to Los Angeles, where a great "outpouring" of the Spirit occurred in 1906 in an abandoned African Methodist Episcopal church building located on Azusa Street. This Azusa Street revival spread quickly and served as the foundational event for a movement known as Pentecostalism (from Acts 2).

---

[1] For example, Abdel Ross Wentz' *A Basic History of Lutheranism in America*, Revised Edition (Philadelphia: Fortress Press, 1964), presents a continual movement toward ecumenical unity.

The Pentecostal movement was initially confined to smaller independent congregations and organizations. In 1914, over 300 like-minded Pentecostal pastors and leaders formed the Assemblies of God, which remains the largest association of Pentecostal churches. The movement would affect mainline Christianity from mid-century until the present in the form of the Charismatic Movement (see later in this chapter).

Isolation or Insulation

In Europe, the Roman Catholic Church maintained prominence, but no was longer was perceived as leading world Christianity. The skillful statesman pope, Leo XIII (1810-1903, pope 1878-1903), was succeeded by a humble parish priest, Pius X (1835-1914, pope 1903-1914). Pius X tried to secure a stronger hold especially in France, but his efforts only created a greater hostility between state and church so that the French government took possession of all church property and only state-approved organizations could rent church property from the state. In 1907, Pius declared both in a decree, *Lamentabili sane* ("lamentable results"), and in an encyclical, *Pascendi dominici gregis* ("feeding the Lord's flock"), that all forms of modernism—whether in scientific or biblical studies—were condemned and to be repressed. A sense of this Catholic isolationism continued for another decade.

On the other hand, in the United States, the same concern for modernism was countered with a form of insulation. Toward the end of the first decade of this century, two successful Christian businessmen, Lyman (1840-1923) and Milton (1838-1923) Stewart, sought to support conservative Christian ideas against the modernist liberal views which were encroaching upon many mainline denominations. Their solution was not to isolate as much as to insulate Christians from false views with clear biblical teachings. Between 1910 and 1915, they financed the publication of twelve small volumes of essays, known as *The Fundamentals: A Testimony to the Truth*. Herein were popular explanations of basic Christian teachings clearly based on God's authoritative Word and focused on salvation through Christ alone (see sidebar). Evangelistic emphases dominated the last volumes with specific articles against many of the common "-isms" of the day. In the 1920s, these books served as a thematic reference for the gradual development of what became known as "fundamentalism," a dispensational premillennial and Biblicist approach to the Christian faith and life.

> **The Five Fundamentals**
> 1. Inspiration and inerrancy of Scripture
> 2. Deity of Jesus Christ
> 3. Virgin birth of Christ
> 4. Substitutionary atoning work of Christ on the cross
> 5. Physical resurrection and personal bodily return of Christ to the earth
>
> These teachings were originally articulated by the Presbyterian General Assembly in 1910, but are now associated with the twelve-volume set of essays by noted conservative scholars. Curiously, dispensational pre-millennial ideas were not promoted, although they would become hallmark features of subsequent "fundamentalism."

Coupled with this significant publishing event was the notorious "Scopes Trial." John Thomas Scopes (1900-1970), a substitute high school teacher in

Tennessee, had reportedly taught evolution, which at the time was not permitted in the state. The trial was set up partially as a publicity stunt by the ACLU to highlight the emerging Fundamentalist-Modernist Controversy and to test the state law's constitutionality. The arguments between the famous lawyers, William Jennings Bryan (1860-1925) and Clarence Darrow (1857-1938), improperly pitted religion against science. Throughout the trial, media coverage was extraordinary. Although John Scopes was found guilty, he was acquitted on a technicality. However, the impact of this event cannot be underestimated. The resulting rift between the Bible and science became set for most of the century.

World War I and the Bolshevik Revolution

In the summer of 1914, "the war to end all wars" began. Britain, France, Russia, and, shortly thereafter, the United States joined as Allies against the strong Austro-Hungarian and German allies, known as the Central Powers. Portrayed as a "holy war," good against evil, God against the devil, the combatants were sometimes identified as the antichrist (as the Russians had labelled Kaiser Wilhelm II of Germany (1859-1941)). Anti-German sentiment in the United States resulted in many organizations and churches to cease using German as their official language. Many Christians, particularly among Orthodox groups in Greece, Armenia, and Assyria were victims of wholesale massacre and extermination (the term "genocide" was not coined until the 1940s) by the Ottoman Empire, which had secretly allied with Germany. The famous Russian novelist and social critic, Aleksandr Solzhenitsyn (1918-2008), later asserted that such atrocities occurred because man had forgotten God!

During this same time, in 1917, a revolution, known as the Bolshevik or October Revolution, overthrew the ruling Russian tsar and established councils (Russian: "soviets") of urban laborers. Under the subsequent leadership of Vladimir Lenin (1870-1924), all church property was seized and atheistic or Marxist communism was imposed. The strong Russian Orthodox Church which had claimed nearly a quarter of the world's Christian population was for all practical purposes obliterated and atheism dominated the Soviet Union for over half a century. Many members of Russian Orthodox congregations fled to Europe, Asia, and America, where they established churches in exile.

Ecumenical and Missionary Conferences

Held for the first time in Edinburgh, Scotland, in 1910, a gathering of over eleven hundred leaders of missionary societies provided impetus for global missions and ecumenical hopes. Although previous meetings over the past century had occurred, this event gave a new momentum to ecumenical and evangelistic efforts. The chairman of this conference, John R. Mott (1865-1955), served as a guiding light for half-a-century of interdenominational missions. In the last decade of the nineteenth century, Mott had been involved in the YMCA, which was oriented toward evangelism, particularly through its Student Volunteer Movement for Foreign Mission. Mott organized and led the World's Student Christian Federation (1895), which trained many women and men for world leadership among young people. In 1921, he chaired the important International

Missionary Council. This Council encouraged the formation of national church groups, especially among the youngest churches in the Orient, India, and Africa. Considered the "father of the ecumenical movement," Mott worked tirelessly to bring about evangelistic activities through cooperative partnerships of many Protestant denominations. We will come back to his work a little later in this chapter.

As a result of World War I, several Lutheran groups in the United States organized a National Lutheran Council in 1918 to represent themselves before the government and to cooperate on common social issues facing the members of their congregations. Between 1923 and 1935, three international Lutheran World Conventions were sponsored by the National Lutheran Council. In 1930, several Lutheran synods merged to form The American Lutheran Church and several others created a less formal federation, The American Lutheran Conference.

During this decade, a significant number of related Protestant denominations merged to form the General Council of Congregational-Christian Churches of the United States (1931), emphasizing their unity in practice rather than in doctrine. Similar organizations were constituted in Switzerland (the Swiss Church Federation in 1920), in Germany (the German Evangelical Church Federation in 1921), and in Scotland (1925), to name a few. In 1934, the Evangelical and Reformed Church was founded as a union between two major German-language American Protestant denominations. Four years after that, The Reformed Church of France (1938) was created from congregations of the Methodist Church, Reformed Evangelical Church, the Reformed Church, and Free Evangelical Churches. In the United States several Methodist Episcopal groups combined to form the Methodist Church (U.S.A.) in 1939.

A significant international voice in ecumenism came from the Swedish Lutheran scholar and bishop, Nathan Söderblom (1866-1931). A leader among the Student Christian Movement, he organized several international conferences to encourage social and ethical involvement of the church in the world. He believed that churches working together could do much more than individual denominations. Organizing a Universal Christian Conference on Life and Work in 1925, his energetic activities led to the formation of a Council in 1930, which focused on social as well as theological activities globally. His ecumenical influence through the Augustana Lutheran Church would be realized over fifty years later with the formation of the Evangelical Lutheran Church in America.

Other Lutherans in America sought corporate unity through a clearer declaration of doctrinal agreement. In 1932, the Lutheran Church—Missouri Synod (as it was renamed in 1947) and several members of the Synodical Conference adopted *A Brief Statement of the Doctrinal Position of the Missouri Synod*. Neither external organizational form nor liturgical conformity was to be the basis of unity, but the clear biblical teachings of the Christian faith. After fifteen years of negotiations with the American Lutheran Church (formed in 1930, and as The American Lutheran Church in 1960) and its fellowship partners, the Missouri Synod in convention rescinded its convention resolution seeking closer ties with them in 1981.

Back in 1927, an Episcopalian missionary bishop, Charles H. Brent (1862-1929), following the Chicago-Lambeth Quadrilateral (see sidebar), called upon his denomination to arrange for the first World Conference on Faith and Order in Lausanne, Switzerland. Rather than avoiding theologically distinctive doctrinal issues, the delegates which represented over a hundred denominations found significant agreement and proposed continued discussions on their differences. Just before the outbreak of World War II, an ecumenical conference was held which brought together into one world council the Evangelical concern for "life and work," which represented an alliance founded in 1908 as the Federal Council of the Churches of Christ in America, and the Anglican proposal for "faith and order." Meeting in Utrecht in 1938, a basic structure for a world council was proposed under the leadership of the philosopher, theologian, and later archbishop of Canterbury, William Temple (1881-1944), who served as chairman of the provisional committee during the next decade. Further plans were temporarily halted by the Second World War.

> **Chicago-Lambeth Quadrilateral**
> Towards the end of the 19th century, American Episcopalians sought a way toward union between Roman Catholics and Orthodox communions. In 1886 and again in 1888, the American bishops met in Chicago, where they identified the following four common articles of faith which could serve as a basis for restored unity:
> 1) The Holy Scriptures of the Old and New Testaments, as "containing all things necessary to salvation," and as being the rule and ultimate standard of faith.
> 2) The Apostles' Creed, as the Baptismal Symbol; and the Nicene Creed, as the sufficient statement of the Christian faith.
> 3) The two Sacraments ordained by Christ Himself — Baptism and the Supper of the Lord — ministered with unfailing use of Christ's Words of Institution, and of the elements ordained by Him.
> 4) The Historic Episcopate, locally adapted in the methods of its administration to the varying needs of the nations and peoples called of God into the Unity of His Church.

The Presence of Liberalism

Adolf von Harnack (1841-1930) (see illustration) provided a key document for twentieth century Christian liberalism (see chapter 19). In 1901, Harnack published *What Is Christianity?*, adapted from a series of lectures given in Berlin. The essence of Christianity, stated Harnack, was a proclamation of the kingdom of God, which links humanity with God as Father, and wherein believers practice humility through love. His Lutheran heritage is evident as he summarized the Gospel as the "free grace of God in Christ which makes guilty and despairing men blessed." While his "gospel" seems adequate upon a first read, the rest of his work shows that Harnack reduced Jesus to a human prophet and teacher of social ethics. He asserted that the "kernel" of truth (emphasizing ethical behavior) needed to be separated from "the husk" of later historically influenced dogmas.

The first three decades in this century were the most prolific for Harnack. He produced more than 450 books, reviews, and lectures on specific aspects of the New Testament and early Christian history by the time of his death in 1930. Many of his students (including Karl Barth, see below) found his form of liberalism unworkable. As a result, Harnack's influence diminished over much of the rest of the century.

About ten years earlier in 1921, Princeton Theological Seminary, which had remained a strongly conservative school in the Reformed (Calvinistic Presbyterian) tradition (known as the "Princeton theology"), opened their faculty to several liberal scholars. Under the leadership of J. Greshem Machen (1881-1937), several conservative faculty members left Princeton and formed Westminster Theological Seminary. Doctrinal discord brought denominational division.

The "Social Gospel" and the Niebuhr Family

Already at the end of the previous century, a Baptist minister and theologian, Walter Rauschenbusch (1861-1918), exhibited a strong post-millennial view of Christianity in that he sought to establish Christ's kingdom on earth through social reform. Founding a loosely structured organization in the 1890s, The Brotherhood of the Kingdom, he and his colleagues advocated an earthly social renewal which would engage all denominations to create a new world order. His *Christianity and Social Crisis* (1907) became a kind of manifesto for the movement and, along with his *A Theology of the Social Gospel* (1917), has influenced Christian activism throughout this century as a means not to prepare for eternal life but to transform the present life into a more heavenly condition.

Reinhold Niebuhr

Reinhold Niebuhr (1892-1971) and his younger brother, H. Richard Niebuhr (1894-1962), were among the most prominent American theologians of the early twentieth century, who saw benefits in Rauschenbusch's social gospel. Born to German immigrants about 50 miles west of St Louis, Missouri, both men became outspoken advocates of political and economic ethics. Their father was an Evangelical preacher who had come from the Prussian Union Church in Germany (which formed the United Church of Christ in the United States). Their older sister, Hulda (1889-1959), was a gifted theologian in her own right and became Professor of Christian Education at McCormick Theological Seminary in Chicago.

Reinhold first pastored a German American congregation in Detroit, where he became disheartened by the terrible conditions of many factory workers and spoke out against Henry Ford (1863-1947) and capitalism. During the 1930s, after moving to New York City, although trained in liberal theology, Reinhold gradually rejected many of its central themes and advanced a form of Marxist Social Gospel, especially in terms of a Barthian-type of neo-orthodoxy (see below). He identified sin as a social concern, particularly as manifested in self-centered pride. As a professor at Union Theological Seminary in New York, he influenced many Protestant leaders, including Dietrich Bonhoeffer (1906-1945) and Martin Luther King, Jr (1929-1968). He supported American involvement in World War II—seeing war as justifiable for the sake of peace—but opposed the Vietnam War efforts. His legacy is mixed, since he revised his views on numerous issues, although always seeking a Christ-oriented position.

H. Richard Niebuhr

H. Richard Niebuhr, having the same liberal roots as his brother, retained them in the area of ethical compromise. After his ordination, he taught at Eden Theological Seminary (1919-1922) while earning a master's degree from Washington University in St Louis. He was called as president of Elmhurst College in Illinois (1924-1927) after earning a PhD from Yale University in 1924. He returned to Eden for several years before a study leave took him to Germany and, upon his return, to Yale in 1931, where he remained to teach Christian ethics. Reflecting upon his dissertation subject, Ernst Troeltsch (1865-1923), and influenced by Karl Barth (1886-1968) after his sabbatical in 1930, H. Richard Niebuhr sought to combine their two ways of thinking. He recognized that all history can be relative or at least the views are historically conditioned (Troeltsch), yet he also realized that Christianity needed a foundation from which to view history and that was the revelation of the Christian community (Barth). With that basis, he then advocated considering Christian action not as reflection of the culture of the day, but as a biblical sense of responsibility which would manifest God's reign throughout the world. His book, *Christ and Culture* (see sidebar), continues to serve as a denominational guide to cultural distinctions.

> H. Richard Niebuhr's
> *Christ and Culture (1951)*
> delineated five views, the last of which he believed was required of Christianity:
> Christ against culture (monasticism)
> Christ of culture (Thomas Jefferson)
> Christ above culture (Aquinas)
> Christ and culture in paradox (Luther)
> Christ transforming culture (Calvin)

World War II (1939-1945) and Alternatives to Liberalism

With the rise of Hitler's National Socialism, many Christians found themselves facing a conflicted circumstance—to support a corrupt Nazi government or to rebel against divinely ordered authorities. As the militaristic practices and programs of persecution by the Third Reich slowly became openly hostile to the church, some Christians engaged in passive resistance. Others, as will be noted below, were actively involved in clearly opposing the demonic governmental powers at work in the world. Sometimes recognized as a dark moment in Christian history because of the supposed silence of those who were aware of the events, countless Jews, Christian leaders, and non-Aryan Europeans were carried off to concentration camps, where many were surreptitiously murdered.

Karl Barth: The Word and the World

In 1934, a pastor/theologian, Karl Barth (1886-1968) authored *The Barmen Declaration*, which encouraged Protestant leaders in Europe to reject the Nazi ploy of a superior Germanic Christianity. After refusing to swear allegiance to Adolf Hitler (1889-1945), Barth moved from his post at the University of Bonn and returned to Switzerland, where he taught at the University of Basel and became a leader in the Confessing Church.

Rejecting the liberalism of his early theological training in Germany, yet not following the traditional conservative approach that was in vogue at the time, Barth set out to clarify the reality of God's love in Christ for the world. Influenced by the writings of Søren Kierkegaard (1813-1856) as well as the propaganda of religious socialism, he wrote a commentary on *The Epistle to the Romans* (1918), while still a parish pastor in Switzerland.

Barth's chief work was his thirteen-volume *Church Dogmatics*, (1932-1967) in which he detailed—particularly through massive footnotes—his thoughts on all aspects of the Christian faith. His theological approach was to use dialectics—finding opposites which draw ideas together—to articulate the faith of Scripture. A Calvinist by tradition, his thinking has been labelled "neo-orthodoxy" (new orthodoxy), although he rejected that term. His central theme was a return to the Word of God. Four major topics are central to his dogmatics—the Word of God as revelation, the reality of God and His election, creation of the world, and reconciliation in Christ. Barth's rejection of inerrancy caused some to question his theological substance, yet he argued that the chief authority was Christ, the Word made flesh and reconciler of the world.

Costly Discipleship

Among the many theologians influenced by Barth and H. Richard Niebuhr, Dietrich Bonhoeffer (1906-1945) most closely exemplifies the paradoxical approach to Christ and culture (see above). Trained in liberal theology at Tübingen and Berlin, where he earned doctorates in 1927 and 1929, he rejected liberalism in favor of a more Barthian approach with a clear Lutheran perspective. Rather than looking at the human qualities of religion (the liberal approach), Bonhoeffer recognized the need to get back to the Word of God as source and fountain for Christian faith and life. After reading much of Barth's writings, Bonhoeffer met Barth in 1930 and they became close friends as well as mutual opponents to the German "Christian" cultural religion (promoted by the Nazi regime). However, Bonhoeffer criticized Barth's personalistic and pietistic approach to God's involvement in the world. That same year, Bonhoeffer had the opportunity to study in New York's Union Theological Seminary, although he was critical of their empty theologizing. Traveling to several other countries, he became aware of the ecumenical nature of Christianity and in 1931 was elected as a youth representative to the World Alliance for Promoting International Friendship through the Churches, a forerunner to the World Council of Churches.

Bonhoeffer is best known for his work, *The Cost of Discipleship*, a work which has captured the hearts and minds of both conservative and liberal Protestants. That cost was exemplified in Bonhoeffer's early opposition to the Nazis, and particularly its practices of euthanasia and genocide, which resulted in Bonhoeffer's imprisonment and ultimately his martyrdom (death by hanging) just two weeks before the Allies entered Germany. In 1964, he was commemorated with his picture on a stamp in Germany (see illustration).

The Influence of Mass Media

Already noted above with the Scopes Trial, the use of media increased significantly in this century. With the invention of the radio at the end of the nineteenth century, by the 1920s the medium of radio began to influence more and more of the population in Europe and the Americas. A Congregational minister, preaching in Brooklyn, New York, S. Parks Cadman (1864-1936) was the first to utilize the radio for his preaching in 1923. Shortly thereafter, the Pentecostal revival preacher, Aimee Semple McPherson (1890-1944), already familiar with the advantages of attracting newspaper headlines, used the benefits of radio for her media savvy ministries in 1924. Her Angelus Temple in Los Angeles, California, became a center of her radio broadcasts and her International Church of the Foursquare Gospel.

A creative Catholic theologian from Illinois, Archbishop Fulton Sheen (1895-1979), was the first Catholic to broadcast a weekly radio show, "The Catholic Hour," each Sunday, starting on March 2, 1930, and running through 1950, when he went to television. Seven months later, The Lutheran Laymen's League committed to fund a radio program for a year, called "The Lutheran Hour," and engaged Walter A. Maier (1893-1950) as featured speaker. The program's success is evident in the fact that the Lutheran Hour is presently the longest running religious broadcasting program in the world. Ten years later the Lutheran Hour began a broadcast in Spanish with Andrew Melendez (1902-1999) as speaker.

Although television began in the 1930s, only after the Second World War did it become widespread. Christians recognized the benefit of such a mass-media communication tool. Many denominational communications organizations adapted from radio broadcasts to television broadcasts in the early 1950s. Probably the most well-known were Bishop Fulton Sheen and Oral Roberts (1918-2009); later to be followed by Billy Graham (1918-), Jimmy Swaggart (1935-), Jerry Falwell (1933-2007), and Robert Schuler (1926-2015), to name a few.

Ecumenism after World War II

Globally, the hiatus on a worldwide organization of Christians was lifted after the war. Instead of reviving the Lutheran World Convention, a meeting was organized in Lund, Sweden, in 1947, to form the Lutheran World Federation, which officially began in 1948. The next year delegates from almost 150 different church groups from all over the world met in Amsterdam to bring to fulfillment the hope for a World Council of Churches (see below). And the following year, seven inter-denominational agencies merged to form the National Council of the Churches of Christ in the U.S.A.

The same kind of federation was formed in Germany. Already in 1921, the German Evangelical Church Federation was created. After the war, this group was abandoned, but reconstituted themselves as a federation of Lutheran, Reformed, and Union territorial churches, known as the Evangelical Church in Germany (EKD). A similar federation of Baptists, Evangelicals, and Methodists was established. Several other groups in France, Switzerland, Spain, and Scotland joined together for the sake of cooperative work, particularly for reconstruction efforts after the war.

World Council of Churches

The World Council of Churches is the best known world-wide church federation. Initially, it worked toward greater cooperation among denominations, particularly through theological and ecclesiastical discussions. Their ecumenical purpose is evident in their constitutional description: "The World Council of Churches is a fellowship of churches which accepts our Lord Jesus Christ as God and Saviour." This ecumenical purpose was demonstrated in their New Delhi Statement of 1961 (see sidebar). However, during the more turbulent sixties, concerns shifted from evangelism to social issues of human rights, world hunger, racism, and the advocacy of violence to bring about social change. Issues of global poverty and service to the world increased and discussions on faith and order broadened to include many smaller denominations as well as Orthodox churches.

> **The New Delhi Statement**
>
> The World Council of Churches stated: "We believe that the unity which is both God's will and his gift to his Church is being made visible as all in each place who are baptized into Jesus Christ and confess him as Lord and Saviour are brought by the Holy Spirit into one fully committed fellowship, holding the one apostolic faith, preaching the one Gospel, breaking the one bread, joining in common prayer, and having a corporate life reaching out in witness and service to all and who at the same time are united with the whole Christian fellowship in all places and all ages in such wise that ministry and members are accepted by all, and that all can act and speak together as occasion requires for the tasks to which God calls his people. It is for such unity that we believe we must pray and work."

Formation of new or merged denominations increased significantly in the next decades. The United Church of Christ (combining several Reformed and Evangelical groups) came into existence in 1961, several Lutheran bodies merged in 1960s and again in the 1980s, Presbyterians joined together in 1950s and again in the 1980s, in 1961 the Unitarian and Universalists merged, and several Methodists groups came together 1968 in the United States. At the same time in

Canada, several other Protestant groups formed the United Church of Canada. Catholics however remained outside those conversations until mid-century, asserting that unity can only be found under the papacy.

In 1962, a Consultation on Church Union, which consisted of Congregational, Disciples, Episcopal, Methodist, Presbyterian, and Reformed churches, began to work on the formation of one ecumenical denomination. The idea was to create a "catholic, evangelical, and reformed" church. However, with the societal upheavals of the seventies, the growing optimism for such a church diminished until there was little activity at the turn of the century. In 2002, a renewed effort resulted in the formation of Churches Uniting in Christ.

Roman Catholicism's Ecumenism and Vatican II

By mid-century, Roman Catholicism began to emerge from its isolationist posture. But before that occurred, a significant dogmatic statement, *Munificentissimus Deus* ("most beautiful God"), was made by Pope Pius XII (1876-1958, pope 1939-1958) based upon his 1946 encyclical. On November 1st, 1950, he declared that Mary was bodily assumed into heaven. After a millennium and a half of prayers offered to Mary, the Roman Catholic Church formally created a theological rationale for such prayer. That same year his encyclical, *Humani generis* ("of the human race"), warned against any modern departures from the traditional Tridentine faith, particularly through secularization. Strongly anticommunist and antifascist, he was criticized for not speaking out openly against the Jewish holocaust, yet his supporters assert that he acted so as to prevent harsh reprisals on German Catholics by the Nazis.

Perhaps no pope had a greater impact on global Christianity in the past millennium than Pope John XXIII (1881-1963, pope 1958-1963) (see illustration). While serving as a papal nuncio in Turkey and Greece at the time of World War II, he intervened to aid Jews and others escaping the German holocaust. In 1959, just a few months after his election as a supposedly transitional pope, he called for an ecumenical council (officially the twenty-first such event) which changed the face of Catholicism for generations. Pope John XXIII died in late spring 1963 of stomach cancer before the opening of the second session of the Council and was succeeded by Pope Paul VI (1897-1978, pope 1963-1978), but his influence remained.

Vatican II (1962-1965) is noteworthy for several decisions (and documents) produced over the four sessions held each fall of the year. Most of them had a significant impact on Christian communities beyond the Roman Church itself. An overarching theme was a desire for "updating" (Italian, *aggiornamento*) of the Catholic Church; a process of reformation which would not be easy or easily carried out.

The first document of the Council was on the liturgy, the Constitution of the Sacred Liturgy (*Sacrosanctum Concilium*), which encouraged greater participation by the laity in the Mass and the conduct of the liturgy in the language of the people (in contrast to the requirement of Mass being in Latin since the sixteenth century). More Scripture was to be included in the services so a revision of the Bible passages for reading at worship resulted in a three-year series of Scripture selections, a practice followed by many non-Catholic denominations throughout the rest of the century.

Another product of Vatican II was *Lumen gentium* ("Light of the Nations"), the Dogmatic Constitution on the Church. Here the Roman Church asserted that the fullness of the one, holy, catholic, and apostolic Church subsists only in a society governed by the pope and bishops under him, although it recognizes some elements of sanctification and truth in other Christian groups. This document used the phrase, "the People of God," to refer to the members of the Roman Church, noting that they were part of "a common priesthood of the faithful," a concept which Martin Luther had rediscovered three-and-a-half centuries earlier. Sensitive to its attempted ecumenical focus, this document included strong affirmations of Mary's place in the life of the church.

> *Lumen gentium*
> ¶14: "Whosoever, therefore, knowing that the Catholic Church was made necessary by Christ, would refuse to enter or to remain in it, could not be saved."

Dei Verbum (Word of God), the Dogmatic Constitution of Divine Revelation, reaffirmed the Catholic Church's reliance on both Scripture and tradition, although trying to emphasize the importance of modern scriptural studies for all. Other documents included declarations on the duties of bishop, education for the priesthood as well as for all Christians, religious freedom and missions, and ecumenism, as well as a more favorable attitude toward non-Christian religions. The final document of a total of sixteen which were officially promulgated dealt with the church in the modern world is known as *Gaudium et Spes* ("Joys and Hopes"). This document affirmed the Roman Catholic Church's desire to be in conversation with the world—culturally, socio-economically, and ultimately spiritually—for the sake of peace and continuing ecumenical dialogue.

Liberal Catholic Theology

A French Jesuit and philosophical theologian, Pierre Teilhard de Chardin (1881-1955), provides a unique perspective on the transformation of Catholic theology, particularly in the intersection of modern science and theology. An avid paleontologist, de Chardin participated in several significant archeological discoveries in China, including the Peking Man. He accepted the theory of evolution and used it in his theological writing, arguing that all of creation is directed purposefully (teleologically) toward unification with Christ. In one of his books, he entitled this directional evolution, *The Omega Point* (omega is the last letter in the Greek alphabet). Although his views had initially been condemned under the label of "philosophical immanentism," his writing gained popularity and acceptance in the last half of the century, particularly when Pope Benedict XVI (1927-, pope 2005-2013) spoke approvingly of several of his ideas. His influence is reflected in both of the following theologians.

Karl Rahner, S.J. (1904-1984) was one of the most influential Roman Catholic theologians of the century. Joining the Society of Jesus (Jesuits) in 1922, he demonstrated a theological depth in keeping with the spiritual discipline of Ignatius. Studying at the University of Freiburg from 1934-1937, his academic advisor refused to approve his dissertation because of the heavy influence of the philosophy of Martin Heidegger (1889-1976).

> **From *Lumen gentium***
>
> Rahner's "anonymous Christians" is expressed in this document of Vatican II, when it states in ¶15 that those "who no fault of their own, do not know the Gospel of Christ or His Church, but who nevertheless seek God with a sincere heart, and moved by grace, try in their actions to do His will as they know it through the dictates of their conscience—those too may achieve eternal salvation."

Transferring to the Jesuit University in Innsbruck, Rahner taught there (except for a decade during the Nazi era when he taught in Vienna) and in Munich and Munster until his death. He was appointed as a theological expert by Pope John XXIII to Vatican II and later worked with Joseph Ratzinger (Pope Benedict XVI), although they later differed on several doctrines, particularly his view of salvation outside the Roman Catholic Church and even for non-believers, whom Rahner called "anonymous Christians." (See sidebar) He was a prolific writer and editor, particularly on several encyclopedias on Catholic doctrine.

Hans Urs von Balthasar (1905-1988) is known for his popular poetic style of theology. He spoke of love as being more important than rational thought. In contrast to de Chardin's evolutionary approach, von Balthasar thought of the world as suffering a Hegelian-type of dialectic conflict, which ultimately would result in a spiritual unity. His *Theology of Love* gave a romantic voice to the ecumenical outlook among Catholic theologians at the end of the century. In his sixteen volume systematic theology (1961-1985), which he called a "trilogy" he showed his aesthetic approach to theology, when he wrote, "Before the beautiful—no, not really *before* but *within* the beautiful—the whole person quivers. He not only 'finds' the beautiful moving; rather, he experiences himself as being moved and possessed by it," and as he labeled parts two and three, *Theo-Drama* and *Theo-Logic*.

Several other Catholic theologians could be added to this list, including the following noteworthy individuals: Henri de Lubac (1896-1991), John Courtney Murray (1904-1967), Yves Congar (1904-1996), and Edward Schillebeeckx (1914-2009). These men promoted a Catholic theology which was directed toward the broader context of global Christianity. Their goal was to be ecumenical by engaging other Christians in their conversations.

Liberal Protestant Theology

As a refugee from Hitler's Germany, Paul Tillich (1886-1965) came to America, where he presented his mature thinking in his multivolume *Systematic Theology* (1951-1963). Born into a Lutheran pastor's home, he was trained in the Romanticism of the nineteenth century, but after serving as a chaplain in World War I, he found that his philosophical training in Berlin, Tübingen, and Halle was inadequate. After the war, he taught in Berlin and met Karl Barth and Martin Heidegger. He was greatly influenced by Heidegger's existential views as evident in his teaching in Marburg, Dresden, Leipzig, and finally Frankfurt. With Hitler's rise to power, he was barred from teaching in Germany and emigrated to the United States, where he took a professorship at Union Theological Seminary from 1935-1955. While at Union, he completed the first volume of his systematic theology. He then taught at Harvard University (1955-1962), where he published the second volume (1957), and then moved to the University of Chicago and completed the third volume of this work (1963).

Recognizing the powerful effect that post-War secularism was having on Christians, Tillich proposed using non-theological language about God. God, he wrote, is the "ground of Being" and through Christ, "the New Being," humanity can become reconciled to God as the "New Creation." He sought to address existential questions with theological answers in a way that bridged philosophy and theology into a dialectic synthesis. Rejecting what he saw as the rigidity of Lutheran orthodoxy, he tried to maintain what he called "the Protestant principle" of justification by grace through faith in a way that he deemed was palatable to the modern mind.

Another voice which sought to speak in a more contemporary fashion was James H. Cone (1938-), who is recognized as the founder of "black liberation theology" in America. His book, *A Black Theology of Liberation* (1970), followed his first publication, *Black Theology and Black Power* (1969). Raised in and ordained by the African Methodist Episcopal Church, he returned to teach at his undergraduate school, Philander Smith College, in Arkansas, after receiving his bachelor of divinity degree from Garrett Evangelical Theological Seminary in 1961. Since 1970, he has taught at Union Theological Seminary in New York. Influenced by Barth (the subject of his doctoral dissertation) and Tillich's view that theology must reflect its social context, Cone says that God must be viewed as caring for and bringing liberation to the oppressed, particularly among Black Americans. (See more on liberation theology below.)

A powerful speaker, Martin Luther King, Jr. (1929-1968), followed the liberal theology of Rauschenbusch. Born to a Baptist pastor, Michael King, Sr. (1899-1984), who changed his name to Martin Luther King, Sr. after visiting Germany, the younger King graduated from high school and entered Morehouse College at the age of 15 in 1944. He received his Bachelor of Divinity degree from a liberal Baptist school, Crozer Theological Seminary in Pennsylvania. In 1955 he received his PhD from Boston University. It was at Boston that he studied the works of Rauschenbusch, Niebuhr, Barth, and Tillich. At the end of 1955, the bus boycott of Montgomery, Alabama, elevated King to prominence as he served as the elected community leader. After visiting Gandhi's birthplace in India in 1959, King saw the benefit of non-violent protests, which he advocated for the rest of his life. His speech, "I Have A Dream," at the 1963 March on Washington had a lasting impact on the civil rights movement (see illustration). Denying many of the basic Christian teachings, such as the virgin birth, the bodily resurrection, and the return of Christ, King maintained that one had to reinterpret biblical stories from their pre-scientific worldviews to contemporary applications.

Instead of only fighting for the cause of racial justice, several voices were raised in protest against other injustices, particularly against a perceived diminution of the role of women in the world. A feminist Catholic scholar, Rosemary Radford Ruether (1936-) advocated for the ordination of women to the priesthood and several other teachings which are contrary to Roman Catholic doctrine. Trained in early Christian history, Ruether's method reinterpreted earlier Christian teachings in light of liberation and liberal theology. Based upon her non-literal reading of Scripture, she understood the Bible and Catholic tradition, such as the 1968 papal document *Humanae Vitae* ("of human life"), as being patriarchal and limiting of women's roles. Her continuing concern remains with ecology as evident in her advocacy of "ecofeminism." The ordination of women did occur in several mainline denominations, including the Lutheran Church in America (1970) and the Episcopal Church (1989).

Conservative Challenge

In response to the undermining of basic Christian teachings and biblical authority, and as an alternative to the fundamentalist insulation of the first quarter of the century, several strong voices challenged post-war Christians to stand their ground confidently on God's Word. Carl F. H. Henry (1913-2003), a journalist by training, graduated from Wheaton College. While pursuing his M.A. at Wheaton and a ThD from Northern Baptist Theological Seminary, he helped launch the National Association of Evangelicals. In 1947, his book, *The Uneasy Conscience of Modern Fundamentalism*, became a sounding board for the new Evangelicals, as they became known. That same year, he and several other leaders helped the radio-evangelist, Charles Fuller (1887-1968), establish Fuller Theological Seminary. Henry was a popular speaker and prolific writer, editing the evangelical magazine, *Christianity Today* for over a decade. His most significant work was the six-volume dogmatic response to liberalism and fundamentalism, *God, Revelation, and Authority* (1983).

Another evangelical leader and classmate of Carl Henry was William Franklin Graham, Jr. (1918-). "Billy" Graham became the public voice for many Protestant conservatives as he preached a decidedly Arminian theology to the great American populace in city-wide rallies that were reminiscent of Billy Sunday. Beginning as a radio preacher in Chicago-land in 1940s, he was selected as president of Northwestern Bible College in Minneapolis at the age of 30 in 1947. His first crusade was conducted that year in Michigan. Over the next fifty-five years, he would preach to live audiences of over 200 million people in more than 185 nations in addition to the millions who heard or saw him through other media. (See illustration) Curiously echoing a

Rahnerian view of Christianity near the end of his life, Graham seemed to hold the view that people without explicit faith in Jesus could still be saved.

During the 1950s and early 1960s, America was more churchly than it had ever been in the past or would experience in the following decades. Sunday attendance and church membership were at an all-time high, particularly among the mainline denominations (Baptists, Congregationalists, Disciples, Episcopalians, Lutherans, Methodists, and Presbyterians). Much of this was a response to the uncertainties of the war years and a desire for traditional values.

In contrast to this popular American Christian optimism, several cultural movements caused concern among conservative Christians. In 1962, the Supreme Court of the United States ruled that a prayer used in New York schools was unconstitutional. Madelyn Murray O'Hair (1919-1995), an avowed atheist and communist sympathizer, had pressed for the elimination of Bible reading in public schools and in 1963 the Supreme Court agreed that such practices violated the Establishment Clause of the First Amendment. This era also saw the "Death of God" proposal by Thomas J. J. Altizer (1927-) and others. Altizer's book, *Gospel of Christian Atheism* (1966), suggested that secularity should replace the Christian deity.

Although the promotion of a secular perspective remains a populist view, the Austrian-born American sociologist Peter Berger (1929-), who earlier championed the idea, abandoned it as being inconsistent with cultural developments globally. There is now an increasing recognition instead of plurality or multiculturalism which has affected American religious scene. For example, Asian religions and new religious movements, such as the International Society of Krishna Consciousness (founded in 1965) and Transcendental Meditation, founded by Mararishi Mahesh Yogi (1918-2008), provided a greater voice for diverse religious views. Many of these groups appealed to younger people. Yet, among the vocal youth culture of the 1960s and 1970s, many Christian young people expressed themselves in the Jesus Movement with its hippie cultural trappings and simple focus on Jesus as the Giver of the Spirit.

Mid-Century Biblical Studies

Perhaps no one figure influenced twentieth century biblical studies more than did Rudolf Bultmann (1884-1976). Educated in liberal German biblical scholarship, he became Professor of Theology at Marburg in 1921, the same year he published *History of the Synoptic Tradition,* which revolutionized biblical research. Wanting to find a middle ground between Barth's neo-orthodoxy and the earlier liberalism, Bultmann initially proposed, with three other collaborators, an approach to biblical studies called form-criticism. Although he was supportive of the Confessing Church and disagreed with Hitler's National Socialism, he remained a-political and avoided any open opposition to Hitler's activities.

After World War II, Bultmann became a key figure in Protestant biblical studies. Twenty years after his first major work, Bultmann's book *New Testament and Mythology* (1941), introduced the concept of "demythologizing" of the biblical records. He proposed that the historical critical method had uncovered the errors of previous views of New Testament narratives, which now had to be reduced to a more common and existentially acceptable form—the myth. For the next several decades his views were heralded as providing great innovations for New Testament studies, especially through the publication of several more influential texts in the 1950s. From within the "Bultmann school" come several notable scholars—including Ernst Käsemann (1906-1998), who questioned the historical Jesus; Ernst Fuchs (1903-1983), who denied the ability to discern a historical Jesus and advocated instead that all biblical writing was a "language event" through which "faith happens;" and Gerhard Ebeling (1912-2001), who, with Fuchs, proposed "the new hermeneutic" by which they encouraged a study of the function of words and their historical breadth. Thus, they opened the way for a variety of interpretations of the biblical narratives.

Biblical Discoveries and Translations

Archaeological discoveries which provided new insights into Christian history already occurred in previous centuries (for example, the 1897 discovery of the *Oxyrhynchus Papyri*, included fragments from biblical books and an example of early Christian music). However, in the twentieth century, several significant finds were made. Near Nag Hammadi, Egypt, a Gnostic library of over a dozen Coptic papyri was found in 1945. Toward the end of the century, Israeli archaeologists found a stone inscription with "King of Israel" and "House of David" in Aramaic and inscriptions with the name of King Herod at Masada.

Perhaps no more significant discovery affecting biblical studies over the past millennium occurred at the middle of this century. The Dead Sea Scrolls were discovered in 1946, apparently by Bedouin shepherds in some hillside caves near the Dead Sea, known as Qumran. These ancient parchment and papyri scrolls

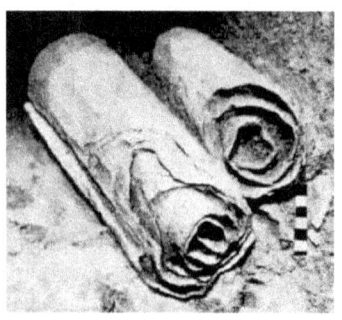

were copies of most Old Testament books and other manuscripts providing information on the community which prepared them. Because they date from the Second Temple Period, that is, the time of Christ, and are thus almost a thousand years older than any other extant ancient manuscripts of the Old Testament, they bore greater insights for both Jews and Christians. These manuscripts and fragments, which continue to be studied, have influenced Bible translations and interpretation ever since.

In addition to the scholarly contributions offered through the study of these scrolls, many popular Bible translations were prepared during this century. Already at the end of the last century, a *Revised Version* of the King James translation was made and shortly thereafter, in 1901, *The American Standard Version* was released. Throughout the first half of the century, almost fifty translations came off the press, either by individual translators (Edgar J. Goodspeed [1871-1962], James Moffatt [1870-1944], J. B. Phillips [1906-1982], Kenneth N. Taylor [1917-2005]) or by scholarly groups and Bible societies (*Jerusalem Bible [1966], Good News Bible [1976]*). In 1978, the New York Bible Society produced the *New International Version*, which had significant support for almost a quarter of the century as a very readable translation in American English. Although not receiving the same acceptance, in 1982, a *New King James Version* and a *Reader's Digest Bible* also were prepared for special interest groups.

Controversy over the Bible's authority came to the fore during the third quarter of this century, but gave witness to the ecumenical nature of many conservative American church groups. In 1976, Harold Lindsell (1913-1998) wrote a book, *Battle for the Bible*, which rallied many Protestants by warning that neglecting the teaching of biblical inerrancy was undermining the very fabric of biblical studies. Although the controversy began in the late 1940s, it came to a head in the 1970s. Several Protestant denominations saw splits occur over the authority of Scripture, including The Lutheran Church—Missouri Synod. In 1978, the International Council of Biblical Inerrancy prepared a document, "The Chicago Statement on Biblical Inerrancy."

The Charismatic Movement

The Pentecostal emphasis on the immediate working of the Holy Spirit on individual Christians had remained limited to small groups outside of mainline Christianity for the first half of this century. As noted above, the largest official denomination was the Assemblies of God. The televangelist, Oral Roberts (1918-2009), was one of the few Pentecostals to bring his healing ministry and "prosperity gospel" to the general public through his international faith-healing crusades and weekly television broadcasts.

When on Easter Sunday 1960 an Episcopal priest in California, Father Dennis Bennett (1917-1991), announced his ability to speak in tongues to his congregation, this was the first evidence of the spread of Pentecostalism's appeal into mainline Christianity. Within a few years, several denominations, particularly Lutheran, Reformed, and Roman Catholic, witnessed the same phenomenon among some of their members and pastors. In order to distinguish this movement from earlier Pentecostalism, the biblical term, "charismatic," was used, referring to the gifts of the Spirit (1 Corinthians 7:7; 12:1-11, 31).

The Jesus People, as noted above, in the sixties and seventies as well as the Vineyard Church Fellowship in the eighties, show the continuing attraction to this phenomenal emphasis upon the activity of the Holy Spirit in a very ecumenical and evangelistic context. The cult-like International House of Prayer in Kansas City with its 24-hour prayer services has developed into a strong influence on young people since the eighties and demonstrates how theologically extreme this movement can depart from traditional and biblical Christianity.

Liberation Theology

Around the middle of this century, a cry for help and hope in the name of Christ was sounded, this time from South America. Suffering social, political, and economic hardships, the poor in many of the developing economies of Latin America were being neglected while the wealthy prospered. Sensitized by Marxist theories and the social gospel, several Roman Catholic priests began to speak out against the perceived mismanagement both in the government and in the church.

At a 1968 conference in Medellin, Colombia, the Conference of Latin American Bishops prepared a document which decried the "sinful" socioeconomic development of their nations in the southern hemisphere by the North American and European powers at the expense of the poor and underprivileged.

In 1971, a Peruvian theologian and Dominican priest, Gustavo Gutiérez (1928-), published his *Teología de la liberación* (Theology of Liberation), in which he popularized the phrase, "preferential option for the poor." His work, which he had developed over several years, became a seminal work for the movement. A Franciscan priest, Leonardo Boff (1938-) of Brazil, wrote a similarly influential work, *Jesus Cristo Libertador* (1978), as did a Spanish Jesuit, Jon Sobrino (1938-), *Jesus the Liberator: a historical-theological reading of Jesus of Nazareth* (1993). Sobrino remains the subject of Vatican criticism for his militant political views and outspoken attacks on the church's hierarchy as well as his overemphasis upon Christ's humanity.

> From *Theology of Liberation*
> An essential clue to the understanding of poverty in liberation theology is the distinction, made in the Medellín document "Poverty of the Church," between three meanings of the term "poverty": real poverty as an evil—that is something that God does not want; spiritual poverty, in the sense of a readiness to do God's will; and solidarity with the poor, along with protest against the conditions under which they suffer.
> --Gustavo Gutiérrez,

Returning to their grassroots "base communities," a term utilized by the movement to describe their Bible study and working groups instead of congregations, these theologians continue to speak a word of caution to the world as well as a word of hope to the poor and oppressed. Several popes have been cautiously critical of their work, although Pope Francis (see chapter 21) has shown some openness to their desire for more active care for the poor.

Global Evangelism and Ecumenism

In 1974, a renewed approach, under the able leadership of Carl F. H. Henry and Billy Graham, saw the Lausanne movement for global evangelism take on a more evangelical, albeit still ecumenical spirit, as they adopted as their motto a very ecumenical theme: "the whole church taking the whole gospel to the whole world." Evangelism and socio-political involvement were affirmed as part of the Christian's duty. In addition, the over two-thousand delegates from more than 150 nations and 150 denominations reaffirmed biblical authority and salvation through faith in Christ alone. Delivering the key note addresses was Billy Graham.

The following year, the World Council of Churches met for their fifth assembly in Nairobi, Kenya, focusing their attention more on liberation theologies and concern for the oppressed. A conservative presence was evident as one report was unanimously approved, "Confessing Christ Today," although the future impact of the WCC would no longer demonstrate the strong commitment to unity through doctrinal accord.

At the same time, a consumerist approach to evangelism arose. Market-influenced approaches to church membership and growth were espoused, especially among Evangelicals. Popular teachers from Fuller Theological Seminary promoted a return to the camp-meeting style of worship from earlier

American revivalism along with this consumerist approach. Worship practices became a central feature of such consumerism as the focus of worship shifted from God to the audience and worship as entertainment was promoted. People were encouraged to pick and choose from a smorgasbord of denominational (or more often non-denominational "community church") options for membership. The Vineyard Movement, founded by the charismatic preacher John Wimber (1934-1997), eventually became a denomination with its characteristic informal worship and musically dynamic sounds. Around the same time, Willow Creek Community Church in suburban Chicago promoted a "seeker-sensitive" style of worship for the unchurched, removing all elements which suggested traditional church life.

Since then, several other preacher-oriented congregational associations have arisen. Many denominational congregations seek to mimic these "successful" mega-churches (see chapter 21) through what has become known as a contemporary-style of informal worship. Curiously at the same time, and by way of contrast, a movement known as "convergence" has sought to bring together charismatic Christians with Anglican, Orthodox, and some Lutherans on the basis of a more liturgical (and early Christian) practice of worship.

With the dissolution of the Soviet Union at the end of 1991, Russian Orthodox Christians experienced a resurgence of membership and participation in the liturgy. Already under Mikhael Gorbachev (1931-), some relaxing of suppression and persecution of Christians and reopening of several Orthodox buildings—monasteries and cathedrals—was experienced. Much of this revitalization was a result of the support from Russians living in exile, particularly in the United States. Already in 1962, the mutual excommunications between the Eastern Orthodox and the Roman Catholic churches were cancelled by Pope Paul VI and the Ecumenical Patriarch of the Orthodox Church, Athenagoras I of Constantinople (1886-1972). A Paraguayan stamp commemorated that event (see illustration).

A Global Consciousness

Toward the end of this century, a greater global consciousness centered in non-European and non-North American nations, most of which had reclaimed their independence from colonial governments and exhibited renewed interest in Christianity in their own cultures. As one church leader said, "Today, a historic shift is occurring. Christianity is moving away from the Global North (primarily Europe and North America) to the Global South (Africa, Asia, and Latin America)." Africa has seen a significant growth in Christianity in recent years. Until the middle of this century, many African nations were colonial territories of European nations and had nominally followed their European Christian models. After colonial control was removed, many thought native religious practices would rise. However, with less than ten percent of the population of African nations being Christian in 1900, Christians were estimated to be almost 50 percent of the more than four hundred million Africans at the end of the century. Indigenous Christian churches emerged with a strong connection to biblical and early Christian practices, including a strong Pentecostal influence, along with continuing ties to mainline denominations.

This same Pentecostal influence is seen in several South American nations. Analysis of such influence shows Pentecostalism's openness to cultural adaptation to a less literate environment, focus on the oral message, and strong emotional spirituality as effective elements. The Pentecostal population in South America increased from about 4% to over 25% of the population (almost 75% of Protestant groups) over the last quarter of this century.

Christianity had long been part of the Asian culture and experience, particularly in the Philippines. The Catholic Church remained strong in the Philippines, although Protestant groups continued mission work there for decades. More notable in growth is Korea. At the beginning of the century, less than 1% of the population was Christian. At the turn of the millennium, nearly a third of the population claimed membership in a Christian organization, many of them Presbyterian or Pentecostal. One of the most well-known of the Korean congregations is the Yoido Full Gospel Church in Seoul. The Korean churches have begun mission work globally, sending several thousand missionaries worldwide each year.

After the rise of Communism in mainland China under Mao Zedong (1893-1976), Christianity experienced a decisive blow in that country. During Mao's "Cultural Revolution" (1966) mainland China was closed to Christian missionary work for a decade. However Christians in underground house churches maintained a presence in spite of government persecutions. Since then, several official churches have been recognized by the Chinese government and, with the economic contacts from Western business and tourism, a Christian influence is slowly returning.

Similar experiences have occurred in South East Asia (from Burma—now Myanmar—to Vietnam), where Christians are far outnumbered by Buddhists and Muslims. Pentecostal charismatic Christianity has been particularly influential among the upwardly mobile Chinese in this region. In the last quarter of this century alone, among ethnic Chinese Christians in South East Asia, membership has increased from 10 million to 135 million. [2]

Still Seeking Ecumenical Consensus

The World Council of Churches, meeting in Lima, Peru, in 1982, prepared a document which expressed what they called an "ecclesiology of communion." The document, *Baptism, Eucharist, and Ministry* (BEM), was a way for the WCC to "realize the goal of visible Church unity," as noted in the Preface. The following year, an Eastern Orthodox/Roman Catholic Consultation offered their critique, published in 1984, noting agreement in some areas, but others

---

[2] Juliette Koning and Heidi Dahles, "*Spiritual Power: Ethnic Chinese Managers and the Rise of Charismatic Christianity in Southeast Asia*" are cited in "Understanding the rapid rise of Charismatic Christianity in Southewat Asia" in *Knowledge@SMU* (5-31-2010) http://ink.library.smu.edu.sg/cgi/viewcontent.cgi?article=1241&context=ksmu

"require further clarification." In 1985, the LCMS published its response, finding the topics as very important, but raised the concern of ambiguous language and a non-biblical basis for unity. Ten years after the initial publication of BEM, *An Evangelical Response*, prepared by the World Evangelical Fellowship, lauded some points of general agreement, but found the whole approach to sacraments and a defined ministry as being too restrictive. On the other hand, BEM has been the basis for the "mutual recognition" of various participating groups ever since.

Mergers

Several denominations of similar backgrounds did merge toward the end of the century. The Presbyterian Church in the United States of America and the Presbyterian Church in the United States formed the Presbyterian Church (U.S.A.) in 1987. Several Lutheran groups established the Evangelical Lutheran Church in America (ELCA) in 1988, but later experienced several splinter groups breaking away. In 1992, these two merged-denominations (PCUSA and ELCA) along with the Reformed Church in America, and the United Church of Christ declared that they were in full communion fellowship with each other. This fellowship was based upon "consensus," a shared understanding and acceptance of differences, rather than an agreement on doctrine.

Roman Catholicism

In 1992, Pope John Paul II (1920-2005, pope 1979-2005) announced the publication of *The Catechism of the Catholic Church*, on the thirtieth anniversary of Vatican II. The Vatican saw this as a tool for unity to help Christians understand the central moral and theological doctrines of the Roman Church. One of the interesting features of this catechism is the return to a medieval approach to biblical studies, using the "four senses." Dialogue between Roman Catholics and Protestant denominations continued as evident by the papal publication in mid-2000 of *Dominus Iesus: On the Unicity and Salvific Universality of Jesus Christ and the Church*. Seen as a step toward ecumenism, it calls non-Catholic churches "not Churches in the proper sense," thus reaffirming the only way to unity would be to unite with Catholic communities under the papacy.

Joint Declaration on the Doctrine of Justification

In 1999, representatives of the Roman Catholic Church and the Lutheran World Federation agreed on a *Joint Declaration on the Doctrine of Justification*, suggesting that one of the key divisive issues of the sixteenth century (see chapter 16) between Lutherans and Catholics had been settled. The document stated that the excommunication of Lutherans at the Council of Trent no longer applies, since newer understandings by both churches have been discovered. The Roman Catholic leaders offered an *Annex*, which questioned several key Lutheran teachings, such as human beings being "simultaneously saints and sinners." Only seventy-five percent of the Lutheran participants voted for the document. The Wisconsin Evangelical Lutheran Synod stated forthrightly that the document "should be repudiated by all Lutherans." Similarly, LCMS theologians have called the document "a betrayal of the Gospel."

Throughout this century, attempts to unite Christians sometimes succeeded in a limited way through the idea of "reconciled diversity" (that is, agreeing to disagree), but were never fully realized.[3] Faith in Christ is certainly foundational throughout Christian history. Doctrinal clarity and confessional commitment remains a continuing hope through the next century.

For Review and Discussion
1. How does the theme of ecumenism flow throughout this century?
2. What problems did liberal theology address as well as create?
3. Who do you consider five of the most influential individuals mentioned in this chapter and why?
4. How has the use of modern media affected both the church and society?
5. Why has the goal of complete unity among all Christian groups not been achieved when so many different groups set ecumenical goals?
6. Why have liberalism and its conservative responses not always addressed the real issue of proclaiming Christ to the world?

For Further Reading
Abbott, Walter M. *The Documents of Vatican II*. Boston: American Press, 1966.
Alberigo, Giuseppe. *A Brief History of Vatican II*. Maryknoll, NY: Orbis Books, 2006.
Baepler Walter A. *A Century of Grace: Missouri Synod 1847-1947*. St. Louis: Concordia Publishing House, 1947.
Barth, Karl. *Dogmatics*. New York: T&T Clark International, 1957 ff.
Bartsch, Hans Werner, ed. *Kerygma and Myth: A Theological Debate by Rudolf Bultmann and Five Critics*. New York: Harper & Row, 1961.
Bultmann, Rudolf. *Jesus Christ and Mythology*. New York: Charles Scribner's Sons, 1958.
Burgess, Joseph A., ed. *In Search of Christian Unity: Basic Consensus/Basic Differences*. Minneapolis: Fortress Press, 1991.
Dau, W.H. T., ed. *Ebenezer: Reviews of the Work of the Missouri Synod during Three Quarters of a Century*. St. Louis: Concordia Publishing House, 1922.
Chardin, Pierre Teilhard de. *The Future of Man*. Norman Denny, trans. New York: Harper & Row, 1964.
Chardin, Pierre Teilhard de. *The Phenomenon of Man*. Bernard Wall, trans. New York: Harper & Row, 1961.
Gutiérrez, Gustavo. *A Theology of Liberation: 15th Anniversary Edition*. Caridad Inda and John Eagleson, trans. Maryknoll, NY: Orbis Books, 1988.

---

[3] Joseph A. Burgess, ed. *In Search of Christian Unity: Basic Consensus/Basic Differences* (Minneapolis: Fortress Press, 1991), illustrates the fundamental issues which have stymied Christian unity and church fellowship between Anglican, Lutheran, Orthodox, Reformed, Roman Catholics, and Wesleyan Methodist traditions.

Harnack, Adolf von. *What Is Christianity?* New York: G. P. Putnam Sons, 1908.
Henry, C. F. W. *The Uneasy Conscience of Modern Fundamentalism.* Grand Rapids, MI: William B. Eerdmans, 1947.
Kerr, Fergus. *Twentieth-Century Catholic Theologians.* Malden, MA: Blackwell Publishing, 2007.
Latourette, Kenneth Scott. *Christianity in a Revolutionary Age.* Volumes IV and V. New York: Harper and Row, 1961-1962.
Lindsell, Harald. *Battle for the Bible.* Grand Rapids, MI: Zondervan, 1977.
Livingston, James C. and Francis Schüssler Fiorenza, et. al. *Modern Christian Thought.* Volume II: The Twentieth Century. Upper Saddle River, NJ: Prentice Hall, 2000.
Meyer, Carl S. *Log Cabin to Luther Tower: Concordia Seminary during One Hundred and Twenty-five Years toward a More Excellent Ministry 1839-1964.* St. Louis: Concordia Publishing House, 1965.
Meyer, Carl S., ed. *Moving Frontiers: Readings in the History of The Lutheran Church—Missouri Synod.* St. Louis: Concordia Publishing House, 1964.
Niebuhr, H. Richard. *Christ and Culture.* New York: Harper & Brothers, 1951.
Rahner, Karl. *Foundations of Christian Faith: An Introduction to the Idea of Christianity.* William V. Dych, trans. New York: Seabury Press, 1978.
Rauschenbusch, Walter. *A Theology of Social Gospel.* New York: Macmillan Co., 1917.
Tillich, Paul. *The Protestant Era.* Chicago: University of Chicago Press, 1953.

21. Post-Modern Potentialities

The Twenty-first Century

"The future is now." What this next century will bring for the Christian community is uncertainty in the midst of certainty. We cannot see into the future, but we know Who holds the future. For the first decades of the twenty-first century, several themes have already become obvious—secularism, ecology, and terror dominated the media, which itself is a phenomenon of unprecedented and relatively untapped potential for Christianity. Another phenomenon has been labelled post-modernism.

This chapter will be the briefest, yet also the most significant for those of you who have read or at least skimmed through the rest of this volume. It will, in one way, also be more sermonic in theme as we anticipate our Lord's promised return "on that day and that hour which no one knows" (Matthew 23).

Impact of "9-11"

Perhaps no one event affected American Christianity than the terrorist attack on September 11th, 2001. Seeing the twin towers of the International Trade Center in New York City collapse remains vivid for those who first heard of the seemingly impossible event. Almost immediately after that tragic occurrence, churches throughout the United States saw a great increase in attendance. People needed the assurance of God's presence in their lives.

For those who continue to view the news videos of that historic event, there may be incredulity at such evil devastation from religiously zealot masterminds. Yet, the fact remains that it happened. Explanations continue to be offered. Through it all, a deeper understanding of the theological viewpoint made by Martin Luther in the sixteenth century is helpful. He spoke of the "theology of the cross," in the midst of suffering we see our Savior, Jesus Christ. God does not always remove suffering from His people, but gives us the perspective that recalls a higher goal of eternal life with Him. Through faith in Jesus's life, death, and resurrection, there can be hope for those who seek to be holy in the world.

Secularism and Postmodernity
Secularism

As noted in the previous chapter, secularity seems to be a dominant fact in American and European Christianity. Yet, we see in Africa, South America, and the Asian Pacific that secularism is not as virulent and Christianity is growing in profound ways. Religious life, since the beginning of Christianity, has always faced some issues of living "in the world, but not of the world" (John 17). Some scholars have spoken of the end of Constantinian Christianity in which the culture accepts the Christian worldview. However, that has never been a constant as seen through out the past chapters and as Reinhold Niebuhr (see chapter 20) so clearly articulated.

Postmodernism

Postmodernism has been characterized as deconstructing all that can be identified as modern. Some Christians return to the roots of Christianity and seek a more mystical experience of God through meditation and experiential worship. Others seek to create new contexts for Christian witnessing, whether it is through the internet or through personal relationships. Dialogue rather than proclamation characterizes their approach. Uncertain of Scripture's authority, post-moderns emphasize a plurality of interpretations, which they claim can be enjoyed through the simple authentic repetition of the biblical narratives. For them, Christianity is a matter of conversation and involvement in the world.

While secularity and postmodernism pose legitimate concerns, the clarity of the gospel continues to shine a bright light of God's truth in Him who is "the Way, and the Truth, and the Life" (John 14:6). Keeping the focus on Him will help clarify the reality of God's love for the whole world.

Ecology

One interesting emphasis which began in the last century is the role of Christianity in global ecology. Christians have long been involved in the scientific study of nature, recognizing that it is God's creation and is an object of inspiring awe and worthy of respect. However, the biblical mandate to "have dominion over the earth" (Genesis 1) has sometimes been misunderstood at best or misrepresented at worst to promote an uncaring consumption of natural resources and the destruction of natural habitats in the name of technological progress and economic growth. Christians understand that "the whole creation groans…for the redemption of sons" (Romans 8:19-23), which suggests that Christians of all religious groups should be most involved in conservation and environmental biodiversity.

Sally McFague (1933-) (see illustration), although a liberal feminist theologian, is noted especially for her strong emphasis upon eco-Christianity (sometimes more broadly labelled as "ecotheology"). Using a questionable approach to interpreting scripture solely as metaphor and speaking of "God as mother," she argued in her book, *The Body of God: An Ecological Theology* (1993), that Christians should care for the earth.

Her dubious biblical base and panentheistic views have resulted in a less than widespread acceptance of her legitimate concerns.

Catholic, Reformed, and Orthodox theologians have voiced similar calls for Christian care. To help their members, the Episcopal Church in 2005 prepared *A Catechism of Creation: An Episcopal Understanding,* and The Lutheran Church—Missouri Synod produced in 2010 *Together With All Creatures: Caring for God's Living Earth,* prepared by its Commission on Theology and Church Relations. Other denominations have study documents available. The issue of caring for creation and Christian stewardship of the environment will continue to be a strong theme throughout the first half of this century.

Catholic Papacy Remains a Force

Pope Benedict XVI (1927-, pope 2005-2013) was elected in 2005 at the death of John Paul II, after one of the longest pontificates in recent centuries. Serving as a respected German university theologian, Joseph Ratzinger (1927-), he became an archbishop with little pastoral experience in 1977 and four years later was promoted to several prominent offices in the Vatican. Prior to his papal election, he held the highest position among the College of Cardinals, Prefect of the Sacred Congregation for the Doctrine of the Faith. He was trained in liberal Catholic theology, but in most of his service and in his pontificate he advocated a return to traditional doctrines and practices, including (as pope) allowing a return of the Tridentine Mass. In 2001, several years before his election, Ratzinger had advised John Paul II (1920-2005, pope 1978-2005) to address the issue of sexual abuse by clergy, and after his election took strong action in several cases.

With the unusually rare resignation of Benedict XVI, the Roman Catholic Church saw the election of Pope Francis I (pope 2013-) (see illustration), the first Jesuit and the first to come from South America. The Argentinian archbishop and cardinal, Jorge Bergoglio (1936-), was a strong advocate for the poor and oppressed. He was recognized for his humility and commitment to social justice and continues those themes in his papacy since 2013.

Islam

With the increased awareness of and contact with Islam, Christianity has seen an increase in Muslim extremist groups. More Christians were martyred for their faith in the twentieth century than in all previous centuries (see earlier chapters of this book). This attack on Christianity will not wane in this century. Although Islam claims the name stands for peace, the word in Arabic means "submission and obedience," and is a requirement for all people to submit to Allah and obey Mohammed's teachings. Of the three major Muslim sects—Sunni, Sufi, and Shi'ah—Sufi's have demonstrated the most peaceful dimensions of Islam, with the Sunni holding the majority of members in most Muslim countries.

Islam is more than a religion. It is a worldview, which includes the totality of a member's life—political, social, and familial. Christianity is seen as a decadent form of Western monotheism. The majority of Muslims assume that Islam will ultimately triumph over all other religious systems and are taught to seek that goal.

Globally, Islam has increased its influence and power significantly. In America, for instance, the Muslim population at the beginning of this third millennium was just a little under four million, although Muslim organizations suggested that it was closer to seven million. (See illustration of the Islamic Center

in Dearborn, Michigan.) A Pew Research Center report projected that the Muslim population will grow twice as fast as the general population and will be nearly as numerous as Christians in the world by 2050.[1] Because of their strong family ties and a sense of community, reaching out to them with the love of Christ can be difficult. Yet, the legalism and enslavement that characterizes most Muslim sects will provide opportunities to show the full and free forgiveness and reconciliation with God through His own Son, Jesus.

Internet and Megachurches

No one event or invention, since the printing press with moveable type in the sixteenth century, has influenced Christianity as much as the internet. Although the World Wide Web first began in the latter years of the previous century, its impact will be most striking in this century. With information overload, finding the truth—and Him who is the Truth—is often diminished or deemed impossible. Relativism and atheism have equal voice to the Christian verities.

The internet has been a significantly beneficial resource for many churches and mission agencies. Use of the internet has enabled missionaries and

---

[1] Michael Lipka and Conrad Hacket. "Why Muslims Are the World Fastest Growing Group." http://www.pewresearch.org/fact-tank/2015/04/23/why-muslims-are-the-worlds-fastest-growing-religious-group/ (Accessed 7/11/2015)

mission-oriented groups to maintain contact across great distances. Local congregations are able to "visit" mission sites and get information for the support of various missionary endeavors. This social networking will only increase this century.

Congregations identified as "megachurches" are those Christian churches that have over 2000 persons attending Sunday services. These large churches, which date back to the nineteenth century, became influential toward the end of the twentieth century through the use of media. Robert Schuller (1926-2015) and his "Crystal Cathedral" in Garden Grove, California, was recognized for years as a one of the first modern megachurches. Although these large congregations will be able to provide a multiplicity of services, they will never replace the smaller community-oriented churches.

Evangelism

Perhaps at no time in history has evangelistic efforts been more necessary. With world populations growing and European and American culture becoming increasingly secular, the world provides a great opportunity to share the Good News of God's grace and mercy in Christ.

One of the interesting phenomenon of this century is the fact that Christians from other nations are coming to the United States as missionaries and evangelists. A few years ago, the United States was identified as the third largest mission field for Christian evangelism, only behind China and India.

While we live in a highly skeptical, almost agnostic society, the need for relationship building is a key to bridging the gap. Many people are seeking spiritual depth and desire to have a spiritual relationship as well as personal relationship with others. In addition, our very individualistic society provides an opportunity for a sense of community through a vibrant congregation where Christ is the center. Conversion is the work of the Holy Spirit, but we are His instruments through whom He will accomplish the great task of calling the world to faith in Christ so that we can truly be holy in the world.

For Review and Discussion
1. How does the impact of the destruction of the Twin Trade Towers in New York City on September 11, 2001, affect a Christian perspective on the world today?
2. What impact does secularism and postmodernity have on local Christian congregations?
3. Why is ecology a theological issue (see Paul's letter to the Romans, chapter 8)?
4. What benefits does the Internet provide for Christian congregations globally?
5. How is Islam both a threat and an opportunity for Christian witnessing in the world?
6. Describe the future of Christianity as you foresee it from your perspective in this twenty-first century.

For Further Reading

Caputo, John and Brian McLaren. *What Would Jesus Construct? The Good News of Postmodernity for the Church.* Grand Rapids, MI: Baker Academic Press, 2007.

Penner, Myron B. *Christianity and the Postmodern Turn: Six Views.* Ada, MI: Brazos Press, 2005.

The Lutheran Church—Missouri Synod. *Together With All Creatures: Caring for God's Living Earth.* A Report by the Commission on Theology and Church Relations. St. Louis: LCMS, 2010.

Veith, Gene Edward. *Postmodern Times.* Wheaton, IL: Crossway Books, 1994.

Wuthnow Robert. *Christianity in the 21st Century: Reflections on the Challenges Ahead.* New York: Oxford University Press, 1993.

General Bibliography

The books listed here are helpful for most chapters of this textbook. Several of these resources cover multiple centuries and are therefore included. Books related to specific topics or centuries are normally included in the chapter section "For Further Reading," although a few are repeated here for convenience.

Ahlstrom, Sydney E. *A Religious History of the American People*. New Haven, CN: Yale University Press, 1972.
Baillie, John, John T. McNeill, and Henry P. Van Dusen, eds. *Library of Christian Classics*. 26 volumes. CD-ROM edition. Louisville: Westminster John Knox Press, 2006.
Bainton, Roland H. *Christendom: A Short History of Christianity and Its Impact on Western Civilization*. Volume I: From the Birth of Christ to the Reformation. Volume II: From the Reformation to the Present. New York: Harper & Row, 1966.
Bauer, Walter. *Orthodoxy and Heresy in Earliest Christianity*. Philadelphia: Fortress Press, 1971.
Bercot, David W., ed. *A Dictionary of Early Christian Beliefs*. Peabody, MA: Hendrickson Publishers, 1998.
Benedetto, Robert, ed. *The New Westminster Dictionary of Church History*. Louisville: Westminster John Knox Press, 2008.
Bettenson, Henry, and Chris Mauder, eds. *Documents of the Christian Church*. Fourth Edition. New York: Oxford University Press, 2011.
Bloickmans, Wim, and Peter Hoppenbrouwers. *Introduction to Medieval Europe: 300-1550*. Isola van den Hoven, trans. New York: Routledge, 2007.
Chadwick, Henry. *The Early Church*. New York: Penguin Books, 1967.
Cory, Catherine A. and David T. Landry, eds. *The Christian Theological Tradition*. Upper Saddle River, NJ: Prentice Hall, 2000.
Dowley, Tim, ed. *Eerdmans' Handbook to the History of Christianity*. Grand Rapids: Wm. B. Eerdmans Publishing Co., 1977.
Farrar, Frederic W. *Lives of the Fathers: Sketches of Church History in Biography*. New York: Macmillan and Co., 1889.
González, Justo L. *Church History: An Essential Guide*. Nashville: Abingdon Press, 1996.

González, Justo L. *The Story of Christianity*. Volume 1: The Early Church to the Dawn of the Reformation. Volume 2: The Reformation to the Present Day. New York: HarperSanFrancisco, 1984 & 1985.

Greenslade, S. L., ed. *The Cambridge History of the Bible*. Three volumes. New York: Cambridge University Press, 1975.

Gritsch, Eric W. *A History of Lutheranism*. Minneapolis: Fortress Press, 2002.

Hageman, G. E. *Sketches from the History of the Church*. St. Louis: Concordia Publishing House, 1950.

Hagen, Kenneth, ed. *The Bible in the Churches: How Various Christians Interpret the Scriptures*. Third Edition. Milwaukee: Marquette University Press, 1998.

Kiecker, James G. *Martin Luther and the Long Reformation: Response and Reform in the Church: Pentecost to the Present*. Milwaukee: Northwestern Publishing House, 1992.

Krauss, E. A. W. *Lebensbilder aus der Geschichte der christlichen Kirche*. St. Louis: Concordia Publishing House 1930.

Lane, Tony. *A Concise History of Christian Thought*. Grand Rapids: Baker Academic, 2006.

Lietzmann, Hans. *A History of the Early Church*. 4 volumes. Bertram Lee Woolf, trans. London: Lutterworth Press, 1961.

Lindberg, Carter. *A Brief History of Christianity*. Malden, MA: Blackwell Publishing, 2006.

Lueker, Erwin L., ed. *Lutheran Cyclopedia*. St Louis: Concordia Publishing House, 1954.

Marty, Martin E. *A Short History of Christianity*. New York: The World Publishing Company, 1959.

McBrien, Richard P. *Lives of the Popes: The Pontiffs from St. Peter to John Paul II*. New York: HarperSanFrancisco, 1997.

McGrath, Alister E. *Christian History: An Introduction*. West Sussex, UK: John Wiley & Sons, Ltd., 2013.

McManners, John, ed. *The Oxford Illustrated History of Christianity*. New York: Oxford University Press, 1992.

Miles, Margaret R. *The Word Made Flesh: A History of Christian Thought*. Malden, MA: Blackwell Publishing, 2005.

Nelson, Clifford E. *Lutherans in North America*. Philadelphia: Fortress Press, 1975.

Pelikan, Jaroslav Jan. *The Christian Tradition*. Five volumes. Chicago: University of Chicago Press, 1973-1990.

Platinga, Harry, ed. Grand Rapids: Christian Classics Ethereal Library. http://www.ccel.org/

Qualben, Lars P. *A History of the Christian Church*. New York: Thomas Nelson and Sons, 1958.

Roberts, Alexander J., ed. *The Ante-Nicene Fathers*. 10 volumes. New York: Charles Scribner's Sons, 1899.

Schaff, Philip. *History of the Christian Church*. 8 volumes. Grand Rapids: Wm. B. Eerdmans Publishing Company, 1910; 1973 reprint. http://www.ccel.org/s/schaff/history/About.htm

Schaff, Philip and Henry Wace, eds. *Nicene and Post-Nicene Fathers of the Christian Church*. First Series: 8 volumes. Second Series: 14 volumes. Grand Rapids: Wm. B. Eerdmans Publishing Company, 1952.

Schmidt, Alvin J. *Under the Influence: How Christianity Transformed Civilization*. Grand Rapids: Zondervan, 2001.

Seeberg, Reinhold. *Textbook of the History of Doctrines*. Two volumes. Charles E. Hay, trans. Philadelphia: Lutheran Publication Society, 1905.

Smalley, Beryl. *The Study of the Bible in the Middle Ages*. Notre Dame, IN: University of Notre Dame Press, 1964.

Urban, Linwood. *A Short History of Christian Thought*. Revised and Expanded Edition. New York: Oxford University Press, 1992.

Van Voorst, Robert E., comp. *Readings in Christianity*. Second Edition. Stamford, CT: Wadsworth, 2001.

Walker, Williston and Richard A. Norris, David W. Lotz, Robert T. Handy. *A History of the Christian Church*. Fourth Edition. New York: Charles Scribner's Sons, 1918, 1946, 1985.

Wilson, Brian. *Christianity*. Upper Saddle River, NJ: Prentice Hall, 1999.

Index

Abelard, Peter – 145-148, 150
Abraham – 20, 22, 52, 89-90, 288
Absolution – 83, 245
Act of Supremacy – 239
Acts, book of – 1-4, 6-7
Adalbert, Bishop – 124
Ad fontes – 190, 210
Adiaphora – 228-229
Adoptionism – 14, 99-100, 109
Adventist – 300
Africa – 6, 8, 25, 28, 62-66, 68, 73, 77, 82, 87, 92, 97, 158, 196, 201-202, 292, 302, 310, 326-327, 331
African Methodist Episcopal – 278, 302, 307, 320
Agricola, John – 225, 228
Agricola, Mikael – 225, 227
Albertus Magnus – 165
Albigenses – 143, 153, 162, 163, 181
Alcuin of York – 100, 108-109
Alexander II, Pope – 132
Alexander III, Pope – 143, 152
Alexander V, Pope – 187
Alexander VI, Pope – 195-196, 206, 243
Alexander of Alexandria – 40-41
Alexander of Hales – 165, 167
Alexander the Great – 5
Alexandria – 5, 22, 25, 32, 40, 42, 61, 92, 101
Allen, Richard – 277
Altizer, Thomas J. J. – 322
Ambrose of Milan – 47-48, 50, 51, 53
American Bible Society – 290
American Lutheran Church – 310
Amsdorf, Nicholas von – 229
Anabaptism – 237, 238-239
Andreae, Jakob – 229-230, 235

Angels – 29, 59, 64, 80, 81, 82, 90, 91, 92, 150, 159, 168, 273
Anglican – 239-240, 256, 266, 272, 273, 275, 290, 297, 311, 326
Anglo-Catholic – 291
Anselm of Canterbury – 136-138, 146
Anselmic theory of atonement – 138
Ansgar – 116
Antony, Saint – 44
Anti-Trinitarian – 234, 261, 262
Antichrist – 184, 216, 217
Antinomianian – 180, 225, 228
Antioch – 3, 15, 17, 27, 30, 34, 57, 77, 92, 101, 135
Apocrypha – 290
Apologists – 20, 24, 26, 38
Apology of the Augsburg Confession – 223
Apostasy – 31, 295
Apostles – 1-4, 8, 10, 13-15 19, 21-24, 31, 33, 35, 69, 147, 158,
Apostles' Creed – 30, 60, 66, 103, 112, 191, 311
Apostolic Fathers – 13, 14, 21, 290,
Apostolic Tradition – 29-30
Aquinas, Thomas – 165-167, 175, 176, 181, 189
Architecture – 149, 169, 206
Arianism – also see "Arius" – 42-45, 47, 48, 52, 75, 77, 87
Aristotelian – 77, 102, 148, 149, 165, 166, 167, 168, 170, 174, 205, 243, 251
Aristotle – 20, 95, 148-149, 164, 165, 168
Arius – also see "Arianism" – 40, 41-42, 46, 48, 59, 61
Arles, Council of – 40, 42
Armenian Church – 61, 77, 182, 193

Arminianism – 250, 253, 273, 274, 298, 300, 321
Arminius, Jacob – 235, 253
Arndt, Johann – 230, 250, 251, 257
Asbury, Francis – 273, 275, 278
Asceticism – also see "monasticism" 43-45, 53, 79
Athanasius – 42-45
Atheism – 9, 16, 283, 286, 287, 289, 309, 322
Atonement – 137, 147, 250, 253, 289, 301
Attila – 68, 69
Augsburg Confession – 222, 223, 230, 271, 302
Augsburg Interim – 227
Augustana Lutheran Church – 310
Augustine of Canterbury – 83, 85, 89
Augustine of Hippo – 40, 49-52, 62-70, 75
Augustinian Canons – 138, 142,
Augustinian Friars (Hermits) – 161-162, 177, 214, 215, 218
Avignon – 174, 176-177, 180-182
Awakening – 142, 194, 270; the Great – 274-275; the Second – 293, 296, 299

Babylonian Captivity – 174, 180, 216, 237
Bach, Johann Sebastian – 252, 278
Bacon, Francis – 208, 261
Bacon, Roger – 167
Baptism – 3, 14, 15, 19, 26-28, 30, 32, 33, 35, 47-49, 57, 60, 63, 65, 66, 71, 83, 94, 99,100, 107, 151, 185, 166,191, 193, 203, 213, 237, 238, 311,
Baptism, Eucharist, and Ministry – 327
Baptist – 250, 257, 262, 272, 274, 2752, 278, 292, 293, 300, 312, 316, 320, 321, 322
Barnabas – 3, 242
Barnes, Robert – 240
Barth, Karl – 288, 312-314, 319, 320, 322
Bartholomew – 8, 235
Basel, Council – 192
Basil of Caesarea – 45-46,
Basilides – 17
Battle of Hastings – 130, 132
Battle of Tours – 97

Baur, F. Christian – 286-287, 303
Bede, Venerable –83, 89, 99
Becket, Thomas – 151
Beethoven, Ludwig van – 278, 279
Beguines – 178, 180-181
Beghards – 180, 181
Bellarmine, Robert – 245-246, 250, 251, 260
Benedict XI, Pope – 174
Benedict XII, Pope – 181
Benedict XVI, Pope – 318-319
Benedict of Aiane – 110
Benedictines – 81, 89, 109, 116, 123, 128, 136, 138, 144, 148, 152, 165, 182, 206,
Benedict of Nursia – 77-79, 82
Bennett, Dennis – 324
Berger, Peter – 322
Bernard of Clairvaux – 141, 143-145, 147-148, 150
Beza, Theodore – 234-235
Bible – see also "Scripture" – 1, 7, 17, 32, 52, 58, 66, 67, 70, 84, 108, 113, 150, 162, 164, 183, 186, 191, 204, 205, 224, 234, 239, 250, 257, 258, 261, 269, 285, 290, 297, 298, 300, 309, 318, 321, 322, 323-324, 325,
Bible interpretation – 6, 10, 14, 23, 32-33, 48, 50, 216, 220, 234, 236, 237, 261, 300, 321, 323, 332
Biel, Gabriel – 176, 189
Black Cloister – 214
Boethius – 74
Boff, Leonardo – 325
Bohemian Brothers – 188
Bologna – 164, 187
Bolshevik Revolution – 309
Bonaventure – 162, 167
Bonhoeffer, Dietrich – 312, 314-315
Boniface VIII, Pope – 173-174
Boniface, missionary – 97-99, 104, 105
Bondage of the Will – 219-220
Book of Common Prayer – 240, 275,
Book of Concord – 230, 251, 252, 302
Booth, William – 292
Bora, Katherine von – 220
Borgia (family) – 195-196, 206, 210
Boyle, Robert – 261
Brazil – 202, 325
Brent, Charles – 311
Brenz, Johann – 230

Brethren of the Common Life – 179, 185, 189, 190
Bridget of Sweden – 180
Brief Statement – 310
British and Foreign Bible Society – 290
Broad Church movement – 290
Brück, Gregory – 223
Bucer, Martin – 223-224, 234
Bugenhagen, Johannes – 223-224, 226, 227
Bullinger, Heinrich – 237
Bultmann, Rudolf – 322-323
Bunyan, John – 259
Byzantine – 76, 81-82, 88-89, 92, 101, 103, 105, 110, 111, 113, 119, 127, 129, 132, 153, 156
Caesar – 1, 16, 37, 38, 40,
Cajetan, Thomas Cardinal – 215, 242
Caliphates – 91-92, 101, 102, 111, 127
Calixtus, Popes – 29, 142, 193
Calixtines – 188
Calov, Abraham – 252
Calvin, John – 233-237
Calvinism – 205, 230, 235-236, 240, 246
Cambridge – 164
Camp meetings – 275, 296-297, 325
Campbell, Alexander and Thomas – 297
Canada – 276, 292, 297, 317
Canon of Scripture– 21
Canon of the Mass – 189
Canon law – 114, 116, 149, 188
Canons Regular – 142, 160, 185,
Canterbury – 83, 89, 132, 151, 156, 169, 183, 239, 311
Capitalism – 312
Cappadocian Fathers – 45-47, 64
Capuchins –242, 292
Cardinal, College of – 128, 132, 133, 143, 154, 182, 187, 243, 333
Carey, William – 272
Carlstadt, Andreas Bodenstein von – 216, 218, 225, 237-239
Carthage, Councils of – 31, 39-40, 63
Cassian, John – 65, 69-70
Cassiodorus – 79-80
Catechism, Small and *Large* – 221, 295
Catechism of the Catholic Church, The – 328
Catechisms – 203, 227, 234, 237, 245, 256, 302, 333

Cathars – 152, 160, 162-163
Cathedrals – 89, 138, 146, 149, 150, 151, 168-169, 257
Catherine of Sienna – 179
Catholic – 48, 63, 65, 66, 67, 73, 74, 77, 81, 83, 84, 85, 87, 89, 115, 116, 145, 149, 152, 154, 155, 159, 163, 164, 165, 166, 176, 181, 193, 203, 205, 206, 208, 215, 216-218, 221-225, 227-230, 233-246, 249-253, 257-261, 268, 271, 270, 280, 290, 291-292, 293, 294, 297, 308, 311, 315, 317-319, 321, 324, 326, 328, 333
Celibacy –77, 95, 112, 123, 128, 129, 179, 186, 239, 270, 291
Cerinthus – 17
Cerularius, Michael –129
Chalcedon, Council of—60-61, 76, 77, 93
Chalcedonian Definition – 61, 69
Charismatic movement – 308, 324, 326, 327
Charlemagne – 88, 100, 103-106, 107-110, 112, 115
Charles V, Emperor – 200-201, 203, 216-218, 220-222, 226-227, 243
Charles Martel – 97, 98, 101, 103-104
Chaucer, Geoffrey – 183
Chemnitz, Martin – 226, 227, 230, 245
Chicago-Lambeth Quadrilateral – 311
Chiliasm – see "Millennialism"
China – 93, 97, 203, 242, 260, 271, 318, 327, 335
Christian III, King – 223
Christian Church, Disciples – 297, 317, 322
Christian Science – 299, 301
Christological teachings – 58, 74, 76, 84, 102, 104, 239
Chrysostom – 57-58
Church and state – 63, 63, 107, 131, 174, 209, 268, 277, 283
Church of England – 239, 249, 272, 273, 276
Church of Jesus Christ of Latter Day Saints – 299-300
Churches Uniting in Christ -- 317
Chytraeus, David – 230
Cistercians –136, 138, 143, 144, 152
City of God – 63-65
Clement of Rome – 10, 13

Clement VII, Pope – 218, 221, 224, 243
Clericis Laicos, bull – 173
Clovis – 71, 73, 88
Cluniac reforms – 122-123, 136, 138
Cluny, monastery – 119, 122, 123, 143, 145, 147
Coke, Thomas –275
Colet, John – 190
Columba, missionary – 85
Columbanus – 85
Columbus, Christopher – 202
Commission on Faith and Order – 311
Conciliar movement – 187, 195
Concordat of Worms – 142-143
Cone, James H. – 320
Confession Tetrapolitan – 223
Confessionalism – 246, 249-250
Confirmation – 99, 166, 193, 258
Confutation – 223
Congregational churches – 255, 257, 266, 274, 275, 279, 292, 293, 297, 310, 315, 317, 322,
Constance, Bishop – 237
Constance, Council of – 187, 192, 223,
Constantine the Great – 38-42, 48, 54
Constantinople, Councils – 33, 40, 76, 104
Consultation on Church Union -- 317
Convergence—326
Copernicus, Nicolaus – 207-208, 229, 260-261
Coptic Church – 61, 77, 323
Cornelius – 2; Bishop – 32,
Cosmology – 17-18, 208
Cotton, John – 255
Coverdale, Miles – 205
Cranach, Lucas – 192
Cranmer, Thomas – 234, 236, 239-240
Creed – 23, 24, 30, 34, 41, 46, 48, 60, 74, 272; see also "Apostles' Creed" and "Nicene Creed"
Cromwell, Oliver – 256-269
Cromwell, Thomas – 239
Cross –2, 3, 4, 10, 15, 18, 21, 28, 48, 70, 71, 78, 94, 109, 136, 145,151, 153, 159, 161, 185, 259, 308
Crusades
    First – 133-136, 141
    Second –145-148
    Third – 154
    Fourth – 156

    Children's –156-157
    Later – 161, 162, 163, 169, 170, 187, 193, 241
Crypto-Calvinistic controversy – 228
Cur Deus Homo (Why God Man?) – 137-138
Cyprian, Bishop – 31
Cyril (Cyrillos) – 113, 124
Cyril of Alexandria – 59
Cyril of Jerusalem – 48-49

Danish Evangelical Lutheran Church – 224, 225, 269, 270, 288
Dante – 174, 177
Darwin, Charles – 287
Deaconate – 10, 14, 15, 31, 35, 40, 41, 42, 81, 95, 99, 108, 121, 150, 155, 162, 203, 272, 274,
Deaconesses – 16, 35, 284
Dead Sea Scrolls – 5, 6, 323
Decius, Emperor – 30, 31, 32, 38
Declaration of Independence – 277
Defensor pacis – 174
Deism – 267, 268
Demiurge – 17, 18
Denmark – 89, 111, 116, 123, 218, 223, 253, 302
Denominations – 65, 239, 249, 257, 271, 275, 278, 293, 294, 296, 297, 299, 301-302
Descartes, Rene – 261, 262
Deutsche Messe ("German Mass") – 220
Dictatus papae – 133
Didache – 13-14, 34-35
Didascalia Apostolorum – 34-35
Diderot, Denis – 267
Diet of Speyer – 220, 221
Diocletian –37-39
Dionysius the Areopagite – 80, 110, 114, 168, 191
Disciples of Christ – 297
Dispensational Premillennialism – 308
Docetism – 17, 18, 21
Dominicans – 159-162, 164, 165, 174, 175, 177, 178, 179, 182, 185, 196, 202, 214, 234, 242, 292, 325
Dominus Iesus – 307, 328
Domitian, Emperor – 9
Donations of Constantine – 101, 112, 190
Donations of Pepin II – 105

Donatism – 39-40
Dort, Synod of – 252, 253
Duns Scotus – 166-168, 175, 189
Dürer, Albrecht – 192
Dutch Reformed Church – 252, 266, 274

Easter controversy – 23
Ebionites – 19, 22
Ecclesiastical History – 40
Ecclesiolae in ecclesia – 258, 271
Eck, Johann Maier –216, 217, 222
Eckhart, Meister –177-178
Ecology – 332-333
Ecumenical – 280, 298, 302, 307, 309, 310, 311, 314, 316, 317, 319, 324, 325, 326, 327
Ecumenical Councils – 54, 76, 84, 93-94, 100, 104, 111, 143, 180, 187, 243, 291, 317-318
Ecumenical creeds – 24, 112
Eddy, Mary Baker --301
Edict of Milan – 38
Edict of Nantes – 235
Edward VI, King – 240
Edwards, Jonathan – 274
Eisenach – 190, 218, 278
Eisleben – 190, 213, 226
Elizabeth I, Queen -- 240
Emperor worship – 9-10.
Encyclical – 308, 317
Epiphanius – 19
Episcopacy – 10, 37, 47, 85, 295
Episcopalian – 275, 311, 317, 321, 322, 324, 333
Epitome – 230
Erasmus Desiderius of Rotterdam – 179, 190, 205-206, 214, 219-220
Eriugena, John Scotus – 110, 114
Erfurt – 177, 189, 213-214
Estienne, Robert – 205
Essenes – 5, 6
Eucharist – see "Lord's Supper"
Eusebius of Caesarea – 7, 38, 40, 41, 45, 52
Eusebius of Nicamedia – 41, 42
Eutyches – 74
Eutychianism – 94
Evangelicals – 217, 221, 227, 285, 293, 294, 295, 296, 302, 303, 310, 311, 312, 316, 317, 321, 328
Evangelism –77, 157, 309, 316, 325

Evolution – 290, 309, 318, 319,
Ex cathedra – 291
Excommunicate – 18, 28, 42, 77, 78, 101, 112, 113, 129, 133, 134, 143, 156, 169, 176, 183, 233, 234
Extreme Unction – 166
Exurge domini 216

Falwell, Jerry – 315
Farel, William –233, 234, 241
Federal Council of Churches in Christ – 311
Felix of Apthungi – 39
Felix of Urgel – 100, 109
Ferdinand of Aragon – 194, 200, 201, 241
Feudalism – 115, 128, 135, 138, 142, 193, 200, 201, 203
Feuerbach, Ludwig – 286, 288
Filioque – 84, 112, 146, 192
Finland – 225, 227
Finnian, missionary – 85
Finney, Charles G. – 297-298
Flacius, Matthias – x, 228-229
Flagellants – 178, 182
Fliedner, Theodor – 284
Florence, Italy – 185, 188, 189, 191-194, 196, 201, 206
Florence Nightingale – 284
Foreign mission societies – 266, 290, 309
Foreknowledge – 146, 149, 176, 177
Forensic justification – see "justification"
Formula of Concord – 228, 230, 282
Fox, George – 256, 260
Foxe, John – 240
France – 8, 68, 71, 73, 88, 97, 103, 110, 114, 119, 122, 128, 135, 136, 138, 143, 145, 151, 152, 153, 156, 157, 158, 160, 162, 163, 168, 169, 173, 174, 175, 181, 182, 185, 189, 190, 193, 196, 200, 218, 224, 233, 235, 241, 243, 254, 255, 258, 259, 265, 276, 280, 283, 291, 292, 301, 309, 310, 316
Francis de Sales – 246, 250
Francis of Assisi – 157-159, 167, 177, 180
Francis I of France – 216, 218, 220, 221, 222, 235, 243

Francis I, Pope – 325, 333
Franciscans – 161, 162, 164, 167, 168, 175, 176, 181,182, 195, 196, 202, 203, 241, 242, 292, 325
Francke, Hermann – 258, 269, 270
Francke, Gotthelf August – 270
Franck, Sebastian – 238
Frederick the Wise, elector – 192, 220
Freemason – 279
Frelingheusen Theodore J. – 274
French Revolution –265, 280, 283
Fronto –52
Fundamentalism – 308, 309, 321
Fundamentals, The – 308,

Galerius – 37-38
Galesburg or Akron Rule -- 303
Galilei, Galileo – 207, 208, 250, 260, 261
Gallican Confession – 235
Geneva – 233, 234, 236, 246
Gerhard, John – 230, 251, 252
Gerhardt, Paul – 252
German Baptists – 275
German Bible Society – 290
German, language – 108, 191,195, 218, 219, 223, 224, 250, 267, 295, 310
Germany – 98, 103, 104, 110, 113, 116, 119, 120, 121, 128, 131-135, 142, 145, 148, 155, 156, 160, 162, 178, 182, 187, 189, 190, 192, 195, 200, 204-207, 210, 213, 216-220, 228-230, 243, 251, 253-255, 270, 271, 273, 278, 279, 284, 286, 287, 291, 292, 294, 302, 303, 309, 310, 312-317, 319, 320, 322, 333
Germanus, Patriarch – 101, 102
Gerson, Jean de – 176
Gibbon, Edward – 268
Glossa ordinaria – 150-151
Gnesio-Lutherans – 227-229
Gnosticism – 9, 17-19, 21-22, 24, 163, 323
Gospel of Thomas – 21, 22
Gothic architecture – see "Architecture"
Gottschalk – 114-115
Graf, Karl Heinrich – 289
Graham, Billy – 315, 321, 322, 325
Gratian's *Decretals* – 149, 164
Great Awakening – see "Awakenings"

Great Commission – 158
Great Schism, The – 119
Great Western Schism – 185, 187, 271
Greek, culture – 4-6, 8, 9, 11, 28, 50, 74, 88, 95, 148, 149, 165, 185, 191,
Greek Orthodox – 84, 156, 192, 271
Gregorian calendar – 267
Gregory II, Pope – 92, 101
Gregory III, Pope – 101, 104
Gregory VII, Pope – 133-134, 139, 186
Gregory IX, Pope – 159, 164, 165
Gregory XI, Pope – 182, 183
Gregory, the Great (I), Pope – 77, 79-84, 87, 88, 89, 94, 103
Gregory the Wonderworker (Thaumaturgus) – 33-34, 48
Gregory of Nazianzus – 45, 46, 52, 125
Gregory of Nyssa – 45
Gregory of Rimini – 177
Gregory of Tours – 84
Gregory Palamas – 180
Groot, Geert de -- 179
Grosseteste, Robert – 167-168
Gustavus Adolphus – 253
Gustavus Vasa (I) – see "Vasa, Gustavus"
Gutenberg, Johannes – 191
Gutiérez, Gustavo – 325

Hadith – 90
Hadrian I, Pope – 100, 104, 105, 108
Hadrian VI, Pope – 218, 243
Hajj – 90
Halle – 258, 269-271, 290, 319
Hamilton, Patrick – 221
Handel, George Frederic – 279
Hanseatic League – 204
Harald Bluetooth – 123
Harms, Claus – 294
Harnack, Adolf von – 303-304, 311-312
Harvard – 255, 293, 320
Hasidism – 258
Hauge, Hans Nielsen – 285
Haydn, Franz Joseph – 279
Hegel, George – 285-286, 287, 288, 289, 319
Hegira – 91
Heidelberg Catechism – 237
Heidelberg Theses – 215
Helvetic Confession – 237

Hengstenberg, Ernest Wilhelm – 294
Henkel, Paul and David – 302
Henry, Carl F. H. – 321, 325
Henry IV, Emperor – 131, 133, 134
Henry VIII, King – 201, 206, 218, 223, 224, 239, 240
Heresies—see specific doctrine or heretic
Herman of Alaska – 272
Hermeneutics – 323; see "interpretation"
Hermits, monastic – 43, 44, 52, 77, 116, 138, 161, 179, 242
Herod Agrippa – 4
Herod the Great – 2, 5,
Herrnhut – 270-271
Hesychasm – 125, 180
Hexapla – 37
Hieronymus of Prague – 187
High Church – 290, 294
Higher criticism – see "Bible interpretation"
Hildebrand – see "Gregory VII, Pope"
Hildegard of Bingen – 148
Hincmar – 114
Hippolytus – 29
Historical Critical method – see "Bible interpretation"
Historical-grammatical method – see "Bible interpretation"
Holiness – 39, 69, 73, 170, 179, 274
Holy Club – 272
Holy Communion – see "Lord's Supper"
Holy orders – 146, 166
Holy Roman Empire – 106, 121, 127, 142, 153, 169, 200, 201, 222, 243, 281, 283
Holy Spirit – 1, 2, 14, 16, 21, 23, 27-30, 33, 34, 40, 41, 46-47, 48, 54, 63, 85, 112, 125, 126, 146, 152, 228, 257, 297, 316, 324, 335
Homoiousios – 40-43, 45
Homoousios – 41-43, 45, 71
Hooker, Thomas – 255
Hort, F. J. A. – 290
Hospitalers – 141, 153,
Hrabanus Maurus – 109, 114
Hugh of St. Victor – 142, 148
Huguenots – 235, 246, 283
Humanism – 174, 189, 192, 199, 201, 204, 206, 207

Humbert, Cardinal – 129, 131
Hume, David – 267
Hungarian – 113, 119, 120, 135,
Hus, Jan – 184, 186-188
Hutter, Leonhard – 252
Hypostasis – 45, 58, 61, 77, 102

Icon – 93, 100, 101-104
Iconoclasm – 101-102, 218, 240
Ignatius of Antioch – 15-16, 35
Immaculate Conception – 175, 291
Incarnation – 60, 71, 95, 99, 102, 150, 153, 163, 166
Index of Forbidden Books – 229, 245
Indulgences – 141, 174, 182, 183, 187, 195, 214, 215, 216, 236, 241, 245
Inerrancy – 308, 314, 324
Innocent I – 58
Innocent III – 155-156, 158, 160, 161, 162, 163
Inquisition – 162, 164, 194, 241, 242, 243
Inspiration of scripture – 294, 308
Investiture – 121, 131, 133, 142, 143, 146
Iona, monastery -- 85
Irenaeus – 20-24
Irish-Celtic Christianity – 89
Isabella of Castile – 194, 201, 241
Isidore of Seville – 87-88, 95, 112
Islam – 40, 87, 89-95, 97, 100, 133, 135, 148, 169, 182, 218, 221, 333-334; see also "Muslim"
Italy – 4, 51, 69, 73, 74, 77, 79, 82, 84, 85, 95, 97, 101, 105, 108, 109, 110, 115, 119, 120, 127, 128, 129, 132, 134, 136, 145, 146, 153, 157, 159, 160, 161, 167, 169, 179, 182, 185, 187, 191, 192, 194, 196, 199, 201, 204, 207, 210, 242, 243, 291
Ivan the Terrible – 209

Jacobites – 77, 182
Jansen, Cornelius – 259
Jansenism – 258-259, 262
Jefferson, Thomas – 293, 313
Jehovah's Witnesses – 300-301
Jerome, Saint – 49, 51-54, 58, 62, 66-68, 108,

Jerusalem – 2, 4, 6, 7, 9, 22, 48, 53, 67, 77, 91, 92, 101, 127, 134-135, 139, 141,145, 153, 156, 159
Jesuits – 201, 202, 224, 230, 241, 245, 246, 249, 251, 255, 258, 260, 271, 292, 318, 319, 325, 333
Jesus – see individual chapters
Jesus People – 324
Jesus Prayer, The –180
Jihad – 92, 135
Joachimites – 152
Joan of Arc – 193
John, Apostle – 8, 13, 22, 27, 125, 179, 303
John Calvin – see "Calvin"
John Cassian – see "Cassian"
John Chrysostom – see "Chrysostom"
John Climacus – 80-81
John Frederick I, elector – 223-226
John of Beverley – 99
John of Damascus – 102, 104
John of the Cross – 242
John Oldcastle – 186
John Paul II, Pope – 328, 333
John Scotus Eriugena – see "Eriugena"
John the Baptist – 19, 157
John the Steadfast, elector – 220, 222,
John XII, Pope – 120-122
John XXIII, Pope – 187, 317, 319,
Joint Declaration on the Doctrine of Justification – 307, 328
Jonas, Justus – 222-223, 226
Josephites – 209
Josephus – 6, 7, 11
Judaism – 1-11, 14, 16, 18, 19, 20, 22, 23, 26, 27, 32, 52, 75, 90, 91, 97, 100, 112, 145, 148-149, 170, 182, 185, 194, 225, 241, 258, 268, 286, 287, 288, 313, 317, 323
Jude, apostle – 8
Julian the Apostate – 43
Julius II, Pope – 206-207, 243
Julius III, Pope – 244
Justification – 189, 217, 223, 225, 226, 227, 229, 241, 244, 245, 274, 289, 300, 307, 320, 328
Justin Martyr – 20, 24
Justinian I – 74, 75-77, 81

Ka'abah – 90
Kaiserwerth – 284,
Kant, Emmanuel – 260, 268, 286, 289

Kappel, battle – 237
Kempis, Thomas à – 185
Kepler, Johannes – 207, 208, 260
King James Bible – 250
King, Martin Luther – 320-321
Kierkegaard, Søren – 287-288, 314
Knights Templars – 141, 144, 153, 181
Knox, John – 236
Koran – See "Qur'an"
Krauth, Charles P. – 303

Las Casas, Bartolomé de – 203
Lateran Councils – 142-143, 149, 152, 156, 160, 163, 181, 241
Laud, William – 256
Laurence, Saint – 31
Lausanne – 311, 325
Lefevre d'Etaples –see "Stapulensis"
Leibnitz, Gottfried Wilhelm von – 262
Leipzig – 177, 216-217, 227, 278, 294, 320
Lenin, Vladimir – 309
Leo I, "the Great", Pope – 60-61, 69
Leo III, Pope – 101-102, 107, 108
Leo IX, Pope – 128, 129
Leo X, Pope – 214, 216, 239, 241, 243
Leo XIII, Pope – 308
Leonardo da Vinci – 191, 207, 206, 215
Lessing, Gotthold – 260, 269
Liberal arts – 87, 108, 164
Liberalism –284, 291, 292, 303, 311-314, 321, 322
Liberation theology – 321, 324-325
Licinius – 38
Lightfoot, Joseph Barber – 290
Liturgy – 31, 34, 35, 58, 83, 84, 88, 94, 95, 99, 103-104, 108, 112, 113, 120, 138, 227, 240, 245, 268, 279, 290, 294, 310, 317-318, 326
Locke, John – 263
Loehe, William – 294
Logos – 8, 58, 61, 77, 102
Lollards – 186
Lombard, Peter – 150, 165, 168, 175
Lombards – 73, 77, 79, 81, 82, 97, 104, 105, 106, 108, 115, 120, 160, 162
Lord's Prayer – 14
Lord's Supper – 2, 4, 14, 15, 21, 23, 28,39,44, 49, 60, 78, 94, 95, 103, 115, 116, 129, 151, 163, 164, 166, 183, 188, 189, 192, 193, 219, 220, 222, 224, 117, 228,

230, 237, 238, 239, 240, 244, 245, 270, 273, 302, 311, 328
Low Church – 290
Loyola, Ignatius – also see "Jesuits" – 224, 241
Luke, Evangelist – 1-2, 18, 21, 22
Lumen gentium – 318, 319
Luther, Martin – 75, 138, 150, 162, 176, 177, 178, 179, 187, 189, 190, 196, 200, 204, 205, 206, 213-230, 233, 236-243, 257, 273, 278, 286, 294, 296, 313, 318, 331
Lutheran – 115, 194, 206, 208, 218-219, 220, 223, 224, 225, 227-230, 235, 239, 242, 243, 244, 245, 249, 250, 253, 255, 257, 258, 259, 269, 270, 271, 275, 277, 279, 284, 285, 286, 287, 288, 289, 293, 297, 301, 302, 303, 310, 311, 314, 315, 316, 319, 320, 322, 324, 326, 328
Lutheran Churches – 224, 225, 271, 293, 295, 296, 302, 303, 310, 321, 328
Lutheran Church—Missouri Synod, The – 294, 296, 302, 310, 315, 324, 333
Lutheran Confessions – see "Book of Concord"
Lutheran Orthodoxy – 251-252, 278
Lyon – 20, 152, 162, 166, 169

Macedonian heresy – 46-47
Machiavelli, Nicolo – 194
Magdeburg Centuries, The – x, 229
Magna Carta – 156
Magnus, Albertus – 165
Maier, Walter A. – 315
Maimonides – 149
Major, George – 229
Manichaeism – 50, 62, 75, 152
Mantua, Council of – 224
Marburg Colloquy – 221, 222, 223, 237,
Marcion – 18-19, 21, 22
Marozia – 121-122
Marquette, Jacques – 255-256
Marriage – 29, 53, 122, 133, 143, 146, 180, 193, 194, 196, 220, 239, 245, 288, 300, 301
Marsilius of Padua – 174

Martyrdom – 4, 7, 15, 16, 20, 24, 25-27, 29, 30, 31, 32, 35, 37, 45, 67, 74, 98-99, 144, 218, 240, 255, 315, 333
Marx, Karl – 286, 288-289, 309, 312, 324
Mary, Blessed Virgin – 1, 28, 30, 53, 59, 60, 61, 67, 91, 114, 167, 175, 178, 213, 214, 226, 245, 249, 291, 317, 318
Masada – 7, 11, 323
Mass – 83, 103, 108, 161, 163, 189, 214, 217, 219, 220, 240, 245, 279, 318
Mather, Cotton – 266
Mayflower Compact – 255
Maximillian I – 200, 215-216
McFague, Sally – 332
McPherson, Aimee Semple – 315
Medici – 191, 196, 204, 210
Megachurches – 334, 335
Meister Eckhart – 177
Melanchthon, Philip – 207, 216, 221-223, 224-226, 227-228, 234
Melendez, Andrew – 315
Mendicant friars – 155, 157-162, 165, 170
Mennonites – 238
Merovingian dynasty – 88, 105
Methodism – 272-275, 278, 292, 310, 316, 317, 322
Methodius – 113, 124
Michelangelo – 192, 206-207, 245
Millennialism – 278, 300-303, 308, 312
Miller, William and Millerites – 300
Miltitz, Karl von – 215
Milton, John – 261
Missions – 3, 4, 7, 15, 34, 70, 85, 89-90, 93, 94, 95, 97-99, 103, 113, 116, 119, 123-124, 151, 159, 182, 185, 196, 199, 202, 203, 242-243, 249, 255, 256, 257, 258, 260, 261, 269-273, 275, 285, 290, 291, 292, 294, 295, 300, 302, 303, 304, 309, 311, 318, 327, 335
Modernism – 308
Moffat, James – 323
Monarchianism – 27-28, 29, 34, 40
Monasticism – 44, 45, 51, 53, 54, 66, 67, 69, 70, 71, 77, 79, 80, 82, 85, 103, 104, 105, 108, 110, 114, 116, 119, 120, 122, 123, 125,

127, 130, 136, 137, 138, 141-148, 152-153, 155, 157, 160, 161, 164, 180, 181, 183, 194, 202, 203, 204, 205, 206, 209, 210, 236, 239, 242, 268, 270, 313, 326
Monophysite – 60, 61, 76, 77, 84, 93
Montanus – 19
Montesinos, Antinio – 202-203
Monte Cassino – 77, 79, 134, 165
Moody, Dwight L. – 298
Moravian – 113, 188, 257, 268, 270, 271, 272, 293
More, Thomas – 190, 194, 205, 206, 239
Mormons – see "Church of Jesus Christ of Latter Day Saints"
Mott, John R. – 309-310
Mother Ann Lee – 277-278
Mother of God – see "Theotokos"
Mozarabic rite – 88, 99
Mozart, Wolfgang Amadeus – 279
Muhammad – 87, 89-92, 95
Muhlenberg, Henry Melchior – 271
Müntzer, Thomas – 219, 238
Muratorian Fragment – 22
Muslims: Shi'ah, Sufi, Sunni – 32, 63, 76, 87, 88, 91, 92, 97, 99, 101, 102, 107, 115, 119, 127, 132, 134, 135, 136, 139, 141, 145, 148, 157, 158, 161, 162, 169, 170, 182, 194, 201, 209, 218, 241, 327, 333, 334
Mystical theology – 17, 18, 80, 81, 94, 114, 142, 148, 167, 168, 177-180, 184, 188, 238, 242, 258, 332
Mysticism – see "Mystical theology"

Nag Hammadi – 17, 323
Napoleon Bonaparte – 280, 283
National Council of the Churches of Christ – 316
National Socialism – see "Nazi"
Nazi – 313, 314, 315, 317, 319, 322
Neo-orthodox – 312, 314, 322
Neo-Platonism – 80
Nero – 7, 9
Nestorianism – 59-60, 61, 74, 93, 99, 182
Nestorian Stele – 93
New Lights – 266, 274
Newman, John Henry – 291
Newton, Isaac – 208, 261,

Newton, John – 271, 290
Nicaea, Council of
Nicene Creed – 41-43, 46-47, 54, 58, 61, 84, 94, 112, 192, 311
Niceno-Constantinopolitan Creed – see "Nicene Creed"
Nicholas I, Pope – 113-115
Nicholas II, Pope – 132
Nicholas of Cusa – 188
Nicholas of Lyra – 168
Niebuhr, H. Richard – 313-314, 320
Niebuhr, Reinhold – 312-313
Nietzsche, Friedrich – 289
Nightingale, Florence – 284
Ninety-five theses – 214-216, 236, 257
Nonconformists – 257, 280
Norway – 123-124, 128, 285, 302, 303
Novatian of Rome – 31
Nuremberg – 99, 192, 208

Ockham, William – 166, 175-177, 183, 189
Odo of Cluny – 123
Oecolampadius – 233
Olaf II Haraldsson – 128
Olga of Kiev – 119, 124
Orange, Synod of – 75
Oratory of Divine Love -- 242
Origen of Alexandria – 32-34, 48, 51, 52, 58, 67
Organ, instrument – 103, 252, 278
Original sin – 49, 65, 75, 244, 249, 291
Orthodox Church, Eastern – 75, 93, 94, 102, 104, 111, 125, 146, 163, 180, 192, 193, 209, 260, 271, 309, 311, 316, 326, 327, 333
Orthodoxy, doctrinal – 17, 21, 22, 24, 25, 33, 34, 36, 40, 42, 45, 47, 48, 58, 59, 61, 69, 71, 73, 74, 215, 113, 114, 166, 178, 194, 251-252, 258, 278, 284, 294, 320
Osiander, Andreas – 208
Ostragoths – 74
Otto I, emperor – 119-121, 124
Ottoman Empire – 200-201, 309
Ousia – 45
Oxford – 164, 167, 168, 175, 176, 177, 183, 186, 187, 235, 272,
Oxford movement – 291
Ozman, Agnes – 307

Pachomius – 44

Pantheism – 177, 234, 263
Papacy – also see individual popes – 69, 73, 84, 89, 97, 101, 104-105, 107, 108, 115, 119, 121, 122, 123, 127, 128, 131, 141, 156, 160, 163, 168, 174, 177, 184, 186, 190, 194, 210, 241, 243, 253, 283, 317, 328, 333
Paraclete, convent – 146
Parham, Charles – 307
Pascal, Blaise – 262
Pastor aeternus – 291
Pastoral care – 15, 34, 58, 62, 65, 82, 123, 145, 162, 168, 202, 258, 294, 303,
Patrick, Saint – 70-71, 85
Patripassianism – 28
Paul, Apostle – 1, 3-4, 7, 10, 13, 15, 18, 21, 22, 23, 35, 49, 65, 80, 128, 150, 168, 179, 191, 241, 286, 287,
Paul III, Pope – 243
Paul IV, Pope – 245
Paul V, Pope – 249
Paul VI, Pope – 317, 326
Paul of Samosata – 27-28, 34,
Paula – 53
Pax Romana – 4, 64
Peace of Augsburg – 249
Peasants' Revolt – 204, 219, 224
Pelagius – 64-65, 67,
Pelagianism – see "Pelagius"
Penance – 31, 35, 74, 83, 135, 141, 166, 193, 216, 244
Penn, William – 256
Pentecost – 2, 3, 19
Pentecostalism – 302-308, 315, 324, 327
Pepin I, II, and III, emperors – 88, 97, 103, 104-105, 107, 109, 110
Perichoresis – 102
Perpetua – 25-26
Persecution – 3, 4, 6, 9, 10, 13, 15, 16, 19, 20, 24, 25, 26-27, 30, 32, 32, 34, 35, 37-40, 42, 43, 54, 74, 75, 111, 182, 186, 240, 256, 313, 326, 327
Peter, Apostle – 2, 3, 10, 13, 30, 69, 89, 101, 147, 179, 186, 195, 214, 291
Peter Damian – 128, 131, 133
Peter the Hermit – 135
Peter the Venerable – 148, 152

Petrarch – 174, 190
Petri, Laurentius and Olavus – 219
Pharisees – 5, 6
Philip of Hesse –221
Philippists – 227
Philo – 5
Photios, Patriarch – 111, 112, 113, 119, 129
Pia Desideria – 258
Pietism – 258-259, 260, 261, 263, 268, 269-272, 273, 274, 278, 284, 287, 289, 294, 314
Pisa, Council of – 187
Pius II, Pope – 195
Pius IV, Pope – 244, 245
Pius VI, Pope – 280
Pius VII, Pope – 283
Pius IX, Pope – 291
Pius X, Pope – 308
Pius XII, Pope – 317
Plague, The – 112
Plan of Union – 293
Plato / Platonic – 17, 20, 75, 205
Pneumatomachians – 46
Polycarp – 13, 16, 20
Pope, Alexander – 267
Pope – see individual names
Polygamy – 91, 95, 223, 238, 299
Polytheism – 6, 8, 9, 91, 267
Pornocracy – 121
Post-millennialism – see "Millennialism"
Postmodernism – 331-332
Praxeas – 28
Predestination – 114-115, 146, 150, 176, 177, 186, 235, 246, 253, 273, 303
Pre-millennialism – see "Millennialism"
Presbyter – 10, 15, 20, 35, 51, 57, 95, 236, 257,
Presbyterians – 236, 257, 266, 274, 275, 293, 296, 297, 298, 308, 312, 316, 317, 322, 327, 328
Priesthood of all believers – 258
Princeton Seminary / University – 266, 293, 302, 312
Prophet / Prophetic office – 5, 10, 11, 14, 19, 21, 23, 30, 35, 42, 47, 48, 90, 91, 128, 149, 175, 178, 297, 300
Proslogion – 136-137

Prosopon – 61
Prosper of Aquitaine – 66, 75
Protestant Episcopal Church – 275
Protestant – 194, 200, 205, 214, 221, 223, 228, 230, 233, 235-241, 243, 245, 249, 250, 253, 254, 268, 270, 278, 285, 289, 291, 293, 294, 307, 310, 312, 313, 315, 317, 319, 320, 321, 322, 324, 327, 328
Prussian Union Church – 295, 312
Pseudo-Isidorian Decretals – 112
Pseudo-Dionysius – see "Dionysius the Areopagite"
Purgatory – 83, 166, 177, 192, 195, 214, 216, 236, 245
Puritan – 240, 255-257, 259, 262, 263, 274
Pythagoras – 20

Quakers 256-257, 260, 275, 278, 292
Quatrodeciman Controversy – 23
Quenstedt, Johann – 252
Qur'an – 90-91, 148

Radbertus – 114-115
Radical reformation – 238-239, 240
Rahner, Karl – 319, 322
Raikes, Robert – 266
Raphael – 192, 206, 207
Rationalism –267, 268, 284, 285, 291, 294, 296
Ratisbon – see "Regensburg"
Ratramnus – 114-115
Ratzinger, Joseph – see "Benedict XVI, Pope" – 319, 333
Rauschenbusch, Walter – 312, 320
Rebaptism – see "Anabaptism"
Reformation – see chapters 16 A, B, and C
Reformed Church – 224, 225, 235, 237, 251, 253, 266, 268, 274, 292, 293, 294, 301, 310, 312, 316, 317, 324, 328, 333
Regensburg – 100, 225
Regula fidei – 23, 28, 30, 33,
Relics – 67, 83
Renaissance – 149, 185, 190-192, 195-196, 199, 204, 205, 207, 243
Restoration Movement – 196-197
Reuchlin, Johannes – 189, 206
Revivalism – 297-298, 302, 326

Ricci, Matteo – 203, 242
Ritschl, Albrecht – 289, 303
Roberts, Oral – 315, 324
Roman Catholic – see "Catholic"
Romanticism – 278, 283, 284, 294, 319
Rosary – 160
Rule of Faith – see "*Regula fidei*"
Rule of Saint Augustine – 162
Rule of Saint Benedict – 123, 138
Ruether, Rosemary R. – 321
Rufinus of Aquileia – 32, 51, 67
Ruggieri, Michele – 203, 242
Russell, Charles Taze – 300
Russian Orthodox Church – 209, 260, 309, 326

Sabellius – 28, 43
Sacrament of the Altar – see "Lord's Supper"
Sacramentarian controversy – 221, 224, 239
Sacraments – 14, 28, 39, 48, 63, 65, 100, 115, 140, 148, 150, 151, 153, 163, 166, 178, 189, 193, 218, 227, 237, 240, 244, 273, 292, 296, 300, 301, 311, 328,
Sadducees – 5, 6, 7, 29
Saints – See names
Salvation Army – 292
Samosatenes – see "Paul of Samosata"
Saracens – see "Muslim"
Satan – 23, 63, 133, 262, 300
Savonarola, Girolamo –196, 241
Schaff, Philip – 301
Schism – see "Great Schism"
Schleiermacher, F. D. E. – 261, 268, 284, 285, 287, 289
Schmucker, Samuel S. – 302, 303
Schuller, Robert -- 335
Schwenkfeld, Kaspar – 239
Science – 87, 167, 207-208, 259, 261, 266, 309, 318
Scopes Trial – 308-309, 315
Scripture – 23, 44, 48, 50, 53, 58, 62, 66, 67, 79, 84, 90, 93, 103, 123, 133, 137, 147, 150, 165, 167, 168, 176, 179, 183, 188, 205, 209, 214, 216-218, 220, 226, 228, 229, 234, 236, 241, 244, 251, 261, 262, 285, 296, 301, 308, 311, 314, 318, 321, 324, 332
Seabury, Samuel – 275

Secularism – 210, 317, 320, 322, 331, 332, 335
Semi-Arianism – 43
Semi-Pelagianism – 70, 75
September Testament – 218
Septuagint – 5, 32, 67
Sermon on the Mount – 13, 238, 286
Servetus, Michael – 234
Seventh Day Adventists – 300
Seymour, William – 307
Shakers – 278
Shepherd of Hermes – 14, 22
Sic et Non –147
Sigismund of Germany – 187-188
Silence – see "*Hesychasm*"
Simon Stylites – 69
Simons, Menno -- 238
Simony – 128, 131, 133, 143, 181, 183, 195, 210
Smalcald Articles –224, 243
Small Catechism – 221
Smith, Joseph – 299
Smythe, John – 250
Sobrino, Jon – 325
Social Gospel – 312, 324
Society for the Propagation of Christian Knowledge – 258
Society for the Propagation of the Gospel I Foreign Parts – 266
Society of Friends – see "Quakers"
Society of Jesus – see "Jesuits"
Socinianism – 252, 263
Söderblom, Nathan – 310
Solid Declaration – 230
Song of Roland – 107-108
Soul – 16, 17, 33, 48, 52, 61, 65, 74, 78, 82, 90, 113, 126, 144, 148, 161, 167, 177, 178, 181, 195, 214, 241, 242, 274, 294,
Spener, Philp Jakob – 252, 258, 259, 269, 270, 271
Speyer, Diet of – 220, 221
Spirit – see "Holy Spirit"
Spiritualism – 180
Spiritual Exercises -- 241
Spurgeon, Charles – 292
Stapulensis, Faber –241
Staupitz, Johann von – 214
Stephan, Martin – 294-295
Stewart, Lyman and Milton – 308
Stone, Barton W. – 297
Strauss, David Friedrich – 287

Substitutionary atonement – 137, 301, 308
Summa Theologiae – 166
Sunday School – 266, 298
Suso, Henry – 178
Sweden – 116, 123, 180, 218, 219, 223, 227, 254, 302, 316
Swiss Brethren – 238
Symeon the New Theologian – 124-125
Synagogue – 5, 10
Syncretism – 6, 8, 9, 10, 275
Synergism – 228
Synodical Conference – 303, 310
Synod of Orange – 75

Taborites – 188
Tatian – 21
Tauler, Johnannes – 178
Temple, Jerusalem – 2, 4-7, 10
Ten Commandments – 4, 13, 150, 241
Tennent, William – 274
Tenskwatawa, "The Prophet" – 275, 297
Teresa of Ávila – 242
Tertullian – 27, 28-30, 34, 40, 64
Tetzel, John – 214
Teutonic Knights – 153
Textual criticism – 290
Theatines – 242
Theodora, Empress – 111
Theodora, noblewoman – 121-122
Theodora, Queen – 75
Theodore of Mopsuestia – 58, 76
Theodorus of Tarsus – 89
Theodosius the Great – 46, 54,
Theologia Deutsch – 179
Theology of glory – 215
Theology of the cross – 215
Theotokos – 59, 60-61
Thirty-nine Articles – 240
Thirty Years' War – 242, 249, 252-254
Thomas á Kempis – see "Kempis, Thomas á"
Tillich, Paul – 319-320
Tongues, speaking in – 324
Toleration Act – 257
Toleration, Edit of – 38
Torgau Articles – 222-223,
Torah – 4, 6, 149
Tractarians – see "Oxford movement"

Tradition – 4, 7, 8, 21, 22-24, 59, 66, 93, 175, 183, 218, 227, 230, 244, 263, 267, 283, 290, 293, 297, 298, 312, 314, 317, 318, 321, 333
Trajan –16
Translations, Bible – 5, 32, 52, 67-68, 70, 183, 205, 218, 223, 224, 227, 234, 235, 244, 250, 257, 259, 269-270, 290, 323-324
Transubstantiation – 163, 165, 176, 184, 239, 240, 244
Treaty of Verdun – 110
Trent, Council of – 225, 227, 243-246, 328
Trinity – 28, 34, 40, 45, 64, 71, 74, 75, 84, 99, 102, 109, 112, 146, 150, 152, 166, 181, 234, 286, 300
Tryggvasson, Olav – 123
Tübingen – 189, 208, 286, 287, 289, 314, 319
Tudor, "Bloody" Mary, Queen – 240
TULIP – 253
Tyndale, William – 205-206, 224

Ulfilas – 70
Union Theological Seminary – 301, 312, 314, 320
Unitarian Universalist Church – 316
Unitarianism – 287, 293, 298
United Brethren of Bohemia – 188, 270
United Church of Christ – 312, 316, 328
Universities – 160, 162, 164-168, 177, 181-183, 186-190, 205, 207, 213, 214, 218, 219, 224, 225, 226, 230, 233, 235, 245, 251, 258, 266, 270, 286, 288, 293, 294, 302, 303, 304, 313, 314, 319, 320, 333
Urban II, Pope – 134, 135, 139, 141
Urban V, Pope – 180, 182
Urban VIII, Pope – 250, 259
Utraquists – 188

Valentinus – 22
Valentius – 17
Valerian – 31
Valla, Lorenzo – 101, 190-191
Vasa, Gustavus I – 218-219
Vatican Councils – 245, 291, 317-319, 325, 328,
Verba – 237

Verbal inspiration – see "Inspiration"
Vespasian – 7
Via antiqua – 175, 189
Via moderna – 175
Vikings – 111, 115, 119, 123, 124
Vincent of Lérin – 66
Vineyard Church / movement – 324, 326
Virgin conception and birth – see "Mary, Blessed Virgin"
Visigoths – 63, 66, 68, 77, 87, 97
Voltaire – 267, 268
Vulgate – 32, 67, 108, 191, 205, 244, 250

Waldensians –143, 152, 162-163
Waldo, Peter – 152, 162
Walther, C.F.W. – 294-296
Washington, George – 277
Watts, Isaac – 260, 279
Wellhausen, Julius – 289
Wenceslas IV – 187
Wesley, Charles and John – 272, 273, 275
Wesleyans – see "Methodists"
Westcott, Brooke Foss – 290
Westminster Confession – 256, 274
White, Ellen Gould – 300
White, William – 275
Whitefield, George – 272-274,
Willibrord, missionary – 89, 98
Wittenberg Concord – 224
World Conference on Faith and Order – 311
World Council of Churches –314, 316, 325, 327
World's Student Christian Federation – 309
Worms, Diet of – 217-218, 223
Women, ordination of – 321
Worship, Christian – 13, 16, 18, 10, 23, 26-27, 39, 41, 46, 47, 64, 65-66, 67, 99, 100, 102, 103, 104, 108, 120, 123, 143, 209, 219, 220, 253, 257, 270, 275, 278, 290, 295, 296, 298, 302, 318, 325-326, 332
Worship, Emperor – 11, 12, 16
Worship, heretical – 48, 59, 180,
Worship, Jewish – 7, 10, 149
Worship, pagan – 19, 91, 260,
Wycliffe, John –183, 184, 186, 188

Xavier, Francis – 241

Yale University – 266, 293, 313
Young, Brigham – 299
Young Men's Christian Association – 298, 309,

Zinzendorf, Count Nicolas von – 270-271, 279
Zumárraga, Juan de – 203
Zwingli, Ulrich – 190, 220, 221-222, 223, 228

κοινός, "common" + βίος, "life"), where individuals resided in a community of like-minded ascetics. These cenobites were called monks (Greek, μοναχός, "single, solitary") and their community a monastery.

The *Life of Anthony*, chronicled by Athanasius, portrayed this early hermit as a faithful hero of the Christian faith. Anthony (c.251-356) was an Egyptian who had been raised in a Christian family. At twenty years of age, both of his parents died. Attending the Divine Service, he heard the words of Jesus, "sell everything and give it to the poor" (Matthew 19:21). Immediately, Ahntony sold all of his parents' possessions, placed his sister with a community of Christian virgins, and set out to live an ascetic life. Initially, he learned this life from a local hermit. Following this, Anthony took up residence in some nearby tombs that were considered the habitation of demons and evil spirits. Their attacks upon Anthony were ruthless and unrelenting: they appeared as wild beasts and uttered unbearable sounds and shook the walls of the tombs. Athanasius reports that Jesus watched over Anthony and delivered him from this torture.

Antony rigorously exercised his Christian faith throughout his life. His sparsity of food was contrasted by his multitudinous prayers. He sought an eremitic solitude, but often he was sought out by or led into the company of other Christians, for whom he performed miracles and provided spiritual guidance. During the Arian controversy, he marched a troop of Egyptian ascetics into Alexandria to condemn Arianism and confess that Jesus was the "Eternal Word."

Another Egyptian, a military officer named Pachomius (c.290-346), was converted to Christianity when he was twenty years old. Initially, he also became an eremite, but was frustrated with its lack of order. Consequently, he became a cenobite, forming a community along the Nile River in southern Egypt. His first attempt failed dismally when the monks complained that his ascetic demands were too rigorous. Dismissing the lot, he began anew, increasing his ascetic requirements for the monks.

Pachomius developed the first "rule" or set of instructions for an ascetic community. His rule detailed the many components of the ascetic's life, and it was to be followed by all in the community. The structure of the community was a familial-like hierarchy: an abbot (Latin, *abba*, "father") was the father-figure of the community and the monks were seen as brothers. Their clothing was a simple uniform: white, sleeveless garments that were sewn from a coarse material, including a hood or cowl. General activities were regimented: individuals cooked, cleaned, and cared for sick in service the community; food and possessions, speech and sleep were kept to a minimum. Spiritual activities were strictly ordered: daily reading and memorization of Holy Scripture, regular prayer both communal and private, reception of the Lord's Supper on Saturday evening in town and on Sunday morning at the monastery.

Pachomius's cenobitic monasticism ultimately fared well with his general principles of obedience, devotion, and useful labor. By the end of his life, he oversaw nine monasteries of men and two of women.

uniting the baptized with the crucified Christ and clothing the baptized in the glorious attire of his resurrected Son.

In the mystagogical homilies, Cyril debriefed the newly baptized. Even though they had received extensive catechesis prior to their baptism, anointing, and reception of the Lord's Supper, they could never be fully prepared for what they would experience and receive in these sacred rituals. Having been submerged in divine mercy through baptism, Cyril sought to explain what had just happened to them:

> For as in the night one no longer sees, while by day one is in the light, so you during your immersion, as in a night, saw nothing, but on coming up found yourselves in the day. In the same moment you were dying and being born, so that saving water was at once your grave and your mother. (Cyril, *Mystagogical Homilies*, 2.4)

Cyril masterfully preached the Christian faith to catechumens. He both explained the biblical content and utilized vivid imagery to paint pictures of spiritual realities that transcend explanation. Of greatest import, Cyril preserved the doctrine and practices of Christianity through his faithful proclamation of Jesus and the message of the Gospel.

The Latin Theologians

While there was much work done in the East, two significant theologians arose toward the end of this century—Augustine and Jerome. Both of them had a great influence on the theology of Western Christianity as they wrote predominantly in Latin. We will look at their work in the next chapter, but we conclude this chapter with a review of their early lives.

Augustine's Early Life

From a seeker to a saint describes Augustine's incredible transformation at the close of the fourth century. Born on November 13, 354, in Tagaste, a small town in northern Africa, to a pagan Roman official, Patricius, and a Christian mother, Monica, Aurelius Augustinus (354-430) became one of the most influential theologians of early Christianity since the time of Saint Paul. Some say his conversion to Christianity was nothing short of miraculous. (See illustration of Monica taking Augustine to school.)

Augustine was not baptized as a child, since in those days it was felt that baptism should be saved until after one "sowed his wild oats." This Augustine certainly did. In observing little children, Augustine noted the selfishness of an infant, which he considered as clear and obvious evidence of original sin. He also told of how with some friends he had stolen some unripe fruit in an orchard, illustrating the human enjoyment of wanton destruction. Something not even animals do, noted Augustine.

> I stole a thing of which I had plenty of my own and of much better quality. Nor did I wish to enjoy that thing which I desired to gain by theft, but rather to enjoy

Jerusalem." His sense of purity was still from an outward understanding rather than seeing the purity of Christ within.

While still in Rome, Jerome had promoted a very rigid form of the monastic and ascetic life. There he became a spiritual leader, teacher, and spiritual counselor for a group of wealthy and aristocratic women—Albina (+387), whose palace they used, and her daughter, Marcella (325-410), Ambrose's sister Marcellina (c.330/335-c.398), and Paula (347-404). With them he studied and commented on Scripture, a practice which he continued for the rest of his life (see illustration).

One of the reasons for his abrupt departure from Rome was his rigid insistence that a rigorously ascetic life, particularly virginity, was superior to marriage. He argued in *Against Helvidius* and later *Against Jovinian* that Mary, the mother of God, was a model ascetic, because she maintained her virginity throughout her life. He also boldly attacked the comfortable life of the Roman clergy and nobility. On one occasion, he preached against the worldly women of Rome, saying that they "paint their cheeks with rouge and their eyelids with antimony." He continued:

> Their plastered faces, too white for human beings, look like idols; and if in a middle of forgetfulness they shed a tear, it makes a furrow where it rolls down the painted cheek. Women to whom years do not bring the gravity of age, load their heads with other people's hair, enamel a lost youth upon the wrinkles of age, and affect a maidenly timidity in the midst of a troop of grandchildren.[2]

Is it any wonder that the nobility of Rome, particularly the wealthy women, were happy to see him depart?

Jerome echoed the fears and frustrations of Christianity's new-found and already-entrenched acceptance of the culture of his day, recognizing that the softness of Christianity was also its potential downfall. Therefore, he sought to return to what he thought was the purity of earlier Christian living. After his flight to Bethlehem in 388, he established two small monastic communities for himself and several women, Paula (+404) and her daughters Blesilla (363-384) and Eustochium (c.368-419/420). Paula supervised the monastery for women and Jerome headed the men's monastery. In a letter to Eustochium laying down some severe rules for women, Jerome includes this telling paragraph:

> I praise wedlock, I praise marriage, but only because they produce virgins for me. I gather the rose from the thorns, the gold from the earth, the pearl from the shell. *Does the plowman plow all day to sow?* (Is. 28:24) Shall he not also enjoy the fruit of his labor? Wedlock is more honored, when what is born of it is more loved. Why, mother, do you envy your daughter? She has been nourished with your milk, she has been brought forth from your womb, and she has grown up at

---

[2] From *Butler's Lives of Saints*, cited in www.catholic.org/saints/saint.php?saint_id=10.

St Patrick

Patrick (c.385/9-460/1), an intriguing historical figure and missionary, became associated with Ireland as he brought the gospel to that isle of green. Little is known of his early years, although in his autobiography he reports that his father, a Roman official named Calpurnius (c.350-c.400), was also a deacon. As the Roman legions were departing to defend the continent, Irish pirates (called Scots) began to attack settlements along the English (British) or French (Brittany) coast, plundering the lands and securing slaves for their lands. Among the slaves was the young sixteen year old lad, Patrick (probably named Maewyn Succat until his ordination), who was forced to serve as a swine herder. As he watched over the pigs he prayed for deliverance. Escaping the herd of pigs, he reports that he came to the coast where a cargo ship needed someone to care for their cargo of dogs when they sailed to France. Volunteering to assist, Patrick fled his captors. After gaining his freedom and coming in contact with some French monks, he returned home to England. However, he had a dream about unborn Irish children needing the Gospel. He returned to a French monastery for training, remaining there fourteen years. Finally, he secured approval from Pope Celestine (pope 422-432) and was ordained as a bishop, enabling him to return to Ireland around 432. There he baptized many of the inhabitants, establishing congregations in the north and west. He found strong opposition from the traditional religious leaders, the Druids.

Among the famous works attributed to Patrick is his Christo-centric affirmation of the Trinity in his famous "Breastplate":

> I bind unto myself today the strong name of the Trinity
> By invocation of the same, the Three in One and One in Three.
> I bind this day to me forever, by power of faith, Christ's incarnation,
> His baptism in the Jordan River, His cross of death for my salvation,
> His bursting from the spiced tomb, His riding up the heavenly way,
> His coming at the day of doom, I bind unto myself today.
> Christ be with me, Christ within me.
> Christ behind me, Christ before me,
> Christ beside me, Christ to win me, Christ to comfort and restore me.
> Christ beneath me, Christ above me, Christ in quiet, Christ in danger,
> Christ in hearts of all that love me,
> Christ in mouth of friend and stranger. (*Lorica*)

The faith of Patrick was clearly directed to Christ as the one who saved by grace alone. It was faith in Christ alone that he proclaimed wherever he traveled. Patrick died quietly around 461 at one of the monasteries he founded in Ireland.

Near the end of the century, the date was Christmas Day in 496 to be precise, the leader of the Franks, Clovis, was baptized into the Christian faith. As

Justinian also enhanced the architecture of Christian churches through his rebuilding of Hagia Sophia in Constantinople in the great basilica style. According to Procopius (c.490/507-c.560/565), a noted Byzantine historian of that era, the dome of this magnificent edifice "hangs as from a golden chain from heaven." Dedicated on Christmas Day, 538, this impressive building served as a model for generations of Christian congregations.

Between 548 and 565 Emperor Justinian was also instrumental in the construction of what is now the oldest Christian monastery, Saint Catherine's Monastery at the base of Mount Sinai in Egyptian peninsula. This monastery has remained active ever since, although it was briefly captured by Muslims.

Fifth Ecumenical Council (553)

Under Justinian's leadership a second Council of Constantinople was called (553) to deal with the continuing question of Christ's natures. Thinking that he could draw together dissident groups who had rejected Chalcedon, Justinian planned to attack, not the definition, but three Antiochene theologians in the controversy of the "Three Chapters." The "three chapters" were actually three authors' works—Theodore of Mopsuestia (see chapter 3), and his two students, Theodoret of Cyprus (c.393-c.458/466) and Ibas of Edessa (bishop 435-457) who sent a letter explaining their understandings of Christology to Maris of Persia. Ibas' strongly stated writings about Christ's two natures had been used and affirmed in Chalcedon. By condemning these works, Justinian intended to mollify the Monophysites and bring them into closer agreement with him.

> **Ecumenical Councils**
> During the first centuries of the Christianity, special meetings were held to discuss theological (and sometimes political) issues. These assemblies were legally convened by either the Emperor or one of the church leaders and were composed of members of the church hierarchy. Their purpose was to carry out judicial and/or doctrinal functions, through careful deliberation so that regulations and decrees would have the authority of the whole assembly. The first seven, which are recognized by most mainline Christian groups, are the following:
> First Council of Nicaea (325)
> First Council of Constantinople (381)
> Council of Ephesus (431)
> Council of Chalcedon (451)
> Second Council of Constantinople (553)
> Third Council of Constantinople (680)
> Second Council of Nicaea (787)

This Fifth Ecumenical Council tended to confuse the issue further by giving some concessions to Monophysite views. That approach did not draw the empire together as intended. At this council, a proposed compromise between the encouraged to consult the other brothers in the monastery on issues of grave concern. Breaking of the rule resulted in reprimands, first privately, but if repeated infractions occurred, publicly. Excommunication was the next step, which meant not only not being allowed to take Holy Communion, but also not eating with the rest of the monks. Whipping and expulsion from the community could follow, yet even these were not permanent and a repentant monk could return to the community up to three times.

Besides these three vows, the *Rule* designated three activities which were to occupy the monks' lives: the daily office (seven devotional services throughout the day and one at night), manual labor (usually in their vast farm holdings), and scriptural reading and meditation (called in Latin, *lectio divina*). Believing that "idleness is the enemy of the soul" (*Rule* 48), Benedict gave form to the life of the monks. All of this was under the general Benedictine principle of *ora et labora* ("prayer and work").

A daily schedule for a Benedictine monk would be something like this, with its particular emphasis on the devotional *opus dei* (work of God): Arising at about 2 a.m. the monks would assemble for Matins (a night service of the Word which included the chanting of several psalms) then go to their cells for private meditation until around sunrise when they would assemble to sing Lauds (a simple

service of praise). For the next four hours they would study, perhaps stopping briefly for Prime (in which they would pledge their loyalty to God). At around nine in the morning, after a brief devotion (Terse) they would go out into the fields for three hours of agrarian labor. At noon (our English word comes from the Latin term for the ninth hour, *nona*, although technically this was the sixth hour, *sext*), the monks would eat one meal after a short devotional time recalling Jesus' suffering on the cross. (The actual ninth hour was 3 p.m., since the day began at 6 a.m., but Benedict realized men could not labor effectively without food earlier in the day.) An hour of rest was allowed after which manual labor was once again required. At three another brief devotional break was allowed for prayer (the actual office of None), along with a second meal during the winter months. The day ended in the late afternoon with a service of Vespers, which followed the evening meal in summer months. After preparing for sleep, a service ending the day (Compline) was conducted and the monks would silently go to bed soon after sunset.

Monasteries were self-sustaining, having their own tillable fields, a clean well for drinking water, and sufficient areas for poultry or rabbits or fish. Food was somewhat meager, even for these communities, since they would normally eat only bread and wine, vegetables and some meat (usually fish or poultry). Beef was reserved only for the weak. Benedict, however, did not promote an extreme asceticism, since he allowed for two meals a day with two cooked dishes at each, along with fresh fruit and vegetables as available. Bathing was a luxury and property was held in common. These institutions were not established for the comfort of the community, but for the glory of God.

Along with their land holdings, the Benedictine order established schools which were necessary for instructing the novices interested in prayer and Scripture. Benedict died in 550 after predicting his own death six days earlier. The death of King Totila (ruled 541-552), the last great Ostrogothic ruler, occurred two years later, as predicted by Benedict. When the Lombards plundered the Monte Cassino monastery in 586, most of the monks fled to Rome where the future Gregory the Great would come under their influence. The lasting legacy of Benedict is in his *Rule*, which is still used today in many monastic communities.

Cassiodorus, the Statesman Monk

Cassiodorus (c. 485-580) was a statesman turned monk and contemporary of Benedict, who also wanted to establish a monastic life. After serving King Theodoric as a statesman (senator), he founded a monastery in Vivarium in extreme-southern Italy as a center for biblical and humanistic learning.

The illustration at right is from an eighth-century Bamberg manuscript of Cassiodorus's *Institutions* and depicts the site of this ideal world. Cassiodorus described the monastery rather vividly:

> The site of the monastery of Vivarium conduces to making provision for travelers and the poor, since you have irrigated gardens and the nearby river Pellena full of fish--its waves threaten no danger, but neither is it despicable for its size. It flows into your precincts, channeled artificially where it is wanted, adequate to water your gardens and turn your mills. It is there when you want it and flows on when no longer needed; it exists to serve you, never too roisterous and bothersome nor yet again ever deficient. The sea lies all about you as well, accessible for fishing with fishponds [*vivaria*] to keep the caught fish alive. We have constructed them as pleasant receptacles, with the Lord's help, where a multitude of fish swim close by the cloister, in circumstances so like mountain caves that the fish never sense themselves constrained in any way, since they are free to seek their food and hide away in dark recesses. We have also had baths built to refresh weary bodies, where sparkling water for drinking and washing flows by. Thus it is that your monastery is sought by outsiders, rather than that you could justly long for other places. These are the delights of temporal things, as you know, not the things the faithful hope for in the future; these things shall pass away, but those shall abide without end. But placed here in the monastery, let us be in the power of those desires that will make us co-regents with Christ. (*Institutions* 1.29.1)

Among the emphases of Cassiodorus's monastery was academic transcription of the classic works by Cicero, Ovid, and Virgil. The copying of manuscripts required not only the self-discipline of the monk, but a significant financial cost—a single treatise written on parchment (animal skin) sheets would require a whole flock of sheep or goats. While his monastic model was not successful in his lifetime, his ideas as expressed in his book *Institutions* set a vision for future monasteries in the West which would follow his model of scriptural study with classical education.

Emphasizing the grace of God in Christ, Cassiodorus described the Christian's continuing vocation—not merely monastic, but throughout one's life, in his work *On the Spirit*: "In Christ's service no heart which gives itself wholly up to Him is ever found untouchable, nor can it fail to see what it seeks, nor can it lose what it is given in reward for loyalty." (*De anima* 17.33-36). Similarly, Cassiodorus interpreted the Psalms as being centered in Christ—either speaking of Him or His speaking through them.

Dionysius the Areopagite and John of the Ladder

Two curious figures from this century need to be introduced. Taking the name Dionysius (c.470-c.532) (also spelled Denis or Dennis), an Athenian disciple of Paul mentioned by St. Luke (Acts 17:34), this monk's Greek compositions were considered authentic products from the hand of a prominent disciple of Paul. In the ninth century, his works on hierarchy were translated into Latin, when they became a standard by which various bishops and popes claimed their superior authority over other clergy and, certainly, over the laity (see chapter 9). Because of its later origin, the incorrect attribution to the first century Dionysius is usually clarified by calling this monk, pseudo-Dionysius (the false Dennis).

This prolific Syrian monk prepared several detailed descriptions of angels and their orders and their application to the church life of his era. These influential works were entitled, *On the Divine Names*, *On Mystical Theology*, *On the Ecclesiastical Hierarchy*, and *On the Heavenly Hierarchy*. The latter two became standard works among mystical thinkers in the high middle ages. Gregory the Great accepted them as being authentic works from the first century. Dionysius' basic premise was that as monks contemplated the three triadic ranks of angels, they could acquire an ever-increasing closeness to God. Following a Neoplatonic way of thinking, he described a negative way of coming into God's presence—the Greek word is *apophatic*—by which one does not seek to understand qualities or characteristics of God, but rather one emptied simself of knowledge so that he experiences only spiritual things and

estates be utilized to aid the poor. Another noteworthy political accomplishment of Gregory was establishing a treaty with the Lombards in Italy, enhancing the influence and power of the Roman see over against the ever-weakening Byzantine patriarch.

As bishop of Rome, Gregory preached regularly in the numerous churches of the city. He also extended his pastoral and political influence through correspondence with leaders in Spain, Gaul, and even Africa (over 850 letters have survived). Although these efforts were not always successful, his prolific writing has resulted in his being called "the Great."

Gregory (see illustration) is counted among the "Doctors of the Church." As a teacher (*doctores*) he wrote several influential books, particularly his *Book of Pastoral Care,* directing the bishops to be especially faithful in their watching over their spiritual flocks. The work, which described the bishop as a physician of souls whose main responsibility was to preach and enforce church discipline, became a standard guide for the bishops of the medieval church. His *Morals on Job* explored the monastic life of work and contemplation. Likewise, his *Dialogues on the Life and Miracles of the Italian Fathers* described the work of Benedict of Nursia and other monks. In both these latter works, Gregory's theological ideas took concrete form.

A strong promoter of monasticism, Gregory saw the potential in using monks to help expand the church's influence in the world. He himself had loved the monastic life, yet when he became pope he was shocked into action. In one of his sermons on Ezekiel, he recounts the biblical patriarch Jacob in Genesis 29. Jacob had two wives; Rachel was beautiful (depicted as the contemplative life) and Leah was fertile (depicted as the active life). In one of his sermons on Ezekiel, Gregory said he thought of himself as being married to Rachel when he was a monk, but said that being pope was like waking up in the night to find oneself in the arms of Leah...a shock, but a necessary and productive shock.

An oft repeated story about Gregory's early years is perhaps apocryphal, but it recounts his first experience of seeing three young blond men from England. Gregory asked the nationality of these boys and was told, "They are Angles." He continued, "They are accurately named, since they have faces like angels." In response to his question of their country of origin, he was told, "De Ire" (from Ireland). "*De ira* (Latin for "from wrath") they are indeed," said Gregory, "for they have been called from God's wrath to His mercy. Who is their king?" "Aella," was the answer he received. "Alleluia? Then God's name must be praised in that land." Thus, Gregory became concerned with those who were outside the general contact of Roman citizens.

In 597, seven years after his accession to the papal throne, Gregory sent forty monks under the leadership of the prior of Gregory's own monastery.

potentiality of distorting the work of the Holy Spirit. The tension between the two churches began to increase significantly in the next centuries.

Monastic Outreach

Monastic activities continued in the British Isles after the work of Patrick (see chapter 5) and Augustine of Canterbury. In Ireland, Finnian (c.495-589) established a monastery from where his student, Columba (521-597), and twelve companions conducted missionary work on the Scottish island of Iona around 563. Both of these men were instrumental in expanding the Christian faith throughout the British Isles and beyond. These monastic communities were organized as religious as well as cultural centers and their structure resulted in a kind of church hierarchy which was more tribal than episcopal.

Born into an Irish Christian family, Columba was educated in the ways of the land and the people he would serve for over fifty years. While completing his training in Dub Linn (later Dublin), a devastating plague forced him to go out into the world to conduct the priestly ministrations for which he had been trained. Having an eloquent voice and a poetic heart, Columba crafted inspiring sermons and songs for his congregants. After a dispute with both his teacher, Finnian, and with his king, Columba left Ireland for Iona, where his monastery became a missionary center for future generations. Columba returned to Ireland periodically, particularly for ecclesiastical meetings. The day before he died, he had been copying biblical texts and had completed the verse, "They that love the Lord shall lack no good thing." He looked up and said, "Here I must stop; let Baithin do the rest." Baithin (c.536-c.599), his successor, continued the missionary and educational work begun at Iona.

Another monk from the Irish abbey of Bangor (which means "monastery"), Columbanus (543-615), founded a new monastery in Gaul around 590. In Gaul his rigorous Irish Catholic faith countered the more lax faith of the Frankish clergy. In a controversy over the date for the celebration of Easter, Columbanus insisted on an older dating system. As a result he had to flee to Italy, where he founded another monastery in Burgundy and from which his disciple, Gall (c.550-c.646), later founded a monastery in Switzerland (St. Gall).

Throughout this century, God's people worked to develop a greater contact with the world. Although distortions and errors crept into the official dogmas of the church, the Gospel was being carried out into the world through a variety of enterprising individuals and communities.

His encyclopedic *Etymologies* provided a collection of ancient and current understandings of agriculture, astronomy, medicine, and religion. Through this twenty-volume work, Greek philosophical thinking was preserved (until the Arabic sources brought them back through translation in the twelfth century) along with much understanding of the shape of the world. Isidore was the first to propose, for example, that the earth was round—or at least disc-like. From his understandings, a map of the world was developed which is sometimes called the T-O map, since the Mediterranean Sea was drawn so that it divided the world like a T (see illustration). In his *Etymologies*, he cited over 150 authors, including Greek and Roman classical writers. The work remained an important textbook for almost a millennium.

Similarly, his *History of the Goths, Vandals and Suebi* (the latter were a Germanic people who had swept into France and Spain) along with his *Chronicle*, which covered world events from Creation to 616, laid the groundwork for future historical records of these early Middle Ages. Although his biblical and dogmatic works were merely compilations of previous materials, they exhibited a selective approach exemplary of life in Spain at that time. Isidore is also credited with preparing the final form of the Hispanic liturgy, which became known as the Mozarabic Rite after the Muslims took over the Iberian peninsula.

Growth in Christianity

The successors of Pope Gregory I were not as powerful or spiritual as Gregory. Boniface III (pope 604-607), for example, assumed the title "universal bishop," which Gregory had rejected as antichristian and blasphemous and which the patriarchs of Constantinople also claimed.

The Merovingian (Gallic) dynasty (named after Merovech [+453/457] a barbarian warlord of the Salian Franks and father of Clovis—see chapter 6) of the Frankish kingdom remained strong for the first part of this century. With the death of Dagobert I (c.502-639), however, the Merovingian line slowly degenerated. In the next century, a new political power arose in the person of Pepin II (c.714-768) and his illegitimate son, Charles (see Charlemagne [c.742/748-814] in chapter 8). This new dynasty was interested in reunifying the Frankish lands and defending their various frontiers from pagan raiders.

In the East, Emperor Heraclius (ruled 610-641) led Byzantine Christians in several victorious battles between 622 and 628 against hostile forces encroaching upon Constantinople from the East and the West. His highly trained army withstood the attack on his capital by two kingdoms, the Persians and the Slavic Avars, but they were not able to check the advance of the Muslim hordes which gradually encroached upon the Empire (see below). He did, however, rebuff the Persians sufficiently to regain Syria, Palestine, and Egypt for his imperial rule.

Little is known of Muhammad's childhood and early years. He seems to have had some contact with both Christians and Jews and their Scriptures. In addition, the influence of a monotheistic movement in Arabia, known as Hanif, is apparent in his spirituality. His father died before Muhammad was born. He and his widowed mother resided in the Arabian city of Mecca, approximately forty miles east of the Red Sea. They were members of the prominent Quraysh tribe,

which served as custodians of a sacred shrine, the Ka'abah (cube). This pagan temple, which housed a supposedly sacred black stone (perhaps a meteorite) and several hundred idols, has continued to be held as sacred by Islam (see illustration). The *Qur'an* (literally, "the reading" or "the reciting") provides Muhammad's moral injunctions, but gives almost no information on his life. His most reliable biographers wrote over a hundred years after Muhammad's death, leaving much room for speculation and exaggeration. As a youth, Muhammad tended sheep and goats outside of Mecca and developed a deep appreciation for the poetic aspects of the Arabic language. At some point, he participated in caravan travel to Palestine, Syria, and Yemen. From that experience, he was invited to manage the caravan trade of a wealthy widow named Khadija (558-620). Because she was a distant relative, she asked him to marry her, although she was fifteen years his elder. This provided him with ample time to spend in contemplation and ultimately to receive his call.

Around the beginning of the second decade of this century, he claimed to have received a call from the archangel Gabriel and began to preach, declaring himself to be a new prophet. Muhammad's message was simple: God, or Allah, is one. He is all-powerful and all-knowing. Unconditional submission to Allah is the essence of this religious system, and thus the name of the religion is Islam (which means "submission" to Allah's will). Muhammad received several more divine revelations which were subsequently recorded in the *Qur'an* (also spelled *Koran*). These revelations told of good and evil angels and the immortality of the soul, which would be judged and rewarded or punished according to one's obedience to the five obligations ("pillars of Islam")—confession of faith, prayers five times daily, various forms of fasting (including the holy month of Ramadan), almsgiving for charities, and a once-in-a-lifetime pilgrimage (*hajj*) to Mecca. Islam also teaches that other prophets had come before Muhammad, including Adam, Noah, Abraham, Moses, and Jesus, but Muhammad was the final messenger who provided God's last and ultimate word. The *Hadith*, a collection of traditions from Muhammad, along with a body of laws (*Ijma*) are also part of the *Qur'an*. The religious actions and comments by Muhammad as recorded by his companions make up a second source of religious truth in Islam, called the *Sunna* or Path. One of the major sects of Islam, the Shiites, disputed the authority of this source in favor of additional guidance from Muhammad's successors.

Muhammad's youngest daughter Fatima [c.605-632]). His caliphate was much contested and many battles resulted from the power struggle between him and other tribesmen. The ultimate split between Sunnis and Shiites came with Ali's son, Hussai.

Among the characteristic features of this new religion was the use of force. Muhammad had purportedly asserted that "the sword is the key of heaven and hell; a drop of blood shed in the cause of Allah, a night spent in arms, is of more avail than two months of fasting or prayer; whosoever falls in battle, his sins are forgiven, and at the day of judgment his limbs shall be supplied by the wings of angels and cherubim." The idea of a holy war (*jihad*) against all infidels served to motivate many Arab followers as these military leaders became civil governors of the occupied areas. By the middle of this century, three of the five centers of Christianity—Antioch, Jerusalem, and Alexandria—were seized by Islamic forces.

During the initial century of their existence, Islam's dramatic conquest of many Christian regions, including Palestine, Syria, and Mesopotamia and the African lands that bordered the Mediterranean Sea from Egypt to the Atlantic

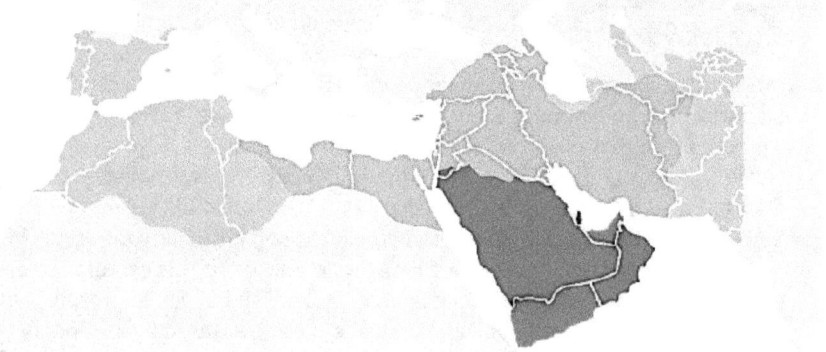

Ocean, caught most Christians by surprise. (Map displays expansion: dark gray: 622-632; medium gray: 632-662; lighter gray: 661-750.) The weakness of the Persian and Byzantine kingdoms coupled with the strong military solidarity of the Muslims explains some of these conquests. The territory conquered or controlled by Muslims was known as "the house of Islam" (*dar al-Islam*) in contrast to the *dar al-harb* ("the house of war") which meant that warfare was encouraged for the expansion of Islam. Thus, within a few decades most of the centers of Christianity—Antioch (638), Alexandria (641), Carthage, Damascus (635), and Jerusalem (638)—were under the control of Islamic caliphs. A major geographic shift was occurring in Christianity.

Internal strife among the various Muslim leaders continued throughout the final years of this century. Upon the death of Ali, his eldest son, Hasan (625-670), was poisoned after abdicating his power. Ali's youngest son, Husain (626-680), was killed shortly thereafter, but established a rift in Muslim rule. The followers of Ali are known as Shiites (*Shi'a* means "party" or those belonging to Ali) and continue to hold sway predominantly in southern Iraq and Iran.

Christianity in China

Although Christian tradition suggests that the apostle Thomas brought Christianity to India and some also claimed he came to China and even preached in Xi'an, no evidence of a Christian presence was evident that early in Chinese history. However, in the early seventeenth century a large stone monument was discovered, which describes events from the second quarter of the seventh century. Known as the "Nestorian Stele," (see illustration) this ten foot high limestone block was erected in 781 and describes 150 years of Christian activity. During the Tang Dynasty (618-877), China seems to have been open to Christian missions. The inscription on the stone tells how Nestorian Christian monks from the Assyrian Church of the East came to the area and were given a public hearing by officials, who approved of the general principles of this "illustrious religion."

In the year 638, a public proclamation acknowledge the work of a bishop Alopen (or Olopun), known only from this stele. Alopen brought the Christian Scriptures and, apparently, some icons. He was given administrative responsibilities for several congregations which the emperor sponsored. In addition, Alopen prepared a Chinese book about Jesus, which recent historians have given the title, *The Sutra of Jesus the Messiah*, a mixture of Christianity and some Buddhist philosophy.

The presence of Christianity in China continued throughout the Tang Dynasty, but subsequently disappeared, most likely through the strength of Buddhist philosophy and Islamic pressures.

Sixth Ecumenical Council (680-681)

As noted above, Emperor Heraclius (610-641) had resolved a major issue for the Empire by defeating Slavic raiders who had attacked the very walls of Constantinople, and regained land from Persian forces in Syria, Palestine, and Egypt. Through several brilliant campaigns between 622 and 628 these lands were once again restored in the eastern Empire. Feeling the blush of victory, Emperor Heraclius proposed a compromise position between the Monophysites and the Orthodox Christians in order to build a more solid political and theological union against the increasingly hostile Islamic forces. Although seemingly settled at Chalcedon and subsequently at the fifth ecumenical council, the Third Council of Constantinople, in 553 (see chapter 6), this Monophysite view continued to trouble the church, a position which claimed Christ had one nature.

In the East, this compromising view was promulgated by Patriarch Sergius I (patriarch 610-638), and in the west by Pope Honorius I (pope 625-638).

life in 754, Boniface resigned his ecclesiastical office and returned to Frisia as a missionary. There the following spring, after gathering several dozen candidates for a Christian confirmation, which included baptisms, he was martyred by Frisian bandits, who had hoped to acquire gold, but only found Boniface's manuscripts and books.

Venerable Bede's *History*

Beda venerabilis

The original chronicler of England, Venerable Bede (673-735), studied in Northumbria and wrote on chronology, grammar, biblical exegesis, and history. For the most part, he lived his entire life from age seven to his death exclusively in the monasteries of St. Peter in Wearmouth and St. Paul in nearby Jarrow. Following a devastating plague in which all the monks of the monastery died, only the young lad, Bede, and the abbot survived. Bede reports that Abbot Coelfrid (or Coelfrith, c.642-716) and one boy (Bede?) conducted all the services of the Divine Office together until more monks could be enlisted. Ever since, Bede found the regular routine of daily worship stimulating for his own spiritual life (see illustration from the *Nuremberg Chronicle*). He was ordained a deacon and later a priest by John of Beverley (+721), whom Bede reports taught a deaf person to speak (*Ecclesiastical History*, Book 5, chapter 2).

His *Ecclesiastical History of the English People* remains a classic exposition of the early years of Christianization and missionary work as it coalesced in England. Noted for citing his sources, Bede sought facts rather than legends as the basis for his history. His calendric interest led him to date events on the basis of Christ's birth, *anno domini* ("in the year of our Lord"); the first to do so. In Book 1, chapter 2, he dates the Roman contact with England both from the founding of Rome, the usual way of dating events at that time, and also in relation to the birth of Christ.

Adoptionism

A seeming recurrence of an earlier heresy, known as Nestorianism, arose in this century in central Spain around the major city, Toledo. The Archbishop of Toledo had responsibility to oversee the theological teachings in his region. Having rooted out a heretic identified as a certain Migetius, the Spanish archbishop, Elipandus of Toledo (c.715/717-805/808), proceeded to argue that the man Jesus was united with the second person of the Trinity by way of "adoption" (*filius adoptivus*). This understanding may perhaps have been proposed as a way to explain the incarnation to the Muslim invaders and to maintain the oneness of God. Elipandus had used this term from the "Mozarabic" (Spanish) liturgy to emphasize the unity of Christ with all of humanity. The question was whether Christ was the divine Son of God in human form by nature or by adoption.

Elipandus suggested that, as Christ was adopted as the Son of God at his baptism, so each believer was adopted into God's family at baptism. Elipandus's views were supported and articulated most clearly by the Frankish bishop of Urgel, Felix (+816).

The problem with his explanation is that he made Christ into two distinct persons—one divine and one human, one from the Father and the other by adoption. The other problem is that the divinity of Christ was questioned along with the actual humanity of the Son of God. The first to raise concerns about this view was a monk, Morgan Beatus of Liebana (c.730-c.800), who wrote a two-volume work with his friend, Etherius (c.750-c.800), bishop of Othma, condemning Elipandus. Elipandus responded with threats to banish them both. When Charlemagne (742/47-814) heard that this view was held by Felix of Urgel in his newly acquired region, he convened a meeting in Regensburg in 792. Although initially recanting his position, Felix returned from Regensburg by way of Rome, where his recantation was accepted, and then to Spain, where he repented of his recantation! Several Spanish bishops then sent letters to the Emperor and Pope Hadrian I (or Adrian, c.700-795), requesting that they endorse the Adoptionism of Felix and Elipandus.

Most significantly, the English scholar, Alcuin (735-804), opposed Elipandus and Felix. Initially absent from his post in Frankfurt, Alcuin sent letters encouraging Felix and Elipandus to change their views for the sake of Christian love. He composed a treatise against the adoptionist view, which Charlemagne sent to various religious leaders, including the pope. Officially, adoptionism was condemned in 794 at the Council of Frankfurt. However, Felix was brought to a Synod at Aachen (Aix) in 799, called by the emperor, where Alcuin persuaded him to cease using the term, although privately he held this view until his death. Alcuin stated what would become the accepted formulation, "when God assumed fleshly form, the human person disappeared, but not the human nature."

Iconoclastic Controversy

The last ecumenical council, which is recognized by nearly every Christian group, dealt with a topic which had heated up and nearly boiled over for almost a century—icons. An icon (see illustration) is a stylized two-dimensional tempura painting on wood of a biblical figure, saint, or of Christ. Little objection to such drawings was evident in the early church, especially when one considers the many drawings and paintings in the catacombs depicting the sacraments and biblical stories, including pictures of Christ.

However, over time, questions had been raised whether icons were being worshipped or were merely adored. With the rise of Islam and the continuing influence of Judaism with their rejection of any depictions of humans, Christian leaders debated the appropriateness of such paintings, especially in Christian churches.

The iconoclastic (Greek, εἰκονοκλάστης, "icon/image" + "breaker') issue came to a head in the second decade of this century. After the horrific onslaught of the Muslim troops on the Byzantine Empire, Emperor Leo III (717-740) and his son, Constantine V (741-775) founded the Isaurian dynasty (named after the region around Mt Taurus in Asia Minor). Leo defeated Caliph Omar II (717-720) at Constantinople, reasserting Roman control of Asia Minor. But, in so doing, he also abolished all veneration of icons—whether painted or sculpted—of Mary or Christ or saints. He also removed the patriarch of Constantinople, Germanus (c.634-733), who opposed Leo's ban. Pope Gregory II resisted the mandate and rejected the emperor's policy as exceeding lay authority; a move which was both political and theological. Because Leo's military control over the Italian peninsula was weak and ineffectual, Gregory could take such a contrarian stand. His successor, Gregory III (pope 731-741), holding the same respect for icons, declared that anyone who profaned a sacred image should be excommunicated; in effect he was excommunicating Leo. Because of his distance from Rome, the emperor could do little with Rome itself, but finally confiscated the papal estates in Sicily and southern Italy.

Gregory III sought political support against the domination of the emperor in Constantinople and pleaded (albeit unsuccessfully) for the support of Charles Martel against the Emperor in Constantinople. However, another form of support arose.

Around the middle of the century, an unusual document suddenly but quite appropriately appeared, the *Donation of Constantine*. This document was based upon a popular legend that Emperor Constantine had been cured of leprosy by Pope Sylvester (+335). In gratitude for this miracle, Constantine is said to have given over all the patriarchates of Antioch, Alexandria, Jerusalem, and Constantinople, declaring that "more than our empire and earthly throne, the most sacred seat of St. Peter shall be gloriously exalted... [and] the city of Rome and all the provinces, districts and cities of Italy or of the western regions" be given

to the papacy. This forgery would have an enormous influence on papal powers over political leaders for almost a millennium. Not until the fifteenth century was this document finally recognized and identified by Lorenzo Valla (1407-1457) as a forgery prepared by an early medieval papal secretary.

In 754, Leo's iconoclastic son, Emperor Constantine V (718-775, ruled 741-775), at the Synod of Hieria, not only forbade the use of all icons in church, condemning anyone who defended their use, but also destroyed an image of Christ above one of the gates to the imperial palace in Constantinople. (See illustration their duty in the confines of their private chapels, usually for specific causes or people and for a financial fee. Slowly a distinction between the laity and the clergy became more and more apparent.

The first evidence of the modern version of the Apostles' Creed is recorded by the missionary monk, Pirminius (c.700-753), in his collection of quotations from Scripture and Church Fathers. The first report of a church organ occurred when the Byzantine emperor, Constantine V (718-775), sent an organ to King Pepin III (714-768), in 757 for use in his chapel. In the next century, Charles [Charlemagne] would request that a similar organ be placed in his Palatine chapel in Aachen in 812. In 826, a priest from Venice named George built a calliope-sounding organ at the palace chapel of Louis the Pious (778-840, ruled 814-840)

at Aachen. (The illustration above is from the *Utrecht Psalter*, c.830.) Chanting, usually attributed to Gregory the Great (540-604), probably developed during this century as a combination of Gallic and Roman worship practices and spread through France, Germany, and England. Under Bishop Chrodegang (bishop c.742/8-766), a close political advisor to Charles Martel, a monastic rule for cathedral clergy was prepared which featured chanting of the Daily Office.

Pepin prescribed the Roman liturgy for his realm in 754 and Charles the Great (747-814) made the Roman Rite standard for his whole empire in 789. That same year, Pope Hadrian (c.700-795, pope 722-795) sent a Gregorian sacramentary (texts used by priests for various worship services) to Charles. Charles added several liturgical texts from Gallican-Frankish liturgies, since he noted in his preface that Hadrian's was deficient. Gradually, the liturgical life of the community became increasingly elaborate and formalized.

The Seventh Ecumenical Council: Council of Nicaea (787)

Returning to the issue of icons, some important distinctions were being made toward the end of this century. Serving as co-regent with her son, Constantine VI (771-c.804, ruled 780-797), Empress Irene (c.752-803, ruled 797-

court scholar and historian, Einhard (c.776-840) wrote a comprehensive biography, *Vita Karoli Magni*, detailing Charlemagne's personal and professional life and his noble character. In addition, many nameless monks copied and embellished exquisite manuscripts in their scriptoriums (see illustration). These copyists of classical authors provided the only access later generations would have of the original thinking of these masters.

Much of the educational reform in the empire was a result of the able leadership of Alcuin who had come from Northumbria (England) and whom Charlemagne had met in Italy. Alcuin was a careful Christian thinker, who wrote several commentaries and philosophical treatises, including a work dealing with the nature of God, entitled *On the Trinity* (*De Trinitate*). He also wrote convincingly *Against Felix*, a Spanish priest who argued for "Adoptionism," a heresy which alleged that Jesus' humanity was only adopted by the Son of God (see chapter 8). He joined Charlemagne's court in 781 and remained a strong influence throughout Charlemagne's reign. As a result of Charlemagne's support, many scholars seeking to use their Christian vocations in a Christian context moved into the empire.

Noteworthy is the Benedictine monk, Hrabanus Maurus (780-856), who later became the Archbishop of Mainz. Hrabanus began his studies at Fulda, but was recognized for his intelligence and was sent away to Tours to study with Alcuin. Around 804, he returned to Fulda after studying with Alcuin for two years

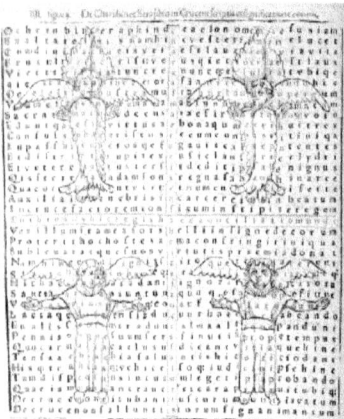

and, then, a decade later was ordained into the priesthood. After traveling to Palestine, he returned to Fulda and from 822-842 served as abbot, where he prepared commentaries on many biblical books. Near the end of his life, he was elected Archbishop, but felt his greatest service was in his literary production, such as his *De rerum naturis*, "of the things of nature." He is remembered for a peculiar form of poetic-art in which poems were composed of 36 letters and 36 lines on a grid often superimposed with a religious image (see illustration at the left). Among the poems were those honoring the holy cross, *In honorem sanctae crucis*. His hymn, "Come, Holy Ghost, Creator Blest," is still sung in many Christian churches.

Charlemagne's Successors

Charlemagne's second son was named Carloman (770/773-810) after two of his relatives, but, when he was crowned king of Italy in 781, he changed his name to Pepin, after his grandfather and older half-brother (c.767-811), who had been banished to a monastery in 792. Several months after a long, but unsuccessful siege of Venice in 810, he died, always ruling under the imperial authority of his father.

Pepin Carloman's younger brother, Louis the Pious (778-840), was given Aquitaine in 781, but then was named co-emperor in 813 by his father, sustaining the power and growth of Charlemagne's empire. One of Louis's noteworthy acts, besides continuing his father's political and educational endeavors, was to receive a copy of Pseudo-Dionysius' writings from the Byzantine emperor, Michael II (770-829), and send it to the abbot of the French monastery of Saint Denis, who claimed its author was their patron. This gift was translated thirty-five years later into Latin by John Scotus Eriugena (c. 810-877), although it was not widely used until the twelfth century.

Another policy, begun by Louis's father, was the restoration of monastic discipline. Through Benedict of Aniane ([751-821] not to be confused with the earlier Benedict of Nursia [480-547]), Louis restored order as well as a sense of piety in the monasteries. Benedict promoted his regulations in the *Concordia regularum* (Harmony of Rules) and *Codex regularum* (Book of Rules) over the next few years. The resulting monastic presence in which all the monks followed the same Rule provided a sense of peace and concord in a very troubled and socially disordered world.

After a series of internecine wars, the weakening of the empire became increasingly apparent. Upon his death according to Frankish tradition, Louis's three sons divided the kingdom, diminishing the Carolingian influence and power further. After a series of legal and military disputes, the Treaty of Verdun was formally accepted by the sons in 843. This date is often used to mark the beginning of the separate histories of Germany and France. Louis (804-876) received the eastern area by which he was given the nickname, "the German"; the youngest son, Charles the Bald (823-877), was given the western region (present day France); and the eldest son, Lothair I (795-855), took the strip of land between them, from the Netherlands to northern Italy. Subsequently at his death, Lothair's land was subdivided into three more regions and eventually the area became a string of insignificant principalities (see map below).

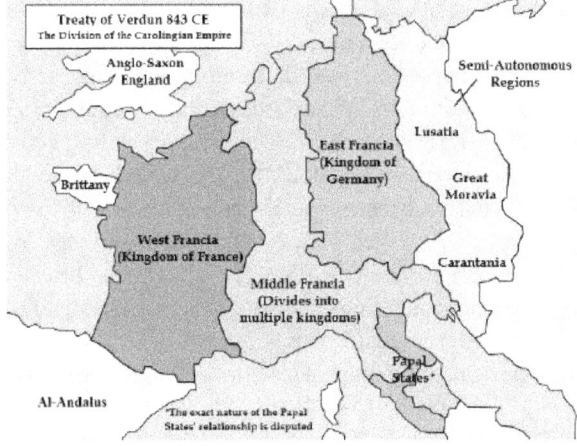

purposes, his reign was merely the nominal ending of the great Carolingian era which had ceased almost a century earlier. (The map below gives approximate locations of the various kingdoms toward the end of the tenth century.)

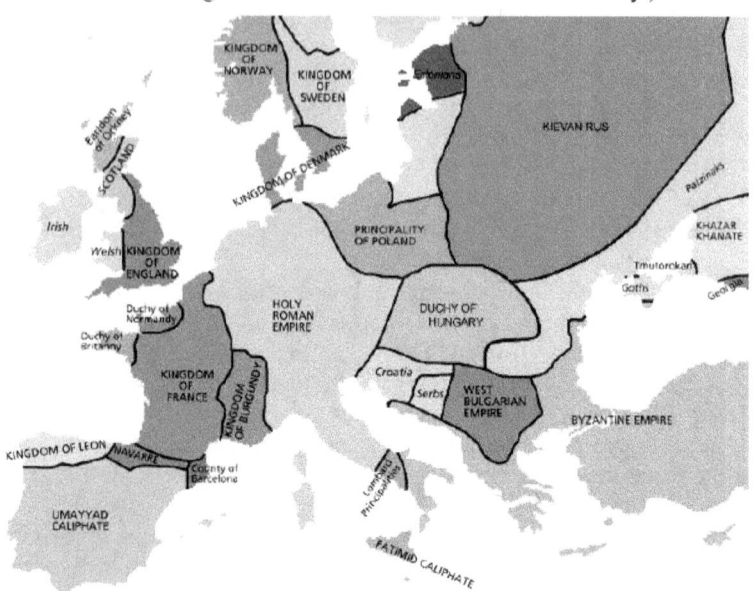

Emperor Otto I had expanded the German territories a few years earlier, following the election of his father, Henry the Fowler (919-936), as the first German emperor. Otto worked very closely with the German bishops and abbots, providing land, special privileges, and military protection. In return, these ecclesiastical leaders supported his expansion of the empire against the various hereditary noble families in and around Saxony. He also initiated a renewed sense of liturgical worship and ecclesiastical art, evident in his establishment of a very important monastic scriptorium for manuscript illumination at Quedlinburg Abbey. As his kingdom extended, he wielded greater control over the papal lands which had suffered under the Roman and Italian political chaos.

In 951, Otto entered Italy and declared himself king of Lombardy. He also acceded to the request to marry Adelaide of Italy/Burgundy (931-999), who had succeeded her husband, Lothar I of Arles (c.926/8-950), as ruler over Italy. This alliance proved extremely beneficial to the church, since they now had military support, which though somewhat distant was sufficiently strong to protect it from local interference. However, because of political intrigues, Pope Agapetus II (pope 946-955) did not declare Otto emperor; something Otto had to await for another ten years, during which time his own soldiers acclaimed him emperor as a result of his defeat of the Hungarians in 955.

In 961, Otto returned to Italy. This time he came at the invitation of Pope John XII (c.930/937-964, pope 955-964), a much weaker pope than those before. In February of 962 in St. Peter's Basilica, Pope John crowned Otto successor to

Charlemagne and Emperor over the Holy Roman Empire along with Empress Adelaide. From this date (until 1250), every German ruler would receive the crown from the hands of the pope in Rome. This recognition of the papacy was at the cost of the papacy losing its sole ecclesiastical power in the election of future popes. Every pope had to be approved by the emperor before being elected. This practice is known as *lay investiture*.

Shortly after his coronation, Pope John XII was deposed by Emperor Otto for turning against the emperor. The pope was then summarily replaced by a layman, Leo, whose consecration remained suspect. Pope Leo VIII (pope 964-965) was installed into his papal office through an unusually swift and highly dubious process. Normal procedures would be that a man was ordained into the various "ordered ministries"—porter, exorcist, lector, subdeacon, deacon, priest, bishop—over a series of years or at least months of on-the-job training or at least some practical experience. Leo, as a layman with no ecclesiastical training (although he had worked in papal administration for several years), was made pope by Otto within one twenty-four hour period. No sooner had Otto left Rome, but Leo was deposed and John was restored. When John XII died in 964, Pope Benedict V (964) was placed in the papal office, but without imperial consent. Therefore, Otto returned to Rome, banished Benedict to Germany, and restored Leo and his successor, John XIII (c.930/935-972, pope 965-972). These personal appointments by the emperor continued until the great Investiture Controversy (see chapter 11) in the next century.

Papal Pornocracy

Perhaps the hallmark of this century is the concept of *pornocracy*, which literally means "the rule of the illegitimates/prostitutes." Also known in Latin as *saeculum obscurum* ("dark age"), it refers to the papal office holders of almost half the century in which papal power was wielded by the mistresses and concubines of the popes, particularly by the noblewoman, Theodora (c.870-916), and her daughter, Marozia (890-937).

Corruption of the papacy had been going on for several decades, but under Pope Sergius III (c.860-911, pope 904-911), the papal quarters declined to an extremely low moral plane. Gaining control of the Lateran Palace with armed troops, after being deposed and exiled in 897, Sergius was acclaimed pope early in 904. Denying the validity of several of his predecessors, he immediately had his predecessor, Pope Leo V (pope 903-904), and his opponent, an antipope named Cardinal Christopher (antipope 903-904), strangled in prison. His sexual liaisons with fifteen year old Marozia, produced at least one son (later to become Pope John XI, see below). Sergius III was succeeded by two puppet-

England, became king of Norway in 995 that Christianity was fully established in his realm.

Probably the most significant missionary achievement in this century was the conversion of the Russian people, centered in its capital city, Kiev. Swedish Vikings had taken control of the waterways between the Baltic and the Black Sea and their descendants now ruled the region. As traders continued to come to Byzantium with their western goods, Christian missionary work was also progressing into the territory.

After her husband Igor's (ruled 912-945) death by an eastern Slavic tribe, the Drevlians, Princess Olga (c.879/890-969) was converted to Christianity in mid-century (see illustration by Roerich). Prior to her conversion, the *Primary Chronicle*, a Slavic history of this era, indicates that she took drastic steps to avenge her husband's death— burying some Drevlian ambassadors alive, burning others in a bathhouse, and finally killing several thousand at a feast given in her husband's honor. After her conversion she rejected missionary envoys sent by Bishop Adalbert (c.956-997) from Otto I probably recognizing them as having political implications for her own rule. Her son, Svyatoslav (942-989), with whom she served as co-regent from 945 until 963, rejected her Christian faith, but allowed her to practice it privately. Her grandson, Vladimir I (989-1015), on the other hand, expanded Christianity from Kiev into the northern area of his realm and continued his grandmother's legacy.

After the Magyars were defeated by Otto I in 955, the Great Prince of the Magyars, Géza (c.940-997), allowed Christian missionaries to work among his people. He was baptized sometime within the last quarter of the century, but continued several pagan practices as well, claiming he was wealthy enough to sacrifice to both old and new gods. His son, Stephen (c.970-1038), who became the patron saint of Hungary, advanced beyond his father's toleration of Christianity and worked hard to evangelize his people with the assistance of Slavic missionaries from Poland and Bohemia. These Slavic missionaries had undoubtedly been converted as a result of the work of Cyril and Methodius (see chapter 9).

Around this same time, Otto I had brought Bohemia under his rule and within several decades Duke Boleslav II (967-999) established Prague as a center for Christianity in Poland. Clearly, the light of Christianity was beginning to enlighten the darkness of paganism.

Symeon the New Theologian

Born to a well-to-do aristocratic family of Galatia around 949, Symeon (c.949-1022) was sent to Constantinople for his early education as an imperial plow to cut the soil and flip it over as well as to plow deeper. This innovation (see illustration) greatly reduced the time required to plow a field, since previously the fields had to be crisscrossed in order to accomplish the same effect. Wheels also increased productivity in the northern regions with heavier soils. Oxen were used for millennia in plowing.

Horses, not having as large a shoulder for harnessing a plow, were not used until the invention of the horse-collar. Horses were twice as fast as oxen and were capable of a variety of farming functions.

Crop cultivation had become more efficient as the Arabs also introduced summer irrigation. Instead of only planting during the spring and fall, lands which had normally lain fallow for the summer were able to be used for more production of grains and leafy vegetables. Fertilization from animal manure aided in this expanded use of the lands. Wheat, barley, peas and oats, along with vegetables, vineyards and fruit orchards were the mainstay of this agrarian economy. Medieval monasteries experimented with various techniques for improving crop production, although the communication of these techniques and the suspicion of changing practices did not influence farming to any great extent. The church, while requiring a tithe from its landholders, also stored excess grains and in times of drought or famine, regularly opened its storehouse for the poor and needy.

Towns were growing as more and more people were able to be sustained by surplus food. Fulltime artisans were able to survive in these towns as others exchanged food and produce for the specialized work of leather workers, blacksmiths, thatchers, bakers, butchers and carpenters. Trade was expanding, too, as surplus food was exchanged for handcrafts in other cities. London and Brussels, for example, became significant trading centers.

After the Norman's captured England at the Battle of Hastings (see below), the arable land on local estates shifted their farming techniques. Previously, they had farmed one area near the villages during the summer, allowing their cattle to roam in more distant areas. In the winter, they would bring their animals nearer their village or estate (a natural source of fertilization). The new method was to leave one of three fields fallow for each of three years, allowing the sheep and cattle to graze the land and the soil to regain its fertility. On the other two fields, wheat (for bread), barley (for beer), oats, or other crops such as peas or beans could be grown in a simple rotation. The grains were normally planted in the fall and, if the winter was not too severe, harvested in the spring. A second crop was then planted in spring as early as possible and harvested in the fall. Flax and hemp were planted for clothing and rope production. Normally, a bushel of grain was planted with the hopes that up to a half-dozen bushels could be harvested of the same grains.

Medieval fields were divided into strips of roughly an acre, which was about the area one could plough in a day. Each villager would farm a few of these strips scattered around the three fields. The heavy, iron-shared plough, pulled by a team of oxen, could cut a furrow of roughly a furlong (a term derived from the joining of "furrow" and " long") before the team had to stop to rest.

Reforming Papacy

The election of Pope Victor II (1018-1057, pope 1055-1057) was rather unusual in that he was elected by the Roman clergy, but was German and the obvious appointee of Henry III. His election removed the Italian families from wielding control over the papacy as they had in the past. But it did not completely eliminate the interference of the emperor, something the reforming movement had been working for. After the death of Henry III, Victor cared for Henry's six-year old son, Henry IV (1050-1106), so that he had power over both church and state. But that convenient arrangement was short-lived with the death of Victor.

Young Henry IV (king of Germany 1056-1106, emperor 1084-1105) (see illustration), under the regency of his mother, Agnes of Poitou (c.1024-1077),

was powerless to become involved in the election of the next pope. As a result, the Italian clergy, once again having the power, elected Frederick of Lorraine (c.1020-1058) as Pope Stephen IX (1057-1058). Cardinal Humbert's treatises against simony were published at this time. Although not everyone agreed with Humbert (including Peter Damian (1007-1072), who still favored lay investiture), his positions on reforming the church prevailed. This became evident at the death of Stephen when the Roman nobility, headed by Count Gregory of Tusculum, elected John of Velletri (+1073/1080) as Benedict X (antipope 1058-January 1059). Prior to his death, Stephen had secured from the Roman clergy a promise not to elect a successor until Hildebrand had returned from his negotiations with the German imperial court. Upon Hildebrand's arrival in Rome, the reformist clergy elected

Gerard of Florence (c.1000-1061), who took the name Nicholas II (pope 1059-1061), and declared Benedict X's election invalid.

Shortly after his election, Pope Nicholas II called a council at his Lateran Palace in 1059 which determined that only cardinals could elect a pope, who in turn would name new cardinals. This procedure removed lay involvement completely in the selection of the pope and remains in place to the present time. As a result, reforming of the church continued, but papal power was being solidified in the Roman curia. To support this ecclesiastical power, Nicholas secured the perpetual support of a Norman army (at the time, serving in southern Italy) under the pope's direct command.

The Battle of Hastings in 1066

When Pope Alexander II (pope 1061-1073) was duly elected by the cardinals, he was opposed by powerful Roman families as well as the German nobles, including Empress Agnes (c.1025-1077), who helped set up a rival pope, Honorius II (antipope 1061-1072). A revolution against Agnes gave political power to the archbishop, Anno I of Cologne (c.1010-1075, bishop 1056-1075), who sided with Alexander. However, in order to gain greater political support, Alexander sanctioned the historically monumental invasion of England by Duke William of Normandy (c.1028-1087).

At the decisive, Battle of Hastings in 1066 (see illustration from the Bayeaux Tapestry, with the Latin words "William, Leader, the Great"), England fell under French rule. Papal influences spread throughout the English church, particularly when the pope's appointment, Lanfranc (c.1005/10-1089), became Archbishop of Canterbury. As

"the Conqueror," William acknowledged the spiritual superiority of the bishop of Rome; however, he said such rule was by royal approval. In the meantime, Henry IV came of age and was crowned king in 1065. Securing the support of the German clergy through his own selection of bishops, he presented land holdings to them as repayment.

Shortly after this significant invasion and change of power in western Europe, Muslim forces under the Seljuk Turks defeated the Byzantine forces of Emperor Romanus IV of Constantinople (1032-1072, ruled 1068-1071) at Manzikert in Armenia in 1071. Having lost much land to the Muslims over the preceding decade, this battle is most memorable in the fact that it set a series of destabilizing losses for the Christian East. After appealing to Rome for help, prospect of keeping all that they plundered, including the land and property reclaimed in the Holy Land.

Pilgrimages had always been popular. Since the seventh century they had been imposed as penance for wealthy sinners. With the Seljuk Turkish control of Jerusalem, the prospect of such a spiritual pursuit had ceased, particularly with the destruction of significant holy sites. Yet, those so moved by the greater spirituality of penance, desired to continue the pathway of penance. This coincided with the Muslim accumulation of significant income earned through pilgrimage activity. Such a promise of a holy war against the infidels seems also to have mirrored the Islamic ideal of *jihad*.

The response to Urban's proposal, as recorded by the chroniclers of the time, was almost immediate. The crowds reportedly shouted, *"Deus lo volt"* (medieval Catalan, "God wills it!"). Among the initial responses was the popular preacher, Peter the Hermit (c.1050-1115), a monk from Amiens, France, who mobilized large groups of peasants in the spring of 1096 in what is sometimes called the Peoples' Crusade. Although these reckless bands often took recourse to plundering the German and Hungarian countryside through which they travelled, they got as far as Nicaea where the Turkish troops destroyed them completely.

The real First Crusade began in 1096 and was conducted by the feudal nobility of Europe. Four individual armies were mustered by French, English, and Italian knights. They arrived at Constantinople in the winter, causing Alexius I concern, since they would not swear allegiance to him. In the spring of 1097, they laid siege to Nicaea. After severe losses to hunger and thirst during the summer, the Crusaders laid siege to Antioch in the fall. Not until June of 1098 was Antioch taken by the Crusaders, only to suffer a severe setback when the Turkish troops tried to regain the city. Finally, in June of 1099 they approached Jerusalem and, in the middle of July, recaptured it for the Christian community.

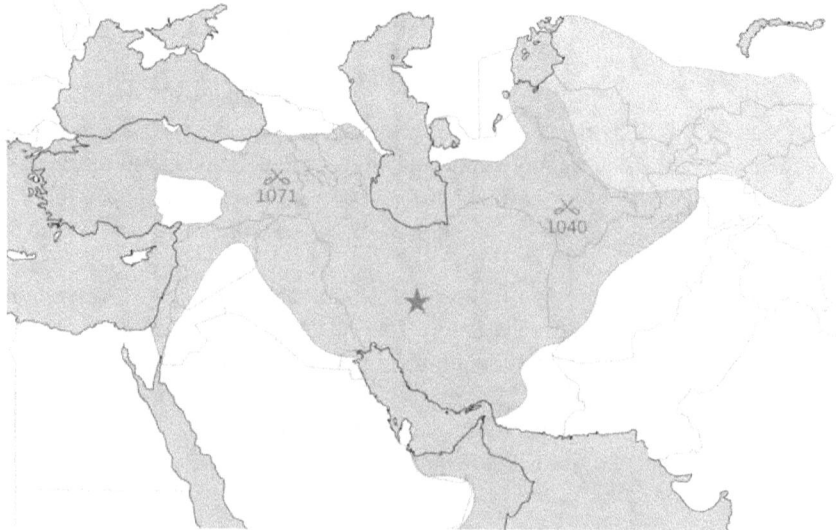

daughter of a nobleman. Because of his mother's untimely death during his childhood, Bernard resolved to enter a monastery early in his life. When given the opportunity to enter the Cistercian monastery in 1098, he not only took his vows quickly and confidently, but he brought several friends and family members. When a new monastery was founded at Clairvaux, Bernard was immediately appointed abbot.

Bernard served as the conscience of the church. Strongly affirming the necessity of rigorously obeying the Cistercian Rule, Bernard influenced many other abbeys as well as bishops to reform their monasteries or congregations from their worldly emphasis on wealth and to reinvigorate a spiritual fervor for the Lord's kingdom-work. Among the Cistercian practices which influenced Bernard was the replacement of the *Christus Victor* image (the Lord in majesty) with a corpus of a suffering Savior. As a result, one of the most cherished meditations in western contemplative Christianity was penned by Bernard in 1127, entitled "The Love of God" (*De Diligendo Deo*), which depicts the soul's desire for God (see text box below). He composed this while serving as abbot at Clairvaux after settling several political disputes, particularly one between the pope and the city of Milan.

> **Bernard: *On Loving God***
> In this life, I think, we cannot fully and perfectly obey that precept, "Thou shalt love the Lord your God with all your heart, and with all your soul, and with all your strength, and with all your mind" (Luke 10:27). For here [on earth] the heart must take thought for the body; and the soul must energize the flesh; and the strength must guard itself from impairment; and by God's favor, must seek to increase. It is therefore impossible to offer up all our being to God, to yearn altogether for His face, so long as we must accommodate our purposes and aspirations to these fragile, sickly bodies of ours. Wherefore the soul may hope to possess the fourth degree of love, or rather to be possessed by it, only when it has been clothed upon with that spiritual and immortal body, which will be perfect, peaceful, lovely, and in everything wholly subjected to the spirit. And to this degree no human effort can attain; it is in God's power to give it to whom He wills. Then the soul will easily reach that highest stage, because no lusts of the flesh will retard its eager entrance into the joy of its Lord, and no troubles will disturb its peace. May we not think that the holy martyrs enjoyed this grace, in some degree at least, before they laid down their victorious bodies? Surely that was immeasurable strength of love which enraptured their souls, enabling them to laugh at fleshly torments and to yield their lives gladly. But even though the frightful pain could not destroy their peace of mind, it must have impaired somewhat its perfection.
> From chapter X: *"Of the Fourth Degree of Love: Wherein Man Does Not Even Love Self Except for God's Sake."*

At about the same time, the monastic order of the Knights Templars were recognized by the Synod of Troyes in 1129 due to Bernard's strong advocacy of their function as well as his own composition of their rule. The men in this new order took vows of chastity and obedience. Poverty was their symbol and providing food for the poor was their vocation, along with the practice of fasting for great lengths of time. The seal of the Knights Templar (see illustration) was an image of two

(1092-1156), he and Bernard were officially reconciled and Abelard was taken to St. Marcel where he died.

Monastic Theologians

Although not as well known or as notorious as Bernard or Abelard, Hugh of St. Victor (1096-1141) left a lasting legacy in Christian theology. Around 1134 he published his *De sacramentis Christianae fidei* (On the sacraments of the Christian Faith) in which he discusses over thirty sacraments and sacramentals for the Christian believer. Although the work focuses on sacraments, it became the first complete scholastic text which utilized the dialectical method to present topics from creation to the last things. Hugh has been called one of the most influential theologians of the twelfth century. His biblical commentaries straddled the fine line between mystical allegory and literal application of texts.

About the same time, a Benedictine abbess, Hildegard of Bingen (1098-1179), established several convents in Europe and built her own convent in Bingen, Germany (1147-1151). Hildegard is best known for her musical compositions and mystical poetry. She wrote the first extant morality play, *Ordo Virtutum* (Order of Virtues), in which the human soul is depicted as struggling between the devil and the divine virtues. Her writings included a wealth of letters to various leaders throughout the church and government, corresponding with kings, prelates, and at least one emperor. Yet, she was much more than a writer. Hildegard also was a visionary, claiming to see visions of heaven [see illustration], which she dictated to her loyal scribe. In addition to her spirituality, she was very interested in holistic healing and the effects of a variety of natural herbs and plants for medical purposes.

Muslim and Jewish Philosophers

Just before the Second Crusade, the Cluniac abbot, Peter the Venerable (c.1092-1156), had prepared a translation of the *Qur'an* into Latin (1143). Two centuries earlier, an Arab philosopher, Ibn Sina (Latinized as Avicenna, 930-1037), had introduced Greek learning, particularly Aristotle's metaphysics to Islamic scholarship. Near the end of the eleventh century, the Muslim philosopher and *Mujaddid* (renewer of the faith), al-Ghazali (1058-1111), tried to reconcile faith and reason. But, prior to his death, he wrote *The Destruction/Incoherence of Philosophers* in which he argued that the two ways of thinking were truly antagonistic. A half-century later, a young Muslim scholar in the Iberian peninsula, Ibn Rushd (Latinized as Averroes, 1126-1198) proposed a kind of "double truth" in which theology and philosophy are on parallel tracks. It was through the work of Avicenna and especially Averroes that Aristotelian philosophy again entered into western thinking. Within a century, Aristotle would dominate most academic studies in the West as we will see in the next chapter.

A Jewish philosopher, Moses Maimonides (1135-1204), was also instrumental in promoting Aristotelian philosophy among Christian scholars. He served as a prominent rabbi and successful physician in Spain, Egypt, and Morocco, where he read Aristotle in Arabic. His commentaries on the Torah and Mishnah (Jewish code of law) are still held in high regard. He is best known for his work on Jewish ethics and law (Torah), particularly his essay *The Guide to the Perplexed*, which he wrote in Arabic.

> **Maimonides's**
> *13 Principles of Judaism*
> 1. God's existence
> 2. God's unity
> 3. God's spiritual incorporeality
> 4. God's eternity
> 5. Worship only God
> 6. God's revelation through prophets
> 7. Moses as preeminent prophet
> 8. God's Mosaic law
> 9. God's Torah is immutable
> 10. God foreknows human acts
> 11. God rewards good and punishes evil
> 12. Jewish Messiah is coming
> 13. The dead will be raised

Architectural Innovation

One of the major medieval architectural innovations was the use of the ribbed vault (see illustration). Thin ribbings of stone were placed diagonally, transversely, and longitudinally, running from the pillars to the second innovation, the pointed ceiling arch. To support the walls, side pillars, known as "flying buttresses," were constructed outside the building. These architectural approaches enabled the walls to be thinner and the ceilings higher. The overall effect was that these grand buildings were much brighter and provided greater openness of space. The name for this style was labeled "Gothic" (a pejorative term suggesting it was barbarian) in the fifteenth century because it had been a departure from the classical style of earlier Greeks and Romans, which the Renaissance was seeking to restore.

During this century, construction began on the Cathedral of Notre Dame in Paris (1160), the Laon Cathedral (1160) and the Chartres Cathedral (1194).

Gratian's Decretals of Canon Law

Known as the "Father of Canon Law," an almost unknown monk and jurist named Gratian (c.1100-c.1165) assembled a concordance of various ecclesiastical laws from the earliest Christian era to the Lateran Council. The book, *Concordia discordantium canonum* (a harmony of discordant canons), followed a principle of harmonization. Gratian sought to unify the interpretation of several thousand seemingly contradictory laws by classifying the different explanations which had been presented. The result was a textbook for church lawyers to analyze church law and formalize the various practices associated with church discipline. It was used in the Roman Catholic Church until 1918 as the basis for all church legal decisions.

By the end of this century, and drawing on the work of many anonymous theologians, the *Glossa ordinaria* became a standard text for theological study. As the biblical explanations lengthened and as longer discussions of theological topics were introduced, the *Gloss* gradually took the form of a biblical commentary. The biblical text would be situated in the middle of the page (see illustration of a page from Genesis) and the comments of various theologians would be placed around it.

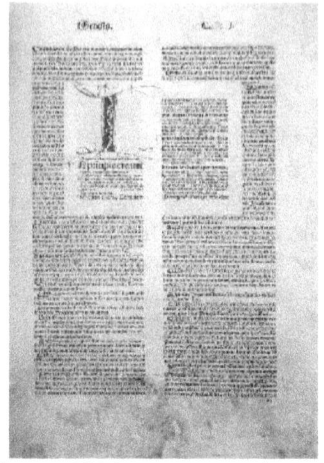

Thomas Becket

As a very gifted young man, Thomas Becket (c.1118/20-1170) was educated in England and France. Attracting the attention of the Archbishop of Canterbury, Thomas was enlisted for several important political and ecclesiastical missions. Because of his administrative skills, he began service to King Henry II (1133-1189, ruled 1154-1189) as Lord Chancellor in 1155. In 1162, Becket became archbishop of Canterbury. His amicable relationship with the king quickly deteriorated, as he withstood attempts by the king to diminish clerical autonomy. Within two years he had to flee to France after refusing to follow the Constitutions of Clarendon, a set of sixteen articles designed by Henry II to restrict the power of the church. (See the 14th century illustration of Henry II and Thomas.) Eight years after becoming archbishop, he was assassinated by four French knights in the Canterbury Cathedral (whether or not they were under orders from Henry has remained uncertain). Three years later he was declared a saint of the church and his grave became an important site of pilgrimages.

Heresiarchs

During the first half of this century, unrest among both clergy and laity began to increase. Strange teachings began to be promulgated. Many of the teachers were labelled heretics, religious teachers or leaders who firmly held and defended teachings contrary to Roman dogma. (The originators of these teachings were identified with the term, *heresiarch*.)

A popular preacher, Peter de Bruys (c.1087-c.1131), for example, attacked devotion to the cross and images; he suggested that infant baptism was useless; and he taught that communion bread and wine only represented Christ's body and blood in the Sacrament. Much of this concern came as a result of the corruption of the clergy and the privileges and property rights usurped by the

13. Church Theologians and Mendicant Movements

The Thirteenth Century

With the enthronement of Pope Innocent III (1161-1216, pope 1198-1216) at the end of the twelfth century, the Roman Catholic Church's power became firmly established in medieval society in the thirteenth century. This century also marks one of the high points for scholastic theology. Yet, the mendicant (begging) orders come of age in this era as reforming agents not only for the monasteries but also for the church itself. The century opened with a call by Innocent II for another crusade.

Innocent III

Probably one of the most powerful popes of the middle ages, Lotario de Segni (1160/61-1216, pope 1198-1216) was made a cardinal-deacon at the age of

twenty-nine by his uncle, Pope Clement III (1130-1191, pope 1187-1191), and upon the death of Celestine III (1106-1198, pope 1191-1198) was elected pope at the age of thirty-seven, taking the name Innocent. His papacy was noteworthy both for his political powers as well as his desire for reform. He asserted that as the moon is related to the sun, so the political system is related to the universal church. After securing a strong power-base in Rome, he became involved in one of the first major political coalitions. With the death of Henry VI of Germany (1165-1197), Otto of Brunswick (1175-1218, ruled 1209-1215) and Frederick of Sicily (1194-1250, ruled 1220-1250) vied for the position. Because Otto promised to support the expanded papal area which Innocent had acquired, the pope chose Otto. Once in power, Otto reneged on his promise and Innocent deposed him, giving the political authority to Frederick.

In 1224, Francis went to Mount La Verna (Alverno) in the northern Apennines of Italy to meditate more deeply on Christ's sufferings. During this

time of nearly complete isolation, only one colleague, Brother Leo, had contact with him, bringing him food occasionally. On September 14, the Feast of the Holy Cross, a seraph (Isaiah 6:2 describes such an angel as having six wings of fire) presented an image of the crucified Christ before Francis, which imprinted on Francis Christ's marks of crucifixion and the lance wound. Brother Leo claimed he saw a "ball of fire" come down to Francis and return to heaven (an angel?) and the *stigmata* (simulations of Christ's wounds) appeared on Francis' body. (See illustration of a fifteenth century painting by Bernardo Strozzi.)

Upon his return to Assisi, Francis visited the Poor Clares, but experienced some kind of a terrible eye disease along with severe headaches. The story continues that he went into seclusion and darkness for fifty days and was tormented by mice during the whole time. Finally, cauterization was tried (a hot iron was inserted into his sinuses), but this failed to cure his eye pain and headaches. Francis died on October 3, 1226 and within two years was canonized by Pope Gregory IX.

Popular legends surrounding Francis' life are recorded in the *Fioretti* ("little flowers"), a fourteenth century composition. Among these anecdotes are several about his care for all of creation, where Francis would refer to animals and even the sun and moon as "brothers" or "sisters." (His "Canticle of the Sun"—*Laudes Creaturarum,* "Praise of Creation"—appears in many church hymn books as "All Creatures of Our God and King.") Thus Francis was named the "patron saint of ecology" by the Roman Catholic Church in 1979.

The overall goal of Francis was to seek Christian perfection in this life. Three approaches were taken by Francis: (1) to unite with God through prayer, (2) to take up the apostolate—missionary work, and (3) to imitate Christ literally and perfectly. The Franciscan life was simple: become like Christ by imitating Francis. As wandering evangelists, the Friars Minor also practiced their respective trades—often taking the role of teachers. The Rule required that the friars give up all possessions. Modeling themselves after the description of Christ in Philippians 2:7 which says that Christ "emptied Himself," the Franciscans became exemplary illustrations of the mendicant movement.

The Dominicans: Order of Friars Preachers

In contrast to the Franciscans, yet consistent with the mendicant movement, a young priest named Dominic de Guzman (1170-1221) followed the *vita apostolica* (apostolic life) by rejecting possessions for the sake of spreading the gospel. His newly founded order, named after him, was focused on study and eradicating heresy through proclamation of the truth. Born to a well-to-do family around 1170 and trained in the Augustinian order as a canon regular in Castilian Spain, Dominic was moved to preach against the Cathari and Albigensian heresies early in the thirteenth century (see below).

Recognizing the need for an educated clergy, Dominic established several monastic schools. In 1206, he established a female convent to safeguard  the women of the region from heretical teachings and crusader contact. In 1215, the community which had formed around him was recognized by the papacy at the Lateran Council specifically for the propagation of true doctrine, good morals, and the extinction of heresy. A year later, Dominic provided an official rule for his Order of Friars Preachers but more commonly known as Dominicans. The "Black Friars," as they were also known from their habit made of black wool, were placed directly under the pope of Rome, rather than under local bishops or abbots. (See illustration by Fra Angelico illustrating Dominic's black habit over his white cassock.) A pun on their name in Latin, *Dominicanus*, was that they were the "Lord's watchdogs" (*domini + canis*).

The following year, Pope Honorius III (1150-1227, pope 1216-1227), who succeeded Innocent III, sent several Dominicans to Paris to supervise the university faculty. In order to keep Dominic at the Lateran, Honorius appointed him as his theological advisor with the title, "Master of the Sacred Palace," a position traditionally held by Friar Preachers ever since. Around this time, tradition suggests that Dominic developed the prayers used for reciting the Rosary. Somewhat later Dominic sent the members of his small community to various schools not only to supervise, but also to become better educated. In the meantime, he himself traveled throughout France, Spain, and Italy, helping the poor and preaching repentance. By 1220, the Order had grown to eight provinces: Spain, Provence, France, Lombardy, Rome, Germany, Hungary, and England.

As mendicant preaching-friars, the Dominicans relied heavily on financial and physical support by residents of the growing cities. This new class of urban citizens had sufficient wealth to supply the needs of these itinerant preachers, who were developing the art of sermon-making. An early master general of the Dominicans, Humbert de Romans (c.1190/1200-1277) provided useful advice for the preaching task in his book, *On the Formation of Preachers*. Key to the sermon, he asserted, was an emphasis upon life-applications and a positive recognition of various vocations which carried out their Christian responsibilities in the world.

Although Dominic died on August 6, 1221, his administrative ability created a strong, yet efficient organization through representative governance. In addition, the colleges and seminaries which the order founded, served not only their members, but also produced some of the great medieval theologians, such as Thomas Aquinas (see below). This is in line with their rule, which stated, "Study is not the end of the order, but is most necessary to secure its ends, namely ordinance. Many of the other precepts adopted at this momentous council are still binding on Roman Catholics (such as the Easter obligation of making a confession and receiving Holy Communion at least annually).

Inquisition

Begun as a measure to control heretical teachings of specific groups in 1231, Pope Gregory IX (1145-1241, pope 1227-1241) placed the inquisitors, mostly Dominican and Franciscan friars, directly under his jurisdiction. He collected earlier papal decretals and canonical decisions, following the style of the Gratian *Decretals* (c.1140), to create a definitive statement of canon law for the church. Gregory's papal bull, *Excommunicamus*, initially required that heretics be banished and their earthly goods confiscated, although the death penalty was also carried out on occasion. The institution of inquisitors was permanently established in 1252 by Pope Innocent IV (c.1195-1254, pope 1243-1254). Among the sanctions encouraged by him was the use of torture. The death penalty by burning at the stake was required for persons holding heretical views considered dangerous. Later inquisitions, particularly the Spanish (from 1478-1520s) and the Protestant (from the 1560s through the mid-seventeenth century), followed a similar goal of wiping out an opposing heretical religious group.

Theological Philosophy

The thirteenth century is marked as one of the greatest theological centuries since the era of the apostolic fathers. With the rediscovery of Aristotle (chapter 12), a new interest was raised in explaining the Christian faith in philosophical terms. In addition, the rise of universities provided a venue for promulgating such new teachings. These schools were originally formed as guilds of scholars—students and teachers—who sought to standardize and certify professional competencies in their several academic fields. Most schools offered basic education in the liberal arts, but some schools tended to specialize. For example, medical students would go to Montpelier (1220) or Salerno (9th century), law students attended Bologna (1088) and Cambridge (1209), and the centers of theological studies were Oxford (1167) and Paris (1150).

The method of learning was mostly lecturing and disputations. Disputations were technical questions (*quastiones disputatae*) posed by a

---

A Medieval University Education:
An aspiring theologian would be required to begin his studies in philosophy and the humanities with the Faculty of Arts and then proceed to the Faculty of Theology where he would become an "auditor" (hearer). He would then progress through the following levels: first as a "Bachelor of the Bible," then a "Bachelor of the Sentences." He would move on to become a "Formed Bachelor," and a "Licensed Master," who could teach underclassmen, and finally he would achieve the highest level, a "Doctor of Theology" (Teacher), giving him ecclesiastical responsibility for teaching the faith. Similar steps would be required in medicine and law.

---

professor, which the student was then required to answer, based upon a reasoned and logical presentation of Scriptural evidence and the support from ancient writers. Such an approach reached a high level in the *summae*, most particularly by Thomas Aquinas (see below).

lighter stone vaulting, and tall towers. The thinner walls were supported by flying buttresses (exterior supports) which also allowed for larger stained glass windows.

Besides the Chartres Cathedral, representative of this period include Notre Dame in Paris; Reims Cathedral, Strasbourg Cathedral in France, Antwerp Cathedral in Belgium, Cologne Cathedral in Germany, Salisbury Cathedral, Canterbury Cathedral and Lincoln Cathedral in England, and several in Austria, Italy, Spain, and Portugal.

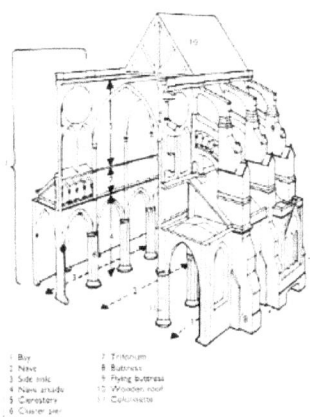

The Last Crusades?

Pope Honorius III (1150-1227, pope 1216-1227), who had come to the papal throne in 1215, authorized the last official crusade (the Fifth) to receive papal approval. Crusaders were sent against the Muslim stronghold in Egypt in 1217. Four years later, in 1221, they had to flee Cairo after severe flooding of the Nile prevented their continued military activities.

In 1228, Emperor Frederick II (1194-1250, ruled 1220-1250) of the Holy Roman Empire led a sixth crusade to the Holy Land. Having knowledge of the Arabic language, he was able to gain jurisdiction over most of Jerusalem (except for the Temple Mount which the Muslims considered sacred). As a result, he assumed the title, King of Jerusalem. Frederick was subsequently excommunicated at the First Council of Lyons (1245) for trying to make the church part of his imperial territory. This same Council instigated a crusade (1248-1254) led by Louis IX of France (1214-1270, ruled 1226-1270), which failed miserably. Initially relying upon diplomatic maneuvering, Saladin (see chapter twelve) and his allies moved from northern Iran into the center of Jerusalem to the Church of the Holy Sepulcher, where innocent victims who were seeking asylum were murdered.

Louis IX of France (1214-1270, ruled 1226-1270) set out in 1248 to eradicate the Muslims in Egypt, but was captured at Mansura, so that seventh crusade also failed. His armies had suffered both financial and physical decimation due to an exorbitant ransom demanded by the Muslims and severe dysentery experienced by thousands of his soldiers. His second crusade, the eighth crusade, ended with his death in 1270. As a result Islamic troops slowly but surely overpowered the last of the Latin territory, the city of Acre.

For the next several centuries, crusades were invoked against the Muslims or Turks until the sixteenth century. Only occasionally were they carried out with any actual military endeavor. Thus, for all practical purposes, the thirteenth century saw the last of the crusades.

Holy Land Abandoned

After the fall of the city of Acre to the Muslims in 1291, the last crusaders departed from the Holy Land. The consequences of the crusading centuries are

never was granted full teaching privileges as a doctor. In 1323, a couple of years

after his graduation, the chancellor of Oxford filed charges of heresy against him and Ockham was summoned before the pope in Avignon to defend himself. No formal action developed from the charges, but he remained in Avignon, becoming involved with the dispute among the Franciscans over whether they should possess property or not. Finally in 1329, he publicly opposed Pope John XXII's (1224-1334, pope 1316-1334) toleration of property ownership by the Franciscans. The Pope excommunicated him and Ockham fled Avignon for Munich. He died twenty years later, probably of the Black Death.

Ockham was a fiercely independent scholar and original thinker who followed in the Franciscan tradition, although was a critic of both Aquinas and Scotus. He is most exemplary of the philosophical view known as "nominalism," from Latin word for "name." Nominalists believed that ideas are only names of concrete things. Truth is attained only by investigating those specific things, using reason.

Advocating Scripture as the single and sufficient source and norm for church teachings, he attacked transubstantiation as a rationalization of something which should be accepted by faith alone. Also parting ways with Aquinas who taught that God necessarily followed the dictates of high reason, he followed Scotus' idea that God's freely ordained plan of salvation included some human participation. God will save everyone who does their best (*facere quod in se est*, "do what in you is"). As a result, he said that a person could perform works which God could consider good; that is, they were congruent with natural human abilities (*de congruo*). God would then reward such actions with the gift of grace (*de condigno*), thus enabling believers to do the good works which earned salvation. Ockham also rejected Scotus' idea of predestination, arguing that predestination was always based upon God's foreknowledge of the works (or lack of good works) which a person performed. These teachings would remain in Roman Catholic piety and dogma.

> Ockham's "Razor"
> The simplest version of his decisive statement, also known as the economy of explanation, states: *Numquam ponenda est pluralitas sine necessitate*, "Plurality is not to be postulated without necessity." In other words, one should always strive to consider or accomplish something using the least number of assumptions. The simplest explanation is best. All knowledge is intuitive, he believed. One knows something because it is either observed or revealed in Scripture. There are no independent "universals" as earlier Christian theologians had postulated, following the ancient Greeks.

Although never forming a specific theological "school," Ockhamist thought continued in Europe for several more centuries under the "nominalist" perspective. Advocates included the French theologians Pierre d'Ailly (1350-1420) and Jean de Gerson (1363-1429) and the German scholar, Gabriel Biel (1420-1495), whose teachings would influence Martin Luther in the sixteenth orthodox using Augustinian and Thomistic terms. Unfortunately, the pope found twenty-eight heretical ideas among Eckhart's sermons and he was ultimately condemned two years after his death.

Johannes Tauler

Another German Dominican and disciple of Eckhart, Johannes Tauler (ca.1300-1361) was more cautious in his preaching, although just as popular, especially in light of the devastating consequence on society of the Black Plague (see below). As Eckhart, Tauler also emphasized faith and the working of the Spirit to create that faith. Even the sacraments require faith to be beneficial, he proclaimed. Tauler did emphasize the idea of the "spark" in one's soul, but he differed from Eckhart in that he identified it as being God-given. Tauler asserted that clergy and laity were equal before God and the elevation of priestly authority was unscriptural. He is credited with elevating the role of Mary as a mediator before God and her Son, Jesus. Two centuries later, Martin Luther found Tauler's sermons attractive as a source of "pure theology," but not his mysticism. In Tauler's stress on self-denial and suffering, he demonstrated the human need for God's grace.[1]

Henry Suso

Another mystic of this century was Henry Suso (c. 1295-1366). His *Little Book of Eternal Wisdom* was printed in Germany around 1325. In this practical guide, Henry presented a mystical treatise on how to meditate on Christ's Passion.

Such meditations became popular sources for personal devotions, especially among the cloistered nuns and Beguines (See sidebar below) who had spiritualized the ideal of absolute poverty by emphasizing interior self-sacrifice. Henry's sermons accentuated God's love which motivated people to return that love back to Him. Such expressions of love, he said, were in the form of suffering, which he practiced throughout his life by starving himself and even administering bloody flagellations. (See medieval illustration of flagellants.)

---

[1] Martin Luther referred to Tauler early in his teaching ministry; the phrase is from his letter to Spalatin. See LW 25 "Lectures on Romans: Glosses and Scholia," ed. Hilton C. Oswald (St Louis: Concordia, 1972), 366; LW 31 "Explanation of the Ninety-Five Theses," ed. Harold J. Grimm (Philadelphia: Fortress Press, 1957), 128-129, 178; as well as LW 48 "Letters," ed. Gottfried Krodel (Philadephia: Fortress Press, 1963), 35-36 "Letter to Spalatin, December 14, 1516."

"mystical betrothal" to Christ (see illustration of Giovanni de Paolo's painting of her mystic marriage) and began to devote her activities to care for the poor. She is most remembered for her letter writing campaign to most of the European leaders from around 1374 until her death. She claimed to have received the "stigmata" as had Francis of Assisi, but only invisibly. During the Babylonian Captivity, she decried the activities of the church as "stink in my nose with the stench of mortal sin."

Bridget of Sweden

Bridget of Sweden (c.1303-1373), a wealthy widow, who after her husband's death in 1344 claimed that she received many visions of Christ. These "heavenly revelations," as they were called, were written down in Latin. Performing great acts of charity in Rome, she worked for the return and restoration of the papal seat in Rome. In 1370, shortly before Pope Urban V's (1310-1370, pope 1362-1370) return to Avignon, he recognized a new community of nuns which followed Bridget's Order of the Most Holy Savior for their works of mercy and service to the poor.

Hesychasm

Mystical ideas were not limited to European Christianity. Orthodox Christians in the East also experienced an increase in mystical writings and practices. Most significant in this century was a controversy over a special form of meditation, *hesychasm* (Greek, ἡσυχασμός "quietness, inner stillness, or silence"). This experiential prayer practice may involve body postures and quiet breathing, similar to some yoga methods, although the prayer is never to

> **The Jesus Prayer**
> This simple prayer, "Jesus Christ, Son of God, have mercy on me a sinner," continues to be prayed, along with quiet breathing and meditation. It is a popular model for *hesychastic* prayer.

be considered a mindless mantra. Gregory Palamas (1296-1359), a monk from Mt. Athos and later archbishop of Thessalonica, defended the monastic practice during a decade of controversial synods held in Constantinople between 1341 and 1351. *Hesychasm* is an official dogma of Orthodox Christianity. The "Jesus Prayer" is one of the most popular forms of *hesychasm* still practiced by many Christians.

Call for Reform

A fifteenth Ecumenical Council, the Council of Vienne (1311-1313) was called by Pope Clement V (c.1264-1314, pope 1305-1314) to respond to the cries for reform both from within and from outside the church. One of the decrees issued by the council was against the "abominable sects" of Beguines and Beghards, who were accused of three major errors: "antinomianism" (repudiating divine law), "spiritualism" (eliminating any outward aids for worship), and

power among the several Italian city-states—Florence, Milan, Naples (known as "the Kingdom of the Two Sicilies"), and Venice.

Regrettably, the other significant action taken by the Council was the condemnation of Jan Hus. After hearing the case against him, he was handed over to civil authorities and burned at the stake on July 6, 1415 (see illustration from the 1485 *Spiezer Chronik* manuscript), in spite of having been given safe passage to and from the Council by Sigismund. As a result, he remains a national hero of the Bohemians. Wycliffe was also condemned posthumously and his bones were disinterred and burned.

Five years after the Council, the Bohemian followers of Hus prepared a common statement to be implemented by several conflicting groups. The "Four Articles of Prague" demanded that God's Word be the basis of all preaching; the laity be given the communion cup along with the bread; apostolic poverty be practiced; and both clergy and laity live a strict life in conformity with Scripture. The three groups which joined together were known as the Utraquists (*utraque*, Latin for "both," indicating that both bread and wine were used in communion), the Calixtines (*calix*, Latin for "cup," for those who only wished to receive the chalice), and the Taborites (named for the fortress of the more political group of Wycliffe and Hus disciples). The Taborites and Utraquists, along with a group of Waldenses formed the *Unitas Fratrum* (United Brethrens of Bohemia), which became the spiritual ancestors of the Moravians.

Humanistic Scholars
Nicolas of Cusa

Born to lowly peasants, Nicolas of Cusa (1401-1464) studied canon law, mathematics and astronomy at the University of Padua. Although not an actual humanist, he did not follow the traditional scholastic approach to knowledge either. His views have been called "Neoplatonic mysticism," and first appeared in his 1440 philosophical treatise, *De docta ignorantia* (On Learned Ignorance). There he stated that God unites all things in Himself and all things come from Him. This unity of all things is not recognized by using discursive reasoning, but is only a result of a kind of intelligent-intuition, which he called "learned ignorance." He asked, "How is it that knowing is not-knowing?" By use of a variety of metaphors and mathematical analogies, he believed humans could appreciate God, although not understand Him.

and land holdings in Rome for centuries. Using philological and historical methods, Valla proved without a doubt that this supposed fourth century document was a forgery from around the 8th century. He also proved that the writings attributed to Dionysius the Areopagite, the supposed follower of Paul, were unauthentic. He demonstrated that the Apostles' Creed was not a composition dictated section by section by each of the apostles, but rather a product of early Christian baptismal formulations.

Perhaps no one invention has been more accurately credited with creating an all-encompassing transformation in culture than the moveable type 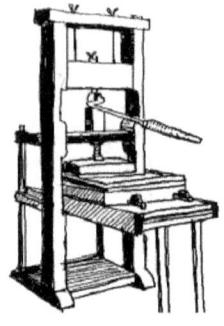 printing press (see illustration) of Johannes Gutenberg (c.1398-1468). It was in 1450 that he produced the first Bible, the Latin Vulgate, on such a press. Within a half-century over two hundred printing establishments had arisen in Europe, providing opportunities for the dissemination of Renaissance learning and (later) Reformation teaching in large quantities and at reasonable prices. Estimates suggest that more than thirty thousand publications were issued before 1500. By the end of the century, ninety-two editions of the Vulgate were printed, in addition to complete Bibles in German (1466), Italian (1471), French (1478), Spanish (1478, although initially burned, 1492 republished), and Czech (1488 and 1489).

Art and Artists

Artistic expressions are perhaps the most visible characteristic of the Renaissance, especially as this was disseminated from the heart of Renaissance thought in Italy. Painting expressed a grander presentation of true perspective, anatomical accuracy of human forms flourished, impressive sculptures, which reflected earlier Greek and Roman influences, were produced on an extravagant scale, and architectural advances transformed the great cities of Europe.

Florentine Artists

Consider the following artists who came into prominence during this century: Donatello (1386-1466) sculpted and painted in Florence and was a key  in making that city a center of humanistic art. Botticelli (1444-1510), born as Alessandro di Mariano di Vanni Filipepi, characterized the golden age of Florentine art. Most of his works were religious in character, although his most popular work, the "Birth of Venus" (*La Nascita di Venere*, 1486) was commissioned by the Medici. Leonardo da Vinci (1452-1519) born near Florence, Italy, was the epitome of the "Renaissance man." Besides several captured Constantinople in 1453, the reality of union was permanently lost. Attention to and the influence of Eastern Christianity slipped away until it reemerged in Russia two centuries later. One other feature of the Ferrara-Florence Council was an agreement in 1439 with the Armenian Orthodox Church in which, for the first time, the Roman Catholic Church officially listed the seven sacraments—baptism, confirmation, communion, penance, last rights, ordination, and marriage.

Pope Nicholas V (1397-1455, pope 1447-1455) among his many humanistic endeavors, founded the Vatican library and desired to make Rome the center of humanistic culture and art. His plans for St. Peter's basilica represented the full flowering of papal powers and humanistic grandeur. His successor, Calixtus III (1455-1458), ignored the humanistic tendencies of his predecessor and focused, however briefly, on trying to organize a crusade to remove the Turks from Constantinople.

Wars, Nationalism and Spirituality

The Hundred Years' War (1337-1453) (see chapter 14) between England and France ended in somewhat of a stalemate, yet feudalism had significantly faltered and finally failed. Before the end of this series of wars, France, under King Charles VII (1403-1462, ruled 1422-1461) had secured relief from papal interference and especially taxation. His successor, Louis XI (1423-1483, ruled 1461-1483), secured sovereign rule over the lower nobles, thereby eliminating feudalism in France and establishing a centralized state for his successor, Charles VIII (1470-1498, ruled 1483-1498). The church in France was largely under royal control.

For thirty years between 1455 and 1485 two royal families in England claimed the throne, each with an insignia of a rose. The House of York (white rose) and the House of Lancaster (red rose) vied for control. Thus, the name of this conflict is "the War of the Roses." When Henry VII (1457-1509, ruled 1485-1509) came to power, the English people sought stability through a strong government in order to avoid further civil war. Indeed, the Catholic Church had come under the English sovereign's authority.

Joan of Arc (1412-1431)
A French peasant girl with visionary messages aroused the French people to a national fervor. Known as "the maid of Orleans," she captured the hearts and ideals of her compatriots. After leading a victorious battle against English and Burgundian troops to save her city, she was captured by them, tried as a heretic, and put to death for witchcraft and false teachings.

security—both physically and spiritually. Popular devotional practices often expressed a great fear of death and the devil in the face of the lingering results of the plague. Witchcraft increased as superstitious spirituality spread throughout Europe. In 1484, Pope Innocent VIII (1432-1492, pope 1484-1492) produced a bull declaring that Germany was full of witches. In 1489, two self-proclaimed inquisitors prepared a celebrated work, *The Hammer of Witches* (in German, *Der Hexenhammer*), which argued for the existence of witches and then told how to overpower them.

Renaissance Papacies

With the papacy of Pope Pius II (1405-1464, pope 1458-1464), a reclamation of papal powers occurred. Although prior to being elected pope, he had been an advocate of the conciliar movement, early in his pontificate, he promoted his bull *Execrabilis* (1460), which prohibited any further appeals to church councils over against papal powers. Any such proposal for a council by a non-pope would be considered heresy. Pope Paul II (1417-1471, pope 1464-1471) continued the humanistic tendencies of the age, particularly as an avid collector of antiquities. A semblance of sanctifying sanity is seen in his papacy, as he sought to curb simony (selling church positions for money), restore a more conservative life-style among the Curia, and only appoint men of high spiritual caliber to papal offices.

A Franciscan friar and scholar was elected pope in 1471, Sixtus IV. However, he had greater political interests and sought to make Rome the center of Italian life. As a scholar, he reorganized the Vatican library and attracted many scholars and artists to Rome. His Sistine Chapel (named after him) is only one of many building projects which he funded through higher taxes during his extravagant pontificate. He was also known for his political ambitions and his unabashed practice of nepotism. In 1476, he introduced as the official article of faith that indulgences could be purchased for souls even in purgatory.

Innocent VIII (1432-1492, pope 1484-1492), the next pope (see illustration), was anything but "innocent." Prior to his ordination as a priest, he had been married and fathered several illegitimate children along with one son (some scholars suggest he had fathered sixteen children in all). His appointees as cardinals lived as worldly princes—hunting, gaming, and womanizing. His political activities included receiving generous "gifts" from a Turkish sultan for keeping a rival brother imprisoned in Rome.

In 1492, the successor of Innocent VIII was Alexander VI (1431-1503, pope 1492-1503). Intimately acquainted with papal administration and intrigue, Rodrigo Borgia, was an extremely wealthy Spanish nobleman who had purchased the chair of Peter. He did much to improve the city and culture of Rome, encouraging an expansion of the already wide-spread development of the city. He was also notorious in his personal conduct and used his children as pawns in ecclesiastical procurements and national alliances. His son, Cesare Borgia (1473-1507), was similarly unprincipled, having been appointed cardinal as a teenager, a position he later rejected in order to develop his political ambitions of leading Italy. Caesar's sister, the pope's daughter, Lucrezia Borgia (1480-1519), was given in marriage several times, all for political purposes.

While embodying the fatal flaws of the papacy, these popes did represent the Renaissance of Italy.

An Italian Reformer

From the city of Florence came an interesting itinerant preacher, Girolamo Savonarola (1452-1498) (see illustration). After studying to become a 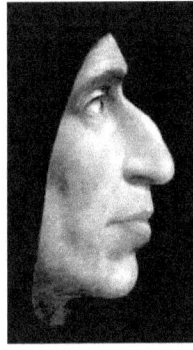 medical doctor, he entered a Dominican monastery in 1475 where he experienced some kind of mystical vision. He became prior of the Florentine monastery, San Marco, which he restored as an "observant" congregation. Feeling compelled to be an itinerant missionary, his superiors gave him leave of the monastery, although he had little initial success on his missions. After several more years of preaching and teaching, his message settled on three key themes—the church needed to be punished for its corruption, the church will be renewed, and such reforming events are imminent. In 1480, the great Florentine nobleman, Lorenzo de Medici (1435-1488), "the Magnificent," called him back to Florence. In spite of his own scandalous life-style as a "Renaissance man," Lorenzo failed to reverse Savonarola's reforming movement and died in 1488 with Savonarola's blessing.

When Charles VIII of France drove Piero Medici (1472-1503) from Florence in 1494, Savonarola's popularity increased, since it appeared to be the apocalyptic tribulation he had predicted. Savonarola tried to turn the city into a Christian democracy. The new republic of Florence, freed from French domination, provided him with a great opportunity to carry out his reform. During the carnival seasons of 1496 and 1497, Florence experienced "the bonfires of the vanities"—the public burning of games and cards, extravagant wigs and colorful cosmetics, gaudy baubles and ornate jewelry, lewd pictures and bawdy books. Upon hearing of Savonarola's activities, Pope Alexander VI placed him under a papal ban, particularly because of his denunciation of papal authority. The following year, Savonarola was falsely condemned as a heretic, hanged, and then burned at the stake and his ashes thrown into the river. Luther would later commend Savonarola for his piety and evangelical teaching.

The Century Ends in Explorations

In 1488, Bartolomeu Dias (c.1451-1500) named the tip of southern Africa, the Cape of Good Hope, as he sought a navigational route to India. Exploration of the world continued to expand as the now famous "discovery" of the Americas by Christopher Columbus (1451-1506) in 1492 and excursion of work. The age of reformation was beginning to be evident on the surface as well as the soul of society.

Nationalism

No one form of government existed throughout the sixteenth century. From loosely connected federations of villages to local principalities under a duke or prince; from kingdoms to free imperial cities, a diversity of political constellations held sway over the growing populations of what later became Europe.

The Holy Roman Empire was slowly disappearing. What remained in name of the feudal rule which had dominated the scene for centuries was disintegrating as peasants, merchants, and princes began to grow stronger. The Holy Roman Empire was more Germanic than it was European—emperors were chosen by seven electors, all but one from Germany, and almost all emperors after the thirteenth century were chosen from the Hapsburg dynasty in Vienna. Through political and marital alliances, these emperors had consolidated much of European political control.

Five emperors served as dynastic rulers during the sixteenth century of the Holy Roman Empire. Beginning his reign in the late fifteenth century, Maximillian I (1459-1519, ruled 1493-1519) was succeeded by his son, Charles V (1500-1558, ruled 1519-1530). Charles's tumultuous imperial rule is noteworthy both in the person of Martin Luther and the rise of the Reformation as well as the fact that the Ottoman Turks besieged his capital in 1529, giving greater need for unity among the European nations, and the rise of Protestantism. We will read more about his Reformation connection in the next section of this chapter. Charles was succeeded by Ferdinand I in 1556 (1503-1564, ruled 1556-1564) and Maximillian II (1527-1576, ruled 1564-1576), who ruled only a dozen years and was followed by Rudolph II (1552-1612, ruled 1576-1612).

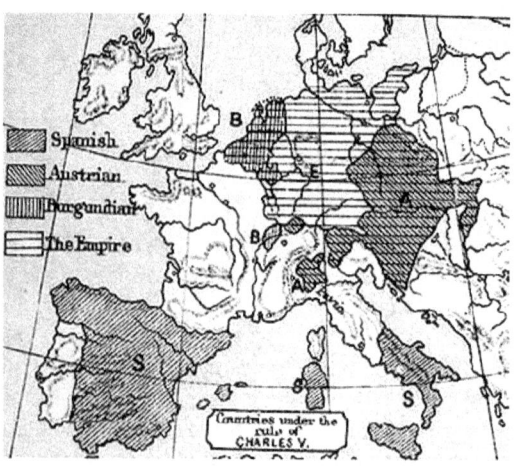

Although a political reality first in the nineteenth century, several nascent nation-states were emerging during the sixteenth century—France, England, Spain, Portugal and the Netherlands. Each of these nation-states developed a professional army, equipped with new fire-power in the form of recently imported gunpowder. France had experienced strong dynastic leadership for almost a half-millennium and only in the sixteenth century did it lose some of its influence to Spain. In contrast, following the War of the Roses (1455-1485) and the consolidation of political power under Henry VII (1457-1509), who had married a son to Catherine of Aragon (1485-1536, queen 1509-1533) and a daughter to the king of Scotland. his successor, Henry VIII (1491-1547), inherited a prospering English empire. Charles V also ruled as Charles I in Spain, succeeding Ferdinand and Isabella, until abdicating to his son, Philip II (1527-1598, ruled 1556-1598) in 1556, thereby continuing the Spanish hegemony over the seas, particularly in the New World. Italy remained divided into numerous city-states and Germany struggled to unite several strong feudal states as the Holy Roman Empire grew weaker by the decade. Yet, the process was set in motion for greater national autonomy.

Cities grew in population and a new urban middle class arose, the *bourgeoisie* (French, "borough-dwellers," as distinct from the rural peasants). These city-dwellers were very much aware of what was needed politically, economically, and culturally. Merchants and guilds of craftsmen became prominent community leaders, often competing with various ecclesiastical bureaucrats for revenue and influence. Cities such as Lisbon and Seville, Brussels and Antwerp became more important than the great Italian cities of Venice, Florence, and Genoa, which had been reduced by Turkish incursions.

The Ottoman Empire (see map) posed a decisive danger throughout most this century. Holding lands around the south and eastern shores of the Mediterranean Sea, these Muslims maintained a constant threat to the remaining Christian regions of Europe. In 1571, at the Battle of Lepanto, the papal fleet reduced the Turkish power permanently.

Discovery

Humanism and nationalism were at the heart of the great geographic discoveries of the century. The Portuguese had long been the leaders in exploration, particularly moving down and around the African coast as well as crossing the Atlantic to a new world. Coupled with the humanist desire for discovery, these navigators established Christian outposts at many of their trading sites which were built around the western coast of Africa and, finally after 1497, in India.

Exploration of the New World began in earnest during the first years of the sixteenth century. In 1500, the Portuguese nobleman and explorer, Pedro Cabral (1468-1520), sailed to South America and claimed the region which would  later be Brazil. Around 1510-1513, the Spanish explorer, Vasco de Balboa (1475-1519), crossed the Panama isthmus and reached the Pacific Ocean (see illustration). Another Spaniard, Ponce de Leon (1474-1520) arrived in Florida around 1513, seeking the proverbial "fountain of youth." By 1541, Hernando de Soto (1497-1542) explored much of South America for Spain and then directed his attention to what became southern United States, particularly the region around the Mississippi River, where he died. By 1555, the Portuguese had established a significant number of trading posts in Brazil and along the coast of Africa. In addition, they founded settlements all the way to India and what became known as the East Indies and then further East to Japan.

The Spanish discoveries in the New World, following the initial successes of Christopher Columbus (1451-1506), provided a unique development in the life of the church. One of the objectives of his exploration into the New World, claimed Christopher Columbus, was the conversion of the Amerindians. During the first years of the sixteenth century, the popes allowed the Spanish sovereign to have enormous authority. In a little more than a decade, Hernán Cortés (1485-1547) overthrew the Aztec state and founded Mexico City (1521), Francisco Pizarro (1478-1541) entered Peru (1532) and established a base for Spanish conquest in South America.

These Spanish conquests ignored papal influence and the colonial church instead came under the appointees of the Spanish crown. As a result, many of the bishops sent to the New World were politicians with little spiritual strength or pastoral concern to direct the development of this mission field. Enslavement and cruelties were not only tolerated by the church, but often were carried out in her name.

Yet, in the New World there were monastic missionaries accompanying the explorers. The Franciscans, Dominicans, and later Jesuits, who came with each ship, often stayed with the indigenous people in the New World, living with them and helping them develop in the face of disastrous European settlements. For example, Dominican Antonio Montesinos (+1545) in Santo Domingo preached a sermon against the European exploitation of the indigenous peoples there. As Justo Gonzalez reports:

> The system of *encomiendas*—trusts—was the main abuse against which the Dominicans protested. It was forbidden to enslave the Indians. But, supposedly in order to civilize them and to teach them Christian doctrine, groups of them were "entrusted" to a settler. In exchange for the settler's guidance, the Indians were to work for him. The result was even worse than outright slavery, for those who held trusts—the *encomenderos*—had no investment in the Indians, and therefore no reason to be concerned for their well-being. (*The Story of Christianity*, 1:382)

After hearing Montesinos's sermons, Bartolomé de Las Casas (1474-1566), the first priest to be ordained in the New World, realized that the Christian faith was incompatible with holding individuals as "trusts." He released the enslaved Indians under his care and began a lifetime of protest against the practice. He died at the age of ninety-two, having failed to make a significant change in the actual colonial culture, but at least protesting the handling of the native peoples.

In New Spain, the name given to the Aztec empire known now as Mexico, the Spanish conquistador, Cortés, introduced a Catholic presence. After seeing how the non-monastic priests often looked only for the comforts of home, he requested a dozen Franciscan priests from Emperor Charles V. Although these priests sometimes performed mass baptisms with little instruction, they lived among the people and provided contact points for the people.

In 1536, the first bishop of New Spain was ordained, Juan de Zumárraga (1468-1548). Recognizing the need for reform through education, he brought the first printing press to the western hemisphere to publish Christian material for the communities. In 1539, he opened the minor orders of the Catholic Church to Amerindians, although not those of deacon, priest, or bishop. In 1588, the king of Spain issued an order declaring that Amerindians could enter priestly and monastic orders. Bishop Zumárraga, later to become archbishop, became concerned with heresy and in a period of less than ten years, almost 150 people were tried for false doctrine. In 1573, Spain adopted a policy of pacifying rather than conquering the New World peoples. Conversions to Christianity were to be voluntary and peaceful, not coerced.

Two Italian Jesuit missionaries traveled from India to the Portuguese colony of Macau in the latter quarter of this century. From that peninsula of China, Matteo Ricci (1552-1610) and Michele Ruggieri (1543-1607) entered mainland China around 1582, settling in Zhaoqing in southern China. There they prepared a Chinese catechism and a Portuguese-Chinese dictionary for future mission workers. (See illustration depicting Ricci with Xu Guangqi, who helped establish Christian work in China.)

Along with the practical, political, and mercantile causes associated with the magnificent land acquisitions by the European nation states, the Gospel was being carried "into all the world." Yet, as the historian, Kenneth Latourette, noted about this century, "If a Christian motive entered into the initial voyages, results followed which were a tragic contradiction of that motive" (*Christianity Through the Ages*, 164).

Commerce

Coupled with nationalism and discovery was the increase in commercial activities during this century, sometimes referred to as "the Commercial Revolution." Feudalism as an economic system (as well as a form of governance) declined as both peasants and townspeople gained some fiscal independence.

published, known as the "Polyglot Bible" (Greek, "several" + "languages"), containing Hebrew, Latin, and Greek texts of the Old Testament, an Aramaic Targum of the Pentateuch with a Latin translation, and the entire New Testament in the Greek with the Latin Vulgate.

Perhaps one of the most outstanding teachers at the University of Paris, Jacques Lefèvre d'Étaples (1455-1536), advocated the Scriptures as the sole authority for Christian doctrine and life. As a Bible teacher, he encouraged his students to return to a more primitive New Testament style of Christianity along with a revived Aristotelianism and restored Platonism. To that end, he worked tirelessly to translate the Latin Vulgate into French, producing a commentary on the Psalms with five different Latin versions in 1509 and a complete French New Testament by 1523.

Another Parisian-born humanist was the printer, Robert I Estienne (Robertus Stephenus) (1503-1558), who late in life converted from Catholicism to Calvinism. Besides his print shops' extremely high quality typography, he is remembered as the first printer to introduce verse numberings into the Greek New Testament in 1551.

Desiderius Erasmus of Rotterdam (1466-1536), undoubtedly the most gifted Renaissance scholar of the century, was recognized as the humanist's

humanist. An exceptional linguist, he loved Latin, but also worked proficiently in Greek and Hebrew. His publication of a critical edition of the New Testament in Greek in 1516 provided a magnificent resource for the Protestant Reformation. In 1511, he prepared a satirically critical social commentary, *In Praise of Folly*. The Greek title, *Moria Encomium*, was a pun on his friendship with Thomas More. (See below and chapter 15.) Erasmus's humanistic qualities led him to reject the amassing of scholastic details. Instead, he advocated an emphasis on Christian morality as the key to a revitalized Christianity. Eschewing the superstitions which had enveloped the piety of the church, Erasmus saw true piety as resting in the ethical teachings of Christ. We will discuss Erasmus more in the part B of this chapter.

In 1526 William Tyndale (c.1494-1536) published an English translation of the New Testament, using Luther's 1522 Testament as a guide. Because he was declared a heretic, it had to be printed in Germany. He was assisted by Miles Coverdale (1488-1568) in translating the Old Testament and a complete Bible was printed in 1535. The following year, Tyndale was kidnapped from Antwerp, which was then a "free city," that is, a non-aligned city-state, and taken to a castle in present-day Belgium where he was tried as a heretic, and condemned to death by strangulation. His body was then burned.

Tyndale's strongest opponent was Sir Thomas More (1478-1535), another English humanist. More never joined a monastic order, but was always a strong proponent of papal authority and Roman Catholic doctrine. Although a friend of Erasmus, he took strong actions against Tyndale and the rise of any potential Lutheran influences. As a lawyer and statesman, he held political positions under King Henry VIII, but opposed the king when he ventured too far away from papal authority. More was beheaded for high treason in 1532. His major contributions were political, particularly his creatively imaginary, *Utopia*, a land with an ideal political system and no lawyers, since the laws were simple and self-evident.

A German humanist with more political than theological interests was Ulrich von Hutten (1488-1523). Trained in a Benedictine monastery, he fled that environment and sought a less sedate humanistic lifestyle. Recognized for his poetic ability, he wrote satirical poems against many social, political, and religious individuals and circumstances. Most recognized was his contribution (if not authorship) of *Letters of Obscure Men* (*Epistolae Obscurorum Virorum*), which supported Reuchlin against his scholastic and monastic opponents.

Architecture and the Arts

Under the pontifical aegis, art and architecture found significant patrons. Pope Alexander VI (1431-1503, pope 1492-1503) supported architectural and civic improvements in Rome, especially encouraging many artists through patronage from his vast personal and ecclesiastical wealth. Having fathered several children most of whom were illegitimate, he openly gave preferential treatment to his sons, especially Caesar Borgia (see chapter 15). Alexander's successor, Pius III (1439-1503) died after less than a month in office. His successor, Julius II (1443-1513, pope 1504-1513), led the efforts to construct a new St. Peter's Basilica in Rome in 1506. This masterpiece of humanistic architecture was finally completed 120 years later, having been underwritten by twenty papacies. Other architects of this era include Donato Bramante (1444-1514), recognized in Milan for his unique adaptation of ancient classical Roman style and also in Rome for his exquisite design for Julius II's basilica and several other churches.

Michelangelo

Combining architecture and art are the three great masters of this age—Leonardo da Vinci (1452-1519) (see chapter 15), Michelangelo (1475-1564), and Raphael (1483-1520). Flowing with the vigor of Italian humanism, Michelangelo grew up in Florence, where he often returned, and was a recognized rival of Raphael. Michelangelo combined the versatile skills of a sculptor, painter, inventor, and architect. He also wrote over 300 sonnets in Italian. His *Pieta* (see illustration) and *Statue of David* are classical in style, yet exemplify the high publication in Nuremberg. The Lutheran theologian, Andreas Osiander (1498-1552), prepared a preface for the work in which he suggested that new theories are certainly worthy of consideration as long as they have scientific support. Copernicus's major work, *De revolutionibus orbium coelestium* (On the Revolutions of the Heavenly Spheres) (see illustration) was finally completed and, according to some biographers, the final pages were given to Copernicus on the day he died at the age of 70.

Galileo Galilei

Galileo Galilei (1564-1642) has been called "the father of modern observational astronomy." Although coming from a pious Catholic musical family, his father allowed him to study mathematics after a few years of medical training. As we will see in chapter 17, his discoveries supported a heliocentric understanding, which resulted in serious controversies with the church.

Johannes Kepler

Johannes Kepler (1571-1630), although not a direct student of Copernicus, was an astronomer and an assistant to Tycho Brahe (1546-1601), who himself advocated a geo-heliocentric universe. As a child, Kepler was intrigued by a great comet (1577) and a lunar eclipse (1580). As a university student at Tübingen, he was convinced that Copernicus's view was correct. After studying for the pastoral ministry, he received a teaching position in mathematics and astronomy at the Lutheran school in Graz, where he published his first astronomical work, *Mysterium Cosmographicum*, (Cosmographic Mystery or Secret of the Universe) in 1595. Later, he introduced a key concept, his laws of planetary motion, which in turn influenced Isaac Newton's (1642-1727) concept of universal gravitation.

Francis Bacon

Besides these astronomers, Francis Bacon (1561-1625) encouraged the use of observation of God's creation through the natural sciences. As a British philosopher and scientist, Bacon advocated a careful and meticulous scientific method of inductive experimentation rather than merely following the philosophical assumptions of the ancients. He had three goals for his life—to uncover truth, to serve his country and to serve his church. He sought

In July, 1505, Luther entered the Black Cloister of the Order of the Hermits of Saint Augustine in Erfurt as a novice (see portrait). He continued his

academic studies at the University of Erfurt after his novitiate, but changed his focus from law to theology. He was ordained into the priesthood in April of 1507 in the Erfurt cathedral of St. Mary and celebrated his first Mass the following month. In 1508, he was sent by his superior, Johann von Staupitz (c.1460-1524), to teach philosophy at the fairly new university in Wittenberg. After another year in Erfurt, Staupitz sent him back to Wittenberg in 1511, this time with the added responsibility of earning a doctorate (1512) and becoming an official teacher of the church.[1] The following year, the affable Pope Leo X (1475-1521, pope 1513-1521) was elected to the chair of Peter in Rome.

The Ninety-five Theses

Recognizing his own spiritual needs and having a gift for communicating clearly and winsomely, Martin Luther spoke to the hearts of thousands of people when he raised the issue of indulgences (a process whereby sins were forgiven through an act of mercy or a gift of money) in sermons he preached toward the end of 1516 and early 1517. Nailing his "Ninety-five Theses" or propositions to the door of the Castle Church in Wittenberg on October 31st of that year, Luther broached the question whether the papacy had the power and right to extort money from the laity for forgiveness. He drew the attention of the people to the full and free forgiveness assured by God through Jesus Christ as reported in the Scriptures. Addressing a spiritually vexing need among the laity, this document,[2] and the consequent communications that it enlisted, became the precipitating event for the Protestant Reformation. As Erasmus stated later, "Luther sinned in two respects, namely, that he attacked the crown of the Pope and the bellies of the monks."

> **Indulgence Sales**
> A Dominican friar, Johann Tetzel, was an outstandingly successful salesman of indulgences and was engaged by Albrecht, Archbishop of Mainz. His method was to enter town with a fanfare and preach three sermons—on hell, on purgatory, and on heaven. Without the purchased indulgences, he proclaimed, individuals and family members would suffer the torments of hell or purgatory. For the simple purchase of indulgence document, forgiveness was granted from a theoretical storehouse of merits. "When a coin in the coffer rings, a soul from purgatory springs," he claimed. Luther's protest over such arrogant claims was sent to the Archbishop, whom Luther incorrectly thought was unaware of Tetzel's activities.

---

[1] Martin Luther, *Luther's Works* 49:48. Luther said of Staupitz, "It was through you that the light of the gospel first began to shine out of the darkness into my heart."

[2] The official title of Luther's academic proposal was "A Disputation on the Power and Efficacy of Indulgences." Such a disputation was apparently never held, but the subsequent consequences were earth- and church-shaking.

Luther's "breakthrough" had come as a gradual clarification for Luther over several years, contrary to some scholarly proposals. Sometime during his class preparations for his biblical lectures on Psalms (1513), Romans (1515-1516), Galatians (1516-1517), and Hebrews (1517-1518), Luther came to realize that the phrase of Paul in Romans 1, "the righteousness of God," was not only a characteristic of God and a requirement of humanity, but it was a gift which God bestowed on all who believed and trusted in the life, death, and resurrection of Jesus, the Messiah and God's Son. With that understanding, heaven opened for him, he said.[3] Salvation was not something earned, but a free gift of grace, received through faith, because of Christ. Luther thereby reversed the longstanding medieval idea that good works made a person acceptable to God. Rather, because one is declared acceptable by God because of Christ, one can perform good works. Salvation is not achieved but received.

In May of the next year, 1518 (the same year Leonardo da Vinci was born), Luther met with his Augustinian brother-friars at Heidelberg for their chapter meeting. He was asked to defend his theses. Instead of defending them, which he had done in print, he presented a completely new set of theses, later known as *The Heidelberg Theses,* in which he spoke more clearly about a

distinction between a theology of glory—which sought the hidden things of God and elevated the manifestation of God's goodness in people's lives—and the true theology of the cross—God is always present in our sufferings. Later that year and almost a year after the posting of his *Ninety-five Theses,* the Roman Catholic theologian and papal legate, Cardinal Thomas de Vio Cajetan (1469-1534), met with Luther for three days in Augsburg. Cajetan demanded that Luther recant, that is, withdraw his teachings from public discourse, and his condemnation of indulgences and the questioning of papal infallibility (see illustration, with Cajetan at the table and Luther standing). Luther refused and left town. But Cajetan had uncovered the sensitive issue of ecclesiastical authority, one which would become more central to the papacy than the morality of selling indulgences.

In early January of 1519, Luther was visited by another papal representative, Karl von Miltitz (c.1490-1529), who orchestrated Luther's agreement to support papal authority in temporal matters. The short-lived concord disintegrated when Emperor Maximillian (1459-1519, ruled 1486-1519) died and his replacement became a political issue throughout the continent. In early

---

[3] Martin Luther, *Luther's Works* 34:337. "I felt that I was altogether born again and had entered paradise itself through open gates."

summer of 1519, deliberations began for Maximillian's replacement as the electors were enticed by the chief candidates, Francis I (1484-1547, ruled 1515-1547) and Charles V (1500-1558, ruled 1519-1556). On June 28, Charles was elected, much to the dismay of Pope Leo, who had supported Francis, but also had delayed in dealing with Luther.

The day before Charles's election, a debate was held between Luther and the Roman Catholic theologian, Johann Maier von Eck (1486-1543), in Leipzig. Originally scheduled to be between Luther's colleague, Andreas Bodenstein von Carlstadt (c.1480-1541), on the topics of grace and free will, Luther quickly stepped into the fray as the topics touched on the critical issues of indulgences and then penance, purgatory, and papal authority. Along with 200 students, Carlstadt and Luther were accompanied by a new Wittenberg faculty member, Philip Melanchthon (1497-1560). Although both sides claimed victory, Luther demonstrated most clearly his commitment to Scripture alone as his ultimate authority—neither Councils nor popes were infallible, he declared.

Significant Documents of 1520

The following summer, on June 15, 1520, Pope Leo X published his papal bull (an official statement from the Vatican marked with a lead seal known as a *bulla*), *Exurge domini* ("Rise, Lord") (see illustration of the cover page) condemning over forty teachings attributed to Luther or drawn from the *Ninety-five Theses*, and requiring that he recant all these teachings. About this same time, Luther wrote his treatise on *The Papacy in Rome* in which he asserted that the papacy's claim to divine origin based upon Matthew 16:18-19 was a faulty interpretation and that, because of such self-acclaimed status, the papacy was indeed "the true Antichrist" and the "scarlet whore of Babylon."

That same year, three significant documents stated Luther's position most clearly—*To the Christian Nobility of the German Nation*, *On the Babylonian Captivity of the Church*, and *On the Freedom of a Christian*. Each of these works, produced at this critical time in the course of the Reformation, illustrated a significant idea in Luther's thinking and emphasized an important aspect of the Gospel, which was the sole motivation for Luther's call for reform.

In the first treatise, *To the Christian Nobility*, Luther emphasized the right and responsibility of the Christian nobles to live out their vocations as spiritual priests. Papal authority was limited, he stated, to spiritual things and even Scripture itself was to be recognized as being over the pope. He concluded that document by requesting a church council to address the ecclesiastical problems recognized by so many.

The second work used the seventy-year captivity of the people of Israel in Babylon and also the fiasco of the papal duplication in the fourteenth century as its starting point, known as *The Babylonian Captivity*. Luther argued that the detailed style of academic discourse, Luther critiqued Erasmus's ideas with stronger evidence, demonstrating from Scripture that Erasmus had adopted the humanist view which was neither biblical nor even Christian. Luther concluded that humans were indeed bound by sin and only Christ could loose them from this bondage. Although Erasmus responded again to Luther, Luther refused to continue the debate. Their previously cordial relationship had ended.

Practicing the Faith

Luther's protector, Elector Frederick the Wise, died in late spring of 1525 and was succeeded by his brother, Johann (1468-1532), known as John "the Steadfast" (ruled 1524-1532). Fearing for his life and acknowledging his own inadequacies as a husband, Luther reluctantly yet confidently entered into marriage on June 13, 1525 at the age of forty-one. His new wife was Katherine von Bora (1499-1552), a twenty-six year old nun who had escaped from her Nimbschen convent with a dozen others a year earlier. "Dr. Katie," as he often affectionately referred to her, provided the strength and stability that Martin needed to be free to carry on his academic and theological pursuits, calling her "Katie, my rib," in reference to Eve's complementary role. Their first child, Hans (1526-1575), would be born a little more than a year later.

Early in 1526, Luther issued his *German Mass and Order for Public Worship*, which he had prepared for the Wittenberg worshipers the previous December, entirely in German. During the busyness of teaching and preaching, Luther prepared several commentaries on the Old Testament books of Jonah, Habakkuk, and Ecclesiastes. In the meantime, Emperor Charles and Francis I signed a peace treaty ending their five-year conflict and Charles turned his attention to Germany. Toward the end of June, an imperial diet was held in Speyer, although Charles could not attend. This allowed the Lutheran princes to form an alliance, the League of Torgau, and suspend the earlier Edict of Worms and decide the religious allegiance of their region, thus providing a great advantage for the reformation movement.

Further Unrest

Controversy between several of the reformers began to erupt around this time. Swiss theologians, Ulrich Zwingli (1484-1531) and Oecolampadius (1482-1531), did not always agree with Luther's scriptural interpretations, particularly on the Lord's Supper. In 1526, Luther published a strong pamphlet against the views espoused by Oecolampadius in *The Sacrament of the Body and Blood of Christ—Against the Fanatics*. "Fanatics" for Luther were those who denied the real presence of Christ and only held a spiritual view. In seeking to ameliorate the issue, Luther actually exacerbated the situation for the next several years.

By the beginning of 1527, political issues began to emerge again as a significant influence on the reformation. The Islamic forces of Sulieman defeated King Louis (ruled 1516-1526) in Hungary as the Turkish threat extended further into European consciousness. At about the same time, Francis I with the support of the papacy moved against Charles V, but the Charles's imperial armies not only defeated him, but also sacked the city of Rome. A treaty was negotiated between Charles and Pope Clement VII toward the end of the year.

Forging a Stronger Church

During this same year Luther composed his famous Reformation hymn, "*A Mighty Fortress Is Our God,*" perhaps in light of the political and theological unrest of the time. Luther began to experience severe health issues, which would become more chronic over the next years as he worked tirelessly to forge a stronger church. Through a series of pastoral and ecclesiastical "visitations," Luther and his colleagues promoted a critique of the evangelical congregations, ascertaining what they needed as well as how to address those needs. The key to a strengthening the church, Luther recognized, was better educated pastors and laity. The following year, Philip Melanchthon (1497-1560) prepared (with Luther's encouragement and approval) a series of "Visitation Articles" by which clergy and congregations could be evaluated. It was in that same year, 1528, in Scotland that Patrick Hamilton (1504-1528) was burned at the stake for advocating Luther's teaching, an event which only fueled the Reformation in that country.

Along with the Visitation Articles and regular preaching on the central doctrines of the Christian faith, Luther finally completed a task he had proposed earlier—the preparation of a catechism for both pastors and parents. In 1529, Luther published both his *Small Catechism* for the heads of the households and his *Large Catechism* for pastors. The *Small Catechism* came out in the form of a set of posters (see illustration), which families could use as a household teaching aid. Around that same time, a second Diet was called at Speyer, but this time the Catholic leaders prevailed. When the reformers protested the actions of this diet and appealed to the Emperor, the term "Protestant" was first applied to them.

It was later in this same year that the Sacramentarian Controversy was addressed during the Marburg Colloquy from October 1st to the 4th. Philip I (1504-1567, ruled 1518-1567), Landgrave of Hesse, desired political stability and unity in his region and so called the meeting of the leading reformers at his castle in Marburg. Among the dozen representatives, Ulrich Zwingli and Martin Luther were the chief spokesmen for the two groups. Consensus was attained on fourteen of the fifteen issues in discussion, later known as the *Marburg Articles*; however, over the understanding of Christ's presence in the Lord's Supper, Luther maintained that Christ was present in the bread and wine, while Zwingli continued to hold that the elements were only symbolic representations. As Luther left the meeting, he stated: "We are not of the same spirit."

The 1530s and the Augsburg Confession

At the end of 1529, Emperor Charles had defeated Francis I and received a papal promise to be recognized as the head of the Holy Roman Empire. At the same time, Suleieman was marching toward Vienna with a force of almost a quarter of a million soldiers. Charles saw the need for political unity and called for a meeting to be held in Augsburg to settle the religious disputes and form a military alliance against the Turks.

In March 1530, Elector John "the Steadfast" of Saxony received word of the diet at his castle in Torgau and called upon Luther, Melanchthon, Johannes Bugenhagen (1485-1558) and Justus Jonas (1493-1555) to prepare a statement which reflected both agreements and disagreements with the Roman Catholic Church. Known as the *Torgau Articles*, these doctrinal statements served as a basis for the subsequent diet. In the meantime, Johann Eck had sent Charles *404 Articles*, which he claimed were held by Luther and were heretical.

Because he was still under the imperial ban, Luther had to stay in the castle at Coburg from April through August, rather than attend the assembly at Augsburg. In June, Luther learned of the death in May of his father, who had been ill since February and to whom Luther had sent a letter of encouragement. From Coburg, Luther relied on Philip Melanchthon to prepare and present a clear statement of the doctrinal positions to the Emperor and princes at this diet and

After Luther

After an imperial meeting was held in Augsburg in 1548, an official statement, *The Augsburg Interim*, offered several concessions to the new Evangelicals—clergy could marry and laity could receive both bread and wine in communion—however, the Evangelical Lutherans were required to accept most of the traditional Catholic teachings, including the seven sacraments. While Melanchthon's irenic spirit saw this as a beneficial solution, most of the Lutheran theologians and princes rejected this "compromise." An alternate position was drawn up the following year and was known as the *Leipzig Interim*. This time, the Catholic position was compromised; Lutherans could retain their teaching on justification by grace through faith because of Christ, but were required to give up some of their less central practices. Those who supported this Leipzig Interim became known as "Philippists," followers of Philip Melanchthon, while those who opposed it were known as "Gnesio-Lutherans" (Greek, "genuine").

From the fall of 1553 through most of 1554, Martin Chemnitz again was in Wittenberg, teaching philosophy and serving as an assistant to Melanchthon. He began to study theology on his own and was ordained by Bugenhagen as a Lutheran pastor in 1554, being recognized for his theological acumen. Shortly after the Council of Trent was concluded (see the third section of this chapter), Chemnitz prepared a four-volume critique of those proceedings, showing carefully and critically the biblical basis for Lutheran positions.

Also in 1554, Luther's student, Mikael Agricola (1510-1557), was named Bishop of Turku, Finland, but his influence on Finnish Lutheranism had already begun with his preparation of a basic catechism in 1543. Agricola published prayer books, liturgical books, and a New Testament in Finnish a few years later. Work on the Finnish New Testament, *Se Wsi Testamenti* (see illustration of the cover page), had taken his team of scholars a little more than a decade to complete. Respected by the Swedish King, Gustav I (1496-1560, ruled 1523-1560), he was sent on several diplomatic missions to Sweden and Russia. It was on such a trip to Russia that he fell ill and died in 1557. Besides being instrumental in bringing Lutheranism to Finland, he is considered the founder of Finnish literature because of his prolific translation work.

Finally, a lasting political and theological peace was worked out in 1555 in the city of Augsburg. Emperor Charles granted to all princes the right to determine the religion of their own region—Catholic princes would enforce Catholicism and Lutheran princes could establish Lutheran lands. The principle, "whose rule, his religion" (Latin, *cuius regio, eius religio*), was thereby introduced. The *Peace of Augsburg*, as it became known, also promised that religious issues would no longer be grounds for political battles.

controverted issues and possible solutions, which he had learned in part from his teacher, Johann Brenz (1499-1570). Since the early years of the Reformation, Brenz had spent considerable effort to meet with Calvinists over controversial issues. Martin Chemnitz encouraged Andreae to publish his conclusions, which he prepared in a series of sermons in 1573. Shortly thereafter, a professor from the University of Rostock in northern Germany, David Chytraeus (1530-1600), revised Andreae's document with the guidance of Chemnitz and prepared the *Swabian-Saxon Concord* in 1575. The following year, a colloquy was called by Elector Augustus I (1553-1586) of Saxony and Württemberg in the town of Maulbronn to resolve a Calvinistic view of the Lord's Supper being taught in Wittenberg. The resulting document was known as the *Maulbronn Formula*.

The documents from Maulbronn along with the *Swabian-Saxon Concord* were revised by Andreae, Chemnitz, Chytraeus, and others in 1576 in the town of Torgau and became known as the *Torgau Book*. It was accepted as the *Bergen Book* and became the expanded version of the *Formula of Concord*, called either the *Solid* or *Thorough Declaration*. A summary had been adapted from Andreae's work as a short extract or *Epitome* for the *Formula of Concord*.

Finally, in 1580, at the fiftieth anniversary of the reading of the Augsburg Confession, the Lutheran doctrinal statements were gathered together into the *Book of Concord* (see illustration). Over eight thousand pastors and fifty political leaders attached their names to the work as a distinct witness to the Lutheran tradition.

Two years later, Johann Gerhard (1582-1637), one of the most influential Lutheran theologians of the next century, was born in Quedlinburg, Germany. After a critical illness as a youth, he found great comfort from his pastor, Johann Arndt (1555-1621). Shortly thereafter, in 1599, he entered the University of Wittenberg to study theology. We will investigate these two men in greater detail in the next chapter.

For the last quarter century, Catholic presence remained weak in German lands, although Jesuit activities gradually led to the physical hostilities in the next century. For Protestants, advances in southern Germany were more in favor of Calvinism, especially as the Lutherans experienced their inner doctrinal conflicts. Secular authorities had followed many of the Protestant teachings, although Catholic prelates continued to dominate the German Reichstag (parliament). As the century ended, unrest seemed to be about to boil over into public displays of hostilities.

For Review and Discussion
1. How did Luther's early years prepare him for his call for reform?

16 C. The Protestant, Catholic, and Radical Reformations

The Sixteenth Century: Part 3

Luther and his colleagues in Wittenberg were not the only ones working on reforming the church. Voices had been raised both within the Roman Catholic Church and outside of it for over a century. In this section of chapter 16, we will look at the several reformations which were occurring simultaneously among European Christians. Three particular areas will be presented—the Protestant reformers, the Radical reformers, and the Roman Catholic reformers.

John Calvin

John Calvin (1509-1564, baptized "Jehan Cauvin"), probably the most outstanding systematician of the Protestant cause, was trained as a humanist  lawyer at various French universities. As a result, his understanding of Christianity sought to organize his biblical ideas, particularly about God's sovereign will, as well as ecclesiastical practices, into clear categories. After a conversion experience of some kind, he left the University of Paris in 1534 when he became aware that his evangelical views were unacceptable in that environment. Moving to Basel, he became acquainted with the reformer, Johannes Oecolampadius (1482-1531). Around that same time he began to prepare his theological masterpiece, *The Institutes of the Christian Religion*, published in 1536, a work which increased in size with each edition.

On a journey to Strassburg, Calvin was sidetracked through the Swiss city of Geneva, which had recently been emancipated from France. There he met William (Guillaume) Farel (1489-1565), a local reformer, who had read Calvin's work and effectively demanded his help to establish the reformation in that city. Because of his legal training, Calvin proposed a legislated reformation there, emphasizing the need for true believers to demonstrate their faith or be excommunicated. This disciplined approach, while well-intended, was not accepted by the citizens of Geneva and he and Farel were banished in 1538.

Calvin's teachings began to spread quickly. Most significantly, John Knox (1514-1572), born near Edinburgh, Scotland, converted from Catholicism to Protestantism over a period of years. Influenced by significant reforming preachers in the early 1540s, he was released from a brief imprisonment and travelled to England, where he met Thomas Cranmer. With the regency of the Catholic Queen Mary (1516-1558, ruled 1553-1558) in 1553, he fled to Europe and came in contact with John Calvin. Returning to Scotland in 1559, he remained there, advocating the evangelical faith of Calvin. In 1560, he issued the *First Book of Discipline*, establishing an austere form of Calvinism and a presbyterian form of church governance (presbyter, Greek, "elder."). He was the most famous of the Scottish Reformers and his legacy is in the present-day Presbyterian churches.

Ulrich Zwingli

Ulrich Zwingli (1484-1531) or Huldrychus Zwinglius as he preferred to be called, younger and more revolutionary than Calvin, had read Luther, but insisted that his own reformation ideas came independently through his careful reading of Scripture.

For Zwingli only a radical shift in one's life and a re-interpretation of Scripture which removed the "Catholic" substance of the faith were acceptable. Trained as a humanist prior to his ordination in 1506, his study of Scripture led him to reject papal authority, along with monasticism, purgatory, and many other practices associated with his Catholic upbringing. After serving for a decade as a parish priest in the Swiss town of Glarus, and around the same time as Luther's *Ninety-five Theses* were publicized, Zwingli declared that papal authority was only of human origin. Then in early 1519 he moved to Zurich where he denounced indulgences and monastic vows from the pulpit. That date is often given for the beginning of the Swiss Reformation. A few years later, he defied his local bishop

Although ordained a priest, he soon left the priesthood and married. Influenced by Luther and then by the Anabaptists, he was intrigued by the more spiritual reformers and finally settled on "inner experience" as the foundation for one's faith.

Kaspar Schwenkfeld (1489-1560), a Silesian nobleman, was initially attracted to Luther's reformation rhetoric, too. However, he followed Carlstadt and Müntzer more closely, and soon became a popular preacher under their influence. During the Sacramentarian Controversy, he parted company both with Zwingli and Luther, proposing a "heavenly flesh" idea, which resulted in a weakened Christology. Although closely associated with Anabaptists, his followers, who were exiled from Silesia, formed a new denomination named after him.

The Anglican Reformation

Unusual was the reform that occurred in England, since it had much more of a political than a theological basis. Reformation, and particularly Lutheran,  ideas had come to England early in the 1520s. When Henry VIII wrote a book against Luther's view of the Lord's Supper, Pope Leo X (1475-1521, pope 1513-1521) awarded him the title, "Defender of the Faith." By the end of that decade, Henry had also rejected papal authority and, partially because of his desire to marry a second wife, declared himself head of the English church.

In 1532, Thomas Cranmer was named Archbishop of Canterbury and two years later Parliament passed the "Act of Supremacy," whereby all English citizens had to acknowledge Henry as head of the Church of England. Thomas More (1478-1535), longtime humanist statesman, social philosopher, and councilor to Henry, was subsequently beheaded when he refused to back Henry's "reformation" in defiance of papal authority. After a three-year hiatus of the Parliament, Henry called for a committee to decide on doctrinal issues in light of a visit by several Lutheran theologians. The result was Parliament's passing *The Six Articles* in 1539, which affirmed the Catholic teachings on transubstantiation, clerical celibacy and vows of chastity, private masses, auricular confessions, and withholding the communion chalice from the laity.

For the next ten years, a slow development of a protestantized Catholicism emerged. Monasteries and other church properties were turned over to the English crown. Thomas Cromwell (1485-1540), Henry's faithful political advisor was executed by beheading, presumably for his failure to support the *Six Articles* and his perceived support of several "Lutheran" heretics. Cromwell had encouraged Bible reading in 1536, but Henry changed that law in 1543, limiting Bible reading only to the nobles. Around the middle of 1540, Henry had his marriage to Anne of Cleve (1515-1557) annulled in order to marry Catherine

Howard (c.1521-1542), whom he beheaded a few years later. As noted in chapter 16 B, he also had Robert Barnes (c.1495-1540) burned at the stake.

Upon Henry's death in 1547, his nine-year-old son, Edward VI (1537-1553, ruled 1547-1553), exhibited a stronger Protestant attitude and promoted reform from a Calvinist orientation. A Reformed iconoclasm soon spread through much of the English countryside. A real reformation was in the air. In 1549, the first *Book of Common Prayer* was released, but was not widely accepted. Within three years a revised version was issued which completely eliminated any "Catholic ideas," especially that of the sacrifice of the Mass. The "black rubric" in the *Book of Common Prayer* remained, which directed people to kneel for communion, in order to provide an orderly distribution of the sacrament, yet many considered it overtly Roman. It was removed in the 1559 edition.

Edward's reign was short-lived. When Henry's only surviving daughter by Catherine of Aragon, Mary Tudor (1516-1558), came to the throne, her Catholic proclivity returned much of England temporarily to the Catholic fold (ruled 1553-1558). Besides having Cranmer burned at the stake, many other leaders with Protestant allegiances left England for Europe. After 1555, the so-called "Marian persecutions" broke out and almost 300 Protestants were executed, giving Queen Mary I the well-known moniker of "Bloody Mary." Although she thought she was pregnant with her successor, she died during a severe influenza outbreak, with her younger half-sister, Elizabeth, assuming the throne.

Upon her accession to the throne in 1558, Queen Elizabeth I (1533-1603) (see illustration) provided a restored structure to the church under the queen's  governance and mediating position. Two acts of Parliament re-established the church's independence from Rome and restored Edward's *Book of Common Prayer*. In 1563, the *Thirty-Nine Articles*, an adaptation of Thomas Cranmer's *Ten Articles* (1536), were published, delineating doctrines which were distinct from the Roman Church, as well as from the radical reformers, as a kind of middle way—a stance which remains to the present in the Anglican communion. Denying Roman Catholic transubstantiation and Zwinglian symbolism, Anglicans remained open to a range of interpretations regarding Christ's presence in the Lord's Supper between Luther and Calvin. That same year John Foxe's (1516-1587) *Christian Martyrs of the World* came to print, which gave vividly detailed accounts of the Protestant executions under Mary as well as many that had occurred during the early Christian persecutions.

While the English reformation was "complete," there remained those who felt the reformation had not gone far enough. This group became known as Puritans, for their desire to have a "pure" and completely restored church free from anything "Catholic," such as vestments and liturgy. We will see more of this movement in the next chapters.

Working hard to learn the Japanese language and culture, his efforts were met initially with very little success. He died in December of 1552 just before a planned journey to mainland China, where Matteo Ricci (1552-1610) and Michele Ruggieri (1543-1602) carried out mission work thirty years later (See chapter 16 A).

New Monastic Orders

Besides the Jesuits and the attempted reforms among some of the major orders, such as the Dominicans and Luther's Augustinian Hermits, over a half-dozen new orders were given papal approval during this century.

The Theatines

The Theatines (1524) or the Congregation of the Clerks Regular of the Divine Providence was founded by Cajetan of Tiene (1480-1547) to combat Lutheran influences in Italy through preaching, along with the reorganized and strengthened Inquisition. The order emphasized prayer and established the famous Oratory of Divine Love as well as several hospitals and mission sites in the next century.

The Capuchins

The Capuchins (1528), a strict order of Franciscan friars, first arose in the early 1520s as a reform of the more lax order of Franciscans. After being given refuge by a group of monks in central Italian mountains, they adopted the hood (Italian, *cappuccio*) worn by those hermits as a mark of their order.

The Clerics Regular of Saint Paul

The Barnabites (1530) or the Clerics Regular of Saint Paul were founded in Milan by three nobles in protest of the moral laxity in the church. The popular name was derived from their first church, St Barnabas.

The Carmelites

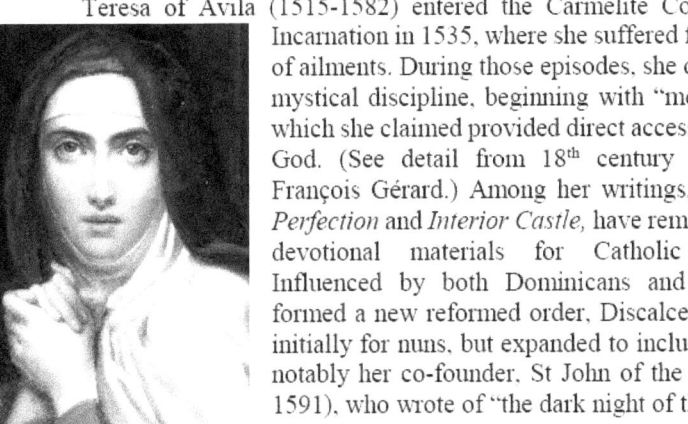

Teresa of Ávila (1515-1582) entered the Carmelite Convent of the Incarnation in 1535, where she suffered from a variety of ailments. During those episodes, she developed her mystical discipline, beginning with "mental prayer," which she claimed provided direct access to visions of God. (See detail from 18th century depiction by François Gérard.) Among her writings, *The Way of Perfection* and *Interior Castle*, have remained popular devotional materials for Catholic spirituality. Influenced by both Dominicans and Jesuits, she formed a new reformed order, Discalced Carmelites, initially for nuns, but expanded to include men, most notably her co-founder, St John of the Cross (1542-1591), who wrote of "the dark night of the soul."

continued by Popes Julius III (1487-1555, pope 1550-1555) and Pius IV (1499-1565, pope 1559-1565), no pope ever attended in person.

The three assemblies, held between 1545-1549, 1551-1552, and 1562-1563, dealt with significant doctrinal as well as practical issues facing the Roman Catholic Church at this time. After procedural matters were addressed in the first three sessions, session four took up Scripture and tradition as being equally authoritative for the church and the Latin (*Vulgate*) translation as the only authorized text. The doctrines of original sin and the sacraments of the church were also clarified at that time. The key issue during this first assembly was the doctrine of justification. In six sessions, over a dozen decrees and 33 canons were approved by the council in clear and deliberate opposition to Lutheran teachings. While asserting that sinners are justified through Christ by grace and by faith (chapters 3, 7 and 8 of the Decree on Justification), such faith is only the beginning. Faith "cooperating with good works" (chapter 10) increases one's justification. As far as the Roman Catholic Church was concerned, the Lutheran "heresy" was forcefully and finally condemned (the Greek word, *anathema*, means "cursed" or "condemned to hell") as evident in several of the official canons of the Council. (See sidebar on the next page with canons 9 and 14.) The "chapters" of the decrees stated the Catholic doctrines in positive terms and the "canons" were formed in the negative. These canons of the Council have never been rescinded and are the official teaching of the Roman Church to the present time. (See illustration from a session.)

During the second assembly, under the scandalous pontificate of Julius III (1487-1555, pope 1550-1555), the Catholic sacraments of communion, penance, and last rites were discussed and over two dozen decrees and thirty canons approved, including a reaffirmation of the teaching of transubstantiation two-year pontificate and was followed by Pope Urban VIII (1568-1644, pope 1623-1644).

Personal piety began to overshadow doctrinal concerns. Already in 1605, the Lutheran theologian, Johann Arndt (1555-1621), published the first book of his four-volume work, *True Christianity*, in which he emphasized a more interior piety and personal introspection. During the next decades following Arndt's publication, an emphasis on individual spirituality continued to expand among several confessional groups. Francis de Sales (1567-1622) published a work in 1608 which would become one of the most popular works of Catholic spirituality, *Introduction to the Devout Life*. He later founded a religious order for persons with disabilities which had kept them from membership in other orders.

The following year, 1609, saw the publication of the first part of the English translation for Catholics of the Latin Vulgate, the Douay-Rheims Bible. The same year, John Smythe (c.1570-1612), an exiled Englishman in Amsterdam, baptized himself and established the Baptist churches as distinct from both Catholics and Protestants. Another Englishman, Lewis Bayly (1565-1631) published *Practice of Piety* in 1611, which was translated into German in 1628 and by 1636 had seen 36 English editions. Several Baptists returned to England in 1611, following the teaching of Jacob Arminius (1560-1609) and established a congregation there as "General Baptists." Two decades later a group of these English Baptists began to teach the Calvinist idea of limited atonement and were called "Particular" or Calvinistic Baptists. Such diversity in religious expression only led to further explorations in non-dogmatic experiences.

1611 marks the date of the first edition of the King James Version of the Bible (see illustration of front page), the culmination of a seven-year project. King James I (1566-1625, ruled 1603-1625) had authorized this translation in 1604 as a revision of the Bishops' Bible in consultation with other English translations as well as the Hebrew and Greek manuscripts. As a scholarly project it involved over fifty scholars and continues to be praised for its literary beauty.

Perhaps one of the most significant events in the early years of the seventeenth century was an initial inquisitorial investigation of Galileo (see below) by Robert Cardinal Bellarmine (1542-1621). This occurred in the year, 1616, the same year Shakespeare died. Although no definitive condemnation was given against Galileo, ecclesiastical concerns were officially raised. Twelve years after Bellarmine's death, Galileo was again summoned before the church and was forced to recant his theories of a heliocentric universe.

Finally, in 1630, Gustavus Adolphus of Sweden (1594-1632) landed in northern Germany and, with the help of some French and many of the Protestant German states, drove the imperial armies out of Germany in 1631. Unfortunately, he was killed in a victorious battle against Wallenstein. In addition to these national military conflicts, the plague continued to devastate citizenries in much of Europe. One Bavarian town, Oberammergau, in gratitude for divine protection from the bubonic plague instituted a celebrative event, a city-wide production of the *Passion Play*, in 1634.

Three years later, Spain moved against the Swedish armies in Nordlingen and defeated them, forcing the Protestants out of southern Germany. This could have resulted in the end of the war. However, fearing political encirclement, France re-entered the fray in 1635 and declared war on Spain. From this point, the battles had lost their religious nature and were motivated purely for political reasons.

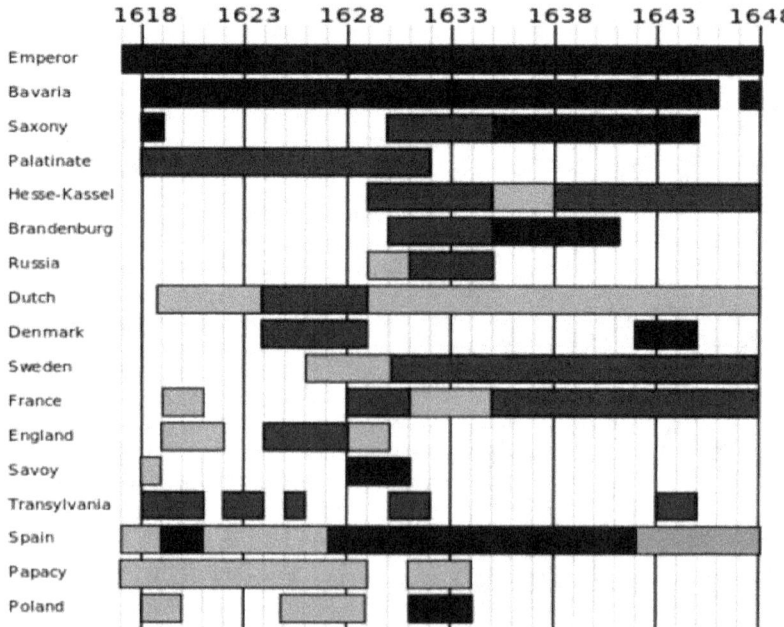

For the next dozen years, the great political powers of Europe—Spain, Sweden, France, and Austria—were contending for control of German lands. The military maneuvers were characterized by their astoundingly horrific atrocities as the mercenary troops sought to appropriate confiscated resources as payment for services. By some estimates, half the population living between Pomerania in the northern Baltic region of Germany and the Black Forest were killed in battle or died as a result of hostilities. Finally, in 1643, the French won a decisive victory over Spain in Rocroi. Two years later, the Swedes defeated the imperial armies in

Jankau. These military activities marked the ending of the major battles and the final determinations for peace.

In 1648, the Peace of Westphalia ended the Thirty Years' War. Establishing the principle of *cuius region illius religio* ("whose region, his religion"), Germany's devastating war came to an uncertain, yet definitive conclusion. The sovereignty of the German princes was recognized in this treaty, weakening the power of the Emperor. Holland and Switzerland were given independent status. The Hohenzollern elector of Brandenburg garnered great land territory, eventually leading to control over the kingdom of Prussia at the end of this century. Besides the war, famine and plague had decimated the population by over five-eighth of its citizenry. Spain was weakened significantly. France became much stronger and more influential, which may have contributed to the French Civil War (1648-1652), which began the same year.

New World Advances

In the meantime, in North America, the Mayflower Compact was drafted in 1620 as the Mayflower landed in Plymouth, Massachusetts. This colony was founded by Puritan Separatists, known as "pilgrims." Fifteen years later, in 1635, the Massachusetts Bay Colony Congregationalists founded Harvard College. Five years after the pilgrims settle in Massachusetts, the Jesuit missionary, Jean de Brébeuf (1593-1649) traveling with the French explorer, Samuel de Champlain (1574-1635), brought the Christian message to the Huron peoples in Québec. Regrettably, he died a martyr's death at the hands of some Iroquois raiders, who destroyed their Huron mission village.

In 1626, the Dutch explorer and colonial governor, Peter Minuit (1580-1638), purchased Manhattan Island from a Native American tribe, the Lenape, for 60 guilders (under $1000 today). Lutherans from Germany and other European countries were already living in the surrounding territory. Ten years later, in 1636, Roger Williams (1603-1683) founded Providence, Rhode Island, as a community for religious refugees. That same year the Puritans published the first hymn book ever printed in America, *The Bay Psalm Book*. More emigrants came to Massachusetts by 1638, under the leadership of John Cotton (1584-1652) and Richard Mather (1596-1669). Later, Thomas Hooker (1586-1647) helped establish religious services in Connecticut under the congregational polity of Puritanism.

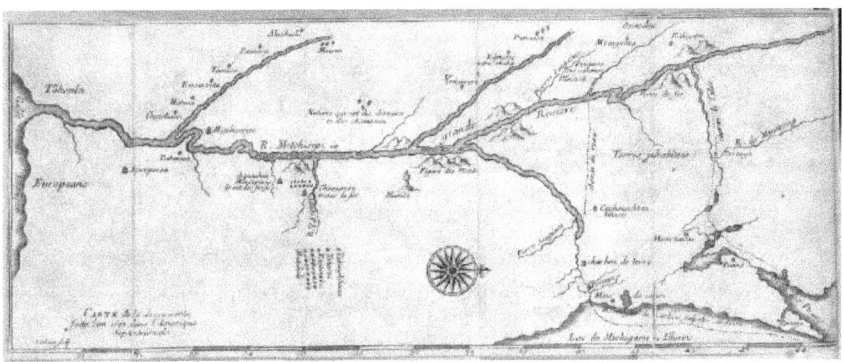

reading of the Bible in devotional assemblies, known as "little churches in the church" (*ecclesiolae in ecclesia*), realization of the priesthood of all believers in practicing the Christian life, a limitation on confessional polemics, a reforming of the traditional pastoral training toward piety instead of doctrine, and parish preaching for edification of the inner person instead of indoctrination.

It was during his theological studies in Strassburg between 1651 and 1659 that Spener (see his portrait below) first expressed his concerns for what he  saw as the rigidity of orthodox theology as well as the less-than-exemplary discipline of Lutheran clergy. He visited several Calvinist communities, where he found the regulatory nature of the teachings and a more mystical dimension of religion attractive. In 1666, Spener was named senior pastor in Frankfurt, where he developed a strong social program for the poor and introduced a more thorough catechetical program for the young by introducing the practice of confirmation instructions. He became the head preacher in the Dresden court in 1686 and in 1691 was called to Berlin, where he served Frederick III of Brandenburg (1657-1713; later Frederick I of Prussia) and influenced the new University of Halle. Hostility to Spener's views increased over the years, so that by 1695 the Wittenberg faculty prepared a list of almost 300 errors attributed to Spener. He died in Berlin in 1705 after preparing a defense of his teachings in his *Theologische Bedenken* (Theological Reflections, 1700-1702).

Hermann Francke (1663-1727), student and successor to Philipp Spener, personified Pietism as he embodied the goals articulated most ardently by Spener. Having experienced a crisis of faith as a student, such a "conversion experience" became a key element in subsequent Pietist practices. Francke was an incredible organizer. After having been placed by Spener as a language professor in the new Prussian university of Halle, Francke established an orphanage, a publishing house, an apothecary and science laboratory, along with various academic institutions—a school for Scripture study and translation, a teachers college, a seminary-type institute, and a variety of schools for students of different abilities and skills. His entrepreneurial nature led him to develop a strong missionary movement. (See chapter 18.)

Pietist Influences

The influence of Pietism was trans-denominational, affecting both Roman Catholic mysticism and Puritan devotional piety. Even the eighteenth century Jewish movement, Hasidism (Hebrew, "pious ones" promoting a mystical spirituality), was influenced in some ways by the personal, individual spirituality of Pietism.

Although Jesuit influence on the Counter-Reformation was significant, a Pietistic-type counter-movement, known especially in France as Jansenism, showed some marks and tendencies similar to Pietism. Originating as a reaction

18. The Age of Reason and New Awakenings

The Eighteenth Century

No era had higher expectations for the future of humanity than the eighteenth century, yet this century ended with less than glorious conclusions. Scientific discoveries, enlightened thinking, global consciousness, and a renewal of spiritual vitality all marked the first decades of this period.

In one sense the architectural style known as Rococo characterized this century (see illustration of the Bavarian Ottobeuren Abbey basilica). Its elaborate ornamentation came into vogue with King Louis XV of France (1638-1715) and disappeared with the French Revolution (1789-1799). In the midst of high hopes and ample possibilities, troubles and difficulties persisted as many Christians wavered in striving to be wholly holy in the world. Wars and rumors of wars raged as theological ideas were wrested from the church by the academy.

many scriptural accounts as well as much of his French Catholic upbringing. For Voltaire, the concept of God was a necessary presupposition for moral behavior and explains his comment, "If God did not exist, it would be necessary to invent Him." Morality became the major focus for those with deist-views.

Edward Gibbon

Another famous Enlightenment thinker was the historian, Edward Gibbon (1737-1794), who wrote one of the most massive accounts of *The Rise and Fall of the Roman Empire* in six volumes between 1776 and 1778. Although his historiography was of a very high quality, he was most remembered for his criticism of all organized religions, especially Christianity for its supplanting of other cultures and reliance on doctrinal authority.

A lesser known event in this century, yet one which had profound consequences, was an act by the still surviving Holy Roman Emperor, Joseph II (1741-1790, emperor 1765-1790). In 1780, he set forth a series of reforms by which both church and state were brought into a more Enlightenment mode. For the church, religious toleration was required for both Protestants and Roman Catholics. In addition, the liturgy of the Catholic Church was simplified, monasteries were closed, and papal power in Austria was limited. For the state, discriminatory laws, especially against serfs and Jews, were removed and a new law code was enacted.

Emmanuel Kant

In 1781, Emmanuel Kant (1724-1804) (see illustration) produced *Critique of Pure Reason* in which he said that all knowledge comes from  experience (empiricism) based upon deduction (rationalism). Such a critique of deism caused the Enlightenment's Age of Reason to begin to sputter toward the end of the century. Having been raised in a pietistic home and attending Pietist schools, he had seen the hypocrisy of religious emotion. Rather than emotion, he said, religion should focus on behavior, especially good, moral actions. In his *Grounding for the Metaphysics of Morals* (1785), he delineated what became known as his "categorical imperative" (*kategorischer Imperativ*): "Every rational person must act as if his behavior was legislating a universal law." In 1788, he published his *Critique of Practical Reason,* which looked not only at behavior, but also at one's motivation and the methods used to teach proper rational morality or the experience of moral "oughtness." Thus, Kantian moralism became a central focus for much of the theology in the next century.

Frederick Schleiermacher

Frederick D. E. Schleiermacher (1768-1834) was born in Silesia, in what is now Poland, into the family of an army chaplain. In 1794, he left the Moravian Church with its Pietist roots to become a minister in the Reformed Church. In

Awakening." Although human nature was viewed pessimistically, holiness was emphasized as a result of God's grace and one being "born again."

Early revivals in local communities began among the Dutch Reformed under the Pietist preacher, Theodore J. Frelinghuysen (1691-1748). In 1736, this American movement was strengthened when William Tennent, Sr. (1673-1745) founded a "Log College," which was established to train Presbyterian ministers in revivalistic and pietistic Christianity. Already present at the turn of the century, Scotch-Irish immigrants had moved out of the original colonies into the frontiers of Kentucky and Tennessee. Needing spiritual connections and stronger religious ties, the Awakening drew these unchurched, yet Christian, laypeople together for fellowship, Christian nurture, and spiritual support.

In New England, Jonathan Edwards (1703-1758), a Congregationalist minister and revival preacher, delivered his famous sermon, "Sinners in the Hands of an Angry God," in 1742. Prior to that, he had described the events of 1734-1735 in Massachusetts as "the surprising work of God in the conversion of many hundred souls" (part of the title of a book he published in 1737). Concerned with the over-emphasis of Arminianism upon human decisions, Edwards emphasized justification by faith alone. His movement spread along the coast to the southern colonies, particularly among Baptists and Methodists. At the same time, some of the Presbyterians were divided about the proper evangelistic methods that were being employed, and the Congregationalists began to split between the "Old Lights," who were suspicious of most revival methods and centered in traditional Boston, and the "New Lights," who pressed for greater revival activities.

Ultimately, it was George Whitefield (1715-1770), (see illustration) the Anglican preaching deacon and Methodist evangelist, who gave voice to this

Great Awakening through his ardent American preaching tours. Not only did he support the Puritan "New Side" Presbyterians (the "Old Side" adhered to a strict subscription to the doctrines of the Westminster Confession for their ministers), but his preaching spread the revival practices into other colonies. He was an eloquent preacher, whose enthusiasm for the gospel resulted in a rapid spread of this Awakening.

The Awakening movement peaked in the early 1740s. But southern colonies continued to be affected by the Awakening, particularly as the New England Presbyterians moved southward. By the 1750s, many Baptists had caught the stirrings and expanded the revival themes with those believers under their spiritual influence. However, as concerns for American independence were increasingly being raised, spiritual concerns diminished among colonists toward the end of the century. In addition, some extravagant practices including dramatic expressions of loud groans and fits of fainting,

The Constitution of the United States was ratified between 1787 and 1788. Three key features relating to religious life were also established there: government neutrality in confessional matters; the free exercise of religion; and the separation of church and state. The following year, George Washington was elected the first President. In 1791, the Bill of Rights went into effect, allowing for religious freedom for all. One result was the disestablishment of existing state churches in the colonies—voluntary denominational membership became the norm, instead of the earlier practice where citizenship was equated with membership.

> The Preamble to the *Declaration of Independence*
> We hold these truths to be self-evident, that all men are created equal, that they are endowed by their Creator with certain unalienable Rights, that among these are Life, Liberty and the pursuit of Happiness. That to secure these rights, Governments are instituted among Men, deriving their just powers from the consent of the governed, That whenever any Form of Government becomes destructive of these ends, it is the Right of the People to alter or to abolish it, and to institute new Government, laying its foundation on such principles and organizing its powers in such form, as to them shall seem most likely to effect their Safety and Happiness. Prudence, indeed, will dictate that Governments long established should not be changed for light and transient causes; and accordingly all experience hath shewn, that mankind are more disposed to suffer, while evils are sufferable, than to right themselves by abolishing the forms to which they are accustomed. But when a long train of abuses and usurpations, pursuing invariably the same Object evinces a design to reduce them under absolute Despotism, it is their right, it is their duty, to throw off such Government, and to provide new Guards for their future security. Such has been the patient sufferance of these Colonies; and such is now the necessity which constrains them to alter their former Systems of Government. The history of the present King of Great Britain is a history of repeated injuries and usurpations, all having in direct object the establishment of an absolute Tyranny over these States. To prove this, let Facts be submitted to a candid world.

After the War

The first African American Episcopal congregation was started in 1787 by Richard Allen (1760-1831) after being frustrated by the limitations placed upon black members by a Methodist Episcopal church in Philadelphia. Ordained in 1799 by Francis Asbury, Allen (see illustration) established several black Methodist Episcopal congregations in Pennsylvania. Finally, with several other black pastors, he formed a new denomination in 1816, the African Methodist Episcopal Church.

Mother Ann Lee (1736-1784), a visionary and self-proclaimed prophetess, set up her first Shaker colony in 1770, known as the United Society of Believers in Christ's Second Appearing. As an offshoot of the Quaker movement in England, they followed the revivalist tendencies along with utopian ideals. Four years later she brought her millenarian communal group to New York, where the movement grew and influenced the frontier revivals of the next century in Kentucky.

Within the last quarter of this century, a Universalist congregation was formed in Massachusetts and a related group, the Society of Universal Baptists, was formed in Philadelphia. Both of these groups sought to unify believers under a non-Trinitarian understanding of God. By 1790, there were over two dozen distinct Protestant denominations among the states of the new nation.

Musical Masters

The musical period known as "classical age" is another key element of this century. Most noteworthy among the classical composers is the first B of the three Bs—Bach (1685-1750), Beethoven (1770-1827), and Brahms (1833-1897), who spanned the cultural shift from Baroque to Romanticism.

Johann Sebastian Bach (1685-1750) (see illustration) was born into a very musical Lutheran family in Eisenach, Germany, where Luther had studied as a young boy. Recognized as a master organist, his reputation in other musical  genres was less appreciated until after his death. For example, he was also a prolific composer of vocal and instrumental music. Although living in a strongly Pietist environment, the theological content of Bach's music was clearly drawn from Lutheran Orthodoxy. While serving as Kantor in the St. Thomas Church of Leipzig, he composed over 300 cantatas, musical compositions usually based upon biblical texts for Sunday services enlisting choirs, soloists, and several instruments, including the organ. His Brandenburg Concertos were composed in 1721; the St Matthew's Passion in 1729, and in 1738, the *Mass in B Minor*, a landmark work of the Baroque period, although it was too long for regular worship settings and considered too Catholic for Lutheran congregations. Bach is now recognized to be one of the most gifted musicians in the world. He communicated his strong Lutheran faith as a teacher as well as through his numerous compositions, frequently placing "SDG" (*Soli Deo Gloria*; "To God be the Glory") at the end of his cantatas.

George Frederic Handel (1685-1759), born the same year and within 100 miles of Bach, never met him. Yet, their Lutheran heritage influenced their compositions greatly. Although a German, Handel lived most of his professional life in London, England, where he elevated a modified form of opera, known as the oratorio, a non-theatrical musical work, to greater prominence. In addition to his vocal music, Handel's orchestral compositions included the *Water Music* (1717), *Music for the Royal Fireworks* (1749). Handel is most remembered for his well-known, familiar, recognizable, and frequently performed work, *Messsiah*, in 1741.

Wolfgang Amadeus Mozart (1756-1791) brought classical music to new heights. A child prodigy, he began composing musical works at the age of four or five. Known more as a court composer, he wrote over sixty sacred compositions,

an unusual and unanticipated emotional shift in society and culture and a new kind of religious fervor, known as Romanticism.

The Industrial Revolution (see chapter 18 and illustration above) took on greater significance in this century. Both positive and negative social consequences became evident. For example, Charles Dickens (1812-1870) gave names and voices to the horrific urban conditions in *Oliver Twist* (1838) and *David Copperfield* (1850). In Germany, Johann Hinrich Wichern (1808-1881) organized what became known as "inner mission work," helping the homeless and poor in the large cities. Similarly, a Lutheran pastor, Theodor Fliedner (1800-1864), founded an organization of deaconesses in Kaiserwerth, Germany, in 1836 to work with recently released women prisoners, a nursery to care for children, and medical facilities for local communities. Florence Nightingale (1820-1910) took her initial training at Kaiserwerth.

Liberalism and Romanticism

The word "romanticism," which is associated with this period of thought, began in Germany but spread throughout Europe and North America. Emphasizing individual freedom, romanticism rejected the mechanical formality of earlier rationalism as well as orthodox theology. Such freedom of the individual led to a greater focus on feelings in religious thought (similar to Pietism of the previous century), yet it had a broader perspective in the sense of a celebration of diversity. Friedrich Daniel Ernst Schleiermacher (1768-1834), for example, wrote in *On Religion: Speeches to Its Cultural Despisers*: "I find that multiplicity of the religions is based on the nature of religion...The whole of religion is nothing but the sum of all relations of man to God, apprehended in all the possible ways in which any man can be immediately conscious in his life...." Thus, a theme of a more personal concern for what was labelled "subjectivity" bore fruit throughout this century in many ways, including the religious.

According to Schleiermacher (see illustration), neither morality nor doctrine alone were sufficient to understand the realm of religion. Rather, he said, one needed to feel the faith as well. Religion as he redefined it was about human experience, thereby removing it from the rational sceptics of the previous generation. But his approach also eliminated its divinely revealed content in Scripture.

A little over twenty years later, he wrote a complete systematic theology based upon his new approach called *Christian Faith According to the Principles of the Evangelical Church* (1821-1822). Here he explained that human experience or faith is being in a relationship with God which he described as "the consciousness of being utterly dependent" (*schlechthin abhängig*). He read the Bible as a human record of human dependency upon God, not as a revelation from God to humanity. Similarly, his view of Jesus was that He recognized most perfectly His dependence upon the Father. Christ's sacrificial death, miraculous resurrection and ultimate ascension were inconsequential to humanity as long as humans experienced a sense of dependency on God, concluded Schleiermacher.

Haugian Piety in Scandinavia

The elements of a spiritual awakening were not only experienced in Europe and America. Scandinavian Protestants soon rejected the cold rationalism of the state churches and adopted a deeper and more personal piety. Noteworthy was Hans Nielsen Hauge (1771-1824), a lay evangelist from Norway, who was committed to spreading the revitalizing message of the Gospel as a personal message. Hauge travelled extensively in Norway, wrote prodigiously (thirty-three books in eighteen years), and revived Lutheranism there. His zeal for personal piety resulted in a missionary movement which spread through the subsequent migration of Norwegians to the American Midwest.

Speculations in Theology and Philosophy

One of the major movements in this century of change, was in the area of speculative theology and philosophy. Besides the work of Schleiermacher, several other individuals had an impact beyond this century into the twentieth century.

Georg Hegel

Although a philosopher of religion by training and productivity, Georg Wilhelm Friedrich Hegel (1770-1831) influenced philosophy and theology quite profoundly in the nineteenth century. He believed that his Lutheran heritage and the Lutheran church (which he called a sect) was the best belief system available in his day. Recognizing the great paradoxes of the ancient faith, Hegel strove to reconcile the various polarities of life into an ideal. These views led to what of the local congregation as the embodiment of the true church, he proposed a unique form of synodical polity. The word, *synod*, from the Greek for "walking together," described the ideal structure. Walther proposed that this new Lutheran denomination seek a balance between lay and clergy leaders, between congregational and denominational authority.

Publishing his ideas in *The Voice of Our Church in the Question of Church and Office/Ministry* (1852) and *The Proper Form of an Evangelical Lutheran Congregation Independent of the State* (1863), Walther spelled out clearly his ideas and ideals. Synod, as an organizing agency, is advisory to congregations who have voluntarily joined the synod. While being somewhat influenced by his historical context, Walther was a faithful student of the Scriptures and Martin Luther's understanding of the gospel. It was the Word of God which was the final authority for faith and life for this group of New World citizens.

Camp Meetings, Revival, and the Restoration Movement
The first significant assembly of evangelical Christians met in a Kentucky frontier setting in 1800 under the "pastoral" leadership of James McGready (1763-1817). Trained as an evangelistic preacher in the 1780s, he assumed pastorates in several south-eastern states, where he emphasized a need to revive the spiritual lives of these frontier communities. The next year what became known as "the Second Great Awakening" began at the Cane Ridge Revival, particularly in response to the steady secularizing of society and the rampant rationalism of the Enlightenment. Characteristic of this movement was an emphasis on a personal conversion experience. Growing out of a Presbyterian practice of outdoor worship services (known as "the sacramental season"), these camp meetings drew ever increasing crowds together, many travelling several days and then expecting to stay for a week of worship and "supernatural" experiences. (See illustration.)

experience" in 1821. Studying under a Presbyterian minister, he questioned some

of the traditional doctrines and moved to New York City, where he attended a Manhattan church known for its revivals. Adapting and expanding the revival techniques he saw there, Finney returned to upstate New York and led revivals throughout the northeastern states between 1825 and 1835. He then moved to Ohio, where he taught at Oberlin College and became a strong advocate of the school's abolitionist movement. From 1851-1866 he was president of the college, which served a key link in the Underground Railroad.

In 1835, Finney described his techniques in *Lectures on Revivals of Religion*, known as "New Measures." Among these activities were women in leadership roles, the "anxious bench" where persons who desired to be converted could "make their decision," using music to prepare people for the message, and employing common, emotional, and persuasive language in preaching. Conversion, he asserted, was less of a miracle and more of a decision of one's free will. Worship should be entertaining and draw people into the assembly. His doctrinal views were published in 1846, *Lectures on Systematic Theology*, demonstrating his Arminian form of Calvinism.

Dwight L. Moody

Toward the end of the century, Finney's techniques were expanded by the lay evangelist, Dwight Lyman Moody (1837-1899), who also understood the need for educational programs. With little formal education, yet a natural ability to communicate, Moody became a leading force for evangelistic work at the end of the century. Born into a Unitarian family in Massachusetts, he became a Christian in 1855 under the influence of an uncle in Boston. Moving to Chicago, he started a Sunday School with a particular focus on the slums and then he began to lead a local YMCA. After losing his home, church, and the YMCA in the Chicago fire of 1871, he resolved to work globally while on a fund-raising trip to New York City. In the next years, as a tireless preacher and aggressive organizer, he set out on many international evangelistic trips, using some of Finney's techniques and adding his own—house to house visits prior to his preaching "crusades," an ecumenical involvement of various church bodies, and musical attractions during the event. In the 1880s he added educational conferences and an institution of higher education, Chicago Bible Institute, renamed in his honor as the Moody Bible Institute.

New Religious Expressions and Inventions

At the end of the Civil War another period of religious revivalism occurred in frontier America, resulting a plethora of novel expressions and organizations. Many of them developed from a renewed sense of living in the End Times or on the last days before Christ's imminent return, a theme which echoed from the Second Great Awakening. Except for the Christian Science, the other three cults continue to outpace mainline Christian groups in membership growth into the present. We can only briefly provide a historical overview of them in this chapter.

The Church of Jesus Christ of Latter Day Saints
    Rejecting the religious fervor of the second great awakening, Joseph Smith (1805-1844) sought to find a true denomination. Claiming to have a vision from the angel Moroni in the early 1820s, he unearthed golden plates which he subsequently translated from a supposed ancient Egyptian hieroglyphic script. This translation, which Smith dictated from behind a screen, was written down and became known as *The Book of Mormon*. It reveals that Jesus, prior to His ascension, visited North America. The lost tribes of Israel had settled in the New World and then, through infighting, lost the true Gospel until Smith rediscovered it.
    With several friends, he founded a new denomination which claimed to be a restoration of the original church of Jesus. The group grew slowly in New York and then, fleeing opposition from various communities, moved to Ohio, Missouri, and then Illinois. (See map of LDS movements) Suspicious of the

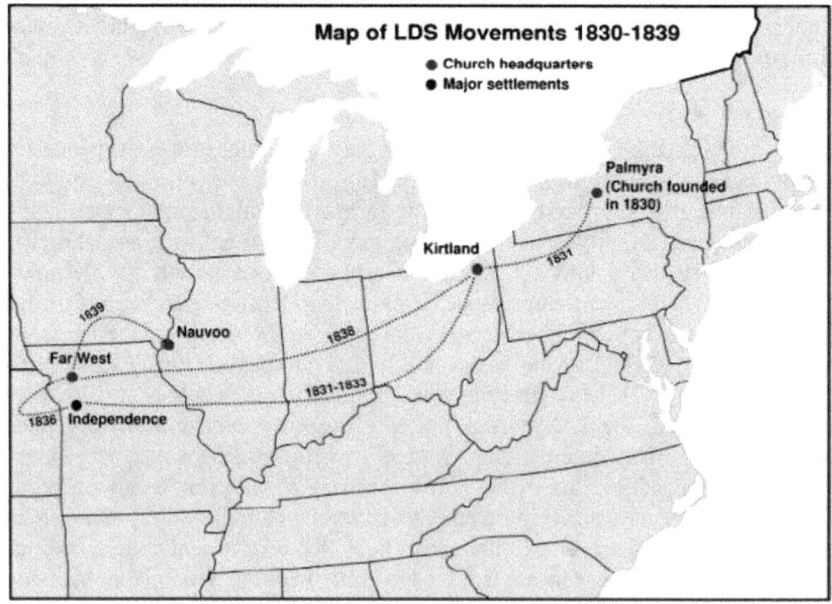

politics of the group, Smith was assassinated in 1844 while incarcerated in Carthage, Illinois. Fearful of further attacks, Brigham Young (1801-1877), close friend and successor to Smith, led a group to the territory around the Salt Lake in Utah. There they formed an independent community, later to become the Utah Territory (1850). They joined the United States in 1896, after repudiating their practice of polygamy.

Michael, the group also denies Christ's substitutionary atonement, but assert that Jesus died only for Adam's sin. Holding a premillennial perspective, they want to establish God's kingdom on earth, where the majority of Witnesses will return and rule after the resurrection on the Last Day.

Christian Science

Mary Morse Baker Eddy (1821-1910), a widow and then divorced spiritualist, gathered friends together after her third marriage and professed to them that she had special spiritual powers (see illustration). She published *Science and Health with Key to the Scriptures* (1875), claiming to have special insights from God about healing. Suffering as a child from frequent illnesses, she sought alternate healing methods. A disciple of Phineas Quimby (1802-1855), she adapted his mesmerism (also known as "animal magnetism") to elements of Christianity and created a kind of spiritual do-it-yourself religion. Rejecting clergy, she emphasized that all members of the Church of Christ, Scientist (founded in 1879) were equally capable of teaching and instructing. She taught that the material world is a "mist" and does not really exist; therefore, illnesses can be overcome by prayer and mental discipline (a metaphysical ideal). While claiming to be a "Christian" organization, Eddy taught that Jesus was a divine healer, but He was not God. God is Father-Mother or the Divine Mind, which alone can cure all through prayer and right thinking.

Christian History and Denominationalism

Philip Schaff (1819-1893), a Swiss-born, German-trained, historian of the Christian church, prepared an eight-volume *History of the Christian Church* (1858; revised 1882 and 1890). Coming to the United States in 1844, he served as a professor at a German-Reformed seminary in Mercersburg, Pennsylvania, until it closed during the Civil War. There at Mercersburg, along with John Nevin (1803-1886), Schaff was instrumental in promoting what became known as "Mercersburg Theology," a combination of historical ecclesiology and sacramentality (more in line with Lutheranism than Calvinism). The latter emphasis resulted in severe criticism of Schaff by his Reformed Church of the United States. Subsequently, he taught at Union Theological Seminary, New York, from 1870 until his death.

In 1857, Schaff reported on "Christianity in America," noting especially that a great variety of denominations coexisted in the context of American religious freedom. Although he would later work toward unity among all Christians, he saw denominational distinctions as a blessing, something he compared to the blessing of having four distinct accounts in the Gospels. Reflecting their historical origins in European Christianity, many American denominations developed as a result of geographic or national distinctions—whether they settled in the East or Midwest or South; or, in what language they

Bonhoeffer is best known for his work, *The Cost of Discipleship*, a work which has captured the hearts and minds of both conservative and liberal Protestants. That cost was exemplified in Bonhoeffer's early opposition to the Nazis, and particularly its practices of euthanasia and genocide, which resulted in Bonhoeffer's imprisonment and ultimately his martyrdom (death by hanging) just two weeks before the Allies entered Germany. In 1964, he was commemorated with his picture on a stamp in Germany (see illustration).

The Influence of Mass Media

Already noted above with the Scopes Trial, the use of media increased significantly in this century. With the invention of the radio at the end of the nineteenth century, by the 1920s the medium of radio began to influence more and more of the population in Europe and the Americas. A Congregational minister, preaching in Brooklyn, New York, S. Parks Cadman (1864-1936) was the first to utilize the radio for his preaching in 1923. Shortly thereafter, the Pentecostal revival preacher, Aimee Semple McPherson (1890-1944), already familiar with the advantages of attracting newspaper headlines, used the benefits of radio for her media savvy ministries in 1924. Her Angelus Temple in Los Angeles, California, became a center of her radio broadcasts and her International Church of the Foursquare Gospel.

A creative Catholic theologian from Illinois, Archbishop Fulton Sheen (1895-1979), was the first Catholic to broadcast a weekly radio show, "The Catholic Hour," each Sunday, starting on March 2, 1930, and running through 1950, when he went to television. Seven months later, The Lutheran Laymen's League committed to fund a radio program for a year, called "The Lutheran Hour," and engaged Walter A. Maier (1893-1950) as featured speaker. The program's success is evident in the fact that the Lutheran Hour is presently the longest running religious broadcasting program in the world. Ten years later the Lutheran Hour began a broadcast in Spanish with Andrew Melendez (1902-1999) as speaker.

Although television began in the 1930s, only after the Second World War did it become widespread. Christians recognized the benefit of such a mass-media communication tool. Many denominational communications organizations adapted from radio broadcasts to television broadcasts in the early 1950s. Probably the most well-known were Bishop Fulton Sheen and Oral Roberts (1918-2009); later to be followed by Billy Graham (1918-), Jimmy Swaggart (1935-), Jerry Falwell (1933-2007), and Robert Schuler (1926-2015), to name a few.

Canada, several other Protestant groups formed the United Church of Canada. Catholics however remained outside those conversations until mid-century, asserting that unity can only be found under the papacy.

In 1962, a Consultation on Church Union, which consisted of Congregational, Disciples, Episcopal, Methodist, Presbyterian, and Reformed churches, began to work on the formation of one ecumenical denomination. The idea was to create a "catholic, evangelical, and reformed" church. However, with the societal upheavals of the seventies, the growing optimism for such a church diminished until there was little activity at the turn of the century. In 2002, a renewed effort resulted in the formation of Churches Uniting in Christ.

Roman Catholicism's Ecumenism and Vatican II

By mid-century, Roman Catholicism began to emerge from its isolationist posture. But before that occurred, a significant dogmatic statement, *Munificentissimus Deus* ("most beautiful God"), was made by Pope Pius XII (1876-1958, pope 1939-1958) based upon his 1946 encyclical. On November 1st, 1950, he declared that Mary was bodily assumed into heaven. After a millennium and a half of prayers offered to Mary, the Roman Catholic Church formally created a theological rationale for such prayer. That same year his encyclical, *Humani generis* ("of the human race"), warned against any modern departures from the traditional Tridentine faith, particularly through secularization. Strongly anticommunist and antifascist, he was criticized for not speaking out openly against the Jewish holocaust, yet his supporters assert that he acted so as to prevent harsh reprisals on German Catholics by the Nazis.

Perhaps no pope had a greater impact on global Christianity in the past millennium than Pope John XXIII (1881-1963, pope 1958-1963) (see illustration). While serving as a papal nuncio in Turkey and Greece at the time of World War II, he intervened to aid Jews and others escaping the German holocaust. In 1959, just a few months after his election as a supposedly transitional pope, he called for an ecumenical council (officially the twenty-first such event) which changed the face of Catholicism for generations. Pope John XXIII died in late spring 1963 of stomach cancer before the opening of the second session of the Council and was succeeded by Pope Paul VI (1897-1978, pope 1963-1978), but his influence remained.

Vatican II (1962-1965) is noteworthy for several decisions (and documents) produced over the four sessions held each fall of the year. Most of them had a significant impact on Christian communities beyond the Roman Church itself. An overarching theme was a desire for "updating" (Italian, *aggiornamento*) of the Catholic Church; a process of reformation which would not be easy or easily carried out.

The first document of the Council was on the liturgy, the Constitution of the Sacred Liturgy (*Sacrosanctum Concilium*), which encouraged greater in his teaching in Marburg, Dresden, Leipzig, and finally Frankfurt. With Hitler's rise to power, he was barred from teaching in Germany and emigrated to the United States, where he took a professorship at Union Theological Seminary from 1935-1955. While at Union, he completed the first volume of his systematic theology. He then taught at Harvard University (1955-1962), where he published the second volume (1957), and then moved to the University of Chicago and completed the third volume of this work (1963).

Recognizing the powerful effect that post-War secularism was having on Christians, Tillich proposed using non-theological language about God. God, he wrote, is the "ground of Being" and through Christ, "the New Being," humanity can become reconciled to God as the "New Creation." He sought to address existential questions with theological answers in a way that bridged philosophy and theology into a dialectic synthesis. Rejecting what he saw as the rigidity of Lutheran orthodoxy, he tried to maintain what he called "the Protestant principle" of justification by grace through faith in a way that he deemed was palatable to the modern mind.

Another voice which sought to speak in a more contemporary fashion was James H. Cone (1938-), who is recognized as the founder of "black liberation theology" in America. His book, *A Black Theology of Liberation* (1970), followed his first publication, *Black Theology and Black Power* (1969). Raised in and ordained by the African Methodist Episcopal Church, he returned to teach at his undergraduate school, Philander Smith College, in Arkansas, after receiving his bachelor of divinity degree from Garrett Evangelical Theological Seminary in 1961. Since 1970, he has taught at Union Theological Seminary in New York. Influenced by Barth (the subject of his doctoral dissertation) and Tillich's view that theology must reflect its social context, Cone says that God must be viewed as caring for and bringing liberation to the oppressed, particularly among Black Americans. (See more on liberation theology below.)

A powerful speaker, Martin Luther King, Jr. (1929-1968), followed the liberal theology of Rauschenbusch. Born to a Baptist pastor, Michael King, Sr. (1899-1984), who changed his name to Martin Luther King, Sr. after visiting Germany, the younger King graduated from high school and entered Morehouse College at the age of 15 in 1944. He received his Bachelor of Divinity degree from a liberal Baptist school, Crozer Theological Seminary in Pennsylvania. In 1955 he received his PhD from Boston University. It was at Boston that he studied the works of Rauschenbusch, Niebuhr, Barth, and Tillich. At the end of 1955, the bus boycott of Montgomery, Alabama, elevated King to prominence as he served as the elected community leader. After visiting Gandhi's birthplace in India in 1959, King saw the benefit of non-violent protests, which he advocated for the rest of his life. His speech, "I Have A Dream," at the 1963 March on Washington had a lasting impact on the civil rights movement (see illustration). Denying many of the basic Christian

teachings, such as the virgin birth, the bodily resurrection, and the return of Christ, King maintained that one had to reinterpret biblical stories from their pre-scientific worldviews to contemporary applications.

Instead of only fighting for the cause of racial justice, several voices were raised in protest against other injustices, particularly against a perceived diminution of the role of women in the world. A feminist Catholic scholar, Rosemary Radford Ruether (1936-) advocated for the ordination of women to the priesthood and several other teachings which are contrary to Roman Catholic doctrine. Trained in early Christian history, Ruether's method reinterpreted earlier Christian teachings in light of liberation and liberal theology. Based upon her non-literal reading of Scripture, she understood the Bible and Catholic tradition, such as the 1968 papal document *Humanae Vitae* ("of human life"), as being patriarchal and limiting of women's roles. Her continuing concern remains with ecology as evident in her advocacy of "ecofeminism." The ordination of women did occur in several mainline denominations, including the Lutheran Church in America (1970) and the Episcopal Church (1989).

Conservative Challenge

In response to the undermining of basic Christian teachings and biblical authority, and as an alternative to the fundamentalist insulation of the first quarter of the century, several strong voices challenged post-war Christians to stand their ground confidently on God's Word. Carl F. H. Henry (1913-2003), a journalist by training, graduated from Wheaton College. While pursuing his M.A. at Wheaton and a ThD from Northern Baptist Theological Seminary, he helped launch the National Association of Evangelicals. In 1947, his book, *The Uneasy Conscience of Modern Fundamentalism*, became a sounding board for the new Evangelicals, as they became known. That same year, he and several other leaders helped the radio-evangelist, Charles Fuller (1887-1968), establish Fuller Theological Seminary. Henry was a popular speaker and prolific writer, editing the evangelical magazine, *Christianity Today* for over a decade. His most significant work was the six-volume dogmatic response to liberalism and fundamentalism, *God, Revelation, and Authority* (1983).

Another evangelical leader and classmate of Carl Henry was William Franklin Graham, Jr. (1918-). "Billy" Graham became the public voice for many Protestant conservatives as he preached a decidedly Arminian theology to the great American populace in city-wide rallies that were reminiscent of Billy Sunday. Beginning as a radio preacher in Chicago-land in 1940s, he was selected as president of Northwestern Bible College in Minneapolis at the age of 30 in 1947. His first crusade was conducted that year in Michigan. Over the next fifty-five years, he would preach to live audiences of over 200 million people in more than 185 nations in addition to the millions who heard or saw him through other media. (See illustration) Curiously echoing a

American revivalism along with this consumerist approach. Worship practices became a central feature of such consumerism as the focus of worship shifted from God to the audience and worship as entertainment was promoted. People were encouraged to pick and choose from a smorgasbord of denominational (or more often non-denominational "community church") options for membership. The Vineyard Movement, founded by the charismatic preacher John Wimber (1934-1997), eventually became a denomination with its characteristic informal worship and musically dynamic sounds. Around the same time, Willow Creek Community Church in suburban Chicago promoted a "seeker-sensitive" style of worship for the unchurched, removing all elements which suggested traditional church life.

Since then, several other preacher-oriented congregational associations have arisen. Many denominational congregations seek to mimic these "successful" mega-churches (see chapter 21) through what has become known as a contemporary-style of informal worship. Curiously at the same time, and by way of contrast, a movement known as "convergence" has sought to bring together charismatic Christians with Anglican, Orthodox, and some Lutherans on the basis of a more liturgical (and early Christian) practice of worship.

With the dissolution of the Soviet Union at the end of 1991, Russian Orthodox Christians experienced a resurgence of membership and participation in the liturgy. Already under Mikhael Gorbachev (1931-), some relaxing of suppression and persecution of Christians and reopening of several Orthodox buildings—monasteries and cathedrals—was experienced. Much of this revitalization was a result of the support from Russians living in exile, particularly in the United States. Already in 1962, the mutual excommunications between the Eastern Orthodox and the Roman Catholic churches were cancelled by Pope Paul VI and the Ecumenical Patriarch of the Orthodox Church, Athenagoras I of Constantinople (1886-1972). A Paraguayan stamp commemorated that event (see illustration).

A Global Consciousness

Toward the end of this century, a greater global consciousness centered in non-European and non-North American nations, most of which had reclaimed their independence from colonial governments and exhibited renewed interest in Christianity in their own cultures. As one church leader said, "Today, a historic shift is occurring. Christianity is moving away from the Global North (primarily Europe and North America) to the Global South (Africa, Asia, and Latin America)." Africa has seen a significant growth in Christianity in recent years. Until the middle of this century, many African nations were colonial territories of European nations and had nominally followed their European Christian models. After colonial control was removed, many thought native religious practices would rise. However, with less than ten percent of the population of African nations being Christian in 1900, Christians were estimated to be almost 50 percent

Her dubious biblical base and panentheistic views have resulted in a less than widespread acceptance of her legitimate concerns.

Catholic, Reformed, and Orthodox theologians have voiced similar calls for Christian care. To help their members, the Episcopal Church in 2005 prepared *A Catechism of Creation: An Episcopal Understanding,* and The Lutheran Church—Missouri Synod produced in 2010 *Together With All Creatures: Caring for God's Living Earth,* prepared by its Commission on Theology and Church Relations. Other denominations have study documents available. The issue of caring for creation and Christian stewardship of the environment will continue to be a strong theme throughout the first half of this century.

Catholic Papacy Remains a Force

Pope Benedict XVI (1927-, pope 2005-2013) was elected in 2005 at the death of John Paul II, after one of the longest pontificates in recent centuries. Serving as a respected German university theologian, Joseph Ratzinger (1927-), he became an archbishop with little pastoral experience in 1977 and four years later was promoted to several prominent offices in the Vatican. Prior to his papal election, he held the highest position among the College of Cardinals, Prefect of the Sacred Congregation for the Doctrine of the Faith. He was trained in liberal Catholic theology, but in most of his service and in his pontificate he advocated a return to traditional doctrines and practices, including (as pope) allowing a return of the Tridentine Mass. In 2001, several years before his election, Ratzinger had advised John Paul II (1920-2005, pope 1978-2005) to address the issue of sexual abuse by clergy, and after his election took strong action in several cases.

With the unusually rare resignation of Benedict XVI, the Roman Catholic Church saw the election of Pope Francis I (pope 2013-) (see illustration), the first Jesuit and the first to come from South America. The Argentinian archbishop and cardinal, Jorge Bergoglio (1936-), was a strong advocate for the poor and oppressed. He was recognized for his humility and commitment to social justice and continues those themes in his papacy since 2013.

Islam

With the increased awareness of and contact with Islam, Christianity has seen an increase in Muslim extremist groups. More Christians were martyred for their faith in the twentieth century than in all previous centuries (see earlier chapters of this book). This attack on Christianity will not wane in this century. Although Islam claims the name stands for peace, the word in Arabic means "submission and obedience," and is a requirement for all people to submit to Allah and obey Mohammed's teachings. Of the three major Muslim sects—Sunni, Sufi, and Shi'ah—Sufi's have demonstrated the most peaceful dimensions of Islam, with the Sunni holding the majority of members in most Muslim countries.

Islam is more than a religion. It is a worldview, which includes the totality of a member's life—political, social, and familial. Christianity is seen as a decadent form of Western monotheism. The majority of Muslims assume that Islam will ultimately triumph over all other religious systems and are taught to seek that goal.

Globally, Islam has increased its influence and power significantly. In America, for instance, the Muslim population at the beginning of this third millennium was just a little under four million, although Muslim organizations suggested that it was closer to seven million. (See illustration of the Islamic Center

in Dearborn, Michigan.) A Pew Research Center report projected that the Muslim population will grow twice as fast as the general population and will be nearly as numerous as Christians in the world by 2050.[1] Because of their strong family ties and a sense of community, reaching out to them with the love of Christ can be difficult. Yet, the legalism and enslavement that characterizes most Muslim sects will provide opportunities to show the full and free forgiveness and reconciliation with God through His own Son, Jesus.

Internet and Megachurches

No one event or invention, since the printing press with moveable type in the sixteenth century, has influenced Christianity as much as the internet. Although the World Wide Web first began in the latter years of the previous century, its impact will be most striking in this century. With information overload, finding the truth—and Him who is the Truth—is often diminished or deemed impossible. Relativism and atheism have equal voice to the Christian verities.

The internet has been a significantly beneficial resource for many churches and mission agencies. Use of the internet has enabled missionaries and

---

[1] Michael Lipka and Conrad Hacket. "Why Muslims Are the World Fastest Growing Group." http://www.pewresearch.org/fact-tank/2015/04/23/why-muslims-are-the-worlds-fastest-growing-religious-group/ (Accessed 7/11/2015)

www.ingramcontent.com/pod-product-compliance
Lightning Source LLC
Chambersburg PA
CBHW071223290426
44108CB00013B/1269